Jennet Conant

MAN

OF THE

HOUR

JAMES B. CONANT, WARRIOR SCIENTIST

SIMON & SCHUSTER

NEW YORK   LONDON   TORONTO   SYDNEY   NEW DELHI

Simon & Schuster
1230 Avenue of the Americas
New York, NY 10020

First Simon & Schuster hardcover edition September 2017

SIMON & SCHUSTER and colophon are registered trademarks
of Simon & Schuster, Inc.

For information about special discounts for bulk purchases, please
contact Simon & Schuster Special Sales at 1-866-506-1949 or
business@simonandschuster.com.

The Simon & Schuster Speakers Bureau can bring authors to your live
event. For more information or to book an event, contact the Simon & Schuster
Speakers Bureau at 1-866-248-3049 or visit our website at
www.simonspeakers.com.

Interior design by Paul Dippolito

Photo credits appear on page 591

Manufactured in the United States of America

10   9   8   7   6   5   4   3   2   1

Library of Congress Cataloging-in-Publication Data

Names: Conant, Jennet, author.
Title: Man of the hour : James B. Conant, warrior scientist / Jennet Conant.
Description: New York, NY : Simon & Schuster, 2017. | Includes bibliographical
   references and index.
Identifiers: LCCN 2017033241| ISBN 9781476730882 (hardback) |
   ISBN 9781476730912 (paperback) | ISBN 9781476730929 (ebook)
Subjects: LCSH: Conant, James Bryant, 1893–1978. | Educators—United
   States—Biography. | College presidents—United States—Biography. |
   Chemists—United States—Biography. | Atomic bomb—United States—
   History. | Manhattan Project (U.S.)—History. | Cold War—Decision
   making—History. | United States—Foreign relations—20th century. | Science
   and state—United States—History. | Technology and state—United States—
   History. | BISAC: BIOGRAPHY & AUTOBIOGRAPHY / Political. |
   BIOGRAPHY & AUTOBIOGRAPHY / Science & Technology. |
   HISTORY / United States / 20th Century.
Classification: LCC CT275.C757 C66 2017 | DDC 370.92 [B]—dc23
LC record available at https://lccn.loc.gov/2017033241

ISBN 978-1-4767-3088-2
ISBN 978-1-4767-3092-9 (ebook)

For my family

CONTENTS

MAN

OF THE

HOUR

CHAPTER 1

Atomic Pioneer

Here sits a man who perhaps is carrying a bit of the atomic
bomb in his waist-coat pocket.

—Vyacheslav Molotov to JBC

Christmas Eve, 1945. Moscow was blanketed under a thick coat of snow. There were almost no cars about. His driver eased down ruined streets that made it look like a country still at war. The winter blizzards had begun before the rebuilding had gotten under way, and now it would have to wait for the thaw. Unfinished buildings stood frozen in time. Stores looked dark and uninviting, and appeared to offer little for sale. Even so, huge numbers of people gathered outside the shops and still more filled the crowded sidewalks, all carrying parcels. Most were poorly dressed, covered heads bent against the swirling white. Over twenty-seven million Soviet citizens died defeating the Nazis, nearly a third of the country's former wealth was gone, but Russia was already on the rebound. There were children everywhere. Babies—so many babies—bundled up within an inch of their lives against the bitter cold. Despite its drab appearance, the capital was alive and teeming with humanity. James Conant was a Yankee from hardy New England stock, but he had to admit he was impressed with the Russians. They were a tough race, tested by war, insurrection, and an unforgiving climate. "There is no foolishness in this nation," he wrote in his diary. "Nothing soft."

As the embassy car approached the gates of the Kremlin, Conant peered up at the gloomy fortress-like complex on the Moskva River that was the seat of the Soviet government. Situated in the heart of old Moscow, bordered by Red Square to the east, and Alexander Garden to the west, it consisted of four palaces, four cathedrals, and some twenty towers enclosed within red turreted walls. The famous citadel had been the imperial residence of the czars for centuries, its opulent interior structures torn down and rebuilt on an ever-grander scale by a succession of monarchs until the Revolution of 1917. Even the Bolsheviks had been unable to resist the urge to glorify their rule. When Vladimir Lenin finally made it his headquarters, he stripped the golden eagles of the old regime from the towers and replaced them with the gleaming red stars of the new Communist order. Now the Russian dictator Joseph Stalin called the Kremlin home, and had chosen the savior's birthday to hold a reception in honor of his victorious allies. Since the atheist Soviet state had banned Christmas as a bourgeois tradition, however, the timing was not nearly as ironic for their host as it was for his guests.

The dinner was held in a cavernous banquet hall. America's secretary of state, James Francis Byrnes, and Great Britain's foreign minister, Ernest Bevin, took their places on either side of Stalin, each flanked by a twelve-man delegation. The Soviet commissar of foreign affairs, Vyacheslav Molotov, was also in attendance, along with various members of the Politburo. The Russians aimed to impress: there were boats of caviar, smoked sturgeon, guinea hen, beef, and lamb and other delicacies, arrayed like a flotilla of silver down the long table, along with oceans of booze—champagne, wine, brandy, and, of course, vodka. As soon as the guests were seated, the toasts began. According to custom, each course was preceded by a toast and a tumbler of vodka, which courtesy required be responded to in kind, toast for toast, drink for drink. One after another, the official toasts were drunk—to their nations, peoples, armies, leaders, and innumerable government functionaries present that night. As each ponderous speech of welcome and good wishes had to be translated by an interpreter, even the short toasts seemed long. Conant, unused to so much alcohol, found it hard to relax. If one of the Russian officials were to drink to his health, he doubted his vodka-soaked brain would be able to formulate a suitable reply.

He was still not sure what he was doing there. Two weeks earlier, he had stopped by his Washington office for a few hours when he received a call that the secretary of state was "anxious to speak to him right away." When he reported to Byrnes's office, he was informed an emergency had arisen. The secretary was leaving for Moscow in two days' time and wanted Conant to accompany him. The main purpose of the trip was to try to talk to the Russians about international control of the atomic bomb. Byrnes, a short, energetic man with sharp eyes, explained that he needed a bomb expert. Vannevar Bush, the director of the Office of Scientific Research and Development, had fallen ill. Conant, the science administrator who along with Bush had led the Manhattan Project, and had been chiefly responsible for overseeing the development of the revolutionary new weapon, was an obvious choice. His distinguished war service, together with his stature as president of Harvard University, meant he would be able to argue effectively with the Soviet experts. Would he go?

Conant was immediately intrigued by the prospect. He knew a great deal was at stake. Since the first bomb fell on Hiroshima in August of that year, America's atomic monopoly had divided their countries and cast a pall over postwar peace negotiations. Conant believed the only way to ensure peace was for the United States and the Soviet Union, which until very recently had been allies, to work out their differences and come to some arrangement regarding atomic energy and weapons of mass destruction. Even though it meant that the United States would have to give up its sole possession of the atomic "secret," the internationalization of nuclear weapons and their production was the only way he could see to prevent an arms race. Nuclear intimidation was not the way to achieve national security. Having had a hand in unleashing this tremendous destructive force, Conant felt a strong obligation to help see it contained. No one understood better than he the need to outlaw the bomb's use in future conflicts, for that way led only to certain disaster and Armageddon.

At the same time, he had no official standing. He was a scientist, not a politician. He had only just returned to Harvard full-time after a four-year absence during the war, and knew accepting another high-profile government assignment would infuriate the university trustees. By then, he had also spent enough time in Washington to worry about what he might be getting himself into by signing up for Byrnes's Moscow mission. There would be a price to pay, either way.

After some deliberation, he decided he had no choice but to accede to the secretary of state's request. He rushed back to Boston and grabbed some winter clothes, and was back in Washington by Wednesday in time to leave with the American delegation from National Airport. They crossed the Atlantic in a special C-47 that was put at the secretary of state's disposal, overnighted in Frankfurt, and the next morning took off for Moscow via Berlin despite a warning that a front was closing in. They flew straight into the snowstorm, veering off course and getting lost. For a hair-raising hour or more, they flew blind, searching for lights—any signs of human habitation—while their fuel was running low. The decision was made that if the pilots could not find the city in the next ten minutes, they would have to turn back. Seconds later, the plane banked sharply, and Conant assumed they were headed for Berlin. Just then, the clouds parted, and the sprawling outskirts of Moscow came into view. Everyone let out a sigh of relief when they landed, even though it was the wrong airport. The Russian officials who met them kept asking why they had attempted such a risky flight. No one had an adequate answer.

The hastily improvised Moscow Foreign Ministers Conference was Byrnes's last-ditch effort at atomic diplomacy. For months, the Soviet leaders had done everything they could to frustrate his attempts to use America's monopoly on the bomb as leverage in the peace talks. The failure of Byrnes's gunslinger-style tactics at the Foreign Ministers Conference in London that fall had been an embarrassment. The negotiations had been fruitless. Rather than treat the bomb with the respect and fear Byrnes expected, the Russians had ridiculed the metaphorical bulge in his jacket in social gatherings while refusing to address it seriously in formal sessions. Stalin had feigned indifference, and issued a statement saying that it was only a weapon to frighten the weak-willed. Molotov, a master at subterfuge and delay, adopted the same line, and delighted in denigrating the bomb at every turn.

President Harry Truman was losing faith in Byrnes, who had been dubbed Roosevelt's "assistant president" by the press, a title that did not sit well with his new boss. Even an old soldier like Henry Stimson, the outgoing secretary of war, warned that the bomb was a game changer, and it was a mistake to use it as a lever of pressure to extract internal political changes and the granting of individual liberties. Such changes took time, and the United States could not afford to delay reaching an agreement on the bomb. "If we fail to approach them now," Stimson argued, "and merely continue to negotiate with them, having this weapon rather ostentatiously on our hip, their suspicions and their distrust of our purposes and motives will increase." They could not afford to waste this chance at world peace.

Desperate to reach some sort of compromise, and in the process score a diplomatic triumph that would redeem his reputation, Byrnes decided to take a more conciliatory approach. He would journey to the Soviet capital and take his case directly to Stalin. With luck, the home turf advantage would make the Russians more amenable to the need for international action so that this unprecedented form of power did not become a postwar threat to the world.

In Moscow, however, things did not go much better. Molotov was as obstructionist as ever. He persisted in making flip remarks about America's atomic ace in the hole, clearly aimed at letting Byrnes know the Soviet Union would not be cowed into making political concessions. As in the Potsdam and London conferences, no member of the Soviet delegation showed any interest in discussing the bomb, or the proposed resolution for the creation of a United Nations commission to control atomic energy. The Soviets never demanded the sharing of the atomic "secret," or objected to the need for an inspection system—something that would not be popular in the United States, let alone in Russia—to police all military and industrial plants to prevent abuses and safeguard against any nation clandestinely stockpiling weapons.

Conant had felt it was imperative the Soviets should know about this radical new method of decisive warfare, and was surprised to find there were no technical questions, no arguments. Although his arrival in Moscow had been covered at length in the local press, not a single Soviet scientist had sought him out. Molotov, during the course of a dinner at which he was host, had suggested that perhaps the great American chemist, who was also president of a great American citadel of learning, should address the University of Moscow on the subject of atomic energy. The following day, however, Molotov withdrew the invitation, stating that he had no authority to make such an offer and was "only trying to be pleasant." If Byrnes had been hoping the presence of the illustrious atomic pioneer at the negotiations would spark debate about the future of the bomb, his ploy fizzled. Conant felt like he might as well have stayed home for all the good he had done. He never suspected that the reason behind the Soviets' apparent disregard was to prevent any chance of an inadvertent leak by Russian scientists that might alert the US delegation that they were feverishly at work on an atom bomb of their own.

Conant had lost count of how many times they had drained their glasses when Molotov, who was acting as master of ceremonies, rose slowly to his feet. Raising a freshly filled glass, a broad grin on his round, bespectacled accountant's face, he proposed to the assembled party that they had all had enough to drink to allow them to "speak of secret matters." Turning to Conant, he said mischievously, "Here sits a man who perhaps is carrying a bit of the atomic bomb in his waist-coat pocket, with which he could blow us all to tiny pieces—"

Before he could finish, Stalin jumped to his feet and broke in angrily, "Comrade Molotov, this is too serious a matter to joke about." After the sharp rebuke of his unruly foreign minister, Stalin explained that although he was no scientist himself and had absolutely no knowledge of physics, he was not prepared to make light of Conant's work. He then addressed the issue of the bomb for the first time. He praised Conant and his fellow atomic scientists for their achievement in creating the weapon that had brought the war to a close. They had rendered "a great service," he continued in his hoarse voice. "We must now work together to see that this great invention is used for peaceful ends." On that solemn note, he raised his glass in honor of the quiet, silver-haired American chemist. "Here's to Professor Conant."

Molotov, whose expression never altered, stood in grim silence. No one dared look in his direction. In the Politburo, survival depended on accurately reading and responding to the generalissimo's moods, and anyone who earned his displeasure could expect there to be consequences. After an awkward pause, Conant stood. Holding his glass aloft, he thanked Stalin for his kind statement, and gamely acknowledged Molotov's "humorous remarks," though in truth he was rather floored by his cavalier attitude. Adding that he felt sufficiently emboldened by their sentiments, and by the "molecular energy of the excellent wine," he offered a toast of his own, addressed to his Russian counterparts at the table. "I have no atomic energy in my pocket," he began a bit sheepishly. "But I can say that the scientists of Russia and those of the other countries represented here tonight worked together to win a common victory. I trust they may cooperate equally effectively in the tasks of peace which lie ahead."

After the coffee was served, and Conant rose to leave, Stalin detained him for a moment. The Soviet leader was much shorter and broader in person than Conant had imagined: not more than five foot four inches tall, he resembled "a shrewd but kindly and humble old peasant." Speaking through an interpreter, Stalin repeated his earlier congratulations and again expressed his hope that the bomb could be used only for peaceful purposes and not for war. Then, referring to Conant's generous toast, he added quietly, "Those were fine words, but were they sincere?"

Later, a few of the Americans and British gathered at Spaso House, the grand neoclassical manor that served as the US embassy, to share their impressions of the astonishing moment when history appeared to have suddenly changed course. Stalin had publicly humiliated his longest-serving deputy at a state dinner, signaling a decisive—if rather impulsive—change in attitude. While the generalissimo could be capricious, he knew what he was doing. Whether his displeasure with Molotov was genuine or staged was hard to tell. But the significance of the moment was not lost on anyone. The sixty-six-year-old Soviet despot, the most powerful and dangerous postwar ruler, was finally ready to incorporate nuclear weapons into his worldview. "There in the banquet hall of the Kremlin, we saw Stalin abruptly change Soviet policy," recalled Charles Bohlen, a State Department aide and subsequent ambassador to Russia. "From that moment on, the Soviets gave the atomic bomb the serious consideration it deserved."

It was the moment they had all "pinned their hopes" on—a sign that the Russians were prepared to cooperate. Stalin's remarks indicated a willingness to work with the United States and Britain to control atomic energy and promote peace through international agreement. The Soviet experts in both delegations fairly hummed with excitement as they analyzed the various interpretations and implications of what had happened. Byrnes saw it as a cause for optimism. He immediately began making plans for the British-American—and now Soviet—resolution calling for the creation of an Atomic Energy Commission to be presented at the upcoming meeting of the United Nations General Assembly in London in January. He would even make arrangements, on his return to Washington, to make a nationwide radio broadcast reporting on the success of his trip.

Conant was not as quick to celebrate. Even in the convivial atmosphere that prevailed by the end of the long boozy evening, he had picked up on some troubling undercurrents. When they had finished dinner, they were escorted from the banquet hall to another room to watch a short film. It was purportedly about the war with Japan, but focused exclusively on the Soviet contribution to victory, even though the Red Army did not join the battle until August 9, 1945, the same day the second atomic bomb laid waste to Nagasaki. There was no hint that the United States and Britain had played any role except for a brief mention of Pearl Harbor and, in the closing minutes, a fleeting glimpse of a Japanese and a Russian general signing a treaty aboard the US battleship *Missouri*. Almost as an afterthought, an image of General Douglas MacArthur flashed by seconds before the end of the film. Irritated, Conant dismissed it as pure propaganda.

When the lights went up, he observed that many members of the American and British delegations were also indignant. Afterward, he could not help wondering at the Soviet's motive in showing them such a "crass nationalistic movie." Was it intended as an "intentional insult"? If so, what were the

Russians playing at? "And no one, literally no one, is on a basis with Russian officialdom to say, 'That was a bit thick, you know,'" he noted in his diary, adding, "This little episode shows a lot."

Equally disquieting was the Soviets' refusal to grant them permission to make Stalin's tribute to Conant and the atomic scientists public. It was a matter of protocol: what was said in the Kremlin, stayed in the Kremlin. Stalin's recognition of America's technical prowess could not be reported to the world. Despite all the talk of friendship between their two countries, the Iron Curtain was as tightly shut as ever. At the time, Conant was chiefly annoyed by the fact that there seemed to be no channel by which they could communicate their frustration to their hosts. Someone cynically suggested the best way to get word out would be to write down a list of their complaints and toss it in the wastebasket—it was certain that the next morning their message would be read in Molotov's office in the Kremlin.

Despite all the "unfavorable evidence" he accumulated during his eleven days in Moscow, Conant remained convinced that the Russians would eventually see reason. Logic dictated that continuing their wartime alliance was the best way to proceed in the interdependent postwar years. If they did not act together to stop the manufacture of atomic bombs before it became widespread, the means of atomic destruction could find its way into the hands of an unexpected and reckless enemy.

In a speech he gave in late November, which was reprinted in the *Boston Globe* shortly before he departed for Moscow, Conant had predicted the Russians would soon get the bomb, giving a rough forecast of between five and fifteen years. He cautioned that the time estimate meant little, as the United States' monopoly on this power was only temporary. There was "time, but not too much time" to evolve a plan for the exchange of scientific knowledge and the creation of an international inspection system. Without inspection there was no way to ensure their protection. Without it no one was safe. Conant startled his audience with this ominous injunction: "There is no defense against a surprise attack with atomic bombs."

> One thing has been as clear as daylight to me ever since I first became convinced of the reality of the atomic bomb; namely, that a secret armaments race in respect to this weapon must at all costs be avoided. If a situation were to develop where two great powers had stacks of bombs but neither was sure of the exact status of the other, the possibility of a devastating surprise attack by the one upon the

other would poison all our thinking. Like two gunmen with itchy trigger fingers, it would only be a question of who fired first. Under such circumstances, the United States might be the loser.

Conant's estimate was slightly off. Exactly four years and one month after Hiroshima, the Soviet Union would explode an atomic bomb, and two countries would be locked in a cold war struggle.

Years later, looking back on that extraordinary Christmas Eve in Moscow, Conant found it hard to believe that as 1945 came to a close, he could have had such faith in the future. He had hoped that the difficulties would disappear and they could proceed to work out a plan to preserve the peace instead of continually preparing for war. "My ascent into the golden clouds of irrational hope can only be explained by my honest appraisal of the worldwide catastrophic consequences of a failure to attain international control," he later reflected. "Some scheme just had to work. And who is prepared to say my basic belief was wrong?"

He wrote those lines in 1969. Toiling over his memoir, safely ensconced in his wood-paneled study in Hanover, New Hampshire, he observed the perilous state of the world, "with American and Soviet aircraft and missiles poised to strike on a moment's notice." America was more vulnerable than ever before, and Conant had lost much of his old certainty, but none of the cold, clear-eyed Yankee pragmatism. A chemist, statesman, educator, and critic, he had had within his grasp all the elements to help forge the new atomic age. Supremely confident, he had acted upon his convictions to shape the kind of world he wanted to live in. He was, first and foremost, a defender of democracy. He had helped design and manufacture weapons of mass destruction in two world wars to protect liberty. He had fought for an open and fluid society, for a fairer system of higher education, for free discussion, a competitive spirit, and a courageous and responsible citizenry. He had occupied the presidency of Harvard as a bully pulpit, and had never hesitated to take daring stands on contentious issues, applying his reason, morals, and high ideals on matters of national import. As a "social inventor," his term for the half century spent in public service, he had tried to find new formulas to keep alive the precarious American political experiment known as democracy.

As a war scientist, however, he knew he had much to answer for. Atomic energy's "potentialities for destruction" were so awesome as to far outweigh any possible gains that might accrue from America's technical triumph in the summer of 1945. Writing as an old man, he acknowledged that these new weapons of aggression had added to the frightful insecurity of the world, and he did not think future generations would be inclined to thank him for it. Yet the nuclear standoff had continued for years—no mean accomplishment given the number and variety of armed conflicts—which suggested that the stakes had become too high and the risks too great. Perhaps there might still be time to moderate the vicious arms race, though that remained for history to decide. "The verdict of history," he wrote, "has not yet been given."

CHAPTER 2

A Dorchester Boy

*He is manly, reliable, and in Physics & Chemistry perhaps
the most-brilliant-fellow we ever had.*
—Letter of recommendation for a scholarship to Harvard

Unlike most who claim to be descended from one of America's first families, James Bryant Conant was not a snob. If anything, he was guilty of a kind of reverse snobbery.

The Conants were an old family, to be sure, with deep roots in New England that stretched back to the earliest days of the Massachusetts Bay Colony. They lived in old towns, hung old portraits of beady-eyed ancestors on their walls, and were buried beneath old stone graves in older cemeteries. Their souls were stamped with those legendary Yankee traits—chilly reserve, frugality, firmness of character—that have been featured in countless high WASP novels and today seem rather quaint, like the outsized footprints of an extinct tribe. Throughout his life, however, Conant resisted being categorized as a true Bostonian or, more pompously, a "proper Bostonian." It is the first assertion, and second sentence, of his remarkably impersonal autobiography, following the bald statement that he was born on March 26, 1893. After all, he would tell people with a smile, the most distinguished Conant was Roger, the founder and first governor of Salem, Massachusetts, who "missed the boat." Roger came to America in 1623, three years after the *Mayflower*, forever denying the family that social distinction.

The Puritan disdain for anything that smacked of aristocracy was apparent early on. A friend remembers visiting Conant when he was a young chemistry professor at Harvard, and finding him in his laboratory busy over a beaker of bright blue fluid. "I'm studying the bluest blood in Boston," he announced, the gleam in his eyes unmistakable behind the steel-rimmed spectacles. As it turned out, the fluid in question had not been extracted from the city's wealthy Brahmin elite, whose indifferent offspring populated Harvard in those days, but rather from several hundred horseshoe crabs, whose blood achieves its distinctive color because it contains copper as an oxygen-carrying pigment. It was a characteristic pose: the man of science, clinically removed from dynastic Boston's exalted self-regard. The sly, dry one-liners were part of the act, Conant's way of skirmishing with the Beacon Hill worthies who never let him forget that he was not quite "their sort." He seldom, if ever, let the cool analytical façade slip. "He had a chip on his shoulder about his background," observed Martha "Muffy" Henderson Coolidge, a cousin by marriage, "so that he was almost allergic to pomposity and pretension of any kind."

Clubby, insular, and impossibly smug, turn-of-the-century Boston had a way of making even its native sons feel like outsiders. Good society, in Conant's youth, was preoccupied with matters of birth and breeding, a legacy of the English colonists that a revolution and over a hundred years of independence had failed to eradicate. Proper Bostonians held vehemently to the notion that there were the "best people"—descendants of a clutch of first families whose names appeared in the *Social Register*—and "everyone else." It was a world so small and well defined that it excluded hundreds of thousands of families as undeniably Anglo-Saxon as Conant's own, at least another million of Irish descent, not to mention all the Italians, Jews, and Poles who peopled industrial Massachusetts. But the snub, in his case, did not take the form of an inhibition so much as an incentive. No matter how firmly planted his family tree, Conant knew ancestry would only get him so far; he put his faith in empiricism. Science was the way to invent a new future, with the promise of change, discovery, and dazzling possibility. "Ever since he was eight years old, he has applied science to everything," his mother told the first reporter who called with the news her son had been tapped to be the next president of Harvard. "Everything, to him, works out by formula."

It did not take the genealogical sleuthhounds on the Boston papers long to figure out that Conant was from the wrong side of the tracks. "Dorchester Boy Will Be President of Harvard at 40," the local rags crowed when his nomination was announced on May 8, 1933. Imagine their astonishment when they learned that someone so young and utterly obscure would assume the throne of the country's oldest and most important university, which its alumni—mostly old Bostonians—had up to then regarded as almost a family concern. That the majestic cloak would now rest on the narrow shoulders of a scholarship kid from an ignoble working-class suburb was unimaginable. Less than five miles from campus, Dorchester "may as well have been a thousand miles from Cambridge," said John B. Fox Jr., a longtime Harvard dean from an old Dorchester family. "Culturally, it was a world apart."

Compared with Milton, a manicured suburb of Boston where wealthy families once rode to city churches on Sundays in carriages, Dorchester was a semirural hinterland where, as one scribe sniffed, "only the most intrepid ventured to escape the summer heat." Though Dorchester had undergone a transformation in the decades since Conant's birth, and could no longer be considered a sleepy backwater on Boston's border, it was still far from fashionable. By the turn of the century, the railroad had created pockets of gentrification known as "country seats," and soon after the trolley brought an influx of workingmen and their families, crowding out the fields and farms and turning Dorchester into a lively commuter neighborhood. While the new "streetcar suburbs" were predominantly working class and heavily Irish, Roman Catholic, and Democratic, the Victorian businessmen who inhabited the older, more bucolic enclaves like Ashmont, where Conant grew up, were solidly middle class, Protestant, and Republican.

Still, in the eyes of Boston's rich, educated ruling class, Conant was a complete unknown, a stranger in their midst. The old guard, whose universe was defined by the Beacon Hill–Back Bay–Cambridge axis, could only shake their heads at the prospect of this new president and mutter disconsolately that he was "a Boston man, but no Brahmin."

His predecessor, A. Lawrence Lowell, an imposing figure who had presided over Harvard for nearly a quarter century, was a member of the eminent Boston family of whom it was said, "The Lowells speak only to the Cabots, and the Cabots speak only to God." Generations of Lowells had beaten a path to Harvard, all serious gentlemen of sound morals and high ideals. Conant's name did not summon the same ancient nobility, nor did his accent—with its missing r's and elongated a's—have the same mellow patrician ring. He was not a product of Groton or St. Paul's. At college, he did not "make" the Porcellian or any of the other clubs that played such an important role in ushering select undergraduates into Boston's tight society. To make matters worse, it was revealed that a search of the college records turned up not "a single Harvard sheepskin" in the family prior to his, which suggested that both the Conant money and cultural endowment were new.* As the *Boston Sunday Post* concluded a week after his nomination was announced, "For Harvard to 'marry' this president was almost as sensational as for the Prince of Wales to join in wedlock with the commoner daughter of a commoner Mr. and Mrs."

From what he wrote and said to family members, Conant was mortified by all the press attention. He had expected a certain amount of handwringing and indignation at his appointment, if not the "boiling" anger expressed by some diehard Lowell loyalists, who did not consider him fit to shine the great man's shoes. Nothing, however, had prepared him for the condescending newspaper stories about his Dorchester childhood. He loathed the drummed-up "color" pieces about his public school days, playing scrub football in vacant lots with kids named "Skid" and "Spike," and cringed at the thought of how the tales would be received on the sunny side of Commonwealth Avenue. Infuriated by the onslaught of prying reporters, Conant wrote his two older sisters, Esther and Marjorie, warning them to circle the wagons. After too many "intimate details" ended up in the *Globe*'s six-part series on his early life, he ordered a stop to all interviews. His sharply worded letter demanding that his relations refrain from gossiping to the press elicited a droll response from Esther, nine years his senior. "You may be sure wherever the family are concerned in publicity in the future—*mum* will be the word," she responded lightly. "On the other hand, no one anybody knows socially reads the old *Globe*—and the Roosevelt family have been painted quite as unappetizingly."

Conant was not ashamed so much as protective of his family. Plain, honest, and hardworking, his Puritan forebears had labored with their hands to make their way in the new world. They were artisans, carpenters, tanners, and cobblers. That he derived his independence and integrity from them he had no doubt. There was also the fierce determination—and doggedness. When he made up his mind, he was absolute in his convictions. "Science

---

* JBC was the first male member of the Conant family to graduate from any college. On his mother's side of the family, however, JBC had an uncle, George Bernard Bryant, who was a graduate of Harvard, as were his two sons, Richard and Philip.

and Puritanism merged in Jim Conant," observed one of his closest friends, the Harvard chemist George Kistiakowsky. "His scientific rigor replaced the Puritan vision of an austere God; his human straightness kept the colonists' sense of equality." But there was an unyielding quality to his character, the atavism of his ancestors' blood reasserting itself, so that for all his wit and warmth it was the cold certainty that people remembered—the arrogance of a prophet. "No matter what he was doing," said John W. Gardner, the president of the Carnegie Corporation of New York, whether it was running Harvard, overseeing the massive structure of the Manhattan Project, serving as high commissioner to Germany after World War II, or reforming the nation's public school system, he was always "a lone eagle."

The family patriarch was certainly a figure of heroic piety, judging by English sculptor Henry Kitson's massive cloaked statue of Roger Conant that stands atop a boulder facing the Salem Common in Massachusetts. When it was first erected in 1913, the giant bronze pilgrim loomed portentously, though in his later years James Conant—the eighth of Roger's descendants born in America—secretly nursed an interest in genealogy, intrigued by the idea that something of the man's indomitable will may have been handed down the generations. For an educator and statesman for whom the founding fathers were both a reference point and a continuing influence, there was no way to avoid the recognition that his own beginning was located in the past. He had little interest in his English antecedents, however, and began his research with the founder of the American line. He was too much the hardheaded scientist to believe in any nobility of birth, only in biology and the "natural aristocracy" of talent that was, in Thomas Jefferson's words, a "gift of nature."

In the first of several family trees he undertook in an effort to understand the hereditary forces that had helped make him who and what he was, Conant determined that apart from Roger—the immigrant—his kinsmen were not inclined to the "pioneer life." Once they settled in Plymouth County, they never strayed far. Roger Conant was born to a fairly well-to-do English family. His father, Richard Conant of East Budleigh, Devonshire, was a prominent farmer, and his mother, Agnes Clarke, was the daughter of a leading merchant. All the Conant boys were well educated and ambitious. Raised Church of England, they were imbued with religious feeling and joined with the Puritans in their endeavor to simplify the liturgy. The youngest of eight, Roger had no hope of inheriting his father's estate. Eager to make his fortune, he followed an older brother to London, completed an apprenticeship, and was made a freeman of the Salters' Company. After six years, Roger packed up his wife and baby, braved the perilous ocean voyage, and struck out into an unknown wilderness on the opposite side of the world. Together with his brother Christopher, they set sail on the *Anne*, the second ship after the *Mayflower*, arriving in Plymouth in 1623.*

Roger did not stay in Plymouth long, however, owing to the differences between his Puritan beliefs and those of the Pilgrim Fathers. In 1625 the Reverend John White of the Dorchester Company invited him to join the company's fishing settlement as governor "for the management and government of all their affairs at Cape Anne." The following year, the Dorchester Company, disheartened by a series of setbacks, decided to relinquish the enterprise and offered free passage to England to all who desired to return. But Roger was not a man to abandon a project he had set his heart on. He led his remaining followers to a more favorable site, known to the Indians as Naumkeag. Roger continued to serve as governor, and his tenacity and commitment are credited with making the new settlement a success. His "prudent moderation" in dealing with the new contingent sent over by the Massachusetts Bay Company in 1628, and willingness to sacrifice his own interests for the public good, even after they replaced him as governor, led the colony to be renamed Salem, or "city of peace."

It was from Roger's youngest son, Lot, who fathered ten children, that James Conant's ancestors descend. Of Lot's five boys, Nathaniel, a cordwainer, or shoemaker, moved to Bridgewater, Massachusetts, making tiny Joppa Village the family base for the next two hundred years. His grandson, John, had three sons, all of whom served in the revolutionary army. The youngest, Jeremiah, took part in the siege of Boston, according to a dramatic 1883 account penned by his son, Thomas, James Conant's grandfather. Thomas was a tanner and cobbler. He took a respectable part in local affairs, became a member of the school board, and was elected to the state legislature. He had three sons: John, Thomas, and James Scott, born in 1844. Two years later, his wife, Esther, died in childbirth. Thomas quickly remarried, but his new wife did not care for his children.

---

* While only Christopher's name is listed as a passenger, it seems probable that he was accompanied by Roger and his wife, Sarah Horton, and their son Caleb, though some accounts speculate that they made the journey on a small trading vessel.

Growing up, Conant's father, James Scott, knew little in the way of warmth and affection. He talked sparingly, if at all, of the past. "The family was poor," Conant wrote in his memoir, and his father's early childhood was "not pleasant." There had been "one bright spot" in his father's life, one person who had been his refuge: "the grand but simple lady across the street, Jane Breed Bryant," Conant recalled. "She had been so good to him as a boy that there was nothing my father would not do [for her.]" James Scott's gratitude would extend to marrying one of the six Bryant girls, and later, making sure his beloved mother-in-law's old age was as comfortable as possible.

The Bryants were a leading Bridgewater family. They were from old Yankee stock and could trace their bloodline back to Governor William Bradford of Plymouth Colony. Jane's husband, Seth Bryant, was a successful shoe and boot manufacturer, and owned a large factory that employed many men in Joppa, including Thomas Conant. The firm of Mitchell & Bryant, which Seth established in 1824, was the largest wholesale shoe and leather manufacturing company in Boston. Though practically retired in 1861 when the Civil War broke out, he set off for Washington, DC, with samples of army boots almost before the guns of Fort Sumter were silent. He took immense pride in furnishing over two hundred thousand pairs of boots to the Union Army—more than $800,000 worth—each stamped with his name as warranty, and "Made on the Massachusetts South Shore."

By the time James Scott Conant proposed to Jennet Orr Bryant in 1880, he was thirty-six and prosperous enough to buy a house almost as big as her childhood home in Joppa. In a strange inversion, by then, Seth Bryant had been wiped out by the Financial Panic of 1873 and was in no position to provide dowries for his many daughters. Required to earn her keep, Jennie had embarked on a career as a teacher, following the example of Elizabeth Peabody, who had established the first kindergarten in Boston in 1870. Almost twenty-nine and on the brink of spinsterhood, Jennie accepted her former neighbor with alacrity. A rather plain brown wren in a large oil portrait, she was intelligent, well read, and exceptionally opinionated and outspoken for a woman of her day.

Conant's parents first met in church, and they were bonded in part by their "special faith." Both from mill village families, they shared the significant distinction of belonging to the same small Protestant sect, the Swedenborgian, or New Jerusalem, Church. The teachings of the eighteenth-century Swedish mystic Emanuel Swedenborg had come to Boston in 1818 as part of the spiritual movement that swept the country, and soon became the center of religious life in Joppa, setting it apart from neighboring communities. Before he was a theologian, Swedenborg had been an accomplished scientist. Following a direct communication from God, he became convinced that his theory of the cosmos made religion compatible with modern scientific thought. Jane Breed Bryant, Conant's grandmother, wholeheartedly embraced Swedenborg's belief in the reality of an unseen world, telling her grandson, "Here was to be found the explanation of the universe." She was such an enthusiastic convert that she renounced her Quaker faith and sent all her daughters away to be educated at the New Church School in Waltham, Massachusetts, that had been established under the auspices of Henry James Sr., the Harvard theologian, and father of William, a noted philosopher and psychologist, and the novelist Henry James. Seth Bryant was equally devout, and was a generous patron of the church's building fund before his troubles.

Compared with his voluble, charismatic father-in-law, James Scott was quiet, serious, and austere—a "massively silent" man in his son's memory. Breaking with Conant family tradition, shoe making held no allure for him. He had a craftsman's skill with his hands but dreamed of becoming a painter. With the Civil War under way, however, he inevitably got caught up in the action. When his older brothers enlisted in the Twenty-Ninth Company of Massachusetts' Volunteers, he tagged along as a captain's boy. After he fell ill and was discharged, he joined the navy and served another year as a deckhand on a Union ship.

On his return from the war, James Scott went to Paris and studied art. When he found he could not make a living as a portrait painter, he went to work as an illustrator and soon became known for the fine drawings he made on wood blocks for the Boston engravers. His work appeared regularly in *Gleason's Pictorial Drawing-Room Companion*, *Ballou's Monthly*, and *Harper's Weekly*. He was one of the first to introduce wood engraving into the commercial field, and the firm of Bricher & Conant, which he helped found in 1870, was for many years the most famous of its kind in the country. A pioneer in his field, he continually experimented with new methods and techniques. Later, as the firm of James S. Conant & Co. expanded, he moved into the new industry of photo engraving. Though he carried on this profitable trade for more than thirty years, James Scott never had his father-in-law's ease with money. All his life, he remained suspicious of prosperity, and the unspoken shame of the squandered Bryant fortune caused him to keep his family to a strict economy. Conant absorbed the lesson, and like his father, would always be extremely cautious when it came to money.

It was only when he was much older that Conant understood what a sacrifice his father had made when he invited his impoverished in-laws into his home as "permanent guests"—especially as the old man's loquaciousness nearly drove James Scott to despair. Always determined to have the last word, Grandpa Bryant penned a thirty-three-page pamphlet about his life and career in the shoe trade, published at his son-in-law's expense. A man of strong opinions when it came to politics, he was a frequent contributor to the newspapers and a source of considerable controversy at home. "The sad fact was that in his declining years my grandfather had become a Democrat," Conant noted in his memoir, a transgression that dated back to the first Grover Cleveland campaign, in 1884, and scandalized his father, who, like many New Englanders, still believed that the words *Republican* and *patriotic* were synonymous. An ardent supporter of William Jennings Bryan, his grandfather famously rose up from his sickbed in 1896 to cast a vote for free trade and free silver. With every passing year, the "heresy" of his grandfather, who died when Conant was five, only increased, which made living under the same roof difficult at times.

Fortunately, the grand old mansion that James Scott bought Jennie on Bailey Street in the Ashmont section of Dorchester was big enough for them all. The large Federal-era house had an old-fashioned feel even then, with long front and back parlors separated by curtains, numerous annexes, and decaying stables. Situated on an airy knoll above the Neponset River, the front yard was shaded by great elms, the broad lawn running down to Dorchester Avenue. The house overlooked the Ashmont Station of the Old Colony Railway line, and the back of the property ran to open fields of considerable acreage. The couple became close friends with their neighbors, including Harold Murdock, president of the National Exchange Bank, and Dr. Edward Twitchell, a popular local physician, and their sons would become Conant's best boyhood pals and Harvard contemporaries.

A late and much-longed-for son, born when his father was almost fifty, James Bryant Conant was a much-adored and coddled child. He was raised by "a regiment of women," presided over by his grandmother Bryant, two sisters, three aunts, and innumerable female cousins. They all doted on the baby boy and read to him by the hour, so that he did not learn to read until he was almost seven. Listening at their knee, he picked up bits and pieces of family lore, as well as the smoldering disputes between his Republican father and Democratic Bryant relations. While his mother was usually gently spoken, he became aware that she, like her father, held strong views that occasionally led to "words of condemnation"—particularly when it came to those who fought under the Confederate Stars and Bars and failed to embrace the abolitionist cause. She and her sisters were also emphatic anti-imperialists. They often excoriated Republican foreign policy, their voices rising to a fevered pitch with Theodore Roosevelt's ascension to the presidency in 1901.

Conant's mother was equally condemnatory of all "Trinitarian doctrines." He could remember her angrily holding forth against a group of churchgoers whose interpretations of Swedenborg's writings she took issue with—a schism that ultimately led to her leaving the church. She held to the basic Quaker tenets, though in later life became a Unitarian. When they were young, she had taken her children to the Swedenborgian church in Roxbury, but never attempted to indoctrinate them; rather, she succeeded in inculcating an early and lasting skepticism of all religion. Conant would usually characterize himself as a Unitarian, though that glossed over his fundamental agnosticism and Puritan hostility for ritual and creed. Whether it concerned politics or religion, however, it was his mother's moral indignation that made a lasting impression.

"What my mother approved and what she disapproved soon became quite clear in the course of conversation," he wrote. "More often than not, the clear opinion which emerged was not that of the majority of our friends and acquaintances. Mother was basically a dissenter." He was raised to believe "dissent was not only respectable but usually morally correct."

Conant's parents, who called him "Bryant" as a child, sought to give him and his sisters every advantage. When it came to the all-important question of education, James Scott decided the overcrowded public school would not do. He joined together with other civic leaders to establish a new elementary school in their neighborhood. Conant began his education at the little Bailey Street School at the age of five, moving to the Henry L. Pierce Grammar School in the third grade. Except for a year he spent in a local private school—in hopes of boosting his reading and writing—all his early education was in public schools, where the rigid teaching methods held little appeal. He disliked the dull curriculum, which made no allowance for any interesting extracurricular activities, and the strict discipline, which consisted of rapping the hands of miscreants with a rattan switch, accompanied by "possible threats" of more severe forms of corporal punishment.

For the most part, however, he enjoyed a happy, sheltered childhood. Ashmont's shady streets were "built for bicycles," he recalled, and in winter the new, mostly empty macadam-paved roads were ideal for sledding. In summer, the Conants journeyed with a number of neighboring families to a rustic vacation colony near Danbury, New Hampshire, making the last plodding leg of the trip from the train station by carriage. The new age of electricity had not yet reached this remote outpost, so he spent several months of every year transported back to the "horse-and-buggy age."

Conant credited his father with shaping his view of the future. James Scott perceived that the recently opened electric trolley line in Dorchester, which provided rapid access to downtown Boston, was an opportunity to be grasped. Anticipating that Dorchester's empty pastures were inevitably going to make way for new suburbs, James Scott went into the construction business as a profitable sideline. His first project was to tear down the old stables on their property and erect a two-story wooden house. By the time little Bryant was in kindergarten, his father's building activities were in "full swing," and James Scott and his partners were aggressively developing the green hills, cutting them into lots along paved streets soon to be lined with two- and three-family housing units. It was only many years later that the once picturesque village, squeezed by masses of low-income construction on all sides, came to regard his father's plain, rather unattractive structures as the "scourge of the community."

Even as a boy of four or five, Bryant had begun to form an understanding of the class tensions in his neighborhood. His best friend lived in the modern row house his father had built next door, and he would have been astonished to hear anyone say a word against it: "Our own homes were far from luxurious," he recalled, "but on the whole represented a higher standard of living than those of the boys with whom we went to school but were not of our 'bunch.' We regarded ourselves as 'top dogs' in the neighborhood but were careful not to let this come to a physical showdown."

He would always remember the brisk fall afternoon his father took him along to inspect a construction site a short walk up the hill from their home. Seeing the new road being built not ten minutes from his back door, Conant suddenly understood that the future was close at hand. His father had told him stories about how the new efficient electric trolley cars had replaced the old horse cars shortly before he was born. Now there was a line that ran from the heart of Boston right through their neighborhood as far as Milton. A new line had just been added, reaching out even further, bringing the distant towns and villages of Plymouth County within reach.

"I must have breathed in the optimistic spirit of the expanding suburb," Conant wrote. Sensing amazing things would soon be possible, his imagination thrilled at the idea that the clang of the electric trolley, which could be heard the length and breadth of Dorchester, would eventually resound in every corner of the country. He could picture the fast trolley car that might one day speed them to their isolated farm in under twenty minutes: "Of this, I was quite certain. Such was progress, which the grownups liked to talk about. The twentieth century, they said, would certainly bring more streets and more electric cars—possibly things called automobiles as well, though I had never seen one."

He was entranced by electricity. Even in its simplest manifestations the spark of current was still something of a "marvel." Few of the homes in Dorchester were wired for electricity. No one he knew had a telephone. The first electrical device he came into contact with on a regular basis was the doorbell, which was then becoming "standard equipment" in the modern homes his father was building. To a small boy, it was irresistible. As the old Ashmont house did not have a doorbell, James Scott brought home an electric buzzer and showed his son how the simple mechanism worked. Soon Conant was "monkeying" with electromagnets, dry and wet batteries, tiny motors, and lightbulbs.

When he was a little older, Conant was allowed to accompany his father to his printing firm, where he watched him execute the complicated steps involved in preparing and developing the glass negatives and beautiful sharp prints. "It may be that my love of chemistry," he later reflected, "resulted from my fascination with the mysterious changes in the plates which various chemicals brought forth." Though his father had no formal training, the same initiative that helped him work his way up in the printing business enabled him to stay abreast of the technical advances in his field. He taught himself both commercial photography and the half-tone process and, for all practical purposes, became "an applied chemist."

A forward-looking man, James Scott encouraged his son's scientific interests. He helped him set up a small shop in one of the downstairs closets, and furnished it with cast-off equipment from his own workbench. Conant's first experiments often went awry. His mother recalled having to roust him in the middle of the night on more than one occasion to do something about the noxious fumes permeating the house. Still half-asleep, he would descend to his lab, dispose of the offending solution, replace the rubber stoppers in any bottles left open, and stagger back to bed. According to his youthful diary, he spent "cold winter afternoons working in the shop," combining ingredients in test tubes. In no time Conant, billing himself a "Young Edison," was putting on shows for all the neighborhood children, who stood and watched in "silent and nose-holding awe" as he staged loud but harmless explosions, created great stinks, and used the nickel ticket fees to buy more equipment.

The long hours Conant spent shut up in his makeshift laboratory worried his mother. While other boys were "out batting a baseball," she recalled, "he printed a sign and stuck it on the door: 'Only two persons allowable in shop at a time.'" Distressed at the idea that she might be raising a lonely "pedant," she enticed him outdoors with rowdy Wild West shows and boisterous treasure hunts. James Scott shared his wife's concern about their bookish son. A brief note from eleven-year-old Bryant begging his father to send his favorite "Sintific [sic] American" (Scientific American magazine) to the Danbury farm, where he was supposed to be enjoying such summer pursuits as swimming and fishing, revealed perhaps an unhealthy focus. In an effort to interest his son in sports, Conant's father taught him to play tennis, chalking out a court on the Ashmont house's expansive front lawn, much to the astonishment of his neighbors. While no athlete, Bryant was growing to be tall and wiry, and was a relentless competitor. Eventually the great lawn became home field for the neighborhood baseball and football games, with young Conant often as not serving as his team's captain. A few years later, James Scott purchased a sailboat, hoping to foster in his son the sturdy qualities—courage, independence, and self-reliance—that had enabled their Puritan forebears to make a life by the sea.

When it came time for him to enter preparatory school, his parents had intended to send him to nearby Milton Academy, a private school, where Esther, recently graduated from Smith College, was a teacher in the girl's division. Their son, however, had other plans. His best friend Roger Twitchell's older brother, Paul, was enrolled in the Roxbury Latin School, a part of the Boston public school system, and had boasted of its separate laboratories for chemistry and physics. From his parents' perspective, it was a far less exclusive and considerably more distant inner city institution, and would require him to commute by trolley. But Conant was insistent. "It was agreed that I had the scientific 'bug,'" he recalled. "My father and mother at least recognized an interest and wisely sought a school where it might be welcomed and encouraged."

Founded in 1645, Roxbury Latin was an old, prestigious academy and, in spite of its name, was indeed known for its strong science department. Under the direction of its science master George Fairfield Forbes, it was the first school to use a laboratory for teaching experimental physics, with special apparatus for demonstration and study he built himself, and would later be used as a model by other schools. All students were required to study both chemistry and physics in their last two years. Although money was not a consideration—tuition was free for Roxbury residents, and those living outside paid a modest fee—admission to its rigorous six-year program was competitive. That spring, ninety applicants sat for the three-hour entrance exams and thirty-five were accepted.

Conant did not make the cut. He returned home in tears after being informed he had flunked the spelling section. His mother, a forceful woman when she wanted to be, went down to the school and had it out with the head, arguing that her son's high scores in math and science more than compensated for a few misplaced *e*'s. In the end, she got her way, on the condition that as a trained teacher she would see to it that his spelling improved over the summer.

When eleven-year-old "Jim" Conant—for that was how he was known from then on—entered the sixth grade of Roxbury Latin in the fall of 1904, he did not immediately impress anyone as a scholar. His classmates were all hard strivers. They were the offspring of doctors, clerics, contractors, factory managers, and small business owners—the new middle class that was just coming into its own. For them, Conant recalled, "college was either for those who had a career in mind or for the rich who attended the private schools in Boston or the nearby boarding schools." That first year, he had to scramble to catch up. His grades were acceptable but not extraordinary. Mathematics was his best subject, music his worst. His spelling was still weak, and his handwriting so poor the headmaster included a warning note in his report card: "Must do work in penmanship." To his classmates and teachers, Conant appeared quiet, self-contained, and rather shy. Never one to make himself conspicuous or push to the head of the line, he generally faded into the background. At first glance, Newton Henry Black, his science teacher, dismissed the "towhead with a Dutch cut and broad collar" as both "undistinguished and unprecocious."

All that changed the following year, when he took Black's elementary science course. It was immediately apparent that Conant showed an unusual level of aptitude, particularly in the final section on chemistry. "N. Henry," as the boys called him when out of earshot, was a gifted young teacher with an infectious enthusiasm for his subject and that rare ability to transfix the most fidgety of pupils. His spirited lectures earned him a devoted following, though he was too exacting and impatient with stragglers to ever be called popular. Conant became one of Black's disciples, joining the small clutch of boys that brought their sandwiches to his laboratory at lunchtime. Sometimes he would stay behind to get advice about some tricky piece of apparatus, once bringing in a homemade induction coil housed in an empty chalk box that was giving him trouble. Black could only smile as he looked over the crudely wound wire, attached to an old electric bell mechanism as a circuit breaker. "You don't expect to make that work, do you?" he asked.

"I've got to make it work," Conant explained, "because my father said he'd buy me a real induction coil if I can get this one to go."

Black was impressed with the boy's spirit and scientific bent. He had been rather ingenious in adapting basic materials to his purpose, and his early efforts showed "prompt signs of facility." Moreover, he possessed the inherent curiosity about how things worked and were made that marked out the best scientific minds. Black was scarcely thinking in terms of the next Edison, but he took a special interest in young Conant.

Black soon learned that Conant's father had carefully nurtured the boy's inventive turn of mind. Not only had James Scott built his son a new, large shop in the lean-to off the kitchen, he had gas—which was supposed to be used for purposes of illumination—piped in so that it was a proper chemical laboratory, complete with a Bunsen burner and stopcock. With the aid of a hot flame—as opposed to the meager output of an alcohol lamp—Conant could now make distilled water, evaporate solutions, and even prepare oxygen gas by heating red oxide of mercury. He befriended the pharmacist at the local drugstore and secured a ready source of chemicals. As an incentive to creativity, James Scott gave his son an allowance of $5 a month, and proposed that for every piece of apparatus he could rig up and make work, he would buy the comparable item. Conant, who liked to get his money's worth, judiciously invested $2.50 in parts and managed to build a balance scale that cost his father $50 new.

His performance at school improved, but while he excelled at chemistry, he was still compiling a number of Bs and Cs. In the academic year of 1905–6, he ranked just sixteenth in a class of thirty-two. Aware of his son's inclinations, James Scott requested that Jim be allowed to keep on with his laboratory work at home, as chemistry would not be part of his curriculum the following year. Black was "skeptical," but suggested a book, Arthur A. Noyes's *System of Qualitative Analysis*, and offered to monitor his progress. It was a fairly daunting tome, however, and Black doubted the boy had the "backbone" to tackle it on his own.

Over the next few months, Conant regularly sought Black out during the noon periods at school, and their relationship evolved into an informal private tutorial. Every week or so, Black would give him a small bottle containing an unknown sample, and Conant would report back when he had managed to identify the contents: silver and tin, for example, but no copper or lead. This process of discovery was "an exciting business," and Conant kept coming back for more "unknowns" to analyze. An avid experimenter, he loved the idea that nature was a puzzle that could be solved, and devoted hours of work after school to his solitary labors. He surprised Black by racing through Noyes's text. He was soon back, asking for a second book. He was seldom defeated by a problem, and systematically worked through the high school laboratory manual on his own steam. It was then that his teacher began to note Conant's "capacity for work," especially for one so young, and extraordinary inner drive. Not only did he like to work alone, he worked fast, completing the equivalent of two years' work in the space of one.

For Conant, the new world of chemistry Black had opened for him captured his imagination. "The experiments were simple but spectacular," Conant recalled. "The knowledge acquired about elements and compounds was so foreign to what was discussed in the daily papers or in general conversation that it seemed a passport into a strange and secret land." His boyish zeal is almost palpable in a 1908 letter to his sister Marjorie, who was studying painting in Paris. Written on March 29, three days after his fifteenth birthday, he gushed about his new favorite teacher while unapologetically trying to finagle another present:

By the way about the book that you said you were trying to find for me. If you are really going to get one I wish you would get one on *Chemistry*, rather Elementary, though most anyone would do, in *either German*, or *French*.

> Mr. Black is the instructor in Physics and Chemistry as you perhaps know and is quite a friend of mine. We had him out for Super [sic] last Sunday night and I showed him my shop etc.

While Conant's ability was not in question, Black could not be certain how much he had really absorbed in the course of his solo studies. As it happened, that spring a group of his graduating seniors would be taking a practice college entrance exam in chemistry, and Black decided to take advantage of the timing to arrange a little experiment of his own. Corralling Conant one afternoon as he passed by the laboratory, Black gestured toward the blue books he had just passed around to the class and casually suggested to the sophomore, "Why don't you try to see what you can do?" After a hesitant glance at the older boys, Conant rose to the challenge. An hour later, he handed back his blue book. Black quickly scanned the answers to the twelve questions. To his astonishment, Conant had aced the exam. Black did not need any more proof of his fifteen-year-old prodigy's "unusual mental power."

It was an important turning point in Conant's life. What had up to then been a youthful passion was now to be a fixed vocation: "My career was now clearly marked," he recalled. "I was to be a chemist."

To give Conant a glimpse of what the future held, Black took him on a tour of Harvard's laboratories, housed in a gleaming white building called Boylston Hall, and introduced him to the famous chemistry professor and department chairman, Theodore William Richards. The memorable day earned an excited mention in the youngster's red-leather diary: "GREAT!!!" Conant knew it was his mentor's deepest wish that he attend Harvard, where Black himself had earned a master's degree in chemistry only a few years before, and it had become his wish, too. He was keenly aware of the competition among his peers, and kept a close eye on the class rankings. If it occurred to him that failure was a possibility, or if he felt in any way burdened by the pressure, the only sign of it was in his redoubled efforts. When he sat down to take the college entrance exam at the end of his junior year in the spring of 1909, the somber pledge he wrote out on the back of the grade card showed his resolve:

"I, James Bryant Conant, on the eve of my Preliminary Exams, testify that, I have in my opinion, done as well as could be under conditions and having nothing to regret during last year's work and I will not blame myself or anyone if I fail to pass."

Conant passed with flying colors. In October Black wrote to Richards at Harvard to plead his pupil's case. Black made the rather audacious request that Conant not only be admitted, but as he had passed the college entrance exams at the end of his junior year of high school, be permitted to skip first-year chemistry and enroll immediately in classes usually reserved for upperclassmen. Before the month was out, Richards replied that the department had decided that Conant, "considering his extraordinary ability," be allowed to take the final exam in Chemistry 1 the following June. If the results were satisfactory, he would be credited with the course. But Black's plans for his prize student did not end there. After thanking Richards for the department's indulgence regarding Chemistry 1, he proceeded to argue that Conant should also be allowed to dispense with Chemistry 3, and hoped the department would accept his word at the end of the year that his pupil had completed the necessary work in qualitative analysis.

From then on, Black dedicated himself to preparing Conant for Harvard. The only hiccup was that there was no official transcript to prove that Conant had achieved a knowledge of physical chemistry, and an understanding of qualitative analysis, both far beyond the school syllabus. To redress this gap, Black designed a concentrated course of study in both chemistry and physics, culminating in stiff final exams. He also gave him access to his own private laboratory—and considerably superior equipment—and guided him through the course work required in Harvard's freshman year.

By now, it was clear to Conant's classmates that their science master was grooming his "boy chemist" for greatness. Black saw to it that Conant received a wide-ranging education in science, steered him into new fields, and exposed him to some of the great European thinkers. He also encouraged him to take three years of German—in addition to five years of both Latin and French—though Conant regarded these subjects, along with English and history, as "just so many hurdles one had to jump." There were weekend excursions to Cambridge, either to stock up on chemicals or attend afternoon lectures at the Lowell Institute, the subjects ranging from astronomy to atomic weights. Black was a frequent visitor to the Ashmont house, as well as the shop off the kitchen, where teacher and student often disappeared after dinner for supervised practice in the art of glass blowing. Over the summer holidays, they often went sailing, the young captain honing his skill at the rudder of a new, faster boat while Black served as "ballast." As Conant observed fondly in his memoir, "I doubt if any schoolteacher has ever had a greater influence on the intellectual development of a youth than Newton Henry Black had on mine."

Black more than reciprocated his pupil's affection and admiration. As the letters of recommendation he wrote to the Harvard authorities in the spring of 1910 attest, he could not have been more proud of Conant than if he were his own son. The degree to which he had mapped out his protégé's future, following very much in his own footsteps, is evident in his argument for a scholarship based more on merit than on need:

> In regard to Mr. James Bryant Conant, I may say that his class, and in Chemistry and Physics is the best student . . . He is looking forward to university teaching as a career. While his family could provide for his expenses at college for a year or two, when one considers the long course of study yet ahead of him, I feel certain that he is decidedly the kind of boy to be helped by a scholarship.
>
> Taking all things into consideration I consider him the most promising boy I have had in science during my ten years here in this school. He is bound to be heard from later as a scholar and a man.

Although Conant recalled that he "practically lived in the library" his senior year, his classmates did not write him off as a grind. He found time for a variety of after-school activities, including serving as editor in chief of the school magazine, the *Tripod*. Like most schoolboys, he perceived that his achievements in the classroom did not count for half as much as those in the field of sports. He played football, though he was slight for a fullback, and rowed crew, eventually becoming good enough to make the second boat. Rowing came naturally to him. He liked the hard labor, and developed his stamina by forcing himself on through the pain and exhaustion of those oft-repeated races. The discipline appealed to his puritanical code, and he derived enormous satisfaction from pushing himself to his limits. The summer before his senior year, he discovered mountaineering, a sport that suited his self-sufficient nature. Hiking and climbing the snowcapped peaks of New England became an integral part of his life, combining his love of exercise with the need to test himself.

His greater confidence also revealed itself on the stage his senior year. He had always taken bit parts in school plays, but in his final turn as Lucille, the heroine of the French romantic comedy *Maître Corbeau*, he stole the show. In the big finale, Conant, sporting a blond wig and frilly pink dress, was preparing to fall into the arms of the leading man—no less than the crew team captain, Charles Crombie—when Crombie accidentally trod on his toes, and instead of cooing, Conant/Lucille swore loudly: "God damn you, get off my foot!" The auditorium erupted. "Lucille certainly made a corking good fiancé," raved the *Tripod*'s critic. "Can you imagine how shocked, mortified, astonished and overwhelmed the Observer was when he beheld his stern, implacable editor-in-chief parading around in skirts and petticoats."

Conant was immensely pleased with his performance, and wrote his sister Marjorie in Paris about his triumph. For someone who had never shone at anything outside of science, he had grown into an unlikely headliner, and he could not help wondering if his sister, who had been away almost three years, would even recognize him on her return. Her reply conveys her genuine pleasure in his success and also the extent to which the whole family was counting on him, not only to better himself but finally pull the Conant name to the front. "Congratulations my very dear boy," responded Marjorie. "I am so proud I can assure you. I feel now that it's no use trying for laurels for one's self when one has such a 'coming' brother. Rush in and win and cover us all with glory—and money. I really mean it—no fooling."

Further evidence of his metamorphosis could be found in the class yearbook. His senior portrait shows a poised young man, blond hair neatly parted to one side, gazing into the future with clear, confident eyes. As the editors noted with grudging admiration: "'Jim' has been with us from the sixth, but up to last year no one suspected him of owning more than his share of gray matter. When, last June, he walked off with 18 points in the 'prelims,' we sat up and took notice." A year later, when it was announced that he was graduating at the top of his class, and was the recipient of one of five Harvard Club scholarships awarded to outstanding students from Boston schools, no one was surprised. He had done splendidly—first in chemistry, second in Latin, and third in German and history—and would be one of twelve boys "headed to Cambridge" in the fall. "We certainly hope he will not blow up the laboratory at Harvard," the yearbook editors added. A late bloomer in a pack of smart, purposeful boys, he was still no one's pick as a future leader. Crombie, the class jokester, predicted at graduation that Conant was most likely to become a druggist, "serving, as a premium on all sales over three cents, a guaranteed chemically-pure prussic acid ferrocyanide milkshake."

Ironically, after all the elaborate, drawn-out negotiations with Harvard's Chemistry Department, Black had been forced to write Richards that Conant would not be available to take the final exam in introductory chemistry, given to Harvard students on the morning of June 16. Unfortunately, the date coincided with Roxbury Latin's closing exercises, and as the "star boy" in his class, he was expected to take part. Noting apologetically that it was "a good deal to ask" that the date of the exam be changed at such short notice, Black nevertheless tried to have it rescheduled. This last request for special treatment was denied, and Conant ended up taking a makeup exam in Chem 1 the following autumn. He got an A.

Black was jubilant. Conant's exceptional results meant that he would enter Harvard with special advanced standing, almost halfway through the four-year-degree program. He could finish up his first degree quickly and plunge ahead with his training as a chemist. Conant's mother, however, was ambivalent about the plan. It worried her that Black's ambitions for his prodigy meant her son would not enjoy the full benefit of a liberal arts education. Jim's two opinionated older sisters, who were both studying painting, shared her "misgivings" about his premature specialization, and narrowing of perspective at such an early age. It was a lingering doubt about his cultivation that never ceased to amuse Conant. "The enjoyment with which I studied chemistry and only chemistry was regarded as a bad omen," he recalled. "Was I going to be nothing but a narrow-minded chemist?"

CHAPTER 3

A Harvard Man

There was nothing more undesirable back at Harvard than to be someone who "sucked up." You did not have to do it if you were the right sort of person.

—John P. Marquand, *H. M. Pulham, Esquire*

W hen Conant crossed the river from Dorchester to Cambridge in the autumn of 1910, he entered a daunting world of wealth and inherited privilege. Harvard, founded in 1636, was a miniature version of an English university, a highly stratified kingdom of rich men's sons, where all the "Grottlesexers"—graduates of Groton, St. Mark's, St. Paul's, St. George's, Middlesex, and the other elite Episcopal Church schools—were admitted without question, private and public school boys knew exactly who was who, and everyone knew his place. In its formative years, the college was as academically inbred as Boston society was biologically, and while it stopped ranking incoming students according to their family pedigree in 1759, a half century later, Harvard president John Kirkland still found it helpful to keep a list of his students "other than alphabetically."

Although they paid lip service to the ideals of democracy, equality, and freedom of choice, Harvard's leaders were always conscious of their obligation to uphold the college's social tone. It was the "heart's desire" of fussy old Josiah Quincy III (president from 1829 to 1845), his son wrote, to make the college "a nursery of high-minded, high-principled, well-taught, well-conducted, well-bred gentlemen." Even Charles W. Eliot (1869–1909), a man with unshakeable faith in science and progress, who did his best during his forty-year reign to transform Harvard from a provincial New England college into a national institution, acknowledged that the school owed much of its distinctive character to the "aristocracy to which the sons of Harvard belonged," those who brought "from refined homes good breeding, gentle tastes, and a manly delicacy." By the time A. Lawrence Lowell took over in 1909, Harvard was so notorious for its snobbishness that he made it clear in his inaugural address that he was going to make some drastic changes, beginning with restoring the "solidarity . . . earnestness of purpose and intellectual enthusiasm" that ought to lie at the basis of university life.

With brutal clarity, a scholarship boy came to realize his first days on campus that Harvard did not make even the slightest pretense to the "collegiate way of living" its Puritan founders had envisioned. One look at the baronial magnificence of Beck Hall was all it took. Built in 1876 by a wealthy law student unhappy with the available lodging in Harvard Yard, the Italian renaissance building was legendary for its lavish furnishings and décor, where upper-crust undergraduate tenants such as Theodore Roosevelt, J. P. Morgan, and John Jacob Astor IV lived in private apartments, attended by butlers and maids. As Samuel Eliot Morison noted in his 1936 book *Three Centuries of Harvard*, "King's 'Guide to Cambridge' grows lyrical over the high ceilings, ash trim, handsome chandeliers, steam-heating apparatus, and marble mantels of Beck," adding that the less fortunate were consigned to the Yard, or to "sundry run-down dwellings and three-deckers in the neighborhood, which were remodeled and let-out at land-office prices."

Acting with "mistaken laissez-faire," Charles Eliot had happily allowed the college's enrollment to expand—the student body soared from fewer than six hundred in 1869 to nearly two thousand by 1909—along with the country's new prosperity, and private capital to address the housing shortage. By Conant's day, the stretch of Mount Auburn Street that was home to the biggest and most expensive of the new private residences, some of which boasted their own swimming pools and squash courts, was known as the "Gold Coast." As George Santayana, the philosopher and essayist, who was both a student and a professor in his three decades as a member of the university, observed, "Divisions of wealth and breeding are not made conspicuous at Yale as at Harvard by the neighborhood of a city with well-marked social sets, the most fashionable of which sends all its boys to the College."

The writer John Reed, who graduated just before Conant arrived, described a college devoid of any sense of community or cohesiveness, in which "the aristocrats controlled the places of pride and power," filled the clubs and societies, and "dominated" the campus. Reed, a moderately well-off doctor's son from Portland, Oregon, had not realized that achieving admission to the highly selective institution in no way guaranteed him acceptance into its superior realms. The college was so stratified, he wrote, it was almost as if those "splendid youths" went to a different Harvard altogether. "They were so exclusive that most of the real life went on outside their ranks—and all the intellectual life of the student body."

Conant's own address at 5 Linden Street, within steps of the Yard, reflected both his lack of means and lowly status. In need of cheap accommodations, he had to make do with a shabby boardinghouse, gray and forlorn, known as Mrs. Mooney's for the aged proprietress who had run the place for more than a quarter century. Students, who paid $100 a year for bare rooms with coal-grate fires and oil lamps, dubbed the establishment "Mrs. Mooney's Pleasure Palace" for its laughable absence of amenities. For those who could pony up an extra $50, she provided hot water and janitor service. If you wanted a bath, an expedition to the Hemenway Gymnasium was recommended. Conant, who was used to roughing it on the family farm, took the Spartan digs in stride, though he was grateful when the building was wired for electricity that first winter. His $200 scholarship paid his tuition fees and covered the cost of his room, if not his board. His father supplemented this with an allowance for books, meals, club fees, clothes, and other expenses, so while not residing in the lap of luxury he was comfortable, and saved from the burden of working his way through school.

Still, the cleavage between the haves and the have-nots was such that Conant could not ignore the social chasm. Only at Harvard could a boy raised in what Boston historian Douglass Shand-Tucci called the "easeful world" of Ashmont be made to feel underprivileged. In a detailed monograph of the college, Harvard dean John Fox faults Conant for what he considers his contrived myth of disadvantage, his "pose as that of an outsider, as someone who had to battle his way to the top from a starting place that was modest, even humble." Yet it is clear that being ushered into adulthood in such an unabashedly patrician city and college, Conant read his experience as that of an uncouth scholarship boy rising up from a common background. He had earned his place at Harvard on merit, not claimed it as a birthright. He took pride in his ability to cope with the challenges of the demanding, at times disorienting, new world his talent had opened up for him. But the inequity between the aristocrats, heedless young men from proper families who only occasionally deigned to open a book, and the scholars, students of proven ability intent on graduate school, rankled. His first encounter with the college's skewed social slide rule was a rude awakening and roused his social conscience. Those early disillusionments, deliberate slights and snubs at Harvard, and the resentments he later harbored, would inform every aspect of his life and career, not only his drive to succeed, but his intense desire to make the education system, and above all American society, more truly democratic.

While later in life Conant suppressed the impulse to write about his undergraduate ordeal, his housemate John P. Marquand was eloquent on the subject. His many short stories and books, including his Pulitzer Prize–winning novel-cum-memoir, *The Late George Apley*, are steeped in the social agony of his college days. For Marquand, a public school boy who won a scholarship to Harvard, and moved into the room above Conant's in the fall of 1911, the gulf between the Yard and the "Gold Coast" was humiliating. The poor relation of a well-off family, Marquand was acutely sensitive to the way class differences colored everything at the college. Freshmen entered in obscurity, and those who lived outside the genteel pale were doomed to remain there. A young man with social ambition needed to be on the "Gold Coast"; without that entrée, he did not have a ghost of a chance of being accepted into Boston society, invited to the best soirees, or asked to join the top clubs.

Harvard's governors and faculty turned a blind eye to the college's increasing social problems, which further diversity in the form of the pioneer representatives of Boston's Irish Catholic, Italian, and Jewish populations only exacerbated. "In vain are freshmen tossed onto the same heap," acknowledged Morison. "Freshmen fellowship, brisk enough in the opening days of College and the first elections of committees, blows away in a whiff of invitations to dances and week-end house parties."

Left out in the cold, Marquand felt ostracized. He was a nobody—"a greaseball," like Jeffrey Wilson, the principal character of his 1943 novel *So Little Time*:

He was part of that grim and underprivileged group that appeared in the Yard each morning with small leather bags containing books and papers. He was one of the boys who wore celluloid collars which you could wash off in your room, and who used the reading room in the Library as a resting place because there was no other place to go, and who ate a sandwich there for lunch, and to whom no one spoke unless it was absolutely necessary.

Unlike Marquand, Conant did not endure a miserable freshman year. He was fortunate in his roommate, Charlie Crombie—the most popular boy in his class at Roxbury Latin—who from the moment he arrived on campus seemed to belong. Big, easygoing, and a gifted athlete, Crombie promptly made freshman crew, one of the surest routes to acceptability. It also helped that Conant entered college with a cluster of close friends from school, and was later joined by Ken Murdock and Roger Twitchell, members of his old Ashmont gang. They may not have mingled with the gilded youth of the Gold Coast or the swaggering Grottlesexers, but their tight circle was a shield against the isolation and anonymity of college life. Despite their limited pocket money, he and his housemates had plenty of fun at the Pleasure Palace.

Conant was the resident prankster. Invariably most of the gags and hijinks revolved around alcohol and Conant demonstrated an early expertise. There was the "morning-after party," only dimly remembered by Crombie, who awoke to find a rubber tube in his mouth and the other end in a nearby punch bowl—basic physics, courtesy of the house chemist. Conant also won accolades for once fielding a baseball while balanced on a beer barrel. But his real claim to fame was for inventing an elaborate drinking game, the Two-Beer Dash, which required them to leave their rooms at staggered intervals, travel by subway to the Holland Wine Company on Essex Street in downtown Boston, knock back two quick ones, and return to Mrs. Mooney's as rapidly as possible. The winner was the one who made the round-trip the fastest. The contest presented myriad challenges, not the least of which was getting served one's drink quotient given the age limit, and they would stay up late into the night arguing the pros and cons of different routes and strategies.

Always feisty and in good form, Conant had "a grand sense of humor," recalled Crombie, who joined the staff of the Harvard *Lampoon*, and enjoyed jousting with his roommate, who was "funnier than most of the fellows" on the humor magazine. He had such a deadpan delivery that his jokes did not always land right away, but when they did, they were lethal. "He would say things that made you laugh when you thought of them later."

Coming from Roxbury Latin, which welcomed a cross section of students, Conant was not prepared for the clannishness that pervaded Harvard. Almost all aspects of college life outside the lecture hall were determined along class lines, including eligibility for the ten so-called final clubs that were the center of Harvard's social existence. The club system was ruthlessly exclusive. The Porcellian and A.D., the top of the heap, recruited their members according to ancestry and affluence, drawing from generations of Cabots, Lowells, Adamses, Saltonstalls, and Lodges. The Hasty Pudding, which had the finest clubhouse though was not technically a club, and whose spring theatrical was one of the most popular social events of the season, had its own fearsome vetting process.

There is no question Conant would have liked very much to be tapped for the Pudding, but it was not to be, and he was far too stoic to indulge in any self-pity in the pages of his diary. It was accepted fact that the number of Harvard students who were "club material" was always 25 percent to 50 percent greater than there were places for them, so the clubs reigned as the ultimate "sophomore sifters." Upper-class spotters kept a watchful eye on aspiring freshmen, who were expected to strictly observe all of the social taboos, which included either too shabby or too fastidious dress, undue athletic exertion, serious literary endeavor, and grades above a C. Of the most presentable models of prep school aristocracy, only a small fraction would then be chosen for one of the "waiting clubs," a steppingstone to the final clubs. Marquand, who was never accepted by a single club, joined the staff of the Lampoon instead and later took vengeful pleasure in satirizing his classmates. Conant fared better. "He was brilliant without being grubby," recalled Marquand, who envied his "ability to learn everything without the slightest damage to his poise and popularity."

Much as he appreciated Marquand's droll humor, Conant did not have the same contempt for his peers, though he shared some of the same instincts as a social critic. He viewed the college's elitist club society as an antiquated caste system designed to prop up the sons of Boston's magistrates and merchant barons, irrespective of their intellect or ability. As much as he personally disliked any system based on unfair advantage, however, he was not prepared to turn his back on it. Conant was not a rebel. Nor was he, like Marquand, a "nose thumber at settled authority." He had too strong a sense of his own self-worth and even a stronger sense of his priorities. Moreover, as Harvard had only ten, he saw the clubs as an important proving ground. Conant cared about being club caliber—making the grade mattered to him. He did not want to end up a "runt": someone who failed to make even the first rung of clubdom and missed out on the life that distinguished the true "Harvard man" from those who merely "went to Harvard."

His freshman diary reveals a self-conscious, self-directed young man bent on bettering himself. While hardly a country rube, he disliked being a gauche Dorchester boy, and worked to smooth his rough edges. At seventeen, he was five foot nine, lean and lanky, with a mass of sandy hair that hung carelessly across his forehead, alert blue eyes, and a wide, sensitive mouth. Though not conventionally handsome, there was an attractive gentleness in both his appearance and manner, and a sympathetic laugh that endeared him to his fellow students. He tried to fit the club mold: he kept his locks neatly trimmed above his collar, purchased his suits from the correct old-line Cambridge tailors, and even worked to lighten his "outer gravity" to an easy affability. An early diary entry includes the emphatic reminder "*Smile*, damn it, *smile!*"

Whenever he had applied himself in the past, he had succeeded, and he set about scaling Harvard's academic and social peaks with the same determination. He looked at the best attributes of his classmates and aimed for an agreeable conformity, but only so long as it did not impinge on his basic integrity. He made friends easily and found a way to get along with a diverse array of acquaintances, developing what a colleague described later as a talent for "handling" people and controversy well. When opinions diverged and testosterone flared, Conant tended to "demur and go his own way," demonstrating a cool rationality combined with an innate prudence. He never needed to raise his voice in argument or prove himself right and others wrong. It was a quiet confidence in his own judgment that was to become his most distinctive trait and earn him a reputation for arrogance, which he once lamented as the "fate of more than one shy person whose aloofness is attributed to pride."

Eager to get on, Conant plunged into the fray. He joined the Boylston Club, a group for students interested in the sciences. His cousin Philip Bryant, a junior, took him under his wing and urged extracurricular activities as a way to expand his outlook and associations beyond the confines of the Chemistry Department. At his suggestion, Conant decided to "go out" for the *Crimson*, the college paper, which wielded considerable influence and was itself a select group. Had it not been for the extra leeway afforded by his advanced standing, the "time-consuming operation" of competing for a spot on the *Crimson* would have been out of the question. Although he made a noble attempt to juggle his studies and story assignments, it eventually got to be too much. On April 7, 1911, Conant's diary entry reads: "FINIS! got fired from the *Crimson* with one other Freshman, last to go! Worked hard in the lab making up back work."

Once he was on firm footing in the laboratory, Conant felt free to widen his scope. He had learned the trick of doing "the minimum amount of work necessary" to get As and satisfy the conditions of his scholarship. He sampled courses in sociology, zoology, and French, but was underwhelmed by some of his professors. He complained that one lecturer wasted the first fifty minutes and got down to business only at the end, so he made it a point to "only be awake the last ten minutes of the hour." He was more impressed with an economics course taught by Frank Taussig, and one in history with the great Frederick Jackson Turner, whose Midwestern American values resonated with Conant's own egalitarian attitudes and firm belief in the Jeffersonian ideal of a classless society.

Conant was also intrigued by the introduction to philosophy he took with George Herbert Palmer. This was the Golden Age of the Harvard Philosophy Department, still basking in the glory of William James, whose great work *Pragmatism* had been published shortly before his death in the summer of 1910. Conant was inspired to seek out George Santayana, one of the most brilliant professors of his day, whose incisive mind, caustic wit, and compelling presence mesmerized students. He was struck by Santayana's doctrine that the function of reason is to dominate experience, and insistence that the goal of man's existence was the struggle for excellence. His ideas made a profound impression, and Conant would continue to be intrigued by metaphysical problems and returned to the subject again and again the rest of his life. But apart from these brief excursions into the humanities, the bulk of his classes were devoted to chemistry and its ally, physics. Conant managed to completely bypass the riches of an English Department that included George Lyman Kittredge, Charles Townsend Copeland, Bliss Perry, and Barrett Wendell, to say nothing of E. K. Rand in the classics and Irving Babbitt in French literature. Despite the expressed wishes of his mother and two sisters, an introductory course in the "Art and Culture of Italy" did not a Renaissance man make.

Having come so close to getting "punched" for the *Crimson*, Conant was not about to give up. He made a second run at the paper his sophomore year, and got so caught up with his deadlines that he "nearly wrecked a half-year of work." In mid-January 1912 he received word from the *Crimson* that he had made the cut, and recorded the hard-won victory in his diary in red ink: "Big Punch! AN EDITOR AT LAST." He enjoyed slaving for "*The Crime*," as it was known to students, and the following year was promoted to assistant managing editor. His success at the *Crimson* gave him entrée to other esoteric circles. He was tapped for Delta Upsilon, a fraternity populated by brainy scholarship boys, the otherwise unclubbable intelligentsia. While the DU carried no social prestige—it rated near the bottom in the club hierarchy and was regarded by Marquand as "beneath consideration"—it had the distinction of having more than its share of members in Phi Beta Kappa. While none of the stray young men who took refuge in the DU's gloomy rooms were typical Harvard clubmen, they were an impressive group of self-starters, including Joseph P. Kennedy, an outspoken Irish Catholic and Democrat, who would go on to become ambassador to England and father of a president; Robert Benchley, who earned fame as a *Vanity Fair* and *New Yorker* humorist and member of the Algonquin Round Table; and authors J. Gordon Gilkey, Robert Duncan, and Clarence Randall. They formed unlikely friendships, wrote and performed plays, and indulged in late-night bull sessions. "Not one of us was genuinely solvent," recalled Randall, "and most of us were on the Harvard dole."

Conant was also invited to join the Signet, the well-established Harvard literary society. Limited to admitting only twenty-one handpicked juniors, the Signet, Conant confided in his memoir, made "all the effort worthwhile." It was there, in the society's handsome clubhouse, gathered around the lunch table with other able students and erudite faculty, that he received the "general education" his mother had wanted for him. Those discussions, which seemed so wonderfully "sophisticated" at the time, did more to broaden his horizons than any of his formal courses in the humanities. He developed a taste for worldly friends and worldly interests, and discovered there were fascinating things going on in the world outside the laboratory. They talked about existentialism, pluralism, ethics, metaphysics, and the meaning of life, and argued campus politics and the issues of the day. Their lively give-and-take was as natural to him as the dinner table debates at Ashmont, and he knew he had finally found his own kind and an intellectual home.

Looking back, Conant always maintained that the most important part of his liberal education occurred outside the classroom. The atmosphere on campus was full of ferment, with students whose idealism—and in some cases, burgeoning Socialism—made them eager to remake the world, starting with the university itself. When the *Crimson*'s editorial board decided to champion President Lowell's new House Plan to end the "class segregation" created by the gulf between the Yard and the "Gold Coast"—declaring in a January 12, 1912, editorial that the distinction had done "more than anything else to harm Harvard in the eyes of the outside world"—Conant felt they had struck a victory in the name of social justice. And when the paper took aim at the most self-centered defenders of gentility and homogeneity, he took a certain satisfaction in seeing the snobs shot down.

Lowell stopped short of moving against the final clubs, stating that he had no intention of wrecking his presidency "like [Woodrow] Wilson did down at Princeton." But change was coming to Harvard's campus. New clubs were springing up that were devoted to more than just drinking beer. There was the Speakers' Club, which gave the future statesman Adolf A. Berle Jr. his first political forum; the Diplomatic Club and its offshoot, the International Polity Club, to discuss international affairs; the Cosmopolitan Club, to bring together students of different nationalities and races; and the Socialist Club, organized by Walter Lippmann and a handful of associates, which invited prominent radicals to Cambridge to lecture. There was even a Harvard Men's League for Women's Suffrage, and Conant, whose mother was a supporter of women's right to vote, marched in a parade in Boston.

For the most part, however, he remained detached from the political and social movements of that progressive decade. The upwardly mobile son of a self-made businessman, Conant had no argument with capitalism. And as an aspiring chemist, he had no desire to rail against the growth of industrialism that was already profiting his profession. While he had little truck with the student agitators, he read their publications, and he would be sufficiently interested in the *New Republic*, a political journal Lippmann helped launch in 1914, to volunteer to sell subscriptions for the fledgling magazine. All the fervor had a liberating influence. Even Conant could not resist what John Reed called "the modern spirit" sweeping the campus, and he took advantage of the new sense of freedom to test his wings and experiment intellectually—to open his mind to new ideas, embrace skepticism, and reject dogma.

Conant had less time for these activities than he might have liked because he was still focused on early graduation. Before he had registered for his first class at Harvard, Black had mapped out his "whole collegiate future," a detailed plan of study in which he would complete the requisite sixteen credits in three years. College may have exposed him to new ideas, interests, and professors, but his high school mentor was still very much a part of his life and a guiding influence. All the more so since Conant now saw his parents only on fleeting visits. His father had retired from business the same year he entered college, selling his business to the Suffolk Engraving Company, and trading the old Ashmont house for a cottage in the fashionable seaside town of Duxbury. While they kept a toehold in Boston—a townhouse on Newbury Street—it was chiefly for the benefit of his older sisters. Conant's diary makes almost no reference to his parents—nothing in the way of fatherly advice or instructions—but the pages are peppered with the initials N.H.B. They often met for dinner and long talks, or mucked about in the laboratory, "fixing up the oscillograp," their relationship evolving into that of friends and, already in his teacher's mind, future partners.

Black had drawn up his blueprint for Conant's undergraduate training based on Harvard's "free-elective system" that President Eliot had implemented in 1886 in the firm belief that students should have the liberty to pursue their own interests rather than be forced to take groups of required courses. "Groups are like ready-made clothing, cut in regular sizes; they never fit any concrete individual," Eliot had argued with the rarefied logic of a gentleman reformer. "Spontaneous diversity of choice" would allow every man to custom tailor his own curriculum. Of course, there was a method to his madness, and the elective system gave Eliot the cover he needed to introduce a whole array of new courses on science, modern foreign languages, and history, hire new faculty, and vastly increase the intellectual resources of the university. Unfortunately, as with all liberties, abuses were inevitable. "C is the gentleman's grade" became a slogan of the Eliot era, with the most boorish athletes and party boys—exemplified by Rodney "Bo-Jo" Brown in Marquand's *H. M. Pulham, Esq.*—exploiting the system by taking only elementary courses. On the other end of the spectrum were ambitious students like Conant, who instead of availing themselves of four years of enlightenment sought to shorten its duration, speeding along a narrow track with the aim of obtaining a professional degree as quickly as possible.

Lowell was determined to raise the bar. "The college," he declared, "ought to produce, not defective specialists, but men intellectually well rounded, of wide sympathies and unfettered judgment." The faculty had already seen the writing on the wall, and by the end of Lowell's first year the elective system was replaced by a plan of "concentration and distributions." Under Lowell's framework, six of the sixteen courses had to be "concentrated" in one field, and another half dozen had to be "distributed" elsewhere among three general groups of courses. The class of 1914 was the first that had to conform to Lowell's requirements, but despite pressure from his dean, Conant held to Black's focused "three-year plan."

Conant's preparation as a chemist, however, did not quite proceed as planned. Black had intended him to train under Richards, who had been Conant's early champion, and become a physical chemist. A professor since 1889, and chair of the department since 1903, Richards was one of Harvard's brightest lights. While still in his twenties, he had earned worldwide renown for his precise determinations of atomic weights, and was sought after by universities. An offer from Germany 's University of Göttingen in 1901 established his reputation, and secured his position at Harvard, where he agreed to remain in exchange for a reduced teaching load. Regarded as an American experimentalist of genius, the forty-three-year-old Richards was at the pinnacle of his career, and still pressing to extend his influence on the developing framework of physical chemistry. Wealthy admirers raised funds to endow a great new facility dedicated to furthering his work, and the Wolcott Gibbs Memorial Laboratory was planned and constructed.

Conant found Richards, with his love for research, and passion for the "grand strategy" of advancing science, awe inspiring, and felt privileged to be able to do his PhD under his direction. Richards believed atomic weights were one of the "primal mysteries of the universe." He was convinced that every one of his research undertakings into atomic weights had fundamental theoretical significance, and exhorted his students to devote themselves to making a lasting contribution. "Unless one aimed at a degree of fame which placed an investigator in the same class as [Michael] Faraday," Conant recalled Richards repeatedly telling them, "one would have set one's sights too low."

Although Richards was a fine lecturer, his character and interests were remote from the contemporary scene. As time passed, Conant could not help finding the genteel, high-minded chemist, with his trim mustache and pince-nez, a trifle old school. At the Sunday afternoon teas Richards hosted for small groups of students at his home on 15 Follen Street, he exalted the German intellectual tradition and made it clear he expected his family— and by extension, his pupils—to be similarly "dedicated to things of the mind and the spirit." For him, the embrace of literature, art, and music was essential to a virtuous life.

His view of scientific inquiry had the same elevated, immaterial quality. As a young man, Richards had studied with Walther Nernst in Göttingen and Wilhelm Ostwald in Leipzig, and was committed to "pure" research, far removed from human affairs. This, too, was part of the "German tradition." While he never criticized those who accepted outside consulting jobs, he left no one in doubt that such prosaic distractions, not to mention working for a paycheck, lowered them in his eyes. His polite reserve brooked no argument. Richards "abhorred disagreement," and his students soon came to realize that he could not stomach even the mildest form of debate.

While there was much to learn from the stringent investigator, Conant found his attitude disappointing, particularly as the chemistry profession was in the midst of profound change. In an era of growing industrial prosperity, big companies were beginning to fund experiments to improve the state of knowledge in emerging fields, opening up new and exciting opportunities for research. Willis Whitney, the founder of General Electric's industrial research facility, had recently given a stimulating lecture at Harvard on the importance of developing commercial applications for new principles, arguing that while GE's trained scientists were trying to perfect the incandescent lightbulb, they were doing original work in chemistry and physics. Already Massachusetts Institute of Technology (MIT) was responding to the changing environment and making great strides in applying the principles of physical chemistry to industrial processes. But Richards would not hear of it. "To him, the advancement of the science of chemistry was an all-absorbing occupation," Conant concluded. "He had no time to give to problems in the area of applied science, which was beginning to assume importance in the first decade of this century."

At the beginning of Conant's third year, another professor turned his head. Elmer P. Kohler arrived at Harvard to teach freshman chemistry, along with a more advanced course in his own field, organic chemistry. At forty-seven, Kohler, who had spent two decades at Bryn Mawr College, was known to be a teacher of great gusto and rigor, with an enthusiasm for his subject that he instilled in his students. Conant was immediately attracted to his straightforward manner and zest for experimentation. Although his résumé did not boast a long list of awards and publications, he had few equals in the laboratory and quickly won Conant's admiration and loyalty. "Only those who have seen him in his shirt sleeves, crystallizing and recrystallizing his precious materials on his own workbench, have known the man," he wrote in defense of the newcomer.

When he first arrived, Kohler had few graduate students of his own, and was not only warmly receptive to the eager young chemistry student who approached him about doing an independent research project, but gave generously of his time and attention. With his help, Conant began working with carbon compounds, and in a few months succeeded in preparing a new organic compound. He was enormously impressed with the results of the experimental undertaking, and even more impressed with his supervisor, in whose skilled hands many complicated mixtures could be separated into pure substances. Kohler was interested in the mechanism of organic reactions, and presented the problems to his students as "a series of scientific adventures" so that it was impossible not to want to tag along. Here was the joy of investigation that had originally drawn Conant to chemistry. Although his entire academic trajectory had been tied to Richards since his days at Roxbury Latin, Conant suddenly began to have doubts. He was no longer sure he "wanted to be a physical chemist after all."

Richards and Kohler could not have been more different, both as scientists and men. If Richards was a "strategist" who sought information that would affect basic theory in a significant way, Kohler was a "tactician" who focused on specific problems and their solutions, and rarely took the time to stand back and consider if they were worth solving. The contrast between the two men's personalities was just as marked. Where Richards saw himself as part of an international fraternity of learned scientists, Kohler was a loner who had few friends among his colleagues. While Richards gave celebrated lectures and published with an eye to ensuring his place on the permanent roll of outstanding contributors, Kohler was indifferent to fame, and almost pathologically afraid of public speaking. But Conant, who sympathized with Kohler's shyness, liked his "solidity" and "commonsense judgments on human problems." He and Kohler also shared a love of mountain climbing, and Conant compared him to the "Swiss guide" who tries to inculcate in novices that "mastery of technique" essential before tackling the ice or rock alone. In terms of who he thought would be a better advisor, both personally and professionally, while he was still learning the ropes as a young chemist, there was no contest.

So when Kohler asked if he was interested in being his lab assistant in the fall of 1912, Conant accepted his offer and became his eager young apprentice. In doing so, he was not simply switching mentors, he was altering the direction of his career. "What was intended as an exploration of a neighboring field," he recalled with wonder, "turned out to be an introduction to my lifework as a chemist."

At the end of his third year, Conant earned his bachelor of arts degree, making magna cum laude despite the accelerated pace. He was also awarded an honorary John Harvard Scholarship for academic distinction, as well as an Austin Teaching Fellowship to assist in Chemistry 5, which carried a salary of $500. The teaching stipend gave him his independence. He would no longer have to ask his father to help support him. He immediately enrolled in the Graduate School of Arts and Sciences, and set to work on his PhD in summer school. Crombie, who that fall moved with him into Thayer Hall, one of the senior dormitories in the Yard, marveled at his roommate's boundless energy and powers of concentration. Conant never seemed unduly burdened by his studies. He never burned the midnight oil. No matter how hard he crammed, he could always be convinced to put aside his books and nip out for a quick game of tennis. Even during midyear exams, they would study until nine and then go "knock the puck around" on the frozen river. "I had to work like the devil to get my degree," Crombie said later. "Whereas Jim took everything in stride and swung without a single panting breath into the first ten of the Phi Beta Kappa."

College and chemistry were evidently not all consuming because Conant also found time to fall in love. The previous autumn had brought the arrival of his old chums Kenneth Murdock and Roger Twitchell, and though he was now an upperclassman, they were soon inseparable. The trio formed the habit of going back to Dorchester for Sunday night suppers at the Twitchells', which brought Conant in regular contact with Roger's lovely older sister, Helen. They had known each other all their lives, and now struck up an easy, flirtatious relationship. Soon she was regularly accompanying the boys to weekend skating outings on the Charles River, concerts and shows in Boston, and Saturday night dances at Brattle Hall. Conant was smitten. His diary for the winter of 1913 is full of praise for Helen. "She is an angel," he swooned, head over heels, on February 8. The following week, she was his date for the big junior dance at the Union. Cocky and self-satisfied, he carelessly dismissed a rumor that he was engaged to a girl named Alice: "Ha! Ha!" he scribbled in a margin, "Oh Lord!" By spring, he was madly in love, courting during long, ardent walks in the park, and torturing himself with jealous thoughts. "Made a fool of myself by getting sore," he confessed at the end of a tempestuous afternoon on May 18. "She kindly forgave me. All's well."

At the end of term, awash in honors and assured of his prowess in his chosen field, Conant proposed. He was full of plans and promises. He took Helen to Duxbury for the weekend to see his sisters and test the waters. An entry on May 25 reads: "She decided to tell her parents. More nervous suspense." It did not go well. Dr. Twitchell, the loyal family practitioner who had helped usher him into the world twenty years earlier, did not give the couple his blessing. Conant was too young to be thinking of marriage. He had years of study ahead and no money. It would be a mistake. Both families counseled them to wait. The diary was abruptly abandoned. He left no record of his disappointment, yet the empty pages speak to the magnitude of the defeat. It was the first time in his life he had set his sights on a goal and not achieved it. He had no doubt that he would amount to something—and something "big"—but he only had his brilliance as a guarantee. The experience only made him more ambitious, and impatient for the opportunity to prove his worth.

CHAPTER 4

No-Man's-Land

Men who would otherwise be eminent in science, in litera-
ture, and in art, are now having their young lives torn out
of them by shells, and it is for the youth of America to take
their place. You are recruited and now in training.

—President A. Lawrence Lowell

When war erupted in Europe during those last, hot days of August 1914, Conant was too entrenched in the laboratory to take much notice. To him, like most Harvard students, the battle lines that had been drawn so rapidly that summer seemed far away, and of less relevance to his daily life than the startling announcement of a major overhaul of the club system. While he stayed abreast of the latest developments, scanning newspaper headlines and taking in the occasional radio dispatch and newsreel, he had little time for foreign affairs. Nothing disturbed the peace of his scientific sanctum. The sound of the Red Cross drive in the Yard, whose volunteers were raising funds for their work in France, barely penetrated the granite bulk of Boylston Hall.

It never occurred to him that Europe's quarrels could in any way touch him or disrupt his carefully laid plans. A confirmed pacifist, he was raised with an aversion to war by his mother, who had instilled in him the Quaker belief that there were better ways to settle disputes between peoples and countries. He favored peace, following the theory that the best way to maintain it was to stay out of the fight. He was not prepared for the fact that when war came, it would obliterate the serene and tolerant world he had always taken for granted. "[It] came with all the blackness and suddenness of a tropical storm," he wrote. "In June there was one climate of opinion, and by September there was another; and with each succeeding month the atmosphere became more electric; the storms more frequent and more violent."

Conant's political awakening coincided with the start of the fall term, and what a *Crimson* editorial described as an outbreak of "pyrotechnic patriotism" on campus. Officially, Harvard pledged to support President Woodrow Wilson's policy of "complete neutrality" for the United States, a position favored by the majority of Americans. To Conant's "amazement," however, his professors all immediately took sides. They did not even try to conceal their sympathy with Britain and France. The brutal invasion of neutral Belgium, and the destruction of the University of Louvain, one of the most renowned in Europe, turned the intellectual community solidly against Germany. The burning of over 250,000 rare books in the ancient library was a crime against civilization.

Many teachers who had admired Germany's strength and intellectual ability were shocked by its ruthlessness, and translated their anger into the worst kind of zealotry, so they were "not only pro-Ally," he recalled, "but violently anti-German." Members of the faculty who had been "bosom friends" became sworn enemies. Even his chemistry mentor, Theodore Richards, who had always spoken highly of his colleagues at Göttingen— that mecca of true science—and extolled their exemplary Kultur, became rabidly partisan. He now "despised all things German" and openly snubbed the few teachers who dared to express solidarity with their native country. The jingoism of his elders offended Conant's moral scruples. "Such reversal of sentiment," he noted scornfully, "brought to the surface all my New England contrariness."

Compared with the faculty, the student body seemed almost a model of impartiality. In an October 13 editorial, the *Crimson* urged members of the university to use nothing but the most extreme caution in "expression of personal opinion in the present crisis," reminding them that it was the college's duty to be impartial and "do nothing in word or speech that shall arouse fruitless passion or personal antagonisms." In the opening stages of the conflict, there was no question of American involvement, and Conant and his friends engaged in lively forums and debates about the European struggle and where their loyalties should lie. By endorsing Britain's blockade of German ports, its confiscation of cargoes headed for the Central powers, and mining of the North Sea to obstruct neutral trade, it seemed to many of them that the faculty was trying to pretend its Allies, aggressive colonial and imperial powers, were entirely blameless. Many of his peers were "highly critical" of the prejudicial remarks of their teachers. "The professors were losing their minds," John Dos Passos, class of 1916, wrote of the ugly mood on campus. "Hating the Huns became a mania."

The more fanatical the faculty became, the more Conant reacted with skepticism. When he learned that a respected instructor of German studies had been "cut dead" in the street by a neighbor, and was later pestered to withdraw from the university, it aroused his indignation. Faced with such hatred and suspicion, he felt compelled to stick up for his convictions. "When I heard someone denounced for an attempt to justify the invasion of Belgium," he recalled, "I became a pro-German apologist." It was not that he was really pro-German, just that he despised the herd mentality induced by nationalism, and the insidious pressure to conform. Everyone acted like a "frenzied rooter at a football game," he recalled, and not to pick one side or another was to incur "a potent blast of criticism from every side."

The college did little to curb the anti-German hysteria, which was further inflamed by the sinking of the RMS *Lusitania* on May 7, 1915. Conant, shunning emotion, clearly saw how public opinion was being manipulated by both an excitable press and exploitive British and French propagandists determined to "swing the sympathy of the young as well as the old in Cambridge to the side of the Allies." But he was swimming against the current. The news that the sleek Cunard liner, en route from New York to Liverpool, had been torpedoed by a German submarine, and that among the 1,198 passengers and crew lost were 128 Americans—5 of them Harvard men— rocked the campus. All at once, the European conflict had become real to Harvard students, and very personal. Most Americans still had little enthusiasm for the war in Europe, but in Cambridge and the rest of the anglophile Eastern Seaboard, they were clamoring for retribution.

Although Conant managed to keep the growing crisis from interfering with his education, it had a profound effect on his ambitions and fortunes. In the spring of 1915, Harvard awarded him a traveling fellowship, and it was with deep regret that he turned it down. He had never been abroad. He had always dreamed of one day going to study in Berlin or Munich— "where the big scientists were"—but this was hardly an opportune moment.

"Nineteen-fifteen was the year it became clear that the great European war was not going to be a short war," he wrote later. "The Germans' plans for a rapid victory had been thwarted. The belligerents had settled down to the horrors of trench warfare, with no end in sight."

At the same time, the drawn-out conflict, and disruptions to international trade, were creating new opportunities for the young chemists of his generation at home. Germany, one of the leading manufacturers of dyes, drugs, and fine chemicals, could not be counted on to resume its exportations anytime in the foreseeable future. With European factories overextended, and the Allies already suffering severe shortages, American industry was stepping up to meet the need for these products, as well as for munitions, metals, oil, and other military goods. In order to produce more materials in a shorter time, new technologies were being developed and new production processes implemented. Suddenly companies of all kinds were knocking on the university's door, he recalled. "Organic chemists were in demand."

As a result of the war boom, that summer brought an unexpected offer of employment. Conant got a call asking if he was interested in working in the laboratories of the Midvale Steel Company in Philadelphia. A few years earlier, Midvale had hired a young Harvard chemistry instructor, George L. Kelley, to head up its research program. Kelley, who remembered Conant from class, offered him a job developing new analytical procedures. It was a chance to get a peek at one of the new industrial labs he had heard so much about, and make a little money in the bargain.

At Midvale, Conant studied the new electrochemical method used in steel production. The research led to his first three publications, authored jointly with Kelley, and covered techniques for the analysis of vanadium, chromium, and nickel content in steel. While the work was rewarding, he took more away from his time at the mill. The engineers did not exactly welcome the intrusion of the Harvard "doctors," and took a dim view of the newfangled ideas they tried to bring to the business of making steel. It was Conant's first practical job experience, and the tension he observed between the hands-on operating men and the research scientists gave him valuable insight into the challenges facing the young marriage of chemistry and industry. "What I learned about steelmaking I forgot in a few years," he recalled. "What I learned about the inner politics of a manufacturing plant stayed with me." At the end of the summer, Midvale offered him a permanent position. Conant wanted his doctorate. He returned to Harvard for his final year, but his view of the possibilities open to a young chemist had been "greatly enlarged."

When he first contemplated earning a PhD, Conant had every intention of pursuing his research with Richards in physical chemistry. But after Kohler's enthusiastic teaching style won him over to organic chemistry, Conant changed course and began his graduate work on fundamental cyclopropane chemistry. Torn between two mentors, he ultimately decided to present a double thesis, a politic solution that involved undertaking a separate research project with each professor. At heart, however, he was already a "committed organic chemist."

Conant's decision to steer a compromise course served him well. He was conducting research on electrochemistry with Richards in his new, almost luxurious laboratory when it was announced that November that the renowned Harvard investigator was to receive the greatest honor that could be bestowed on his profession, the Nobel Prize. It was the first for an American in his field, and recognized not only Richards's contribution to the periodic table—the exact determination of the atomic weights of some thirty elements—but also the new era of analytical accuracy he had inaugurated. Conant, who attended the swirl of celebratory parties at Harvard, had hitched his wagon to the most famous scientist in the country. Given his hatred of the German aggressors, and the all too real dangers of crossing the Atlantic, Richards chose to postpone the trip to Sweden to collect his prize.

Conant, whose admiration of German achievements in chemistry made him more sympathetic to the kaiser's cause, watched with dismay as Harvard's campus became more war conscious with each passing day. More than eighty undergraduates had spent the summer at the Plattsburgh military training camps in New York learning maneuvers, and now marched about the yard in uniform. Drums resounded in the formerly quiet streets. Some of the more gung-ho decided to defy Wilson's warning that the federal penal code barred US citizens from serving as belligerents, and were enlisting in the British and Canadian Expeditionary Forces, the Foreign Legion, and the Lafayette Flying Squad.

In November the *Crimson* reversed its policy of isolation. The student council proposed voluntary military training for all members of the university, and soon afterward General Leonard Wood, a leader of the preparedness movement, announced that he favored the plan. He offered to have the US War Department supply all the rifles, bayonets, ammunition belts, and other equipment, and detail a special officer to drill the volunteers, provided that 400 students signed up within three days. The response was overwhelming, with 922 pledged by the second day. By January 1916, the new Harvard regiment was drilling in the Hemenway gymnasium and the baseball cage. President Lowell, who had been pro-Ally from the start, welcomed wounded French officers as military instructors.

At the same time the regiment was being organized, alumnus and ex-president Theodore Roosevelt, one of the country's strongest proponents of armament, wrote an editorial in the *Harvard Advocate* calling for the college to make military training—not merely drilling—part of the curriculum:

> Harvard ought to take the lead in every real movement for making our country stand as it should stand. Unfortunately prominent Harvard men sometimes take the lead the wrong way. This applies preeminently to all the Harvard men who have anything to do with the absurd and mischievous professional-pacifist or peace-at-any-price movements which have so thoroughly discredited this country during the past five years . . . The pacifist of this type stands on the exact level with the poltroon. His appropriate place is with the college sissy who disapproves of football or boxing because it is rough.

Conant disliked the bullying rhetoric, which was clearly designed to push any waverers into line. Roosevelt had been a boyhood hero, but in the months leading up to the 1916 presidential election Conant's attitude toward him soured. His conversion to Wilson and the Democrats had less to do with their war policy than his feelings that the president's critics had gone too far, and that in their zeal to get elected, Republican politicians such as Theodore Roosevelt and Supreme Court justice Charles Evans Hughes, who surrendered his seat in order to run for office, were "showing more emotion than reason." As a "dissenting youth," Conant noted, "I adhered to the other camp." Of course, it did not hurt that Wilson's platform of noninvolvement meant he could continue to pursue his doctorate without fear of delay. Conant remained focused on his work, and continued to question the logic of America entering the European war, even though his adamant neutrality made him, as one colleague put it, "less than popular in many circles."

As the end of his graduate studies approached, Conant was in a quandary about what to do. He was obsessed with the idea that his professional training would be incomplete without the obligatory postdoc year at a German university, and once again cursed his rotten timing. He briefly considered combining a term at the Swiss Federal Institute of Technology in Zurich, Switzerland, with a stint in the American Ambulance Field Service, but balked when he learned that drivers were required to commit to a full year. He was not prepared to spend that much time away from the laboratory. He took a rather jaundiced view of the patriotic impulse that inspired many of his friends and classmates to volunteer to drive ambulances at the front, among them Ken Murdock and Roger Twitchell. "Though, of course, the Ambulance Service was a noncombatant and in theory neutral, joining it was often regarded as an expression of a strong desire to help the Allied cause," he recalled, "while in fact, in some cases, it seemed far more a manifestation of a desire to come dangerously close to a dangerous adventure without running much risk of becoming a casualty oneself."

Meanwhile, two fellow chemistry majors and DU frat brothers, Stanley B. Pennock and Chauncey Loomis, both class of 1915, approached him about going into business together. Conant had spent a lot of time that winter in the lab with Pennock, a burly football player who was attending postgraduate courses and preparing to follow in the footsteps of his father, a senior executive with Solvay Process Company, the Belgian chemical giant. Their plan was to manufacture certain chemicals and drugs that had previously been imported from Germany, and were now in short supply and fetching fabulous prices. The "famine of all things chemical" since 1914 made the adventure attractive: "On paper, it was easy to calculate that vast profits were in store for those engaged in such an operation," Conant recalled. "Without building a large plant one could, in theory, prepare relatively simple organic chemicals in small batches and sell them without difficulty."

Scores of newly minted chemists were abandoning academe for lucrative jobs in industry. While the new venture with his pals Pennock and Loomis was highly speculative, and both Black and Richards protested he was being diverted from his true calling, Conant had already made up his mind. He promised he would only stay in business until the fighting was over. This was a chance to do something useful. And when he eventually took up a teaching position, he would be that much better off, with a "comfortable bankroll" to supplement what he knew would be a "meager salary." At Harvard's normal snaillike pace of promotion, he would be lucky to earn $4,000 a year by the time he was forty; as a young instructor, he could expect a little more than a quarter of that sum. And Helen Twitchell was still very much on his mind.

His failed courtship had compelled him to face facts. While it was not a requirement that Harvard professors come from money, it was a well-established tradition, and many great academic careers—Richards's included—had been underwritten by family trusts, which rendered their slight wages incidental. Despite his mentors' disapproval, making a brief sojourn into business seemed to him not only pragmatic, it was "a form of pioneering which appealed to both the scientific and acquisitive instinct."

The three Harvard friends set to work in April 1916. They quickly raised the necessary capital to form L.P.C. Laboratories, with Pennock's father as their primary backer, and rented and equipped a one-story building in the Queens borough of New York. By early summer, the plant was up and running. After weeks of experimentation, they managed to develop a new process for making benzoic acid, a popular food preservative and antiseptic manufactured principally in Germany. As soon as they had perfected their formula, a procedure requiring the "cautious chlorination" of toluene, Conant, LPC's twenty-three-year-old director of research, filed for a patent. The company's commercial success seemed assured.

That August, in the early hours of the morning, while he and Loomis struggled to transfer the laboratory-scale procedure to a large-scale plant operation, they accidentally set fire to the building. In no time, the small structure was completely consumed. Although the sight of the building's blackened shell should have discouraged them from carrying on, it did not, nor did their lack of experience with what were very complicated and potentially hazardous chemical processes. They were young and in a hurry, and thought only of their good luck—only days earlier, Pennock had signed an insurance policy for the plant. Within weeks, they were back in business, setting up shop in an abandoned slaughterhouse in the Jersey flats near Newark.

Just as they were preparing to move into their new facility, Conant received a "startling letter" from Harvard offering him a one-year appointment as instructor in organic chemistry. The unexpected vacancy had come about when a young lecturer, Roger Adams, accepted the offer of a professorship at the University of Illinois. The position needed to be filled before the start of the fall term. Harvard wanted an answer at once. Conant could not turn it down: "By what seemed to me a miracle," he recalled, "I had gotten my foot on the bottom rung of the Harvard academic ladder." He begged his partners' forbearance, but opportunities such as this did not come around often and were not refused. The three quickly came to a new business arrangement, awarding Conant an interest in the fledgling company, to be renamed Aromatic Chemical, and he returned to Cambridge.

On Monday, November 27, 1916, Conant was pulled out of an afternoon lecture in Boylston Hall and informed that the Newark plant had burned to the ground. A far more terrible fire than the one at the Queens factory had been triggered as a large tank of benzoic acid was being prepared. The first powerful explosion ripped through the building, killing Stan Pennock instantly. Two other workers—a mechanic, Samuel Welte, and a plumber, Max Stein, who was repairing a pipeline—succumbed to the fumes. Flames and black smoke had shot from the roof, followed by a series of smaller explosions, which shook buildings for blocks around and kept firemen at bay more than an hour. Loomis, who had been in the mixing room when he spotted the first sign of trouble, had desperately tried to stop the reaction. As the air began to vaporize, he quickly shut down the machinery and raced up a ladder to the top of a 110-gallon vat to close the main supply valve when the first blast occurred, hurling him out through the door and into a ditch. His face and eyes scorched by acid, and his clothes ablaze, he managed to save himself by rolling in water. If he had only reached the valve in time, he told reporters from his hospital bed, his eyes still streaming, "All would have been saved."

The tragedy shocked Conant. Pennock, an all-American guard on the Harvard football team for three years in a row, had been a star player and popular student. His sudden, senseless death made all the papers. In the small chemical fraternity, everyone knew Conant was the absent partner. The fact that he had not been there to help his friends see it through made him feel that much worse. The Newark plant had been in only its second week of operation. Loomis and Pennock had spent most of the intervening months fitting up the equipment and had tested the machinery only intermittently to turn out samples of the product. Less than two hours into its inaugural run, it blew. "Because I had not even seen the new plant," Conant castigated himself later, "and had not witnessed the trial run which ended so appallingly, I could not help feeling I had deserted a post of danger."

His subsequent conversations with Loomis, who discreetly held back

Conant's name from the press and from official inquiry into the accident, only deepened his sense of culpability. While the partners were cleared of any criminal negligence, despite the fact that it was an unlicensed factory, Conant felt he had failed to properly assess the risks. The chemical reaction Loomis described had occurred much too soon—and had quickly ignited an explosion. It was not something he had considered possible. "The account Loomis gave me of what had actually happened showed that the procedure had been formulated erroneously," Conant wrote in his own blunt, unsparing postmortem, "which was no one's fault but my own."

The surviving partners sold up and went their separate ways. The stockholders were paid off, thanks to the royalties from the patent based on Conant's work. With characteristic Yankee fortitude, Conant pushed all the guilt and sadness to the back of his mind and buried himself in work. He put on a brave front, but could not bear to speak of the accident that had claimed his friend's life. His reckless foray into free enterprise had left a "permanent mark" and put an abrupt end to his ambitions in industry.

After his disastrous experience with applied chemistry, Conant was grateful to be back in the classroom. He threw himself into teaching. Elementary organic chemistry could be heavy going, and he quickly discovered that holding the attention of a room full of undergraduates was not easy. In the beginning, his "greenness" was all too apparent. Not a lively speaker by nature, he was forced to find ways to improve his lecturing style. He consulted Kohler, who advised him it was not enough to talk in chalk; he needed to develop a sense of showmanship. Conant took his advice to heart. In one particularly dramatic demonstration, he pulled an egg from his pocket, dropped it into a solution he explained would solidify the albumen, quickly fished it out and heaved it at the wall just over his students' heads. There was a collective gasp as they registered that their young instructor was right—the egg bounced. Pleased with his efforts, as well as with the midyear examination marks, Conant was confident he would be reappointed. If everything went according to plan, he hoped to "move up in a year or two."

All that winter of 1916–17, as war fever swept the campus, Conant stubbornly clung to his skepticism about entering on the Allied side. He could not see what good would come from America joining the carnage that had been ravaging Europe for three years. He remained immune to the growing interventionist sentiment, despite the public outcry that had accompanied Germany's renewal of unrestricted submarine warfare and the revelation of the infamous Zimmermann telegram, a secret coded telegram that was sent in January 1917 by the German foreign minister Arthur Zimmermann to the German minister to Mexico offering United States territory to Mexico in return for joining the German cause. Conant's recalcitrance was rooted in his deep dislike of fanaticism, and fear of what joining the melee would do to the country. He was under no illusions about what taking up arms would mean—the consequences when people quit thinking, no longer valued debate and tolerance, but instead devoted all their energies to destruction. He dreaded being engulfed in the unreasonableness of it all. He had nothing but contempt for the faculty's eager embrace of the war: "The spectacle of older men urging younger ones to fight seemed to me far from edifying."

On a wet, raw spring night on April 2, 1917, he had just finished dining at the Harvard Club in Boston when he heard over the news ticker that the president had gone before a joint session of Congress at eight thirty that evening to declare war against Germany. "It is a fearful thing to lead this great peaceful people into war," Wilson told the assembly, which reportedly cheered him as it never had before. The press picked up on the most grandiose line of his battle cry: "The world must be made safe for democracy." As he read the president's words, Conant's spirits plummeted. "The chief reason for my distress was not that Wilson, having been reelected on a platform of noninvolvement, was now asking for complete involvement," he recalled. "It was because of the effect on my own personal plans." He had been anxious to "hang on" to his post at Harvard, but now he felt it slipping away. "Teaching was no place for a young man in wartime. It was going to be a period of painful choice."

CHAPTER 5

The Chemists' War

We were not soldiers, we were chemists dressed up as officers.

—JBC

As soon as Congress voted to declare war on Germany, the country began to mobilize. Almost overnight, Harvard's campus was transformed into a massive recruiting center. So many upperclassmen were leaving for active service or to attend officer training camps that the college moved to begin giving final exams early. By summer, more than half the student body had enlisted. Most of Conant's old crowd from Miss Mooney's already had their marching orders. Charlie Crombie immediately joined the Michigan Naval Militia and was called up on April 6.

"My friends were going to be involved directly in the war," he recalled. "To stand aside was out of the question."

Realizing that war was inevitable, Conant had written George Kelley at Midvale a week before the president's address for advice as to whether he should enlist in the army or navy: "There seems to be a strong opinion among those who should know best that the trained chemists will be more useful in connection with industrial military work than by fighting themselves," he explained. "There is, consequently, both in my mind and in the minds of several of my friends, a great deal of uncertainty as regards what course we had best pursue."

After much agonizing, Conant finally concluded he could not carry on teaching and take his chances with the draft. "To wait until its long arm reached one would be ignominious." There was a job to be done, and once he decided he had to take part, he was anxious to settle the question of where he would be of greater service. "I was not going to stay at Harvard, of that I was certain."

When he informed his parents that he was considering becoming a combat officer, they were horrified. It was his old friend and mentor N. Henry Black who made him reconsider his options. He did not want his protégé ending up as cannon fodder. "When the United States entered the war, Jim wanted to join and shoulder a gun," recalled Black. "I told him: 'That's all right for some, but not for you.'" Black sent him to talk to people in government laboratories in Wilmington, Delaware, and Washington, DC. Ironically, Conant's brief stint in industry now proved advantageous. The pace of wartime research differed markedly from that of academe, and experienced men were needed to lead projects where a high priority was placed on speed, hurried testing, and development with minimum delay. In June, he was offered a job by the Bureau of Chemistry in Washington, and was soon back in an industrial lab trying to manufacture compounds that had previously been made only in Germany.

Sad as he was to quit Harvard, there were also personal reasons for Conant's reluctance to leave town. At a dance that spring, he had fallen for Grace "Patty" Richards, the nineteen-year-old daughter of Harvard's Nobel laureate. "A beautiful vision in a crushed rose dress has made a permanent dent in my heart, I fear," he confessed in his first letter to her, dashed off at the end of the Fourth of July weekend just before he departed for Washington. Despite his romantic flight of fancy, it was hardly love at first sight. He had seen her at least a half dozen times since they met in 1916 at her father's house, sitting quietly in a corner at the Sunday teas to which favored young instructors were invited. She had been no more than a girl when they were introduced, but sometime in the past year she had blossomed into a tall, willowy young woman with high cheekbones, pale-blue eyes, and long, shining auburn hair. She was a painter, possessed of a precocious intelligence and teasing wit. She quoted Keats, Emerson, and Thoreau with ease, and he was charmed by her noble bookishness. Laughingly, she berated him for his lack of sophistication about art, and he vowed to remedy the situation before they saw each other again. "If I can find a copy of Clive Bell's *Art*, I am going to read it and discover the true inwardness of art and the artist," he promised, convinced that in her he had glimpsed his future happiness.

Conant spent the first part of the summer working for the Bureau of Chemistry, and succeeded in finding a more efficient, inexpensive way of producing a scarce drug. Frustrated that his endeavors were "only remotely related to the war," however, he finally made up his mind to join the army as a noncommissioned officer with an outfit being sent to France to train soldiers in the use and repair of gas masks. He was on his way to the enlistment office in Washington when by chance he bumped into James F. Norris, an eminent organic chemist he had known since his undergraduate days, on the street. When Norris heard that Conant was headed overseas, he said, "You're crazy! You could do more good for your country by staying here." Norris, who had been called to Washington to head up the new chemical warfare program, detained him on the busy sidewalk for the next hour and convinced Conant that his talents would be put to far better use producing new poison gases stateside. He did not let up until he had his way, in the end hiring the young Harvard chemist on the spot.

By the time America joined the fight, the Allied scientific effort to combat poison gas had taken the form of both defense and retaliation. The question of morality "rarely" came up, Conant recalled, but "since everything German was being condemned, no one was inclined to justify its first use." The Germans had introduced chlorine gas early in the conflict. On April 22, 1915, a special unit of the German army opened the valves on six thousand steel cylinders of pressurized liquid chlorine that had been secretly installed in the trenches along their defensive perimeter at Ypres, Belgium. Within ten minutes, a huge yellow cloud of chlorine gas rolled down over the opposing French lines, killing more than a thousand soldiers and wounding four thousand more. The "poison bombs," as they were called in newspaper accounts the following day, all but paralyzed the French division, the smoke and fumes causing terror and confusion, and forcing a panicked retreat. Those who did not collapse from choking and convulsions ran, but the gas oozed after them.

Dr. Harvey Cushing, in charge of Harvard Medical School's first surgical unit to serve in France, treated a trainload of victims and reported their terrifying stories in the *Alumni Bulletin* that spring:

The smoke was suffocating and smelled to one like ether or sulphur, to another like a sulphur match times one thousand—to still another like burning rosin. One man said there were about one thousand Zouaves of the Bataillon d'Afriques in the lines, and only sixty got back—either suffocated or shot as they clambered out of the trenches to escape . . . In any event, there's the devil's work going on around Ypres.

The Germans' surprise use of chlorine gas—in flagrant defiance of the Hague conventions of 1899 and 1907 which banned the use of "poison or poisonous weapons"—caught the Allies totally unprepared. General John French, commander in chief of the British forces in France and Belgium, immediately denounced the treacherous gas attack as a "cynical and barbarous" act. It had been cunningly executed, requiring weeks of preparation and careful study of the winds. The German gas initiative marked a turning point in the history of military technology. As a weapon, gas had existed principally on paper; Leonardo da Vinci had described a shell containing fine sulphur and arsenic dust that could be hurled against enemy ships. Other accounts of these novel weapons are scattered throughout history, and by the late 1880s, with the evolution of industrial chemicals such as chlorine and phosgene, dangerous gases existed, but militarily they were unknown and untested. The spirit of Hague I and II had been to prohibit the implementation of new chemical projectiles before they caused unnecessary suffering. When the Germans unleashed gas at Ypres—which they repeated on at least four occasions, causing slow death to five thousand and agonizing injuries to fifteen thousand French colonial and Canadian troops—they not only rewrote the rules of war but also pioneered the use of a weapon of mass destruction.

The German high command had hoped that this shocking new weapon would break the stalemate and bring about a quick victory. It was specifically designed by two leading German chemists, Walther Nernst and Fritz Haber, as a technological fix for static trench warfare, a chemical way of driving the enemy from their dugouts and breaking through the lines. (The pride of German chemistry, including five future Nobel laureates, collaborated on chemical warfare: Fritz Haber, Walther Nernst, Otto Hahn, James Franck, and Richard Willstatter.) When it failed, and the next day enemy troops mounted a successful counterattack and were soon back in place and protecting themselves with improvised mouth pads—usually made of dry or urine-soaked socks—worse toxins followed. Allied scientists immediately rushed to develop protective gear, creating a succession of masks, hoods, helmets, goggles, respirators, and filter boxes.

On December 19, 1915, the Germans raised the stakes, deploying phosgene, an even more powerful lung irritant. When the Allies quickly contained the damage, outfitting troops with improved masks, the Germans invented an even more powerful toxin that could penetrate those defenses. Once it became clear that German scientists would invariably bring all their brainpower and technology to bear on increasingly virulent gases, those on the receiving end—Britain and France—felt completely justified in responding in kind, inaugurating national chemical warfare programs mobilizing their full academic, industrial, and economic resources. Soon both sides were deploying chlorine and phosgene, and developing gas artillery shells that would eliminate dependence on fickle winds for delivery.

The summer of 1917 ushered in a new, acute phase of the chemical war. Beginning in mid-July, just as the first American troops were arriving in France, the Germans launched an overwhelming gas assault. These mustard-loaded artillery shells did not pulverize the barricades, but rather burst with a *plop* and smothered the trenches in poison. Mustard gas—also known as Yellow Cross, for the German shell markings—proved to be a highly effective weapon, causing extensive incapacitating injuries to the eyes, lungs, and skin. Five times more toxic than phosgene, it was deemed an almost perfect battle gas—"king of the battle gases"—so powerful that even minute traces could penetrate protective clothing, even rubber boots and leather gloves. Moreover, it rendered the battlefield uninhabitable for as long as a day—it remained active in the soil for weeks—allowing the Germans to stall Allied advances. The heavy, ground-hugging vapor settled in ditches and shell holes, and remained a persistent hazard for soldiers and their horses, causing many to suffer reexposure in the course of evacuating.

Mustard gas (no relation to the harmless mustard seed) was also insidious, giving off a characteristic garlicky odor that on initial exposure did little more than induce sneezing. When British troops first encountered it in the field, they removed their gas masks because they thought the pungent smell was just a ploy on the part of the Germans to fool them into believing a gas attack was under way. Unlike with cloud gas, they experienced no immediate pain or obvious symptoms on contact, but in a matter of hours were covered in blisters, coughing severely, and vomiting. One of the most distressing features of mustard was that injuries became progressively worse, particularly those to the eyes, so the men became temporarily blind. Its heavy toll—fourteen thousand British gas casualties in the first three weeks, more than all the gas casualties in the entire previous year—shook the Allies' confidence. In a bloody war of attrition, mustard's military value was that it wounded rather than killed, removing soldiers from action for weeks or months, weakening their effectiveness, and tying up large numbers of personnel and medical facilities required for their care. From a morale point of view, it was devastating. For Germany, mustard gas represented a technical triumph. It increased uncertainty and apprehension completely out of proportion to the threat, particularly as the Allies had nothing comparable with which to respond.

The United States entered the war late and unprepared. It lagged far behind both the Allied and Axis powers not only in traditional war materiel, but also in understanding of the technology and tactics of the new generation of chemical weapons. For help in the crisis, the government turned to the one agency experienced with asphyxiating gases, the US Bureau of Mines. By the fall of 1917, James Norris, now an army colonel, was director of both offensive and defensive research, and busily recruiting hundreds of university chemists for the gas warfare program. He immediately put Conant to work on making mustard gas, leading a team of four chemists in Organic Unit No. 1 at the American University Experimental Station (AUES) located on the outskirts of Washington, DC. American University was brand new when the war broke out and had graduated only a single class when its board of trustees offered its campus to President Wilson for the war effort.

By the time Conant arrived, the campus looked like a vast construction site, as dozens of new office buildings, laboratories, and testing facilities were being hastily erected for research into all aspects of the new type of warfare: chemical, psychological, pharmacological, and mechanical. The Harvard Chemistry Department had become practically a section of the War Department: his favorite professor, Elmer Kohler, along with another senior colleague, G. P. Baxter, were developing war gases; Arthur Lamb headed the defensive section and was working on gas masks; and Roger Adams, whose shoes Conant had filled the past nine months at Harvard, came a short time later as another group leader under Norris. More familiar faces arrived every day, which, he wrote Patty, "helps to cheer us up in spite of the gloomy news from Europe."

They spent the first four or five months playing catch-up with the British and French, who were already struggling in the laboratory to repeat the scientific steps taken by the Germans to produce mustard gas, or dichlorodiethyl sulphide. Conant was in touch with Sir William Jackson Pope, whose Cambridge laboratory was one of the first centers of gas research in

England. He knew the British had been hampered in their progress by the shortage of ethylene chlorohydrin, a critical material. Pope tried another method, proposed by William F. Guthrie, starting with sulphur monochloride, but after several frustrating weeks had not gotten much further. A third group, at Manchester, was investigating sulphur dichloride. The French also had three teams tackling the problem, and faced many of the same hurdles. In the end, they were the first to hit on a solution—low operating temperature, precise control of the exothermic reaction, and constant stirring of the reactants—and began producing mustard gas several months before their Anglo-American colleagues.

At the start of 1918, Conant's unit was enlarged. Early on, it suffered the same ethylene supply problems as the British, and Conant devoted significant effort to finding other sources. He even worked on cracking crude oil to obtain mixed olefins from which ethylene could be extracted. After weighing the effectiveness of the different manufacturing processes, Conant opted for Guthrie's "cold" method. It took another two months of studying the optimum conditions for the monochloride-ethylene reaction before the Americans perfected their own manufacturing process. The next step was to do a test run to see if they could produce satisfactory batches of mustard gas. A vast new poison-gas factory was being built at the Aberdeen Proving Ground along the Chesapeake River, and combined with the country's major gas shell-filling plant. In record time, the new federal arsenal in Edgewood, Maryland, was up and running, along with specially constructed roads, railroad sidings, water supply and power station. The first experimental batches were made at Edgewood in early June, and the gas went into mass production in August. From then on, Edgewood churned out an average of thirty tons of mustard gas a day. By the end of the war, the United States was producing more mustard gas than England, Germany, and France combined. According to Ludwig F. Haber, an eminent historian and the son of the German army's director of gas warfare, "It was an extraordinary performance," made possible in part by the "lavish use of manpower"—at the peak of activity, seven thousand enlisted men worked at Edgewood, aided by another three thousand civilians—and by the large pool of skilled chemists drawn from industry and academe.

What began as a civilian job in Washington had quickly morphed into military service when Conant and his fellow chemists were given commissions in the army. Still sounding rather amazed to find himself in uniform, he had written to Patty in early January 1918 that he had been made a first lieutenant in the Sanitary Corps. "Cambridge and Harvard seem a long way (and time) distant in this hurly-burly of war work which we are all struggling with down here," he informed her. "I am attempting (at times, it seems vainly) to help in this hideous business of beating the devil at his own game, or more specifically of 'gassing' the originators of 'gas.' My work is connected with an organic research laboratory which in outward appearance is not so different from the usual organic laboratory, but the substances we brew are a merry collection of devilishness."

Conant's determinedly upbeat tone masked his own unease about his assignment. Mustard gas—actually an oily brown liquid at room temperature—was nasty stuff. Not typically deadly, it was a highly toxic vesicant, or blister-forming agent, that attacked not only the skin but also all tissue it came in contact with, especially that of the eyes and airways. The "brewing," or synthesizing, process was dangerous, exacting, and unpleasant work. Accidents were unavoidable. Pipes would leak, vats would boil over. There was no effective antidote. Protection depended on preventing exposure and immediate decontamination to limit injury. Large basins of soapsuds stood at the ready for anyone who came into contact with the chemical, and each time it happened there would be much frantic dunking and scrubbing and general alarm. As in the coal mines, canaries were scattered throughout the premises to warn workers when gas levels were not safe. Conant could not bring himself to admit, even to himself, how strange it was for the son of a Quaker mother to be tasked with manufacturing such a noxious substance. He revealed only a hint of his misgivings in a grim aside to Patty that he found his new position "rather anomalous," as the Sanitary Corps was "supposed to be connected only with saving life." But then, he noted with resignation, "Everything is mixed up in the army."

In the spring of 1918, Conant was transferred to the newly formed Chemical Warfare Service (CWS) branch of the army, which was in the process of assuming responsibility for all weapons-related research, and made a captain. He wrote to Patty about his promotion, and warned her that it meant he would most likely not be coming back to Cambridge anytime soon. "I will have to postpone the pleasure of seeing you," he added regretfully, "and 'flashing my bars' and displaying my regimentals." As much as he missed the "peaceful shade" of Harvard, he was self-conscious about not seeing any action and worried that she might think less of him for it. Even his sister Marjorie had enlisted in the armed forces, and would be serving with a newly formed group of women artists doing occupational therapy with shell-shocked patients in American hospitals in France. "I certainly envied her," he admitted. "This being a chemist and staying in the USA isn't any sort of job at all for a person my age, particularly with one's friends getting wounded and killed 'over there.' But I guess we'll have to see it through for the present time."

Having perfected a method for making mustard gas, Conant was assigned to a new classified military project about which he was honor bound not to disclose the location or even its very existence. This "highly secret operation," he later recalled, involved the development of the "great American gas which would win the War." As the technological advances in gas warfare accelerated, and new and better defenses made the early toxins less debilitating, Allied and Axis scientists were competing to invent more effective offensive agents. Both sides wanted to claim their chemical weapons were superior.

Captain Winford Lee Lewis, a forty-year-old Northwestern University professor of chemistry working under Conant's supervision, was tasked with creating a new, more powerful chemical agent before the Germans. Lewis was specifically charged with developing a gas that would be effective in small concentrations, capable of injuring all parts of the body, and difficult to protect against. If it could be cheaply manufactured in large quantities, and easily transported, so much the better. An unsigned memo regarding their progress by May 1918 reflects the extreme secrecy surrounding the project:

"Captain Lewis at the Catholic University [in Washington, DC], is making no report, as he has instructions to place nothing regarding his work in writing at this time. Captain Conant is also doing certain work with which you are familiar, and concerning which nothing is said."

Lewis and his team decided to investigate arsenic, an ancient poison. Both sides had experimented with arsenic early in the war and rejected it as not particularly useful as a weapon. While researching the subject, however, Lewis heard about a young priest who had accidentally discovered a poisonous substance while working on his dissertation at Catholic University of America. The Belgian-born Julius Aloysius Nieuwland had attended the graduate seminary at Holy Cross College, was ordained a Catholic priest in 1903, and the following year earned a PhD in chemistry at CUA. (Nieuwland went on to become a famous inventor, recognized for his role in developing synthetic rubber, an acetylene-based product later known as neoprene and marketed by DuPont beginning in 1932.) His thesis, entitled rather banally "Some Reactions of Acetylene," consisted of a long list of reactions between acetylene and seventy-five other compounds, and had been sitting on the library shelf collecting dust for more than a decade. Lewis would never have given it a second look if it had not been for Father John Griffin, Nieuwland's old thesis advisor, who was still on the faculty of CUA. Griffin not only pointed out the relevant section describing an experiment that yielded a highly toxic mixture, he remembered that it caused his student to become "so sick that he was hospitalized for several days."

Intrigued, Lewis read Nieuwland's description of what happened when he bubbled acetylene gas through liquid arsenic trichloride, using aluminum chloride as a catalyst. "The contents of the flask turned black," he wrote, and when poured into cold water decomposed into a black gummy mass. "The tarry substance possessed a most nauseating odor, and was extremely poisonous. Inhalation of the fumes, even in small quantity caused nervous depression." Lewis immediately set to work trying to re-create the toxic mixture, and was fairly sure he was close when the fumes gave him a splitting headache. He placed a tiny drop of the liquid on his hand, which immediately became swollen and painful. In order to identify exactly what the compound was chemically, he and his team attempted to purify it, but the normal distilling process did not work. Every time the mixture was heated, it exploded. When Conant learned of the problem, he suggested using a 20 percent HCl wash to "desensitize" the mixture by removing the aluminum chloride catalyst. That did the trick. The explosions stopped, and Lewis was able to identify three arsenic-containing compounds that came to be known as lewisite 1, 2, and 3. L1 was the most deadly—and militarily, the most desirable.

By the end of June, the basic research phase was complete. Lewis handed his lethal arsenic compound over to Conant, who took charge of the development of lewisite as a weapon of war. Conant worked on evaluating the character and properties of the new gas, ascertaining whether it could be manufactured on a large scale, and devising a method for its preparation. For security reasons, it was decided that the new poison be designated as G-34, using one of the existing mustard codes in the war department's files to throw off any potential spies. In some communications, it was called "methyl," another camouflage name.

Conant shepherded lewisite through the various sections of CWS's research division, which included animal and human testing. After several weeks, the pharmacologists concluded that a man of average weight would be killed by one third of a teaspoon of lewisite applied to the skin. Its chief tactical advantage was that its effects were immediate, unlike the delayed effects of mustard, which made the latter a better defensive than offensive weapon. Using lewisite, advancing forces could move into enemy territory without fear of choking on their own toxic fumes. G-34 was the new American gas, regarded by the Department of Defense as "the premier of them all," and the weapon the Allied forces had been waiting for. General William L. Sibert, the director of the Chemical Warfare Service, was convinced that a surprise assault using lewisite could deliver a crushing blow to the German army and finally bring the war to a decisive end. He ordered that three hundred tons of the toxin, in drums and shells, be in readiness on the battlefield by March 1, 1919.

Getting the new poison gas into mass production in time for the planned spring Allied offensive was going to take a herculean effort. On July 18 Conant was promoted to major and ordered to the top-secret production facility in the sleepy town of Willoughby, Ohio. Exactly one week earlier, on the day Conant's experiments proved G-34 could successfully be produced in the laboratory, Frank Dorsey, a thirty-eight-year-old chemical engineer and colonel at National Lamp Works, one of GE's industrial labs in Nela Park, Cleveland, had been dispatched to find a site for the new lewisite plant. Dorsey had been instructed to take all possible precautions to prevent the Germans from discovering anything about the new gas and developing countermeasures. Scouting for an isolated location within commuting distance of his headquarters, he selected an old, shuttered Ben-Hur Motor Company plant about a mile outside Willoughby, on the banks of the aptly named Chagrin River.

After an eight-hour train ride, Conant arrived in Cleveland on July 20. He was met at the station by Dorsey, an energetic Irishman with a jaunty grin, and Colonel William G. Wilcox, who introduced himself as the new superintendent of the wartime plant. They drove directly to the proposed plant site in Willoughby, about eighteen miles east of Cleveland. As Dorsey turned down Ben Hur Avenue, Conant could see at a glance that they had their work cut out for them. The two main structures appeared terribly run-down. There were no water or sewage systems. The electrical wiring was prehistoric. Conant was hard put to see how the plant could be constructed and fully operational by December 1. Hanging in the balance, however, was the knowledge that American boys were being gassed to death in France every day, and unless they made the deadline there would be no way to deliver enough lewisite for the spring drive.

The first month was spent in a whirl of activity the likes of which he had never known before. Two dozen soldiers were immediately transferred to Willoughby and set to work clearing the grounds. Within days, the eleven-acre site was transformed into a military base, cordoned off by barbed wire, which was later electrified, and patrolled around the clock by armed guards. Searchlights swept the perimeter at night. A herd of local contractors, all sworn to secrecy, labored around the clock in order to get the new construction completed as promptly as possible. The first order of business was the laboratory, which was completed on August 11, and by the following day Conant had all the equipment installed and the research under way. Dozens of chemists and engineers convened at Willoughby over the next few weeks. Most were complete strangers. They knew nothing about each other or the work they were about to embark on. All of their nerves were on edge. Of the 22 officers and 542 enlisted men eventually assigned to Willoughby, Conant was one of only three who knew the entire scope of the mission from the outset.

On reaching the gas factory, the chemists found themselves virtual prisoners, locked up together in an industrial stockade, working seven days a week until the war was won. Complete wartime censorship was enforced. No mention could be made of Willoughby in correspondence or conversation under penalty of court-martial or severe punishment. A Cleveland post office box, lock drawer 426, was used as a mailing address. Security at the plant was so tight that the soldiers dubbed it the "mousetrap"—as in "What goes in never comes out." For the first six weeks, the living conditions were worse than most prisons. The officers camped out in tents while the men crowded together in temporary squad rooms. They had to make do with portable toilets and shower trucks, and no mess facilities, which meant forced marches into town three times a day for meals at the Willoughby Inn, which had been commandeered by the government. Although the local residents were not aware of the nature of the secret work being done at the old Ben-Hur plant, the presence of so many soldiers did not go unnoticed. In an effort to explain away all the activity and the foul odors, Conant told town mayor William Carmichael they were making a "new form of rubber."

A slight, baby-faced, twenty-five-year-old major, Conant had to develop new muscles and learn the qualities necessary for command. He had limited experience outside the laboratory walls, and most of what he knew about organization and management he learned by trial and error. As much as he disliked the strut of army life, he learned to play the part. He rose at dawn, buttoned himself into his uniform, wolfed down breakfast, and arrived at the plant in time to sing "A-a-all up!" into the base's public address system at six o'clock sharp each morning. He rarely left before ten at night, sometimes working until midnight. When things were at full tilt, he slept in his lab, plugging on to the point of exhaustion and then collapsing on a cot for a few hours.

By all accounts, he excelled in his new role, and played a significant part in welding the three distinct groups of scientists into an effective working unit. There were often heated arguments about the best way to proceed, and Conant proved adept at negotiating compromises, dispelling tensions and petty disagreements with tact and his dry, restrained humor. "Everybody respected him and his opinions," the *Boston Globe* reported later. "When he spoke, he was always listened to, because he usually said something worthwhile." Under his energetic supervision, rapid progress was made in the laboratory research, and a number of "revolutionary changes" were made in some of the processes originally planned for the manufacture of G-34. Still hoping to get to France, he had obtained a promise from Norris that he would be assigned to a combat unit after the completion of the pilot plant. "The fields of France look greener every day," he would exhort his crew as they toiled over the tricky five-step manufacturing process, working as fast as they could to get the materiel to the front.

The pace of work at the factory was frenetic, and they all suffered from the mental and physical strain of the wartime production schedule. Conant internalized the stress and began suffering the stomach problems that would plague him the rest of his life. He lost weight and had trouble sleeping. He would lie awake at night going over and over his design of the plant, particularly the ventilation of the fumes. He knew firsthand from his "disastrous attempt" after college that if he overlooked one small, crucial detail, it could all go up in flames again. But a senior engineer had warned him that as project leader he could not betray the "slightest indication" of his apprehensions or it would "destroy the confidence of the men," so he hid his doubts behind an implacable Yankee reserve.

The manufacturing work was hazardous in the extreme. Conant went to great lengths to make sure his crew was well versed in the careful handling of toxic materials, especially arsenic trichloride, which was extremely corrosive and volatile, and could be as lethal for the men handling it as for its intended victims. Gas masks were issued, and in some cases airtight protective suits. Procedures had to be strictly adhered to if they were to avoid the frequent accidents that poisoned factory workers in Britain. Even at the American University research station, many of the men conducting the early testing on lewisite had fallen ill from chemical exposure. Because of the high risks, a sixty-bed hospital was erected on-site. Two doctors were on call night and day. Although there were several accidents, and some men suffered painful lewisite burns, there were no deaths on Conant's watch.

In only four months, working under extreme pressure, he successfully oversaw every stage of development from laboratory to large-scale production. The plant went into operation right on schedule. In November, just as they were about to begin ramping up production, word came that the war was over. The fighting ceased on the entire Western Front at eleven o'clock on Monday morning, November 11, 1918. Exhausted, and outmatched by the better-coordinated and equipped Allies, Germany surrendered. Lewisite had not been needed to force the enemy's hand after all. In a war of awful weapons, the worst would not be used.

The overwhelming reaction of the men at Willoughby was one of relief. The sound of the peace bells meant they could turn off their stewing cauldrons, retire from the black arts, and return to the world. In the weeks that followed, the American chemists were lauded for helping to silence the German guns. On November 28 Conant's face graced the front page of the *Cleveland Plain Dealer* alongside those of Colonel Wilcox and Captain William Henry McAdams, under the headline "Makers of the Deadliest Gas; How They Did It." The article went on to praise their "unbelievable accomplishment," promising that the story, told for the first time since the lifting of wartime censorship, "bests the wildest fiction":

> The most terrible weapon ever forged by man has been placed at the disposal of the United States by American chemists . . . Only the signing of the armistice prevented its wholesale use against the Germans, first users of poison gas in battle. For on the day the armistice was signed a great plant, with eighteen acres under one roof, was ready to swing into operation at Willoughby, and the product would have been twenty tons a day. A single day's product, shot into Cleveland, would depopulate the city.

The *Willoughby Republican* trumpeted the news of its hometown heroes: "Here Is the Big Story of the Great Work of the Soldiers Who Have Been in Our Midst." A week later, the *Independent* chimed in with a similar head-line: "Now We Know What Those Ben Hur Boys Are Doing."

The work at the Willoughby plant did not cease immediately, though the winding down began almost at once. Because of the progressive nature of the manufacturing process, there were batches of lewisite that needed to be cycled through the apparatus before it could be shut down. By early December, most of the work was done, and the soldiers and officers were discharged. A small crew remained behind to begin the laborious task of dismantling and disposing of the equipment. Demolition crews arrived and started taking down the barracks and laboratory buildings. In a matter of weeks, almost every trace of the sprawling wartime factory was gone. Only the formulas—and a few samples—were preserved, carefully locked away in the files of the War Department.

It is not clear how much was ever produced. Conant maintained they were in "pilot production" when the hostilities ended, and "no appreciable quantity" of gas had been produced. In his memoir, he goes so far as to suggest that in the final days "many doubts" surfaced about lewisite's ef-fectiveness in battle, and whether the plant would actually have gone into production was "open to question." However, in the official history of the Chemical Warfare Service published in 1919, Lieutenant Colonel W. D. Bancroft, a chemist in the Research Division, claimed the plant was in "commercial production," which would seem to suggest things were well under way. On April 20 a lengthy feature published in the *New York Times Magazine*, entitled "Our Super-Poison Gas," reported that "ten tons a day" were being produced when the peace treaty was signed, and as the plant was ahead of schedule, "almost enough was on hand to destroy the en-tire people of the United States." The *Times* story, along with many other articles that appeared that spring, contained sensational claims regarding lewisite, including the grossly exaggerated statement that it was "72 times deadlier than mustard." The publicity only added to the growing mythol-ogy about its potency, and lewisite became popularly known as the "dew of death."

For all the planning that went into producing lewisite, very little thought was given to what to do with the leftover supply. In the end, the decision was made to take the huge store of liquid lewisite packed in fifty-five-gallon steel drums to the coast by train and dump it at sea. The military routinely interred leaky munitions and chemical waste underwater or underground, the latter technique commonly known as "burn it and bury it." Soldiers working at the American University Experimental Station (AUES), the center of chemical warfare research for two years, left so much debris in the ground in the leased acres around the Washington, DC, neighborhood of Spring Valley that they took to calling it "Death Valley."*

In May 1919 a vial of lewisite, described as "the deadliest poison ever known," was shown under guard at an exhibit in Washington that highlighted the wartime activities of the US Department of the Interior, part of the ongoing postwar propaganda campaign. Of all the inventions to come out of this vast military industrial effort—the Browning machine gun, the Liberty airplane motor, the depth bomb, the submarine detector, and the radio telephone—lewisite was "first on the list," declared *Harper's* magazine, "not only because in itself it epitomizes the romance of chemistry, but because its discovery has placed forever in the hands of the United States the most powerful weapon of war ever yielded."

In the first flush of victory, there were only accolades for the chemists responsible for lewisite's inception and development. For the last two years of the war, when America was an active participant, poison gas had loomed large in the popular imagination, and stories about its death-dealing properties dominated the newspapers. The general feeling was that Germany had inflicted this heinous weapon on the Allies, and America had risen to the challenge, in the end surpassing the enemy. Lewis, who was credited with inventing the new poison gas, was proud of his work, and became an outspoken advocate for the Chemical Warfare Service: "For quantity, new methods of application and novelty, it epitomized the American war spirit," he declared. "The spirit of an outraged and ingenious people, resolved to spare nothing to crush a criminal idea."

Lewis considered poison gas to be a more humane and "merciful" offensive weapon because only a small fraction of the war's 17 million deaths were caused by chemical weapons—an estimated 90,000 were killed by gas, though a million more were left blind or disabled—as compared to conven-

---

* The discovery of toxic caches at the former military testing site, now one of Washington, DC's most coveted residential zip codes, has resulted in a costly twenty-year cleanup, with the total bill expected to run more than $230 million.

tional weapons. Instead of the grotesque wounds inflicted by bullets and shells, gas could incapacitate the enemy long enough for the battle to be won, but allow soldiers to recover and live to fight again. He believed gas was the weapon of the future: "One pound of chloropicrin or brombenzyl cyanide [tear gas] will dispel a mob, and they will go home tearfully and unharmed," he theorized. "Somewhere out in the undiscovered countries of science, there is a chemical weapon that will anesthetize whole armies."

In the peacetime calm, however, the American people and their servants in Congress did not want to contemplate the future of chemical warfare. As the soldiers returned from the front, and stories about their terrible suffering were widely circulated, everyone from journalists and fiction writers to religious figures and women's groups held up poison gas as a principal example of the evils of war. When the government moved to drastically reduce defense spending, it was the Chemical Warfare Service's turn to face extinction. General Amos A. Fries, the head of the CWS, launched a publicity campaign to try to keep it from being disbanded. Sibert and Lewis were among those who lobbied hard for the continued existence of the program, and expressed disgust and dismay that the postwar revulsion against chemical weapons permeating the Paris peace talks was threatening to endanger the "stupendous" organization they had built with so much cost and care.

In his testimony before a joint Senate and House committee hearing on military affairs in November 1919, Dorsey also vigorously defended the Chemical Warfare Service as vital to the national defense, and argued it would be dangerous to believe such a deadly weapon could ever be completely banned:

"I think poison gas is here to stay for the same reason that high explosives are here to stay, because it is effective. It is effective in killing men, which is the business of war, and no matter what agreement is reached at the peace conference or any agreement that nations enter into, the fact remains that you can conduct experiments on poison gas without anyone's knowledge, no matter if you have an investigator coming around every day looking at you."

Conant, who was not at the forefront of the debate, never had to publicly defend his role in overseeing the wartime production of lewisite. Like his fellow CWS officers, he tended to view the subject of poison gases dispassionately—as basic chemistry and not taboo. Just as tear gas was "a gift" to the forces of law and order, he believed chemical weapons were a valid form of warfare, and did not buy the argument they were somehow more uncivilized. The Marquis of Queensbury rules might be made to apply in the boxing ring but not at the front, and not in a desperate fight to the finish in which all manner of firearms and torpedoes were employed without scruple. "To me, the development of new and more effective gases seemed no more immoral than the manufacture of explosives and guns," he asserted in his memoir. "I did not see in 1917, and do not see in 1968, why tearing a man's guts out by high-explosive shell is to be preferred to maiming him by attacking his lungs or skin. All war is immoral. Logically, the 100 percent pacifist has the only impregnable position."

In the debate that ensued in the postwar period, the prevailing "moral" argument against gas was that it could not be controlled with accuracy, and could blow over towns adjacent to battlefields and result in civilian casualties. A number of prominent members of the defense establishment spoke out against the indiscriminate nature of gas warfare as wantonly "cruel" and "savage," with no redeemable value. One of the chief opponents of the CWS was Army Chief of Staff Peyton C. March, who condemned the use of suffocating gas that "carried wherever the wind listeth, kills the birds of the air, and may kill women and children in the rear of the firing line." Conant, clearly impatient with such sentiments, acknowledged only that the same "chain of reasoning" was used to condemn unrestricted submarine warfare because it attacked civilians. He remained steadfastly unapologetic. Dismissing the moral objections as "old-fashioned" by modern standards, he noted with brutal irony that with the advent of aerial bombing in World War II, "civilian casualties became not only a necessary consequence of bombing, but one might almost say an objective of the fleets of bombers directed by the British, the Germans, and the Russians, as well as by the Americans."

Conant had no stake in the continued existence of the CWS. He was thankful to be through with the "highly unattractive task of producing poisons to be used in combat." A number of the older officers he had worked with urged him to consider a career in the civilian chemical industry rather than return to the sheltered world of academe. But Conant was stubborn. He had nurtured the dream of "carrying the title of 'Professor' at Harvard" for so long he was unwilling to consider other opportunities. On a brief visit to Cambridge over Christmas before being mustered out, he had learned that the college authorities were prepared to make him an assistant professor in order to keep him. It was a bit of a comedown from heading his own research division, but the best they could do, he was told, given his thin résumé—one year as a lecturer, and a short list of publications. He did not care if some people thought he had settled for a humble teaching position. He was going home to Harvard, and to his girl.

At the same time, he knew that after his "strange adventure in applied chemistry," and the unique bond he had formed with so many of his fellow scientists, "it would be hard to stick to a laboratory bench." The war had forced him out of the seclusion of his laboratory. He was not the same person he had been when he first reluctantly donned a uniform in Washington. "As head of a team of chemists and engineers at Willoughby, I had directed the efforts of the key unit of a large undertaking," he reflected. "I came to know both the frustrations and satisfactions of a leader and the excitement which goes with making decisions." The ideal of the dedicated scientific investigator "alone on a high pedestal" no longer held the same appeal. He had glimpsed a new, fascinating world, and "cherished a carefully hidden ambition to try my wings someday in other fields."

CHAPTER 6

Air Castles

*I shan't put to sea like the Flying Dutchman, plying from
nowhere to nowhere. I shall hail from a recognised respectable port, being duly registered and legally owned, in a
word, married.*

—George Santayana, *The Last Puritan*

W hen Conant returned to Harvard in January 1919, he discovered
word of his wartime exploits had preceded him. His former colleagues and
professors had read all about his secret assignment in charge of a poison gas
factory, the months spent cooped up behind barbed wire, and successful development of the deadly lewisite. "Naturally, I was impressed," recalled the
journalist John Tunis, class of 1911, who was astonished that "an unknown
twenty-five-year-old chemistry instructor should be promoted so quickly."
Every time Tunis heard Conant's name mentioned in Washington, he was
being awarded a new commission—bumped up from captain, to lieutenant,
to major—and given new, awesome responsibilities. He remembered going
to visit him at the Chemical Warfare Service, only to find his office empty.
Conant, he was informed, had just been "moved upstairs." The next time
he dropped by, he learned his friend had suddenly left the city, tapped for a
mysterious operation that would earn him a "Commendation for Unusual
Service" and much public acclaim.

The war had made stars of organic chemists. They had played a central
role in securing victory, and were poised to play an even bigger part in the

postwar world. When the American Chemical Society (ACS) first offered its services at the outbreak of the hostilities, the War Department had declined on the grounds that "it already had a chemist in its employ." Now there were thousands of chemists working for the military, carrying the same rank as the medical corps. They had won a new place in society, and were no longer regarded as strange recluses working in obscurity but as scientific warriors, worthy of respect and homage alongside warriors in the field. Thanks to the flag-waving postwar press coverage, many of them were now public figures. "The army and powers that be in Washington no longer think the Chemists' Art is a method of transmuting water into wine, but a system where by patient laborious effort produces those things which are valuable to man for destruction and construction," reported Laurence V. Redman, chairman of the ACS, in a trenchant editorial in the January 1919 *Chemical Bulletin*. "Suddenly, as by magic, this erratic individual emerges with marvelous discoveries, and airy nothingness receives a local habitation and a name."

The new importance of chemistry in both industry and academe was reflected in the many attractive job offers that came Conant's way that winter. Because of his outstanding record with the Chemical Warfare Service, B. F. Goodrich Company, the giant tire and rubber manufacturer, was eager to recruit him for their research division. Roger Adams, who had worked with Conant in Washington, recommended him to Julius B. Stieglitz, chairman of the Chemistry Department at the University of Chicago. "Would you be willing to consider a call as Assistant Professor of Chemistry with a salary of $2,500," Stieglitz proposed in a letter that February, expressing his desire to lure "a promising young man like yourself" out west. When Conant opted to remain at Harvard, Chicago chemistry professor Gerald Wendt chided him for being "so rockbound in your provinciality as to insist on Boston in spite of anything and everything."

Conant was certainly provincial, but he also had personal reasons for wanting to stay put. When he turned down an opportunity with a mining concern in Ohio, they raised their offer and pressed him to accept. After he turned them down a second time, they demanded an explanation. "I'm going to marry a girl who wouldn't care to live in your state," he told them frankly. "And if she did, I wouldn't want to marry her."

It took nerve to court his famous mentor's daughter, but Conant was full of confidence. Almost immediately on his arrival in Cambridge, still wearing his uniform, he presented himself at the Richards home at 15 Follen Street. The last they had heard, he was still a captain, and Patty and her mother, Miriam Richards, made a show of fussing over his major's stripes and telling him he looked "most impressive." Conant regaled them with amusing tales of his mousetrap incarceration, and Patty later wrote in her diary that she was relieved to find that success had not gone to his head. He was the same modest boy she remembered, his manner "very nice and simple." The news from Europe was still coming thick and fast, and he had something to say about everything. "As usual, he just bubbled with ideas on the universe," she wrote. "He talked at a great rate about labor and representation for labor, nonintervention in Russia, and government control of the railroads."

If Conant was a product of the brash new professional middle class, Grace (Patty) Thayer Richards belonged very much to Boston's old cultural elite. While the whole idea of class difference was deeply repugnant to him, Miriam Richards's exhausting attempts to enlighten him as to her daughter's pedigree and antecedents—generation after generation of pious and patrician men—forced him to concede that the family was on both sides intellectually eminent. Patty had been born into what he would later refer to with a tight-lipped smile as Harvard's academic "caste system." Her maternal grandfather was Joseph Henry Thayer, a widely revered theologian at the Harvard Divinity School, biblical scholar, and fellow of the Harvard Corporation, the tiny, self-perpetuating group responsible for the conduct of the university. The Thayers, Miriam liked to remind people, were direct descendants of Percival Lowell, a prosperous British merchant who had crossed the Atlantic and settled in the seaport town of Newbury in 1639. Thayers were for the most part Brahmins and intellectuals, distinguished in some line of endeavor other than making money—be it as statesmen, scholars, scientists, or clergymen. Fortunately, two forebears had married wealthy Greenough sisters, injecting enough money into the line to ensure respectable affluence. There was a strong family resemblance: Thayers were all tall, blond, and blue eyed, with the same set of jaw and aristocratic profile.

Miriam Richards was a singular personality, and Conant could tolerate her only in small doses. Since every time he called on Patty he was expected to take tea with her mother, he saw rather more of her than he would have liked. Miriam had been blessed with beauty and talent. She studied music in Leipzig and could have been a professional pianist had it not been for the fact that women of her day did not, as she put it, "waltz onto the stage." Denied a career, she would not be thwarted in her determination to be a drawing room diva, and delighted in giving performances for guests at every opportunity. Miriam basked in the attention, and to satisfy her need for constant society turned their large, dark-paneled parlor into a genteel salon, inviting well-known musicians, artists, authors, poets, and scientists who were intimate family friends. Patty's father, Theodore Richards, who played the violin, also painted, had a whimsical sense of humor, and radiated warmth and intelligence. The Richards house, close to campus, was always filled with the great and the good, including the writer George Santayana, the art collector Bernard Berenson, and the wealthy financier Charles Loeser. Such learned company attracted William James, the philosopher and psychologist, who, along with his novelist brother, Henry, was a frequent dinner guest. After one party, William James wrote to a friend approvingly of the Richardses, and observed that Miriam, with her "splendid playing and general grace and amiability was proof of how much hidden wealth Cambridge has."

As Conant soon came to realize, the Richardses occupied what Jean Strouse, in her biography of the Jameses's sister, Alice, described as a "highly cohesive, rarified world of independent means and shared assumptions." It was not simply that they were well born and well connected—Boston was full of families that were far grander—but that they inhabited an extraordinarily brilliant and cultivated circle, composed of a group of men who had all been at Harvard together, risen to fame together, and were bound by an almost familial feeling for the college. Adding to the incestuous closeness of their set were the many overlapping marital ties, both to the university and academia. Miriam's older sister, Edith, was married to another fantastically erudite Harvard scientist, Lawrence Joseph Henderson, a biochemist, physiologist, and philosopher of distinction, author of numerous books on organic evolution and teleology, and the first unofficial roving professor at Harvard. Her younger sister, Lucy, was married to an exceptionally learned—he had five doctorates—New Testament theologian, Caspar Rene Gregory, who was teaching at Leipzig when the war broke out, enlisted in the German army, and died on the Western Front in 1917. In addition, Theodore Richards's younger brother, Herbert Maule Richards, was a widely respected botanist and leading authority on the physiology of plants.

There was no doubt the Richards family would make an interesting study in heredity. That two brothers should reach the highest rank in their respective fields of science struck Conant as an anomaly, especially in light of their "unusual" upbringing. Their father, William Trost Richards, was an American Pre-Raphaelite artist, and one of the country's foremost marine painters and watercolorists. He was a follower of the English critic John Ruskin's dictum of artistic truth to nature, and his painstaking efforts brooked no com- promise. His plein air watercolors of the rugged New England coastline, and dramatic oils of the magnificent, wind-battered cliffs near his home in New- port, Rhode Island, were famous for their clarity and meticulous detail, and found favor with the Gilded Age barons of the day. Theodore Richards was raised in an imaginative and unorthodox household, under the watchful eye of his mother, Anna Matlack, a formidable intellect and gifted poet. She homeschooled the five of their eight children who survived into adulthood, creating a rigorous curriculum that included reading, writing, arithmetic, geography, and history, as well as art and music.

At the age of fourteen, Theodore Richards passed the entrance exams for Haverford, a small Quaker college near Philadelphia, never having set foot in school. Three years later, after graduating at the head of his class, seventeen-year-old Richards enrolled in Harvard as the youngest mem- ber of the senior class of 1886. After acquiring a second bachelor's degree at Harvard, graduating a year later summa cum laude with the highest honors in chemistry, he went on to earn a PhD for his investigation of the relative atomic weights of hydrogen and oxygen. It was an extraordinarily difficult undertaking, requiring an absolute commitment to accuracy. The qualities that set Richards's work apart were his excruciatingly exact and laborious repetition of experiments, combined with a certain artistry— an unusually fine manual dexterity and ingenuity—he brought to bear on the problems he encountered in the newly developing field of physical chemistry. Almost as important as his data were his improved apparatus, tricks of manipulation, and mastery of the mercury thermometer. The re- sults of his work were published in a joint paper in 1888 that immediately won him international acclaim. In the same year, Richards produced three other papers based on his study of the atomic weights of copper and sil- ver, as well as one dealing with the heat produced by the reaction of silver nitrate with solutions of metallic chlorides. "Four publications and the young investigator was not yet twenty-one!" Conant would later write of his mentor.

Richards's rapid progress came at a price. In the course of completing his doctorate, he overexerted himself and suffered a breakdown, prompt- ing his mother to move to Cambridge for a time to look after him. "The work had been strenuous," he would later recall, "and my none too vigor- ous physical strength had been severely taxed." After a year abroad, spend- ing a semester training at German laboratories in Göttingen and Leipzig, and another studying in England, Richards returned to Harvard and was promptly appointed an instructor in quantitative analysis. Concerned that a heavy teaching load might lead to a relapse, his parents encouraged him to concentrate on his experiments and provided generous financial support. Richards's career continued to flourish, but his physical and psychological health remained precarious. He suffered from fatigue, hopelessness, and bouts of melancholia. He was prone, family letters reveal, to "morbid views and dark forebodings."

His temperament was decorously referred to as "nervously sensitive," though the turbulent emotions and "dark prospect" were almost certainly symptoms of depression. "He was too bright," his mother would write his fiancée, Miriam Stuart Thayer, in an effort to explain his fragile equilibrium in the face of tremendous expectations. "He has gone too far and too fast— and now the 'wheels of the world of bread-and-butter' have got him, and he cannot escape."

Theodore Richards was twenty-eight years old when he married Miriam, two years his senior, a cossetted, unworldly woman who thought she had found in him a tender soul who shared her love of poetry and music, and understood them to be the "vital elements" in her life. Instead, she discovered his "vital life" existed solely among the "fascinating subtleties of atoms." It proved a less than harmonious union. The young chemist who would soon become known for the painstaking precision of his work was forced to resign himself to the permanent chaos of his household. Miriam was a hypochondriac who took to her bed at the slightest provocation. She was afflicted by a variety of mysterious ailments that her friend Charles Loeser characterized in a letter shortly before her marriage as "your disease of ethics, metaphysics and allied festering and fettering inflictions," problems that, he added reprovingly, "have no raison d'être; their existence is never real; but only in one's making."

The Richardses were a high-strung, overstrung family at the best of times. All three children inherited their parents' intelligence and passion. All three were burdened by too much intensity. A talent for music, art, and poetry was in their genes, and assiduously nurtured from birth. Each was assigned an instrument: Patty, the oldest, played the family's Steinway grand; William (Bill), two years her junior, the cello, a Stradivarius known as "Angelika"; and Greenough (Thayer), the baby by five years, the clarinet. Hours of daily practice were enforced. It went without saying that they were expected to be exceptional. Mediocrity in anything was not to be tolerated.

Patty's mother was a perfectionist. Miriam believed in upholding "standards" and imposed her rigid principles, inhibitions, and mantra of self-improvement on her offspring. Although her father was a man of the church, her only true religion was her unshakeable belief in the Social Register. People of "quality" were distinguished by their genteel conversation and bearing; wealth was not supposed to have anything to do with it. Unlike most women of her day, she was not in the least inclined toward domesticity, and her overweening desire to be recognized for her own talent would influence her children, their grandiose dreams and deep vulnerabilities, at least as much as their formidable father. In her diaries, Patty lamented at being born into a "stern Yankee household," with such a high bar for excellence and scant praise, driving her to ever-greater feats in the futile search for affirmation. She was dogged by the sense she was a disappointment—"an overwhelming sense of my unworthiness"—that in turn inspired hours of lacerating self-scrutiny and martyrdom "as a spur" to do better.

Socially ambitious, both for herself and her children, Miriam increasingly chafed at what she perceived as the shabby gentility of "university people." Raised a proper Victorian lady, she required a phalanx of servants to be at her beck and call. The Richardses employed a cook, a girl to wait on table, a housemaid, a lady's maid, and a succession of European governesses referred to as either "Fräulein" or "Mademoiselle." Although well-to-do by most standards, they could not begin to compete with Boston's new industrial rich, their stately Beacon Hill mansions, steam yachts, stables of horses, and exclusive club memberships. Compared with the Boston "swells" Patty felt like a country bumpkin, dowdy and unfashionable, as if Cambridge, located just on the other side of the Charles River, were a hopelessly provincial hamlet.

For Richards, who resented the "distracting task of making money," the family's mounting debts were a constant source of stress. Few outside the family knew that Richards suffered from crippling bouts of depression. He drove himself hard and desperately fought the descending clouds that threatened to choke his productivity. As Conant observed many years later, "The habit of attempting to foresee all possible contingencies, which was basic to his success as a scientific investigator, placed a heavy strain on his life as a husband and father."

Unfortunately, the infinite pains Richards took over his experiments carried over into his personal affairs and condemned him to a lifetime of worry. Small problems could take on immense proportions. Preoccupied with contamination, in the lab and at home, he compulsively washed his hands. Petrified of illness, he fastidiously guarded against infection, and insisted that anyone who showed any unfavorable symptoms wear a protective mask. A cold was cause for hysteria. When twelve-year-old Patty came down with scarlet fever, he became almost unhinged with worry. He banished her to a back room, draped a sheet over the threshold, and forbade any family member to breach the barrier. Her only human contact for the entire six weeks of quarantine was the plump, gray-haired nurse who was hired to care for her, and the doctor who finally pronounced her well.

Even when her isolation was over, Richards would not hear of Patty returning to school. His own vision was "defective," and he was so convinced her eyes had been weakened by the fever that he insisted on keeping her home rather than risk further damage. For a serious little girl who devoured stories and poetry, it meant relinquishing what she loved best. It was hard, in such a cerebral family, to be so completely sidelined. Patty spent the remainder of that lonely winter confined to the house, seeing only her Greek tutor. "My long imprisonment has told on me," she wrote in her diary, aware that the many months of solitude had made her overly sensitive and introspective. She felt increasingly suffocated and found herself becoming "cross, selfish, and quarrelsome." After missing the better part of a year of school, she got glasses and was allowed to attend classes part-time at Miss May's School in Boston. But Richards continued to fret about the dangers of eyestrain and "overstudy," invaliding her to such an extent that this daughter of an outstanding intellectual family never completed high school and instead settled for a "Certificate of Honorable Dismissal."

After Richards won the Nobel, life became both easier and harder. The award, which included a sum roughly equivalent to today's $1 million in prize money, provided the family with much-needed financial security. The accompanying fame also had an ameliorating effect. The public recognition allowed Miriam to finally realize her greatest ambition: to be universally recognized as the first lady of Cambridge, Harvard's own queen bee. She made herself that much more imperious, if possible, and put on all sorts of airs. All the acclaim had a deleterious effect on her children, who would suffer from the weight of the almost impossible expectations placed upon them. The oldest boy, Bill, hailed as another scientific "genius," was already showing signs of the strain that would mar his high promise.

Meanwhile, Patty, caught between her father's oversized achievements and her mother's aspirations, became increasingly clenched, anxious, and fussy. After she was rejected by Radcliffe College for having too few credits, Richards encouraged her to follow in the footsteps of her famous grandfather, and aunt, Anna Richards Brewster, and become a painter. Patty enrolled in the school run by the Boston Museum of Fine Arts, attending classes three mornings a week. Hungry for accomplishment, she dedicated herself to her drawing. On her days off, she stayed at home and spent hours in solitary effort, working in pencil or charcoal, trying to improve her technique. Life at Follen Street, she wrote in her diary, was a "narrow existence."

She came out socially in the spring of 1916, and her party at the Cambridge Boat House earned a mention in the society columns. She amused herself with serial crushes on the Harvard boys who frequented the house—"chiefly Papa's advisees." It was fully expected that she would find a husband within their tiny fraction of proper Cantabrigian society. But it all seemed fairly humdrum, and she could not look ahead at her narrow horizons without feeling some dismay. "Sometimes I feel as though I'd burst," she wrote. "I've lived here all my life so far, and there's every prospect of my living here till I get married, whenever that may be." She envied her brother Billy and his friends, who were in the ROTC and spent their afternoons drilling and talking of going to fight overseas. Patty felt more "stuck" than ever. "And now, of all times, when such chances are open, and work of all sorts to be done," she wrote. "Oh to get away! To see and do and know at first hand."

When Jim Conant had first turned up in January 1919 on leave, she had listened, wide-eyed and riveted, to his stories. With all the excitement and tumult of events leading up to the armistice, it was impossible not to get swept up in his exalted talk about the principles at stake in Wilson's Fourteen Points, and "all the ardor" that the war and peace seemed to inspire in him. His passionate arguments in favor of the League of Nations, and fury at Senator Henry Cabot Lodge's attempts to undermine it in Congress, highlighted his most compelling qualities—the fierce intelligence, moral integrity, and independent streak.

She had met many of her father's protégés, and was "wholly unimpressed by show-offs," but Conant's brilliance and charisma set him apart. In the beginning, she had not really thought of him as a serious suitor, but he gradually won her over. He was appealingly boyish and earnest—no poses, pretensions, or affectations. He made no bones about knowing anything about art, but seemed to "believe in it, look up to it, and enjoy it," she wrote, "so few people do." His admiration for her talent, and his sympathy with her struggles, were a "great comfort." She liked his air of being extremely sure of himself, of knowing exactly what it was that he wanted and precisely how to go about getting it. Patty began to think marrying Jim Conant might be a way out of Follen Street.

Richards, however, took the position that his daughter was too young and unformed to contemplate marriage. In his view, Conant himself was also far from ready: he owed his current perch at Harvard largely to the war, and was under considerable pressure to prove that he was a good investment. He needed to get on with his experiments and publish some papers if he was serious about establishing his reputation as a research scientist.

Conant wasted no time buckling down to work. He decided to focus on some of the reaction mechanisms he had first encountered at Midvale Steel. In a hurry for a good result, he started down what turned out to be a "blind alley" and had to start over again. It would take more than a year of "wallowing in the laboratory" before he hit "pay dirt." Sensing he was finally making real progress, he wrote Patty that he had "so many irons in the chemical fire" that he was optimistic that he was in for an interesting year. That same winter, N. Henry Black, now an assistant professor of chemistry at Harvard, asked him to collaborate on writing a basic high school textbook. Conant supplied the latest technical information and Black ordered the pedagogical structure of the volume. Eager to help his son's career, Conant's father prepared the photo engraving plates for the illustrations, tables, and charts accompanying the experiments. *Practical Chemistry*, published by Macmillan in the fall of 1920, became a classic in the field and, through successive editions, proved a steady earner for years to come.

By summer, Conant was deeply in love and feverishly counting the days until his visit with the Richards family in Seal Harbor, Maine. He and another young chemistry instructor, Norris Hall, had been invited "down east" for a week's holiday before the start of the busy fall term. Every chance he got, Conant found an excuse to go off alone with Patty, and on the last night confessed his love for her under an August moon. The time they spent together was so heavenly, he wrote giddily on his return, that it must have been "a mirage," adding, "Do let a troubled mortal know, was it real?"

He had thoroughly enjoyed their long talks, particularly the "shout" about politics. He loved to argue, and considered the ability to engage in civilized debate a prerequisite for any friendship. Conant was for Ohio governor James Cox and Franklin Roosevelt in the upcoming presidential election, and argued that the Democrats' support for the League of Nations alone would be enough to defeat Senator Warren Harding, the Republican candidate, notwithstanding the editorials in the *Boston Herald*. "I still have a strong taint of Wilsonian about me," he admitted, playfully warning Patty not to be "too much influenced by the aristocratic and plutocratic atmosphere of Seal Harbor which must be strongly Republican."

Aware that she regarded her sensibilities as more "fine-grained" and discriminating than his own, and that their different backgrounds and attitudes were a cause of concern, he constantly sought to reassure Patty that they were more alike than it might at first appear. "I realize only too well that I am not worthy of you," he wrote. "But at the bottom of our hearts, I know we are in absolute accord on every vital point and furthermore in regard to the superficial affairs of everyday life I'm sure we speak the same language." He returned again and again to the theme of mutual understanding, insisting they would never "clash" on important matters, and the only "possible difference" between them was their point of view on the "relative cheapness of certain people and acts—yours too precious, mine too cheap—but that's such a detail of a detail."

As soon as Patty returned to Cambridge, he called on her at home and asked her to marry him. She was too agitated and indecisive to respond, and put him off, saying she cared for him only a little. Undeterred, he kept up his "paper offensive," bombarding her with letters and begging her to forgive him for his "miserable performance" and allow him another chance to plead his case in person. A few weeks later, he took her canoeing in Concord, Massachusetts. At the end of a golden autumn afternoon, he proposed again. "Accepted him finally," Patty confided to her diary on the evening of September 24. "I really couldn't possibly do better. I glowed all night at the thought of him. He is dear and high-minded, and a joy to be with; and I think I am building my house upon a rock."

Two days later, she called off their engagement. Under her mother's pointed questioning, Patty's confidence faltered, and she filled her diary pages with "dark fears and timid doubts." An objection had been raised having to do with his consumption of alcohol—Theodore Richards was abstemious—and on a recent social occasion, Conant had reportedly "passed the line of decorum." His disgrace was being held up as proof of a tendency toward "cheapness" and "dissipation," her parents' Boston prejudice against his origins. The implication was clear: as a boy from the wilds of Dorchester, whose father was engaged in a grubby commercial enterprise, he did not know how to behave. Deeply shocked, Patty conceded that his conduct only added to her misgivings. Her parents, not persuaded she knew her own mind, decided it would be best if she went away. She was being sent to Washington to stay with close friends. Telling Conant not to worry, she explained she needed time to reflect before "going ahead." He replied warily that he would respect her decision and promised to try to "conquer" his impatience, and not allow the disappointment and uncertainty to get the better of him.

While he apologized for making what he called "a few false moves," he defended himself roundly against the charges that his drinking—undertaken "in the spirit of joviality and blowing off steam"—was somehow evidence of immorality:

> The whole question of ethics and "good taste" (which is aesthetics, isn't it?) is certainly very complex . . . You don't believe, do you, that my judgment in spiritual, ethical, and practical matters is unsound—that I have a weak character? If you do, remove your affections for me, but be sure the evidence warrants it!!
>
> Judgments are largely the products of our past experience, traditions and immediate social pressure. They diffuse as we live and develop. May I hope that one who hasn't made certain errors in judgment (perhaps because of greater social pressure) can still love with all her heart one who has?

Just before Patty was due to leave, Conant persuaded her to meet him for a clandestine rendezvous in Fresh Pond Park. When he escorted her home after a two-hour interlude in the woods, all was forgiven. Resolved to brook no further opposition, he wrote to her the next day, "Let our love for each other shine out and together fight and win."

It would take a good deal of maneuvering on his part to prevail. A "stormy month" followed, in which Patty toured Washington's museums and monuments, and listened while her mother enumerated the many reasons why she should not get married. Conant wrote almost daily, desperately importuning her to keep the faith. "It's no use—I've got to keep on loving you until I get positive orders to stop," he beseeched her on October 15. In the end, his persistence paid off. On October 22, after he dashed to Washington for a clandestine reunion, Patty made a single entry in her diary: "Engaged again for the final time."

For the next six months, Conant assiduously courted her, plying Patty with long, devoted letters, fervent notes, and valentines. He tried to improve himself in her eyes, nightly plowing through the volumes of poetry and Shakespearean sonnets that were dear to her. To help anchor her affections, he sprung for a diamond and sapphire engagement ring he could ill afford and would spend the next few years paying off at the rate of $10 a month. They set the date for the last week of May 1920, but he could not dispel the "vague fear" she might "vanish again." He had hoped for a simple wedding, but Miriam Richards was intent on a large, formal affair, and the ensuing tension only made things more difficult. In mid-March, he dashed to Manhattan in an effort to ward off any last-minute jitters. "A heavenly hour alone together," Patty wrote of seeing Bryant, as his family still called him. "B's tenderness never-to-be-forgotten—in spite of my only half-convinced state."

There is no indication that Conant considered Patty hard work or ever lost patience with her chronic anxiety. She was the beautiful daughter of academic royalty, and he was blind to the family's underlying frailties. Fluent in French and German, with all the taste and polish of her rich intellectual heritage, and many ties within the upper echelon of the scientific community, she would, he believed, prove an ideal partner for someone with his high aspirations. The delight he took in his "excellent match," as his friend Norris Hall called it, is evident in the triumphant letters he penned in the weeks following the announcement of their engagement. After dining at the Harvard Club one night with Ken Murdock and other old friends, during which he came in for a good deal of ribbing for marrying the boss's daughter, Conant crowed to Patty, "Why shouldn't I be looking like a joyful prince? I certainly feel like one—and it's all because of you, dearest!"

According to Harvard historian John Fox Jr., while Conant may not have been so calculating as to court Richards's daughter to advance his cause, there is no way he failed to appreciate what he gained by such an alliance. "There's no question Richards looked out for his career," said Fox. "He would have put in a good word here and there. The skids were definitely greased." As one of Conant's chemical colleagues remarked on hearing the news, "You're certainly one lucky fellow—everything breaks right for you."

As the wedding day approached, Miriam Richards retreated to her sickbed. Owing to her illness, and inability to carry on with the preparations, the elaborate nuptials she had insisted on were canceled. In the end, the couple was married on a gray, rain-soaked Sunday morning, on April 17, 1920, several weeks earlier than planned, in a small ceremony in Harvard's Appleton Chapel. Only two dozen people were in attendance, all of them family save for Conant's best man, Ken Murdock. "It didn't seem dreary in the least, as people had threatened a tiny church wedding would be," Miriam reported to her sister, Edith Henderson. Everyone agreed the bride looked enchanting, her shimmering white satin lace dress simple and elegant, with a veil that swept the ground and a diaphanous cap with a single wreath of orange blossoms that formed "a sort of halo" above her head. The groom, in spite of his "goggles," was dignified. "It was all most lovely," Miriam acknowledged grudgingly, "and without any struggles on my part at all." The newlyweds departed for their honeymoon on June 1, taking the night train to Montreal. A week later, they sailed for the Continent.

The trip abroad, a wedding gift from Richards, was Conant's chance to belatedly make his European tour, considered an indispensable part of a gentleman's education. For Patty, it meant retracing a journey she had taken with her family in the summer of 1911, when Richards had collected honorary degrees and silks from the Oxford, Cambridge, and Manchester universities, as well as the Faraday Medal from the Royal Society. With his regal wife by his side, and an armload of letters of introduction from his illustrious father-in-law, Conant would be visiting Britain's great university laboratories, and paying call on some of the leading names in chemistry: Harold Dixon and Arthur Lapworth at Manchester, Jocelyn Thorpe at Cheltenham, William Henry Perkin Jr. at Oxford, and Norman Haworth at Newcastle. In London, they would be hosted by no less than Lady Rayleigh, the widow of the 3rd Baron of Rayleigh, John William Strutt, the internationally famous physicist who had won the Nobel Prize in 1904 for the discovery, with William Ramsay, of argon.

Conant was on his way, in more ways than one. In her engagement diary, tucked between marital advice from her mother—"always dress attractively, keep an attitude of repose—and snippets of romantic verse, Patty recorded her husband-to-be's bravura visions of the future, which she blithely dubbed "Jim's air-castles." Looking ahead to grand vistas of success, he told her he was bent on achieving three goals in his lifetime: "1. To be the greatest organic chemist in America; 2. President of Harvard; 3. A public servant in some Cabinet position such as Sec. of the Interior." They were a young man's pipe dreams, but Patty wrote them down, preserving them for posterity, she mused, "out of curiosity to see how much will come true!"

CHAPTER 7

The Specialist

Gambling on the stock market is really a quiet life compared with this research business—all ups and downs and ten downs to one up.

—JBC to his wife

Conant returned from Europe in the fall of 1921 with a new outlook and new enthusiasm for his work. Travel, the pilgrimage to scientific shrines, and the chance to rub elbows with many of his chemical contemporaries at an international conference in Brussels, Belgium, had opened his mind and set a rush of ideas in motion. Although he was thrilled to be among the American representatives to the important postwar gathering, he was invited only "with the more or less explicit understanding my name was on the list because of Professor Richards's fame." Nevertheless, Conant, who had a passion for first-rate minds, found himself in his element.

He had a "delightful time" going to all the sessions at the Palais des Academies in Brussels. Patty's fluent French and social connections put them "on the wave at all the parties," and he enjoyed himself immensely despite having to put up with "a good deal of kidding" about his terrible accent and excellent "beau-père." He met with the many distinguished delegates from the victorious Allied nations—including his British contact on the mustard gas project, William Pope, who had been knighted for his services—though Conant was disappointed that the Germans and the Austrians had been excluded on the grounds that they were "tainted by war guilt." He came away encouraged by the interest in him shown by some of the older professors and even managed to "slip in" a little personal business, eagerly flogging a copy of his new journal, *Organic Syntheses*, which he founded and edited with a group of top young chemists he'd worked with during the war. Never having allowed himself such an extended vacation, by August, he was itching to get back to the laboratory.

Within a decade, Conant would make his name known to all the leading chemists on the Continent. The 1920s were a period of extraordinary productivity for him. He published more than eighty papers spanning the field, exploring the mysteries of hemoglobin and chlorophyll, superacids and free radicals, expanding developing areas, and achieving an international reputation at the same time American chemistry was on the way to achieving parity with Europe. He blazed a trail in what would become physical-organic chemistry and—along with its earliest British practitioners, Arthur Lapworth and Christopher Kelk Ingold—helped to establish the new discipline. "Almost alone among American chemists at the time, he quickly assumed leadership on both the current frontiers of organic chemistry: fundamental theory and the structure and properties of natural products," wrote the biophysicist Caryl P. Haskins. "His work was not only of distinction in its own right, but was of national importance in bringing chemical research in the United States in those fields abreast of Europe."

Even as his work flourished, Conant remained a "restless soul." He sought out the stimulation of the wider academic world, spending two semester-long sabbaticals on the Pacific Coast—at the University of California at Berkeley, and the California Institute of Technology (Caltech)—and taking a six-month leave of absence to make a much postponed tour of Germany. The disruptions did nothing to slow his meteoric ascent at Harvard: by 1927, he had reached the highest professorial rank, and two years later became head of the department. With the award of the Chandler Medal in 1932, the *Daily Boston Globe* reported that Conant was now recognized as "one of the most brilliant of the younger organic chemists this country has produced." With stunning efficiency, he had fulfilled his expectations of himself and realized the first of his three youthful ambitions. Looking back, he recalled that the bulk of those days were spent in the happy sameness of research, and would always seem to him to have been "the best years" of his life.

Conant was peculiarly qualified to do pioneering work. His dual thesis with Kohler and Richards placed him in a unique position, and he embarked on his career determined to design experiments that combined his abiding interest in organic chemistry—specifically, the ways in which one organic compound reacted with another—and his training in physical chemistry. His novel, integrated approach bridged the gulf between the two branches of chemistry at a time when it was "almost a point of honor to profess ignorance of the other's field," according to Louis P. Hammett, author of a landmark text on the subject, who had the young Harvard chemist as his lab instructor as an undergraduate. In practical terms, it meant Conant was not wedded to the traditional schools of thought in interpreting chemical phenomena. This freedom bore fruit almost immediately.

It was Conant's "open mind" that had made his chemical gas operation in World War I such a success, observed the historian Paul F. Douglass, "his habit of adventuring to find out, his operating belief that old answers do not solve new problems." Even at this early point in his career, his scientific colleagues recognized him as a "calculated gambler," someone who was "always willing to give a possibly good idea a quick try."

He immediately began doing work of path-breaking importance. Beginning in 1922, Conant undertook a major series of investigations of biological systems by applying the methods of electrochemistry—the use of heat, pressure, electricity, and light—to organic compounds. He constructed his own electrochemical apparatus, which had only been in use a short time, and began measuring the potentials (a measure of the energy per unit charge) of electric cells containing certain pairs of organic compounds. It was a new and competitive field, and before long scientific journals in both Europe and America were full of papers by chemists working along similar lines. Over the next several years and many separate studies, principally with Louis Fieser, Conant investigated the reduction potentials of quinones, elucidated the mechanisms of oxidation-reduction, and showed that the electrochemical behavior of organic compounds was in every way analogous to that of inorganic processes. He correctly predicted the intervention of free radicals (molecules that contain at least one unpaired electron) and went on to study their formation and stability and develop the use of radiocarbon to reveal biochemical processes. "He spanned the whole spectrum of the field," recalled Harvard chemist George Kistiakowsky, "participating in all the areas of importance and anticipating many discoveries to come."

One of his most striking contributions to chemistry was in the study of hemoglobin, the protein that carries oxygen from the lungs to the muscles and other tissues in all mammals. Following in the footsteps of the groundbreaking German chemists Wilhelm Z. Kuster and Hans Fischer, Conant tackled one of the great research challenges of the early twentieth century: the respiratory pigments. With his unerring instinct for important problems, and what his colleagues admiringly called his "scientific imagination," a gift for intuitive guessing, Conant conducted intensive research into the biological pigments hemin (a component of hemoglobin, the protein that provides the red color in blood) and chlorophyll (the green matter in plants). The exact conditions under which hemoglobin combined with oxygen were still being debated, and Conant believed that by using his electrical apparatus he had uncovered a means of studying the oxidation process. All he needed to get started was a solution of hemoglobin. A friend in medical school provided the necessary basic material—a supply of fresh horse blood—that Conant stored in the family ice chest despite his wife's protests.

His experiments soon produced results. "The combination of hemoglobin and oxygen was *not* an oxidation," Conant reported. "If hemoglobin was oxidized, another compound, methemoglobin, was formed. Methemoglobin could not combine with oxygen." Working his way forward with what a colleague described as his characteristic "searching logic," he discovered that methemoglobin could be reduced back to hemoglobin, and when this was done by adding a reducing agent to the solution, the capacity to absorb oxygen was restored. He knew the hemoglobin molecule contained a single iron atom, and concluded that what was involved was "the state of oxidation of this atom." In 1923 he provided new and definitive evidence about the relation of three molecules: hemoglobin, oxygenated hemoglobin (both containing iron in the reduced, or ferrous, state), and methemoglobin (a ferric compound containing no oxygen on the iron). Realizing he had strayed into a "foreign field," namely biochemistry, Conant decided not to submit his paper to the *Journal of the American Chemical Society*, which usually printed communications from his laboratory, but instead sent it to the *Journal of Biological Chemistry*. Conant had added immeasurably to the understanding of the composition of hemoglobin and how it acts. In the world of chemistry, such advances are regarded as every bit as exciting as any discovery by archeologists or polar explorers. Publication of his paper immediately created a stir.

A short time afterward, he was accosted by a well-known biologist, who upon seeing the Harvard chemist rocked back on his heels and exclaimed in frustration, "When I read your paper, I felt like shaking your hand to congratulate you and at the same time wringing your neck with my other hand; I was just on the point of making the same experiments myself!"

While Conant was busy establishing his reputation as an independent investigator, his wife was struggling to adjust to married life. It was a much more modest existence than Patty had anticipated, but she tried to suffer the relative penury of junior professors without complaint. "Teaching is certainly the thing for comfort on a small income," she wrote her mother from her tiny, rented house at 8 Shady Hill Square, where the couple had settled on their return from Europe. Even the frugal Conant had to concede it was "a bit small," but it was only a ten-minute walk from campus, and the best he could do on his salary. With the death of his father in 1922, he could have afforded a larger house, as he took over the management of the estate, a sizable legacy of more than $110,000 in stocks and bonds, and $4,500 in cash, the result of the sale of his engraving business in the last months of his life. Too prudent to touch the capital, Conant drew on the accruing interest to care for his mother and sisters, and insisted on living off his own earnings.

Much to his wife's dismay, his self-discipline and dedication knew no bounds. He disappeared into his laboratory seven days a week, and often retired to his study after dinner to edit his journal articles, despite her attempts to distract him with improving "draughts" of literature. "Jim and I are reading proofs together in the evenings," Patty reported. "It's spicey matter—'520* gr. at 230*, yielding 2½ centimeters'—that sort of thing!"

While their new home's proximity to Harvard was appealing, it also meant they were uncomfortably close to Patty's parents. Conant was on cordial terms with his in-laws but privately resented their constant interference and unsolicited advice. He found himself in the awkward position of being something less than a peer of Richards's, with not only his professional performance subject to scrutiny, but also every aspect of his personal life, habits, tastes, and choice of friends. Try as he might, however, he found it impossible to separate his wife from the entanglements of family. She soaked up their comments, complaints, and quarrels, and he blamed them for upsetting her equilibrium. Both her brothers had inherited their father's nervous susceptibility and were never-ending sources of conflict and upheaval. Bill, who suffered a low period after completing his PhD in chemistry at Harvard, left to continue his studies abroad, first under the famed British physicist Sir Ernest Rutherford at Cambridge University, followed by a term at Göttingen. Over time his native gloominess—which he described as intervals of paralyzing dread and "overapprehensiveness" that had dogged him since the age of sixteen—deepened, and he would scandalize the family by deciding to undergo a long course of psychoanalysis with a "Jewish doctor" in Berlin. Thayer, who dreamed of becoming a naval architect, was puzzlingly erratic and seemed to "borrow trouble" at every turn. Aware of their tendencies, Miriam attempted to run her children's lives well into adulthood.

Patty, the most pliable, had no notion of how to function independently of her mother, whom she insisted on involving in the intricacies of her daily existence. The more Conant tried to set boundaries, the more she slipped back to Follen Street, lonely, bereft, and riddled with anxieties about her ability to be a good wife. A few weeks after she returned from her honeymoon, Patty penned a maudlin letter revealing how desperately she missed her mother—the mere thought of her was "something to weep about"—and counted on her as "the deepest underpinning of life." Describing herself as fortunate to have "the perfect husband," Patty confessed that "he is so devoted to me it almost frightens me sometimes when I think of what I have to live up to—so I simply stop thinking at this point."

Married life did not come easily to her. Unlike the other young professors' wives, she simply could not cope. She filled her diary with lists of things to do and to remember—"be prompt," "do not procrastinate"—but the responsibilities of running a house on a budget seemed to overwhelm her. "Patty did not have a practical bone in her body," observed her niece, Muffy Coolidge. "She had been fussed over by maids her entire life and was not capable of looking after herself let alone anyone else." She took cooking lessons, but the challenge of getting a meal to the table often defeated her, and she despaired of her husband's exacting standards. "Jim wants perfection in food," she fretted to her diary. "Well, I have bent all my energies in that direction—and have tried to be economical to boot."

When Conant finally ventured into the kitchen one night to see what was holding up dinner, he was shocked to find the place an utter shambles. A chemist who always kept his laboratory workbench immaculate, he was appalled by the spectacle of the greasy stove, blackened pots and pans, and sink overflowing with dirty dishes—and at the center, Patty, panting and red-faced from her exertions. Years later, he confided to her cousin Elinor Gregory that he realized then that the disarray was indicative of a more serious problem. What he had viewed in the first flush of romance as his wife's youthful innocence—her vagueness, vacillating moods, and incongruous Victorianism—were symptoms of a deeper fragility. She had absolutely no capacity for self-sufficiency. Without constant support and reassurance, she fell apart. Though he could scarcely afford a housekeeper, Conant hired a woman to come in to clean once a week and retained a kind elderly cook to prepare the evening meal.

It was the beginning of an unhappy cycle of hiring and firing household "help" that would continue the rest of their married life. Threatened by competence, Patty would eventually take against anyone in her employ, convinced that she was the object of gossip and ridicule, or "invidious remarks" about her meanness and penny-pinching. She would lash out in anger, accusing them of taking liberties or being lazy. The maids would either quit on the spot, or answer back and be sent packing. This pattern was only exacerbated by the birth of their first son, James "Jimmy" Richards Conant, in May 1923. Worried about her fitness as a mother, she quickly relinquished the care of the newborn to a nurse. The minute the baby appeared to bond with the nanny, however, Patty dismissed the girl in a jealous rage. Complaining to her parents of the difficulty of finding adequate staff—"the servant question is certainly a burden!"—she would solicit recommendations for a replacement governess, only to abruptly fire her. No one was ever good enough or lasted longer than a few months.

The domestic dramas were never ending. As a succession of cooks, maids, and nannies came and went, Conant begged her to mend her ways. In response to his scolding, Patty vented her frustration in a furious "screed" in her diary: "I have an incorrigible impulse to torment poor little Annie my cook. She is very stupid, piously smug and sanctimonious. On each separate point, I am sure I am in the right: that is *not* the point. I must stop this—it is almost a habit now." Penitently recording her transgressions, a habit dating back to childhood, she reiterated her husband's formula for getting the best out of people. "I must praise more: and only *criticize* when I need to get results by it. Give up the things she can't do; let everything possible pass without notice. I ought to take a little notice of her as a human being." She concluded dolefully, "There's no worse habit than jumping on subordinates, and the children will sense this and imitate if I let them. Jimmy may be ruined by this habit of yours. No excuse for this is valid."

Her sharp tongue also alienated many of the wives in their small academic circle. In 1922, Conant helped form the Shop Club, a monthly dinner society where a diverse group of Harvard scientists, historians, philosophers, and literary critics could meet informally and exchange ideas. Just as he had worked hard as an undergraduate to win a seat at the Signet Society's high table, Conant continued to cultivate relationships with scholars across the university, and relished their wide-ranging discussions as an essential part of his ongoing education. While he impressed many of his colleagues with his lively curiosity and breadth of knowledge—not to mention, for a chemist, a "bantering sense of humor"—what people liked best about Conant was his "straightness," commented John Finley, a Harvard classics professor and close friend, "differences in age and position meant nothing."

They soon discovered his wife was quite the opposite. Conscious of the need to "do my bit as a Harvard lady," Patty tended to lord it over newcomers, playing up her status as an important and sought-after hostess to such a degree that they often decided her hospitality was something they could do without. She could be waspish in regard to the slim pickings among her fellow faculty wives, disparaging the guests at one ladies' luncheon as dowdy and pitifully dull, a collection of "conservative and parrot-minded females, much like those one can see anywhere." Her intellectual snobbery was such that she looked down on professors from other parts of the country, and frequently expressed a horror of their common or "vulgar" standards. Even Conant's old friend Ken Murdock, an English literature instructor at Harvard and frequenter of the Shop Club, found her to be a handful.

Fortunately, as Conant's fame spread, he received countless offers to visit other universities, and both he and Patty jumped at the chance to escape the sometimes suffocating confines of Cambridge. The first of these opportunities came quite unexpectedly in 1924, when his old friend Roger Adams fell ill and asked Conant if he could take over the summer course in organic chemistry he had promised to teach at Berkeley. Eager to gain "a wider view of the American scene," Conant, who had never been west of the Mississippi, accepted with alacrity. The summer school was renowned for its international character, and they soon found themselves hobnobbing with famous European scholars who were participating in the six-week session. Conant felt "too shy" at first to join in, but gradually gained confidence and learned to hold his own in the cosmopolitan atmosphere.

The most memorable part of the trip was their excursion to Yosemite National Park. His Berkeley colleague Joel Hildebrand was an enthusiastic outdoorsman, and like many of the faculty an active member of the Sierra Club, founded by the legendary conservationist John Muir. Hildebrand organized a small climbing party, and they spent a week hiking through the Sierra Nevada Mountains. After so many years sequestered in his laboratory, Conant reveled in the opportunity to immerse himself in nature. He loved the height and scale of the landscape, and the lure of the far horizons. The ease and intoxicating freedom of the months out west whet his appetite for further adventures.

While still in California, he was notified that he had been reappointed assistant professor for another three years. "Which will make eight in all for that," Patty pointedly wrote her father, impatient for her husband's promotion. With his job secure, Conant immediately began making plans for his next trip, an expedition to Germany. Harvard granted him the time off, albeit without salary. He had not been teaching long enough to rate a paid sabbatical. Richards was far from happy about his plans. Why anyone would want to spend time in the country that had almost brought Europe to the brink of ruin was beyond him. But Conant had long been fascinated by the question of how Germany became so dominant in the field of organic chemistry in the half century before the war, and the only way to find the answer was to investigate its universities and laboratories for himself.

Just before they were due to set sail in February 1925, Richards sent over an early birthday present for his daughter: a large check to help cover their expenses, and a packet of letters to the German professors he had known well before the war. "You are a thoughtful, helpful, generous dear to give us so much," Patty wrote her father, aware of what the gesture must have cost him. "It makes us a wonderful easy send-off, and will open all sorts of doors."

They found Germany in the grip of an ugly, brooding nationalism. The Treaty of Versailles had brought peace but not tranquility, and the new Weimar Republic seemed to satisfy no one. The country was reeling from the effects of the devastating postwar inflation, and the general atmosphere, Patty reported in her diary, was of "a most sadly defeated community that is struggling back to normality." Conant, whose German was "fearfully bad," had to rely on his wife, who had studied the language in her youth, to play the part of translator. They took up residence in a shabby but comfortable pension in Munich, the only Americans among a group of impoverished German aristocrats who had been driven from their large homes by the "horrible Socialist burgermeisters."

The Conants were unprepared for the extent of the bitterness about the war. "It seems like dragging up the past to us," Patty wrote, "but to the people here the uneasy present is continuous with that past." Of course, they had been warned that Munich was "the center of discontent," a hotbed of ultranationalists, Communists, anti-Semites, eugenicists, and political extremists of all kinds. To say nothing of the ominous rumblings that accompanied Adolf Hitler's recent return as head of the Nazi Party after his failed Beer Hall Putsch in November 1923. Hitler had been sentenced to five years in prison but was paroled after serving less than nine months by his sympathetic Austrian jailers. Although still barred from making public speeches, he used the time behind bars to write his autobiography, *Mein Kampf*. All in all, it was a very different Germany than the one Conant had imagined.

He argued for hours with his German colleagues over the Treaty of Versailles and who started the war and could not help feeling unsettled by the rabid tone of political discourse. One conversation he overheard was so disturbing in its implications, it left him deeply troubled. He was standing with a group of senior academic and industrial chemists who, in an unguarded moment, were proudly assessing the progress their country had made in the last two years, applauding the stabilization of the mark, withdrawal of the French from the Ruhr Valley, and recent election of Field Marshal Paul von Hindenburg as president. "That's all very well," remarked one of the industrialists, "but let us not forget the debt we owe to those men who went out, revolver in hand, and assassinated those who were leading the fatherland astray!" Unmindful of his presence, or perhaps unaware that he could comprehend their meaning, the men all agreed, wholeheartedly approving the casual reference to the murder, three years earlier, of the foreign minister, Walther Rathenau, a prominent Jewish politician, by members of a right-wing nationalist group. "Such sentiments made my hair stand on end," recalled Conant. "I had never heard assassination justified before. I wondered to myself how a republic could be built on such a foundation of violence."

As he traveled from university to university, visiting Hamburg, Frankfurt, Göttingen, Marburg, Tübingen, Erlangen, Würzburg, Halle, and Dresden, speaking to German scientists at a time "when friendly intercourse had only just been resumed," Conant felt he was learning more about the country's cultural malaise, its political and economic problems, than he was about chemistry. Throughout that spring and summer, he listened to them talk about the present state of German science and lament their past greatness, a time when their country was at the zenith of organic chemistry. He went to the Leipzig laboratory of Wilhelm Ostwald, and came away awed by the list of topflight chemists he had taught, including Richards, who had been one of his students in 1885.

While Conant was not able to fully answer his question about how Germany achieved such a monopoly on organic chemistry in the prewar period, he came away convinced that part of the answer lay in the more formal structure of their university system, combined with high professional standards and an intensely competitive spirit. "The rivalry among universities as well as among individuals had resulted in ruthless intolerance of mediocrity and showmanship," he reflected. "Yet the German system, to an American, seemed heartless."

He was also struck by his discovery of the important role research assistants played in the leading university laboratories. He had always assumed the "massive contributions" made by these institutions were the products of graduate students working under an acclaimed professor. Instead, he learned that German chemists routinely employed research assistants who had already earned their doctorate, and more often than not these trained men remained with them for several years, tackling problems that would be much too difficult for students. At the University of Munich, for example, the "elaborate and tricky" investigations of the structure of chlorophyll and other plant pigments that won Richard Willstatter a Nobel Prize in 1915 had been carried out entirely by research assistants, while the direction of his PhD candidates had been relegated to an associate professor.

Recognizing that this arrangement went a long way to explaining German organic chemists' "impressive output," Conant immediately began contemplating how he might implement a similar setup for his own benefit. He did not have to wait long to find out. That spring, he learned that he had been awarded a grant from the William F. Milton Fund for his hemoglobin work: $3,500 for the first year, and $2,800 for the second. The cash infusion would pay for an assistant and the apparatus. It was not as much as he needed, but it was a start. "[Jim] is simply delighted," Patty proudly informed her parents. "It's work he couldn't do alone, too endlessly complicated; but it's very interesting and now can be really explored. Cheers!"

Before he left Germany, Conant made a trip to the legendary Kaiser Wilhelm Institut fur Physikalische Chemie und Elektrochemie in Dahlem, a suburb of Berlin, and paid his respects to Fritz Haber, who in the seven years since the armistice had become notorious as the "father of chemical warfare." In what Conant recalled as a "cordial" meeting, the two men who had competed to develop more effective annihilating gases politely shook hands and talked shop. Haber's active work on chemical weapons ended in 1918, but not before his lab had investigated lewisite's potential as a weapon and concluded that it was less effective than mustard. It seems unlikely, however, that he would have broached the sensitive subject. Although Haber was proud of his service to his country and had been highly decorated, he had paid a price for his patriotism: his wife, Clara Immerwahr, also a chemist, committed suicide by shooting herself in the heart with his revolver on May 2, 1915, reportedly following an argument over his having personally overseen the initial deployment of chlorine gas at Ypres ten days earlier. His name was an "anathema" to Richards, who was among the many chemists to express his consternation when Haber was awarded a Nobel in 1919—after being passed over the previous year—for synthesizing ammonia.

In Conant's eyes, however, Haber was a pioneer, a quasi-heroic figure from the glory days of German science, before the Kaiser Wilhelm's reputation was tarnished by the war. He was "curious" to meet the brilliant physical chemist and have an opportunity to discuss their common research interests. Conant regaled him with the story of his first attempt at an oxidation reaction using an electrochemical battery apparatus, and his excitement at having made "a great discovery," only to be informed by a professor a few days later that Haber had completed the exact same experiment before the war. No doubt, the fifty-seven-year-old Prussian scientist was flattered by the American's frank admiration. "He paid me the greatest compliment an older man can pay a younger," recalled Conant. "He listened with interest as I spoke."

On his return to Harvard in the fall of 1925, Conant resumed his research with dogged zeal. But after only a year, he was unhappy with his progress. Promotion still eluded him. Moreover, he felt his work was being impeded by the disproportionately heavier teaching load he had to carry as one of the junior members of the department. As the low man on the roster, he also got last pick when it came to graduate students. Adding to his malaise was the deplorable state of Harvard's laboratories, which were an embarrassment compared with those he had toured in Germany. Boylston Hall, built in 1857, had not been remodeled in more than a half century, and was hopelessly dark, cramped, and old-fashioned. Ceilings had collapsed, brought down by floods from above, and the cupboard sashes were so old they gave off a continual rain of iron rust. With the example of German productivity still fresh in his mind, Conant was determined to find a way to improve his situation and opportunities for research. In late 1926, when Arthur A. Noyes of the California Institute of Technology approached him about joining the faculty, Conant was restless and dissatisfied, and ready to make a break.

Eager to recruit a chemist of Conant's reputation, Noyes promised terms and working conditions that far exceeded anything he could expect at Harvard. It was, by any standards, "a most attractive offer": a full professorship, four private assistants, and funding for four fellowships—a financial package totaling $25,000. When Conant made it clear he was underwhelmed by the $7,000 salary, Noyes explained that it was what Caltech paid its physicists, and insisted it would only be for the first year. "The sky's the limit," Conant reported back to Patty. The idea of heading his own laboratory of organic chemistry turned his head. After a two-month sabbatical in Pasadena, California, in the spring of 1927, he had more or less made up his mind to leave Harvard.

When he was finally summoned to a meeting with Lowell, the two staunch New Englanders faced each other awkwardly, "anxious to avoid anything that looked like bargaining." When Conant stated his intention to resign, Lowell responded that he would be "foolish" to throw his lot in with an unknown institution based on uncertain wildcat financing. If he accepted their invitation to go out west, the crusty Brahmin added, "They will end by making you president." To which Conant promptly responded that Lowell, of all people, could "hardly regard such a fate as a misfortune."

Mired as he was in tradition, Lowell had no intention of allowing such a high flier to be poached by a West Coast upstart. Harvard agreed to make him a full professor with a salary of $7,000, effective September 1, 1927. Before he was done, Conant negotiated additional financial support for research, and extracted a number of other concessions, reducing his teaching load and excusing him from tedious administrative chores. He celebrated his promotion by immediately hiring several of Roger Adams's best postdoctorate fellows and assembling his own crack research staff. He set them to work on his next project, determining the molecular structure of chlorophyll.

It was little more than a century since two French chemists, Pierre Joseph Pelletier and Joseph Bienamé Caventou, coined the term *chlorophyll*, combining the Greek words for "green" and "leaf" to describe the mysterious substance in plants that they knew to be essential but did not understand. Six or seven generations of chemists had since tried to crack nature's code. Some of the best scientific minds in the world were involved in the hunt to discover the nature of this vital compound, but progress was slow, and the bypaths and false leads many. Building on the work of his predecessors, Conant was finally able to piece together the complicated mosaic of the green-colored molecule—a vast family of 137 atoms, including those of the elements hydrogen, carbon, oxygen, nitrogen, and magnesium—and establish, at last, the structure of chlorophyll. The number of atoms in chlorophyll and their distribution among the various elements had been known for some time, but he was able to prove the exact arrangement and chemical linkage of the component atoms. He went "neck and neck" with the German organic chemist Hans Fischer, who was working on the same problem—though with a different theory as to its composition—but ended up confirming the Harvard investigator's experimental findings. It would turn out to be among Conant's most significant work, and the contribution that he himself was most proud of, garnering him both the Chandler award and, a year later, the coveted William H. Nichols Medal from the American Chemical Society.*

Just as Conant had anticipated, once his energies were focused exclusively on chemistry, his research output increased dramatically. Convinced that many complex chemical problems would yield to a clever integration of scientific efforts, he sought out ways to integrate his research with that of colleagues in other disciplines, giving rise to a great variety of highly original experimental investigations. Conant's diverse ideas and discoveries had a major impact on the development of science. It is a very technical field, but for example, today the leveling effect of water and similar basic solvents on acidity is accepted as fact, but when he first advanced the idea it was unfamiliar and almost counterintuitive. In 1927, working with his friend Norris Hall, he carried out an investigation of extremely strong acids in nonaqueous solvents, and introduced the concept of "superacidity." Conant went on to develop the concept, showing that sodium acetate, frequently used as a catalyst in experiments, could function as a strong base in acetic acid.

---

* Conant continued to wrestle with the difficult problem presented by the five-membered keto ester ring of chlorophyll. The complete structure of chlorophyll, in all its glory except for the stereochemistry of the ring, was ultimately presented by Fischer and his collaborators in 1940.

And in one of his last major series of studies, he and George W. Wheland initiated a quantitative understanding of extremely weak acids and, using sodium triphenylmethyl as the strong base, were able to determine the acidities of acetophenone, phenylacetylene, fluorene, and diphenylmethane. The generalization of acid-base behavior implied by these experiments was revolutionary for the time, and provided a strong impetus to progress.

Conant also originated, or helped to originate, several other fundamental aspects of chemistry. "He was among the group who applied C-11 (it was the only isotope of carbon then available) to a trail-blazing study of the metabolic pathway," recalled Frank Westheimer, a Conant protégé who later became a professor of chemistry at Harvard. "He and G. B. Kistiakowsky initiated the measurement of the heats of hydrogenation of organic compounds, so as to improve the precision of thermodynamic data relative to those available from heats of combustion. He and Percy Williams Bridgman were the first to investigate the effects of extremely high pressure on the rates of reaction of organic compounds, and discovered the acceleration of polymerization by pressure." And in his work with Paul D. Bartlett on the mechanism of semicarbazone formation, Conant distinguished clearly between kinetic and thermodynamic controls. "That paper alone," exclaimed Westheimer, "exerted a powerful influence on developing theory."

Conant was never satisfied unless he was doing seminal work and moving the boundaries of science. Westheimer, one of Conant's last graduate students, recalled his mentor's brutal appraisal of one of his independent projects. "I described my research project to him. He thought about it for a minute, then he said, 'If you are successful, you'll be a footnote to a footnote in the history of chemistry.'" The remark hit home. Conant's critical evisceration made Westheimer realize that what he had done was "an utterly trial piece of research." But it also had a reinvigorating effect, and he promised himself he would never again do work that was not "potentially important." It had never occurred to him, until that moment, that he might be able to have "a real part in the history of chemistry."

Conant, on the other hand, was clearly chasing history. He produced papers at an astonishing rate, oversaw a busy laboratory, and mentored over sixty young chemists, male and female, many of whom would become future leaders in the field. The places in his laboratory were eagerly sought, as he had what Kistiakowsky recalled as almost a "magnetic attraction for budding chemists."

"He was a very, very energetic, dynamic sort of person," observed

Bartlett, who recalled that Conant led by example. "He expected people to be smart, to get the general idea, plan their moment by moment strategy, and to tell him when they'd found something." If their research turned up something of interest, rather than give instructions on how to proceed, he would ask: "And what are you going to do next?" His expectation that the student would have good ideas of his own was "a constant stimulus toward its fulfillment." At the same time, Conant's absorption in his research was such that he could not always be bothered with the demands of his advisees. Finding him hunched over an experiment one night, a former student remembered presenting him with his study guide to approve and watching as Conant "without ever removing his eye from the test tube, groped with one hand for a pencil, felt for the card, signed it, and pushed it away, never once looking at it or the student."

His work ethic was the stuff of legend, and earned him a reputation for "living in his laboratory." His friends and colleagues were much amused when they heard Conant had swung a deal allowing his family to move into a vacant dwelling on the grounds of the new chemistry building. In the original plan, the dilapidated wood frame house was to have been removed, but when Conant heard it was available for rent, he had it renovated instead. Charlie Crombie, who ran into him on campus, was not the least bit surprised to learn his old roommate was living next door to his lab. Even as an undergraduate, Conant could "never bear to be separated from his experiments," and now those midnight runs to check on his work could be accomplished in robe and slippers.

Conant's unceasing labor was rewarded with rapid advancement. In 1929 he was elevated to the Sheldon Emory Professorship of Chemistry, the pinnacle of academic achievement. In two years, he was made chairman of the department. Ironically, Richards, who had held the same honored title, did not live to see his son-in-law replicate his success. His physical strength began to falter early in 1928, after the death of his brother, Herbert. On March 19 he gave his last lecture. Barely a month later, on April 2, after a final, prolonged bout of depression, he "turned his face to the wall and died." He was sixty. His family was shocked by his sudden death. Miriam plunged into deep mourning. Harvard gave its Nobel laureate a grand send-off. At the memorial service, and later in the biographical memoir Conant penned for the National Academy of Sciences, he made only an oblique reference to his father-in-law's illness, stating that the "nervous load Richards had been carrying for years was too much for the physical organism."

While Patty was distraught at the loss of her godlike father, Conant seemed liberated. Finally free from Richards's censure, he overcame the old man's prejudice against stooping to earn money in nonacademic pursuits. Joining the new breed of "hustling scholars," as Harvard's cultural critic Irving Babbitt dubbed them, Conant took on a number of industrial consulting jobs, including one with the American Petroleum Institute. He embarked on a lucrative relationship with DuPont, which was so eager to keep him that by 1930, it was paying him a monthly retainer of $1,500, more than doubling his annual salary. Conant, who commuted regularly to DuPont's headquarters in Wilmington, Delaware, not only served as an advisor on technical matters but also explored new pharmaceutical products.

His ideas were eclectic and imaginative and, in some cases, ahead of their time. Inspired by the demand for bottled Perrier water in Europe, he even suggested a chemical process for "synthetic carbonated beverages." (Today the industry is based on synthetic ethyl alcohol.) He suggested that DuPont study "the effect of changing the partial pressure of CO_2 and the acidity on the taste," adding that if he was right, carbonated mineral waters could be "put on a scientific basis," and the venture might make a "profitable enterprise." He further supplemented his personal income by producing three more textbooks, including a revised edition of his popular high school laboratory manual with Black, and two influential college textbooks, *Organic Chemistry: A Brief Introductory Course*, and with Albert Harold Blatt, *The Chemistry of Organic Compounds*, which went through several editions and became standard issue in classrooms across the country.

His professional success, coupled with his various moneymaking schemes, largely insulated him and his family from the consequences of the stock market crash and the hard times that followed. Too conservative to ever "play the market," he was horrified by the wild roller-coaster economy, the sudden collapse, and the ongoing eroding effects that slowly diminished his father's real estate holdings. Even in the leanest times, however, Conant never felt the crunch, and actually saw his income rise steadily. "The depression days were affluent days for professors," he recalled, noting that Harvard never cut its salaries and the cost of living was low. "I could read the news of the grim years of 1930, 1931, and 1932 with considerable detachment."

He made it a rule to avoid partisan politics, kept his views to himself, and put off probing questions by joking, "even my closest friends have to guess about how I vote." Although a registered Republican—he hardly if ever voted for a Democrat at the local level—he was far less orthodox when it came to presidential candidates. During the 1920s, he switched his allegiance to the Progressive movement, supporting first Robert La Follette, who earned his respect for his opposition to America's entry into World War I, and later Al Smith, an Irish Catholic Democrat who campaigned as a man of the people. In the election of 1932, he voted for Governor Franklin D. Roosevelt, even though Harvard was heavily for Hoover, and won a bet with a friend that the Republican incumbent would not carry more than six states. He nursed a certain suspicion of Roosevelt's glib charm, but approved of his regulatory expedients and, despite some mixed feelings, supported any New Deal legislation that would help mitigate the runaway inflation and unemployment that had crippled Germany.

His chief regret from his stint as a "professional chemist" was just missing out on the discovery of synthetic rubber, later known as polyethylene, and the financial rewards that would have been forthcoming. During his work with Percy Bridgman, their experiments showed that the polymerization of the hydrocarbon molecule isoprene, the basic unit in natural rubber, was essentially complete in fifty hours at room temperature when the pressure was twelve thousand atmospheres. The end product was a tough, transparent, rubberlike solid. Had he thought to try the effect of high pressure on another hydrocarbon, ethylene, it would have polymerized, yielding polyethylene. As a later edition of Conant's own textbook on organic chemistry explains, polyethylene is a product with important insulating properties, used as a protective rubber coating for making everything from gloves to containers, as well as countless industrial applications. If he had only recognized its valuable characteristics, he and DuPont would have had a "monopoly on the production of a new commercial product now used on every hand." From the point of view of an enterprising chemist, it was the big patent that got away, and even years later he could not read about it without feeling a "pang."

As his fame spread, Conant was sought after by prominent figures for his advice. In 1930 the Rockefeller Institute for Medical Research, in New York, appointed him a scientific advisor to the board of trustees. Impressed by his administrative skills, the institute's founder and president, Simon Flexner, enlisted him in many strategic discussions of how to organize and direct their research, as well as soliciting his opinion on personnel matters. Conant became known for his shrewd counsel and the "sharp insight" with which he attacked problems and assessed people's potential and the best way to get the most out of them. He was adept at raising research funds, and talked the Rockefeller Foundation into underwriting substantial grants for his department. He developed a large network of close friends, many of them dating back to the war, who occupied prominent positions in universities and industry, and their clout was reflected in his swift election to the American Academy of Arts and Sciences and the National Academy of Sciences.

With his rise in the world, and a raft of prestigious awards from his peers, came a new sense of himself, and new social ease. While Patty shrunk from the "overpowering amount of publicity" that came with his prizes, and the endless banquets and newspaper interviews, Conant rose to the occasion. His dry wit and disarmingly informal manner made him a popular figure, and he thoroughly enjoyed participating in professional gatherings. An able lecturer, he spoke lucidly about the broad general aspects of pure science and, according to a journal notice advertising an upcoming talk in Chicago, was that rare chemist who could "refrain from the use of terrifying formulas." Befitting his new stature and prosperity, he invested in some custom tailoring to replace the baggy flannels of his chemistry days. "Jim was the sensation of the day in his new dark blue cheviot suit, with vest and coat and all," Patty informed her mother after one of his latest speeches. "He added a watch-chain across the front, which looked magnificent. He is very proud of passing this milestone."

At the height of his powers in his chosen field, with his towering intellect and deep love of science and thrill of discovery, Conant was an enormously influential figure, and left his mark not only on the school of physical-organic chemists he taught, but on the modern practice of chemistry. "I came to think of Conant as probably the most truly intelligent man I ever knew," Bartlett observed of his mentor. "For him, objectivity seemed to be a natural state of mind, rather than something for which one must strive. The habit of viewing the world as it revealed itself, rather than as he might wish it to be, was fundamental to his professional, political, and administrative life." His "perceptiveness and mobility" meant that he never got stuck on any one problem, but was always looking to the future, to the next new idea or opportunity. "When, with a full range of choice, he repeatedly moved from a field where he had a strong position into something else not always even closely related, it was in pursuit of a bigger challenge, and ever more important activities."

At the time, no one dreamed there was anything more important to Conant than chemistry. Rumors of Lowell's impending retirement were beginning to circulate, but Conant gave no indication he had the slightest interest in the office. He was too young and had too much to do. Already the names of possible successors were being bandied about and Conant's boyhood friend Ken Murdock was whispered to be Lowell's choice as heir apparent. Patty sent the press clippings to her mother about his promotion to dean of the faculty of arts and sciences and speculated cattily about the negative effect of too much advance publicity. "Of course, the more talk in the papers about him there is, the less chance he has of the Presidency, I suppose! Also, if he is marked as Pres. Lowell's choice, that may hurt his cause fatally." But it was all in the way of idle gossip, grist for the mill at Boston tea tables, nothing more.

For the summer of 1930, Conant planned another sojourn in Germany which, given the increasing political tensions, he feared might be the last in a long time. Patty was also in need of a holiday to help restore her health and good cheer. She had suffered two consecutive miscarriages and complained of being worn ragged from minding their two boys, aged seven and four, whom she had come to view as increasingly difficult and "highly strung." He was sending her and the children on ahead to spend a month in the country near Freiburg, on the edge of the Black Forest.

Sharing a small steamer cabin with her sons on the ocean crossing meant that Patty spent a good deal more time alone with them than she was used to at home, where they were relegated to the nursery. She was not reassured by what she saw. Jimmy, her firstborn and favorite, was outwardly a sturdy, handsome boy, but at times his behavior frightened her. "I have been a little shocked to watch him at his rests," Patty wrote her husband from aboard the SS *Cleveland*. "He writhes about as if he were having a kind of fit, a good deal of the time lying doubled up on his back with his legs in the air [she included a small sketch of a flailing figure] and his eyes glaring into space in an intent stare and his lips muttering softly—stories about pirates and wars apparently seething in his brain." He was becoming "fearfully introverted," and, left to himself, sank quickly back into an intense "fantasy life" that did not seem normal. "It doesn't seem quite healthy, do you think so?"

she asked, adding it was probably best to just ignore it and hope he outgrew it. "I am showing no interest, and he will forget this stage soon."

Unlike his brother, little Teddy was a frail, awkward child. He was emotional, spasmodic, and tended, Patty wrote her mother after one of his frequent upsets, to be "a bit neurasthenic." Whereas Jimmy received glowing reports that made her "fairly blush" from his teachers at Shady Hill, a small, private day school founded by the philosopher Ernest Hocking and his wife, Agnes, for the children of Harvard faculty, Teddy did not seem to be profiting from that fine institution. She had often been called to meetings to discuss his "problems," and was afraid he was already exhibiting a defiant streak that marked him out as a black sheep.

In the pages of her diary, she worried that she might be to blame for the "nervous strain" her sons exhibited. She knew she had "irritable streaks," when she was unaccountably angry and cruel, and believed she could see Jimmy already beginning to shrink from her touch. "I pounce on him, hound him, nag him with cutting innuendos," she wrote. "I victimize this helpless, gentle, lovely little soul by my reproaches, which really spring from my own sense of being responsible. He'll learn soon that I'm selfish and full of alibis—then it will be too late to win him back." These fears, stemming from the turbulent spirit that had darkened her family history, she hid from her husband. After a few weeks in Germany, she reported that while both boys continued to be "somewhat unmanageable," it was probably just the tension and excitement of travel, and they would soon settle down.

If Conant shared her concerns about the children, he never mentioned it in his letters. He wrote chiefly about wrapping up his work in his laboratory and how much he looked forward to joining them in Heidelberg in August. Finding himself alone in the Oxford Street house on the long, light summer evenings, he told Patty he had taken up painting as a relaxing pastime. One night, James Phinney Baxter III, a young professor of diplomatic history, dropped by unannounced to take him to dinner and was surprised to find the chemist in a paint-spattered smock. Too embarrassed to admit to his new hobby, Conant led him to believe he had been refurbishing an upstairs bedroom. Later that night, after two glasses of port, Conant came clean and apologized for the deception. "It's all right," Baxter reassured him, "the best submarine captain I know paints pictures."

When Conant finally worked up the courage to show his "collection" to his visiting sisters, they were speechless. "Marjorie withstood the shock pretty well," he wrote Patty of his younger sister, an accomplished painter whose works hung in museums and galleries in Atlanta, where she lived with her husband, Harold Bush-Brown, the head of the Department of Architecture at the Georgia Institute of Technology. Esther, when she recovered her voice, tartly reminded her brother of all his condescending remarks about art being a "queer and unremunerative" occupation. "I hadn't realized I had made such a deep impression as a dyed-in-the-wool specialist," he added, much amused. "Dear, dear."

CHAPTER 8

The Dark Horse

*1933 was quite a year for Germany, America, and me.
Hitler rose to power, Franklin Roosevelt took office, and I
became president of Harvard.*

—JBC

It all started because he had not learned to keep his "mouth shut." Conant had not even contemplated "abdicating from chemistry" in the autumn of 1932 when he was approached by a member of the Harvard Corporation who wanted to pick his brain about the challenges facing the college and the names of scholars capable of directing its fortunes. Naturally he was aware that Lowell, nearing his seventy-sixth birthday, had announced his retirement and that a search committee had been formed and was busy compiling a list of possible successors. But since he was not privy to the inscrutable workings of the Corporation, all he could do was listen to the rumors about the candidates and guess at the outcome like everyone else. So immersed was he in his research, and so far removed from college politics, that when the topic came up at a monthly meeting of the Shop Club, and a list of some fifty likely prospects was read off by one of the members, his name was not among them. Conant had been ill with flu and unable to attend the dinner, but on hearing his wife's account of the proceedings, he could not help feeling "somewhat piqued." After all, he admitted later, "It was a bit hard to be considered beyond the pale of discussion."

The Corporation, cloaked in more mystery and stealth than a papal conclave, met behind closed doors, its deliberations a closely guarded secret. All the intrigue only served to fuel the public and press speculation about the momentous decision: "Harvard Scans the Rolls of Her Sons in Search for President," the *Boston Globe* announced on November 27, 1932. The article went on to explain that the responsibility for naming the new chief rested with the Harvard Corporation, "a little circle of seven men" who made up the "absolute powerful governing body of the university." It was a compact unit that consisted of the current president and six fellows, including Charles P. Curtis, Robert Homans, Dr. Roger I. Lee, Thomas Nelson Perkins, and Henry L. Shattuck. The sixth, and only out-of-towner, was Grenville Clark, a prominent New York lawyer. Final approval of their nominee would have to be obtained from the Board of Overseers, commonly referred to as "the most exclusive club in Boston," a body of thirty members of the alumni that had theoretical veto power over the acts of the Corporation, though it was seldom exercised.

The local papers covered the thrilling business like a horse race, printing the names of the front-runners and handicapping their odds. The betting was that it would be a vigorous young leader, with thirty-seven-year-old Murdock the heavy favorite. But it was a wide-open field with as many as fifty senior professors and patrician luminaries said to be in the running. Adding to the drama, at least three members of the Corporation—Clark, Perkins, and Shattuck—had put themselves forward, despite the apparent conflict of interest. There was no law that it had to be a Harvard man, but it was a precedent of some 260 years standing.

This time, however, there was real pressure to see an "outsider" elected. There was a growing apprehension that Harvard was suffering from what one critic called "the chilling effects of its institutional introspection," and a great many out-of-state alumni were demanding a change from the decades of Yankee stewardship. The principal criticism of the aging Lowell, cast as a kind of "Back Bay Lear" by his detractors, was that he was a tired representative of his class, insular and out of touch. Much of their ire dated back to 1927, when Lowell agreed to head the three-man commission appointed by the state's governor to review the infamous Sacco-Vanzetti case, and determine if the trial and conviction of the two Italian-born anarchists for a 1920 payroll murder had been fair and just, and their execution should take place as ordered. For six years, the plight of the condemned men, Nicola Sacco and Bartolomeo Vanzetti, had polarized people on the right and left, and enraged intellectuals and radicals who believed the pair had been improperly tried.

The liberal Harvard law professor Felix Frankfurter led the movement to reopen the case, presenting a persuasive argument that the judge had been prejudicial and intimidated the jury, only to have Lowell's committee confirm the sentence and send them to their death. "Shall the institution of learning at Cambridge which we once called Harvard be known as the Hangman's House," wrote the *New York World*'s Heywood Broun, a member of the Harvard class of 1910, in a harsh column that caused his fellow alumni no end of distress. Controversy over the Sacco-Vanzetti case continued to hound Lowell for years afterward, convincing most observers that Harvard's highest office was in need of new blood.

All fall and winter, as the various candidates jockeyed for position, Conant's name was never publicly mentioned in connection with the presidency. While he had achieved a measure of distinction in his own field, he was not a figure of popular prestige and was unknown to many of the powerful alumni and officers of the university. Early in the search, Charlie Curtis, the youngest member of the Corporation and a Harvard classmate, had stopped by to canvass his views, and Conant had "declared without question" for Ken Murdock. He was delighted at the promotion he felt sure was coming his old friend's way and had been happy to sing his praises. So that December, when Robert Homans, a recent appointee to the Corporation, requested an informal chat, Conant assumed he was after the same kind of inside dope.

Over tea and toasted muffins in Conant's comfortable black-walled library, lined with thick tomes on history, economics, and philosophy as well as thin volumes of verse, Homans casually sounded him out on a number of issues of concern. Unspoken, but hanging in the air, was the question of whether Harvard was in danger of slipping from her undisputed rank as the foremost American university. Lowell, the greatest brick-and-mortar man in Harvard's history, had achieved his goal of rebuilding the college— overseeing the construction of seven new residential houses, as well as new laboratories, music and museum buildings, and the massive Widener Memorial Library—but had failed to simultaneously shore up its commitment to scholarly distinction. His interest lay in "material rather than intellectual growth," as one critic put it. His twenty-four-year reign had seen a marked drop in Harvard's share of towering academic figures. Gone were Theodore William Richards, William James, George Santayana, Josiah Royce, George Herbert Palmer, George Lyman Kittredge, Frank Taussig, and Frederick Jackson Turner, among others. As the old lions died or retired, they had been replaced by a new type of educator who, while adept at training undergraduates, did not compare to the previous generation in stature and influence.

The university faced new challenges. There were new rivals in the Midwest and California, competing for the best scholars. Important professors had actually turned down chairs at Harvard, something that was unheard of not long ago. Boston was no longer the hub of the universe. The intellectual center of the country had moved to New York, with the result that Harvard, according to H. G. Wells in his most recent book, *The Shape of Things to Come*, was on the verge of becoming a cultural backwater, known for producing effete esthetes and teachings of "elegant impracticability."

Conant, who found Homans to be a good listener, needed little encouragement to air his "negative views." He provided a candid and concise outline of exactly what was wrong with the college, which he believed had suffered from Lowell's persistent efforts to secure a system of individual tutoring. As a direct result, the faculty was being filled with "mediocre men." The college, Conant declared, was going downhill. The crux of the problem, as he saw it, was that the standards for promotion were not high enough. "A university was a collection of eminent scholars," he argued. "If the permanent professors were the most distinguished in the world, then the university would be the best university." Harvard should be a community of "outstanding scholars," he insisted, displaying more intensity than he meant to, and concluding dramatically that anything less was "to betray a trust—to be guilty of almost criminal negligence."

He then made a passionate case for the survival power of universities by referencing the history of Oxford and Cambridge during the Puritan rebellion in the mid-seventeenth century, when their faculties were purged by the royalists and rebels, depending which side was in power. With the restoration of the king, however, both institutions returned to their former greatness, and professors were once again dedicated to the advancement of knowledge and preservation of achievements "the world would not willingly let die."

It was a display of dazzling erudition, disarming earnestness, and naked ambition. For more than an hour, Conant had made a brilliant case for why Harvard needed a scholar of his caliber to lead the university and restore it to its former eminence. Homans was mesmerized. Pausing at one point to catch his breath, Conant apologized for being "unduly critical," but the sixty-year-old barrister merely brushed aside the remark, reached for another muffin, and gestured for him to carry on. When the lawyer finally departed, Conant felt they were of one mind. "The meeting left me with the peculiarly subtle feeling that Mr. Homans and I were kindred spirits," he noted afterward, "and that he was interested in me as a possible candidate."

Nothing had been explicitly said, but Conant came away with the definite impression he had talked himself, if not into the job, at least into being a serious candidate for a position for which he had not previously been considered. It had all happened so quickly, he began to second-guess himself: "I rather doubted my intuitions and was inclined to discount them as the products of an overexcited brain." Patty begged to disagree. Watchful as a cat, she knew better. "My wife, recalling my youthful dream of three lives, which I had forgotten, noted the gleam in my eye when I told her of Homan's interview. She felt fate was closing in on her."

Her instincts were right. Homans had made up his mind then and there that Conant was his choice to be Lowell's replacement. This came as rather a surprise to some, who wondered how the chemist had contrived to emerge from comparative obscurity into a contender. Granted, he had done "well" in the war and had married into a family with impeccable crimson credentials. Still, how was it that this otherwise sedentary, solitary man of science had vaulted to the top of the Corporation's short list?

After Christmas, the other fellows, on one pretext or another, called on Conant in order to size him up. The final selection process took place over a series of dinners that winter. During these stag nights, well-lubricated affairs held in a variety of Boston clubs, the pros and cons of the leading prospects were discussed—as well as the more delicate matters of character and social background—and the list was narrowed down to Elihu Root Jr., a New York lawyer, Henry James (the son of the philosopher and the nephew of the novelist), and Conant. Despite being Lowell's protégé, Murdock had been eliminated after a report reached the fellows' ears that he had been seen "crossing the Atlantic in the company of a woman not his wife."

Meanwhile, they had managed to discover little about Conant's foibles beyond the fact that he preferred beer to strong liquor (on account of a weak stomach) and smoked cigars after dinner, but switched to cigarettes at receptions where women were present. His idea of a holiday was a strenuous week spent climbing the White Mountains of New Hampshire, where he kept a primitive cottage, after which he returned refreshed for work. He was known to have a droll, occasionally mischievous, sense of humor. If he had any religion, he was quiet about it and described himself only as a "deist." It was decided that they needed to learn more. Lawrence Henderson, a close ally of Lowell's and a Conant relation by marriage, was dispatched to do some discreet digging.

While the fellows were generally agreed that Conant had an "attractive personality," several remained unconvinced that he would be able to command with confidence. Despite his obvious achievements and apparent poise, they were leery of his ability to boss what one old hand described as the "hardest boiled alumni in the world." Based on his initial impressions, Grenville Clark, one of the Corporation's most influential members, had his doubts. Writing to Homans on March 8, Clark worried that Conant, not yet forty, was too young, stating that he for one would feel "safer and surer" if they went with "a more mature and more experienced man of greater *demonstrated* ability to take on so many-sided a job." His misgivings were reinforced by a letter Homans received two weeks later from Felix Frankfurter enumerating the chemist's shortcomings:

> The more I think about it, the more distressed I am by the possibility of Conant. Concentration on him seems to me the counsel of despair. If you have read [Alfred North] Whitehead's *Science and the Modern Man*, you will know how much of science is responsible for the mess in which the world now finds itself. From all I have seen of Conant and all I have been able to learn about him cross-examining others, he seems to me an essentially unperceptive mind, however distinguished in its own specialty . . . We need a man and a mind of distinction. A distinguished chemist is not enough."

Still, many were of the view that Charles William Eliot had presided over one of Harvard's golden ages, and when he came to the post, he had been barely thirty-five years old, a failed chemist, and the last choice of everyone on the faculty. Yet this unlikely leader had succeeded in transforming what had been a small, humble college into a great university, adding graduate schools and increasing both the endowment and faculty tenfold. Lowell, it was often said, had endeavored ever since to "rescue the college from the university," rekindling a sense of community through his house plan, and bringing undergraduates and their teachers into closer contact. While the acres of raw red brick were evidence of his building spree, Lowell's hammer had been stilled. The Depression had wiped out many wealthy donors. The days of endless expansion—in acreage, endowment, and enrollment—were over. Harvard was at a crossroads and needed another creative and dynamic president along the lines of Eliot to propel it forward.

Opinion began to shift in Conant's favor after Homans circulated several interviews with admirers, who attested to his outstanding intellect and administrative ability. Toward the end of February, after a brief respite in Atlantic City, New Jersey, Conant began hearing from friends that they had it on "good authority" his name was being considered. "The Cambridge atmosphere since we got back has been thick with excitement," Patty reported to Marjorie in a long letter detailing the developments in the "great game of choosing a president," adding, "Bryant *doesn't* want the job and hopes he won't get offered it. He says, 'The happy days would all be over.' But he apparently feels it couldn't be turned down. He does seem so far from the beaten track as a possibility that it seems impossible he will finally be asked."

A few days later, Grenville Clark summoned Conant to New York and interrogated him at length. Still hoping to derail Conant's candidacy, Clark told him that no offer would be forthcoming. But the previous day, while in Washington at a meeting of the American Chemical Society, Conant had received a note from his wife reporting that Uncle Lawrence (Henderson) had paid her a visit with the sole purpose of gathering details about his family and youth. It appeared the Corporation was having trouble making up its collective mind. Exasperated by the mixed signals, Conant cabled Patty on March 29: ENJOYED YOUR LETTER SUBJECT CERTAINLY GETTING STALE AM GOING TO SUGGEST THEY CONSULT A SPIRITUALIST MEDIUM.

In early April Henderson informed Conant that he had been dispatched by Lowell to explore the possibility of his taking his seat. He also told him Lowell said he would be "a fool" to do it. Conant, who had heard much the same from Lowell before, was unmoved. On a subsequent visit, Henderson disclosed excitedly that Lowell, who had crossed swords with Grenville Clark in the past, felt the lawyer was a "poor choice" and, although he had very little belief in the chemist, was now leaning toward Conant. There were more visits by members of the Corporation, and more questions. Despite all their protestations to the contrary, the presidency was beginning to have the feel of inevitability.

On Monday, April 24, he received a phone call telling him Lowell wanted to see him. A few minutes later, he strode into Conant's office, sat down, and told him stiffly that the Corporation had that morning elected him president. It was a unanimous decision. Formal ratification by the Overseers would take another two weeks, though because of some arcane rule in the charter, it could not be finalized until commencement day in June. There was, he added ominously, no guarantee of their consent. Dressed in his customary old-fashioned morning coat, striped pants, and bright red cravat, the retiring head pledged not to interfere in any way with the new administration, his coolness conveying absolute skepticism. "It was painfully evident," recalled Conant, "that he expected the worst."

Disconcerted by the ungracious reception, and feeling aggrieved, Conant asked outright if his salary demands had been met. Unlike the past two incumbents, he was not a man of means. The expense of maintaining a large official residence was weighing on his mind. But it was not the moment to raise the subject of money, a lapse in manners Lowell punished with a frigid reply. "They said you wanted twenty thousand dollars," he said, "and you shall have it." He added a few well-chosen words about his having *given* to Harvard, not taken, and, with a last withering glance at his successor, departed.

Conant carried on with his day as usual, delivering his final lecture of the semester to his unsuspecting students. As they filed out, he looked around the empty classroom and realized he had just come to the end of his career as a teacher and chemist. He walked quickly back to his home and closed the door, his face wet with tears. He was mourning not only the loss of a subject that had engaged and inspired him since boyhood, but also any dreams of a Nobel, which was now forever beyond his reach. "Parting with chemistry," he reflected later, "was not as easy as I perhaps hoped it would be."

A few days later, after he'd had time to collect his thoughts, he sent Clark a brief conciliatory note. "I hope events will prove that you and the Corporation have not made a mistake," he wrote. "Whatever people may say about the wisdom of your action, they cannot question your courage nor perhaps mine."

When the news of his selection was announced at eleven in the morning on Monday, May 8, 1933, official Harvard let out a gasp of surprise. The reporters who gathered outside University Hall and clamored for a first glimpse of the "dark horse" were astonished to learn he was not present. The professor had kept a long-standing engagement to lecture at the University of Pennsylvania on the abstruse topic of "weak acids and bases."

The slim, boyish president elect immediately shattered two traditions held sacred by his predecessor. First, he happily posed for pictures in his laboratory—even agreeing to hoist a slide rule for the cameras—in stark contrast with Lowell, who, one reporter recalled, "used to flee from pressmen as from a pestilence." Secondly, he issued a brief statement, and agreed to talk to reporters on background. Then he stayed on, chatting and shaking hands like a seasoned politician, impressing the assembled journalists with his "ease, accessibility, and lack of stiff formality," leading the *Boston Herald* to declare that this new man might signal the end of the "stuffed shirt" era.

The Boston papers generally applauded his election. "An admirable choice," opined the *Post*, and the *Globe* agreed. The undergraduates also gave him a friendly reception, with the *Crimson* expressing satisfaction that Conant was "a man who to a large extent has risen from the ranks, and is not a member of that aristocracy represented by the Lowell-Eliot binary." The *New York Times* sounded a more cautious note, calling Conant "100 percent a scientist," and pointing out that he was such an "enigma" that there was no way of anticipating what the future direction of the university might be: "Not only Cambridge, and a family of some 70,000 Harvard alumni, students, and faculty, but probably the entire world of education will now focus its attention on another Harvard experiment."

Patty's family thought he was making a terrible mistake. "I don't in the least see the idea," Bill Richards wrote his sister from Berlin on May 11, 1933, on hearing that Conant had been made president. The news filled him with "horror," and it was quite beyond him to make the expected polite noises about it. "I mean, having to sell one's idea to Teddy Mallinckrodt and the Overseers," he began indignantly. "And pumping the more fatuous of the alumni for that odd, reluctant five dollar bill . . . And weekly speeches to the Harvard Club of Spokane or Little Rock . . . Oh, I suppose plenty of the disadvantages that I can't even imagine have been fought through, to and fro, in your parlour." Richards, by then an assistant professor of chemistry at Princeton University, was appalled at what he saw as the utter waste of talent. "The trouble is that Jim is not only a chemist, an active chemist, but also a very effective one who is by no means nearing the point of exhaustion," he continued, stunned by his brother-in-law's decision to forsake science at the prime of his career. "I've never known Jim to take an unwise step yet—even marrying you, although that looked pretty bad at the time. So I'll just 'have faith,' and admit, meanwhile, that I don't understand the situation."

For his part, Conant had "few illusions" about what lay ahead. Informing his sister Marjorie of his election to what he called "the most thankless job in the USA," he was already bracing for the worst. "You had best enjoy the reflected light while it shines pleasantly," he advised. "You'll have plenty of years of hearing and reading many nasty things about me":

If the president does the right thing, he can count on an almost unanimous howl of disapproval from alumni and others. After all, how many people are there who really understand what a university is for and are interested in seeing things furthered? But that's all part of the contract, and I'm prepared for it, I hope . . . It will be interesting and I hope satisfying but on the whole unpleasant and trying—a very, very lonely job. From May 8th until I retire, it will be very hard to find anyone who will speak absolutely frankly and fully to me about any Harvard matter. But all this is the price of "tyranny tempered by assassination," as Mr. Lowell once described the Harvard system of administration.

I have wept several times at leaving such a pleasant scientific life, but the challenge was simply not to be denied. I have no regrets, and I am sure I shall have none in the future as to the correctness of the decision.

Conant added, "Pray for me, I shall need it."

He told his sister he planned on making no unnecessary enemies, but within days of the announcement of his surprise selection he discovered this would be impossible. Frankfurter was so irritated by Conant's ascension that he told colleagues he wished he had bowed to Roosevelt's request that he become solicitor general, and made up for it by becoming a one-man recruiting agency for FDR's "brain trust." There were grumblings from other graying Harvard eminences who shared Lowell's suspicions of Conant as an outsider. To cap it all off, he received a strained letter of congratulations from Murdock, stating that after much introspection, he found himself "relieved at the outcome," and formally tendering his resignation. Conant read the letter with dismay. He had no intention of letting Murdock go, yet he had a strong foreboding he had just lost the first of many friends.

Within a week of his election, Conant left Cambridge. A family holiday in England and France had been moved forward so he could depart immediately after the announcement. The only problem was that his six-year-old son, Teddy, had just undergone a double mastoid operation at the Boston Children's Hospital, and his wife, who was frantic with worry, refused to leave the boy's side. It was decided that Conant would go ahead alone and spend a few weeks at Oxford and Cambridge studying the much anticipated house plan Lowell had adapted from England's universities.

Conant could not wait to get away. He wanted to avoid the advice of well-meaning colleagues almost as much as the disappointment of his scientific brethren, who believed he was forfeiting his claim to a Nobel. His mother-in-law had been a nightmare. She could not believe he was giving up the "serene mysteries of the laboratory" for what she disdainfully termed "the battlefield of administrative life." In the end, Patty had spent untold hours trying to explain her husband's midlife career change. "You idealize Jim's chemistry," she told her mother. "He wasn't happy in it. He can't be 'happy' in that sense; he is too restless."

Grateful to be making his escape, Conant wrote to his "wonderful wife" from his steamer cabin, thanking her for her fortitude during those last few weeks. "Without you I couldn't possibly face all the troubles ahead!" he admitted. "On the other hand, but for you I should never be asked to face them!"

If he was at all uneasy about leaving her to cope with a sick child, it never occurred to Conant to postpone his trip. Moreover, he fully expected his wife to join him in England as soon as their son was "out of danger." As the new president of Harvard, he would be wined and dined by legions of distinguished dons, and he wanted his "better half" by his side. At his insistence, Patty agreed to leave at the end of the month, packing their oldest off to camp and entrusting the ailing Teddy, who would spend another month in the hospital, to his grandmother's care. As he embarked on his "second life," Conant wrote, it would require they all make some sacrifices. "I am very happy about the summer plans," he concluded with remarkable self-absorption. "I think it will do both Jimmy and Teddy a lot of good. I am sure it will be hard for you at first, but I know you will be courageous and alright."

In the meantime, he discovered there were advantages to traveling alone. He had a lot of thinking to do and relished the time to himself. He realized that his new office demanded "a clear-cut social philosophy," as he later told Henry James, one of the Overseers. One couldn't "handle educational problems satisfactorily in the middle of the twentieth century" without a coherent set of principles and ideals. Unlike Lowell, however, he was not about to "declare war" on his predecessors' policies—despite his rash outburst to Homans—so there was no pressing need to announce his own program for the future of Harvard in a major address. Moreover, as a self-described "cranky New Englander," he was innately skeptical of overblown rhetoric, what he called "the magic of words and beautiful phrases." Being both a scientist and a pragmatist, he preferred to test the soundness of his ideas by seeing what worked and measuring the results, suspending final judgment until all the facts were in. After all, he explained, "education is not something conducted in a vacuum but a social process."

Conant also knew he could not hope to compete with his predecessor's oratory brilliance. At his 1909 inauguration, Lowell unveiled his plans for the college before an audience of some fourteen thousand spectators, an occasion that was marked by two days of festivities and concluded with fireworks. Conant had no desire to stage what amounted to a coronation. He was assuming office in the midst of great uncertainty, shadowed by a banking crisis and deepening Depression. On his return, he recommended dispensing with a formal inauguration. He still had only a vague sense of what he intended to do and was grateful to have "a good excuse" for not making a speech. The truth was he disliked splash, and just wanted the whole thing over and done with as quickly as possible.

On his return to Cambridge in August, he slipped quietly into his new role, eager to attract as little notice as possible. He plunged at once into a busy round of meetings that kept him tethered to his desk throughout the day. He worked at such a ferocious pace, his new colleagues despaired. A reporter from the *Boston Herald*, nosing around campus, heard that Conant tackled the waiting mound of correspondence on his desk with such vigor and tenacity—imparting hours of uninterrupted flowing dictation—that he nearly drove his poor secretary into the ground. When the exhausted girl asked if she could "have a minute" to break for lunch, Conant, glancing at his watch and seeing that it was after three o'clock, assented. "But behind the intimated apology lay a note of impatience at human weakness," wrote the journalist, "and his bowed head, buried again in the welter of work confronting him, was her dismissal." While acknowledging the tale had probably been exaggerated in countless retellings, the *Herald*'s scribe had a point: "The first impression was of a man who spared neither himself or others."

Unlike Roosevelt, who during his first hundred days in office moved with unprecedented dispatch to address the national crisis, Conant assured everyone he met with that he did not have any drastic reforms in mind.

He promised not to do anything hasty that would result in unnecessary upheaval at Harvard, where many of the conservative alumni reviled the emergency measures Congress was hurriedly writing into law. But Conant's mild exterior belied an iron will. He had no intention of being the Board of Overseers's tame chemist. He was biding his time, and it would not be long before he began to implement reforms and innovations every bit as controversial as what was being done in Washington.

Harvard got its first clue of what the new era held in store on the morning of September 23, when the new president addressed the freshman class, appearing on the platform of the New Lecture Hall for the first time since his election. Twenty-three years after the determined boy from Dorchester first passed through the college gates, Conant spoke eloquently of his enduring faith in education as a means of advancement—and, above all, as a way to enhance the store of human knowledge. "Today more than ever, it seems to me, the universities are the custodians of the great spiritual values which the human race has so laboriously won in art, literature, philosophy, and science," he told them. "When you enter a university, you walk on hallowed ground."

Speaking directly to the students, he pointed out that they were embarking on new Harvard careers at the same moment. "You and I are both facing unfamiliar conditions and heavy responsibilities," he said, urging them to make the most of the "free and vigorous intellectual atmosphere," and warning them against the snobbishness, clannishness, and narrowness of outlook that had blighted his school days. "May I suggest that your college career is an excellent time to cultivate a tolerant, skeptical spirit? No one need worry lest he have too few prejudices."

Conant's formal induction on October 9 was almost a nonevent. Only 150 people were invited to see the twenty-third president of Harvard sworn in, and the whole procedure was over in less than fifteen minutes. Before a handpicked audience, standing shoulder to shoulder in the small faculty room in University Hall, Conant, wearing the unadorned black gown of the president, accepted the ancient insignia of the office: the charter, seal, and silver keys to the college. At his request, the modest rites harkened back to Colonial days, when John Leverett was installed as president of the college in 1708. Instead of the traditional sumptuous feast, guests were served what Harvard historian Samuel Morison described with disgust as a "wretched temperance punch." The papers noted that the ceremony, like the man, was unpretentious in the extreme. "No Pomp," they reported a trifle regretfully, while acknowledging that the lack of pageantry was in keeping with the mood of the country.

From the moment he took office, Conant was acutely aware that everyone would be watching to see how he fared. In September he and his family moved into the president's house at 17 Quincy Street, a sumptuous brick mansion Lowell had built for himself and generously bequeathed to the college. Along with it came a large staff, a formidable head housekeeper in the person of Mrs. Beach—who had firm ideas on the subject of etiquette, seating arrangements, menus, and so forth—and the expectation that they play host and hostess to an endless parade of faculty, famous alumni, and visiting dignitaries. The prospect of maintaining the palatial home, and entertaining on such a grand scale, was so daunting to Conant that after some discussion Harvard agreed for the first time in its history to assume the full cost of running the president's house.

Unused to public life, Conant found the social demands onerous. He was not the hearty type. He had little small talk and loathed receiving lines. When bored, or out of his element, he hid behind a chilly exterior that made him seem emotionally detached and, at times, dismissive. More than one old gent was heard to complain that they had got themselves another "cold-fish chemist." He tried his best to fulfill the backslapping, glad-handing duties that came with the job, telling his sister that in "even the most collegiate and football-mad of our alumni there is a spark of intellectual interest," but the effort it took "to fan"—and "not water"—that spark was a strain. His discomfort at a gathering of banking swells aboard the yacht of J. P. Morgan chairman Thomas Lamont was ill-concealed. As one Harvard chronicler noted, "Politically and intellectually, he preferred the yeomanry to the nabobs."

Both Conant and his wife dreaded the frequent embarrassing mentions in the newspapers, and felt enormous pressure not to put a foot wrong. Lowell had been childless, and they hoped the presence of a young family would help "humanize" the imposing official residence. But not long after they moved in, Conant was showing someone through the house and, pointing to his sons' sprawling miniature electric train set on the floor, quipped, "That's what all ballrooms should be used for." The remark was immediately picked up by the press as an example of Conant's unassuming, down-to-earth style—and seized on by critics as both unpresidential and more than a little undignified. "The hard reality is only too apparent," Patty wrote Marjorie of their new life. "It is so 'solemn,' as you say, and sometimes appalling." It was very trying always being watched, living under a proverbial microscope. "The hardest thing for me," she added, "will be to see people continually that I shall enjoy talking to, and yet talk to them without saying anything indiscreet."

In the early months, she slipped up once too often, not quite able to repress the unconscious insolence in her quips and catty asides to friends. Her clever repartee, which amused her dinner companions no end, frequently shocked the other guests and faculty members who happened to be within earshot, until her husband finally had to take her to task. He was horrified that his patrician wife was becoming known for her hauteur and peremptory tone with underlings, especially secretaries and assistants. "Remember! You can never afford to be flip or frank," she wrote in her diary after a stern lecture. "You must not admit the comic side of anyone to whom you have an official relation. You haven't got imagination enough to realize how unguarded remarks can travel. You must remember that you have not got a personal life anymore. Read this over, grit your teeth, & *do not* forget it!"

Patty realized she would not be able to count on her husband to come to her rescue as before. She had grown far too dependent on him and worried she was losing her already fragile sense of herself. "I have been a good deal parasitic mentally—leaning on Jim's perceptions and living in his mind. That has made us very close, but I think it has led me to shirk a little being a complete person." Now that he was "loaded down with cares," she would have to learn to fend for herself. "I see more and more that I am going to need all the resources I can call up in myself," she worried to her diary. "He can't hold my hand anymore."

Unfortunately, Patty's maiden efforts to assert herself as the president's wife usually succeeded in offending one constituency or another. After it got back to Conant that at an advisory board meeting of the Society of Harvard Dames she had held forth on the "Negro question," priggishly siding with the ladies with the most "exaggerated prejudices" rather than "standing up as a champion of tolerance," he was beside himself. "Jim says you were gunning for easy popularity," she wrote contritely after another lecture. "You were making conversation without regard to the responsibility of your position. You tried to draw them out by causal remarks without considering that everything you say indicates the attitude of the Powers That Be . . . The vital essential part of your doing a good job is taking pains conscientiously to be humble and stand for the difficult right thing, rather than to slide along on the surface of charming fatuous popularity (a la Roosevelt!), trading on your position instead of trying to be worthy of it."

Doing the "difficult right thing" was second nature to her husband, whose instincts never led him astray. "Jim has all this that I haven't—the single-minded integrity, fearless humility, common sense and humor," she lamented in her diary, feeling more inadequate than ever. "He always rings true."

Conant cautioned his wife against the corrupting influence of fame, and confusing the deference of Cambridge society with genuine respect and ad-miration. "The only way to keep a sense of proportion is to keep your feet as near the ground as possible," she chastised herself, admitting that she had a tendency to "soar too high" and become intoxicated with her own nobility. "This Mt. Olympus life is bad for you because it erects barriers around your only-too-isolated self."

As the autumn progressed, Conant demonstrated a taste for change and an eagerness to experiment that inspired both optimism and apprehension. One of his first acts was to end the seven o'clock bell, originally instituted in 1760 to announce morning prayers. With unerring logic, he announced that he had "looked into the matter and found no good reason for continuing it," and abolished the antiquated practice. The move was hailed by enthusiastic freshmen as a "New Deal in Harvard's administration." Doing away with such a sacred and venerated custom rankled the old guard, especially when it emerged that Conant's attendance at prayers of any sort was spotty at best. On his first visit to the new Memorial Church, which replaced Appleton Chapel, he reportedly told Willard Sperry, dean of the Harvard Divinity School, that if he ever saw a cross or candles on the communion table, he would "never set foot in the place again."

In the eyes of some, he committed an even graver heresy when he did away with the Latin requirement for the AB (bachelor of arts) degree. Not long afterward, Conant attended the annual dinner of the Signet Society, and the toastmaster, E. K. Rand of the Latin Department, made a point of introducing their honored guest in the dying language, and then painstak-ingly translated his remarks in what was intended as a scholarly rebuke of their uncultured new president. Conant, skilled at this kind of academic sparring, got the better of the Latin professor: "I thought we had come to praise the Signet, not to bury Caesar," he replied with the hallmark asperity that would characterize his approach to Harvard skepticism.

Conant was also the first president to recognize that the lowly day students deserved to have their lot improved, and set aside the ground floor of Dudley Hall so that all the Irish, Italian, and Jewish boys who commuted from Greater Boston would have somewhere to eat their brown-paper-bag lunches. The journalist Theodore White, who was one of them, remembered being grateful for the comfortable chairs now available to lounge in between classes. Conant wanted to make Harvard "something more than a New England school." White was excited by the young president's desire to effect change: "Excellence was his goal as he began shaking up both faculty and student body."

Harvard's administrative system was creaking in every joint, but Conant was too eager, and too inexperienced, to anticipate how controversial his attempts to revitalize the tradition-bound college would prove, especially when coupled with the tough measures necessitated by the financial pressures of the times. As the head of an institution with more than 8,000 students (including all the graduate schools) and 4,200 employees, of which approximately 1,000 were teachers, with an annual budget of $137 million and an endowment of $126 million, he had to manage a vast educational empire. Harvard was solvent, but if the newspaper reports and stock quotations were any indication, it could not continue to operate as it had in the past. The prospects for the future were grim: private giving to the university had plummeted from an average of $10 million a year in the prosperous 1920s to $3.8 million the previous year. A mounting deficit threatened to deplete Lowell's contingency fund and eat into the capital as well. Not even Conant's worst enemies envied him a major endowment drive in the depths of the Depression.

A thrifty New Englander, Conant began belt-tightening across the board. Budgets were slashed and many departments received deep cuts. Of paramount concern was the plight of the undergraduates. More and more families were unable to pay their sons' bills and the number of available scholarships was woefully inadequate. Students were appearing in increasing numbers at the dean's office for aid. Many had been forced to abandon their studies. He felt something had to be done to address the younger generation's disillusionment and growing despair in those dismal Depression years.

In a speech outlining the gravity of the economic catastrophe that same spring, Walter Lippmann said, "There is a limit to the endurance of a democratic people." The line resonated with Conant. The year he had spent in impoverished postwar Germany had convinced him "not to take for granted the continuation of a republic form of government and a prosperous free society." Exploiting the spreading panic in his homeland, Hitler had seized power and imposed a ruthless Fascist regime. The situation in America was not without parallel dangers. The country was in an economic tailspin, with cascading business failures and mounting unemployment. Morale was at rock bottom. The government was divided. Desperate to find a solution, restless groups were urging radical expedients. Despite what Roosevelt had accomplished with his emergency bills, as the months went by and the economy did not get better, the future of democracy in America was also in doubt. "Whether one was a liberal or conservative, young or old," Conant recalled, "one was worried."

It was a disheartening outlook for the new head of the country's oldest university. Despite his early assurances that he had no immediate plans, at his first meeting with the Corporation, Conant did not hesitate to state what he thought should be done. What they needed now, he told them emphatically, "were men, not buildings." Any money raised in the near future should be used for scholarships and professorships. He made no criticism of his predecessor's edifice complex, but it was implicit in his remarks.

What he was proposing represented a bold new departure for the college, and it immediately met with resistance. Given the state of the country, the Corporation was nervous about any appeal for funds. Was it wise to risk stirring up the prominent alumni, many of whom had seen their personal fortunes all but disappear? Brushing aside their fears, Conant pushed them to act quickly, suggesting they use Harvard's upcoming tercentenary celebration to launch a three hundredth anniversary fund. The money would go to new merit-based National Scholarships to enable the most outstanding young men throughout the country to attend Harvard. "We should be able to say that any man with remarkable talents may obtain his education at Harvard," he insisted in his first *President's Report*, "whether he be rich or penniless, whether he comes from Boston or San Francisco." If the Depression continued, he feared Harvard would end up a school for rich men's sons. He was determined to remove any "artificial barriers"—economic or geographic—to receiving a first-class college education. It was the cause, he wrote later, "nearest my heart."

Conant's campaign for scholarships was also a way to begin addressing the age-old problem of Harvard's "exclusivity," which stemmed in no small part from its "exclusively eastern orientation": the fact that 90 percent of the students came from states along the Atlantic Seaboard, and over one half from New England. There were few Catholics and Jews, and almost no students of color. While already thinking in terms of much more far-reaching reforms, his initial scheme for diversifying the student body called for establishing a set of "sliding-scale" scholarships—"the more brilliant the boy, the larger the sum of money"—for a handful of freshmen from a group of Midwestern states. He also advocated awarding much larger stipends. When Conant took office, no students received full scholarships. The average amount allotted—between $300 and $500—did not begin to cover the cost of tuition, room and board, and other expenses, which came to a minimum of $1,100 a year. There were also an array of smaller fellowships and grants beginning at $50 that barely made a dent. Lowell had supported the idea of student employment as a way of building character, but Conant felt many of the boys were working themselves to the point of exhaustion at after-school jobs. He pushed for scholarships paying as much as $1,200 a year to permit them to concentrate on their studies and place them on an equal footing with their peers.

He persuaded the Corporation to allow him to combine some of the meager little grants into a few fat scholarships and begin awarding them in the fall of 1934. It would be done on a trial basis, and in four years they would know if his faith in his ability to recruit gifted freshmen from modest backgrounds—future magna and summa cum laudes—was justified. If his hypothesis was proved correct, and appropriate candidates could be identified, the program would be expanded. In his search for a means of identifying unusually able students, Conant turned to Carl Brigham, a psychology professor at Princeton, who had been instrumental in developing the Scholastic Aptitude Test (SAT), which had been offered by the College Entrance Examination Board since 1926 and seemed "a promising device." He met personally with Edward Lee Thorndike, professor of psychology at Columbia University, to learn about advances in intelligence testing and satisfy himself as to the scientific underpinnings of the research. The latter included three examples of entrance exams Thorndike had constructed for Columbia and Stanford universities, as well as the Army Alpha test used to evaluate recruits in World War I.

After studying the materials, Conant assigned two deans, William Bender and Henry Chauncey, to further investigate the feasibility of using the most successful testing procedures to create a new admissions policy to replace the fusty old college boards, which had a prep-school bias. He had gained entry into Roxbury Latin by competitive examination and wanted to be sure the college's admissions policy assessed aptitude not upper crust advantage. Conant "burned with a fierce disapproval of the old ways at Harvard," observed Nicholas Lemann in *The Big Test: The Secret History of the American Meritocracy*, a book about the groundbreaking educational experiment, "and his first goal as president was to loosen them."

It was the beginning of his interest in a new type of objective examination that could reliably, and with reasonable accuracy, predict academic success, and would eventually lead to his playing a part in the establishment, in 1946, of the Educational Testing Service. He became convinced that standardized intelligence testing was a "science with limitless possibilities," wrote Lemann, who identifies the young Harvard president as one of the founders of the modern American meritocracy. "Conant assumed, in fact, that picking a new elite in just the right way would enhance democracy and justice almost automatically. It was an audacious plan for engineering change in the leadership group and social structure of the country—a kind of quiet, planned coup d'état."

Conant decided to use his first presidential report, a kind of "State of the University" message delivered in January each year, to announce his educational imperatives and make a case for the necessity of his scholarship program. For Harvard to become "a truly national university," he told a New York audience of six hundred alumni, it needed to cast a much wider net in order to bring in men of "exceptional talent," in the form of the most brilliant faculty and the best and broadest student body that could be found. The demands of the present day—and not merely the financial crisis—required sweeping changes. The university had to revise its methods, hiring practices, and organization or risk ending up an antiquated gentleman's club. "If we fail in this regard," he warned, "there are no educational panaceas which will restore Harvard to its position of leadership."

His speech was not a great success. His friends told him he was "too obviously scared." His delivery was too dry. But, at least, it showed conviction. He received widespread publicity and was given good, if not glowing, marks for the first formal presentation of his ideas. In a cover story on him, *Time* magazine declared, "Under James Conant, Harvard is on a manhunt and intends to have the best, whether they have sprung from Boston's Back Bay or Bulltown, W. Va." Realizing the burden of selling his ideas to the public and to prospective donors fell squarely on him, Conant took great pains to improve his performance, aware he needed to do a better job of getting across his message.

In order to promote his new policy, he also had to learn how to publicly defend it, and in the process began to articulate his social and educational ideals. His initial, stumbling efforts to explain the educational and social justifications for his reforms often raised more questions than they answered. When he announced that one of his top priorities was to "swing an axe against the root of privilege" through the expansion of financial aid, Harvard Brahmins got their back up. His constant harping on the need to recruit the "best brains," and insistence on "quality, not quantity," so alarmed the old WASP alumni that he found himself having to soothe ruffled feathers and reassure families that at least 50 percent of the student body would continue to include their offspring. "High character"—an invidious Harvard euphemism long used to distinguish between different classes, religions, and races—would continue to be "essential"; the not so brilliant would not be neglected. When he told yet another reporter he would like to abolish phrases such as "the privilege of higher education" and the very adjective "higher," Harvard historian Richard Norton Smith noted that many in the privileged groups to which Harvard graduates belonged began to harbor reservations about him: "Such fidelity to his own brand of Jeffersonian democracy neatly dovetailed with Roosevelt's proclamation of a new estate for the forgotten man."

His relentless drive for excellence also intimidated members of the faculty. Conant made it clear that hard times necessitated hard choices, stating that it would be "mistaken philanthropy to keep a mediocre man in a university during a time of depression." Too many on the payroll were local boys, related to the Harvard family by blood or marriage. Those crowding the lower ranks of the college hierarchy—the instructors, lecturers, assistant and associate professors—were put on notice that those days were over. Mere teaching talent alone would not be sufficient "to ensure a permanent career at Harvard." He then made good on his threat, gutting the English Department, denying more than a dozen junior instructors reappointment. He pressed Murdock to cull men who had no clear future, and commissioned a study to assess "inbreeding among tenured faculty."

As Conant formulated his agenda, he began to consciously fashion his public image as an educational reformer. Harvard's new president "has a clear vision of what essentially needs doing and a strong will to do it," announced the *New York Times*'s H. I. Brock in an admiring profile. "He learned in the laboratory to deal with facts and deal with them patiently, with the single object of producing results." The particular results he was after, however, would require not only raising standards for tenure, and the "merciless elimination" of unproductive teachers, they would also necessitate "a degree of ruthlessness in the removal of cherished clutter—institutions, practices, and even amiable individuals entrenched in the clutter." Comparing him with the seventeenth-century British statesman and general Oliver Cromwell, a strong leader Harvard's young president especially admired, the *Times*'s writer speculated that Conant, too, might soon find himself labeled "an opportunist or strategist" by critics: "Cromwell had his aims—high ones—and the will to achieve those aims, but so fluid was his mind in regard to the real significance of passing events and current causes—determining which side he stood on at one time and another—that he has been roundly abused for inconsistency and worse."

The parable was not lost on Conant. His prolonged study of Cromwell provided him with many examples of what a leader could expect in a turbulent period, and of "conduct under stress." He knew he would face, soon enough, "the liar, the 'double-crosser,' and the intriguer," he wrote in his memoir, noting that being forewarned was not the same as being well armed. As he waded into his first battles at Harvard, and made his first blunders, it might have been better if his deep reading of history had not taught him "to expect the worst when dealing with other people." If anything, Conant was all too conscious of the fierce opposition he would encounter as he began his assault on the university's incestuous hiring practices and Brahmin power structure. After only a few months of exposure to the constant personal attacks, petty jealousies, and turf wars, he was already regretting his decision to leave the laboratory for the corridors of power. "The presidency is an awful job," he confessed to Miriam in a rare moment of vulnerability. "If you take it, you have got to be willing to knife your best friend." Steeling himself for the fight ahead, he added that he might as well accept that it was part of the job and "stop feeling like a martyr."

Conant missed chemistry more than he had thought possible. The burdens of his office meant he had little time to keep up with the advances in his field. Yet even while confined to Massachusetts Hall, he held weekend conferences with his former chemistry colleagues, encouraging George Kistiakowsky to undertake "a novel investigation of a key metabolic process of the liver." On certain Saturday afternoons, when overcome by longing, Conant would steal away from the president's office and return to his old laboratory to spend a few hours with his first love. Mallinckrodt Hall was locked on weekends, and legend has it that Conant would stand outside, tossing pebbles at the windows until someone let him in. He was eager to keep up with the progress of Emma Dietz, his chief research assistant, who was continuing his work on the chemical composition of chlorophyll, and was on the verge of an important breakthrough. The expected discovery would give the final and complete formulae for chlorophyll a and chlorophyll b, two plant materials of extremely complex nature whose exact composition had never been accurately ascertained. He had earned two medals for his theory as to its composition. It was his last hurrah as a chemist.

That first Christmas at 17 Quincy Street was a subdued affair. They were ten for dinner, including his mother and oldest sister, Esther, as well as Miriam, Bill, and Thayer and his bride to be, Betty. Patty's younger brother, in a rush to be married, had come to ask for help in finding a teaching post at a New England prep school. He was, as usual, in need of financial help, which Miriam blamed on "the times." Conant was exhausted and withdrawn. The economic crisis was growing more critical with each passing month. No one knew what was going to happen. The only thing that was certain, he would joke bleakly, was uncertainty itself.

All his grand plans were on hold. Instead of reconstructing the university, he was retrenching. As was true during the war, when he was worried he could not eat. His stomach was in knots. "He is tense inside although he seems calm," Patty told her mother. "It is the responsibility." She tried to be lively for the children's sake, fussing over all the presents and playing Gilbert and Sullivan tunes on her new phonograph. The boys received enough track for their miniature train set to construct their own "transcontinental railroad," their father observed disapprovingly, though he spent hours on his knees helping to connect it up. But there was no shaking the air of gloom that hung over the holiday. "Jim is so pessimistic," Patty confided. "He says we will only stay six months in this big house."

CHAPTER 9

Unexpected Troubles

To begin with, what place has a scientist as the head of a university?

—Robert Frost

"This is an age of dictators," declared the *New York Times* in March 1934, in a none-too-subtle jab at the current occupant of the White House. In Germany, Italy, and Russia, dictators had all been lifted to the top by revolution or political coup of one kind or another. "But at Harvard," continued the *Times*, "it is different. At Harvard, for three long generations, the president of the university has been czar. He is still czar."

Barely six months in office, the new head was making his presence felt, leading to a widespread acknowledgment both within and without the university that the Lowell era was over and they were living in the "Age of Conant." Given the disintegrating state of the world, it was not a time for timid leaders. Gone was the genteel, leisurely atmosphere, replaced by a new urgency and un-Harvard-like anxiety about the university's relevance in both national and international affairs. Increasingly, Conant found himself caught up in outside events and acrimonious politics, under fire for his handling of everything from Nazis, to New Dealers, to right-wing legislators. Almost everyone had a grievance about his autocratic administrative style. While debates raged in Congress and on campus, he continued to call for the application of reason over emotion in times of crisis, and to defend the importance of a "healthy clash of ideas" as part of the country's—and the college's—proud history. But passions were running high, and lines of division deepening. It got to the point, Conant recalled with chagrin, he could not take to the podium without "unexpected troubles."

In his first commencement address on a hot June afternoon in 1934, Conant spoke out against Hitler's totalitarian grip on education, and reaffirmed his commitment to the principle of academic freedom. The reality of the Nazis' repressive regime was becoming clearer every day as news about the purging of German universities reached across the Atlantic. After Hitler mandated that universities teach only authorized doctrines, thousands of torch-bearing students and professors had paraded through the streets of German cities and college towns laying funeral pyres for the pillaged and impounded books. Praising Harvard's long history of freedom, Conant argued that American universities must be vigilant guardians of liberty—only by doing so could they be of value to their country and worthy of their past. "It will be a sad day for America," he told the thousands of alumni and black-gowned students thronging the Yard, "when either reactionary intolerance or revolutionary zealotry takes possession of our academic halls."

He was nearing the end of his remarks when the air was suddenly pierced by the loud cries of two young female students chanting "Down with Hitler!" "Down with Hanfstaengl!" The hecklers, who had chained their wrists to the stands near the speaker's platform in Sever Quadrangle, attempted to interrupt the proceedings with more catcalls and shouts of "Fascist butchers!" before the police rushed in and led them away. Hesitating only briefly, Conant continued to speak, ignoring the commotion. Half an hour later, turmoil erupted again as seven more student agitators chained themselves to the light poles in front of Lehman Hall, brandishing placards and haranguing spectators.

It was all part of an elaborate demonstration protesting the presence of Hitler's foreign press secretary, Ernst Franz "Putzi" Hanfstaengl, who had been invited to attend his twenty-fifth Harvard reunion that same weekend. Putzi—who never failed to remind reporters that his mother was American and a member of the Boston Sedgwick family—was not only a high-ranking representative of the Nazi regime, he was one of der Führer's close friends and favorite court jester. Ironically, Harvard's notorious alumnus was not even on campus to hear Conant's stirring words, having opted instead to spend the afternoon relaxing at the North Shore mansion of his classmate Louis Agassiz Shaw Jr.

A giant of a man, and hugely gregarious, Putzi was known more for his drinking than intellectual capacity, and for being one of the most popular members of the Harvard class of 1909. Although the foreign correspondent William Shirer described him as "an immense, high-strung, incoherent clown," in his college years he was by all accounts a talented musician and Hasty Pudding star, and much beloved by his peers for his enthusiastic performances at pep rallies, once banging away on an upright piano lashed to the back of a flatbed truck as it steamed through the back streets of Cambridge. The son of a wealthy Munich art dealer and publisher, Hanfstaengl moved in elite circles, was close friends with Theodore Roosevelt Jr., and spent Christmas 1908 at the White House. He returned home after World War I, and his childlike enthusiasm and willing racism made him the perfect partisan for Bavaria's right-wing National Socialist leader, proudly telling his class record in 1922 that he had met "the man who has saved Germany and civilization: Adolf Hitler." The strapping Harvard oarsman was soon serving as Hitler's bodyguard and personal pianist, and the two reportedly collaborated in writing "The German Storm," a Nazi marching song.

On receiving the invitation to be vice marshal of the alumni at Harvard's commencement, Hanfstaengl announced from Berlin in late March 1934 that he was looking forward to it with the "greatest anticipation," and added that he might, "as a surprise," bring a propaganda film which could "show better than any words of mine what we Nazis stand for." After news of his impending visit touched off a storm of protest from Jewish alumni and anti-Nazi groups, he resigned his marshal role and indicated he might not make the reunion, professing to be "flabbergasted" by the negative response.

Not one to surrender the spotlight, Hanfstaengl made news again when he walked into a Berlin bank on June 7, reporters in tow, and requested a draft for 2,500 marks payable to Harvard's new president, James B. Conant. The purpose of the check, he explained, was to endow a $1,000 "Dr. Hanfstaengl scholarship" for study in Germany. Then he handed out copies of a letter he had sent Conant expressing his belief that his gift was a fitting symbol of his "perennial love for Harvard, Boston, and New England."

All the prearrival publicity fueled a growing outcry against his visit. A disgusted Heywood Broun devoted several columns in the *New York World-Telegram* to the disgrace to his old university. "Beware of Nazis Bearing Gifts," warned the *Baltimore Sun* as Hanfstaengl bounded down the gangplank in New York on June 16, carrying in his baggage three busts of German heroes he intended to present to his alma mater.

Conant had never encountered the likes of Putzi before and the Nazi publicist ran rings around him. Hanfstaengl knew he could count on college officials to maintain a dignified silence—Harvard issued a statement to the effect that the reunion invitation was not their doing and solely a matter for the alumni. The Corporation, too important to be inconvenienced by a special meeting, put off ruling on the proffered scholarship until the fall, allowing Hanfstaengl to bask in the role of benefactor. The students also played right into his hands, giving him an unduly warm reception. The youthful editors of the *Crimson* even urged Conant and the Corporation to confer an honorary degree on a son of Harvard who "has risen to distinguished station" in a country "which happens to be a great world power." Meanwhile, Hitler's advance man, flanked by four security guards, created a carnival-like atmosphere wherever he went. During the college's annual Class Day ceremonies, he marched into the stadium and rendered a Nazi salute, which brought a roar of cheers from his friends in the stands.

Conant encountered Putzi only once, when he attended the reunion tea at the president's mansion and shook his hand on the receiving line. "Hanfstaengl appeared large as life," he recalled. As the towering German filed past, he leaned in and whispered, "I bring you greetings from Professor Hoenigschmid." Conant froze. He remembered the Austrian scientist who had studied at Harvard and had been helpful to him on his first visit to Munich in 1925. Conant also suspected that if the two compatriots were on friendly terms, Hoenigschmid was probably now a Nazi. "My response was cold," he recalled. "I did not return his greetings."

Hanfstaengl delighted in his public relations coup, while the university endured a week of embarrassing headlines. In the months following his departure, Conant did his best to mitigate the damage. He pushed for the case against the two women protesters to be dropped. Despite his pleas for clemency, the seven other students were tried and sentenced to six months of hard labor. (They were later pardoned by Massachusetts governor Joseph B. Ely.) When the Corporation met in October, Conant persuaded the fellows to unanimously reject the $1,000 scholarship. Regardless of his personal feelings toward Hanfstaengl, there was nothing that could be done to prevent an alumnus from attending a reunion—all manner of rogues returned to campus all the time. For the same reason, Conant could not stop students and professors from joining in the lavish parties hosted by Back Bay society leaders for the cadets and officers of the German warship *Karlsruhe*, which had docked in Boston harbor a month earlier. But he would not allow the college to accept a financial legacy from such an unacceptable regime.

"To me the answer was clear and simple," he recalled. "Hitler's followers had violated the freedom of the universities; professors had been fired, curricula tampered with." It was equally clear that Hanfstaengl's sole purpose in endowing the scholarship was to promote the new Germany, and what better place to plant its flag than America's oldest university. Convinced that "Hitler's henchmen were trying to use Harvard as an American base to spread approval of the Nazi regime," Conant pushed the Corporation to issue a strong statement.

"We are unwilling to accept a gift from one who has been so closely associated with the leadership of a political party which has inflicted damage on the universities of Germany through measures which have struck at principles we believe to be fundamental to universities throughout the world."

Conant's firm stand finally earned the university some good press, the "Bully for Harvard" headlines far outnumbering the hate mail. "Harvard Rebuffs Dr. Hanfstaengl," cheered the *Daily Boston Globe*, featuring a photograph of the bespectacled college president facing off with the beefy Nazi apologist. Conant took particular satisfaction in a *Herald* editorial that praised his rejection slip as "one of the finest pages in the three centuries of Harvard history." The budding young Fascists on the *Crimson* were affronted and complained that the Nazi's offer did not deserve "so curt and caustic a reply."

While Conant would later dismiss the Hanfstaengl episode as a "public relations problem," some critics view it as damning evidence of his reluctance to sever ties with Germany, despite the book burning and expulsion of Jewish scholars. But at that stage, the National Socialists had been in power for less than eighteen months, and almost no American politicians and very few commentators had the prescience to see where the Nazis' fanaticism and savage philosophy would lead. When Hitler became chancellor of Germany on January 30, 1933, at the head of a shaky coalition, the *New York Times* predicted confidently that the bid by the odd, unprepossessing figure to "translate the wild and whirling words of his campaign speeches into political action" would quickly founder. Even the usually prophetic Walter Lippmann got it wrong. Eager to believe the dictator had only used his strong-arm tactics to hold his disintegrating country together, and would soon moderate his policies, he wrote admiringly of Hitler as the "authentic voice of a genuinely civilized people." Expressing the widespread belief that Nazism was a product of a harsh treaty and ruinous postwar reparations, and fearing what might happen if the German people were made into pariahs, he argued that Germany must not be "morally isolated or politically encircled."

Hitler's withdrawal from the faltering League of Nations less than nine months later was alarming, but not enough for Lippmann and others to advocate action. The United States remained steadfastly isolationist, unwilling to confront the growing militancy of Fascism abroad, and more interested in improving economic conditions at home. With Roosevelt's advisors adopting a policy of watchful waiting, and the leaders of most American corporations and institutions following suit, Conant, as the historian William M. Tuttle Jr. observes, was "not alone in his reticence."

Harvard's young president also aspired to national prominence, and sought wherever possible to avoid what he referred to as the "danger of controversy." New to power, he could be cautious to a fault and was on occasion unwilling to take the risks of leadership. "But as a university president, Conant was not really a free agent," wrote Tuttle. "His constituency was Harvard: her alumni, faculty, and students, and this was a constituency which at times displayed not only ambiguous feelings toward Germany but even pro-Nazi sentiments."

Going back to the spring of 1933, before Conant's election, as the first of thousands of refugee scholars started arriving in the United States, Harvard was conspicuously absent from the ranks of prominent American universities willing to lend a hand and endow temporary lectureships. When the Emergency Committee in Aid of Displaced German Scholars, a humanitarian organization headed by Cornell University's president, Livingston Farrand, approached the outgoing Lowell about inviting a Jewish professor to serve on his faculty for two years, with the promise of a $2,000 stipend from the committee and the Rockefeller Corporation, he was not only unreceptive but responded with unmistakable anti-Semitism. In his view, Jewish organizations were trying to exploit the university for propaganda purposes, and would take advantage of any offer in order to persuade others into following their lead. This example of Harvard's institutional arrogance would have come as no surprise—it had been the university's default mode for decades.

When the Emergency Committee asked the newly installed Conant to reconsider the aid program in the fall, he apologized for not getting to it sooner and agreed to take it up at the Corporation's next meeting in October. Two weeks later, they voted not to participate. Conant, perhaps echoing the Corporation's view, took a hard line. It was one thing to want to help the refugee scholars flooding the academic market, he told Grenville Clark, who favored taking a few, and quite another to "mix up charity and education." Not wanting to sound callous, he explained that in order to hire a professor, there would have to be an opening, but, he added with apparent candor, "I have not seen many men on the list of displaced scholars whom I thought we could use." Conant had vowed to rebuild Harvard's faculty by recruiting topflight teachers, and nothing should stand in the way of achieving that goal. Filling professorships with "imported people of middle age" was not part of the plan and would only discourage their own up-and-coming stars. "The best chance of a brilliant, intellectual future in America," he maintained, "is to give every opportunity for our young men to develop."

Conant's argument at least had the virtue of consistency. His private correspondence on the subject, however, does him little credit, and shows that he was not immune to the latent anti-Semitism that was pervasive at the time. That September, he was contacted by DuPont, soliciting his opinion of Max Bergmann, an organic chemist who had been dismissed from his job at the Kaiser Wilhelm Institute for Leather Research. The company believed that he had a great reputation in Conant's field, but had reservations: "Our London representative states that he is decidedly of the Jewish type and raises the point that his appearance might react against favorable reception in many circles in the United States." Conant responded in the same vein, noting that Bergmann was "certainly very definitely of the Jewish type—rather heavy," and with "none of the earmarks of genius," a view he acknowledged that many American chemists did not share.

Although he had not been asked to make any official ruling in Bergmann's case, Conant added that he was "rather against bringing him over." He reiterated his opinion that "we shall not help the cause of American science any by filling up the good positions in this country by imported foreigners . . . I think a deluge of medium and good men of the Jewish race in scientific positions . . . would do a lot of harm. Needless to say, don't quote me too widely on any of this." By approaching the issue purely as a bureaucratic problem, he hoped to appear disinterested and remain above the fray, but his response suggests a singular lack of empathy for the human dimension of Nazi persecution.

Later that fall, when Bergmann was in New York, Conant did bring him to the attention of Harvard's Chemistry Department but advised Columbia chemist Hans Clarke, with whom the German was staying, "I doubt if we can use him." Clarke pleaded with Conant to help secure Bergmann a post at the Rockefeller Institute, telling him that the outcome "lies entirely in your hands." Bergmann did end up at Rockefeller, though it is unclear if Conant played any part in his getting hired. Harvard eventually took in a number of exiled scholars, including the renowned authority on modern German literature Karl Vietor, psychologist Erik Erikson, art historian Jakob Rosenberg, mathematician Richard von Mises, philologist Werner Jaeger, theoretical physicist Philipp Frank, and Bauhaus architects Walter Gropius and Marcel Breuer.* At the time, however, Conant's single-minded focus on restoring Harvard's eminence prevented him from seeing that an infusion of European talent would revitalize the university, as turned out to be the case at the University of Chicago and other institutions that took in large numbers of Jewish professors. In not exerting his influence to do more on behalf of refugee scholars, concluded Tuttle, Conant's attitude reflected a "failure of compassion and political sensitivity."

Nazi Germany's efforts to score a propaganda victory by exploiting Harvard's prestige continued to test Conant's diplomatic skills. In September 1934, he learned that the University of Berlin would be awarding an honorary degree to the famous dean of the Harvard Law School, Roscoe Pound. There was no doubt that it was a thank-you from Nazi officials. Pound, on a tour of Germany the previous summer, had twice publicly congratulated Hitler for restoring domestic tranquility, and on his return told reporters he had no knowledge of Jewish persecution. Furious that the event would besmirch his "beloved Law School," Felix Frankfurter refused to attend.

Frankfurter vented his spleen over a lunch meeting with Conant, who was understanding but intractable. "We're in a kind of a hole, and I don't see how we can get out of it," he admitted readily. While Conant had nothing but contempt for Pound, whom he called a "pathological case," he argued it would be inconsistent with his belief in academic freedom to interfere

---

* Conant would later laud the refugees' role in American academic life, to say nothing of the important services they rendered in the atomic field, and other weapons projects, that were a "significant contribution" to victory.

with the presentation of the honorary degree. Not only that, but he felt duty bound to attend, explaining he could not stay away without "insulting a friendly government." Frankfurter was not mollified and left after fifteen minutes. As much as Conant privately shared the noble jurist's sense of outrage, he was still too unsure of himself to make a public protest and felt obligated to subject his personal opinions to his official role. "If I were not president of the university," he assured Frankfurter, "I would write the kind of letter you are proposing to send Pound, because I feel about the German situation the way you do."

Although constrained by his position, Conant was not about to allow any pro-Hitler declarations to go unchallenged. As a precaution, the weekend before the ceremony, he and an old friend and classmate, A. Calvert Smith, drafted a short speech that was "not very pleasant" about the Nazi regime. If Conant did not like the tenor of the speeches, he wanted to be ready with a rebuttal. It proved unnecessary, although Pound again praised Hitler's "new order." Conant held his tongue. When photographers asked him to pose with German ambassador Hans Luther and Pound, however, he bristled. "I'm not in it," he snapped, stepping sharply out of the frame. "It's strictly a matter between these two gentlemen. I'm not in it."

In hindsight, Conant realized that Berlin might well have construed his silence for sympathy. His public admiration for German universities was well known, and he had been one of the first prominent scientists to seek a resumption of communication after the war. He had spent considerable time in Germany, had many German friends, and was an ardent admirer of German science. Perhaps his deep personal ties to their country had led Nazi officials to believe he would be "open to their approaches?"

Whether his suspicions were correct or not, Conant knew that after the Putzi debacle, any action Harvard took where Germany was concerned was bound to be regarded by the public as a "judgment on the Nazis." It was no accident that in the spring of 1935, Harvard decided to confer honorary degrees on two famous victims of Nazi persecution: the German theoretical physicist Albert Einstein and the novelist Thomas Mann, both of whom had fled Germany in 1933 after Hitler came to power. The exiled Heinrich Brüning, one of the last chancellors of the Weimar Republic, was also invited to lecture. Brüning, a Catholic who was an outspoken opponent of the Nazi Party, was later offered a place on the faculty. Conant also went out of his way to publicly condemn the forces that threatened free intellectual and political inquiry in speech after speech. "In at least two foreign countries we see brutal and degrading tyranny," he warned in a baccalaureate sermon in June 1935. "In the whole world, reason ebbs and hope for freedom and liberty runs low."

When he denounced Nazism, which he did increasingly in the mid-1930s, Conant was fastidious about confining his remarks to the realm of education, not wanting to enmesh the university in politics. As Harvard's leader, he made academic freedom the fundamental issue. The Nazi threat, as Conant articulated it, was aimed at the very heart of universities, and he was relentless in his attacks on their pernicious educational policies: "The suppression of academic freedom, rigid censorship, the abolition of individual liberty of opinion." Democratic societies had to guard the "spirit of inquiry" against persecution, "or by a series of definite steps we shall find ourselves living in a spiritual prison with an organized mob for our jailors."

Despite his doubts about acquiescing to Nazi authorities, when it came to deciding if Harvard would join in the celebration of the 550th anniversary of the University of Heidelberg, Conant chose not to snub the Nazi-controlled institution, even though he believed "the case for a sharp refusal was easy to make." The once-proud university had been purged of Jewish scholars, and almost one quarter of the faculty had been fired or coerced into resigning. Oxford and Cambridge immediately announced that they would boycott the event, with every other British university acting accordingly, as well as many throughout Europe. American universities, however, did not demonstrate the same solidarity, with Columbia, Cornell, and Yale universities among the two dozen who announced they would pay their respects. Conant argued that Harvard should accept Heidelberg's invitation, both as a matter of principle and practicality. "Even if one despised the regime in power," he maintained, one should endeavor "to build a scholarly bridge between two nations"—if only to give encouragement to those still engaged in the struggle for freedom within Germany.

His memories of the bitter divisiveness that led to the last conflict convinced him the European universities had taken "an unwise step in breaking diplomatic relations" with their German counterparts. "If one allows political, racial, or religious matters to enter into a question of containing academic and scientific relations," he reasoned, "one is headed down the path which leads to the terrible prejudices and absurd actions taken by scientists and universities during the World War." He preferred to honor the "ancient ties" which united them, independent of the current tensions. Conant was also motivated by the fact that Harvard was about to issue invitations to its own three hundredth anniversary, to be held in the fall. He argued that the international celebration would not be complete without the presence of the Germans, so at least a dozen were included on the final guest list. He anticipated that the decision would not be well received in certain quarters, but he was unprepared for the "shower of abuse." Angry letters poured in, many of them excoriating him for maintaining friendly relations with the Reich. Conant resented the implications. It had been a difficult decision. Torn over what to do, he had consulted with the presidents of Columbia and Yale, and together they had "weighed the pros and cons" before sending delegates. Moreover, he considered himself to be "strongly anti-Nazi," his views a matter of public record. "No one seemed to remember our letter to Hanfstaengl," he wrote ruefully of the document that was the "crystallization of resentment" he bore Hitler's regime.

Harvard's academic community abided by Conant's decision, but at Columbia, where President Nicholas Murray Butler's accommodationist stance was already a point of contention, students and faculty demanded angrily he rescind his acceptance of the Heidelberg invitation. After a noisy rally in front of his home, Butler had the student leader expelled and fired faculty agitators. As opposition mounted, he proposed that Columbia, Harvard, and Yale issue a joint statement, or possibly three identical statements, condemning Nazism, and submitted a rough draft of what he had in mind.

Conant responded that he and president James Angell of Yale thought his letter "perhaps too gentle" to serve their purpose. Conant wanted to stress that academic freedom was under siege in many countries. He also felt three identical statements was discourteous. Instead, he favored a joint statement deploring Nazi domination that could serve as a fig leaf of sorts in the event the academic pageant was hijacked by propaganda.

Only minutes into the opening ceremony at Heidelberg, it was apparent the birthday party was going to be a political orgy. The festival was launched by a Nazi military review, the traditional procession of brightly colored silks and academic robes replaced by squads of black-shirted guards and brown-shirted storm troopers. Once a citadel of learning, Heidelberg had been reduced to a factory for Nazi ideas and ideals. The speakers all spouted the same Aryan ideology and fraudulent race science. Repulsed by remarks made by the minister of education, Bernhard Rust, who asserted the supremacy of the Nazi Weltanschauung, or worldview, Angell wanted to publish their statement of protest. Conant conceded that Rust and others "pronounced a lot of nonsense about education and research, nonsense which," he added, "is not only absurd but dangerous." But it could have been worse. For his part, Butler saw nothing terribly amiss. The three university presidents concluded there was no need to disassociate themselves from the proceedings and cowardly withheld their denunciatory statement.

Conant was soon second-guessing himself. Heidelberg had been a shameful spectacle, and he could not deny there had been an element of expediency in his decision to send representatives rather than give offense by refusing the invitation and run the risk of reciprocal boycotts. "What my views would have been if we had not been celebrating our tercentenary, I cannot tell you," he admitted a year later to Princeton's president, Harold W. Dodds, granting that the inopportune timing of their back-to-back academic pageants may have made him more amenable, and he might have been "rationalizing a situation into which circumstances forced us!"

When the issue came up again a year later with a request to attend Göttingen's two hundredth, Conant still clung stubbornly to the hope that contact could be maintained. Given the outcry over Heidelberg, and increasingly distressing news from Germany, Grenville Clark and others persuaded him to turn it down. Rather than decline the invitation outright, however, Conant chose to be noncommittal. Harvard notified Göttingen that it would "endeavor" to send a delegate, leaving it unclear if the university was refusing to participate or simply that no one was available to go. Not yet much of a statesman, he failed to anticipate the hazards of ambiguity. As a consequence, in the weeks that followed, people either attacked or applauded the decision, depending on how they interpreted his intentions.

Looking back two decades later on his strained "diplomatic relations" with Germany, Conant would reflect that the Nazis' emergence as a major force placed him on the horns of a cruel dilemma: "the dilemma of those abroad who had friendly feelings for Germany but detested Hitler." Although criticized for being indecisive and inconsistent, he endeavored to occupy a middle ground that he defined as the international fraternity of scholars. Like most compromises, however well meant, it was hard to defend. The difficulty was that "a friendly act" toward Germany could "always be misinterpreted as a friendly act toward Hitler. On the other hand, a repudiation of Hitler could always be misinterpreted as a repudiation of Germany." It was a dilemma he would continue to wrestle with until the Nazis' escalating "barbarity" made any further concessions impossible.

Ironically, even in his liberty-proclaiming Massachusetts, controversy flared over the issue of academic freedom, catapulting Conant into the forefront of the debate and a role of national leadership. His first year as president coincided with the first year of the New Deal, and everywhere he went, he ran into irate graduates fuming about the "dangerous follies of the current administration." The fact that FDR was one of them, class of 1904, only made it worse. The majority of the Harvard community, young and old, opposed Roosevelt politically and loathed him personally—the standard accusation was that he was a "traitor to his class"—so much so that the Reverend Walter Russell Bowie, FDR's old *Crimson* colleague, was astonished by the "rancorous and almost hysterical political animus that rose against him and what he stood for."

Most of the specific complaints Conant heard were about the radical teaching of economics, specifically the selection of teachers who were advocates of Roosevelt's unsound fiscal policy. Conant vigorously defended the composition of his faculty. Harvard's economists, be they Democrat or Republican, prolabor or laisser-faire, were entitled to their own ideas. But as criticism of the New Deal continued to mount, so did the anger at the men responsible for the reviled political revolution. Roosevelt relied heavily on scholarly expertise, and his alphabet agencies were brimming with Harvard men: Lloyd Garrison, chairman of the National Labor Relations Board; Thomas H. Eliot, grandson of the former college president, who served as chief counsel to the Social Security Board; influential aides Adolf Berle Jr., Benjamin V. Cohen, and Thomas Corcoran; economic advisor Stuart Chase; and roving administrator Archibald MacLeish. "This country is being run by a group of college professors," griped West Virginia senator Henry Hatfield, summing up the common suspicion that "this brain trust is endeavoring to force Socialism on the American people."

Second only to FDR, the Harvard New Dealer they loved to hate was Felix Frankfurter, the president's close friend and ace recruiter. Donors expressed doubts about the outspoken law professor; a letter arrived from one offering a large sum of money if Conant would fire him. Mrs. Charles Francis Adams III, the wife of a Harvard overseer, cornered Conant at a dinner party and "quizzed" him on whether or not Felix Frankfurter was "a dangerous Communist." Try as he might to preserve the appearance of political neutrality, Conant was always on the defensive.

The anti–New Deal sentiment, which continued to grow in the year running up to the 1936 election, reached a crescendo when the foremost liberal in FDR's Cabinet, Henry A. Wallace was chosen to receive an honorary degree in the spring of 1935. As secretary of agriculture, Wallace had devoted himself to carrying out his groundbreaking farm relief program with such ability and fortitude that even the *Crimson* editors grudgingly conceded their admiration. Unfortunately, shortly after he was invited, the once little-known plant scientist kicked his campaign into high gear and took it upon himself to go to New England and deliver a speech lambasting New England manufacturers. The Board of Overseers was apoplectic, with some members hotly demanding the honor be withdrawn. Conant faced them down, and Wallace collected his degree. Taking great care in the wording of the accompanying citation, Conant, who privately approved of the New Deal as a "worthwhile experiment," revealed his sympathies in his description of Wallace as "a public servant of deep faith and high integrity who finds courage to attempt an uncharted journey in our modern wilderness."

His high praise caused institutional nervousness among loyalists of the old order, and the grumbling continued. It had not escaped their notice that Conant often expressed admiration for FDR's goals and gift for lifting the country's spirits, or that he and his wife were among the steady procession of Harvard visitors to sign the White House guest book. With the launching of the Second New Deal in July 1935, and FDR's pushing through his "wealth tax" a month later, the alumni were soon up in arms again.

Some saw Conant's preoccupation with "meritocracy," and endless speeches on equal opportunity and helping the have-nots access a Harvard education, as taking a page straight out of Roosevelt's reform agenda. In his second *President's Report*, Conant had stepped up his rhetoric, explicitly linking the availability of scholarship money to social mobility. In an ardent appeal for more prize fellowships, he argued that the American dream of equal opportunity would soon disappear if nothing was done. The Western frontier that Harvard historian Frederick Jackson Turner glorified had vanished, the huge immigrant migrations of the turn of the century were at an end, and the tremendous changes caused by industrialization were unlikely to find a parallel in the years ahead. "We appear to be entering a static period in our social history," Conant worried. "Many powerful factors tend to force even the most ambitious youths into a groove predetermined by geographical and economic considerations." He was absolutely committed to the idea that a college education, available to everyone, could replace the distinctive democratizing role played by the open continent, and provide a means for every citizen to rise up in the world.

Not only was the increased stratification of American society a problem, Conant believed the search for a few good men capable of rising to the top—based on merit measured by their ability and knowledge—and the chance to provide them with the training necessary to make them leaders in the fields of medicine, law, and science, could make all the difference to the country's future. "The presence or absence of a few outstanding thinkers in a profession may determine for years the whole trend of a branch of human thought and practice." As the Depression illustrated all too clearly, the need for able leaders to help conquer the ongoing crisis had never been more urgent. Conant's "academic New Deal," as the *New York Times* touted it, proposed to put Harvard "in a position to bear her full share of the burden of this responsibility."

Conant's message, like FDR's, assumed a mandate for change that not everyone shared. Conservative alumni blamed their earnest, conscience-stricken boy-president for the university's drift to the left. Their dissatisfaction was hurting the fund-raising efforts for Harvard's upcoming tercentenary, the all-important event that, for better or worse, would be seen as a benchmark of Conant's tenure thus far. Complicating matters was that Lowell, who was pouring all his octogenarian energy into planning his part in the birthday celebration, was an arch foe of the New Deal. Lowell let it be known that he was "less than pleased" that Conant had invited Roosevelt to attend as an honored guest and asked him to address the alumni. Indignant, Lowell said he would not preside over any ceremony at which Roosevelt spoke. With the election less than two months after the Harvard festivities, he was not going to give *that man in the White House* the opportunity to deliver a "stump speech." His annoyance, Conant felt sure, was exacerbated by the prospect of "having to introduce a man he despised to an audience he loved."

Lowell was eventually persuaded that short of a public scandal, a speech by the sitting president was inevitable. Still piqued, he wrote FDR a condescending letter—addressing the chief executive as "Mr. Franklin D. Roosevelt"—suggesting that he limit his remarks to "about ten minutes." Conant, who was caught in the middle, did not care for Lowell's tone, "which was that of a schoolmaster telling a pupil what to say—or rather what not to say." Roosevelt took even greater exception to Lowell's attitude: "Damn," he wrote Frankfurter, and asked for advice on how to respond to the cantankerous old man.

While Conant attempted to soothe Lowell's ego, assuring him that it would be "very bad politics for [FDR] to speak too long" and "he is above everything else a politician," Frankfurter ran interference on the other end, with Roosevelt relying on him to use his "ca'm jedgment" to draft a dignified response. Together they managed to defuse the situation and persuade the feuding aristocrats to play nicely, though Frankfurter later described the correspondence between the president emeritus of Harvard and the president of the United States as "incredible among cultured men and without precedent in this country."

While Conant was busy fending off charges of New Deal indoctrination at Harvard, he was aware of the "increasing suspicion of academic people" generally throughout the country, fueled by the conservative publisher William Randolph Hearst's crusade against "Red professors." Playing on the anxiety created by the increased Communist and Socialist activity during the Depression, Hearst unleashed a wave of editorials charging that some of the country's foremost educators were plotting sedition and deliberately misleading students into being "disloyal to our American ideals." The country was being destroyed by the "Raw Deal," as Hearst called it, and Roosevelt, whose Cabinet was crawling with professors, was a tool of radical intellectuals. The only cure was to root out the Red teachers and propagandists who were corrupting the young.

The controversy came to a head in the winter of 1934, when the Massachusetts legislature introduced a bill proposing a mandatory loyalty oath requiring teachers to swear allegiance to state and federal constitutions. Tired of being pestered to do something about the universities, and Harvard in particular, as "hot beds of radicalism," Conant decided the issue had to be joined. He led the campaign to oppose the teacher's oath bill and wrote to every college president in the state, requesting that they testify against the discriminatory and restrictive measure and help prevent its passage. In a stormy public committee hearing in April, he took to the floor, raising his reedy voice above the chorus of boos and hisses to criticize the assault on academic freedom, which he said was a menacing first step toward a totalitarian society.

In a speech at Amherst College that winter, Conant took aim at the crit-

ics. "It is being said that our higher education has no unity, that the influence of colleges and universities is purely negative, that real problems are
avoided or listlessly discussed by disillusioned old men," he stated. "But I
for one will not admit for a moment that there is any lack of purpose, any
lack of positive faith in the great undertaking in which we are embarked."
Declaring that he would "go down fighting" before giving in to the outside
forces that threatened intellectual freedom, he called for colleges and universities to serve as "an arena for combat" for debate on the highly charged
social, political, and economic issues of the day. And in a nod to the reactionaries on his own campus, he added that for the same reason, "We must
also have our share of thoughtful rebels on our faculties," for it was only in
the "heat of battle" that new ideas and new values were forged.

The *New York Times* hailed the speech as a "kind of academic declaration of independence," and the widespread coverage it received cemented
his reputation as the nation's "defender of free inquiry." Caught up in the
fervor of his cause, Conant made an impassioned plea for educators to be
"more militant" than ever, raising expectations that he would carry the fight
against the teacher's oath bill to the courts. But after the Massachusetts legislature passed the oath bill in June 1935, he decided that further combat was
"hopeless." A semipublic institution like Harvard could not defy the state.
Conant reluctantly informed the faculty members that they had no choice
but to comply. A *Times* headline captured his typically blunt instructions:
"Take Oath or Quit."

Some professors were shocked at how quickly Conant folded his tent.
When Harvard geologist Kirtley Mather—a descendant of the fiery Puritan
minister Cotton Mather—refused to sign the oath, declaring the law un-
constitutional and rallying a group of liberal professors to his side, Conant
hurried back from a trip to set them straight. "It is out of the question for
Harvard as an institution to consider not obeying the law," he told them
in no uncertain terms, calling the statute "unfortunate" but any ensuing
legal controversy more so. Under pressure from Conant, Mather signed
the oath, but he and his followers felt let down. They were dismayed, as
one put it, to see their chief "dunking his promising defense in a tub of
tepid water."

Conant, however, had come a long way in understanding the latitude
available to an astute leader. While compelled to obey the letter of the law,
he quietly negotiated a compromise with the attorney general of Massachusetts, Paul Dever, who agreed that as long as the oaths were signed, he did

not care what reservations the professors put down on paper. That spring, Conant joined the effort to repeal the "obnoxious law," once more rallying the college presidents. Once more they made their arguments in vain.

Still disturbed by the "dangerous precedent" set by the loyalty oath, Conant did not let the matter rest. On March 20, 1936, in a speech in the old Sanders Theatre that was carried on national radio, he outlined the plans for Harvard's three hundredth birthday—six months of public festivities drawing scholars from the world over, culminating in a grand three-day finale in September—and justified the elaborate celebration by underscoring the important role of the university in a democracy: "This is admittedly a time of trouble and depression," he told his listeners, "but it is also a time of peril for the universities of the world."

Pointing to what had happened in Germany, Conant connected the intolerance abroad with emerging fears at home, stating, "Liberty is the life blood of those who are in quest of the truth, and liberty has vanished." In Russia, it had vanished nearly a generation ago. He went on to scold American politicians for taking the "first step in the same direction," and attempting to curtail the universities' independence and freedom of inquiry by enacting the teacher's oath. "No issue of patriotism is here involved; the issue is between those who have confidence in the learned world and those who fail to understand it and hence distrust it, dislike it, and would eventually curb it." While the oath law might seem innocuous, it was "the straw" that showed which way the wind was blowing—a warning of "the havoc of the gale in other lands."

Conant spent the summer preparing for Harvard's big birthday and playing host to thousands of renowned scientists and scholars from all over the world. But "black shadows surrounded all the gatherings," he recalled. "The probability of still another European war was never far distant from our minds." The papers were filled with reports of Italian dictator Benito Mussolini's assault on Ethiopia, including stories of the use of poison gas against civilians. Hitler's troops were consolidating their occupation of the Rhineland, a key industrial region in the west lost to France under the Treaty of Versailles, a sign they were preparing for further territorial aggression. Paralyzed by fear, Britain and France did nothing. Nevertheless, the hum of activity on Harvard's campus, the exchange of ideas and renewal of intellectual ties, buoyed Conant's spirits, making him savor what might be the last truly international academic reunion for years to come. Here, at least, was conclusive evidence that "this country prized triumphs of the mind for their own sake, as well as for their utility."

The Corporation had pressed Conant to take advantage of the tercentenary to present a full-length account of his ideas—"the equivalent of an inaugural address." He spent months carefully crafting his speech. He believed that as president of Harvard, it was his responsibility to help lead the way through those dark days, when the world faced the rising threat of totalitarianism, and he began to reassess not only the role of the university in a democracy but also the uses to which he could put his own increasingly public voice.

Rain, the one detail about the final tercentenary day beyond Conant's control, held off just long enough to allow him to deliver the most important speech of his career without getting thoroughly drenched. At nine thirty on the morning of Friday, September 18, a bugle sounded, and fifteen thousand alumni marched four abreast to the exposed and sopping seats in Harvard Yard, while President Roosevelt, in a silk hat and cutaway, leaning heavily on the arm of a military aide, led a procession of dignitaries across the stage, seating himself in a damp red velvet chair on Conant's right. A crackle over the loudspeakers announced that Conant had consulted a meteorologist who'd forecast that the steady drizzle would last only a half hour. By the time they had gotten through all the dreary salutary orations and Morison's "Early History of Harvard," the rain had stopped, and the college's forty-three-year-old president leapt to his feet. "Such a gathering as this," Conant began, peering anxiously at the sky, "could come together only to commemorate an act of faith . . ."

Warning that a "wave of anti-intellectualism is passing around the world," Conant went on to make a powerful case for Harvard and the liberal arts tradition as a means of ensuring the progress of American society. To bring "order out of chaos" was the educational mission of America's universities, and in order to continue doing that in such a challenging time, he declared, "one condition is essential: absolute freedom of discussion, absolute unmolested inquiry. We must have a spirit of tolerance which allows the expression of all opinions, however heretical they might appear." If his rhetoric did not quite soar, his spirit of defiance more than carried the day, and the prolonged applause showed that the audience was with him.

Just as he finished, a fresh torrent began, and the final convocation was moved indoors to the Sanders Theatre. Relieved that apart from the storm there had been little turbulence, Conant was on tenterhooks waiting to see how FDR would handle the hostile crowd. Smiling broadly, the president purposefully omitted Lowell's name in his opening greeting and immediately addressed his adversaries: a hundred years ago, when Harvard was celebrating its 200th anniversary, Andrew Jackson was president, and the alumni were "sorely troubled concerning the state of the nation," he stated. Fifty years ago, when Harvard was celebrating its 250th anniversary, Grover Cleveland was president, and the "alumni were again sorely troubled," he intoned even more emphatically. "Now on the three hundredth anniversary, I am president . . ." Roosevelt paused midsentence; his meaning clear. Disarmed by his audacity, the thousand loyal sons of Harvard filling the theater burst into laughter.

The soggy celebration was deemed a success. *Time* magazine put Harvard's fledgling patriarch on the cover: "As proud as he might be of his university, which after 300 years has no US peer, many a Harvard man was prouder of the university's new president. Son of a humble Dorchester photoengraver, James Bryant Conant, by his gracious and wise bearing, distinguished himself last week in the midst of a large body of social aristocrats, ably established his membership in the aristocracy of brains."

Conant enjoyed his moment in the sun. But controversy was never absent at the college. He knew the accolades bought him only a temporary reprieve. In spite of Yale president James Angell's gibe about the tercentenary deluge being "Conant's way of soaking the rich," the trustees were unimpressed with the paltry $3 million netted by his national scholarship fund-raising drive, which was well below expectations, inspiring fresh doubts about his sales pitch.

The faculty also took a jaundiced view of his elevated profile. Many tended to agree with the *New Yorker* magazine's conclusion that the "president of Harvard is an autocrat." In an exhaustive two-part examination of his character and career, the Pulitzer Prize–winning journalist Henry F. Pringle elucidated how Conant's fame—and notoriety—now extended well beyond academic circles, and his influence stemmed not only from intellectual leadership but also from the very real exercise of power. In theory, Conant was accountable to both the Corporation and the Board of Overseers, but in practice he nearly always bent those bodies "to do his will." He made himself chairman of the Council of the Faculty of Arts and Science, a representative body of sixty professors that was his "own innovation." By creating a system of ad hoc committees over which he was always chairman, he had a say in naming every permanent member of the faculty—not even an associate professor of pediatrics was appointed without his approval.

What the article hinted at, but did not say outright, was that his imperious manner of imposing his authority needlessly antagonized colleagues. Instead of conferring with an entire department, he tended to consult a handful of figures individually—a strategy he called "polling the jury"— and then reached a decision independently. Early on, Conant alienated senior members of the faculty by flatly rejecting their recommendations. He seemed to take pleasure in flaunting the Harvard way of doing things, and they saw their former role eroding in favor of a central administration. The vigorous application of his "up or out" policy to weed out the deadwood and bring in promising new tenure prospects only added to their disquiet.

Many others on the faculty felt slighted by Conant's obvious lack of enthusiasm for their academic fields. More than once he had questioned if the unverifiable disciplines of psychology, government, and sociology merited the same resources as the natural sciences, disparaging them as "the modern equivalents of astrology." The eminent poet Robert Frost, who had knocked heads with Conant over politics, did not think the chemist could see beyond his precise, quantifiable facts and provable hypotheses to any larger truths. "I told Conant once that it was mighty little he knew about humanities, or about poetry, or even about philosophy—with his nose stuck in a test tube," he recalled. "That's the trouble with scientists. They discount and discredit everything not reducible to an algebraic equation."

There was a growing faction within the college that agreed with Frost's appraisal, even though, according to Arthur Schlesinger, Jr., the poet was "full of petty malice." The discontented regarded Conant as so aloof and calculating in his methods they took to calling him a "slide-rule administrator." The feeling was that he was applying scientific methods to problems that were essentially human, and the people under him were paying the price. His cold-blooded approach, reported the *New Yorker*, has "waves of criticism beating against the doors of the president's office in University Hall," but the man in charge "does not appear to be greatly disturbed." Like Cromwell, Conant regarded reform as a "cruel necessity" and was too preoccupied with achieving his ambitious agenda for Harvard—and himself— to pay any heed to the simmering resentment among the rank and file. In his absolute determination to implement his ideas, he was demonstrating the ruthlessness common to all idealists in the act of realizing their vision.

CHAPTER 10

The Acid Test

A laboratory is not the ideal training field for dealing with complex human relationships.

—*Boston Globe* editorial about JBC

Like most Americans, Conant lapsed into complacency in the summer of 1937. Europe's troubles seemed a long way off. With the Harvard tercentenary finally behind him, he was ready to take a break. Since the first year of his presidency, he had found that the only way he could relax was to get away from Cambridge—the farther the better.

In July he and his family traveled by train to California, where he had rented a cottage on Fallen Leaf Lake, not far from Lake Tahoe. He planned to do some fly-fishing, a sport he had recently taken up, and make several short hiking excursions in the nearby mountains. The trip was suggested in part as a "sop" to his wife's feeling of frustration that she and the boys saw so little of him. His sons, ages eleven and fourteen, had sprouted into gangly, unruly adolescents and needed their father to take them in hand. Patty continued to be plagued by jags of depression and worried she had not been enough of a presence in the children's lives that winter, having followed doctor's orders to concentrate on getting well. Conant gave no sign of being particularly bothered on either account. There was nothing wrong that could not be put right with plenty of fresh air and exercise. In an effort to restore domestic harmony, he promised that this would not be a working vacation. He dutifully informed his friends and colleagues at Berkeley and

Caltech that he would not be attending any meetings, declined all invitations, and retreated from public life.

The first day of their holiday, Teddy came down with measles. A week later, his brother was covered in spots. With his disappointed wife consigned to nursemaid duty, Conant was trying to "make the best of a bad prospect" when he received an unexpected visitor. Francis P. Farquhar, a member of the class of 1909 and an experienced alpinist, had heard Harvard's president was fond of "walking uphill." He proposed that Conant join him on a pack trip in the High Sierra. When he casually mentioned that they might try to scale a peak, Conant immediately protested he was not that kind of climber. But after being assured they would not attempt anything too difficult or dangerous, he agreed to go along.

On August 12 he joined Farquhar and a party of three other men at Parchers Camp, twenty miles from the tiny town of Bishop. The supplies were loaded on a packhorse, and they had a spare animal for the benefit of anyone who could not keep up—presumably the spindly academic. It was rugged terrain, cutting through canyons of granite and black volcanic rock. After reaching the top of Bishop Pass, they slowly traversed a route that ran to the west of the highest peaks, camping every other night in a different spot. By the fourth day, Conant was feeling quite pleased with himself. He was in "excellent condition" and showed no signs of tiring, despite having been laid up for several weeks in March after fracturing his left collarbone in a skiing accident. His confidence quickly faded, however, when Farquhar revealed his true objective. Pointing at the North Palisade, an immense rocky peak 14,254 feet high that loomed in the east, he explained that they could easily capture the summit if they roped up together. It would be a pity, he goaded his important guest, to let such an opportunity pass.

On the first day, Conant felt on familiar ground as they painstakingly negotiated the loose rock and shale. But when it came time to begin the real climb, inching up what looked like a sheer vertical cliff, he struggled to keep his nerve. In theory, he was protected from a serious fall by the belaying rope, but his skepticism about the amount of security afforded by the thin manila cord was equaled only by his mounting terror. As he approached the top, however, he was surprised to discover that not only was he winning his "internal wrestling match with incipient panic," but he was actually beginning to *enjoy* the effort to conquer his fear. The route down was even more hair-raising, but the moment his foot hit terra firma, all his doubts were forgotten. In the rush of triumph, Conant found himself agreeing without reservation to an ice climb in the Canadian Rockies the following summer. "The twenty-four hours which had just passed marked a quantum leap in my psyche," he recalled. "I was ready to become an irrationally enthusiastic mountain climber."

He was hooked. For the next few years, climbing became an obsession. As soon as he completed one expedition he began planning the next. Nothing made Conant's blood quicken like the mental and physical challenges of those arduous ascents. Making it to the top was not about who was fastest or strongest, it was about endurance—and staying power.

He had not seen a newspaper for the entire week he was away, and one glance at the front page made him wish he had remained with his head in the clouds. The international situation was deteriorating at an alarming pace. An undeclared war had broken out in Asia, with the Japanese raining shells down on Shanghai, China. Thousands of Americans were fleeing the fighting. Meanwhile, the war in Spain, which had started in July 1936, was being fought with great ferocity. The dictators in Germany and Italy were openly abetting the rebels' attempt to overthrow the foundering Spanish Republic, supplying guns, tanks, and bombs. German Luftwaffe planes had been spotted in dogfights in the skies over Madrid. There was no telling where the Fascist expansion would end or what the map of Europe would look like when all was said and done.

Beneath his growing anxiety, Conant knew, was an older one: an anxiety about the extremism aroused by the last war. When he heard the strident debates about the Spanish Civil War—the overheated rhetoric, rigid sides formed, and political rebellion cast as a moral contest between good and evil—it took him right back to the emotionally charged scene into which he graduated in 1914. The parallels were unavoidable. Now, as Roosevelt's attempts to preserve peace through "collective security" came to nothing, the threat of rearmament hung over all of Europe. Conant could see that it was a dress rehearsal for war. The key to keeping out of it, he believed, was to prevent the heightened emotions generated in America's collective psyche "by the horror and dread of what we have seen in Europe" from once again consuming the country.

The more immediate problem was how to prevent Harvard from being riven by the "hatreds of the moment"—the rank partisanship and divided loyalties that had swamped Lowell's watch. In an effort to avoid repeating the previous generation's "passionate errors," Conant tried to prepare students for the magnitude of the forces they would soon face. He lectured them constantly on the dangers of demagoguery: the angry crosscurrents of opinion, barrage of self-deluding propaganda, and "welter of words, slogans, and catch phrases" that would be hurled about with the irrational spitefulness of people at a time of war. "The acid test," he once warned the class of 1938, "is whether you yourself indulge in them. If you call everyone who stands to the right of you a Bourbon and everyone who stands to the left a Communist, you are contributing your bit to the confusion." Despite his low opinion of human nature, Conant hoped that educated minds might be proof against such pointless name-calling. Past or present, the problem of contending worlds could not be escaped. For all those caught in epochs like their own, when society was at odds, it was essential to have the intellectual discipline and character to be able to "chart an independent course" and, if necessary, "dare to be alone."

Conant did not set out to sail against the powerful tide of American isolationism, but neither could he hide behind the pacifism he had invoked twenty years earlier. The Germany he had once known and loved had changed beyond all recognition. From the start, he had understood that Nazism meant "gangster rule," and that the suppression of individual freedom and ruthless anti-Semitism would lead to "armed aggression." On his last visit to Germany in the summer of 1930, just as the Nazi Party was beginning to attract widespread support, he had come face-to-face with the fanatic nationalism of the "man on the street." He vividly recalled "not only bitterness in the air but a real spirit of revenge." When he departed, he had known then that there would be no going back. He never expected to see Germany again.

Over the summer and fall of 1937, Hitler had seized the initiative in world affairs, and his lust for conquest was becoming obvious for all to see. As he ramped up his inflammatory speeches demanding that Germans in Czechoslovakia be reunited with their homeland, it seemed clear to Conant that Hitler was never going to be appeased or pacified. The Roosevelt administration, troubled by the violation of treaties and invasions of sovereign countries, appeared to reach the same conclusion. But in October, when Roosevelt suggested boldly that peace-loving nations join with Britain and France to "quarantine the aggressors," Harvard's cautious president was unwilling to go that far. While quick to denounce the spread of totalitarianism, he was not ready to take a stand on the issue that was just beginning to "boil to the surface": namely, whether the United States should help the European democracies restrain Hitler.

"I was neither an isolationist nor an interventionist," Conant recalled of his public stance in the late 1930s. Just as he eschewed any party affiliation, he preferred not to declare himself on a subject that was guaranteed to elicit strong objections from the alumni, who were overwhelmingly antiwar. To do so would invite controversy and risk being branded an extremist. Even if he was right about Hitler's aggressive designs, it was not his place to be a prophet of doom. Conant's strong sense of propriety—of not wanting to transgress the limits of acceptability—still ruled his decision making, and he reverted to what he thought of as his proper role as educator. He also had not forgotten Harvard's rush to respond to the cry "make the world safe for democracy" in 1917, and bitterly reflected on the epitaphs that decision wrote. Though far from sanguine about the course of international affairs, he continued to temper his principled rhetoric, and to remain hopeful that a peaceful way of dealing with the dictator's demands might yet be found.

Conant defended his position in a long, ruminative letter to his friend Archibald MacLeish, whose poem "Speech to the Scholars"—urging academics to join the proxy war being fought against Hitler and Mussolini in Spain—Conant publicly criticized as a premature call to arms. "I believe it is easy to lose the very things one wishes to preserve by declaring war in favor of them," he told the zealous poet in the spring of 1937, noting that the last war to "end war and preserve democracy" would seem a case in point:

I do *not* believe, as you seem to think, that a scholar should see his freedom extinguished before he fights; but I do believe he should hold his fire until he sees the whites of his enemies' eyes. And I am convinced above all that he should be on his guard against being drawn into a "preventive war." I think a scholar should have his gun ready to draw when he is immediately attacked; but his gun should be carefully kept apart from his books all the rest of the time, else the smell of powder corrupts his scholarship. Above all, I believe he must keep himself free from entangling alliances and let the weary world fight around him. In short, I am not a "peace at any price" pacifist but a very suspicious Yankee trader whose policy is "armed neutrality."

He was not surprised that Roosevelt's trial balloon about joint action was immediately hooted down by the isolationists in Congress. Since burying his Republican opponent, Kansas governor Alfred M. Landon, in the 1936 election, the president had squandered much of the goodwill with his efforts to expand the Supreme Court to ensure a pro–New Deal majority. No doubt, Roosevelt knew his quarantine speech was considerably out front of where the nation stood and was simply testing the waters, but the loud criticism it received was a sign of the country's profound reluctance to take any action. Disillusioned over the outcome of the "war to end war," most Americans had come to believe it had been a mistake to intervene in the First World War. To many, appeasement seemed like a perfectly appropriate strategy in a part of the globe with a long history of squabbling over borders and jockeying for power. Anti-imperialist and antiwar sentiment swelled on college campuses, where students favored unqualified neutrality, with most opposed to sending aid of any kind for fear it would bring the struggle to American shores.

Conant had also seen how public opinion had been "poisoned" during the 1920s by North Dakota senator Gerald P. Nye's investigation of the munitions industry, and his committee's insinuations that the British had colluded with greedy arms makers to engineer America's entry into the war. The result was a deep distrust of imperial Britain, and a lingering suspicion that America had been duped into fighting. Isolationists such as Nye and William E. Borah, a senior senator known as the "Lion from Idaho," continued to insist that the United States should stay aloof from the struggle. There was so much popular support for measures designed to keep America from being dragged into another war that Congress enacted neutrality legislation in 1935, 1936, and again in 1937. These acts not only forbade the loaning of funds to belligerents but also authorized a strict embargo on the sale of arms to all participants—aggressors and victims alike—in the event of war.

As the news from Europe continued to worsen, Conant became more apprehensive and pessimistic. After the Anschluss, Hitler's breathtakingly efficient annexation of Austria in March 1938, there was little doubt that the Czech Sudetenland was next. Events in Europe had taken on a dangerous momentum. On August 27, the papers carried the news that the British government would back Czechoslovakia, and the chancellor of the exchequer, Sir John Simon, virtually announced that a German invasion would bring England into the war on the side of France. Returning to Cambridge to prepare for the start of another fall term, Conant was increasingly worried about the possibility of war and the proper course for the United States. But he was still reluctant to take sides in the struggle, writing Walter Lippmann,

"I am beginning to think that any solution which does not involve a general European war would be highly satisfactory from my point of view."

The Munich crisis, which unfolded over the month of September, left him disgusted with appeasement and the feebleness of democracies, including his own. He had hoped Britain's prime minister, Neville Chamberlain, would not give in to German pressure, but, eager to avoid a military confrontation at all cost, Chamberlain capitulated completely. In return for promising not to seek another foot of territory in Europe, Hitler got everything he desired without firing a single shot. German occupation of the Sudeten would begin October 1. Shocked by the diplomatic catastrophe, Conant judged Chamberlain's action to be an almost "criminal error." Britain and France had sacrificed their continental position to procure peace. There could be no future for Europe if no one stood up to brute force. It seemed to him that "the problem of evil was being rammed down our throats by every hourly bulletin from the diplomatic front."

But if he was so convinced of the "cause of stopping Hitler," why had he not spoken out? Did he have a moral obligation to do so? At the same time, "What right had a citizen of a nation that was deeply committed to isolation and neutrality to pass verdict on another country's refusal to risk war?" Yet what was the alternative? "Could there still be an escape from the impending holocaust? And if so, on what terms? Could the claims of honor and justice be satisfied and war avoided?" Was there enough definitive evidence of Hitler's will to expand to justify action? He agonized over the implications of his logic—and the inexorable conclusion. "Like many others," he recalled, "I was tortured by such questions."

After the infamous events of November 9, 1938, known as Kristallnacht—as the Nazis dubbed the looting and destruction of Jewish businesses and synagogues that left German streets lined with miles of shattered glass—Conant joined other university presidents in denouncing the Reich's assault on Jews. The new wave of violent state-sponsored pogroms shocked the world. There was no longer any pretending that Hitler would moderate his racial policies or permit the orderly emigration of those trying to escape persecution. The news of the terrible events stirred Conant to action, and he participated in a radio broadcast in which he condemned the "barbaric spirit of the German government." Hitler's coming to power "struck a note of fear" in him, "lest it should happen here."

The suffering of so many young refugees shook Harvard students out of their apathy. On Friday, November 25, a small delegation of undergraduates, led by a senior named Robert E. Lane, called on Conant to ask for permission to hold a fund-raiser. They were seeking the university's support for their plan to provide twenty scholarships for refugee students through a campaign aimed at raising $10,000 from their fellow students and another $25,000 from faculty. "We went to Conant's office in a mood of nervous preparation for engagement," recalled Lane, now a Yale professor emeritus. The president greeted them coolly, his face unreadable, but before they were done making their case, he surprised them by agreeing to match their efforts "dollar for dollar."

Conant's decision to back the students' refugee initiative received nationwide publicity, as did his ringing endorsement of their cause as a symbol that "the humanitarian basis of democracy is not dead." He did not stop there, but went on to urge that the movement be expanded across the country. A *New York Times* editorial praised Conant's efforts on behalf of academic freedom. Supportive messages arrived from FDR and New York governor Herbert Lehman. Albert Einstein, who had refused to attend the tercentenary because of the presence of pro-Nazi German academics, sent a telegram: "APPRECIATE GREATLY YOUR GENEROUS EFFORT AS AID IN EMERGENCY AND AS HUMANITARIAN AID."

Conant began to cast about for other ways to educate the public about the realities of the European situation and shared his unease with a small group of influential men of similar conviction. For the past year, he had chaired the blue-ribbon Committee on Scientific Aids to Learning, established by the National Research Council, to investigate how new technological advances could be adapted for use in the classroom and advanced research. The membership of the committee consisted of leading scientists turned administrators, including Vannevar Bush, the former vice president of MIT, who had recently become president of the Carnegie Institution of Washington; Karl Compton, president of MIT; Frank Jewett, president of Bell Telephone Laboratories; and Richard C. Tolman, a respected theoretical physicist and dean of Caltech's graduate school. Whenever Conant gathered his colleagues on the committee, their attention turned from technological know-how to technological superiority, and to the question of whether the country should prepare to confront the German threat.

By the time he sat down in early 1939 to compose his autobiographical note for his class's *Twenty-Fifth Anniversary Report*, Conant was more convinced than ever of Hitler's goal to dominate Europe, and he now believed the United States could not allow him to go unchecked. Hitler's ambitions knew no bounds. The dictator had shown repeatedly that he had no respect for the legitimate claims of other countries, no use for compromise, no interest in peace. "With Munich fresh in our minds, and a February crisis apparently brewing as I write," Conant reflected, "it is hard to turn one's thoughts back to the summer of 1914 without having the question arise, must it all happen again? Have the last twenty years been nothing but a fruitless armistice?"

He was in Randolph, New Hampshire, on September 1, enjoying the last leisurely days of his summer holiday, when he heard the radio report that Hitler's panzer divisions had invaded Poland. The news came as a stunning blow. England and France, as allies of the overrun nation, would have no choice but to declare war on Germany. On August 23 Germany and Russia had signed a nonaggression pact, making sure the march into neighboring Poland would go unopposed.

Conant's first call was to Karl Compton, who had just been appointed to the newly established War Resources Board to advise the army and the navy on the nation's preparedness plans: Could American scientists volunteer to aid the Allied countries in their scientific war work? "No," Compton told him; such assistance would violate the Neutrality Act. It was a crime for any individual American citizen to assist the war effort of another nation. With the country strongly isolationist, nothing could be done. But Conant had lost faith in neutrality. Noninvolvement was no longer an option. His instincts told him it was time for action.

Having thrown off his uncertainty and ambivalence, he was frustrated by the American public's reaction to the war. "[It] seems to me," he complained in a letter to Archibald MacLeish, "most ostrich-like, puerile, and pusillanimous. But being the head of an institution with 8,000 men under my direction who may get shot if we go to war, while I shan't, I am a bit estopped from saying much. I don't like the moral dilemma I find myself in," he added, "but my personal emotions are a small matter in these times of world grief." It was much the same dilemma he had faced in the early days of his presidency, and the disparity between his public obligations and private inclination again made it difficult to step forward. A few days later, MacLeish came to dinner and spent the night, and they shared their mutual disgust of academe's dispassionate remove, their earlier feud over MacLeish's poetic call to arms forgotten.

A week after the German invasion, Roosevelt declared a limited national emergency. On September 13 he ordered Congress to convene a special session to revise the Neutrality Act. The neutrality legislation passed during the past few years was too inflexible. By prohibiting the shipment of arms and munitions to all combatants, it particularly hurt the Allies, which were far less equipped to wage war. However, the bill permitted the president to make exceptions at his own discretion if the goods were paid for in advance and if they left America in foreign vessels, known as the "cash and carry" exemption. Roosevelt's proposal to revise the law authorizing him to determine who were the aggressors and victims in a war, and to withhold or supply aid accordingly—in effect enabling the United States to sell arms to Britain and France if they carried them in their own ships—immediately provoked a fierce national debate.

Determined to block FDR's action, the isolationists launched a massive publicity campaign. The night after Roosevelt's announcement, Senator Borah took to the airwaves to point out the risks of such a move and inveigh against the revision or repeal of the neutrality legislation. The following night, Colonel Charles Lindbergh, the reclusive aviator, resigned from his position with the Army Air Corps in order to publicly oppose FDR. Speaking on all three national radio networks, the revered hero from the 1920s made an eloquent case that the United States not involve itself in Europe's eternal feuding. Germany, he averred, was no threat to their democratic society, was moreover entitled to rectify the Versailles injustices, and sending munitions to the allies could never ensure victory but would cost in lives "the best of American youth."

The next up was Hamilton Fish III, a Republican congressman from New York, who delivered a furious isolationist diatribe against all those in favor of repealing the arms embargo. "The paramount issue before the country," he declared, "is to prevent America from being 'eased into war.'" He accused the interventionists of being "smear artists and purveyors of hate," for whom any peace-loving citizen was fair game in their "campaign of hysteria, emotionalism, hatred, untruth, and poisonous propaganda." Worse, those who wanted to sell arms to the Allies had the basest of motives: "blood-smeared dollars."

To rebut this assault, and help overcome the strong isolationist and neutrality sentiment in the public, the administration needed its own "silver-tongued orators" to do battle on the same ground as the demagogues. It enlisted the support of such prominent Republicans as Henry L. Stimson,

President Herbert Hoover's secretary of state, and Frank Knox, the Republican nominee for vice president under Alf Landon. Compton informed the White House that Conant would also be willing to make a statement. He had already given a number of speeches at Harvard decrying the war hysteria and atmosphere of invective and unreason. He believed fear of being labeled a warmonger had cast a "blanket of censorship" on public debate, and the danger was that it could paralyze the democratic process. If he penned a public letter to Landon, the titular head of the party, making a rational argument for modifying the neutrality law to permit the sale of weapons to England and France, it would be sure to garner national attention.

Finally resolved to speak out, Conant wrote to Landon on September 26 proposing what he termed a "one-man minor operation" to make Americans see that if France and Britain were defeated by a totalitarian power "the hope of free institutions as a basis of modern civilization will be jeopardized." He went on to explain that he was not writing primarily about the debate before Congress. "What concerns me most," he continued, was the need for a "clear-headed, realistic discussion" of the "advantages and disadvantages from our own selfish point of view of every aspect of foreign policy." Americans could not allow acrimony and emotionalism to divide the country or dictate decisions. They had to trust that "a democracy can make a rational choice on matters of war and peace as on other phases of national policy." If not, "War has already defeated democracy on this continent. This is to me," he stressed, "the vital point."

Conant had carefully calibrated his approach, critiquing the isolationists' argument while not directly attacking them, but at the same time never going so far as to advocate intervention. He went far enough, however, to receive a flood of angry responses after his letter was reprinted in the national papers. The *Crimson* slammed him for "earning an unenviable place in the road gang which is trying to build for the United States a superhighway straight to Armageddon." Enough of the alumni endorsed his position that Conant felt confident he had done the right thing, but he was not ready to urge a belligerent status for the United States and continued to cling to his uncomfortable perch on the fence.

That fall, when a group of internationalists led by Clark Eichelberger, director of the League of Nations Association, formed an emergency nonpartisan committee to lobby Congress and mobilize public opinion to counteract the isolationists, Conant declined to get involved. The spokesman for their campaign was William Allen White, the venerable seventy-one-year-old editor of the *Emporia* (Kansas) *Gazette*, whose homely editorials and no-nonsense analysis had made him a popular and influential voice for the grass roots of the nation. A staunch Republican, he had reversed his position on the Neutrality Act after Germany attacked Poland, and now backed Roosevelt's efforts to supply Britain and France with arms. White's embryonic organization, the Nonpartisan Committee for Peace Through Revision of the Neutrality Law, quickly recruited several hundred important Americans for the cause. Conant was one of the few holdouts. Although he was "strongly in favor of repeal," he wired in reply, it was his "general policy" not to join committees. The name they wanted on their letterhead was not his but Harvard's, and he could not be profligate in lending it out.

On November 4, after three weeks of harsh and bruising debate, the arms embargo was repealed. The new Neutrality Act that Roosevelt signed into law authorized the sale of arms to belligerents on a "cash-and-carry" basis. Almost immediately, tensions dissipated in Congress and elsewhere. The crisis had passed, and Americans seemed convinced there was no conceivable danger that would warrant their fighting. To Conant's surprise, Hitler did not unleash the Luftwaffe on the Allies. Instead, a stalemate settled over Europe. Having discharged their duty to Poland, France and Britain seemed to have "pulled their punches" on the Western Front, leading Senator Borah to dub the pause in activity a "phony war." He believed it might even presage a peace settlement. Conant was not convinced. "Nobody could be sure another Munich was not in the offing," he wrote. "The strong probability that the phony war would someday become a real war was in everybody's mind." But after his brief foray into politics, he did not trumpet his views. He had to tread carefully. The truth was, by the fall of 1939, he was too busy fighting an offensive on his own turf to devote much attention to events abroad.

While the hostilities in Europe had ceased, at Harvard the battle over tenure that had been brewing since Conant became president erupted with an "almost revolutionary force," as he later acknowledged, nearly blowing him out of office. According to the October 1939 issue of the Harvard *Progressive*, "Resignations are threatened. Rumor and suspicion, bickering and ill-will are rampant throughout the entire faculty." The leftist student monthly was given to exaggeration, but there was no denying his staff was in a murderous mood. "I feel quite as though war has come to Cambridge!" he wrote a friend.

The tenure controversy first broke out in April 1937 with Conant's dismissal of two economics instructors, John Raymond Walsh and Alan R. Sweezy. (Actually, they were served notice that this was their final three-year appointment, and there were no prospects for promotion.) After years of painful budget cuts and aborted appointments, the faculty finally cried foul and banded together to protest. The resentment ran deep. One after another, young teachers had been fired. The lower ranks were completely demoralized. Many saw it as a harbinger of their own fate. Sooner or later they would all be sacrificed to Conant's cost-cutting imperative: "up or out." The students in turn complained they were being cheated. Conant's economizing was depriving them of inspired lecturers in favor of a few big-name scholars with fancy salaries. He was more interested in "crack research men" than in the quality of their education. By the 1939 Easter recess, with the two popular young professors on their way out, the students began issuing news releases, circulating leaflets, and rallying their confreres. The local papers played up the political angle, focusing on the Marxist bent of the terminated economists, both well-known union agitators. Overnight, Walsh and Sweezy became political martyrs, with Harvard's president in the role of high executioner.

Conant issued a hasty press release stating that the decision had been made "solely on grounds of teaching capacity and scholarly ability." The announcement immediately backfired, with most of the Harvard community taking umbrage at the suggestion that the two young men had been dropped because they were bad teachers. Conant quickly apologized, but the protests grew louder. The charge was leveled that the two men were victims of their liberal politics and their academic freedom had been violated. The Harvard Teachers Union signed a petition requesting that a panel of respected senior professors conduct a thorough inquiry into what had become known as the Walsh-Sweezy case.

To quell the faculty rebellion, Conant felt he had "no choice" but to agree to the review and vow to abide by its findings. But his back was up. He did not like being second-guessed. Adding to his annoyance, more than one of the panelists had a bone to pick. Chief among them was Kenneth Murdock, who, aided and abetted by a group of followers known as "the Leverett House gang," saw the inquiry as an opportunity to exact revenge for losing the presidency. Emboldened by the angry clamor, he began plotting with other left-wing dissidents to unseat his old rival and seize the throne that rightfully should have been his.

In early 1938, following an exhaustive review of Walsh's and Sweezy's dismissals, the investigating group, known as the Committee of Eight, exonerated Conant and the Economics Department of any political or personal favoritism, but the president was faulted for poor management. Walsh and Sweezy had been treated badly, and the recommendation was that the case be reopened with an eye to having the pair reinstated. Conant flatly refused. He saw no reason to reverse his decision and rehire them. His adamantine rejection of the committee's opinion further antagonized the faculty. Conant's "stubborn streak," which one Harvard chronicler noted had been "so appealing in defense of unpopular causes and their champions," now only reinforced their impression of him as arbitrary and autocratic.

In March 1939, after spending a year canvassing the grievances of younger instructors, the Committee of Eight released its final report. In response to the 165-page document detailing the flaws in the existing tenure system, Conant agreed to implement a long list of proposed reforms. As far as he was concerned, by endorsing its Magna Charta as a guide to future policy, he was more than doing his part. He would amend his flawed policies and exercise greater "flexibility" in implementing any new rules. But instead of following through on those promises, Conant compounded his earlier blunder by refusing to allow the faculty to weigh in on the report. His invitation to have those with objections write to him was a classic dodge and greeted with the skepticism it deserved. Meanwhile, the faculty's suspicions were confirmed when within ten days of adopting Harvard's Magna Charta, Conant fired ten popular assistant professors. A huge hue and cry followed.

By fall, the entire campus was in an uproar. The faculty, now in full revolt, began holding emergency sessions behind closed doors to debate the affair. There were rumors of challenges to Conant's regime and murmurs of Murdock's triumphant return. In a series of stormy meetings, Conant was assailed over and over again for proceeding hastily and callously, and failing to keep his staff informed. They demanded a reversal of his spring termination of the doomed "ten."

All of the undergraduate publications entered the fray, attacking Conant's disregard for what amounted to a presidential dictatorship. The *Lampoon* published a full-page caricature of Harvard's president dressed as a witch, peering into a crystal ball and cackling, "Mirror, mirror, on the wall, on whom next shall the axe fall?" The *Boston Globe* was merciless in its editorial comment: "A laboratory is not the ideal training field for dealing with complex human relationships. It is more concerned with test tubes than with retorts. The retorts are coming all the time."

The climax came in a dramatic meeting held in University Hall on the afternoon of November 7, a large crowd of Harvard professors and nobles packing the chamber. The faculty was out for blood. Their first move was to abolish Conant's small delegated council. The vote, an overwhelming 140 to 6, was a "slap in the face." Next on the agenda was a hostile motion to reexamine the whole role of the faculty in the governance of the university. At stake was no less than his mandate—the presidency itself. The atmosphere was so strained, recalled Corporation member Thomas Perkins, "you could have heard a pin drop."

Rising to his feet, Conant, new lines etched in his face, and gray at the temples, solemnly laid out the consequences to the motion before them. Instead of coming out swinging as expected, he admitted to the nonplussed members that he had made errors that were largely responsible for the current tensions. He pleaded with them not to punish Harvard for his mistakes, noting that any precipitous step on their part now might adversely affect the university for years to come.

Conant was sticking to the script presented to him by Wallace B. Donham, dean of the business school and one of several close advisors who were convinced that if their combative president went into the meeting girded for a "knockdown fight," as he had confided to friends, he would jeopardize more than just his job. Donham put the facts to him plainly. He had lost the support of the faculty. If he allowed a vote of no confidence to threaten the historic relationship between the faculty and governing boards, he would do Harvard a great and possibly permanent disservice. The only thing to do was offer a sincere mea culpa. Conant shrank from the idea. "I had no stomach for apologizing," he recalled, "particularly when I was under violent attack." But he knew he had miscalculated badly. In the end, after "considerable soul-searching," he swallowed his pride and did what needed to be done.

Conant's frank apology extinguished the opposition. The anger in the room drained away. In the lull that followed, someone moved to table the motion, and it was quickly carried by a vote. Much to Conant's relief, it "sounded unanimous." There was nothing Murdock and his coconspirators could do but look on in mutinous silence.

Conant survived the challenge to his authority, but it had been a close-run thing. His enemies had turned out in force. The mood of the faculty that day, he would bitterly recall, was "close to being vindictive." The episode exposed the political treachery that lurked in Harvard's ivied halls, and underscored the enormous antipathy various factions still bore him for his unlikely ascendance. Although he had saved his job, he would never see Harvard in the same light again.

While Conant appeared to most to be coldly unemotional, he felt things deeply and was, if anything, too thin-skinned. His pride was a form of defensiveness, an almost impenetrable barrier he erected to protect a painful sensitivity. The Walsh-Sweezy debacle wounded him to the core. It was the low point of his career and he brooded over it for years afterward. In later life, he chastised himself for his lapses in judgment, confessing to family members that he had brought all the trouble on himself—he had been too arrogant, inexperienced, and bullheaded. Conant had reacted to the challenge to his authority by becoming even more overbearing. "An accumulation of prejudices" had precluded him from considering that the faculty might be allowed more of a voice, he admitted in his memoir, his adherence to tradition "so dogmatic as to be almost blind."

Conant was too preoccupied during this period to notice that his two sons were busy staging their own rebellion. As they entered adolescence, both Jim and Teddy came to regard their father as increasingly unyielding and oppressive. They held him in awe but at arm's length—his frequent absences and carefully titrated emotions ensured that a certain awkwardness and stiff formality characterized their relations. "We saw so little of him, really," recalled his youngest, "we were sort of strangers living under the same roof." Never a patient man, Conant was often exasperated by his sons' obstreperousness and did not hesitate to use corporal punishment. Far more than his wrath, however, they dreaded his disappointment. Having concluded early on that they were not quite up to the standard that their father expected, each boy felt slighted and acted out in his own way. "When we didn't measure up," observed Ted with a defeated shrug, "he wrote us off."

For his part, Conant found his sons oddly feckless and recalcitrant, and altogether too "soft"—at one point confiscating their stuffed teddy bears because he thought they had clung to them too long. They were always ill or nursing colds and unable to participate in the athletic pastimes he pursued with such vigor. He preferred to go on climbing and skiing out- ings with his hardy graduate students and colleagues, sending his wife and children on "soothing holidays" by the sea. Given their sons' inability to please him, Patty generally found it better to enforce the old dictum that "children should be seen and not heard." At the president's mansion at 17 Quincy Street, she banished them to the third-floor nursery. It became her practice to send the "little savages" away as much as possible, packing them off to their grandmother's or aunt's on weekends and school holidays with little or no compunction, blithely telling Conant's sister Marjorie, "I seem to have to ask people to help me with my young, but that's the way it is."

The ease and frequency with which they were dispatched eventually suc- ceeded in causing hurt. Jimmy, "a Goody Two-shoes" in his younger broth- er's estimation, who for years had desperately sought his father's approval, now alternated between biting sarcasm and sullen silences. Patty thought he seemed dejected and "extremely repressed." On his fifteenth birthday on May 17, 1938, she mourned the changes in his demeanor. His old spontane- ity was gone, and he was "reserved, conscientious, no longer straight from the shoulder, beginning to be torturous in order to conceal his real self, in self-defense." Boarding school was the obvious answer. Plans were made for Jimmy to go to Phillips Exeter Academy.

Their ill-starred youngest son, however, was a problem of a different order. After a "disastrous" fall at Shady Hill, Teddy had left the school by mutual agreement. He was kept home all that winter due to another round of infections and a subsequent operation on his ears. A fresh start at his brother's old school, Browne & Nichols, was a dismal failure. His father had hoped that rowing crew would toughen him up, but instead he contracted pneumonia and fell even further behind in his studies. "Ted is so far from any scholarly proficiency that I regard it as quite out of the picture for years!" Patty confided to Marjorie. "He is a rather dif- ficult though interesting personality. Plenty of temperament (and intel- ligence, too, I *think*) if it can somehow coordinate itself. Unregenerate *no end*."

Bored and unhappy, Teddy's chief form of entertainment was upsetting his parents by engaging in some form of monstrously bad behavior. With a child's discernment, he homed in on their preoccupation with keeping up appearances and took undisguised glee in embarrassing them at every turn.

Sitting in the president's box at the all-important Harvard-Yale football game, he brazenly unfurled a huge blue-and-white Yale banner and waved it for all to see. He relished the *Nation's* description of his father as a "tool of Wall Street" and quoted it so often at the dinner table that Conant finally took a hairbrush to his backside. During the height of the faculty uprising, Teddy frequented a radical bookshop on Dunster Street and brought home armloads of prounion pamphlets. The local papers caught wind of his "Commie" activity and tattled on the Harvard president's baby insurgent. Annoyed by the unwanted publicity, Conant reamed out his son for the foolish prank, calling the stories "bad for business." When the twelve-year-old protested that his father was encroaching on his free speech, Conant was forced to compromise, and in exchange for the boy's vow to steer clear of the Bolshevik den, he paid for a subscription to the *Daily Worker*. It was delivered to the door of 17 Quincy Street, Patty recalled, much to the "horror of the housekeeper."

Teddy's misdemeanors escalated. He had been given a handcrafted shortwave radio set by his uncle Bill (Richards), and soon being a ham operator became a full-blown obsession. He quickly discovered he could put his new technical skills to use in his quest to cause more trouble. With the aid of an 80-watt transmitter, he could sit in the cellar and relay naughty songs like Groucho Marx's "Lydia the Tattooed Lady" into the radio in the front parlor, startling visitors. On one occasion, he fixed the large brass horn of a gramophone under the heating vent of the ballroom and interrupted a reception for the crown prince of Norway by blasting Kay Kyser and His Orchestra's novelty tune "Three Little Fishies (Itty Bitty Poo)." More sessions with the belt followed; more meals alone in his room.

Satisfied that this was a surefire means of getting attention, Teddy continued his sabotage campaign. He established his own amateur radio station and broadcast speeches by the notorious pro-Nazi propagandist "Lord Haw-Haw," featured on the radio program *Germany Calling* which he picked up on his shortwave from London, proudly writing his grandmother that it could be heard "all over the Yard and fairly well at MIT." The last straw was his presentation of a medley of "Hitler's favorites." Lowell had installed a small electrical lift in the house, and Ted lowered the car halfway between the basement and the first floor and began blaring "Deutschland Über Alles"—the German national anthem—just as the dinner guests were arriving. "Ted has been living in melodrama for nearly two weeks," Patty reported to her diary. "For a while a real scandal seemed imminent."

At the recommendation of her mother, Patty took Ted to see Dr. Arlie Vernon Bock, director of the university's Department of Hygiene, who served as Harvard's house shrink. Dr. Bock, who had treated her brother, Bill, thought that Teddy was suffering from an "inferiority complex," Patty informed her mother, his incorrigible behavior a form of retaliation against his distant and formidable father. He was also examined by Dr. Lawrence S. Kubie, a leading New York psychiatrist whom Conant had first met as an undergraduate at Harvard. Kubie recommended sending the lad to Boston's McLean Hospital, where he could receive intensive treatment. Conant, who had little faith in the relatively new science of psychiatry—for the most part, he regarded it as "quackery"—rejected the idea.

Conant believed that mental illness resulted from imperfect self-control. Depression and other psychological disorders were a form of weakness that could be overcome by a disciplined mind. His son's problem was that because he had been so sickly, he had been mollycoddled and overindulged almost from birth. His wife's "intense and continuous solicitude about T's health and happiness" had robbed the boy of any chance to develop normally. What Teddy needed was a rigorous intellectual and physical regimen. Overruling the doctors, Conant sent the "spoiled imp" off to the Dublin School in northern New Hampshire, a rugged academy whose educational philosophy included manual labor as an essential part of the curriculum.

As usual, Patty went along with the plan despite her misgivings. In any "conflict of claims," she admitted in her diary, she put her husband's needs and wants ahead of her children's. While aware that her sons loathed the showy, "tinsel" quality of their Quincy Street existence, and that it was the cause of considerable estrangement, she could not tear herself away from the glamorous social whirl. In recent years, her calendar was so full she had been reduced to little more than "checking up" on the boys, "too busy with place cards," as Teddy once reproached her, to read a bedtime story. "You have definitely changed to the children since this new job began," Patty wrote in one of her frequent, self-lacerating moments of introspection. "You 'lost' them when it came."

Even Miriam Richards could not help notice the scant attention her daughter and son-in-law paid their offspring, confiding her concerns to Dr. Bok. "I think none the less of them for what you have said," the doctor demurred. "They have no private lives." He "understood it all," Miriam wrote in her diary, "the lack of emotion, the attitude which has caught Jim and Patty." But he also confirmed her basic belief: "children do need affection."

Part of the reason Patty did not object to sending her sons away was her deep sense of inadequacy. Just trying to keep up with her demanding husband and do her part in running the presidential mansion—this "mean machine," as she called it—was a "struggle." When it all got too much for her, she "relapsed," just as her mother did before her, retreating to her bed with what she quaintly termed a "spell of the vapors." These bouts were "entirely *negative* in their effect," she knew, but she could not help taking a "masochistic pleasure" in flagellating herself afterward for her nervous weakness and uselessness. She needed to watch out, she remonstrated herself in her diary, if only so her "unworthy, selfish, self-deluding, dishonest thoughts" did not contaminate "subtly but surely the children's thoughts and actions."

In a moment of painful self-reckoning, written in the summer of 1938 while racked with fears that her husband might "never come back" from an ice-climbing trip to the Canadian Rockies, she gave vent to the misery and corrosive insecurity that made her begrudge her young sons any hint of freedom or happiness. "There's poison in my will to power," she confessed:

> I inject a little bit of poison in the conversation, in the advice, to darling dear Jimmy who is much too sweet and tempts me to walk on him; I "pick on" Teddy too often (he deserves it, goodness knows, but if I nag he will learn bad tricks from me). I am almost never the quiet well of love that a mother ought to be . . . They can't retort—but Jim unconsciously—both more or less consciously—store up an impression of grudgingness and bitterness. There is a bitter taste in me—I seem to have given up self-pity and romantic reveries for aggressive tactics—persecution of the subtle sort that matriarchs indulge in.

Conant was aware of his wife's temperamental troubles, writing to her from Jasper Park Lodge that he hoped she would try to take some "vicarious pleasure" in the boys' enjoyment and promising that things would soon look "rosier than they have seemed." He did everything he could to keep her on a "plateau of contentment," urging her to avoid unnecessary "emotional indigestion." Although he tried to bond with his sons, as they grew older and more willful, he blamed them for upsetting their mother. Patty was delicate, and the expense of the angry scenes too great. He never spoke of her condition, giving only a cursory reply to inquiries from concerned colleagues and friends. He tried to keep her close, where she would be under his watchful eye. He thought he could ward off trouble. But the Richards family's virulent inherited infirmities would thwart him again and again. When tragedy struck at the start of 1940, followed by the fall of France in June, Conant's life was again forced off course. "The war engulfed all of us," he wrote, "one way or another."

CHAPTER 11

A Private Citizen Speaks Out

It is not too late, but it is long past time to act.
—JBC, nationwide address, May 29, 1940

Conant was on a skiing holiday in Saint Sauveur, Quebec, when he received word of Bill Richards's suicide on Wednesday, January 30, 1940. He caught the last train out that night and returned to Cambridge at once.

Bill had been found dead in the bathroom of his New York apartment on East Eighty-Third Street. He had been living in the dingy three-room flat since withdrawing from his teaching post at Princeton to devote himself to an intensive course of psychotherapy, supporting himself by working part-time as a chemical consultant. His body had been discovered earlier that evening by the superintendent of the building after he noticed a bottle of milk delivered that morning had remained in front of the door all day. When there was no response to his knocks and repeated phone calls, the police were summoned. They contacted Conant's home in Cambridge after a search of the premises turned up letters mentioning his name. In his absence, Patty took the call. The detective in charge of the investigation told her there was no question that it was a suicide. Bill, dressed in his pajamas, had stepped into the tub, placed a pillow behind his head, and severed the arteries in both wrists with a razor blade.

Patty was devastated. By the time Conant arrived, she had brought her mother to the house and broken the news. Both women were reeling with shock. Stunned, grief-stricken, appalled at the idea of such a tragedy, they huddled together in the parlor of 17 Quincy Street like victims of a shipwreck. Compounding their misery, the New York papers had already learned of Bill's identity, along with his illustrious family connections. The *Times* ran a ghastly story under the headline "W. T. Richards Ends Life: Relative Through Marriage of Harvard Head Suicide Here."

A small funeral was held at Mount Auburn Cemetery on Friday—"family only," Conant noted grimly in his diary. The fewer people present, the less attention it was likely to garner. For his own part, Conant wanted Bill and the sordid details of his death buried as soon as possible. Although there was no denying that Bill "died by his own hand," as reported in his Harvard obituary, Conant endeavored to hush up the more unpleasant aspects, and the Boston papers refrained from publishing the story.

Bill's death was all the more shocking to the family because they had celebrated Christmas together only a month earlier. He had appeared to be in good spirits at the time, almost his old self, a welcome change from the morose state he had been in that fall. Miriam had been so encouraged by his buoyant mood that she wrote to a close friend that he seemed to be making "real progress toward restored health," so much so that "he was so happy and well that for fun he wrote a detective story." Over the holidays, he had amazed them all by disclosing that he had submitted the manuscript to Charles Scribner's Sons, which had "at once accepted it."

It was no secret that Bill had battled dark patches and poor health for years, often self-medicating with alcohol. He used to joke that like every good Bostonian, he had "a card at the Athenæum, a pew at Trinity, a plot at Mount Auburn, and a gurney at McLean's." But no one ever imagined he would succumb to the scourge of depression. It brought back disturbing memories of his father's untimely end, of the impossible demands he had lashed himself with and his private torment. Patty was inconsolable. The depth of her grief frightened Conant, who had come to accept the incongruity of the Richards family's intelligence and psychological impairment, and regarded them as weaker beings. By then, he had concluded, as Ted would later observe, that there was "a fatal flaw in the genetic material."

Bill's old college friends paid tribute to the thirty-nine-year-old physical chemist as "beyond any doubt one of the most brilliant members of the class," but in the memorial notes they also recalled him as tragically uncompromising. "He had a mentality which could be called great," wrote Leopold

Mannes, a fellow musician and scientist. "In his attitude towards life, towards science, towards music—of which he had an astounding knowledge and perception—he was a relentless perfectionist and thus his own implacable judge. No human being could be expected fully to satisfy such standards."

Desperate to avoid any scandal, Miriam Richards penned a serene letter attempting to put her son's sudden passing in the context of a decadelong decline, copies of which she sent to important friends. She implied his death was accidental, writing that he "died of an overdose of a sleeping draught," though whether this was her attempt to draw a veil over his suicide or what she had been told is unclear. No one in the family ever spoke of it.

For reasons he was not prepared to disclose, Conant was worried about much more than just the family's reputation. At the news of Bill's death, he had dispatched their uncle, Lawrence Henderson, accompanied by Patty's younger brother, Thayer, to New York to tidy up any loose ends. A suicide note found beside the tub was promptly destroyed. Conant also arranged for all of Bill's papers and personal effects be packed up and shipped directly to 17 Quincy Street before anyone could go through them. His immediate concern was that his brother-in-law might not have been entirely in his right mind during the last months of his illness. "They thought Bill was a bit gaga at the end," said Patty's cousin Muffy Coolidge. "I think Jim wanted to see what he had been getting up to."

Just as Conant feared, Bill, who had always disdained authority and the narrow scope of his plodding academic colleagues, had been dangerously indiscreet. Among the documents found in his desk was the galley proof for his novel, *Brain Waves and Death*, which was to be published in a few weeks under the pseudonym Willard Rich. Although it appeared to be a conventional murder mystery—albeit with the unusual twist of being set in a modern laboratory where the scientists were working on an experiment to measure the electrical impulses sent out by the brain—Conant could see at a glance that the book was a roman à clef. It amounted to a thinly veiled account of Bill's experiences working at the Loomis Institute for Scientific Research in Tuxedo Park, New York, which had conducted pioneering research on electroencephalography in the early 1930s.

This was the same Alfred Lee Loomis, an immensely wealthy Wall Street tycoon, who had been helping the Nobel Prize–winning physicist Ernest O. Lawrence secure a whopping $1.15 million grant from the Rockefeller Foundation to build a new cyclotron—the great atom smasher he had invented—at his Berkeley laboratory, while Harvard struggled to fund its fledgling program. The same Loomis who had been raiding MIT and other top universities of physicists for the past year to work on a secret defense research project. Harold Urey at Columbia had just written to Conant complaining that Loomis's microwave activities were single-handedly creating a dearth of physics professors to teach college courses. Conant had never met the man, but he had heard enough about his larger-than-life personality to know that no one could fail to recognize that the charismatic figure of Howard M. Ward in Bill's novel was transparently based on the New York financier, who owned and operated a private scientific compound in Tuxedo Park. Loomis was the kind of deep-pocketed patron who had friends in high places and sat on innumerable important boards. The sort of notoriety the novel would bring would be the last thing Loomis would want, especially given the highly sensitive nature of the work in which he was involved.

Conant knew little beyond the broad outlines of Bill's relationship with the influential banker-turned-scientist. Not long after he had taken up a teaching post at Princeton, Bill had received a letter from the Loomis Laboratory inviting him to work at the lavishly funded facility. It was there that he had the opportunity to carry out some of the first experiments with intense ultrasonic radiation, work that inspired subsequent research in American and European laboratories. Bill had recruited his close friend and Princeton colleague, George "Kisty" Kistiakowsky, and both scientists worked as consultants to the Loomis Laboratory for a number of years.

Now a prominent member of the Harvard Chemistry Department—Conant had poached him in 1928—and close friend, Kistiakowsky was still in regular contact with Loomis. As the international situation worsened, he had turned to his old benefactor to help aid scientific colleagues fleeing the Nazi terror. Loomis found many of them jobs, and provided generous research stipends for others, most notably the Italian physicist Enrico Fermi. (When he learned he had won the Nobel Prize in 1938, Fermi, whose wife was Jewish, left Rome with his family and $50 in his pocket and never looked back.) In the process, Loomis had earned the loyalty and respect of many in the scientific community. Kistiakowsky, a tall, urbane, immensely self-assured Russian émigré who had fought in the White Army in the Russian Revolution, had an instinct for trouble and shared Conant's concerns about Bill's book. While in the past he might

have laughed at the witty satire of Loomis as a dilettante and wealthy collector of big brains, the war in Europe had changed everything. In only
the past few months, Loomis had transformed his private laboratory into
a research center devoted to the development of war-related technology,
specifically the radar systems used to detect airplanes. The work he was
doing was so secret, and of such fearful importance, that Richards's parody
of Loomis and his research laboratory struck Kistiakowsky as a reckless
and ill-conceived prank.

Sure enough, Loomis was furious. On the eve of the book's publication,
he was on the phone angrily demanding that Conant use his influence to
have it recalled. He threatened to sue for libel. Conant did not care for
the man's bullying tone, but he bit back his anger. He assured him that
he shared his distress, but the book had gone to press—nothing could be
done. Loomis was an intensely private man and was justifiably outraged
at the betrayal by a trusted colleague. Bill Richards was intimately acquainted with all the players and the goings-on at Tuxedo Park, including
Loomis's extramarital affair with his much younger secretary, caricatured
in the novel as a "brazen hussy." Much to Conant's relief, when the book
debuted in March 1940, it earned respectful reviews but attracted no
additional attention. None of the critics was aware that the author was
already dead or that, in a macabre twist, he had foreshadowed his own
imminent demise, killing off a tall, arrogant young chemist named Bill
Roberts.

Conant and Loomis met over lunch and put their differences behind
them, in large part because of their mutual friendship with Lawrence.
Conant had tried unsuccessfully to hire the brilliant young Berkeley physicist in 1936, but the two had remained close, both personally and professionally. Over the next few months, Lawrence would persuade Loomis
to use his considerable influence to help raise funds to support Harvard's
cyclotron project for biomedical research on neutron radiation and radioactive isotopes, which scientists hoped would lead to a new, inexpensive
treatment for cancer. Lawrence succeeded in getting Loomis so "steamed
up" about Harvard's project that in May Loomis wrote Conant a check for
$5,000 for research in nuclear physics.

While Conant continued to regard the novel as a source of embarrassment, it was the least of the problems Bill had bequeathed him. Far more
troubling was the draft of a short story entitled "The Uranium Bomb."
The slim, typed manuscript, bearing the name and address of his literary

agent, Madeleine Boyd, was clearly intended for publication. As he quickly skimmed the story, he became increasingly perturbed. The opening scene described a meeting between a callow young chemist, clearly Richards, and a zany Russian physicist named Boris Zmenov, who bore an uncanny resemblance to Leo Szilard. A Hungarian refugee scientist, Szilard was currently working on uranium fission with Fermi, a newly established professor at Columbia. Szilard was known to be extremely vocal about the importance of fission research and the danger of delay in a time of war. In a scene that rang especially true, the Zmenov character, who is convinced the Nazis want to build an atomic bomb, explains there has been a breakthrough in atomic fission: the uranium nucleus has been split, with the liberation of fifty million times as much energy as could be obtained from any other explosive. "A ton of uranium," Zmenov warns, "would make a bomb which could blow the end of Manhattan island."

With his unerring instinct for the sensational, Bill had homed in on one of the newest and most controversial developments on the frontier of science: atomic energy's explosive power. For all Conant knew, Bill had plucked most of his ideas from the front page of the *New York Times* or from any one of a number of academic journals. The exciting developments had been widely covered: in December 1938 two German physicists, Otto Hahn and Fritz Strassmann, working at the Kaiser Wilhelm Institute in Berlin, had discovered fission. Lise Meitner, their colleague, had quickly grasped the significance of their finding and calculated that when a uranium atom was hit by a slow neutron, it would split, dividing into two distinct elements and, in the process, releasing an enormous amount of energy. Meitner, who escaped the Nazis by fleeing to Stockholm, rushed to inform the Danish physicist Niels Bohr of the news prior to his departure for America. By the time Bohr arrived in the United States, a telegram was waiting for him from Meitner's nephew, the physicist Otto Frisch, reporting that a test had demonstrated the discovery of uranium fission. Bohr and Fermi announced the results at a conference in Washington, and within the first few days of 1939, experiments confirming Frisch's results were performed in several American laboratories. The uranium atom was so small, however, that the explosion of a single nucleus could not be seen with even the most powerful microscope. No one yet saw how energy in the atomic nucleus could be released in practical quantities.

But as Bill's story set forth in disturbing detail, a few physicists kept exploring the possibility that under the right conditions, a chain reaction could occur. "To make a uranium bomb," he theorized, "each exploding nucleus would have to throw off fresh neutrons, which cause more nuclei to explode, and so on, over and over . . . the successive explosions of atoms follow each other so quickly that a colossal amount of power is generated."

In May 1939 Fermi had published the results of the recent experiments he, Szilard, and others had conducted showing that a fission chain reaction could be made to work. Convinced the Germans would soon recognize the same possibility, Szilard had wanted to take immediate political action. The American scientific establishment needed to be alerted. Steps needed to be taken to guard against the possibility that Hitler's forces could get ahold of this knowledge. Fermi, who was of a more conservative temperament, thought any practical application was still remote and was inclined to "play down" the danger. So Szilard appealed to his old friend and mentor, Albert Einstein, to warn the president of the United States to the potential military applications of nuclear fission. Although also a refugee scientist, Einstein was world famous and had the necessary stature to lend credibility to their cause. In August Szilard, drawing on Einstein's first draft, wrote the final version of the letter they would send to Roosevelt advising him that "extremely powerful bombs of a new type" could now be constructed. A mutual acquaintance, Alexander Sachs, a vice president of the Lehman Corporation, with contacts high in the US government, had promised to see that it reached the president.

At the time, Conant was unaware of the Einstein letter. But when the contents of Bill's desk revealed a raft of letters from Szilard, including several updating the progress of his chain reaction work with Fermi, it was obvious the Hungarian physicist had been a source of information and inspiration. The correspondence indicated that Bill had been in regular contact with Szilard, and had appropriated the cutting-edge science for his dramatic fantasy. If his hypothesis was right, as the scientist in the story boasts, uranium could generate a colossal amount of power—greater than any that science had heretofore known—in a bomb that would "revolutionize civilization."

Conant was skeptical. Bill's doomsday scenario reflected the hysterical tone of the newspaper articles claiming that physicists had unlocked the power of the sun and could now destroy the world in a fiery atomic explosion. He was familiar with Bohr's warnings about the destructive potential of fission but had seen nothing that persuaded him it was anywhere near to being ready for use as a weapon. There was little proof that any of this was feasible. Still, the bomb story made him uneasy. The scientific material accurately represented the facts as they were known—too accurately. None of it was classified, but only because no official secrecy policy had yet been established. All of this would have been unsettling enough, but in March 1940 it seemed demonstrably unsafe. Conant decided to err on the side of caution. He called Madeleine Boyd's office and made sure Bill's story would never see the light of day. He demanded she return all copies of the story to him, and locked them in the bottom drawer of his desk.

That should have been the end of the matter except for his son Ted's "great nose for unusual news." The teenager stumbled across a finished draft of the story tucked in among the boxes of books, technical journals, and radio equipment his uncle had left him. He immediately announced his intention of submitting the story to several science-fiction magazines. Conant rarely lost his composure, but in this instance his temper got the better of him. The story was "outlandish," he snapped. It was "ridiculous" to even consider publishing it. A terrible row ensued. When Ted hotly objected that confiscating the story was a form of censorship, Conant cut him off, stating with awkward finality that it was a question of the "family honor."

"I conceded the argument, but not because I believed him," recalled Ted. "He was not someone who talked in terms of 'family honor.' It was such an odd thing for him to say, so completely out of character, I knew something must be up."

By the time Conant suppressed "The Uranium Bomb," any mention of atomic energy's military significance filled him with unease. While the country was still resolutely isolationist, and most Americans had been lulled into a false sense of calm by the months of "phony war" in Europe, the former chemist was acutely conscious of the need to prepare for the worst. The US Army, in its present ill-equipped condition, was no match for Hitler's military machine. Advances in military technology, from new, more powerful explosives, to the developments in aviation, meant the country was more vulnerable to attack than at any time in its history. Given the superiority of German airpower, America's ocean barriers would not keep it safe. The uncertainty about the war that had plagued Conant was gone, replaced by the conviction that Hitler had to be stopped from controlling Europe. What distressed him was the public's apparent indifference to what was taking place three thousand miles across the Atlantic, and ignorance about the necessity of readying its defenses.

While Congress endlessly debated repeal of the Neutrality Acts, the country continued to sit on its hands: American men could not volunteer for Allied armies; citizens could not make private loans to the Allies; military and aviation secrets were being withheld from Britain and France; and companies were continuing to trade with nations that supplied Germany with strategic materials. As he watched Poland's surrender and the German army's rapid progress in the autumn of 1939, Conant could not believe, in the midst of such a catastrophe, that another academic year would proceed "without pause or interruption." The outposts of democracy were falling one by one, with terrifying implications for free people everywhere, yet Americans—the young in particular—remained aloof. Convinced that noninvolvement was a prescription for disaster, he took to the pulpit of Harvard's Memorial Church in late September to sound the alarm. Another world war was "now at hand," he declared. Intelligent people could no longer "pretend to be neutral":

"Every ounce of our sympathies is with those who are fighting on the French and British side," he argued. "The forces of violence must be beaten by superior violence and yet without engendering bitterness or hate. Reason must triumph over unreason without being converted in its hour of victory to the very thing it would destroy."

Whether or not they agreed, the boys who jammed the church "listened intently," Patty told her mother. Even she found the speech "deeply impressive," she added, "especially as he has always been so temperate in what he has said, and this time he expressed himself so forcibly with intense earnestness."

Now that he was openly speaking his mind, Conant waged a personal campaign to alert the country to the need for preparedness. He also began to emerge as a strong exponent of the view that the United States must move to a belligerent status. Although he stopped short of advocating intervention, he argued that a triumphant Nazi regime would be "so inimical" to American values and interests that "from motives of self-interest alone this nation must be ready to supply arms and implements of war to those who face the totalitarian power." No matter what, the United States could not afford to underestimate such a dangerous enemy. The experience

of the slow-moving civilian committees and cumbersome military bureaucracy in the last war had taught him the need to focus attention on the
"tasks at home": the planning, procurement, and security precautions that
must be undertaken. "Gigantic steps in preparedness will be necessary," he
maintained, "to enable the United States to breathe in peace in a world of
war."

For months now, Conant had been quietly conferring with other scientific leaders and university heads behind the scenes on how to organize
educational institutions, laboratories, and personnel for the war effort. "I
hope you are making progress with that plan for enlisting scientific men of
the country on a research basis for preparedness," he wrote Vannevar Bush,
a shrewd Yankee engineer and inventor who had created the most powerful
analog computers of the 1930s and was now the guiding force behind the
Carnegie Institution, the late Andrew Carnegie's massive investment in the
future of American science. "Let me urge the importance of this step." Bush,
who like Conant had spent World War I battling military policy makers—a
submarine-detection device he invented was never adopted—had been using
his new Washington office to try to influence the army and the navy toward
a more scientific approach to the problems of warfare. He had already begun
sounding out his colleagues about creating a new overall organization to coordinate defense research, and bent Conant's ear on the topic when the two
met on May 24, 1940, at a small informal luncheon in New York.

"We were all drawn together by the one thing we deeply shared—worry,"
Bush recalled. The phony war had ended in April, and in the course of only
two weeks, the German blitzkrieg had torn across the flatlands of Belgium,
Holland, and France, and reached the shores of the English Channel. The
British expeditionary forces, on the brink of annihilation, were miracu-
lously being evacuated from Dunkirk by a makeshift armada of fishing
boats and other scrounged vessels. But Hitler's panzer divisions had poured
into France, and the occupation of Paris was imminent. On May 10 the
British prime minister, Neville Chamberlain, had resigned in disgrace, and
Winston Churchill had taken over, promising his country "blood, toil, tears,
and sweat." The swift events transpiring in Europe drove home the need for
action. Conant, Frank Jewett, and the others present at the lunch that day all
shared Bush's conviction that it was going to be "a highly technical struggle,"
that America was woefully unprepared, and that the military system as it
existed, and had operated in World War I, would never be able to produce
the weapons they would need.

"We all agreed it was high time for America to wake up," recalled Conant, noting that the unanimity of opinion around the table spurred him to resume his role as an outspoken interventionist. The best the British could hope for fighting alone was an armed truce. Only American intervention could turn the tide.

However, the mind-set of his scientific colleagues differed sharply from that of his Harvard associates. Conant found many of his fellow academics glum and defeatist—persuaded that it would be a short war, and the outcome was already a foregone conclusion. When he told William Claflin, Harvard's treasurer, that he was considering making a speech urging the United States to "get in and help," Claflin responded, "No, be realistic. Hitler's going to win; let's be friends with him."

The common sentiment seemed to be that Britain did not have a chance. The island would not be able to withstand the first German assault. Better by far to start building a relationship with the future power. Conant was appalled by the pessimism. It was a "bad point of view," he wrote in his diary, "but typical of the business appeasement group." What depressed him more was how little they understood about the real issue: that a military and naval victory for Germany would endanger the institutions of democracy in the Western world. America's security was inextricably linked to Britain's independence and Allied control of the Atlantic. People needed to be educated about what was at stake. Three days later, he ignored his long-standing injunction against joining committees and became a charter member of William Allen White's newly rechristened Committee to Defend America by Aiding the Allies, which advocated lending military material support to Britain as the best way to keep the United States out of the war.

On May 29, 1940, as three destroyers loaded with troops were sunk off Dunkirk, and the Nazis' armored divisions closed in on Paris, Conant went on national radio to urge "immediate aid" for the Allies. Distancing himself from Harvard by stating that he would be presenting his personal views, Conant went on to argue clearly and forcefully that the country must "rearm at once." Hitler's war machine had to be stopped. A Nazi victory in England and France was but a prelude to world domination. "I shall mince no words," he stated. "I believe the United States should take every action possible to ensure the defeat of Hitler. And let us face honestly the possible implications of such a policy. The actions we propose might eventuate in war. But fear of war is no basis for national policy."

"It is not too late," he warned, his own tardiness in alerting the country to the Nazi menace adding weight to his words, "but it is long past time to act."

His speech had the desired effect and made the stand in support of neutrality "not an easy one to uphold," an editorial in the *Crimson* conceded grudgingly. "From that moment," observed historian Paul F. Douglass, "Conant became the foremost voice urging total American involvement. He became honorary chairman of White's committee and its most effective publicist. From his deep personal conviction, he kept hammering on one theme: 'Fear of war is no basis for national policy.'" It was his favorite refrain, and the one he became known for as he increasingly became the public face—and voice—of the interventionist cause.

Having appealed to Americans to "Let your voice be heard" and write to the president or their congressman in favor of war aid, Conant followed up with his own telegram to Roosevelt on June 5: "VENTURE TO WIRE YOU PERSONALLY IN SUPPORT OF VIEWS SET FORTH IN MY RADIO TALK OF MAY 29 PARTICULARLY URGING THAT ALL PLANES WHICH CAN BE SPARED WITHOUT ENDANGERING OUR SECURITY BE RELEASED QUICKLY TO ALLIES."

The message to the president had been motivated by his desire to take an even more prominent role in speeding up the process of rearmament. After the invasion of France, public opinion had begun to shift. Conant was delighted by the reception to his broadcast. A bulging bag of fan mail arrived at his office in University Hall, along with a congratulatory cable from White telling him the government was following his recommendations and releasing large amounts of aid: "WAS SEMI-OFFICIALLY ASSURED 200 PLANES LEFT NEWFOUNDLAND SATURDAY TO FLY TO ALLIES. MORE SOON. WASHINGTON IS FEELING THE IMPULSE OF OUR WORK."

FDR, grateful that the Harvard president was willing to lend his authority and prestige to oppose the isolationists, sent a brief, appreciative reply stating that he had been "thinking along these lines" for several months.

For the most part, the Cambridge constituency was "very favorable," Conant noted in his diary, adding dryly, "much abuse from illiterates." At a Corporation meeting in Boston, he put up with some needling from Charles Coolidge, who wondered if he was "coming out for FDR for a third term?" Conant asked, "No, why?" "Well," came the fulsome reply, "You do so many unexpected things!" After seven years in the hot seat at Harvard, Conant had learned not to let those kinds of comments get under his skin. He had grown accustomed to slings and arrows from his enemies, not to mention the occasional poison dart from a friend. He expected only "sneers" from the *Crimson*, which was shrill in its condemnation of preparedness, as well as the "barrage of dead cats" from the isolationists. Far from withdrawing in the face of enormous domestic opposition, Conant was girded for battle, taking pointers from other high-profile interventionists such as Grenville Clark and telling Archie MacLeish pugnaciously, "I am getting used to the volleys from both right and left."

He was also enjoying the limelight. All the press attention flattered his ego, as did the frequent tributes to his "intellectual leadership." He was absurdly pleased to find himself voted the "fifth best-dressed man in America" by the Custom Tailors Guild of America, edging out sartorial stars such as bandleader Guy Lombardo, ex–New York mayor Jimmy Walker, and the actor Adolphe Menjou. The *Crimson* tweaked him for losing his "common touch in this sudden access of fame," and the *Boston Herald* ran a cartoon speculating that if Harvard's president abandoned his academic tweeds altogether, it would cause "colds in Cambridge—and economic instability on the British isles."

After so many years slogging away in the administrative trenches at Harvard, the opportunity to rally the American people on the vital issue of national defense gave Conant a renewed sense of purpose. He stepped eagerly into the fray, inserting himself into the preparedness debate in speech after speech. Conant deftly worked his war message into commencement addresses and university lectures, talks to the alumni and awards dinners, exploiting every occasion to educate the public about the paramount need to rearm the Allies. It had taken a mere six weeks for the German forces to defeat the French army. Europe was collapsing, Conant warned, and the time had come for America to start to develop a fighting force of the magnitude it would need in the days to come.

On June 10 Roosevelt gave an address at the University of Virginia announcing that the United States would extend to "the opponents of force" the material resources of the nation and at the same time, "harness those resources," in equipment and training, necessary for national defense. To reach this goal, the nation would "not slow down or detour. Signs and signals called for speed—full speed ahead."

On June 12 Conant took up the same theme: "We as a people have awakened to the imminence of a threat," he asserted in a speech to the Jewish War

Veterans in New York. "There may still be dispute as to the course of immediate action, but there is hardly a citizen who does not realize that liberty on this continent is now in danger." He praised FDR's speech, and seconded his call for immediate military training and compulsory service. A peacetime draft—an unprecedented measure—was enormously unpopular, but urgently needed. Aware that this was a thorny issue for FDR, who was loath to alienate isolationist voters, Conant did the advance work for him. There was "no time to lose," he warned, drawing a frightening picture of a "complete totalitarian triumph" and urging Congress to stay in session to enact the controversial conscription law "this summer."

Two days later, Bush called to say that Roosevelt's right-hand man, Secretary of Commerce Harry Hopkins, had arranged a meeting with the president, and it was "all fixed" for a new federal agency to mobilize American science for military research. Hopkins had instructed Bush to present the plan for the National Defense Research Committee (NDRC) on a single sheet of paper, and after listening for less than ten minutes the president had signed it: "OK—FDR." The NDRC would be set up by executive action, with funds of its own to be allocated from the substantial sum Congress was about to place at Roosevelt's disposal.

"Will you be a member?" asked Bush. He was a tough, imposing figure from an old seafaring family, and Conant could think of no one better suited to lead the war effort. Since he had "urged the committee" on Bush for months, he was, of course, prepared to accept. This was a job of immense significance—the kind he had always imagined for himself and had intimated to Patty during their courtship. He had just two questions to put to the engineer, who was a long, lean, plain-talking Yankee of similar ilk, and whose ruggedly independent views and dry sense of humor had made them fast friends: "Is it real?" and "Are you to head the committee?"

On June 18, the "four horsemen" of the NDRC—Vannevar Bush, James Conant, Frank Jewett, and Karl Compton—gathered for their first informal meeting at the Carnegie Institution's massive neoclassical headquarters at Sixteenth and P Streets, in the heart of Washington, DC. Also present was Richard Tolman of Caltech, who, like Conant, was an early advocate of preparedness and had come to Washington for the summer to offer his services. The other scientific member was Conway P. Coe, the commissioner of patents. It would include two delegates from both the War Department and the Navy Department, and two from the National Academy of Sciences. Rear Admiral Harold G. Bowen of the navy and Brigadier General George

V. Strong of the army were already on board. In addition, Bush had drafted Carroll L. Wilson, a recent MIT graduate, as his assistant, and Irvin Stewart, a political scientist, as executive secretary. Bush had moved so rapidly that by the time they met, he had enlisted the ten of them over the telephone, and the president had signed the letters of appointment.

As they gathered around the table in Bush's office that morning, Conant recalled, "The mood was anything but relaxed." The NDRC had come into existence almost overnight, at a time when "many people looked at the future with fear." It seemed almost nothing could be done to stop Hitler from conquering Western Europe. For all they knew, the invasion of England might be only weeks away. Conant raised the question of what, if anything, the new agency could do about helping the British withstand a frontal attack. There was not only the question of legality—a federal statute barred any such assistance—but also the issue of military security. General Strong opined that anything they did to help the British would be "the equivalent of helping the Germans," since it was only a matter of time before Great Britain shared the fate of France.

"Hurry as they might," Conant realized, by the time they had the rearmament program up and running in three or four months, there might be "no free and independent British nation with whom military men and scientists could talk." He was so rattled by the general's dire forecast that he decided to redouble his efforts to promote "immediate aid to the allies."

A week later, Conant was back in Washington for a second NDRC meeting. Wasting no time, Bush announced who would lead the different divisions of operation. He asked Conant to direct all the chemical work—what would be known as Division B—including bombs, fuels, gases, and chemical problems. Tolman would serve as chairman of Division A, dealing with armor and ordinance; Jewett would head Division C, communications and transportation; Compton, Division D, radar and allied matters; Coe, Division E, patents and inventions. Each of them was responsible for establishing as many sections as necessary to handle his division's specific military problems, and these would be the real working groups. They began drawing up a select list of forty scientists whom they hoped to recruit. Conant put forward the names of Roger Adams and other chemical warfare colleagues to lead sections under him. All the candidates would have to be cleared by the army and the navy. He was all too familiar with the frustrating delays caused by having to obtain security clearances for individuals who were to have access to classified wartime information. It was 1917 all over again.

Conant spent that night at the suburban Washington home of the lawyer Dean Acheson, former undersecretary of the Treasury until a row with FDR returned him to private practice. They dined with Archie MacLeish. With the 1940 Republican convention only two days away, the evening was given over to politics. No one thought the president wanted to run for a third term, but what was the alternative? Both Acheson and MacLeish were for Roosevelt "faute de mieux" (for want of a better alternative), as Conant put it in his diary, and very much against Senator Robert A. Taft, a conservative from Ohio. As usual, he kept his opinions to himself. Privately, he was rather taken with the Republican candidate Wendell Willkie, an ex-Democrat and Indiana farm boy made good, but would never have said so. The next morning, he took the nine o'clock train to New York for a meeting with White's executive committee to discuss the military training bill, offered to poll other college presidents on the incendiary issue, and caught the five o'clock Federal Express to Boston.

As much as he loved trains, Conant realized with an inward groan that he was going to be spending twenty to thirty hours a week riding the rails, commuting between Boston, New York, and the NDRC headquarters in Washington. He broke the news to Patty that his new job, while an exciting challenge, would undoubtedly be time consuming. It meant his life was no longer his own. "Jim will definitely have to be in Washington part of each week—for as far as we can see," she wrote her mother in mid-July. "He says his work in Wash. is extraordinarily interesting, even if it seems like turning back the clock 23 years. And of course it has got to be done. On the whole, this last week he feels a good deal has been accomplished. If England can only hold out through the summer, he feels the world may possibly pull through. But that is a big 'if.'"

On June 27 Conant convened a meeting with Harvard scientists at University Hall to tell them about the creation of the NDRC, still a week away from being publicly announced by Roosevelt, and to ask for their cooperation. He had already written to fifty academic institutions with extensive facilities for advanced research, explaining that the NDRC would be using federal money to fund immediate wartime research in the fields of physics and chemistry, electrical and mechanical engineering, and metallurgy. Bush had come up with an ingenious scheme to get around the great bulk of bureaucratic roadblocks they had encountered in the last go-around. Instead of slapping civilians in uniform and putting them to work in large military plants, scientists were to be mobilized for the defense effort in their own laboratories. Bush's plan ensured that this time a significant portion of the weapons research would be contracted out to investigators, working in their own facilities, with small handpicked staffs, doing what needed to be done rather than what the military thought should be done. It was, in Conant's view, nothing short of "revolutionary."

On July 2 he was back in Washington for the first formal meeting of the NDRC. The day was spent passing resolutions, issuing press releases, and posing for photographers. The following day, Conant testified before the Senate Military Affairs Committee on the Selective Service Bill. He came on just before noon, when they adjourned for lunch, and a number of senators were already rising to leave. Although he was not inclined to feel sorry for himself, he had to follow Colonel William J. "Wild Bill" Donovan of the famous "Fighting Sixty-Ninth" Regiment, who gave a rousing presentation. Conant read his statement but "felt ill at ease," complaining to his diary later that he was "not used to this type of audience." It was an inauspicious beginning of his official life. He felt much cheerier the following morning: the *New York Times* ran his testimony in full, and it inspired two editorials, including one in the *Boston Herald*.

Any plans he might have had for a real holiday that summer were put on hold because of his NDRC work. A much-anticipated expedition to the Canadian Rockies was scratched. With the Fourth of July weekend approaching, he flew to Boston and drove to Randolph, New Hampshire, his favorite retreat in the White Mountains, for a few days of relaxation. Unable to resist the temptation to get "above tree line," he scaled the side of Mount Washington with a few friends. Just as they completed their descent, Conant felt something go in his back. He crept home in agony, afraid he would "never straighten up." A doctor taped his back and prescribed plenty of rest, but his rock climbing days were over. He got "no sympathy" from Patty, who disapproved of the dangerous sport.

While laid up, Conant was besieged by calls from politicians, journalists, and celebrities asking him to join one front committee or another and "go on the air" with their concerns. The Harvard-educated newspaper columnist Joseph Alsop, now with the *New York Herald Tribune*, made a long and highly emotional pitch about the plight of the British refugee children and how the president would not modify the rules easing entry into the United States until public opinion demanded it. "He said Cousin Eleanor, i.e. Mrs.

FDR, very interested," Conant jotted in his diary. "Told him to tell her to talk to her husband. I declined flatly. Have talked enough!"

He had good reason for wanting to keep his powder dry. There were more important battles to fight. Conant needed to "save himself" for the NDRC, though he agreed to join an influential pro-Allies citizens committee that came to be known as the Century Group after the Century Association, the New York club where it held its meetings. An exclusive, invitation-only gathering of twenty-eight establishment figures, led by the lawyer Grenville Clark, its members included politician and diplomat Lewis W. Douglas; Council on Foreign Relations executive Francis Miller; Admiral William Standley; *Time* publisher Henry Luce; journalist and historian Henry Agar; Bishop Henry Hobson; theologians Henry P. Van Dusen and Henry Sloane Coffin; columnists Joe Alsop and Elmer Davis; bankers Will Clayton and James Warburg; and lawyers Allen Dulles and Dean Acheson. Aware of the need to mold public opinion, the group used press releases, personal influence, and pressure tactics to undermine isolationism and advance the cause of armed resistance. While Conant considered the majority of the members "extremists" for publishing a statement demanding that the United States declare war on Germany immediately —putting them "four jumps ahead" of White's committee—the two groups worked together closely to outflank the isolationists and lead the reluctant nation on the path to war.

On July 25, key members of the Century Group, determined to get aid to Britain, presented FDR with a legal brief outlining the idea for the destroyers-for-bases agreement that the president announced on September 3. The deal furnished Britain with fifty overage destroyers in return for permanent rights for air and naval bases in British possessions along the Atlantic Coast and a pledge to never surrender its fleet to Germany. Conant hadn't taken part in the negotiations to persuade Congress to stretch the arms ban—he was so busy he failed to attend any of the group's early meetings—but he applauded the "great scheme" and happily joined in signing the public statement, giving his unqualified endorsement of the president's action.

While the destroyer-bases deal was a blow to isolationists, they were still a powerful political force. Conant saw the impact especially on Harvard students, who were so bombarded by propaganda that all they had left were their suspicions and intellectual doubts. In Sweden, writer H. G. Wells had spoken of "this utterly aimless war" and summed up the feelings of a generation. Their convictions had been undermined by appeasers such as

Joseph Kennedy, the US ambassador to the Court of St. James's, who called for cooperation with the misunderstood Germans; by Fascist sympathizers such as Charles and Anne Morrow Lindbergh, who hailed totalitarianism as the "wave of the future"; by the pro-Nazi rants of the Catholic priest Father Charles Coughlin, whose weekly radio show stirred up anti-Semitism in Boston's Irish population; and by the cynicism of Senator Nye, who attacked the idea of bailing out "British plutocrats" and banged on about how the Allies were just waiting to sell the United States down the river.

Conant had every reason to be dismayed by the skepticism and disillusionment of the young. At the Exeter graduation of his oldest son, Jim, that spring, he had listened as the seventeen-year-old delivered a cynical speech praising the "cold-blooded efficiency and the daring of the Germans," and "Hitler's ruthlessness . . . initiative, and resourcefulness." Having come of age in an era of brutality, he and his peers were "without the rose-colored glasses of our parents." They had been well-schooled in broken covenants, lawlessness, and betrayal by their allies. The logic of events had driven them to a new realism: "Today the machine gun rules; the only thing that counts when the chips are down is force," he stated. "[O]ur destiny will be decided, not by treaties or by international law or by diplomatic gestures, but by bombs and hand-grenades, and bayonets."

The fact that he seemed to have only scorn for his father and the "older generation" with their "florid phrases of nineteenth-century moral indignation" added an undercurrent of adolescent rage to his diatribe. Although there were echoes of Conant's own ideas in his son's truculent oration, he did not acknowledge them in his diary, observing only that many of the pro-Ally parents in the audience considered it "quite shocking." But then, most fathers and sons were split on the issue of the war. His cursory review found the schoolboy analysis wanting: "an overstatement of 'hard-boiled' younger generation's point of view. Said they 'saw no moral issues, admired Hitler in spite of themselves.' Don't think he really believes it," he added with exasperation, "and 'moral issues' a battle of phrases!"

The increasingly antagonistic debate had also marred Harvard's usually joyous commencement, when a member of the class of 1915 made a prowar speech and was roundly "booed and hissed." In retaliation, those who supported the war almost drowned out the class orator, who denounced aid to Britain as "fantastic nonsense." There was no escaping it. With each passing week, the arguments between interventionists and isolationists seemed to escalate until the atmosphere on campus practically crackled with tension.

"Harvard was in bitter contention," recalled Arthur Schlesinger Jr., whose memoir vividly conveys the "searing personal impact of those angry days."

By mid-August, Nazi Germany's long-awaited assault on England had begun in earnest. "Mass airplane attacks," Conant noted in his diary, adding with guarded optimism, "so far British doing well." Many experts had predicted that the Luftwaffe would make quick work of the Royal Air Force as a prelude to a September invasion. Day after day, German planes bombarded Britain's shipping centers, air bases, factories, and, finally, its cities. Despite being vastly outnumbered, the RAF frustrated Hitler's hopes for a quick victory. The Luftwaffe was beaten back by the tenacity of the British fighters as well as their advanced Chain Home air-warning system. The US Army and Navy were only just becoming aware of the crucial role of what would soon be known as radar—radio detection and ranging—in securing Britain's triumph over Germany in the skies. Bush and Compton knew already that British scientists had developed a means of detecting enemy planes, and in early summer had organized a secret project and commenced research on a portable microwave detection system for night fighters and antiaircraft guns. The NDRC had scored its first victory. "The importance of physicists for weapon development was rapidly recognized," recalled Conant. "From then on, there was no chance of Dr. Bush's committee being ignored."

Conant responded to the growing urgency of England's plight by shifting his NDRC activities into high gear. He galvanized the Cambridge chemists, and began assigning research projects. He assigned his Harvard protégé Paul Bartlett to lead the unit investigating new methods of manufacturing lewisite, the poison gas he had pioneered in World War I, commandeering a laboratory in Wolcott Gibbs so he could keep close tabs on his progress. Both he and Bush were vexed by the delays in security clearances caused by "the stupidity of the FBI." Despite still suffering from a very bad back—heat and massage treatments were providing little relief—Conant made repeated trips to Washington to meet with army and navy research groups, lay the foundation for a constructive working relationship, and review the problems they would be sending his division. With explosives everyone's first priority, he arranged a conference at Carnegie to discuss a "fundamental physico-chemical study of high explosives (the atom bomb in miniature)."

When not occupied with scientific problems, Conant was increasingly involved in formulating political strategies to circumvent domestic opposition to the war, while at the same time converting it through a process of education. He spent hours a week consulting with members of White's committee devising tactics—some quite devious—to deal with the isolationists. He went to see Sumner Welles, the undersecretary of state, about their "next moves," and afterward wrote up five or six points of revision of the neutrality laws to be pushed after England proved it could ward off a frontal attack. He helped Grenville Clark in a relentless four-month propaganda campaign to build support for the Selective Service Act, which was finally signed into law on September 16, and which military historians later credited as one of the most important of America's defense measures prior to Pearl Harbor. Conant lobbied hard for, and won, a provision granting deferments for men in certain scientific and medical fields, as well as language protecting students training for those professions in colleges and universities.

At the same time, he was also working on a private scheme of his own to provide emergency relief to Britain. While "pretending to be away from Cambridge for the summer," Conant was actually busy raising money and making plans to send a Harvard Public Health unit to England to open a field hospital and fight the spread of disease in the bombed-out cities. Motivated by his "almost overpowering emotional reaction" to the blitz attacks, Conant maneuvered around the legal obstacles posed by the neutrality acts and eventually pooled his resources with the American Red Cross for maximum effect.

With the Battle of Britain in full fury, Conant felt the time had come to try to sway the defeatist sentiment. The climate of opinion was changing. With every Nazi attack, public opinion polls showed that American admiration for Britain in its "finest hour" was growing, along with support for a military rescue effort. He was determined to build on that momentum and try to unite all shades of interventionist opinion—whether pro-Roosevelt or anti-Roosevelt—in a unifying "aid to allies" message he would deliver at the opening of the college year. "I certainly put my heart into the preparation," he noted of the speech that emphasized his belief that the American way of life was worth defending, and chided the country for its lack of courage.

"What is the worst possibility which confronts us—war?" he demanded, deliberately working to strike a responsive chord in the crowd of fresh-faced young men determined this was not their fight. "So many people think, but I venture to disagree. War is not the worst possibility we face; the worst is the complete triumph of totalitarianism."

On October 2 he dined at the Cosmos Club in New York with Bush, who looked inordinately pleased with himself. He divulged that at Loomis's Tuxedo Park laboratory that weekend there had been a secret meeting with the British Technical and Scientific Mission, led by Sir Henry Tizard, an influential defense scientist. After weeks of tense negotiations, Churchill had secured an agreement for the British and Americans to swap military secrets after the US Navy's reluctance to share its new weapons had finally been overcome. It had been "a real exchange of information," Bush reported, a grin splitting his long, leathery face. The haul of secret developments, which far exceeded expectations, showed that the United States was "five years behind on detection of planes."

The British scientists had unveiled a resonant cavity magnetron, a small device that could generate extremely short radio waves. The magnetron, emitting radiation in the ten-centimeter, or microwave, region, would increase the power available to US technicians by a factor of a thousand. "Navy and Army faces very red when they learned this!" Conant exulted in his diary, adding, "Very important. A special lab exclusively for the NDRC should be set up to speed this research."

Compton appointed Loomis head of the new radar laboratory. On November 1 Loomis moved his operation from Tuxedo Park to MIT's campus in Cambridge and went to work developing the magnetron into an airborne intercept system that would transform England's defenses. The secret enterprise was named the Radiation Laboratory, like Lawrence's cyclotron lab at Berkeley, in an attempt to mislead any German spies into thinking that MIT's physicists were engaged in something as academic and remote from the war as nuclear physics. In short order, Lawrence himself was drafted to help Loomis get the "Rad Lab" under way with all due speed.

In a desperate bid for the isolationist vote, Wendell Willkie began to assail the president as a warmonger. He criticized the conscription bill and destroyers-bases deal, protesting lamely in the latter case that FDR should have sought Congress's approval. When that did not work, he accused the president of trying to secretly lead the nation into World War II, forcing FDR to make the rash promise "Your boys are not going to be sent into any foreign wars." Willkie's partisan shots at the administration's foreign policy did not do him any good. Disappointed by his candidate, Conant decided at the last minute to cast his vote for Roosevelt, noting in his diary that not even his wife knew, "thus preserving political neutrality!" FDR won by a clear margin, but the country was more divided on the war than ever before.

On November 20, following the German bombing of Birmingham, Conant addressed the nation by radio on behalf of White's committee. He had been sick as a dog the previous day, but this could not be postponed, so at ten at night he went straight from his bed to the WEEI radio station in Boston. Worried that Willkie had set back the interventionist cause, he went even further than he had at Harvard, arguing that America's free way of life could be preserved only by defeating the Axis powers, which now included Japan. Speaking again as a "private citizen," he explained that the opinion of the experts was that such a defeat could be achieved only if America pledged all its resources, including men, to the Allies "without reservation." It would then be purely a matter of strategy when, and if, that aid would take the form of direct military assistance. He had heard the younger generation's reservations and now responded with a plea for definite action he hoped would dispel their doubts:

"We shall be rightly condemned if we needlessly become involved in a war and squander life and treasure. But we shall be yet more guilty in the eyes of the descendants if we fail to preserve our heritage of freedom—if we fail because of timidity or lack of farsighted resolutions. The decision is momentous. Those who feel as I do believe the future of human liberty is at stake."

Conant's militant speech incensed Harvard students and sparked a number of angry protests. In the six months since his first "aid the allies" radio broadcast, undergraduate opposition to the war had grown in both size and decibel level. The *Crimson* accused Conant of dangerous folly—"the best we can hope for is a stalemate victory"—and the *Lampoon* ran a cartoon of him beating war drums. On November 23, during halftime of the Harvard-Yale football game, three students rushed onto the field and staged a skit portraying the college president engaged in a solitary military drill, driving boys away from their books and into battle with a wooden-bayoneted rifle. Conant was spared the embarrassment of sitting through the burlesque by a bad cold, but he summed up the animus directed at him with the terse diary entry "No fan mail."

No other college president so candidly and forthrightly identified himself with rearmament, though many agreed with him. "So large a proportion of President Conant's constituency feels that he is going too far in his advocacy of immediate participation in the war," wrote Dartmouth College's president, Ernest M. Hopkins, an interventionist and fellow Centurian. Such strong talk disturbed people. Privately, Hopkins was in line with the

Harvard man but took the view that he was out front of most Americans on the issue, and that his attitude could not be "advantageously insisted upon at the present time." But Conant was done weighing the risks and would not remain silent.

In December he wrote a personal note to Roosevelt urging him to warn the nation that total victory now lay within Germany's grasp. In the postelection slump, the White House had been strangely silent. Worried that Britain's defenses were on the point of cracking under the strain, and an all-out assault by the Germans in the spring would finish England, Conant beseeched the president to step up aid to Britain. "I am much disturbed by the lethargy," he began, "and defeatist attitude in certain quarters which asserts that nothing we can do can be of assistance in the critical months ahead." He suggested a series of nationally broadcast "radio addresses" to alert the public to how the defeat of Britain would "jeopardize the future of free institutions in this country." Hoping to persuade the president that he must act decisively, Conant implored, "But for your bold stand during the crucial days of last spring and summer, Great Britain now would be in the position of France. I believe the American people will respond as readily to your leadership at this time as they have in the past."

Another letter would soon follow bearing the names of a great many eminent fellow citizens: "168 signees more to come," he noted in his diary. The interventionist circular, drafted with Lewis Douglas and dubbed the "Conant-Douglas round-robin," would be endorsed by those of the White committee who had moved beyond the position of all aid to Britain "short of war" and now believed that military assistance by the United States would be necessary—and, at a minimum, would involve the use of naval convoys. America had to maintain the "lifeline" that was the sea route from the Western Hemisphere to England. As for White, who still clung to his original slogan—"aid to the Allies short of war"—and thoroughly opposed intervention, Conant recommended he be "muzzled." But he used his influence to persuade other committee members against removing their namesake, who was tired and ill, and run the risk that their internal row became public and weakened their objectives.

Many people throughout the country were still in sympathy with the isolationists, and he was concerned that the America First Committee, founded that autumn by a group of Yalies, was gaining a nationwide following for its platform that a Europe dominated by Germany could peacefully coexist with the United States. Charles Lindbergh was its headline speaker. The most important thing was for their side to maintain a "united front," Conant stressed, taking over the reins of leadership from White, who would resign shortly. "Publicly, I think the efforts of all of us should be to back the president," he added, though "a certain amount of private pressure" should be kept on Roosevelt "to see that he goes farther still."

The day after Christmas, Conant wired their "round-robin" statement to the White House urging the president to "make it the settled policy of this country to do everything that may be necessary to ensure the defeat of the Axis powers." But FDR, who had just received a desperate request for more ships, bombers, and munitions from Churchill, did not need any more prodding. On the very day he received Conant's personal letter, he broached the idea of Lend-Lease at a press conference with a folksy parable about a man lending his garden hose to a neighbor to put out a fire. He approved of the Harvard leader's counsel that he should "inform the American people concerning the grave implications of the present situation" and wrote Conant of his intention of making "a radio address along the line you propose before the end of the year." But more important, Roosevelt added, he deeply appreciated the "tenor and spirit" of his advice.

Just before nine o'clock on the evening of Sunday, December 29, Conant sat down in the opulent parlor of 17 Quincy Street—the Corporation had turned down his request to move to a more modest residence as a wartime sacrifice—and waited anxiously for Roosevelt's "fireside chat" to begin. At that very hour, bombs were raining down on London, a night of terror planned to divert world attention from the president's announcement of whether the United States would remain neutral or support the effort to defeat Hitler. In a moving speech, rounded and warmed by his familiar reassuring tone, Roosevelt called for the United States to become the "great arsenal of democracy." America, he told his radio audience, would furnish the British with the weapons they needed, "the planes, the tanks, the guns, the freighters which will enable them to fight for their liberty and for our security."

Conant thought FDR's speech was "magnificent." Before he turned in for the night, he patted himself on the back for his part in keeping the country on the right track and advancing an idea that would become the basis of the Lend-Lease legislation to be introduced in Congress in the New Year. The president's radio address was "very effective," he noted with satisfaction, and while not going quite as far as he would have liked, it was "as far as he could go probably."

The press and popular response to the president's speech was better than he dared hope. "I have been very encouraged," he wrote "Grennie" (Grenville) Clark, adding that publicly FDR deserved their support until he had played his entire hand. "It takes time for a democracy to move, and we must be patient, or so it seems to me."

Conant's confidence in the democratic process was matched by his faith in America's ability to rise to the challenge ahead. He shared Roosevelt's belief, expressed in his memorandum creating the NDRC, that "this country is singularly fitted, by reason of the ingenuity of its people, the knowledge and skill of its scientists, and the flexibility of its industrial structure, to excel in the arts of peace, and to excel in the arts of war if that be necessary."

Few of his academic colleagues shared his optimism. In a private conversation one rainy Saturday afternoon, Princeton's president, Harold Dodds, admitted to being "pessimistic about the long as well as the short run." Conant agreed that the next five years would be difficult but was confident enough of the future to offer to check in with Dodds in 1950. "Expressed my views on U.S.A. armed to the teeth, belligerent, and running the world," he asserted in his diary. "A Pax Americana like the Pax Britannica of the 19th Century."

Conant knew exactly what he was doing when he stepped into the political arena and was committed to seeing his rearmament efforts through despite the naysayers on his own doorstep. By now, those with isolationist views among the alumni had already marked him as a "dangerous man." He turned a deaf ear to the complaints about his extracurricular crusade against Hitler, as well as the carping about his appointment to the NDRC, frequent absences from Cambridge, and neglect of his academic duties. In spite of his critics—or perhaps to spite them—Conant was arranging to have his interventionist radio addresses published as a booklet. It would make "no reference to Harvard." He began delegating administrative responsibilities to what he called his "heavy deans" and quietly made plans to appoint the historian Paul H. Buck as the university's first provost. His actions might well put him at odds with some members of the Corporation, but the faculty uprising had sufficiently soured him on academe that he was willing to take the risk. He had already begun to "wonder" to his diary how he would be able to continue to juggle his war work "as well as Harvard and speaking as a private citizen."

For Conant, there was never any real choice. The world was again at war. And once again, a new kind of industrial warfare would yield deadly results. Chemistry beckoned, and he was going to answer the call whether Harvard liked it or not.

CHAPTER 12

Mission to London

*To the sorely pressed British, he symbolized the might of
America pausing on the brink before plunging in.*

—Vannevar Bush

AM SAILING FOR ENGLAND TOMORROW VIA LISBON ON OFFICIAL
SCIENTIFIC MISSION AT THE REQUEST OF THE PRESIDENT OF THE
UNITED STATES RETURNING EARLY IN APRIL AM DELIGHTED AT
THIS ASSIGNMENT NEWS WILL BE RELEASED TOMORROW PATTY
IS A GOOD SPORT.

Conant cabled his sister Marjorie at the last possible minute, waiting
until just before he kissed his wife good-bye and boarded a train bound for
New York. The following morning, Saturday, February 15, 1941, he made
his way to the New Jersey pier where the American Export liner *Excalibur*
was docked. He was accompanied by two NDRC associates—Carroll Wilson and Frederick L. Hovde—who would be sailing with him, as well as his
assistant, Calvert Smith, who had come to see them off. The terminal was
packed with holiday travelers. Most of his fellow passengers were embarking on a two-week voyage to Lisbon via Bermuda, and Conant was amused
by the "gala" atmosphere—"might well be the gay 20s with everyone off on
a Mediterranean Cruise." Just as he stepped onto the gangplank, relieved
to be getting away unnoticed, a swarm of reporters appeared out of nowhere and chased on board after him. Dismayed, Conant and his compan-

ions decided on a "dignified though conservative policy of 'laisser-faire,'" he noted in his travel diary, "[We] would neither seek nor avoid the flash of the photographic bulb."

They were quickly cornered on the ship's deck and inundated with questions. It turned out the White House had blown their cover, issuing a press release the previous evening announcing that Conant had been ordered to England and would be reporting directly to Washington "recent scientific information of importance to national defense." It was all in the morning papers, one of the reporters told him, flourishing a copy of the *Sun* with the banner headline "Conant Heads Mission to London." Their curiosity piqued, the newshounds demanded to know the exact nature of his expedition. Would he be studying all of Britain's defensive and offensive weapons, including its long-range bombers, blind-flying technology, and newly developed devices to curb night raids? Conant, dressed in a heavy wool coat, his dark felt homburg at a rakish angle, attempted to retain an air of mystery. "As president of Harvard University, I'd love to talk to the press," he replied, "but as head of a government mission, my mouth is closed."

The Nazis, who had targeted the Harvard chemist for his widely publicized pleas to stop Hitler, put out the story that he had been dispatched by Roosevelt to help the British start a gas war. Like most propaganda, it was no less effective for being untrue.

Conant had managed to steal away from Cambridge unobserved, having disclosed his impending departure to only a handful of deans. The members of the Corporation had greeted the fait accompli with a dumbfounded silence, and when they recovered showed "little or no enthusiasm" for his presidential errand. A few days before he left, the *Crimson* was informed of a scheduling conflict and printed the standard announcement canceling the open house at 17 Quincy Street: "No Conant tea: President and Mrs. Conant will be unable to be at home to students on Sunday."

On the following Monday, the paper reprinted the same announcement with the witty addendum: "Winston: 'One lump or two, Jim?'"

Conant was thrilled to be charged with such an important and prestigious assignment. He had been angling for the job since November, when he heard that Vannevar Bush was planning to dispatch a member of the NDRC to establish a London office, and mounted a strenuous argument as to why he possessed both the wisdom and finesse to head the liaison mission. "I feel very strongly that the person chosen should not be too young," he wrote Bush, "and must have had sufficient 'worldly experience' to be able to get on with our strange British friends and find his way around what must be a pretty distracted atmosphere." Aware that the NDRC chairman believed it "ill-advised" to send a senior member of the committee across the submarine-infested Atlantic to a city under siege from nightly bombing raids, Conant made a strong case that he was uniquely qualified to carry on the complicated negotiations:

> I feel that this may be very vital in one area with which I am par-
> ticularly concerned, namely, chemical warfare. If either side should
> suddenly start to employ this weapon, it would be very important
> that we obtain information rapidly. I have, I am afraid, grave misgiv-
> ings as to the proper functionings of regular channels in this regard.
> So, whoever is to be the permanent officer, I feel that he should be
> accompanied initially by a member of the committee itself and one
> who knows his way around England and has sufficient standing to
> be able to make the initial contacts and make them "stick."

Conant said nothing to Patty of his "conspiracy" to go to London as he continued to lobby stealthily for the job. He had read accounts of wartime London from returning newsmen and listened to Edward R. Murrow's radio broadcasts, but longed to be closer to the action. He wanted to see for himself what the "war from the skies" was really like—"a whole nation not liter-ally under arms but participating in a strange way in a continuous air battle." Unlike many of his chemical warfare colleagues, he had never been sent to the front and as a result always felt he had not pulled his full weight in World War I. He was determined that this go-around he would not miss confront-ing the reality of war firsthand. A letter of commiseration from Frank Jewett, who had also been kept stateside during the Great War and sympathized with his frustration, provided little solace, especially since he sided with Bush against the Harvard president taking such a hazardous assignment.

Conant replied at once in a letter downplaying the danger—"probably not more than one in a thousand of my being put permanently out of the picture"—and insisting that he could not let this opportunity pass. "I believe actions speak louder than words," he argued. For months, he had urged a belligerent policy on the country's young men, and it was time to back up his position by showing he was "willing to take risks."

In the end, he got his way. Roosevelt, pleased that the head of his alma mater had been selected as his special emissary, expressed his confidence that Conant would do a "grand job." FDR trusted Conant, and thought his endorsement of collaboration with British war science was bound to have great impact. Even the *Globe* approved, tipping its hat in an editorial congratulating Conant for demonstrating to his young students that he, for one, had the "courage of his convictions."

On the morning of February 1, he went to the White House to meet with the president and obtain his formal approval and any last-minute instructions. He had expected to discuss the details of the upcoming scientific interchange, which had begun haltingly with the Tizard mission the previous September, but could hardly get Roosevelt to focus on the trip, as he was preoccupied with the congressional brawl over Lend-Lease. "He was very anxious to outline the political strategy," Conant griped in his diary, annoyed to find himself being coached by FDR on the "important points" of the bill rather than what needed doing in England. On several occasions, the president's secretary poked her head in the door to announce that the next visitor had arrived, and it was only with difficulty that Conant finally interjected that perhaps the president should invite him officially to undertake the mission. "Yes, of course, I shall be glad to do that," Roosevelt replied distractedly. But when Conant left the Oval Office an hour later, he still did not have a letter of introduction to Churchill—or any scrap of "proof" empowering him to share US military secrets with the British.

In the weeks prior to his departure, Conant had become conspicuous on the national scene, proving a tough, authoritative, and fearless foot soldier in the president's campaign to send vast amounts of weapons and war materiel to Britain. After Roosevelt introduced his Lend-Lease legislation to Congress in January 1941, Conant fought valiantly to get the arms program passed despite furious opposition from the isolationists. His metamorphosis into the champion of the interventionist movement was so complete that it was widely rumored that he would become the new head of the White committee, the bipartisan pressure group. Pointing out that he was the first to call for all-out aid to England, and the first to call for universal conscription, the *New York Times* observed that the crisis had brought out the best in Conant, and his role as captain, organizer, and catalyst had made him the rearmament camp's D'Artagnan, the youngest and most formidable of the musketeers: "He has made some of the most forceful speeches of the year," the paper observed, "and often these have been psychological shock troops that made holes through which the administration has driven to attack the inertia that is presumably behind the majority of the country's isolationists."

The America Firsters mounted a massive effort to defeat Lend-Lease, lining up an imposing array of prominent figures who attacked the measure before the House and Senate committees and kept the debate going full blast for nearly two months. The opponents of the bill claimed Lend-Lease would only prolong the eventuality of British defeat. "It is like granting a man who is sinking money with which to buy a lifebelt," declared Luther Johnson, a congressman from Texas. Some critics repudiated the bill as simply another attempt by Roosevelt to seize dictatorial powers. Calling it a "dictatorship-war-bankruptcy bill," Representative Hamilton Fish contended that it was a "slick device to further regiment America" and a "betrayal of constitutional power." Senator Burton K. Wheeler of Montana, the head of the opposition, ratcheted up the political invective, assailing "the New Deal's triple A foreign policy" as likely to "plow under every fourth American boy," and attacking Conant personally as "one of the same old crowd . . . who are too old to go to the front line trenches" yet "urge a war that somebody else is going to have to fight."

Conant increasingly became a target of isolationist broadsides, indicted alternately for being a "stooge" of the British government and a captive of the college's wealthy Jewish benefactors. He kept a cool head and never wavered, despite the venomous assaults on his character, and proved such a loyal defender of the president's program that the administration chose him, along with Wendell Willkie and Mayor Fiorello La Guardia of New York, to be one of three final rebuttal witnesses before the Senate Foreign Relations Committee. Charles Lindbergh, who filled stadiums with tens of thousands of flag-waving "Fortress America" fans, would be the isolationists' star witness.

At ten o'clock on the morning of February 11, Conant strode purposefully to the front of the ornate marble caucus room, took his seat at the witness table, and addressed the assembled senators and representatives, and a packed gallery of more than 1,200 raucous and profane spectators, the largest turnout in history. His testimony, which tilted toward a hostile audience, took direct aim at the isolationists' wish for a compromise peace, and gave heart to Americans and their allies who wanted to vanquish Hitler.

Taking the contentious issue and breaking it down into plain, simple terms, Conant proceeded to give a ninety-minute lesson in why there could be no compromise with the Nazis. "Hitler's soldiers are proponents of a literally soulless creed," he explained, taking pains to emphasize that this was not an imperialistic war in the old sense but more closely resembled a "religious war" being waged by fanatics. "They are well armed by modern science," he warned. "They are hard to stop by force of fighting; impossible to stop by fair words or bribes, by talks of trade, or by a negotiated peace." The argument between the isolationists and interventionists, he concluded, "comes down to this diagnosis of the Nazi state. If those of my belief are right, our only hope as a free people lies in a defeat of the Axis powers."

"Suppose it required us to go to war to do it," countered Michigan senator Arthur H. Vandenberg, an ardent isolationist. "Would you go that far?"

"I should," Conant replied without hesitation, "if it were absolutely necessary as the last step."

Conant withstood a barrage of questions from senators eager to impugn his testimony. He calmly parried the queries and warmongering insinuations, and reiterated again and again that Germany, with its philosophy and armed might, must be defeated to preserve America's "free way of life." When he finally left the stand, the crowded committee room gave him an ovation so prolonged that it brought a warning from the chairman that if such a demonstration was repeated, he would have the room cleared.

Three days after the hearings, Conant embarked on his mission. The only route to London in the winter of 1941 was by air from neutral Lisbon. There were only six planes a week to the embattled island, carrying only eight passengers at a time, and they were constantly overbooked. Snagging a seat on the KLM flight was a matter of priorities, controlled tightly by the RAF. Through the usual sort of mix-up, the paperwork for his companions, Hovde and Wilson, had not come through, and they were stranded temporarily. Conant decided to go on ahead and found himself on a plane carrying the new ambassador to the Court of St. James's, John "Gil" Winant, and his advisor, Benjamin V. Cohen. Winant, a former governor of New Hampshire, was replacing the defeatist Joseph Kennedy, who had resigned following a series of disastrous newspaper interviews in which he declared "Democracy was finished" in England, praised Lindbergh, and vowed to spend all he had to keep America out of the war. Kennedy had many fans in Boston, but Conant, repulsed by his talk of appeasement, was not one of them.

Whether Winant had arranged for his seat on the British ferry plane because of a note Conant had sent to his hotel in Lisbon, he never knew, but he felt lucky to be traveling in the diplomatic party. The flight was swift and smooth, though a German Fokker swooped by on its way to Switzerland. He felt luckier still when they landed in Bristol and learned there was a special train waiting to whisk them to London. When it stopped for an hour at Windsor Castle, he watched as the rather rumpled-looking Winant, his hat clenched nervously in one hand, was welcomed by King George VI, spiffy in the full dress uniform of a field marshal. The king dispensed with protocol and greeted the new envoy on the station platform with an outstretched hand—reportedly the first time he had ever done such a thing—and then took him home for tea with the queen.

Conant was not keen on royalty. He was naturally suspicious of the British Empire and opposed to the long-run objectives of its colonial policy. Early in the war, his "New England caution" about their overseas cousins had separated him from the unabashedly anglophile members of the Century Group. Even now he felt a certain wariness of the "subtle flattery" of which the English aristocracy were "masters." But these reservations quickly gave way to admiration for their grit and courage during his first few days in the rainy, blacked-out British capital. He had never seen such devastation: the destroyed buildings, streets pocked with bomb craters, and whole neighborhoods obliterated. An evening visit to an air-raid shelter revealed the horrors of the murderous blitz, with the city's poor crowding into narrow, fetid, underground corridors for protection. "I saw a stouthearted population under bombardment," he recalled. "No one could tell you how the British proposed to survive as free men. But the will was there; there was no talk of negotiations, no faltering, no whimpering. Whenever I feel depressed about the quality of human beings, I recall with emotion the picture of England under fire."

He could not help but be deeply moved by the warm welcome he received from the inhabitants of the beleaguered nation. Everywhere he went, people expressed gratitude for his belligerent speeches and Lend-Lease testimony, grasping his hand and shaking it as if they would never let go. The warrior educator was feted at banquets, invited to address the House of Commons, given honorary degrees from Cambridge and Bristol universities, as well as the keys to the village of Southwark—from whence John Harvard had emigrated. Bush was pleased to see that he had sent "the ideal emissary." Conant's reception signified far more than just an exchange of technology: "To the sorely pressed British," Bush wrote, "he symbolized the might of America pausing on the brink before plunging in to aid a struggle to suppress an assault that threatened all of life as it had been built up over the centuries in the two countries with a common speech and common ideals."

From the moment he arrived, Conant was hailed as a "messenger of hope." It made him feel all the more keenly the burden of responsibility to make real progress and get meaningful projects under way. "The job is really important, and I'm sure I was the one man to undertake it," he wrote Patty at the end of the first busy week, adding that he was "embarrassed" by the effusive praise and attention. "It is a comfort to be able to do something besides talk to senators!"

His lunch with the prime minister in the bombproof basement dining room of 10 Downing Street on March 6 was a success, despite getting off to a bumpy start. Churchill was late, so Conant had a chance to air his strong views in support of the United States becoming a full partner in the fight against Hitler, ingratiating himself with the other guests, including Mrs. (Clementine) Churchill; Charles Eade, editor of the *Sunday Dispatch*; and Frederick Lindemann, a leading physicist and science advisor to the British government. When their host finally arrived, he was "obviously tired and grumpy," and Conant surmised his bad temper stemmed from the uncertain future of the Lend-Lease Bill. It had passed the House on February 8 by a vote of 260 to 165, but was getting hammered in the Senate and had sustained a number of damaging amendments. The hopes of those pushing the bill were reportedly at their "lowest point."

Churchill rather "let himself go" on the subject of Lend-Lease, his irritation rising as he spoke. "This bill has to pass!" he bellowed. "What a state it would leave all of us in if it doesn't; what a state it would leave the president in; what a failure he would appear before history if this bill is not passed!" he exclaimed, working himself up into quite a lather. "What would happen in the United States if the bill was rejected? Would the president resign?" And if so, "Who would become president, the vice president?"

Conant was taken aback by Churchill's vehemence. Could the prime minister really have "such a profound ignorance of the American constitutional system?" Tactfully as possible, he pointed out that the United States did not operate under a parliamentary system, and an American president, unlike a British prime minister, was not obliged to resign after a major political setback. Emboldened, he suggested that perhaps something more than an arsenal of democracy was needed. Perhaps America needed to send troops? "We don't want your men," Churchill grunted. "Give us the tools, and we shall finish the job." Conant recognized the phrase, having already observed the PM's "habit of quoting from his own speeches even in casual conversation," but was unpersuaded by the facile disclaimer.

He was treated to a display of the legendary Churchillian wrath when, at one point in the well-lubricated lunch, Clementine reflected that perhaps the good citizens of Britain, who offered tea and cigarettes to downed Luftwaffe pilots, could never work up a really deep, abiding hatred of the Germans. Churchill pounced on the remark and growled that before the war was over, the British would be hating their enemies, all right. According to Churchill biographers William Manchester and Paul Reid, his "calculated quotient of righteous anger" was entirely for Conant's benefit. The Germans had just dropped a four-thousand-pound "monster bomb" on Hendron, instantly killing eighty civilians. "To address such dastardly technologies and tactics with an overly generous heart would undermine Churchill's status as warlord in front of an important luncheon guest," they wrote. "He had to appear resolute yet not bloodthirsty."

At that point, Charles Eade asked if the big German bomb contained "any new form of explosive." His query, which was more on the money than Conant cared to admit about a journalist, sparked a lively conversation about the ingenious new instruments of death being invented by scientists in what Churchill sometimes referred to as the "Wizard War." Lindemann, an eccentric Oxford physicist commonly referred to as "the Prof," and known as the PM's "pet scientist," appeared to be following his own train of thought and began to ruminate aloud about uranium, saying, "Uranium is continually halving itself. Why is there any uranium left on earth?"

The little-known element meant nothing to most of the guests at the table, but the Harvard chemist immediately grasped its significance. Bill Richards had fantasized about a uranium bomb and the possibility that a multiplying chain reaction might explode with force. Conant still thought it far-fetched, though, at Bush's invitation, he had attended a Conference on Applied Nuclear Physics at MIT the previous fall. He had listened to an interesting presentation by Fermi on nuclear fission and was familiar with the outlines of the theory of the use of uranium for power. He understood there were several promising approaches to separating the uranium-235 isotope from the heavier, far more abundant uranium-238. One was to place the unseparated uranium in a "pile," or reactor, with graphite or heavy water as a moderator (a way of slowing down the neutrons) to increase their chances of being captured by another atom of uranium-235, thereby increasing the chances of a chain reaction. Calculations indicated that if one gradually increased the size of the pile, a self-sustaining nuclear reaction would take place. But all the diffusion methods presented great difficulty, and Conant did not believe the many obstacles would be overcome anytime soon.

Roosevelt, prompted by Einstein's letter, had turned over the problem to a secret Advisory Committee on Uranium headed by Lyman J. Briggs, director of the National Bureau of Standards, and then asked Bush to take it on as part of his NDRC responsibilities. The subject had come up in a number of NDRC meetings, but Conant recalled the discussion was always about "exploiting uranium fission as a source of power rather than a means of destruction." At the time, he had questioned squandering men and money on atomic energy. Priority had to be given to weapons likely to be of practical value in the current war, not the next. In any case, uranium was not part of his London portfolio, and he put Lindemann's comment out of his mind.

The luncheon conversation bothered Conant for other reasons. He did not think Churchill had been entirely frank—though in his view, "no responsible statesman was required to be completely candid"—but the PM's gloomy frame of mind was extremely disturbing. Even though he suspected it had been, at least in part, a performance to stir him up, Churchill "had succeeded." Conant was so agitated that on his return to his hotel, he immediately cabled Calvert Smith demanding to know if the White committee and other proponents were doing all they could on behalf of Lend-Lease: "AMERICAN NEWS VERY DISCOURAGING IS EVERYONE GIVING ALL AID RAPID PASSAGE."

On Friday, March 7, he received Smith's cabled reply informing him that final passage of the bill, without hobbling amendments, was expected within days. The president signed it into law on March 11. All of London seemed to celebrate. The British understood what most Americans did not: that the real significance of Lend-Lease was that it brought the United States one step closer to war. Roosevelt was heaped with praise. "Your great president" was all Conant heard, over and over again. From then on, he noted in his diary, all bureaucratic obstacles to scientific exchange disappeared as "the gratitude of the British for this act swept all difficulty away before us."

At his next meeting with the prime minister, a luncheon at Chequers, a big, drafty house an hour's drive from London that was his official country retreat, Churchill was in excellent spirits. There were a number of American guests present, including Ambassador Winant, Major General Harry J. Malony, and Averell Harriman, FDR's special envoy to Germany who had arrived a few days earlier to take charge of the Lend-Lease operation. All the uneasiness Churchill had displayed ten days earlier was gone, and he was relaxed, witty, and voluble. Putting aside the subject of Anglo-American relations, he held forth on the battles of the American Civil War, proving well versed on the subject. When he came to the Reconstruction period, he remarked sagely that "the men who can win a war can never make a peace." Somebody suggested there might be *one* exception. No one vied for that flattering trial balloon.

Conant was very impressed with Churchill. He was even quite likeable in his way, despite being too bombastic and given to making provocative statements. What sealed their friendship, however, was the discovery that they shared the hobby of painting, though neither had any time for it now. Many years later, Brendan Bracken, the prime minister's chief advisor on public relations, told Conant that Churchill was initially appalled at the prospect of entertaining the president of Harvard. "What shall I talk to him about?" he had asked, according to Bracken, who recounted the story with glee. "He thought you would be an old man with a long white beard, exuding learning and academic formality." Instead, in walked the surprisingly informal, boyish American sporting, of all things, "a tweed suit."

On Wednesday, March 12, Conant had an audience with King George at Buckingham Palace, where he could see through a window where a bomb had knocked down one small wing. As they chatted before an open fire, the king, a "friendly soul" who greeted him without formality, proved not only up-to-date on radar, then a highly secret defensive weapon, but also knowledgeable about the recent introduction of a device that could identify whether a spotted plane was friend or foe, known as IFF. After a quarter of an hour, "the maximum time an ordinary individual should take of His Majesty's day," his time was up, and Conant amused himself by seeing if he could comport himself in the recommended manner and exit "without turning his back on Royalty." The maneuver was easier than expected.

There was almost constant rain. The cold and damp of wartime London eventually got the better of him. Conant was forced to spend a day in bed, curled up with a hot-water bottle, catching up on his correspondence and sending cables. In a long letter to Patty, written later that evening in the midst of an air raid, he described with genuine excitement hearing the sirens sound at a quarter after eight and experiencing his "first real Blitz":

> About 8:30 the guns began to bark, and you could hear the planes overhead very plainly. The waiter who was bringing me dinner assured me it was German planes, and from the racket of the guns, I believed him . . . Here sounds one now! As though it were going to land in the courtyard! They say the noise of the guns is very comforting, but I haven't learned yet how to tell a gun from a bomb.
>
> Probably I haven't heard any bombs, but I would swear I heard two in the last hour *whistling* (they do, you know) and then exploding, but there was no concussion in the room and only a slight shaking of the windows, so I may be wrong.

Clearly relishing his brush with danger, Conant tried to analyze the sound in order to determine the distance of the bombs from his room at Claridge's, telling his wife that the explosions sounded like a "cross between fireworks at the [Boston] Braves' field heard from Quincy Street and a thunderstorm in the 'Massif Central' [mountainous region of southern France]."

In a follow-up note, he reported, "Six bombs dropped within a quarter of a mile of Claridge's. The worst raid on this part of London since October. So you see, living through a raid isn't such a bad business," he added jauntily, explaining that he was including a clipping that showed "how large a city London is and how small the chances are" of being killed. The American embassy had furnished him with a "lovely but heavy" US Service gas mask and tin helmet. He did not tell her that the post-Christmas lull in the Luftwaffe's aerial attacks, which Londoners dubbed the "lullablitz," was over, and the nightly punishment had begun again. What amazed him the most was that through it all his British hosts insisted on dressing for dinner, and seemed to regard his lack of proper attire as a greater crisis than the possibility of being blown up, forcing him to rent a set of tails from Moss Bros. in Covent Garden.

Conant spent the next month establishing liaison at the highest levels of the British government and defense establishment, arranging for a broad-based exchange of secret scientific military information. He toured Porton Down, the chemical warfare proving ground, and Woolwich, home to the Royal Arsenal, which manufactured guns, cartridge cases, shells, and bombs. He met with Sir Henry Tizard, and visited airfields, antiaircraft emplacements, and coastal defenses. After inspecting a radar unit while it was tracking enemy planes, Conant came away so impressed that he immediately proposed a "wild idea" to Harriman and Colonel William Donovan, who was in London on a special intelligence mission of his own: Why not send a group of American reserve officers with physics backgrounds to England to learn how to operate these "most important and highly complicated gadgets?" This "electronic battalion," which came to be known as the "Conant scheme," would serve two ends: the United States could supply the British with much-needed additional operators, and at the same time ensure that if and when America entered the war, it would have radar specialists trained in the use of the advanced equipment.

Having been in the weapons business before, Conant listened with an ear attuned to the hard-won advances and insights that came from front-line experience. The British had nine months of fighting under their belts and had learned some valuable lessons. "One thing they do better here," he stressed to Bush in an almost illegible letter written in haste in order to make the next morning's diplomatic pouch, "is to keep their scientists connected with a project from start *to the finish*." Conant was all for it. He remembered the value of feedback from the field while working on mustard gas, and emphasized the importance of having scientists carry their work through all stages of development and deployment, collaborating closely with the men actually operating the weapons, "or else much of our usefulness comes to an end at a critical point."

As more work on immediate battle problems was a priority, he advised exporting manpower from the United States to England. Unceasing effort had to be made to maintain technical superiority in the air, and England had exhausted its supply of physicists. First-rate American scientists and engineers—"not many men but much talent"—should be dispatched to England to familiarize themselves with explosives, war gases, radar, rockets, fuses, and antisubmarine devices under actual combat conditions. A dozen or two, working "right here," where they could do the most good, would make an "enormous difference." The burden of more long-term research projects, such as completing the development of the British-designed proximity fuse, improving antiaircraft shells and rockets, along with totally new weapons, should be shouldered by America, because they would become a factor only if the conflict dragged on for some time.

"If you accept this line of argument," Conant told Bush, he should further accept that this class of weapons might turn out to be the "determining factor" in the length of the struggle. "We in the US must be willing to take the long gamble," he argued, "do the long-range research as insurance against a war lasting four years or longer."

As a result of Conant's recommendations, twenty-six American scientists would travel to England over the next nine months to exchange secret data and forge close ties. But this was more than just pooling scientific reports and eliminating needless duplication of effort—the men of each country would help to stimulate one another's thinking, giving rise to new ideas for weapons. "Here he was ahead of his time," Bush observed of Conant, noting that his approach "speeded work on both sides of the water."

For the most part, however, his duties were more diplomatic than scientific. His brief was to launch the NDRC's London base, make contact with as many "brass hats" as possible, and along the way assess Britain's capabilities and requirements, not to engage in detailed discussions of technical matters. But when Lindemann asked to meet with him alone for a private lunch at a London club and again raised the subject of uranium fission, Conant realized he was "clearly conveying secret information." He found it curious that the military potential of uranium should keep coming up in conversation. Only days earlier at a Cambridge University laboratory, Conant had met the French physicist Hans von Halban, who had fled Paris with a supply of heavy water, a gram of radium, and a record of his research investigating a chain reaction that might be harnessed to power submarines or possibly a bomb. When the Frenchman began to confide concerns about his work, Conant had quickly cut him off. "Look, you're not supposed to talk to me about this thing," he told him. Halban was obviously speaking "out of channels," and Conant, mindful of the "need to know" principle governing classified material, terminated the conversation.

Lindemann was also way out of bounds, but he was an influential figure and a key member of Churchill's inner circle. Out of respect, Conant let him finish. Still, he did not trust the motives of the arrogant science minister, an unabashed elitist, who made no effort to conceal his contempt for his social inferiors or devotion to the idea that the British Empire should rule the world. Conant told Lindemann point-blank that while atomic power might have its uses someday, he did not like to waste precious resources on "distant objectives," adding, "too distant for us to take seriously in these frightening days."

Lindemann would not be so easily dismissed, however. A large man with heavily set features, he leaned in and said portentously, "You have left out of consideration the possibility of the construction of a bomb of enormous power."

"How would that be possible?" Conant asked.

"By first separating uranium-235," he explained, and then arranging for two portions of the element to be brought together suddenly "so that the resulting mass would spontaneously undergo a self-sustaining reaction" of tremendous force—in other words, an atomic bomb.

As Conant recalled later, this was the first he had heard about "even the remote possibility of a bomb." Until then, he had considered it an unproven concept. He had not known that atomic energy's use as an explosive had been "made evident"—certainly nothing of the kind had been disclosed in the NDRC meetings he had attended. But, then, Bush was a stickler for going through channels, viewing it as a "grave offense" when people exceeded their authority, and uranium was Briggs's bailiwick. No doubt both men were aware of the uranium studies being done in England and, because of the "supersecrecy" of the project, had decided to keep him in the dark. He also assumed Lindemann was dropping hints for reasons of his own: perhaps believing the need to enlist the Americans had become urgent and hoping the Harvard scientist had the ear of the president. "Feeling that this was entirely an unofficial and private communication, and represented a highly speculative scheme," Conant did not pursue the topic further. He decided it would be prudent to keep it under his hat and wait for an opportune moment to tell Bush about the backstairs whispers.

By the end of March, he was sick again. He blamed a long, cold day in Dover inspecting the fortifications. Despite a "bad throat," he visited the site of the Harvard–Red Cross Hospital in Salisbury. The next morning, he took a few minutes to see the Salisbury Cathedral, the tallest spire in England, and it looked so beautiful and proud in the quiet town that he felt his throat—which was better—constrict again. "If I were to stay here long (and out of bed and warm), I might easily become a sentimental Anglophile," he wrote Patty. "It is hard to get this country in focus these days—such a mixture of war and peace, of the normal and the abnormal, of life and death." He had stayed longer than planned, but two months was not long enough to do half of what he would have liked to do. "I've tried to cover so many fronts, all necessary," he worried. "I believe I've done some good. I hope so."

On April 10, the day before his departure on Pan Am's new flying-boat service, he called on the prime minister at Downing Street for the last time. A meeting with a group of high-level officers was breaking up, and the maps they had been consulting hung on the walls obscured by protective coverings. Churchill insisted he join him in the Cabinet Room and divulged that the topic of conversation had been the impending debacle in Greece. The retreating Italians had called in the German army, and it would soon overpower all resistance. Over a two-day period, hundreds of German bombers had dropped thousands of pounds of bombs on Yugoslavia and Greece, pulverizing their ancient cities. The battle on the ground was almost certainly lost. Brigadier General Erwin Rommel's armored divisions had already driven General Archibald Wavell's weary, underequipped forces back three hundred miles, and would not stop until they reached the Suez Canal. The British troops there were doomed. Churchill was somber. "Here we are," he said, "standing alone. What is going to happen?"

There was no adequate reply. Whatever words Conant muttered were forgotten in the hours that followed and the terrible realization of the massacre to come. All he could remember later was the "intensity of my feelings as I left London."

He was filled with an overwhelming sense of urgency. Conant's "immediate objective" was to go home and tell all his friends—everyone he knew in a position of influence—of Britain's desperate predicament. Everything he had seen and heard only confirmed his belief that America had to intervene at once. He despaired not of England's will but her ability to survive. An American delay of even a month, he feared, might be too late. It might mean the war "could not be won at all."

On April 25 Conant met with the president and provided an overview of the mission while they ate lunch on trays in the Oval Office. Roosevelt was particularly encouraged by what he had to say about British advances in radar. Conant seized the opportunity to obtain approval for the scheme he had pitched to Harriman about sending American reserve officers to Britain to gain practical experience in the "radio magic" apparatus to detect enemy aircraft. Astonished to discover that the commander in chief was "almost totally ignorant" about the functioning of radar, Conant found himself tutoring him on the fundamentals of the war-winning technology that had played such a critical role in the Battle of Britain. FDR was so pleased with this bit of military know-how that he sailed into his Cabinet meeting that afternoon full of enthusiasm for the "marvelous progress" the British had made in "what was called radio but was not radio," and ordered Secretary of War Henry Stimson to act on Conant's proposal immediately.

A few days later, Conant met with Stimson. He felt awkward about having gone directly to Roosevelt with his pet scheme, bypassing the secretary of war and placing him in the embarrassing position of hearing about the novel project for the first time from the president. Nevertheless, Stimson saw to it that Conant's "Electronics Training Group" was quickly made operational. In August the first 350 Signal Corps officers—there would be 2,000 in all—were sent to England for radar apprenticeships. They would prove indispensable to their country in the months after Pearl Harbor.

During his talk with Roosevelt, the discussion had inevitably turned to the pressing problem of the isolationists. Conant mentioned that at the annual meeting of Harvard Overseers the week before, he had been dismayed by the number of diehards in the group. "As one Harvard graduate to another," he could not hide his contempt for the many prominent alumni who continued to insist the war might soon be ended by a negotiated peace if it were not for the stubborn and intransigent Churchill. With Britain on the brink of defeat, one muddle-headed individual had asked, "Why shouldn't all of us urge them to come to terms with Hitler?" Conant, barely able to remain polite, replied that no one in Britain was in the mood to bargain with Hitler. The board members' blasé attitude, he admitted, had been "difficult to take."

Roosevelt's reaction surprised him. "The president in turn recounted the extreme neutralist sentiment of certain men we both knew well," but did so "without the slightest rancor or other emotion." Roosevelt was supremely confident of his salesmanship and believed he could move America in the direction he desired it go, if and when circumstances demanded it. In the meantime, he was waiting on events, "trusting to luck," as his biographer James MacGregor Burns put it, and to his "long-tested flair for timing."

Convinced there was not a moment to spare, however, Conant was impatient with the administration's dawdling approach to full involvement. On May 4 he gave another major radio address, this time on behalf of the Fight for Freedom (FFF) Committee, a new pressure group formed by the militant wing of the Century Group, which openly endorsed war as the quickest and surest path to peace. "If we would preserve our freedom," Conant told his radio listeners in an impassioned speech, "the question before us is not 'Shall America fight?' The question before us is 'When Shall America Fight?'

I believe," he declared, his voice betraying his deep emotions, "we should fight now."

On May 27 the president gave a dramatic radio address declaring a national emergency and authorizing American ships to escort British convoys in the combat zone. Germany had dispatched its massive battleship *Bismarck* to the North Atlantic, where it had promptly sunk the British battle cruiser *Hood*, sending all but three of its 1,418 crew to a watery grave, and then skulked away. The German U-boat campaign had already been fearfully effective, and the crippling losses were sapping Britain's strength. Americans could not allow the Nazis' chief opponent to go under and let control of the Atlantic fall into enemy hands. The president presented the "cold, hard facts" to the country: the war was approaching the brink of the Western Hemisphere, would place portions in immediate jeopardy, and ultimately threaten the United States itself. To ensure friendly control of the seas, the United States would have to "give every possible assistance to Britain and to all who, with Britain, were resisting Hitlerism."

Roosevelt was inching toward war. He had made it plain that the Nazi threat was a threat to national security, knowing it was the only way to budge public opinion. The speech was largely symbolic, but it lifted Conant's spirits like nothing had in weeks, and he wired FDR a message of support. "Friends of freedom everywhere rejoice," he wrote. "The people have been overwhelmingly behind you in the steps which you have taken. I am convinced you will have their support in whatever steps you may find it necessary to take in the future."

A month later, the war suddenly veered east, in a new direction. On June 22 Hitler repudiated his nonaggression pact with Joseph Stalin and invaded the Soviet Union. Even though the prospect of Russia as an ally resuscitated the isolationists, Conant agreed with Churchill, who eagerly embraced "any man or state who fights on against Nazidom." Despite finding Communism and Nazism "equally detestable," Conant believed only the latter posed a real threat to the nation's security. Not only was there no danger in lending aid to Russia in its war with Germany, such aid was vital, since "the major concern of the United States must be to secure the military overthrow of Nazi power."

But the great debate about isolationism seemed to lose steam that summer. With Senator Wheeler, former president Hoover, and others wanting no part of the death struggle between two totalitarian powers, and Lindbergh railing against the godless and barbaric Russians, public interest in

foreign policy flagged. Americans seemed content to watch the two dictators duke it out on the Eastern Front. "The thing that worries me most,"
Conant confided to Grenville Clark, "is that if we do not start shooting by
September, the British-American relations will deteriorate rapidly and leave
a long trail of bad feeling for the future." Like many politicians, he had come
to believe that only another major shock would impel the country to action.

While most Americans waited resignedly for the inevitable, Conant radiated a martial spirit, and his constant clamoring for defeat of the Nazis
continued to make news. "No voice is louder urging our entry into the war,"
observed the *Globe* in late July. He was spending so much time in Washington—making on average two trips a week—and working so closely with
administration officials that the *New York Times* reported the "persistent
rumor" that he would be stepping down as head of the university to devote
all his time to the national defense program. Harvard authorities had no
comment. Conant, as usual, was out of town, and had his hands too full to
respond to a reporter's inquiries about his future.

By the fall of 1941, his political views were conditioning his educational
philosophy and found expression in the reasons he gave for wanting to review the undergraduate curriculum. When the faculty debated his modest modifications and then refused to make American history and "certain
great authors" required subjects, Conant redefined his agenda, claiming that
the central purpose of education was the "continuation of the liberal and
humane tradition." Compelled by the rise of Fascism, the masses of young
men entering the armed services, and the critical role of a small number of
scientists at work on advanced weapons, he pressed ahead with his reforms,
convinced that the educational strength that would help them win the war
would also win the peace. What America needed now, more than ever, was
brains.

Conant also sought ways to inculcate democratic values in the educational system that had as its first priority the identification and development
of the talented few—what he like to call "Jefferson's ideal"—the educated
elite who would be the next generation of leaders. Arguing that a good
grounding in mathematics and the sciences, combined with an ability to
read and write, was not sufficient background in "our common heritage"
to foster a strong sense of common citizenship, he urged a broad general
knowledge of the arts, history, literature, and philosophy to create a coherent national culture. "The primary concern of American education today is
not the development of the appreciation of the 'good life' in young gentle-

men born to the purple," he asserted in advancing what came to be known as a core curriculum, but rather to cultivate "an appreciation both of the responsibilities and the benefits which come to them because they are American and free."

On the eve of war, he appointed his trusted advisor, Paul Buck, and a dozen faculty members to undertake a major study of the aims and content of undergraduate and secondary education across the country in anticipation of the future, calling it the Committee on the Objectives of a General Education in a Free Society. But even as Conant moved to inaugurate his innovative ideas, the ominous developments in Europe drew his attention away from education to military defense and the increasingly pressing demands of public service.

CHAPTER 13

War Scientist

*You say you are convinced of the importance of these fission
bombs. Are you ready to devote the next several years of
your life to getting them made?*

—JBC to Ernest Lawrence

Almost as soon as he returned from England, Conant learned he was
being given a much more daunting assignment. It had all been arranged,
and President Roosevelt signed the executive order before Harvard's board
was given a chance to protest—not that it really could have under the circumstances. There was a tacit understanding that, as a scientist, Conant felt
duty bound to serve his country as best he could, and that his resignation
was always on the table.

In May 1941, with the country moving closer to war, Bush persuaded
Roosevelt to establish a new, vastly larger agency to oversee the mobilization of science for military purposes: the Office of Scientific Research and
Development (OSRD). Bush would have the title of chairman and greatly
enhanced powers—specifically, the authority to green-light the production
of new weapons from preliminary model to prototype. As the defense work
was fast outgrowing the president's emergency funds, Bush would also be
given direct access to the Treasury. Since he could not head two agencies at
once, Conant would assume leadership of the NDRC, which would function
as an advisory body responsible for making recommendations on the new

developments coming out of the laboratories, and serve as Bush's deputy at the new organization.

It would prove to be an exceptional partnership. The two flinty New Englanders had forged a deep mutual respect while engaged in various battles as rival college presidents. Each had come to rely on and trust the judgment of the other, so much so that Bush would say later that he could not remember that they ever disagreed through five tense, tumultuous years. Together they were able to provide the united, tough leadership necessary to persuade a skeptical government and military to make use of their scientific knowledge, and the country's technical resources, to create a modern organization for waging a modern war. Bush and Conant "won the confidence of President Roosevelt at the beginning of the national emergency," Secretary of War Stimson noted in his memoir, and "set a standard of effort which in its combination of soundness and daring left open . . . no intelligent course but full and hearty collaboration."

As soon as Conant's appointment was official, Bush took him into his confidence about the sorry state of the government's classified uranium research project. The Briggs Committee, which had been appointed by the president in October 1939 to fund further uranium research, had become hopelessly bogged down. For his part in jump-starting the program, Leo Szilard had been awarded $6,000 to continue his experiments, and various funds had been appropriated for further research, but overall there had been little progress. Meanwhile, Bush was being pestered with complaints from Ernest Lawrence and other leading physicists who were frustrated by the committee's leisurely pace and increasingly anxious that the Germans were exploring the possibility of an atomic weapon.

During the short two months Conant had been abroad, a great deal had happened in the field of nuclear physics in America, causing a considerable stir and a spurt of new activity. At Lawrence's Rad Lab in Berkeley, a team of young physicists—Glenn Seaborg, Emilio Segrè, Joseph W. Kennedy, and graduate chemistry student Arthur Wahl—had begun experiments with U-238 in the cyclotron and in February demonstrated that, after bombardment with neutrons, U-238 eventually transformed itself into an isotope of element 94, soon to be called plutonium. By March, Seaborg's experiments had confirmed that the new element, like one of the uranium isotopes, underwent spontaneous fission. The theoretical implications were striking: already physicists in the United States and England were whispering that the large-scale production of fissionable plutonium might prove the essential step in producing an atomic bomb. Lawrence, who was working on separating uranium by electromagnetic means, began pressing for a rapid expansion of the fission program and begged Conant, who had taken over its supervision when the OSRD was formed, to "light a fire" under the slow, conservative Briggs.

Lawrence had made such a nuisance of himself that Bush enlisted Arthur Holly Compton, a Nobel laureate and professor of physics at the University of Chicago, and as highly regarded a figure as his older brother Karl, to review the uranium program. Conant's reaction after reading Compton's May 17 report was "almost completely negative." The prospect of a bomb was "only hinted at," and "nowhere in the document was there any specific statement about how one started an uncontrolled reaction," which Lindemann had disclosed in London. Higher on Compton's list of military applications was the possibility of radioactive materials for use over enemy territory, and atomic-powered ships and submarines, though even the latter was thought to be years off.

In a private conversation with Bush, Conant voiced grave reservations about the uranium project. With no real military applications in sight, he questioned the assumption that achieving a chain reaction was "so important" that it warranted a large expenditure of both money and manpower. He advocated putting the uranium research project under wraps for the duration. They needed to concentrate all their energies on improving the immediate military power of the United States and Britain. "To me, the defense of the free world was in such a dangerous state," he wrote in his memoir, "that only efforts which were likely to yield results within a matter of months or, at most, a year or two were worthy of serious consideration." With the suffering he had seen in London fresh in his mind, Conant was impatient with arguments presented by some of the physicists who "talked in excited tones about the discovery of a new world" in which power from a uranium reactor would one day revolutionize industrialized society. "These fancies," he recalled, "left me cold."

Bush, who had by his own admission the "rough job" of determining defense research priorities, rather welcomed Conant's cranky opposition to a bomb—especially since it could prove to be a wild-goose chase. Between them, they tried to reorient the irrepressible Lawrence. For the present, they needed the prodigiously talented experimentalist to focus his "prime efforts" on the submarine antiwarfare program at San Diego, which interested him far less than the explosive potential of nuclear power. Lawrence had made that much abundantly clear when all three of them had discussed the matter a few weeks earlier at Harvard, where the Berkeley physicist had collected an honorary degree. He had been very exercised about the fact that the Germans were also working to release the atom's power. They had no cyclotron, though both Bohr's in Copenhagen and Frédéric Joliot-Curie's in Paris had fallen into Nazi hands. There was also strong evidence the Germans were doing advanced work on atomic piles, using uranium moderated by Norwegian heavy water. If a plutonium bomb was feasible, and Germany developed it first, the outcome of the war would be decided. Lawrence, who was competitive under normal circumstances, was almost frantic at the idea that the enemy might have had a head start. Germany could not be allowed to win.

Bush was aware of Lawrence's enthusiasm for fission studies, but time was precious and good physicists few and far between. "I have been putting a lot of thought on the uranium matter," he wrote Lawrence on July 14, adopting a conciliatory tone and complimenting him on his fine work in helping to launch the radar lab. By asking Conant to take charge of the Uranium Committee, he expected a more vigorous assessment of the problem and to begin moving toward a solution. The practical-minded Harvard chemist had already added two engineers to Compton's panel to serve as a reality check. "I rather hope Conant will find it possible to make this one of his primary interests at the moment to get the whole thing fully on track," Bush added, though "just how the matter can be worked out I am not at all sure."

Conant also maneuvered to have two trusted chemists—William Lewis and George Kistiakowsky—placed on Compton's committee. Because Bush felt bound to respect the military's security protocols, he imposed a strict policy of compartmentalization on his wartime agency, which meant no one—scientist, engineer, or technician—was allowed more information than necessary for the performance of his or her task. The atmosphere of secrecy was such that Conant had been unable to confer with Kistiakowsky, who in the last year had turned himself into the NDRC's explosives expert, about what he had learned from Lindemann. Now he brought his friend up to speed. Kisty was already familiar with the research work on separating uranium-235. "When I retailed to him the idea that a bomb could be made by the rapid assembly of two masses of fissionable material," Conant recalled, the Russian émigré looked dubious. "It would seem a difficult undertaking on a battlefield," he replied—his attitude, Conant noted, like his own—every bit that of a "doubting Thomas."

A few weeks later, when they met again, Kistiakowsky's doubts had vanished. "It can be made to work," he reported with certainty. After reviewing the principles of the method, he was "one hundred percent sold." Like Lawrence, Kistiakowsky argued that if a wartime bomb was within reach, they had to find out as fast as possible. He, too, had heard that German physicists at the Kaiser-Wilhelm Institute were hard at work on uranium for military purposes, and was making an independent study of the status of their research for Alfred Loomis. Conant had "complete faith" in Kistiakowsky's judgment, and allowed himself to be converted by his urgent affirmative. Conscious of the responsibility that came with being chairman of the NDRC, however, he decided to keep his "reversal in attitude" to himself. He would wait for Compton's final recommendation.

In Conant's view, even "more significant" support for the prospects of a bomb came from the British. Two leading German physicists, Otto Frisch and Rudolf Peierls, working in England after having fled the Nazis' anti-Jewish campaign, authored a highly influential memorandum confirming the feasibility of an atomic bomb and the force of its explosion. As a weapon, they argued, the bomb would be "practically irresistible," and they urged their colleagues to develop a similar device, if only as a "counter-threat." Instead of being measured in tons, as Bohr and all the other leading investigators had calculated previously, they estimated that the "critical mass"—the minimum material necessary for a self-sustaining chain reaction—of pure uranium-235 could be measured in pounds, not only making a bomb achievable but also making the cost of a plant to produce the explosive insignificant compared with the cost of the war. "We have now concluded," they stated in their report, "that it will be possible to make an effective uranium bomb which, containing some 25 lb of active material, would be equivalent as regards destructive effect of 1,800 tons of T.N.T."

Frisch and Peierls convinced their own secret uranium committee, operating under the code name MAUD, that a weapon of that size could be carried in a number of existing aircraft and would result in an explosion of "unprecedented violence."* The MAUD Report—which Briggs received in March and unaccountably locked in a safe without showing to

---

* The code name MAUD was reportedly inspired by a cryptic reference—"MAUD RAY KENT"—in a cable the Austrian physicist Lise Meitner sent to a British physicist. Convinced it was an anagram, the British used the mysterious code as the name of their secret nuclear weapons committee. Only after the war did they learn that it was simply an attempt to send greetings to Niels Bohr's governess, Maud Ray, who was then living in Kent, England.

anyone—favored purifying uranium though the method of gaseous diffusion, a process by which gaseous uranium was forced through fine mesh barriers, eventually separating the lighter U-235 from the heavier U-238. But the magnitude of the operation, and the investment—estimated at $25 million—virtually prohibited the British from undertaking the work. They urged the Americans to take it on, arguing that the evidence was sufficient to "justify the scheme being strongly pressed."

"With the news from Britain unofficially in hand," Conant recalled in a detailed chronicle of the project's beginnings he made for his own records, "it became clear to the director of the OSRD and the chairman of the NDRC that a major push along the lines outlined was in order." Bush took the first step, Conant noted, and during July had a discussion with Vice President Henry Wallace "about the question of spending a large amount of government money on the uranium program."

In August Mark Oliphant, director of physics at England's University of Birmingham, flew across the Atlantic in an unheated bomber on radar business and to make "discreet inquiries" as to why the United States had not begun that push based on the *MAUD Report*. Although he knew that America did not share England's sense of urgency about the war, Oliphant was "amazed and distressed" to learn that Briggs had buried the report. He raised the issue over dinner with Conant in Washington and then in a brief meeting with Bush, who did not respond well to pressure tactics and spared him only twenty minutes. Neither of the OSRD leaders let on they knew all about the findings in the *MAUD Report*. "Gossip among nuclear scientists on forbidden subjects," was how Conant characterized Oliphant's unofficial pleading for more zealous action. But he later credited the vocal British scientist with helping to change the direction of the American atomic effort, listing him first among the "all-out advocates of a head-on attack on the uranium problem."

A few weeks later, Conant traveled to Chicago, where he and Lawrence were to receive honorary degrees as part of the University of Chicago's fiftieth anniversary celebration. He had been invited to stay at Arthur Compton's home while in town and, rather to his annoyance, found himself subjected to an "involuntary conference" on the atomic bomb, with Lawrence as the surprise guest speaker. So on a cool September evening, he sat in front of the fireplace in Compton's living room, sipping coffee and listening to the two make a passionate case for pressing ahead with the development of the bomb.

Lawrence was especially upbeat about the latest results from England.

He was certain that an atom bomb could be made using only a few kilograms of fissionable material, either uranium-235 or plutonium, the new chemical element discovered in his lab. He supported all the experimental methods for extracting these elements—Harold Urey's gaseous and thermal diffusion separation at Columbia, Jesse Beams's centrifuge experiments at the University of Virginia, and his own, expensive magnetic separation—arguing that pressing forward on these processes was a matter of critical importance. The more Lawrence talked, the more worked up he got. The Germans had access to the same theoretical data, and there was every reason to believe they were already working along the same lines. Imagine the consequences to the world if they succeeded!

Conant had heard the rumors of a Nazi bomb program before—usually from physicists lobbying for more funding—and was inclined to discount them. Still, he could not rule them out altogether. "Though the factual evidence was slight," he recalled, "the terrifying thought that the Nazis might make an atomic bomb within the next year or two could not be shoved aside." Sensing Conant's skepticism, Compton rallied to Lawrence's side. He confirmed his interpretation of the new scientific findings indicating the "practical feasibility" of a bomb, and provided estimates of its destructive power. He echoed Lawrence's concerns that the Germans had embarked on their own major atomic program, arguing they would not have done so in the midst of a war unless they believed they might succeed. "We just [cannot] afford to let the Nazis beat us to the making of atomic weapons," Compton insisted. It would be "inviting disaster."

Conant played his characteristic devil's advocate role and tried to poke holes in their argument. Finally satisfied, he agreed that prudence dictated they do everything possible to prevent the enemy from achieving the bomb first, allowing Compton and Lawrence to believe their arguments had brought him around. Acknowledging that he had long been of the opinion that the uranium project should be dropped from the crowded wartime agenda, Conant admitted he now thought there was a reasonable chance of producing something militarily useful for the war in progress. "If such a weapon is going to be made, we must do it first," he told them. "We can't afford not to. But I am here to tell you," he said flatly, "nothing significant will happen on such a job as this unless we get into it with everything we've got."

Having sat through Lawrence's fervent lecture on how it was vital that the nation's scientific talent be focused on the uranium project, Conant put his big talk to the test by asking if he was prepared to step up. "Ernest, you say you are convinced of the importance of these fission bombs," he said, turning his laser focus on the forty-year-old Berkeley physicist, who, in addition to his war work, was directing an ambitious program of research on his giant cyclotron. "Are you ready to devote the next several years of your life to getting them made?"

The question brought up Lawrence with a start. For a few seconds, he sat staring at Conant, his mouth half open. Compton could almost see the giant brain whirring, calculating the consequences of such a huge commitment. Lawrence hesitated for only a moment before replying, "If you tell me this is my job, I'll do it."

By the end of the fall, Bush, who had been reassessing his own position, had come to the same conclusion. He had been urged on by Conant, whose recounting of his pivotal exchange with Compton and Lawrence in Chicago factored heavily in the OSRD chief's growing conviction that they had to get to the bottom of the bomb question as quickly as possible. On October 9, 1941, Bush met with Roosevelt and Vice President Henry Wallace and obtained the go-ahead for a major attempt to determine whether a fission weapon could be developed in time for use in the current war. There is no record of the meeting, save for a memorandum Bush sent to Conant later the same day, but all indications are that the president's approval was both instant and sweeping. Recognizing the need for security measures far beyond the norm, Roosevelt decided that all knowledge of what they were doing should be confined to himself and five others: Wallace, Stimson, Army Chief of Staff George C. Marshall, Bush, and Conant, soon to be known as the "Top Policy Group." Whether or not it was wise to reserve such heavy responsibility to a chosen few, the minute Conant learned of the president's directive, he knew it meant he was about to become "deeply involved in the atom bomb project."

In the last days of November, Bush sent Roosevelt the third report submitted by Compton's committee. Unlike the others, this one explicitly addressed whether a fission weapon could be achieved in time to affect the outcome of the war. The conclusion was unequivocal: "*A fission bomb of superlatively destructive power will result from bringing quickly together a sufficient mass of element U-235.*" Compton added a physicist's proviso: "This seems to be as sure as any untried prediction based upon theory and experiment can be." It was only a matter of time and cost. A weapon using uranium fission would very likely determine "military superiority." On the basis of Compton's report, the recommendations of the MAUD Committee, and Kistiakowsky's projections of its effectiveness, the members of the Top Policy Group decided to commit several million dollars to a crash program to see if a U-235 bomb could be made.

On December 6 Bush summoned Conant, Compton, Lawrence, and Briggs to his wood-paneled Washington office and told them the president had approved an "all-out" American effort. To meet this challenge, Bush had again overhauled the bureaucratic machinery. Conant's job would become more important than ever as he took charge of the new, strengthened Uranium Section, designated Section S-1, of the OSRD. As the intermediary between the physicists and Bush, Conant would be responsible for expediting the research into the feasibility of a fission weapon. If in six months their findings were favorable, they could expect authorization to proceed with all the resources that the nation could make available.

Nothing about the journey to this point had been easy, none of the steps taken lightly. Perhaps Conant, as some of his critics maintained, was slow to comprehend the meaning and potential of fission. But as atomic historians Richard G. Hewlett and Oscar E. Anderson Jr. point out, it is difficult in retrospect to appreciate the position of the men who held "high responsibility" for the decision to make the atom bomb: "No scientist, no engineer held as much as Bush and Conant. Conceivably, they might have moved earlier . . . But [they] had to look at uranium in the light of the entire role science might play in the emergency. They had to turn a deaf ear to blue-sky talk of nuclear power plants and think of weapons. They had to navigate between the Scylla and Charybdis of excessive pessimism and soaring optimism. They had to set a course by the Pole Star of fact."

It was ironic that the day after Conant learned the decision had been made to proceed "full steam ahead" on the development of the bomb, the Japanese struck Pearl Harbor. The surprise attack of December 7, 1941, wiped out the better part of America's Pacific Fleet, anchored snugly at its Hawaiian base and largely unmanned in the early hours of Sunday morning. News of the devastating raid reached Conant a few minutes before four o'clock, just as faculty members and their wives were arriving for the customary afternoon tea at 17 Quincy Street. He and Patty gathered around the radio with stunned colleagues and listened to the first dispatches of the destruction. It was announced that the president would be meeting with his Cabinet and then congressional leaders later that evening. He would certainly ask for a declaration of war, and Churchill would be right behind him.

In the big, cold parlor, there was a palpable dread of what was to come: a grim struggle on two fronts. After a bulletin reported the Espionage Act had been invoked, several German professors who had escaped Nazi persecution became distraught, afraid that the United States would be swept up in a wave of nationalism, and they would be ostracized or even interned. Feeling helpless, Patty plied them with cups of tea and murmured words of comfort, but there was little she could say that did not sound trite. No one knew what the future held in store.

The following evening, Conant addressed a wildly cheering crowd of six thousand students and teachers who jammed Sanders Theatre and several specially wired lecture halls, as well as Memorial Church, to hear Harvard's apostle of interventionism call for a "speedy and complete victory" over the enemy. Japan's treachery had ended the debate over the war. But Pearl Harbor was too great a tragedy—Roosevelt that morning had called it "a date which will live in infamy"—for Conant to feel anything but a "rush of hot anger" at the way America had been forced into the fight. His speech was simple and direct, every word addressed to the students whom he hoped to inspire and fortify for the severe trials that lay ahead. The majority—like his son Jimmy, a freshman at the University of Michigan, and enrolled in a naval officer training corps—would soon be uniform.

"Some defeatists have said that a democracy could not fight a war and still stay free," he stated, powerful emotions pushing through the prepared sentences. "By our deeds and words, may we show that this nation can pass through the flames of war and emerge victorious and free." A great shout rose up from the boys, and the roar grew rapidly and built to a crescendo, spreading to the hundreds of students standing outside in the chill night air and echoing in the old Yard.

When he was able to resume speaking, Conant pledged all the resources of Harvard to help the country achieve what he described as the twofold task before them: achieving total victory and preserving the American way of life. As everyone in the audience knew, these were not just fine words; the first surge of patriotic feeling that followed the outbreak of hostilities. Conant had commandeered their ivied halls for defense work months ago. The campus was already dotted with buildings where research on everything from explosives to radio detection was being done. In the hours after the Japanese attack, he had taken the precaution of tightening security, and extra watchmen had been posted outside a number of laboratories contracted to the military.

Immediately after Pearl Harbor, Conant moved quickly to put the university on a wartime footing. By the time students returned from Christmas vacation, they found their college altered drastically and already well on its way to becoming a military training camp. With the draft age lowered to twenty and likely to go to lower within a year, the number of men in uniform would soon outnumber those in mufti. Conant revised the academic calendar, putting it on a year-round schedule and adding a twelve-week summer semester that would enable students to earn their baccalaureate degree in three years. He expanded the curriculum to include courses in navigation, camouflage, meteorology, and map reading, as well as other military subjects. With the graduate school enrollment dwindling, he created a dozen or more special schools for the army and navy, accepting three thousand officers. He readied the Overseers to expect wartime deficits and shrinking enrollments. "The mobilization of young men for the fighting forces," he wrote in his annual report, presented in January 1942, "must be the key to the immediate future of our educational institutions."

As head of the NDRC, Conant immediately began funneling war projects Harvard's way. He expanded the university's Radio Research Laboratory, a spin-off of Loomis's Rad Lab at MIT, into a $16 million project concentrating on countermeasures, and organized an $8 million Underwater Sound Laboratory to focus on a new submarine-detection device called sonar (sound, navigation, and ranging). He signed more than a hundred government contracts for research—a total of $33.5 million, exceeded only by MIT and Caltech. He met with Bill Donovan, who was "organizing some kind of a superintelligence service for the government," soon to be known as the Office of Strategic Services (OSS), and helped find "just the people they were looking for." By the end of summer, Time dubbed Harvard's wartime transformation "Conant's arsenal." With so many on the faculty engaged in classified research, and much of the physical plant leased to the military, the old easygoing college atmosphere was gone. "Of what goes on behind closed doors," Conant acknowledged, "no word may now be told."

The war emergency opened Harvard's doors to women, but not because Conant wanted to blaze a path to coeducation. It was economic necessity, not enlightenment, that forced him to overcome his conviction that it should remain a men's college. As he memorably put it, "The last thing in the world I desired when I took office was to open Harvard College to young ladies." But with the pool of professors shrinking, Conant instructed Paul Buck, his judicious provost, to find a solution to the wasteful practice of having Harvard teachers give duplicate lectures at Radcliffe. Buck worked out an agreement by which the university would assume responsibility for educating Radcliffe students in exchange for the lion's share of their tuition, but recalled that when he tried to tell Conant about the radical departure from tradition, the latter was so immersed in his secret reports he hardly looked up. Once he changed his mind, however, he resolved to see it through. When the Overseers later tried to block the decision by the Medical School to admit women, Conant threatened to go public if the motion was not passed.

His experience of the blitz in England had convinced Conant that the task of winning the war came first. The role of colleges must be to "forward the national goal of victory, not shelter youth essential to the country's defense." His hard line was an outgrowth not only of his ardent interventionism but also of his growing awareness of the danger to the nation posed by the possibility of an enemy atomic bomb. As he came to understand its destructive potential, he developed the fierce conviction that they could not leave the country so exposed. If a bomb could be built, they had to beat the Germans to it. They had to overwhelm the enemy's advantage with innovation. They had no choice.

Only days after Pearl Harbor, Conant was spelling out the "catastrophic possibilities of a German bomb" to Harvey Bundy, a mild-mannered Boston estate lawyer who was Stimson's special assistant and chief liaison to the OSRD. Lying in bed with a bad cold, Conant, swaddled in a robe and pajamas, had roused himself for the meeting. Bundy was still shaken badly by the crippling blow the navy had received, as well as reports of the shocking damage and casualties that were circulating throughout Washington. He was deeply pessimistic and spent a considerable amount of time "spreading the gloom" about the long job ahead for Britain, the United States, and the Soviet Union.

And there was no doubt that it would be a long, grueling struggle. They had underrated the strength and ambition of the Japanese, and now faced the staggering task of building up enough of a navy to root them out of their own waters, while needing enough of an army to vanquish the Germans in Europe. The immediate reality was that they did not have a striking force ready—such defensive weapons that were available had been diverted to Britain—so they could expect a run of losses in the Pacific. The task was so monumental, and the outlook so bleak, Bundy admitted that he did not see "how the devil we [are] going to win the war."

Conant, a stalwart optimist, stated he was confident they would eventually defeat the Axis armies. As history amply demonstrated, military reversals could be overcome. "The Germans can never win this war," he assured Bundy. The "one possibility" that gave him pause, he said, was that the Nazis were ahead in the development of the atomic bomb. As Stimson's assistant, Bundy had been briefed on S-1, but until that moment he'd never given serious thought to the danger of Nazi scientists beating them to the punch. Even his most pessimistic appraisals of the air, land, and naval battles that lay ahead paled in comparison to this new nightmare. Instead of feeling better, Bundy recalled, he left Conant's bedside that December afternoon literally sick with worry.

Now that America had plunged into war, Conant felt it was crucial that the country shake off its defensive posture and "learn to think offensively." Convinced that the Maginot Line mentality had been fatal to the French, and that the United States could not afford to hold back its firepower or aggressive fighting spirit, he was one of the first prominent leaders to declare that America's goal must be the "unconditional surrender" of Germany, Italy, and Japan. Making use of the podium provided by the New England Society, he delivered what was surely the most bellicose speech in the organization's genteel history. "To ensure the defeat of the Axis powers, there must be no limitation on our commitments." Total victory required total commitment.

Without revealing the atomic quest on which the country had embarked, Conant went on to explain that this war was in many ways "a race of scientific developments and devices." These new weapons would not be limited to defense only and could play "a decisive part," just as poison gas and tanks might have in the First World War if used in sufficient quantities at the outset. He insisted on the need for a complete victory, warning that any compromise settlement would be dangerous, given that they were dealing with "a state ruled by a dictator, covered by a gestapo, where new weapons can be devised, developed, and manufactured in utmost secrecy."

Looking ahead to when the fighting was over, Conant saw the need for ongoing vigilance. The United States would have to assume leadership in establishing an "armed alliance of free societies" to secure the postwar world. Unconditional surrender did not mean that the victors should impose a vindictive resolution, but until Germany and Japan had been transformed by "hard circumstances"—into smaller agricultural states or societies with no lust to conquer—there could be "no hope of eventual disarmament of other countries or of an enduring peace."

Returning to Washington on December 18, Conant convened the first full meeting of the members of the reorganized S-1 Section. "The country had been at war nine days," he recalled, "and the atmosphere was charged with excitement." The members included Briggs and others from the old Uranium Section, as well as a half-dozen new faces. The scientists engaged on the bomb problem were to be grouped under three program chiefs—Compton, Lawrence, and Urey—all Nobel Prize winners. Conant reviewed the specific assignments: Urey would continue working on the diffusion and centrifuge methods of separating uranium isotopes; Lawrence was given the go-ahead to see if his electromagnetic separation method could be made practical on a large scale; Compton would begin work on the design of the bomb itself. "There will be no need to worry about money," Conant told them. They were to spare no effort, no expense, in developing an atomic weapon at the earliest possible date.

During the first few months of 1942, Conant was primarily occupied with assessing the order and importance of the different methods of obtaining several hundred pounds of fissionable material: either uranium-235 or plutonium. One disagreement cropped up immediately after Bush announced the decision to push the atomic project. After the December 6 meeting in Washington had adjourned, he, Bush, and Compton went for lunch at the Cosmos Club on Lafayette Square, and the subject of plutonium came up in conversation. Compton, who had intentionally omitted it from his final report—apparently for tactical reasons—now spoke up in favor of producing the new element as a substitute for uranium-235. He advocated moving ahead rapidly with the construction of a pile to start producing large amounts of plutonium. This would be achieved by a steady nuclear reaction with ordinary uranium, resulting in a small fraction of the U-235 being transmuted into Pu-239, at which stage it would be chemically extracted from the uranium.

While Conant had come round to believing the atomic bomb was feasible, he could not hide his qualms about what the Chicago physicist was proposing. Compton was asking for money they badly needed for other things in order to produce plutonium, which had "not yet been seen except in microscopic amounts," using a nuclear reactor that existed only in his imagination. In addition to the obvious fact that extracting plutonium from uranium had not yet been shown to be possible in the laboratory, Conant noted that the chemistry of the new element was "largely unknown." What if the separation process was complicated by intense radiation? It could take years to make it operational.

Compton did not conceal his irritation at having a wrench thrown in his plans. His testy recollection of the exchange was that "this was Conant, the expert chemist, speaking from experience." His response to his esteemed colleague's many objections was that further research would produce the necessary knowledge and that Glenn Seaborg was confident that "within six months from the time plutonium is formed [by chain reaction], he could have it available for use in a bomb."

"Glenn Seaborg is a very competent young chemist," Conant scoffed, "but he isn't that good." He intended that to be the last word on the matter, but his usual authority was somewhat undermined when in the midst of the discussion, he took a large gulp from a glass of milk only to discover it was buttermilk—which he detested—and began angrily spluttering and swearing. While this short burst of profanity amused Bush, it offended the straitlaced Presbyterian Compton. In any event, Compton went on to argue the point with such gusto that by the time the coffee arrived, Bush was swayed by his "near certainty" about producing plutonium by a chain reaction. Compton maintained it was a win-win strategy: if for some reason it turned out that plutonium was not ready to be used in a bomb, the construction of self-sustaining chain reaction would still be a "magnificent achievement." It was indicative of the ad hoc way they were working, Compton would later observe, that as a result of a conversation that was "really an afterthought," developing a nuclear reactor was added to the bomb project.

Despite the occasional skirmishes and flashes of ego, it was remarkable how quickly everyone pulled together as a team. Differences of opinion were put aside for the common goal: defeating Hitler. Within weeks, Compton was overseeing a highly secret project at the University of Chicago, the aim of which was the construction of a chain-reacting pile to test the feasibility of producing plutonium. To speed their research, he decided the various groups of physicists should work together under one roof and organized the Metallurgical Laboratory, usually referred to as the Met Lab, yet another misleading name meant to delude enemy spies into believing it was just another boring metals research facility. Fermi, considered the best man in the field of nuclear physics, agreed at once to take time away from his experiments at Columbia to help initiate the Chicago reactor. Eugene Wigner from Princeton helped coordinate the research and experimental and theoretical aspects of the chain reaction. Szilard pitched in, helping to secure pure materials such as graphite and consulting on the whole enterprise. They began building small crude piles, stacking graphite bricks in columns and studying what happened to the neutrons, collecting data for a larger nuclear reactor.

At the same time, Lawrence and his group continued to apply themselves to the electromagnetic separation method at Berkeley. In a stroke of brilliance, he disassembled his famous thirty-seven-inch cyclotron and modified the magnet to develop a new device, the calutron, which facilitated not only the separation of small amounts of material but also might work on large-scale production. By mid-February, as the operation of the calutron improved, they were able to prepare three samples of material enriched to 30 percent U-235 for the Met Lab. Urey, meanwhile, continued to have high hopes for the gaseous diffusion and centrifuge approaches being tested at Columbia. The design and construction of the bomb would be a major task, but it seemed pointless to move ahead with that part of the project until they were reasonably confident that the fissionable material could be produced in sufficient quantities. They could not be sure which was the best method. All they could do was follow every viable lead.

Every two weeks, Conant convened the members of S-1 to take stock. The meetings were "exciting events," Compton recalled. Enthusiasm and optimism reigned. In these early days of the atomic race, there was an enormous amount at stake: convincing evidence of the bomb's feasibility within three to four years had to be found. Major decisions had to be made quickly, even though they might affect the entire course of the atomic program. In April Conant was confronted with just such a choice when the French scientist Hans von Halban came from England and presented results from his experiments indicating that a natural uranium pile could be made quickly if heavy water, deuterium, was used as a moderator. Harold Urey also strongly favored this approach. But based on the encouraging results from the Chicago pile, Conant decided they should concentrate on Fermi's method of making a chain reaction by using a combination of natural uranium and graphite. Heavy water would be used only as an alternative, and, as a contingency measure, he ordered it put into production on a small scale.

During this critical period, Compton considered the S-1 scientists fortunate to have Conant at the helm. If the wrong choice had been made then, or at any number of other junctures, the program could have been sidetracked and seriously delayed. "In guiding these discussions, drawing them to prompt and definite conclusions, and stating the conclusions in a concise form, Conant was superlative. No time was wasted." He brought to the task not only his deep knowledge of science and wide acquaintance with many of the individual scientists but also "an unusual ability to avoid confusion and entanglement in minor complexities, and to cut through quickly and decisively to the fundamental issues involved."

By February, with growing optimism about the results of their tests, it became clear that Conant would soon have to make decisions about the construction of production plants—decisions that would involve very large amounts of money. There were still plenty of uncertainties and many hurdles that had to be surmounted, including the means to handle such large quantities of radioactive material. But all the evidence pointed to there being a workable road to a bomb. At the forefront of his mind at all times was the "recurring question" of how great an expenditure was justifiable in view of the other demands of the war effort. Bush knew he was placing "a heavy burden" on Conant, but for reasons of economy and efficiency, he was hoping the chemist would be able to pick one or perhaps two of the alternative methods of producing fissionable material.

Unfortunately, as the deadline neared, there was still no way to judge which one was superior. Historian James Phinney Baxter described the enormity of the decision Conant faced: "When called on in May to produce a budget for the next eighteen months' operations, Conant found five horses running neck and neck. There was little to choose between the centrifuge, diffusion, and electromagnetic methods of separating U-235 and the uranium-graphite pile and uranium-heavy-water pile methods of producing plutonium."

After considering the pros and cons, Conant recommended "betting heavily" across the board: "All five methods." The president should authorize construction programs based on the assumption that they were backing five competing schemes in the race, right up to the final lap. "Anything less," he reported to Bush, "will mean either the abandonment or slowing down of one of the . . . methods." The decision was going to be difficult. "While all five methods now appear to be about equally promising, clearly the time to production [required] by the five routes will certainly not be the same but might vary by six months or a year because of unforeseen delays. Therefore, if one discards one or two or three of the methods now, one may be betting on the slower horse unconsciously."

Either way, this was not a wager they could afford to lose. Conant's reasoning turned on his appraisal of the military risk involved if one side developed a dozen bombs before the other. If the Nazis dropped their entire haul on England, the new weapon would be the "determining" factor in the outcome of the war. While the Allies had only imperfect intelligence about the Germans' activities, the most recent intercepted communications showed that they were interested in making a bomb. "They cannot be far behind, since they started in 1939 with the same initial facts as the British and ourselves," he worried, "and they may be ahead of us by as much as a year." He could not ignore the implications of his own analysis: speed was imperative. "Three months' delay might be fatal."

At nine thirty on Saturday morning, May 23, Conant called an important meeting of his three program chiefs, as well as Briggs, and Eger V. Murphree, a chemical engineer with the Standard Oil Company, who was head of the Planning Board and overseeing all the engineering plans and the pilot-plant phase. After several hours of discussion, they agreed with Conant's plan to start along five parallel tracks. The cost would be staggering: an estimated $80 million, with an annual operating cost of $34 million. The program, they believed, would yield a small supply of atomic bombs by July 1, 1944, give or take a few months.* Conant was not happy about the production schedule and pushed them to do better. "Why nearly two years' delay?" he demanded, wanting to speed up construction.

Murphree cut off the debate. "Dr. Conant," he replied, "you can't spend that much money any faster."

By five o'clock, the meeting was over. Conant gathered up his notes of the group's recommendations, which he had been jotting down on a lined yellow tablet. He had the rest of the weekend to prepare himself before submitting his extraordinary report to Bush on Monday morning.

It was not what Bush wanted to hear. But Conant had given him ample advance warning, so it came as no great surprise that the members of S-1 were unable to endorse a single approach. Bush agreed to sign off on summary of the costs and estimated time of the program and submitted it to Roosevelt's Top Policy Group. With their approval, Bush then brought it to the president on June 17. The document, with another "VB—O.K.— FDR"

---

* Their estimate was overoptimistic by one year.

scribbled at the bottom of the page, became invaluable, Conant recalled, "when necessary to prove to an incredulous high-ranking government official that what was contemplated was authorized by the president of the United States himself."

The time had come to let the army in on their deep, dark secret. The president's order to go ahead with the Bush-Conant plan to manufacture atom bombs was transmitted to Lieutenant General Wilhelm D. Styer, who would be the army's point man on S-1: "Take the necessary action."

With the atomic quest entering a new phase, Conant realized he would have less time than ever for academic life. The decision to pursue all the methods meant that the program would need to expand greatly, requiring far more manpower and materials. It also meant even more of a personal sacrifice on his part. He would be stepping up an already strenuous schedule: working five days a week in Washington, commuting back to Cambridge when necessary, and making frequent inspection trips to NDRC installations scattered across the country. But he was hardly alone. After Pearl Harbor, anything one could do seemed "all too little." The dire emergency impelled many of the scientists and technical men he knew to outdo themselves. "Like the need for speed," he said later, "the emotional drive of war created a highly abnormal situation."

A worrying consideration was what to do about his wife. Conant assumed his wartime burdens as a matter of course. The notion of duty was dear to him, as was the Jeffersonian idea that the country should look to the "natural aristocracy" of the talented for leadership. But it was asking a lot of Patty, who did not like that her welfare always came second to that of the nation. While he had never been busier, she was bored and lonely, too much on her own now that her sons were away at school. Apprehensive that he was neglecting her needs, he recruited close friends to look after her, invite her to dinner, and generally keep her distracted and happy. His two sisters, along with her cousins Eleanor and Lucy, were loyal coconspirators in his campaign to keep her on an even keel. Surrounded by hand-holders, and occupied with the ladies of the Harvard Wives Club, she would not, he hoped, grow too resentful of his absence and preoccupation with world affairs, as she was sometimes wont to do. But in her journal, a dispirited Patty copied out a quote from Thoreau: "At what expense any valuable work is performed! At the expense of a life!"

James B. Conant, Harvard's newly elected forty-year-old president, poses solemnly with a slide rule for the reporters clamoring for a first glimpse of the obscure young chemist who had emerged as the university's surprise choice.

By his senior year of high school, Jim Conant had distinguished himself as one of the most brilliant boys in his class and had won a scholarship to Harvard.

2

3

A Dorchester boy, Conant, shown with his parents and two older sisters, grew up in a streetcar suburb of Boston that Harvard's Brahmin governing class regarded as being on the wrong side of the tracks.

4

When the United States entered World War I, Conant was recruited by the Chemical Warfare Service to make mustard gas and a new, more dangerous toxin to be manufactured in a top secret military facility.

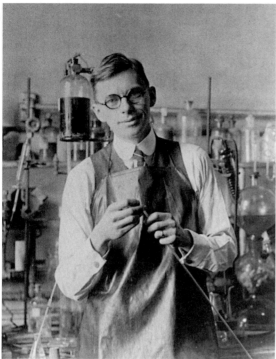

In the 1920s, Conant quickly made a name for himself as an innovative, pioneering chemist, winning awards and international acclaim at the same time American chemistry was on its way to achieving parity with Europe.

Conant's mentor, the Nobel Prize–winning Harvard chemist Theodore William Richards, was a gifted experimentalist who drove himself hard, brooked no compromise, and suffered from bouts of melancholia and a "dark prospect."

7

It took nerve to court his famous mentor's daughter, but Conant was determined to marry the lovely, blue-eyed Grace "Patty" Richards despite her father's reservations.

8

Miriam Richards, a frightful snob, achieved her ambition of becoming queen bee of Harvard and was socially ambitious for all her children.

9

Patty and her brothers, Bill (*standing*) and young Thayer, were all expected to be exceptional. The Richardses were a high-strung, overstrung, family, and both boys would suffer from depression and commit suicide.

10

Throughout her marriage, Patty struggled to live up to her husband's high standards and was dogged by morbid fears and "an overwhelming sense of unworthiness."

11

Conant told his fiancée that he had three ambitions: to be the greatest organic chemist in America, to be president of Harvard, and to be a senior public servant in "some Cabinet position."

Conant—shown here with Albert Einstein, a victim of the Nazi persecution of Jews in Germany—took every opportunity to condemn the repressive regime in Germany and affirm his commitment to academic freedom and individual liberty.

At Harvard's tercentenary celebration in 1936, both presidents—Franklin D. Roosevelt (*far left*) and Conant (*front row*)—sat stoically through the rain. One attendee quipped that it was the reform-minded Conant's way of "soaking the rich."

The young couple found the social demands of the Harvard presidency trying: Patty was terrified of putting a foot wrong, and Jim, who was not the hearty type, loathed receiving lines.

Conant, on the summit of the North Palisade in California, could only relax when far from Cambridge.

Patty had little time for their two sons, Jim (*right*) and Teddy (*left*), who were relegated to the third-floor nursery of the president's mansion.

Convinced America had to join the fight against Hitler, Conant took to the airwaves in the spring of 1940 to urge "immediate aid" for the allies, and became a leading interventionist.

When Conant headed a scientific mission to London during the blitz in 1941 he met Winston Churchill. The British prime minister showed his gratitude by later paying Conant a visit at Harvard.

Patty, whose two sons were serving in the Pacific, found volunteering on the psych ward of a Boston hospital upsetting and had to quit.

Conant (*front center*) at a meeting at the Radiation Laboratory, where some of the country's leading scientists agreed to support Ernest Lawrence's (*far left*) giant cyclotron, aware they might soon be at war. Also present are Arthur Compton (*left*), Vannevar Bush, Karl Compton, and Alfred Lee Loomis.

21

The leaders of the Manhattan Project: (*left to right*) Vannevar Bush, James B. Conant, and General Leslie Groves on a trip to inspect the Hanford, Washington, plutonium production site.

22

J. Robert Oppenheimer, the director of the Los Alamos Laboratory, looked on Conant almost as a father figure and depended on him for advice and support.

Anxiety was high as the "gadget" weathered a storm during its last hours atop the Trinity tower prior to the first detonation of an atomic bomb on July 14, 1945.

9.0 SEC.
N

⊢——⊣ IOO METERS

Conant, lying on the sand seventeen thousand yards from point zero, saw a burst of white light that seemed to fill the sky "like the end of the world."

At a loss for words, Conant and Bush acknowledged the test's success with a handshake, and they later reenacted the moment for a *March of Time* newsreel.

At the White House in May 1948, a beaming President Truman awarded the Medal for Merit and the Bronze Oak Leaf Cluster to Conant and the Medal for Merit to Bush for their work on the bomb.

After the war, the leading bomb scientists became atomic statesmen and President Truman's principal advisors on the nation's nuclear future. Conant and Oppenheimer opposed a crash program to build the Super, or hydrogen, bomb.

28

Conant and Oppenheimer on a trip to Los Alamos with members of the Atomic Energy Commission's General Advisory Committee, the agency tasked with overseeing the peacetime development and control of atomic energy. Standing next to them on the tarmac at the Santa Fe Airport are General James McCormack, Hartley Rowe, John Manley, I. I. Rabi, and Roger S. Warner, Jr.

Conant and Bush at a press conference, alerting the public that it will take more than the atomic bomb to deter Soviet aggression and calling for the mobilization of a large army and universal military service.

29

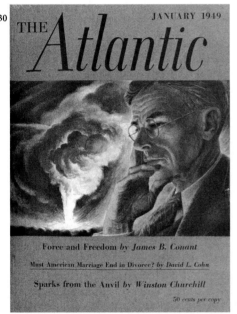

30

THE *Atlantic*

JANUARY 1949

Force and Freedom *by James B. Conant*

Must American Marriage End in Divorce? *by David L. Cohn*

Sparks from the Anvil *by Winston Churchill*

50 cents per copy

Conant, who feared the country was on the brink of World War III, wrote an article arguing against a "preventive war" with Russia.

31

Harvard was shocked by the news he was resigning to become president-elect Eisenhower's high commissioner for Germany, but Conant was eager for one last big challenge.

A newspaper cartoon spoofing President Eisenhower's decision to turn to the warrior educator to find a solution to the problem of a divided Germany.

The new U.S. envoy to West Germany meeting his wife at Frankfurt airport before traveling to their official residence in the new capital of Bonn.

President Eisenhower, Conant, Secretary of State John Foster Dulles, and West German chancellor Konrad Adenauer at a White House meeting to discuss the huge numbers of refugees escaping from the Communist East.

35

CBS news correspondent Edward R. Murrow's interview with Conant in front of Berlin's Brandenburg Gate was disrupted by a group of Communist protesters from the Soviet-controlled Eastern zone.

36

Conant (*far right*) clashed with Senator Joseph McCarthy (*left*) during a Senate appropriations subcommittee hearing in 1953, and refused to be bullied into impugning the loyalty of several Foreign Service officers on his staff.

Conant believed the best way to beat the Soviets was to show that democracy was better than dictatorship, and a strong, educated citizenry required a public school system that enabled all Americans to advance.

37

38

Hoping to be remembered for his contributions to education not weaponry, Conant served on President John F. Kennedy's committee on youth unemployment to address the problems facing the next generation.

Conant's public school reforms landed him back on the cover of *Time*. A fourth appearance, the editors noted, was "a rare record" for someone never elected to public office.

39

40

In later life, Conant relished the role of grandpa, shown here with the author.

In order to simplify their lives as much as possible, Conant informed Harvard that as part of the wartime austerity measures, he would vacate the presidential mansion—leaving it to the navy for use as an administrative headquarters—and make do with the unpretentious little yellow frame house next door at 11 Quincy Street. He also took a voluntary pay cut. The move almost came as a relief to Patty. In the past year, she had found running the large official residence increasingly taxing. The war had made it impossible to find good help. The cook and parlor maids had quit, and with the defense factories taking every halfway decent pair of hands, she told her mother, "only a few elderly and difficult personalities and a collection of slack Irish biddies remain." In Washington, where he was spending the bulk of his time, Conant kept a comfortable four-room apartment in a dormitory building at Dumbarton Oaks, the magnificent eighteen-acre Georgetown estate gifted to Harvard by the diplomat and philanthropist Robert Woods Bliss two years earlier.

Then there was the still fraught question of what to do with Ted, who had run afoul of the headmaster of the Dublin School. He had spent much of the spring term in the "doghouse" and was refusing to return in the fall. There was no question of the troubled teenager remaining at home with his mother. After much deliberation, and more visits to doctors and psychiatrists, Conant settled on another small rural New England boarding school known for taking the wayward offspring of Boston families. A former teacher at Shady Hill, Carmelita Hinton, had left in 1935 to start the Putney School in Vermont, based on the progressive educational ideas of John Dewey. It was an experimental farm school where students were permitted to learn at their own pace while milking cows and mucking out stalls. At this point Conant, who had all but given up on his youngest, was in favor of anything that would keep the boy out of sight and mind.

The summer of 1942 soon presented other challenges. July in Washington was no one's idea of fun, and Conant had been counting the days until he could get away, when he found himself roped into the rubber controversy—one of the most contentious issues in the capital during the first anxious year of war. For months, the newspapers had been filled with furious screeds about the "inefficiency, mismanagement, carelessness, politics, waste, and extravagance" of Roosevelt's bungled mobilization plans. There had been no fewer than seventeen separate congressional hearings, and the printed copies, filled with conflicting reports and suspect testimony, measured well over a foot and a half when stacked one upon the other. The raging battle pitted powerful industrial and commercial interests against one another, generated a struggle between the executive and congressional branches over which would have the authority to allocate vital materials for war production, and sparked more than one public brawl. The most infamous altercation was between *Washington Post* publisher Eugene Meyer, whose paper ran an editorial accusing Secretary of Commerce Jesse H. Jones of mistakes that brought on the crisis, leading the two distinguished millionaires to come to blows at the exclusive Alfalfa Club.

While there was plenty of greed and incompetence to go around, the ominous truth was that the Japanese had struck at the most vulnerable spot in the American economy. In the first half of 1942, the Japanese, in their aggressive conquest of the South Pacific, had captured 90 percent of the crude rubber in the world and 97 percent of the American supply. Despite this calamity, the United States had to find a way to meet the requirements not only of its military forces but also those of its allies, to say nothing of its own essential civilian needs. If new supplies could not be found, the military would exhaust the remaining crude stocks before the end of the next summer. Rumors swirled about impending shortages and nationwide rationing of rubber and gasoline. All the stories about the dire straits the country was in were beginning to cause a public panic.

The only solution was to develop a synthetic rubber and do it quickly. On July 27, 1942, the *New York Herald Tribune* published a strong editorial about the rubber scandal, criticizing Chief Justice Harlan Fiske Stone's reluctance to head a commission to clear up the crisis, and stating that Conant was the obvious man for the job. The Harvard chemist was "fearless, independent, and technically wise," and could be counted on "to bring order out of the present chaos."

Faced with mounting criticism, Roosevelt vetoed a farm bill to produce rubber from grain-based alcohol and instead announced the formation of an independent committee to "investigate the whole rubber situation" and restore public confidence. The president turned to three wise men to sort out the mess: Bernard Baruch, who had run the War Industries Board in World War I and would serve as chairman, Conant, and Karl Compton. Conant, who already had too much on his plate, accepted the appointment with some trepidation but felt flattered at being asked to come to the nation's—and the administration's—rescue. He could not help being "a little bit disappointed," however, that it was Baruch, and not he, who would be "calling the shots." Not at all sure how he would like working with the legendary

Wall Street speculator, he had lobbied hard for the selection of Compton, just in case he would need "powerful reinforcement."

The president's Rubber Survey Committee (RSC) met for the first time on August 3, three days before he sent his veto message to Capitol Hill, at Baruch's home in Port Washington, Long Island. The wily seventy-one-year-old financier, whose business acumen was equaled only by his ego and love of the spotlight, announced immediately that he would deal with the politics and press. "Let me handle the senators and fellows on the Hill," Baruch asserted in his patronizing avuncular manner. "Very important. I'll do that sort of thing. You young fellows will do the work."

Conant could not help worrying about what it meant for a man in his position to be taking on what the *Tribune* called a "thankless task." Whoever conducted the inquiry could expect to be attacked by all sides, and he was putting not only his good name on the line but also Harvard's. The issue had become so controversial, Conant feared that if his verdict was not well received, as was Lowell's experience with the Sacco-Vanzetti case, he would never live it down. Before leaving his colleagues that afternoon, he remarked that he had no illusions about the ticklish nature of their assignment. "No, sir," drawled Baruch, who liked to play up his "country boy" roots in South Carolina, "this job is a porcupine and a skunk all rolled into one."

Roosevelt's appointment of the expert board quieted the clamor for a month. The public seemed to breathe a collective sigh of relief on hearing that a survey of the situation was in competent hands. "Unquestionably, the very best formula for synthetic rubber is the one President Roosevelt has hit upon," the *New York Times* noted in an editorial. "It comprises Baruch, Conant, and Compton. The finest ingredient for producing any mixture is brains."

Bearing in mind the president's request that they report back as soon as possible, the RSC began at once to compile data. Conant arranged for them to move into temporary quarters at Dumbarton Oaks, and dispatched a battalion of chemists to investigate commercial alcohol plants, whiskey distilleries, petroleum refineries, and Department of Agriculture experimental stations. If the fundamental purpose of the RSC was, as Baruch was fond of saying, "getting the mostest rubber fastest," the first thing they needed to find was a suitable manufacturing facility. Over four sweltering weeks in August, they listened to testimony from dozens of government officials, industrialists, and technical advisors. Baruch, who liked to sit in the sun for his health, insisted on holding so many meetings in Lafayette Park, close by his rooms at the Carlton Hotel, that the hardworking trio became known as the "park bench committee."

The three men delivered their findings to the president on September 10, after several arduous days spent writing the seventy-five-page report in an unair-conditioned office suite. Presuming the RSC's first duty to be the creation of a steady rubber supply that would "keep our armed forces fighting and our essential civilian wheels turning," they recommended that this could be best done by "bulling through" the present synthetic program as rapidly as possible, and by "safeguarding jealously every ounce of rubber in the country." The committee supported all efforts to expand rubber supplies, but in the interest of speed recommended moving ahead with the butadiene-from-petroleum program instead of the alcohol process favored by Henry Wallace and the farm lobby. The headline-making part of the report found the "existing situation to be so dangerous" that sweeping corrective measures had to be implemented, including speed limits, rationing, recapping tires, and reclaiming scrap rubber. "Discomfort or defeat, there is no middle course," the report warned in blunt language that sounded very much like Conant's stern advocacy of conservation.*

The committee's acceptance of the government program Jones had contracted did not prevent the RSC from taking a swing at the architects of the rubber scandal. It denounced the "overlapping and confusing authority" that had resulted in delays and unwise decisions, and urged the appointment of a "rubber administrator" to have sole responsibility for the government program.

The press applauded the RSC's constructive program of action. "The incantations of a prestigious authority," observed a political scientist, had elicited public acceptance of rationing, a policy on which Americans had been sharply divided. As an unexpected bonus, Conant and Compton came away with a burnished image, their performance enhancing the status of scientists as cool, trained minds who, with their objective methodology, were capable of solving almost any problem.

The president was greatly pleased. He declared the Baruch-Conant-Compton report "excellent" and said that the government was indebted to the trio. It put to rest many embarrassing questions and paved the way for a

---

* The RSC's decision gave birth to a massive new synthetic rubber industry, and by the war's end, the United States was the world's largest exporter of rubber, all of it man-made—an outcome Conant told Baruch in 1944 "almost seems too good to be true."

new industry that would eliminate the country's dependence on imported rubber. More important, it gave FDR the moral authority to ask for new and necessary wartime sacrifices, including nationwide gas rationing, a painful task on the eve of congressional elections. Still unresolved, however, was who would fill the position of rubber czar. "What about you, Dr. Conant?" Roosevelt suggested during a convivial meeting in his office. Oh no, Conant demurred; he had no experience running an operation of that magnitude. "Well," the president replied, "you run a pretty big show up in Cambridge, don't you?"

Given the opening, Conant could not resist plugging his idea for a military training corps, a rational deferment and training system he had been in the midst of negotiating with the army and educators when he was commandeered for the rubber survey. He had "a plan," he began quickly. But Roosevelt turned away and changed the subject, brushing aside any more of Conant's bright ideas for the moment.

As he left the White House, a reporter asked the weary war scientist if there was anything he would like to add to the report. "It's all in there, and it's a lot," he replied. "Now for some sleep." He did not mention that when he finally put his head down, it would be in a Pullman car. Conant was on his way to catch a train for California to inspect Lawrence's electromagnetic separation operation at his Berkeley lab.

CHAPTER 14

A Colossal Gamble

To my mind, it is this fear that the Germans may be near
the goal which is the prime reason for an all-out effort now
on this gamble.

—JBC to General Leslie R. Groves, December 9, 1942

The transition from planning phase to design and construction on any large project can be trying, but embarking on five different ones simultaneously proved an exercise in frustration. The summer of 1942 was one of missed deadlines, delays, and disagreements, as the bomb project became mired in confusion. Conant had warned Bush that proceeding with pilot-plant development for each of the competing methods of producing fissionable material would be a gigantic task, surpassing the greatest military campaigns of all time. The "grand scale" of the program he envisioned would require multiple sites, a mass of machinery, and tens of thousands of workers, in addition to the procurement of tons of vital raw materials—high-purity graphite, uranium ore, copper, and steel—already in short supply. But he had ended by insisting that this "Napoleonic approach," as he summed up his Yankee horror at the wretched excess, was dictated by the "desperate need for speed" in the race to find the shortest route to an atomic weapon.

Conant did not believe the OSRD could create the enormous construction organization that would be needed, and assumed it would be handed over to the army. With national survival at stake, those in the scientific establishment would have to work with the military whether they liked it or not. He knew Bush had raised the possibility with Roosevelt back in 1941, and all three of them were agreed that for reasons of security it made sense to limit the assignment to just one of the services. Having seen the army erect huge poison gasworks during World War I, Conant believed it capable of building the pilot plants and taking over production. From his experience with lewisite, he could also attest to the army's ability to maintain absolute secrecy. He even suggested that some top scientists should be commissioned as officers in the new US Army Corps of Engineers to smooth the way for a cooperative effort. Reluctant to give up control over the research, however, he proposed creating an advisory committee on the "scientific aspects" so that the OSRD could remain involved in the project at every stage. Bush disagreed, deciding it would be better to have "the whole thing in one package," and dropped it in the lap of the army.

If Bush and Conant felt any relief at yielding responsibility for the vast program, they soon regretted it. Established as the Manhattan Engineering District in June 1942 by the temporary commanding officer whose main office was in New York City, the hastily cobbled together setup ran into problems from the start. The army officers had no time to prepare for the massive assignment and lacked the necessary technical experience. None had a working knowledge of atomic energy.

At the same time, Bush and Conant were unsure how to exert their authority in a military organization far removed from their official sphere of influence. While they'd had extensive dealings with the War Department in the past, once the bomb project was formally ushered into the army, they suddenly found themselves on the outside looking in. Because they had failed to adequately define their roles beforehand, routine matters became unexpectedly difficult to handle. Worse still, they had made no provision for a higher power to resolve conflicts. As a result, months were wasted haggling over construction plans, with some issues, such as the selection of a site in Tennessee, passed back and forth like a hot potato until it almost slipped through their fingers. With the two camps battling over which projects should have top priority, Conant became the bearer of bad news, repeatedly going to a harried Bush with reports of postponements that "threatened to negate" all the radiant estimates of the spring.

The transfer to military jurisdiction also took a toll on morale. Many of the scientists were extremely disheartened to learn that their work was being snatched from their hands just as they were on the verge of real breakthroughs. There was an underlying feeling among many that they had earned the right to see the historic undertaking through to the end. The younger men, in particular, chafed at the idea of being under military control. Their antagonism was exacerbated by the fears of some of the senior refugee scientists who had fled totalitarian regimes and had frightening memories of the military. Compton faced a "near rebellion" from members of his staff, and in a tense confrontation on a hot June evening in Chicago barely managed to persuade them that they could not accomplish their goal of beating the Germans if they were divided among themselves.

The cleavage between the scientific and military organizations was such that by the end of the summer, Conant realized that if something did not change soon, the bomb would never be ready in time. The difficulty of procuring manpower and materials, compounded by bureaucratic rivalries and suspicion, had resulted in one setback after another. Given the critical shortages, the army's top officers did not want to go ahead with five ways of producing plutonium and U-235. They were completely focused on winning the ground war: preparing for the upcoming North African offensive, supplying its own arsenals and proving grounds, equipping its soldiers abroad, and housing and training the thousands of recruits pouring into induction centers. To them, the bomb was at best a long shot, and while the scientists fiddled, they had to make sure the battle was not lost.

On August 26 Conant called a meeting of the S-1 Executive Committee, the small leadership council that replaced the S-1 Section that had grown too large and had been pared down to Briggs, Compton, Lawrence, Urey, and Murphree. Their backs were to the wall. They desperately needed to solve the priority problem. Under enormous pressure from the army, the committee members pleaded with him to reduce the number of production methods. It looked like the electromagnetic method would probably be the first to yield fissionable material, but it was not necessarily the best approach. They debated whether to throw everything they had at it at the expense of the others. Had the time come to abandon their overambitious strategy?

With the committee teetering on the brink of an imprudent decision, Conant, according to his colleagues, "raised a steadying hand." He reminded them that in June he had said no sound basis existed for eliminating any of the five processes, and it was still "too soon by one or two months" to make a decision. To bet on one method and lose might cost the war. He convinced the committee to stick to his original plan. But he warned Bush that they had to find a way to win the army's support. Unless it was a full partnership, they would not prevail.

Fed up with army resistance, Bush decided it was time to reboot the project's leadership. What he had in mind was a sort of board of directors to advise the Manhattan District's new director, with both him and Conant as balancing members, ensuring that the civilian scientists had a say in any decisions. As part of the arrangement, Bush expected his new board to hand-pick the commanding officer who would be in charge of the bomb project. But this proved to be another failure in communication with his military counterparts. So when a portly, aggressive, and supremely self-confident colonel by the name of Leslie R. Groves swaggered into his office on the afternoon of September 17, Bush gave him a "cool reception," dismissing his claims that he had been given the job and refusing to answer most of his questions.

As soon as the cocky officer was out the door, Bush was on the phone to army headquarters. Much to his irritation, it turned out that Groves had indeed been appointed and, through some oversight, Bush had not been informed. Convinced that the West Point graduate, who had earned a formidable reputation overseeing the massive Pentagon construction project, was a disastrous choice, Bush sent Conant a note expressing his displeasure. Having seen Groves only briefly, Bush groused that he was "very seriously" bothered, and considered the colonel "abrupt and lacking in tact." Groves was old school: tough, uncompromising, and impatient. Bush worried that his brusque manner would rub the scientists the wrong way. Although he was on record as being against it, he told Harvey Bundy that it looked like a done deal, adding resignedly, "I fear we are in the soup."

On September 23 Conant had an opportunity to size up the man for himself at a meeting in the secretary of war's office to discuss the reorganization of S-1. His first impression was also not particularly favorable. Stimson agreed to Bush's proposal for a new Military Policy Committee to supervise the atomic effort, and suggested it be composed of seven or nine high-ranking representatives from the army, navy, and OSRD. Even though Groves was the most junior man present—having received his promotion to brigadier general only that morning—he objected immediately, arguing strenuously that such a large group would be "unwieldy" and that any more than three committee members would be more of a hindrance than help. This was rather awkward for Conant, as it meant that either he or Bush would have to be eliminated. Fortunately, Stimson intervened and solved the problem by proposing Bush as chairman and Conant as his alternate, so that both indispensable scientists would have a voice. Admiral William R. Purnell would serve as the navy member. After Groves excused himself, announcing he had to catch a train to inspect the Tennessee site, Stimson chose Lieutenant General Styer, an experienced engineer, to represent the army.

With Groves in charge, the pace of the work quickened. The general was a force to be reckoned with: obstacles crumbled at his feet, and orders came hard and fast and were followed through. Despite himself, Conant developed a grudging respect for the way he got things done. After only forty-eight hours on the job, Groves acquired the Tennessee site and cleared up the priority problem that had hampered them all summer. He had a quick mind, keen sense of how to motivate people, and his compelling presentations moved industrialists to "perform miracles." Conant did not doubt that without Groves's ferocious energy and drive, the second phase of the operation would never have gotten off the ground.

For his part, Groves took an immediate liking to the blunt, no-nonsense chemist. He appreciated his honesty and directness. Bush was more circumspect, more political, and had an acerbic edge. He preferred to rely on Conant to keep him informed of the goings-on in Washington. The general was also keenly aware that outside of the OSRD, Conant wielded enormous influence. "Conant had always been on a level far above Bush," he recalled, repeating the old line that "if you said something about the president in Boston, you did not mean the president of the United States. You meant the president of Harvard."

Relieved of some of the management burdens, Conant spent most of his time bird-dogging the different separation processes and keeping Bush informed of problems or new developments. His province encompassed the Harvard and MIT research labs in Cambridge and the Met Lab in Chicago, extending to the new Oak Ridge site in Tennessee and westward to Lawrence's Rad Lab in Berkeley, with many stops in between.* As he crisscrossed the country that fall, he searched for signs of success—experimental results showing that one of the competing processes had emerged as a surefire winner. He needed solid evidence before committing all their resources to one method.

---

* The Tennessee site was originally called the Clinton Engineer Works because of its proximity to the small town of Clinton, but it later became known as Oak Ridge, which was officially adopted after the war.

At an S-1 meeting at the Bohemian Grove Lodge, an exclusive camp-ground just outside San Francisco, in mid-September, a gung-ho Lawrence pushed his calutron as the best bet to produce uranium-235 before the end of 1944. It was impossible not to admire his spirit and dedication, and some excited committee members were so carried away by what they had seen on "Cyclotron Hill" high above Berkeley's campus that they advocated con-centrating everything they had on the electromagnetic process. Although expensive, it promised to be a shortcut to victory. Conant, who had learned to steel himself against Lawrence's infectious enthusiasm, was more judi-cious. He wanted to wait and see how the other methods fared before elimi-nating one that might eventually prove better and cheaper. But he and the committee were sufficiently impressed to recommend expediting work on a calutron pilot plant and making a start on a portion of the full-scale sys-tem in Tennessee. In the weeks that followed, Conant continued to receive encouraging reports from Lawrence, Compton, and Urey, but he worried that their judgment might be distorted by their extravagant hopes and the excitement of the chase.

By late October, with time running out, Conant knew he had to narrow the field. He told Bush that the centrifuge method was the "weakest horse" and could be dropped, despite the angry protests from its supporters. The high-speed centrifuges built to separate U-235 required huge amounts of en-ergy, and the machinery kept breaking down, making them unsuitable for in-dustrial production. Positive results coming from the gaseous diffusion tests confirmed it was a promising approach to separating U-235 on a large scale, but it might be difficult to complete in time. He still considered Compton's pile program to be the wildest gamble, and "boggled" at its problems and complexities. There was no experimental proof that his hoped-for nuclear chain reaction would actually occur, as a result of which a small fraction of U-238 would be transmuted into plutonium-239. And the recovery of the plu-tonium from the highly radioactive material had been accomplished only on a microchemical scale. Conant remained so dubious about the pile's chances of succeeding that he offered to treat all the members of S-1 to a "champagne dinner" if the project attained full production by January 1, 1945.

Compton was understandably anxious to demonstrate the chain reaction to the skeptical Conant, who would determine the fate of his pile project. He was also eager to prove that it could be done safely to the doubtful officials of the DuPont Company, the colossus of American explosives Groves had approached about taking on the design, construction, and operation of the full-scale pile project. Compton, along with many of the talented, independent-minded scientists at Chicago, had been reluctant to accept the idea that they needed outside assistance. Conant, who had worked as a DuPont consultant, admonished him against trying to hunt "elephants with a peashooter," arguing that he was underestimating the magnitude of the challenge. They were going to have to accept the army's insistence on an immense production operation, by private industry under military supervision, to provide fissionable material in quantity. They were no longer talking about building one bomb and counting on the overwhelming psychological advantage to weaken the enemy's resolve. Total victory would require them to turn out bombs on an assembly line. They were all going to have to start thinking in much bigger terms.

Earlier that fall, Compton had informed him they were almost ready to attempt building a large pile. Conant had expected that the dangerous experiment would be conducted at the Argonne Forest Preserve outside Chicago, which had been carefully selected for the purpose. The army had completed plans for a structure suitable for housing the nuclear reactor, but was running behind schedule due to labor disputes. Compton was frustrated by the holdup. In early November, acting on his own initiative, he agreed to Fermi's urgent request that they brook no delay and begin assembling the pile right there on campus. Space was found in a building formerly occupied by the squash court under the west stands of Stagg Field, the university stadium. Without waiting for blueprints, Fermi and his team set to work stacking heavy graphite bricks and uranium-oxide units on a wood frame, constructing a sphere some twenty-six feet in diameter. Unused to manual labor, the physicists emerged at the end of each day exhausted and as black as coal miners from the carbon dust.

Fermi had assured Compton that he could make the controlled chain reaction safe. According to his calculations, which Compton checked carefully, a small fraction of the neutrons associated with the fission process was emitted a few seconds after the reaction occurred. These "delayed" neutrons gave them a small window in which they could make adjustments so the reaction would always be under full control. The only reason for worry was if some new, unforeseen phenomenon occurred that might result in the release of nuclear energy that far exceeded their figures. While they did not really see how a true nuclear explosion could occur, they were pinning their safety on only "a marginal fraction"—less than 1 percent—of all the neutrons. Elaborate precautions were planned to keep the pile within the proscribed limits. Fermi would only permit the reaction to grow very slowly to avoid any chance of its "breaking out of control." If the intensity of the reaction exceeded the preset limit, a cadmium control rod (which absorbed neutrons) would be reinserted to stop the process.

At a November 14 meeting of the S-1 Executive Committee in Conant's office in Washington, Compton mentioned, with studied casualness, that his team had constructed the pile on campus and was preparing to test the chain reaction. When Conant realized he meant to perform the crucial experiment "in the middle of Chicago," his face went white. If the pile exploded, there was no way to know how great an area would be affected. An accident could be catastrophic. Groves rushed to the nearest phone and demanded to know how soon the Argonne site could be made ready. Compton maintained that Fermi and the other senior physicists were quite certain there would not be a runaway reaction. Although Conant and Groves were "disturbed," neither of them put a stop to it. They were both persuaded that work on the pile was so advanced, it was "too late" to halt it. And there was no doubt it would save time. In the end, after much discussion, they accepted the element of danger, which Compton rationalized as a hazard of war.

But privately, Conant was appalled by Compton's rashness. Threatened with elimination, or a low priority rating, he had acted on his own authority, bypassing both army and university approval, and violating just about every rule of OSRD protocol. Even though luck had been on Compton's side, Conant noted that in retrospect there were those who would always feel the Met Lab leader had taken an "unwarranted risk."

If that morning's disclosure had not been enough to undermine his confidence in Compton, the news Conant received over lunch from the British technical chief, Wallace T. Akers, shook him to the core. Akers informed him that a British study had concluded that plutonium might not be a practical fissionable material for a bomb because the impurities in it might spoil the weapon before it could be completely assembled. Scarcely able to believe what he was hearing, Conant checked with Lawrence, who admitted he was aware of the possibility.

That evening, Conant met with Compton and Lawrence and demanded an explanation. He learned that scientists at both Berkeley and Chicago already knew about the problem and were looking into a chemical process to meet the British specifications. Furious, Conant ordered a complete review of the entire S-1 program. Almost more worrying than the prospect of meeting the new purity requirements was the implication that Compton and his team could not be trusted to supply accurate data. Reprimanding them for the "rather fuzzy state" of their thinking, Conant drove home the need for absolute candor and clearheaded feasibility reports at this critical stage. "I should very much hate the record to show," he added pointedly, "that American scientists lost their critical acumen and failed to be realistic and hard-boiled about the chance of success."

"Now is the time for faith," a desperate Compton wrote Conant at the end of November, urging him to continue to support their venture into the unknown despite the recent blunder.* He had taken that Saturday off and driven to a friend's log cabin in the woods northwest of Chicago to get some rest and reassess the situation. While there, he had penned the letter addressing the purity crisis and sent it special delivery to the head of S-1. But Conant was not inclined to look to heaven for inspiration. Preferring tangible signs of progress, his answer was short and to the point: "It isn't faith we need now, Arthur. It's works."

December 2, the eve of Chanukah, was fated to be the day of the demonstration. It was Fermi's show. From the balcony of the squash court at Stagg Field, where twenty members of his team were observing the operation and monitoring instruments, he ordered all the control rods to be removed from the pile. They were drawn out gingerly, a little at a time. The nerve-racking process took all morning and, after Fermi insisted on a break for lunch, much of the afternoon. At 3:20 p.m., he ordered the last rod to be pulled out, and the pile became critical. It performed exactly as he had said it would: a slow, self-sustaining chain reaction. After a few minutes, the increase in radioactivity required him to shut it down.

Conant was in his Washington apartment waiting for news. He had tried to work but found it difficult to keep his mind from imagining all the things that could go wrong. Nothing was harder, he agreed with Groves, than standing by and staying calm in the face of events over which he had no control. The afternoon light was beginning to fade when the phone finally rang. He snatched it from the cradle in time to hear Compton say, "Our Italian navigator has just landed in the new world."

"Is that so," Conant responded, excited but uncertain. All the hours of

---

* It later transpired that the apparent discrepancies in purity requirements were the result of confusion caused by the tight security barriers between England and the United States rather than incompetence.

pent-up fear and apprehension went into the question that immediately formed on his lips: "Were the natives friendly?"

There was no prearranged code, but Conant had immediately fallen in with the subterfuge and wanted Compton's assurance that there had been no complications. "Everyone landed safe and happy," said Compton, clearly elated.

It was definitely one for the books. The nuclear reaction was now established fact. The success of the Stagg Field demonstration brought plutonium production to the fore of the atomic program. The Chicago team submitted a report stating that with full support for their project, 500 grams of plutonium could be produced and separated in 1943, and the first plutonium bomb would be ready in 1944. The S-1 Committee recommended the pile be developed at once at full scale at the Argonne site. But significant as it was in the history of science, and as proud as everyone in Chicago had a right to be, the experiment, in practical terms, only confirmed Compton's prediction of a year earlier.

Conant found the result reassuring, but it did not fundamentally alter his opinion that a plutonium weapon was a much more iffy proposition than a uranium bomb. He continued to fight stubbornly for the electromagnetic process, supporting Lawrence's claim that he might be able to get sufficient U-235 from his calutrons for a bomb by the end of 1944. Even though the review committee found the production process to be slow and full of difficulties, Conant believed it was crucial they know by that date whether or not the uranium bomb design worked. All he needed was enough fully enriched uranium for one test explosion. Ever present in his thoughts was the "time schedule of the enemy"—the possibility that the Germans were a year or even eighteen months ahead. The knowledge that the Berkeley group had a workable weapon might make all the difference to the Manhattan Project scientists' morale, especially if the Nazis produced "an effective bomb" while theirs was still in the pipeline.

The report Bush sent to the president on December 16, 1942, was a blueprint for action. Conant and his S-1 Committee cut the number of methods to three. They proposed going ahead with a full-scale uranium gaseous diffusion plant and a plutonium plant, costing $150 million and $100 million respectively, and, in a compromise won by Conant, a medium-size experimental electromagnetic plant for producing uranium costing $10 million, to be expanded as necessary. Another $20 million was allotted to produce heavy water for use as a moderator in a chain-reacting pile. At the same time, the design for the bomb had grown more complicated, and a new estimate doubling the amount of fissionable material they needed for a weapon was going to increase both the production costs and timescale. Groves was ready to put the $400 million enterprise in motion, having already negotiated contracts with four of the nation's largest corporations to design, construct, and operate the giant industrial complex. If all went according to plan, the Military Policy Committee predicted there was a small chance that bomb production could begin as early as June 1, 1944, though a better possibility was January 1, 1945, with "an uncertainty either way of several months."

Conant, always on guard against false optimism, thought it unlikely they would have a bomb ready to use much before the summer of '45. Unable to single out one horse as superior, he had asked the president to commit to backing three rivals, despite the staggering sums. It would be a race to the finish. And time was against them. "To my mind, it is this fear that the Germans may be near the goal which is the prime reason for an all-out effort now on this gamble," he wrote Groves. "This being so, it is clear that nothing short of a full-speed, all-out attempt would be worthwhile." The boldness of his proposal later led Groves to remark, "Conant has the gambling spirit of New England pioneers—a calculated gambling spirit."

Conant's determination to expedite the bomb project was reinforced days later when, during a meeting with Bush in Stimson's office, he was confronted with an alarming intelligence report from General Marshall that Germany was planning to use poison gas against the Allies. Even though Hitler, who had been gassed in World War I and blinded temporarily, had promised to never use the weapon, none of them could be sanguine that the Nazis would not resort to chemical combat. There were rumors that German scientists had solved some of the problems that had made mustard gas so difficult to deploy in World War I and found a way to make it more tactically effective on the battlefield. Tanks of the lethal liquid were reportedly being shipped to secret depots in Algeria and the Mediterranean region, as well as a more forward cache near the Italian theater.

Although chemical warfare had been universally condemned by the civilized world after the last war, and progress had been made toward outlawing the use of asphyxiating gases per the Geneva Protocol of 1925, Conant feared German research programs could have developed far more powerful biological weapons and more sophisticated delivery systems. Fears of gas warfare—of the horrific casualties and psychological effects should Germany strike first—prompted a major expansion the US Chemical Warfare

Service—the budget rose from $2 million in 1940 to $1 billion in 1942—and both offensive and defensive weapons were developed. Stockpiles of aerial bombs filled with mustard and phosgene gas were readied should the need arise to retaliate against any use of gas by an Axis power. While Conant felt it necessary to take these precautions, he and the Allied generals had no inkling that Germany had made major advances in chemical weaponry—developing new, rapid action, extremely toxic nerve agents called tabun and sarin—for which the biological weapons expert Jonathan B. Tucker has shown they were "totally unprepared." Or that the Nazis had begun to employ another gas, Zyklon-B, a formulation of hydrogen cyanide (also known as prussic acid) to facilitate the mass murder of millions of Jews and defenseless civilians in extermination camps.

Conant was opposed to the use of gas for anything but reprisals, less for moral reasons than for concerns about resistance from the public, which was still haunted by the memory of the uncontrollable choking clouds. He would never forget the bitter censure heaped on those who helped create this new type of industrial death, and had confided to his assistant Calvert Smith that he counted himself fortunate that "lewisite was first discovered in [Winford Lee] Lewis's lot and not mine!" He would not have wanted that stain on his name.

The threatened escalation in the scientific war was very much on Conant's mind when he gave an emotional address in the New Year to a midwinter graduating class being pressed into service. He had watched the college's classrooms empty as the country's armies grew in strength. A generation of young men was marching off to war, but the question was for how long. "How many years before the end?" Explaining why they needed to prosecute the war with ever-increasing vigor, he told them, "This is for the country an hour of need:

"Every day the war continues prolongs the agony of civilization; every month adds to the chaos with which the postwar must deal; every year increases the hazards liberty must encounter when the war is won. Therefore, to ensure victory in the shortest span of time, no sacrifice can be too great."

With their course set, the focus of the Manhattan District shifted from the laboratory to the production plant, and Conant's role altered again. In recent months, he had found himself functioning more and more as Groves's scientific advisor, and in January 1943 the appointment was made official.

While he had initially been wary of the blustery, abrasive forty-six-year-old general, they worked well together. But Conant knew Groves's bullying style had done nothing to lessen his colleagues' fears about military control, and many regarded the general with "jaundiced eyes."

Anything but diplomatic, Groves had managed to alienate the physicists at the start by expressing his dismay at the paucity of proven theory. A career officer, he had been hoping for a prestigious post overseas and made no secret of the fact that he did not relish leading an endeavor that, as he put it, was "founded on possibilities rather than probabilities." Moreover, he was unused to "long-haired scientists," with their oddball personalities and idiosyncratic ways of working. He was forever trying to instill discipline, irritably barking at the division chiefs that if they wanted to command respect, they should make their men address them by the title "Doctor," or at the very least "Professor," and avoid using first names. This did not go over well. Conant, who kept an ear to the ground for rumblings of trouble, quietly advised Groves to consider appointing himself and Richard Tolman, a respected physicist and vice chairman of the NDRC, as dual advisors as a way of alleviating some of the resentment. Recognizing the "soundness of his reasoning," Groves acted on Conant's suggestion.

In the transition from OSRD to army control, the issue of security had also become a growing source of friction, and Conant was forced to pay new attention to the Manhattan Project's procedures. The president had repeatedly stressed the need for extra security restrictions despite the inconvenience. This continued to be unpopular with the scientists, many of whom were averse to any kind of supervision and believed they were capable of policing themselves. But in a war in which new technology might prove decisive, Conant agreed with Roosevelt that this project had to be "more drastically guarded than other highly secret developments."

Conant's concerns about security, reflected in his correspondence with Bush and Groves, were fueled by a number of alarming—if unsubstantiated—reports warning of an imminent German threat. On July 15, 1942, an agitated Compton, prompted by Szilard and the increasingly frantic refugee physicists in Chicago, had passed on allegedly "reliable information" from Switzerland that the Germans had achieved a self-sustaining chain reaction and were on the verge of producing an atomic weapon. "We have become convinced," Compton wrote, "that there is a real danger of bombardment by the Germans within the next few months using bombs designed to spread radioactive material in lethal quantities." Conant wrote the American embassy in London, which sent a paraphrased version of his letter to the Directorate of Tube Alloys (code name for the British atomic bomb program). The British responded that they had it on good information that the German uranium bomb program was being directed by Werner Heisenberg, a brilliant physicist and fervent nationalist, but their own informants did not believe he had accumulated enough heavy water to sustain a chain reaction. Could Conant please tell them more about Szilard's source and try to "verify" his tip? What is unmistakable in the flurry of jittery cables that followed is the very real fear that the Germans might get there first.

From the outset, Conant was as apprehensive about internal leaks as he was of foreign espionage, and went to great lengths to restrict the knowledge of his role in the bomb project. His experience with Bill Richards had taught him to trust no one—not even his wife or closest Harvard associates—with even the vaguest suggestion of his top-secret assignment. Though his son Ted suspected it was a military project of some importance when the army came and ran a special telephone line up the long dirt road that led to their isolated summer cottage to ensure constant communication with the White House, Conant kept his family in complete ignorance. Rather than worry constantly about relaxing his guard and letting something slip, he found it easier to lie. "The amount of bare-faced lying that was done in Washington in those days is beyond estimate," he recalled. "Military secrets of all sorts were closely guarded. One just didn't ask an old friend whom he met at the Cosmos Club what he was doing. A statement that a person was working for the government was sufficient sign to change the conversation."

One of the biggest problems facing the Manhattan District leaders was deciding who would take charge of the next critical phase of the project: developing a method for making the actual bomb. While it had been demonstrated theoretically, the bomb's design and size had yet to be worked out, as well as such practical problems as how it would be detonated. They could still not do much more than make an educated guess at how much force an atomic bomb would exert. Both Bush and Conant felt it was imperative they begin drawing up detailed plans. Per their request, Compton had organized a study group at Berkeley in June 1942 to begin work on the problem. To help with the calculations, he recruited J. Robert Oppenheimer, an outstanding theoretical physicist and a specialist in the problems of nuclear physics. It became clear from their preliminary studies that working out the mechanics by which a mass of fissionable material would suddenly become critical and explode would require extensive exploration, and would by necessity have to be carried out in a secluded location.

Groves, who inherited all his other laboratory directors when he arrived on the scene, realized it would take a unique individual to lead the bomb laboratory, and he was determined to find the very best man for the job. He asked Bush and Conant for nominations, and talked to them at length about the technical expertise and administrative skills the enterprise would require. Oppenheimer was not at the top of anyone's list. Given the importance of the project and the extreme difficulty of the task, it went without saying that it would go to a Nobel Prize winner—someone of the caliber of Compton, Fermi, Franck, and Lawrence.

Oppie, as he was known, was a comparative latecomer to the bomb project. He had come to Berkeley in 1929, where he earned a reputation as an inspiring lecturer with a devoted following, and rose swiftly to become head of the Theoretical Physics Department. He was a great friend and frequent sounding board of Lawrence's, and had accidentally overheard him in conversation with Mark Oliphant about the possibility of Anglo-American cooperation on building an atomic bomb. Once the cat was out of the bag, Oppenheimer knew too much to be excluded from the project, and Lawrence—after being reprimanded by Conant for spilling official secrets—convinced everyone it would be better to have him inside the tent than out.

Lawrence was eager to involve his brilliant friend in the weapon's research but was not helped by Oppenheimer's apparent determination to carry on with his left-wing political activity, including an array of Communist causes. While Oppie appeared earnest in his desire not to let anything interfere with his ability to "be of direct use" to the government, he attended various labor union meetings, as well as a fund-raising event for veterans of the Spanish Civil War, despite Lawrence's advice to do nothing that would give anyone in Washington a reason to find fault with him. But it was a cause that was close to the heart of his wife, Katherine "Kitty," whose late husband, Joseph Dallet, an active member of the US Communist Party, had been killed in the struggle in 1937. It was also guaranteed to attract the "parlor pinks" with whom the couple socialized regularly, as well as a good number of the high-level Communist organizers that the FBI suspected of aiding the Russians in their intelligence-gathering efforts. At the event, Oppenheimer was introduced to Gregory Kheifetz, reportedly an agent for the NKVD, the forerunner of the KGB, and agreed to meet him for lunch the following day—during which the physicist discussed Einstein's letter to Roosevelt, as well as a secret wartime project that involved the country's leading scientists. Why Oppenheimer persisted in such risky behavior, which he knew full well would invite further suspicion, is open to debate. It was just one in a series of mystifyingly inconsistent, self-indulgent, and reckless acts that would make the extraordinarily gifted and enigmatic physicist such a controversial figure.

The FBI and military counterintelligence agents first opened a file on Oppenheimer in the wake of the Oliphant episode, but by early 1942, his cavalier attitude goaded them into compiling a thick dossier. Newly alert to the threat of German and Soviet espionage, they were particularly disturbed by some of the circles Oppenheimer traveled in and some of the prominent Communist intellectuals he called friends, including a left-leaning Berkeley professor of French literature named Haakon Chevalier. Far from denying it, when asked to fill out a government security questionnaire, Oppenheimer reportedly told them, "I am not a Communist, but I have probably belonged to every Communist-front organization on the West Coast." Not surprisingly, his initial clearance application was rejected. Though Oppenheimer was not yet officially part of the bomb project, and technically was not supposed to even know about it, according to his biographer Ray Monk, he was working on it more or less full-time, having been allowed in "through the back door" by Lawrence.

At the same time, Conant, still troubled by the security breach that led to Oppenheimer's hearing about the bomb project, worried that security precautions at Berkeley might be a bit lax. On January 30, 1942, he wrote Lawrence and the other program chiefs that he would be instituting new security restrictions, calling them "a necessary nuisance to all this work." As an additional safeguard, he and Bush had decided that everyone working on the bomb project, no matter how small a detail of the problem, must have their names submitted for clearance to the intelligence services. Apologizing in advance for the additional paperwork, he promised that this would "in no way slow down or hamper" their work but would provide them with a record of "all the people who are in any way concerned with even a small fragment of the investigation."

As a college president, Conant was well acquainted with the propensity of the young to buck authority, and he wanted to know if other Berkeley researchers were gossiping freely about forbidden subjects. In February he recruited First Lieutenant John Lansdale Jr., a recent Harvard Law graduate working for the US Army Military Intelligence Service, to go undercover as a student and investigate whether the physicists were talking out of school. At their first meeting in his NDRC office, Conant gave Lansdale a capsule summary of the race against Germany for the bomb, telling him matter-of-factly, "Whoever gets this first will win the war." In less than a month, Lansdale managed to fill a notebook with atomic scuttlebutt and even filched a blueprint of a spectrograph from the cyclotron lab. One law school dean had been so obliging as to point out the great E. O. Lawrence to him as the man who was trying to "split the atom" for use as an explosive. Conant listened to his report in grim silence, punctuating the most flagrant lapses in security with a murmur of pained incredulity: "Oh! . . . Oh! . . . Oh my goodness!"

He ordered Lansdale to return directly to campus in uniform and read the Berkeley crowd the riot act. Loose talk would not be tolerated. Under the new security restrictions, there was a "complete ban" on discussing nuclear fission with anybody not officially involved in S-1, and corrective action would be taken. Their conduct was undermining the cause of secrecy. The Bush-Groves policy of strict "compartmentalization"—which limited the information given to individuals and small units to no more than that which was required for the performance of the work—was to be enforced, with Lansdale, soon to be promoted to captain and put in charge of project security, as chief enforcer.

It was probably with mixed emotions that Conant received a glowing letter from Lawrence on March 26, 1942, urging him to consider "the desirability of asking Oppenheimer" to serve as a member of S-1: "I think he would be a tremendous asset in every way. He combines a penetrating insight into the theoretical aspects of the whole program with solid common sense, which sometimes in certain directions seems to be lacking, and I am sure you and Dr. Bush would find him a useful advisor."

Any hesitancy Conant might have felt about including a potential security risk in the secret project was overridden by the unstoppable Lawrence, who prevailed on Compton to make Oppenheimer a member of the Chicago group. After so many months waiting on the sidelines, Oppenheimer reveled in his new title, coordinator of rapid rupture, and surprised Compton with the "wisdom and firmness" he demonstrated on both policy and personnel issues. By the end of the summer, after receiving rave reviews for his dynamic leadership of the Berkeley study group, where he guided nine of the country's most distinguished physicists in complex theoretical discussions about the fission bomb—as well as the more speculative *fusion* weapon, a thermonuclear hydrogen bomb—Oppenheimer had more than proven himself. Even Edward Teller, a strong-willed Hungarian-born physicist who often clashed with his colleagues and had long regarded Oppenheimer as a dreamy eccentric, had to admit that he had "showed a refined, sure, informal touch." Hans Bethe, the highly regarded thirty-six-year-old Cornell physicist, was even more enthusiastic about the spirit of cooperation and spontaneity that set those sessions apart as an "unforgettable" experience. Bethe, whose tome on nuclear physics was referred to as the "Bible," was half-Jewish and was a much beloved figure. He left Nazi Germany in 1933 after the first wave of anti-Semitic legislation. His opinion carried weight. He could now attest to Oppenheimer's "intellectual power" and how by the close of the meetings he had transformed himself into "the unquestioned leader of our group."

Conant received Oppenheimer's report on the results of the Berkeley study group at an S-1 meeting at the end of August. The essentials of fast-neutron fission had been worked out, and under the heading of "Status of the Bomb," he noted that the group estimated the fission bomb would explode with "150 times energy of previous calculation." Unfortunately, such a bomb would require more U-235 than previously estimated—about 30 kilograms, or 66 pounds—and more precise values would require further experimentation. This news paled in importance compared with the startling revelation that a much more powerful reaction than nuclear fission might be produced by the thermonuclear fusion of deuterium, the heavy-hydrogen isotope. A 66-pound uranium bomb was equivalent to 100,000 tons of TNT. But Oppie's report suggested that if the same bomb was used to ignite a fusion explosion of two to three tons of liquid deuterium, it would explode with the force of 100 million tons of TNT. "Estimate devastation area of 1,000 sq. km [or] 360 sq. miles," Conant scribbled. He immediately sent off the new status report to Bush, with the S-1 Committee's conclusion: "We have become convinced that success in this program before the enemy can succeed is necessary for victory. We also believe that success of this program will win the war if it has not been previously terminated."

Groves met Oppenheimer for the first time when he visited Berkeley on October 8, 1942, to discuss the recommendations of the summer study group. The whip-lean, wild-haired Oppenheimer, with his love of literature, poetry, and erudite pursuits—he was studying Sanskrit in order to read the Bhagavad Gita in the original—did not seem like someone the hard-nosed general would take to, but Groves appreciated his quick mind and "tremendous intellectual capacity." That and the fact that Oppenheimer, as he put it, "knew everything that was then known" about how to make a bomb. Groves grilled him for hours on his conclusions, as well as the methods by which he had reached them, later telling Compton that he was "strongly impressed by Oppenheimer's intelligence and grasp of the problem."

Groves had come to Berkeley expecting to request that Lawrence take charge of Project Y, the name he had given to the classified weapon's laboratory well in advance of its existence, but the general was forced to accept that he could not be spared from his work on electromagnetic separation. Instead, Lawrence recommended his protégé Edward MacMillan, but he was an extremely modest man and did not have the forceful personality Groves had in mind. A number of eminent physicists' names were floated—Teller favored Bethe, and Eugene P. Wigner, the Hungarian theoretical physicist who had been with the project since its embryonic beginnings—but they were not long out of Europe. Groves was not about to name a foreigner as head of a top-secret American military project. By comparison, Oppenheimer was a relatively junior member of the project and a theorist, not a hands-on experimentalist, and if ever there was a job for an experimental physicist, this was it. Groves was tired of theory and speculation. He wanted someone who could talk about the "down-to-earth" problems—such as "how to detonate the bomb, or design it so that it could be detonated"—and how to tackle them in practical terms.

At the same time, there was something about the charismatic thirty-eight-year-old Oppenheimer that caught the general's eye. Groves had just come from a strained meeting with the Chicago scientists, who were openly hostile to the idea of a military laboratory, especially the querulous Leo Szilard, whom he loathed almost on sight. Groves had little sympathy for the armchair critics, considered them long on talk and short on action. "None of them were go-getters," he groused. "They preferred to move at a pipe-smoking academic pace." Oppenheimer, on the other hand, agreed that the heart of the problem lay not in theory but in the lack of good experimental data. He believed the time had come to make a major change in the organization of the project, and proposed consolidating all their scattered research operations in one laboratory where they could come to grips with the chemical, metallurgical, engineering, and ordnance problems that had so far received scant consideration. He expressed the same sense of frustration at the snail's pace of the project, and emphasized the need to eliminate the waste, errors, and duplication caused by all the security constraints and compartmentalization if they were to get the fast results they needed des-

perately. If the most efficient way to accomplish this was in a military establishment, it was fine by him. He was willing to be adaptable.

Groves was so relieved to have finally found someone capable of the
kind of pragmatic thinking the job required that he asked Oppenheimer
to meet with him again in a week. He would be back in Chicago, and asked
the Berkeley physicist to accompany him, along with Colonel James Marshall and Lieutenant Colonel Kenneth Nichols, on the train back to New
York. The overnight run would allow Oppenheimer ample opportunity to
expand on his ideas. By the time the 20th Century Limited pulled into
Grand Central Terminal the next morning, the four of them—sitting knee-
to-knee in the tiny compartment—had come up with a plan for a single
centralized laboratory, located in an isolated region, and small enough to
be under strict military watch, where the scientists could go about their
business and converse freely, completely protected from outsiders and
enemy spies.

Within a month of the train trip, Oppenheimer had talked Conant and
Groves out of using the Oak Ridge site and into "a lovely spot" in a part
of the country that held special significance for him: the Jemez Mountains
of northern New Mexico. As soon as Groves saw the barren, windswept
mesa, empty except for a small cluster of buildings and crude log cabins
that belonged to the Los Alamos Ranch School, he reportedly said, "This
is the place." The mesa, a strip of land that was two miles wide and eight
miles long, was as isolated and inaccessible as imaginable. Steep canyons
formed the north and south boundaries, and the open sections could easily
be fenced and patrolled. The nearest railhead was in Santa Fe, twenty miles
to the southeast, but the bad road connecting the city with the mesa, with
its hairpin turns and precipitous drops, discouraged all but the most determined travelers. Conant, who remembered Los Alamos from a brief visit to
see if the rigorous boys' academy would benefit his sickly son, agreed that
they would be hard put to find a better location. Groves acted quickly to
acquire the site and surrounding property. On December 4 the secretary of
war notified the owners it was being taken over. The sale was arranged in
complete secrecy and the documents sealed. It could not have worked out
better for Oppie, who knew the area like the back of his hand and just happened to own a ranch in the nearby Pecos Valley, on the other side of the
Sangre de Cristo Mountains.

While Oppenheimer threw himself into the preparations for the new
laboratory, acting as the de facto director of Los Alamos, Groves could find

no one who "showed any great enthusiasm" for his choice. There was nothing in the Berkeley physicist's background or résumé that indicated that he was prepared for such awesome responsibility. He had a mystic streak that raised eyebrows, and sometimes told stories or acted in ways that struck his colleagues as foolish. "To most physicists, it came as a surprise," observed Isidor I. Rabi, putting it mildly. In truth, the formidable Columbia University physicist who was the associate director of the MIT Rad Lab, considered it "a most improbable appointment." The consensus, Groves learned, was that Oppenheimer lacked the necessary "prestige among his fellow scientists"—he had never won a scientific award of any kind—and that many did not believe he could carry the development through to a successful conclusion.

As the selection process dragged on, Groves asked each member of the Military Policy Committee to give him the name of someone who could possibly be a project leader, but "it became apparent we were not going to find a better man." In the end, with Lawrence's assurance that he would take over if the project faltered, Groves went with his gut instincts and asked Oppenheimer to undertake the task. His plan almost immediately hit a "snag," as he delicately put it, when military intelligence refused to clear Oppenheimer. "His background included much that was not to our liking, by any means," Groves acknowledged later, but he and Conant—who had reviewed the contents of his FBI file—had concluded that Oppenheimer's potential value outweighed any security risk. They did not think his brief flirtation with Communism should bar him from doing vital war work. The army's reservations did not go away, however. The letter formalizing his appointment, signed by Groves and Conant, would not be sent until February 1943, and problems over his clearance would continue for months to come.

In the meantime, Oppenheimer set to work trying to put together the nucleus of the new organization, writing to Conant for advice and assistance. He began by catching him up on the results of recent scientific work and then addressed the real purpose of his letter: namely, the difficulty of recruiting men of the first rank to come to a remote military outpost for what was vaguely described as the "duration of the war." Oppenheimer knew rounding up the talent he needed was not going to be easy. Rumors abounded that the bomb project was a giant boondoggle: a sideshow to the bloody struggle in progress. Lawrence and Loomis had already raided the physics departments of the top Eastern universities for the radar lab, and everyone else in the field was already fully engaged in war work. He was going to have to poach talent from existing projects, incurring the wrath of the other program chiefs, but confided to Conant that he was "inclined not to take too seriously the absolute nos with which we shall be greeted."

Oppenheimer could not afford to stand on ceremony. "The job we have to do will not be possible," he stressed, "without personnel substantially greater than that which we have now available, and I shall only be misleading you and all others concerned with the S-1 project if I were to promise to get the work done without this help."

Always a quick study, Oppenheimer recognized that the fifty-year-old Harvard president was regarded as an elder statesman of the scientific community, and modeled himself after the veteran wartime leader and Washington insider. Conant's administrative ability, intuition, quiet sense of humor, and cool determination to keep the project moving and the men in good spirits were qualities he sought to emulate. But it was the cool Yankee's political savvy he envied most. "Oppenheimer saw this faculty of Conant and wanted to learn from it," recalled John Manley, an experimental physicist at the Met Lab who became Oppie's assistant. Over time Conant became Oppenheimer's "mentor in national policy matters," and evolved into a kind of worldly father figure on whom he relied heavily for sympathy and wise counsel in his battles with government and military bureaucracies.

Aware that the success of the bomb project—and the outcome of the war—might very well rest on Oppenheimer's inexperienced shoulders, Conant took it upon himself to help the Los Alamos director get established as quickly as possible, cleaning up his messes, straightening out misunderstandings, and fielding complaints during his shaky first few months on the job. There was a low moment in late December 1942 when Oppenheimer's overzealous recruiting tactics sparked so many complaints within the NDRC and OSRD that Conant wrote Groves that both he and Bush were "wondering whether we have found the right man." To keep peace in the family, Conant decided it would be better if he rather than Oppenheimer made the initial approach, telling Groves that he would personally speak "to the top man in each organization who was likely to kick" and smooth the way for the new laboratory leader, who would then talk to the scientist in question and "try to sell him on the idea."

Conant also had to run interference on the loaded issue of whether the Los Alamos laboratory should be militarized. Oppenheimer had been so eager for the top job that he had readily embraced Groves's plan to induct the scientists into the army. He had agreed to assume the rank of lieutenant colonel—and had even ordered his uniforms. A number of the senior physicists he wanted to recruit thought he had been naïve to agree, however, and both Rabi and his Rad Lab colleague Robert F. Bacher were adamantly against it. They had spent the last two years in the successful radar lab and saw no need to impose a rigid military hierarchy at Los Alamos, which they believed would only stifle creativity and productivity, divide personnel, and damage morale. They told Oppenheimer in no uncertain terms that if he went ahead with the plan, "None of us would come."

After a heated meeting in Washington on January 30, 1943, and afraid he was facing an insurrection, Oppenheimer again asked Conant to intercede on his behalf. After listing all the Rad Lab scientists' conditions, "the discussion of which you were a witness in the early stages," Oppenheimer admitted that he was unsure how Groves would respond to the ultimatum that the project be demilitarized. He also asked Conant to use his persuasive powers on Rabi, but worried they risked losing more than just his cooperation. "I believe that the solidarity of the physicists is such that if these conditions are not met, we shall fail not only to have the men from MIT with us, but many men who have already planned to join the new laboratory will reconsider their commitments." If they were forced to come with real misgivings, he doubted they could "carry on the work with anything like the speed required."

Although he had donned a uniform during his chemical warfare service in World War I, and considered it a mere formality, Conant now sought to defuse the growing dissension. The compromise he negotiated with Groves took the form of an open letter, bearing both their signatures, which Oppenheimer could share with the men he was trying to recruit. The letter, dated February 25, stated that the laboratory was to be run "on a strictly civilian basis" during the early, experimental stages, with the military assuming control later, when the dangerous ordnance work began. At that point in time—but not before January 1, 1944—the scientists would become commissioned officers and take their orders from the army.* To assuage any fears they had about the isolated laboratory losing its "scientific autonomy," the authors assured the scientists that they would be exempt from the usual wartime restrictions that prevented them from learning what was going on in the other research facilities. They also asserted rather arrogantly, "Through Dr. Conant, complete access to the scientific world is guaranteed."

---

* In the end, the scientists prevailed, and the transition to army control was never implemented.

The letter went a long way to easing tensions and overcoming the misgivings of potential recruits, and Groves gratefully acknowledged Conant's "great experience in, and understanding of, the academic world, particularly its scientific elements." But Conant's word was not enough to erase everyone's doubts about the army and Oppenheimer's selection. Rabi declined the offer to become associate director of the Los Alamos laboratory—he was unwilling to abandon his crucial radar work for a project whose overall odds were fifty-fifty at best. In response to Oppenheimer's cajoling letters, however, he agreed to send some of his ablest men. Still, they had cleared a difficult hurdle, and physicists at MIT, Chicago, and elsewhere were hanging up their lab coats and heading west to join the new venture. Hans and Rose Bethe's decision to throw in their lot with the Los Alamos group meant that many others would want to come and would make the job of recruiting personnel much easier. It was a victory, and an important vote of confidence.

Conant praised Oppenheimer for his "patience, courage, and determination" during the trying formative months of the project, and forgave him his trespasses. "Don't worry about all the trouble which your activities may have caused me," he wrote with evident warmth and goodwill. "I am only sorry that I can't press a button and produce the men that I know you need and want." Conant had once led a group of men in a risky, highly speculative experimental endeavor, and probably knew better than anyone the pressure Oppenheimer was under. The kinship he felt with the intensely cerebral young physicist quickly developed into a genuine friendship, with the reserved Conant reciprocating to an unusual degree, so that in their frequent correspondence, Oppie soon felt comfortable addressing the NDRC chairman as "Uncle Jim."

Oppenheimer had been given his marching orders. In the February 25 letter, which served as a sort of charter for Los Alamos, Conant and Groves explicitly laid out the task ahead. "We are addressing this letter to you," they began, "as the scientific director of the special laboratory in New Mexico in order to confirm our many conversations on the matters of organization and responsibility." Oppenheimer would report to Groves, who had overall responsibility for the project and its security. Conant, as the general's chief advisor, would supervise the scientific and technical aspects of the work. Oppenheimer would be in charge of a small, highly secret community of scientists living and working under constant stress in a compound surrounded by a high fence and secured by troops, and would have to manage the politics and personalities as well as technological problems. They detailed it all in the letter, spelling out his duties in black-and-white, putting it all on the record so there would be no room for misunderstanding. But there could be no confusion about the ultimate objective: Los Alamos, they asserted, "will be concerned with the development and final manufacture of an instrument of war."

For Conant, who could never find enough hours in a day to stay on top of all the people and programs vying for his attention, the spring of 1943 offered a chance to catch his breath. As he sat back and took stock that May, he noted with satisfaction that the basic experimental program had been completed, and his—and OSRD's—responsibility for the uranium program was nearly at an end. The arrangements were all in place. The president had approved their plans. Now the fate of S-1 rested with Oppenheimer and the scientists and engineers toiling in obscurity on a distant mountaintop, perched on the cone of an extinct volcano.

In the brief interlude, Conant took a moment to reflect on the things he had seen and heard over the last eighteen months. As a way of ordering his thoughts, he began writing out in his scratchy hand a detailed account of the atom bomb project from its inception, describing it as a "fragment of a strange scientific history." At the start, his tone is upbeat and brisk, charged with the excitement of the endeavor and the power of science itself. "This highly secret war effort has moved at a giddy pace," he wrote. "New results, new ideas, new decisions, and new organization have kept all concerned in a state of healthy turmoil.

> The time for "freezing design" and construction arrived a few weeks past; now, we must await the slower task of plant construction and large-scale experimentation. The new results when they arrive will henceforth be no laboratory affair; their import may well be world shattering. But as in the animal world, so in industry: the period of gestation is commensurate with the magnitude to be achieved.

Although Conant was fully committed to the atomic program, there was a part of him that held out hope that the bomb would never become a reality. It was not so much that he dreamed of failure—his worst nightmare was of some "unforeseen block" that might stall the project—but that he dreaded the idea of science being used for such destructiveness. He was repulsed by the idea that the thrilling discovery of a fast-neutron self-sustaining chain reaction would be dedicated to this terrible new force rather than making abundant atomic power for peaceful purposes a reality. "How many times in all the scientific conferences of the last two years has it been said, 'I hope the thing won't work, but we must be sure it won't,'" he recalled, adding that "everyone concerned with the project would feel greatly relieved and thoroughly delighted if something would develop to *prove* the impossibility of such an atomic explosion."

But this was a deeply personal plea; a private hope in a private history that he kept locked away in a special safe in his office. Conant knew, of course, that not all the project scientists felt the same way. In fact, many thought only of the moment the bomb would end the present suffering in Europe, and peace and the right to freedom were restored. But he was already filled with foreboding about the future: of the day that Germany, Japan, or some other aggressor harnessed the power of the atom, and the world was never free of the fear of such weapons again. "What the future a year hence has to say is still another story," he wrote. One thing was certain: he was far from finished with "this scientific delirium tremens."

CHAPTER 15

Uneasy Alliances

The price of greatness is responsibility.
—Churchill at Harvard, 1943

"President Conant of Harvard has the balanced lucid mind of a research addict, and is deliberately turning from physical science to educational and administrative work," observed H. G. Wells. "Ever since I met him, I have been asking whether there are more like him and why he is not running for the White House." Wells actually advanced the idea of Conant as a candidate for high office on a visit to the United States five years earlier, but *Fact* magazine reprinted his prophetic comment in May 1943 given the wartime leader's relevance to the current political scene. "A good many million fellow Americans should—if not in 1944—then in 1948 answer this question at the polls with a bang," opined the magazine. "A man of such varied gifts, such practical ability, such profound insights and such buoyant courage is a man to honor and watch."

Until the spring of 1943, Conant had hardly dared think beyond the country's safety. It almost seemed like "tempting fate" to talk about the state of the nation after the war was won. But the issues were too important for him to overlook. Distressed by the shortsighted election-year debate about America's place in the postwar world, he felt compelled to wade into the public discussion, speaking his mind forcefully in an article in the May 1943 issue of the *Atlantic Monthly*, entitled "Wanted: American Radicals." Conant wanted to get on with the constructive business of planning the "post-victory era" as much as the next man. However, he did not share the idealists' faith that the United States would automatically assume leadership of the world. It was important to point out that the problems the country would face when the fighting was over would not merely be those engendered by it, but would be a manifestation of the "larger maladjustment" of which the war itself was a part. America could scarcely play a leading role in international affairs until it got its own internal affairs in order, and decided exactly what kind of country it wanted to be: the land of plenty or the land of the privileged few.

His contention was that the war had irrevocably altered the domestic political landscape. The old-fashioned conservative—who believed "when it is not necessary to change, it is necessary not to change"—was gone. For after years of living in a total war economy, where everything was dictated by military necessity, "who is to be found who does not believe that change is necessary once the war is won?" Given a choice between the reactionary, who wanted nothing more than to return to prewar status (or an even rosier time), and the radical, who wanted a completely different situation, Conant argued for the rise of a new American radical—rooted in native soil, endowed with earthy common sense, and firm in the belief that every man deserves an equal chance. This "hypothetical" American radical of the 1940s, he suggested, might not be the answer to all of the country's problems, but his "voice was needed" if they were going to find a way to fix their stratified society:

> The American radical traces his lineage through the democratic revolution of Jackson when Emerson was sounding his famous call for the American Scholar. His political ideal will, of course, be Jefferson: his prophets will be Emerson and Thoreau; his poet, Whitman . . . He will be lusty in wielding the axe against the root of inherited privilege. To prevent the growth of the caste system, which he abhors, he will be resolute in his demand to confiscate (by constitutional methods) all property once a generation. He will demand really effective inheritance and gift taxes and the breaking up of trust funds and estates. And this point cannot be lightly pushed aside, for it is the kernel of his radical philosophy.

Conant's message, apart from its intentionally provocative tone, was simple: mass conscription had leveled the playing field. Unless the United States began taking steps to help the returning soldier—a job for everyone, universal educational opportunity, and the promise of social mobility—before the demobilization of the armed forces, "we may well sow the seeds of a civil war within a decade." The best defense against another war and the growing threat of Communism was upholding the basic ideals that had always sustained American democracy: "life, liberty, and the pursuit of happiness." When Jefferson wrote that famous line into the Declaration of Independence, Conant added cheekily, he did not write "life, liberty and *property*." Conant swung his axe at the root of privilege only so that a greater number might be free to carry the responsibility as well as enjoy the benefits of modern civilization. But he was careful not to press his utopian vision to its logical conclusion. His political alter ego was "respectful but not enthusiastic about Marx, Engels, and Lenin." A capitalist at heart—if a "peculiar North American brand of doctrine"—his American radical believed in equality of opportunity, not equality of rewards, and would be "quite willing in times of peace to let net salaries and earnings sail way above the $25,000 mark."

The editors of the *Atlantic Monthly* were so proud of the essay, they instructed their readers that it was a "splendid successor" to Conant's oft-quoted article in the May 1940 issue, "Education for a Classless Society," in which he argued for "more equitable distribution of opportunity for all the children of the land," and drew attention to the "continuity of [his] thinking" which was "worthy of note."

He might as well have lobbed a stink bomb into a meeting of the Harvard Corporation. The idea that the president of an institution heavily dependent on its wealthy benefactors would endorse such extreme sentiments stunned the trustees. Conant had expounded on his favorite theme of an American meritocracy before—in terms of admissions, testing, scholarships, and the selection of professors—but this was the first time he had extended it to society as a whole. His sharp challenge of the status quo, and his call for a redistribution of wealth, was more than some of the Brahmin members of the Corporation could bear. Several demanded his head on a platter. One outraged trustee observed scathingly that since the educational problems of the postwar world would doubtless be extremely demanding, perhaps the president might be well advised to leave the problem of inherited wealth alone. Another took exception to his hiding behind a hypothetical figure, sniffing that "this is not a dignified or sportsmanlike way to put yourself on the record." The alumni resonated with indignation. Protest letters and telegrams poured into Conant's office.

One of the most vociferous critics was Thomas W. Lamont, class of 1892, a generous financier and philanthropist who had already pledged millions for a new undergraduate library at the end of the war. By Wall Street standards, Lamont was a liberal and had even supported aspects of the New Deal. But this time he felt Conant had gone too far in chasing the moneychangers from the temple. Calling his American radical "a destructive sort of chap," Lamont penned an eight-page critique of Conant's ill-considered scheme, arguing that it would deliver a "death blow to individual enterprise."

In a spirited reply, Conant wrote that he suspected their disagreement came down to their very different views about the seriousness of the disease afflicting the country: whereas for Lamont it was nothing more than a "disagreeable cold," for him it was "pneumonia with possible prognosis of death." The only hope was reform, and drastic reform at that. He expanded on his argument over seventeen pages, explaining that if the eleven million soldiers, most of whom were under twenty-five, came back to a country that did not live up to its promise of advancement determined by merit, talent, character, and grit, and instead found that advancement depended on "accidents of geography and birth," many would become discontented. More pessimistic in his appraisal of their society than most, Conant admitted to being frankly fearful that "the clash between the 'haves' and 'have-nots' will destroy freedom in the postwar world unless a majority of the American people *believe* in the *reality* of the American dream—equal opportunity for all." He acknowledged his use of the word *confiscate* in relation to property may have caused unease but assured Lamont this was just the attitude of his radical in an "extreme mood," and not meant to be taken literally.

Harvard may have been hostile to his argument, but Conant's lively article scored with many critics. The *Wall Street Journal* applauded his desire to reinvigorate the discussion of America's future, hailing Conant as a "potent and refreshing political voice in this country." His appeal for change and a "more fluid society" was direct and practical. He seemed to have a clear view of the horizon at a time when to most Americans the path ahead appeared murky and sketchily charted. "President Conant speaks at a moment when this country really needs new ideas of future policy," continued the *Journal's* editorial, adding that he had done much to redeem Harvard for its "doubtful contribution to national life"—a dig at Roosevelt and all those who "followed Frankfurter" to Washington. "When we survey the field of possible choice, we find many good alternatives to a fourth term. But most of the prospective candidates have done little thinking about national problems" and had "much to learn from this schoolmaster."

A flurry of "Conant for President" editorials ran in local papers across the country, which was amusing and of little import—except to the extent to which they helped quash the old boys' coup attempt at Harvard. "The stew continues," an exasperated Conant wrote Patty in late June, reporting that he had received a memo from Lamont, "or rather the returns about the stew continue to come in":

> Apparently I have "offended" some of my good friends . . . In other words, they didn't realize just where I stood *in re* the troubles of our times. In fact, a good deal of the difficulty arises from the fact that these people don't admit there are any real troubles except those caused by Hitler and Roosevelt. Lick one on the battlefield and the other in the voting booth, and everything will be O.K. In short, I now have evidence that my diagnosis of American reactionaries was all too true, and the number included several of whom I should not have suspected. It is partly a matter of age. But enough of that!

Lamont respected Conant and had been measured in his response, but he reported to a friend that the president's progressive rhetoric had "stirred up a hornet's nest," and "the Harvard crowd was generally buzzing with the whole thing." Whether it really reached the level of a full-blown "crisis," as implied in a late-in-life interview of Provost Paul Buck, seems questionable. No doubt, those in charge of Harvard's rich endowment impressed on Conant the gravity of his error. He had violated the sacred tenet of fundraising—never bite the hand that feeds you—and strayed far beyond his office's well-fenced precincts. At one point, Henry Shattuck, the influential former treasurer of the Corporation, suggested that perhaps the busy scientist take a leave of absence and appoint Buck in his place. But Conant had less and less tolerance for these college flaps. He had no intention of being hustled out the door at such a critical hour, and after alluding darkly to the "important work" he was doing in Washington, Shattuck dropped the idea. There was enough opposition, however, to make Conant more guarded in expressing his ideas.

What may have finally quieted the controversy on the Charles was a well-timed visit from his famous friend across the Atlantic. "By the time you read this, you will have seen in the papers that a certain historian 'who has written a glorious page of British history' is now in Canada," Conant wrote Patty, then vacationing in New Hampshire, on August 7, alerting her to the possibility that Churchill might come to Harvard to collect an honorary degree before heading home from his Canadian trip, effectively canceling their plans for Labor Day weekend. "If such an event occurs, would it be worth your while to return to Cambridge for a day?" he inquired teasingly, as he knew full well she would never miss out on all the parties and pageantry that would accompany such a celebrated guest. "I shall let you know details if and when there are any. All of which is *secret*, of course, and may be wrong."

Conant had reason to worry the prime minister might decide to pass them by, however, confiding "it won't hurt my feelings if he does." His anxiety, occasioned by a rocky period in the atomic partnership between their two countries, was understandable. Eager as he had once been to come to Britain's aid, almost from the moment the bomb went into production, Conant had instinctively sought to curtail the amount of classified S-1 data that was being passed to their ally. At first, it was simply out of concern about the ability of the Brits to keep their secrets. The Australian physicist Mark Oliphant had slipped up more than once, and the clumsy scientific interchange with the innumerable and hopelessly byzantine British ministries did nothing to allay his fears. His doubts had intensified as plans for their common military effort had progressed, complicated by their divergent strategic interests, as well as the profound postwar consequences of controlling such an important military and industrial asset.

Beginning with the Tizard mission in 1940, the British had offered their most-prized technical information to the United States as an overture to what they hoped would blossom into a reciprocal relationship, and not as part of any bargain. Conant's mission to London in February 1941 had established the machinery for Anglo-American collaboration, and their combined work on radar—which was given top priority—had paved the way for the ensuing combined effort. At a decisive meeting in October 1941, Roosevelt and Churchill had first broached the issue of a cooperative nuclear effort, and two days later the president wrote him a letter proposing that the undertaking be "coordinated or even jointly conducted." The two nations agreed to pool their uranium research in the genial atmosphere of a June 1942 summit in Hyde Park, New York, FDR's lifelong home, and Churchill was "very glad" when Roosevelt said America would take on the job of manufacturing the munitions. The discussion was in very general terms, however, with no formal written agreement. Afterward, FDR sent a note to Bush that he and the prime minister were "in complete accord," though there is no evidence he ever told anyone exactly what he thought had been settled, and it seems the two may have come away with different impressions of whether their joint enterprise included equal sharing of the results.

The whole tenor of the enterprise altered when the Anglophobe Groves took command in the fall of 1942. The American bomb program was militarized, and with the change in personalities and policies, many of the differences and disagreements between the atomic advisors for the two sides became magnified. A hard-driving administrator, Groves made speed an imperative. With a weapon now in sight, compartmentalization of information was enforced even more rigidly, and the attempts to integrate their experimental efforts became more problematic. When Sir John Anderson, chief administrator of the British atomic program and a member of Churchill's War Cabinet, put forward a plan that August for a uranium gaseous diffusion plant of their own, Bush and Conant rejected it on the grounds that it was too late to add another horse to the already crowded field. They did not have the money or resources to spare. The British found themselves being edged out of the Manhattan Project, a bitter irony given the importance of the *MAUD Report* in bolstering American confidence that the weapon could be made in the first place.

With America doing most of the work and putting up all of the capital, Bush and Conant became increasingly reluctant to share the fruits of their efforts. Too much was up for grabs—the line between research and development was already "nebulous," and there was no common policy on patents, and no plan for the future control of nuclear energy, the supervision of production, or the supply of raw materials. At the same time that Conant was clamping down on security measures for US scientists working on S-1, he resisted the idea of sharing secret data with their English colleagues who were not "essentially responsible to anyone in this country." Possessive of their atomic program, and of the enormous economic and strategic benefits it would yield, they advised Roosevelt to restrict the exchange of technical information except when it was absolutely necessary to advance the military effort. Needless to say, this provoked a good deal of resentment across the pond.

Realizing England was being frozen out, Churchill tried to redress the balance. In late November he sent Wallace Akers, the head of the British uranium program, to Washington to move foward with the discussions on linking their national efforts, only to have Conant stonewall the negotiations. Akers, who took it as a point of national pride that the British be part of the nuclear program they had helped to initiate, insisted that the understanding between Churchill and FDR entitled Britain to unlimited access to the entire American effort. But he had nothing to substantiate his claim but a handful of vague oral and written statements. Conant, aware of how little Akers had to trade, refused to compromise on secrecy. He saw no reason to allow British scientists near the electromagnetic and plutonium processes, which were strictly American operations, and was emphatic that the bomb-design laboratory at Los Alamos should be off limits. His priority was getting a bomb as fast as possible. To the extent the British could help with that, he welcomed their participation, but he was not going to hand over information they might well exploit to great advantage after the war.

By his third meeting with Akers, Conant's initial unease about British demands for a merger of their atomic efforts had intensified. He suspected Akers of having a hidden agenda. A former research director of Imperial Chemical Industries, Akers had demonstrated an unseemly interest in the large-scale production facilities that would be most beneficial in rebuilding Britain's industry. Was he interested in furthering their joint war effort or furthering his small island's postwar prospects? Conant was so difficult and unaccommodating that Akers reported to London that he was "wasting his time" talking to the self-important bureaucrat, dismissing him as little more than a human "post-box" who hoarded policy decisions.

Conant shared his concerns with Bush and then put his views on paper, laying out his argument in a carefully reasoned memorandum on the future of America's nuclear cooperation with Britain. Coldly stated, the president had three choices: he could end the S-1 interchange; permit complete interchange, not only in research but also development and production; or pursue a middle course and allow a carefully restricted exchange. Conant, convinced that Akers was already eyeing the commercial potential of nuclear energy, favored the latter. But he took a characteristically hard line: if the British pressed them to extremes, he advocated cessation.

Bush sent a report to the White House summarizing each country's position, incorporating Conant's analysis almost word for word, and attaching a letter from Akers listing his objections. It landed on the president's desk in late December just as he was recovering from the staggering news of an Anglo-Russian agreement for the exchange of new weapons, negotiations he had not been privy to. Stimson, who was old enough to have seen every trick in the book, regarded the weapons pact as bad policy. It could endanger the secrecy of any future technical discoveries shared with the British. Furious that Churchill was playing politics with the war effort, Roosevelt approved the decision to reduce the flow of scientific secrets to Britain. Roosevelt may have just been looking for an excuse to turn off the spigot, but if so, he found it. Limited interchange became the order of the day.

At the start of 1943, Conant began preparing a memorandum on the new policy of limited interchange, spelling out the strict rules and regulations. Before he had a chance to complete it, Akers learned of its content. Anderson was outraged by Conant's terms and reported to Churchill that the memo had "come as a bombshell and is quite intolerable." Now it was the British scientists who felt alarmed. Conant's recommendations were clearly designed to give the United States a postwar monopoly on atomic energy. Not to be outdone, Akers refused Groves's request that the British send a group of experts to the United States to help with the design and construction of a diffusion plant. He also held off on sending two of Britain's top physicists, James Chadwick and Rudolf Peierls, for the final technical discussions about the bomb. The gambit backfired, however, when Conant and Groves decided they could get by without their assistance and told Akers Britain would have to abide by the new rules. Conant sent Akers another letter inviting Chadwick and Peierls, but by then, all cooperation had broken down. Britain had put pride before the prosecution of war. Interchange ground to a standstill.

By the spring of 1943, distrust of each other's motives, exacerbated by a series of disputes—including the scramble for Canadian uranium ore and heavy water—had made it impossible to ignore the growing competition for control of atomic power during and after the war. As tensions escalated, Churchill became seriously ill with pneumonia in Carthage, Tunisia, and spent ten days in his sickbed fixated on the problem. The deepening rift could have disastrous consequences on their conduct of the rest of the war. He wrote Harry Hopkins, the president's troubleshooter, in late February that the restrictions Conant outlined were correct in principle but violated the spirit of Roosevelt's concept of a coordinated effort. He repeatedly nagged and prodded Hopkins to get the original Hyde Park agreement restored. On April 1 he cabled Roosevelt's top aide that it would be "a sombre decision" if the two countries had to do the work separately. Hopkins consulted Bush and Conant, but they defended their position. The matter dragged on until the end of the month, when Churchill decided to make another visit to Washington.

On May 25, the last day of the Trident Conference, Roosevelt told Churchill what he longed to hear, promising a full scientific interchange and a share in the finished product of the Manhattan Project. The prime minister went home happy, thinking they had at last resolved the arguments between their advisors. For some reason, however, no one saw fit to inform Bush, who spent that afternoon conferring with Frederick Lindemann, now Lord Cherwell, who freely admitted that the main reason Britain wanted access to atomic information was in order to build its own nuclear weapon after the war. It was only when the president invited Bush to lunch at the White House on June 24, a month later, and learned of Cherwell's "astounding" admission about Britain's postwar military plans, that Roosevelt realized he may have overstepped the mark. He kept quiet about his promise to Churchill, perhaps regretting his impulsiveness, and nodded vigorously at Bush's suggestion that they should "sit tight" on British relations.

On July 9 the prime minister again pressed for action. Hopkins reminded Roosevelt he had made a firm commitment to Churchill. After procrastinating for weeks, FDR finally wrote Bush on July 20 that he should "renew, in an inclusive manner, the full exchange of information with the British Government regarding tube alloys."

Meanwhile, Bush had gone to London on submarine business and found himself called on the carpet of 10 Downing Street, confronted by a fuming Churchill. (Neither of them was yet aware of Roosevelt's new instructions.) The PM complained about Conant's memorandum and spent fifteen minutes "bawling him out" on the whole interchange business: "it was unfair, it was unreasonable, it did not make sense, he did not like the arrangement." When Churchill came to the end of his tirade, Bush told him that American atomic energy development fell under the auspices of the army, and he would have to take it up with Secretary Stimson, who happened to be in London. "Very well," snapped Churchill, who had no intention of allowing the Americans off the hook. "We will have a full-dress discussion."

In the interim, FDR's letter had arrived at Bush's OSRD office at 1530

P Street in Washington, where Conant intercepted it. He immediately cabled Bush, but the message was garbled in the coding and decoding. Bush thought it said the president wanted him to "review"—instead of "renew"—the interchange. Since this was more or less what he was doing, he did not alter his course.

The full-dress session, which followed a few days later with Stimson and Bundy in attendance, as well as Lord Cherwell and Sir John Anderson, turned out to be a healthy airing of grievances. When Churchill asserted he was "interested only in fighting this war" and was not trying to strengthen their postwar position, Bush countered with Conant's charge that Akers was already exploring the commercial possibilities of atomic energy. Churchill said nothing but seemed nonplussed. He again insisted he did not "give a damn" about any postwar advantages. After a few more rounds, Churchill changed his tone. He paused, looked at the ceiling, and then said, "I will make you a proposition." He proceeded to reel off a set of perfectly reasonable proposals to be signed by himself and Roosevelt governing the joint atomic enterprise.

When Bush returned to Washington the weekend of July 30, he read Roosevelt's letter ordering him, in effect, to accede to the British position. But in London, Churchill had practically conceded the American position. Convinced a full interchange along the lines of the original agreement would cause "all sorts of trouble" after the war, Bush decided not to follow FDR's instructions to the letter.

He informed Conant of the diplomatic snarl, and the two of them set to work trying to sort it out. They met with Sir John Anderson at the British embassy and spent the next four days turning the suggestions the prime minister had sprung on them into a formal nuclear agreement. Their expanded version began with a Churchillian preamble stressing the importance of Anglo-American cooperation in order to bring the bomb project "to fruition at the earliest possible moment," and followed with pledges that neither would ever use the weapon against the other and would never communicate it to or use it against a third party except after mutual consent. It restored "full and effective collaboration," but included Churchill's disclaimer on postwar commercial advantages, as well as other concessions they had wrested from the British. It also provided for the creation of a combined policy committee to coordinate the work being done by each country and adjudicate conflicts.

Conant declared himself satisfied with the new arrangements. Many misunderstandings had been cleared up, cooperation resumed, and they could once more focus on the war effort. Moreover, American interests had been protected, and the pesky Akers, whom he had taken exception to, was out. The British physicist Sir James Chadwick was made head of the British mission in Washington, and mutual respect and trust restored. If Conant was unduly harsh in his dealings with the British, the historian McGeorge Bundy (son of Harvey), an expert in foreign policy and former national security advisor to both presidents John F. Kennedy and Lyndon B. Johnson, speculates it may have been because of his "heavy sense of responsibility for the secrecy of the program."

It may also have been because, more than the others, he foresaw the danger of allowing the bomb to be used as a diplomatic bargaining chip in the foreign policy disputes between the two nations. The rift indicated the problems that could easily erupt as a result of their failure to spell out clearly, or even to understand fully, their long-term aims. As it was, even though the British negotiators' apprehensions about being supplanted drove them to make misguided demands, the breakdown in relations did not have much of an impact on the American effort. "But if Bush, Conant, and Groves had been less cool and confident than they were," McGeorge Bundy concludes, "it might have had truly damaging results."

All in all, Conant did not think the eight-month interruption had seriously delayed the project. But he could breathe easier now that it was over. Feeling more lighthearted than he had in some time, he wrote Patty that he had had "a most interesting though strenuous week in Washington," adding maddeningly, "when the war is over, remind me to tell you about it."

On Monday, August 9, draft versions of the new nuclear agreement were sent to the two heads of government. Ten days later, at a secret military conference in Quebec, Roosevelt and Churchill met at the Citadelle, overlooking the Old City, and signed the Articles of Agreement governing their secret collaboration on the atomic bomb. They made only one alteration to the section on interchange, naming the members of the new Combined Policy Committee: Bush, Conant, and Stimson were to serve for the United States; Field Marshall Sir John Dill and Colonel J. J. Llewellin, the United Kingdom; and Clarence D. Howe, Canada's Minister of Munitions and Supply, represented his country. "The Quebec Agreement was an effort to resolve a basic conflict of interest, a conflict as intricate and divisive as any in the long annals of Anglo-American discord," wrote Hewlett and Anderson in *The New World*. "Fortunately, the dispute took place behind the ironbound doors of wartime secrecy, and popular passions were not a factor." Even so, the issue had menaced the alliance against the Axis powers, and an understanding was reached only after months of hard bargaining. Both Churchill and Roosevelt knew that "the stake of their diplomacy was a technological breakthrough so revolutionary that it transcended in importance even the bloody work of carrying the war to the heartland of the Nazi foe."

Churchill was magnanimous in reconciliation. He fully accepted the American strategy to launch a major invasion in northern France on May 1, 1944, after having repeatedly wavered on the cross-Channel attack. (The date for the invasion, codenamed Operation Overlord, was later changed to June 6.) As the Quadrant Conference wrapped up, there were still many differences between them on military and political issues, from Britain's efforts to save its empire in the Far East to its postwar relations with Russia, but nonetheless an atmosphere of confidence prevailed. Victory in Europe now seemed within reach.

Conant cabled Patty that the party for the PM was on. He canceled his vacation plans and hurried back to Cambridge. At the last minute, Harvard sent out invitations—marked "Confidential"—stating that an honorary degree would be conferred at an "Academic Meeting" on September 6, but withheld the name of the recipient. No public announcement was permitted, for reasons of security. The censorship extended to the printing of the programs, which were run off by the Harvard University Press late at night. The submitted copy omitted the name of the honoree, which would be filled in later. The only clue as to the identity of the distinguished guest was that the program closed with "God Save the King!"

On September 6 Churchill arrived in Cambridge on a private train from Washington, together with his wife, Clementine, and their youngest daughter, twenty-year-old Mary, who during their prolonged stay in the capital had become the darling of the American press. The party disembarked on a special sidetrack in Allston Yards, where the Conants, accompanied by the state governor, Leverett Saltonstall, greeted them and took them back to the modest yellow house that was their wartime residence. Although he was running a fever, Churchill had spent the overnight journey working on his speech, proudly telling them he had completed it at a quarter to three in the morning. After only a brief rest, he struggled into his Oxford scarlet, borrowed from Princeton for the occasion, and reluctantly abandoned an almost untouched cigar as they hastened him off to Sanders Theatre. At precisely noon, with the fanfare sounded by the Boston Symphony Orchestra, Conant, almost ascetic looking beside the jolly-built British leader, proceeded to the platform while a capacity crowd of 1,400 applauded wildly.

With a slight bow to his audience, Churchill began his speech. "I am once again in academic groves—groves is, I believe, the right word," he said, grinning at his own joke, a sly reference to the name of the American general who was Conant's partner on the secret bomb project. Their names were not yet linked in the newspapers, so most people missed the pun but laughed politely at what they took to be an obscure English witticism. The next day's *New York Herald Tribune* had the PM saying, "I am once again in academic robe—robe is, I believe, the right word."

Churchill went on to tell the story of how in the winter of 1941, when "the blitz was running hard," he had conferred honorary degrees on Ambassador Winant and, in absentia, on Conant, who had rushed back to Washington to plead for the defense of Britain. The night before that academic ceremony, the bombing in Bristol had been heavy, with hundreds killed. But the university officials "pulled on their robes over uniforms begrimed and drenched," Churchill recalled, and presented the diplomas with faultless decorum, and it left him with a very strong impression "of the superiority of man over the forces that can destroy him."

Now that America had risen to become a leading country, he continued, it could not avoid taking a stand against world anarchy. "The price of greatness," he declared, "is responsibility." He then made a moving plea for their two English-speaking countries, bound by "ties of blood and history," to continue their military partnership to preserve the peace once the war was won: "I am here to tell you whatever form your system of world security may take, nothing will work soundly or for long without the united effort of the British and American people. If we are together, nothing is impossible. If we are divided, all will fail."

After the ceremony, Conant led Churchill to the steps of the Memorial Church, where he greeted a cheering throng of nearly ten thousand, including more than six thousand army and navy cadets and officers in parade formation, and almost as many students, faculty, staff members, and guests. The afternoon was stiflingly hot, and the PM wisely ditched his academic gown. He was now a familiar figure in his short black jacket, gray trousers, gray waistcoat, and polka-dot bow tie, a cane in one hand and the other flashing the famous victory sign. The day was long and exhausting, and Conant was grateful to be done with what he called his "national public relations job." A photographer had caught him and the prime minister side by side, and as Churchill made the V sign, Conant was pushing back the sleeve of his jacket to steal a surreptitious glance at his watch. *Time* magazine observed that the pose was "typical" of both men.

Churchill was visibly touched by his reception. At the end of the ceremony, he stumped eagerly into the living room, where Clementine and Patty were waiting, and, turning straight to his wife, asked, "How did I do, Mother?" She told him that the speech was "one of his best," and he beamed at them all with pleasure. He charmed the college trustees, who were once again favorably inclined to Conant, who got the credit for the surprise visit. It would long be remembered in Harvard history and reaffirmed his own reputation as the country's leading educational statesman, who, like the English historian, had risen to the challenge of the war and helped martial the country's defenses in the cause of freedom.

It was no coincidence that Churchill chose Harvard's stage to proclaim that "the empires of the future are the empires of the mind." To Conant, his meaning was clear: "The twentieth-century struggles over ideology, technology, and markets" had replaced the nineteenth-century wars over territory. In the fierce struggles of the future, whether for profit or aggrandizement, weapons would be of prime importance. Self-preservation demanded they confront the nuclear age standing "shoulder to shoulder."

Bush told Conant he was also feeling encouraged. Based on what he had heard in London, he was convinced the technological battle in the Atlantic had reached a turning point. Thanks to OSRD advances in radar and sonar, and new tactics and techniques, they were making inroads against the deadly German submarine. (The code breakers at Bletchley Park, a secret decryption facility outside London, had also reworked the British convoy code so that the Germans could no longer pinpoint their locations.) The Allied high command had white-knuckled it through the worst winter of the war, afraid the U-boat campaign might sever virtually all communication between America and Europe. But advances in subsurface weaponry now had the Germans on the run. In the last ten days of March, U-boat sinkings of cargo ships had dropped dramatically by two thirds. With each passing month, as the Rad Lab got more devices into the field, the numbers were continuing to decline.

This was especially heartening to Conant, as his son Jim, who had earned his bachelor's degree and naval ROTC reserve commission from the University of Michigan at nineteen, was on active duty with the submarine service. The last he had heard, Jim had been assigned to the USS *Halibut* and was in a "safe portion" of the Pacific. But the *Halibut* was a sub hunter, and it would not be long before he went back out on patrol. Conant did not tell his wife that it had one of the highest casualty rates in the armed forces: one in five submariners that went to sea did not return. She was already beside herself with worry, and that spring had thrown herself into volunteer work with the injured at the Chelsea Naval Hospital outside Boston, where Joe Kennedy's son, Jack, Harvard class of 1940, was recovering from back surgery for an injury he had sustained when his boat, PT-109, was attacked by a Japanese destroyer in August 1943. Many Harvard wives were helping out by providing coffee and doughnuts and a welcome diversion from the dreary hospital routine. But the twice-weekly stint as a sketch artist in the psychiatric wing soon proved too much for Patty. Seeing so many trembling, emotionally fractured boys left her upset and depressed for days afterward, and Conant finally put an end to it.

In an attempt to keep her spirits up, Conant reported from Washington that Bush was "most optimistic" the war would soon be over:

"[His] feeling is that Germany will be licked in six months . . . All agree that it will take 6 to 18 mos. longer for Japan. I stick to Xmas '45 for the entire show. Only two things can possibly save the Germans, anyhow, one is a miracle, the other Joe Stalin. And personally I'm not betting that either savior will appear!"

That "miracle" was much on his mind when he boarded the Chief in Chicago in late November for the sixteen-hour trip to Lamy, a lonely whistle-stop in New Mexico, where an army car would be waiting to take him up the long, torturous route to Los Alamos. Groves would not allow any of the key members of S-1 to travel by plane because of the risk of a crash. Conant, who loved trains, did not mind the inconvenience nearly as much as Bush and Lawrence did. To the astonishment of his colleagues, he had mastered the art of sleeping sitting bolt upright in a coach and would arrive well rested even when it was impossible to get a Pullman berth.

Now that the atomic partnership with the British had been patched up, he was taking a delegation from Tube Alloys on a cross-country tour of the large-scale laboratories. They had already been to Oak Ridge, where Lawrence's electromagnetic separation process was proving to be painfully slow, producing only tiny amounts of enriched uranium, and raising concerns about whether he would ever be able to deliver enough material in time. The other uranium separation process, gaseous diffusion, was becoming more important by the minute, and they needed all the help they could get from the British in designing and building the new plant at Oak Ridge, as well as a giant complex at Hanford, Washington.

The first group of scientists the British had sent over was small in number—about twenty—but large in talent. Perusing the list, Conant noticed that only a handful were actually English born and bred, and knew that would aggravate Groves. Nevertheless, they would be of tremendous assistance. Rudolf Peierls, whose pioneering work had contributed to the *MAUD Report*, was sent straight to New York to consult with the isotope-plant designers at Columbia before moving to Los Alamos. His group also included Otto Frisch, as well as a shy, courteous young German theoretician named Klaus Fuchs. Mark Oliphant and a half dozen who worked under him were assigned to the electromagnetic operation. Conant worked with Sir James Chadwick and Groves to arrange their transfer to different parts of the Manhattan Project, putting them to work wherever they would be most useful.

It was also under British auspices that Niels Bohr and his physicist son, Aage, would soon be making a trip to the bomb laboratory under a cloak of secrecy. The elder Bohr had barely escaped from Nazi-occupied Denmark, a now-legendary feat that began with him hiding on a fishing boat bound for Sweden and then being smuggled into England in the bomb bay of a Mosquito fighter, briefly losing consciousness when he failed to hear the pilot's instructions to use the oxygen mask as the plane gained altitude. The fifty-eight-year-old physicist arrived in London on October 5, 1943, none the worse for wear, began a series of debriefings about the German bomb program, and was promptly appointed a consultant to Tube Alloys. Within weeks, he was on his way to America. Oppenheimer hoped that the eminent Nobel laureate, revered as the wise old man of nuclear physics, would be an inspiring presence for the young project scientists. Groves, however, worried that the great Dane, already publicly identified as the inventor of "atomic explosions," and an important figure in the Allied war effort, would attract exactly the kind of attention they had to avoid if they were to keep the laboratory's existence secret from the Germans.

The approach to Los Alamos always took Conant's breath away. As the twisting road slowly wound its way up the mesa, the terrain changed from the vast, sparse red and brown southwestern desert to pleasant aspen forests, and in the distance was a splendid view of the majestic snowcapped Sangre de Cristo Mountains across thirty miles of the Middle Rio Grande Valley. Where the road leveled, there was a tall wooden sentry tower with a small guardhouse built into the base, which constituted the first checkpoint for the army post. More checkpoints followed. Conant's reception on arrival was not notable because the security guards were alerted in advance to expect him. Each time, he produced his identification and gate pass, and once cleared was waved through. The high fence and barbed wire brought back memories of the year he had spent in the primitive military compound outside Cleveland, as did the rows of barracks and ugly, raw look of the place.

Oppenheimer and the first group of scientists had gone out to Los Alamos in mid-March to begin setting up the laboratory and establish a rudimentary community on the desolate plateau. When they went up to "the Hill" to inspect the construction site, it was a mess. The army crews were behind schedule, and the bulk of the housing, along with the main administration building (Tech Main) and five laboratories were unfinished. The most basic equipment they needed to get to work was either not ready or had not arrived. Even food was in short supply. On top of that, one unreliable and noisy Forest Service line provided the only means of communication with the project office in Santa Fe. Any conversation more complicated than a few shouted instructions required a face-to-face meeting, involving an eighty-mile round-trip commute on the execrable road. But they had no choice except to make the best of it, bedding down in nearby ranches at night and camping out on the mesa by day, sustained by boxed lunches and Bunsen burner coffee.

Vividly recalling his miserable first few months in the Mousetrap, when hot meals and showers had been hard to come by, Conant assured the unhappy scientists that conditions would improve soon. In truth, their comfort did not overly concern him, except to the extent that it affected their performance. He worried that Oppenheimer underestimated the difficulty of organizing and running what amounted to a small town, complete with all the usual problems of providing housing, sewage, electricity, and fresh water, only compounded by the fact that it was completely cut off from the outside world, and no one could know they were there. He worried that the somewhat ethereal Berkeley physicist would be overwhelmed by all the mundane difficulties and housekeeping duties, that the scientific work would suffer, and he would fall behind the schedule they had set for him. Mostly, Conant worried that the project would end in failure.

It did not help matters that the laboratory's associate director, Edward Condon, whom Groves had urged on Oppenheimer to help ease the administrative burden, and keep the peace between the scientists and soldiers, up and quit after only six weeks. While his letter of resignation never gave the real reasons for his departure, it seemed he was primarily motivated by the belief that the project would not be successful. Neither Conant nor Groves had any tolerance for naysayers. They were both acutely aware of what would happen to them after the war if the $500 million investment went belly-up, and often joked grimly among themselves that they should consider purchasing homes near Capitol Hill, because if the bomb did not work, they would both be condemned to spend the rest of their lives testifying before angry congressional committees.

But remarkably, by the April conference at Los Alamos, which marked the official opening of the laboratory, Oppie had assembled some thirty scientists, and they made rapid progress in laying out the theoretical and experimental problems and deciding what needed to be done. Robert Serber, Oppie's former student and frequent collaborator, gave a series of introductory lectures on the state of knowledge about the nuclear bomb, which he called "the gadget." It was not that much. He covered it in five concise hour-long lectures, summarizing the theoretical calculations and experimental data, and giving an overview of the main areas for study: energy release, chain reaction, critical size, fission cross sections, possible ways of assembling fissionable materials, and damage. He also briefly discussed the hydrogen bomb, dubbed "the Super," and the far more powerful explosion that might result from a thermonuclear reaction in deuterium, a possibility that had emerged during the Berkeley study group. Serber's tutorials were so good, they were immediately compiled and mimeographed, and a copy, known as *The Los Alamos Primer*, was required reading for all new recruits.

Oppenheimer, on Rabi's advice, organized the laboratory into separate divisions, a system that had worked extremely well at the MIT Rad Lab. Rabi refused to join the bomb project but agreed to act as a senior consultant, and he came out with Robert Bacher to help them block out the program of research. The conference members created four divisions to tackle the

technical work: Bethe took charge of theoretical physics; Bacher took experimental physics; Joseph W. Kennedy, a twenty-six-year-old disciple of Seaborg's, took chemistry and metallurgy. Because of Kennedy's extreme youth,
Groves and Conant provided backup in the form of Charles A. Thomas,
an industrial engineer with years of experience at the Monsanto Chemical
Company, who would coordinate the work in the division with the other
related Manhattan Project efforts. British-born Cyril Smith, another veteran
industrial scientist, was responsible for the metallurgical work. Since none
of the Berkeley physicists had any experience with explosives, they brought
in Commander William S. "Deak" Parsons, an outstanding naval officer
who had spent much of his career on battleship gunnery duties and devoted
the last few years to developing and field-testing the proximity fuse, to take
charge of the ordnance work.

The original idea was to make an atom bomb based on the "gun method":
an arrangement by which one mass of fissionable uranium was fired, using
a miniature gun, at another mass of fissionable uranium, which served as
a target. As long as these two hemispheres were apart, the bomb was inert.
When the projectile and target came together, they would exceed critical
mass, and the bomb would explode. The assumption was that the design
of the bomb would be essentially the same whether the fissionable material
was uranium-235 or plutonium made in a pile. Even though much less was
known about the new element—for example, it had not yet been established
that fissioning Pu-239 emitted enough neutrons for an explosive chain reaction—it held out great promise. A plutonium bomb required less fissionable
material, and it seemed possible they would be able to produce Pu-239 more
rapidly than U-235. While Fermi's successful chain reaction in Chicago had
demonstrated that the basic nuclear process in fission could create an explosion, many experiments had to be carried out to confirm their deductions
about the nature and speed of the reaction, size of the critical mass, and
destructive effect. Any one of these factors could affect the success of the
weapon.

A second way of making a bomb had been proposed by Seth H. Neddermeyer, a thirty-six-year-old Caltech physicist who offered theoretical
analysis that demonstrated the feasibility of the "implosion method." In his
strategy, high explosives were grouped in a spherical shell around a solid
core of fissionable material. When compressed symmetrically with great
force, the active material was squeezed together until it reached a critical
mass and detonated. He was unable to convince his fellow physicists of its

merits, which was not surprising, since it involved a far more difficult design and had never been done before. Oppenheimer polled his men and found most opposed to allotting laboratory resources to implosion, which meant veering off into an unknown area where they might encounter all kinds of obstacles and insoluble problems. Parsons doubted implosion would ever be reliable enough for field use. The gun assembly was the sounder method and involved tried-and-true technology. Oppenheimer agreed but at the same time felt they could not neglect such a novel approach. Neddermeyer, who was something of a loner, was left to pursue his intriguing idea on his own.

Despite all the gaps in their understanding, the physicists were very confident when it came to the theory. The gun model seemed fairly straightforward, and they anticipated that the work ahead would essentially be, as Bethe put it, "engineering."

At the start, Oppenheimer had envisioned a small, dedicated bomb laboratory staffed by fifty scientists, with perhaps up to fifty assistants, supported by an equal number of technical, shop, and administrative employees. But even before the spring planning sessions were over, it was apparent he had considerably underestimated the size of the job. The scientists found it hard to explain the need for all the costly changes to Groves, who was obviously insecure around so many brilliant minds, and was more obnoxious and oppressive than ever. Even though he had them under lock and key, he vehemently objected to Oppenheimer's weekly colloquia, where classified topics were discussed openly among members of the laboratory. The dispute quickly blew up into a full-fledged crisis. It took two letters from the White House, one drafted by Conant, to convince the incarcerated scientists that Groves was not a petty tyrant and that they had to tolerate the extraordinary restrictions. Oppenheimer, who fought hard for free discussion, succeeded in preserving the democratic organization of the laboratory. In deference to the security-conscious Groves, however, he agreed to limit those eligible for the colloquia to qualified members of the laboratory.

Although they could see that Groves was dedicated and efficient, he annoyed his minions with his displays of egotism and insistence on throwing his not inconsiderable weight around. Early on at Los Alamos, he got up on a podium and announced, "The reason why I am here today is to introduce you to your boss's boss's boss," meaning himself. The young graduate-student theoreticians—the average age at Los Alamos was all of twenty-five—such as Richard Feynman and Philip Morrison, rolled their eyes at his posturing. Conant, hoping to lessen the friction, created another bureaucratic buffer between the general and his sensitive charges. He suggested to Groves that it might improve his working relationship with the laboratory staff if he appointed a committee to review their progress. That way any suggestion would come from their peers and would be readily accepted, whereas if it came from him "it might be regarded as interference." Groves, who had no objection to committees as long as he appointed them, went along with the idea.

The Review Committee gave the Los Alamos research program the thumbs-up on May 10. After going over their report, Conant and Groves decided that the investigation of the theoretical aspects of the "superbomb" should continue—its potential was too great to overlook—but the atomic bomb, as the practical military weapon, had priority. They also concurred that chemistry/metallurgy and ordnance were the least developed and needed to be pushed. Kennedy's division was ordered to take over the purification process for plutonium—by which it was transformed into a metal and refined to a high level of purity to ensure it would reach critical mass and not melt down—an arduous, multistage task that would require additional facilities as well as a large force of chemists, analysts, and assistants. Then Parsons announced that he would need his own laboratory and ballistics range, along with a team of two hundred ordnance experts. These changes effectively doubled the size of Los Alamos. They were just the first in a series of expansions that added greatly to Conant's indigestion in the months to come.

By his November 1943 visit, several crucial questions had been answered. Compton had made good on his promise to master the process for separating plutonium from the contents of the pile. In July Glenn Seaborg delivered the first microscopic speck of plutonium, detectable only by its radioactivity, which he brought to Los Alamos from Chicago in his suitcase. From only traces of the new element, they were able to conduct the first nuclear experiments that established that not only did plutonium emit neutrons on fusion, but also the number was greater than in uranium. Finally, here was proof of plutonium's "intrinsic explosibility." They all breathed a huge sigh of relief. Conant and Groves were especially thankful because it justified the massive $350 million plutonium pile already under construction at Hanford, Washington. Because of the need to optimize every approach, they had rushed ahead on the expensive reactor without waiting for the studies to be completed. The go-ahead signal had been given on scant evidence, and Conant had sweated the huge sums riding on what amounted to Compton and company's confident bet.

That fall, Conant received another piece of news that added to his peace of mind. Robert Wilson, a young Lawrence protégé who had secured the use of Harvard's cyclotron for Los Alamos and now headed up the cyclotron group, confirmed that most of the neutrons emitted from fissioning U-235 were "fast" neutrons, generated in less than one billionth of a second. This was evidence that the neutrons were being transformed at an unbelievable speed. It provided ample margin for an efficient explosive reaction. Success of the gun-assembly weapon was now a near certainty.

With the basic physics out of the way, they could get on with the nuts-and-bolts work of designing the bomb itself. Parsons immediately set to work on a plutonium gun. Tests on the small amounts of plutonium available had shown that it had a much higher rate of spontaneous fission than uranium; consequently, they would need a much faster gun, or there was a chance it might predetonate, reducing the bomb's efficiency. They needed to develop a miniature, high-velocity cannon that could fire the subcritical projectile mass into the target sphere fast enough to keep the weapon from fizzling out, but at the same time was small enough to fit into a bomb casing—which in turn had to fit into the belly of a B-29 bomber. To achieve a more compact mechanism with greater muzzle velocity, they could try welding two guns together. Once the designers got the plutonium gun to perform, the uranium model would be comparatively simple. Taking over one of the old homesteads, called Anchor Ranch, Parsons and his team began an elaborate testing program to perfect the gun requirements. Since these were not your run-of-the-mill howitzers, and no military arsenal made anything that suited their purposes, he got the Naval Gun Factory in Washington, DC, to fabricate them from strong high-alloy steel.

While they waited for the guns, the alternative way to detonate plutonium suggested earlier by Seth Neddermeyer suddenly took on a new importance. The Hungarian mathematician Johnny von Neumann, who happened to be visiting Los Alamos that autumn, was convinced that not only could implosion be made into a precision weapon, but also that the higher implosion velocities would eliminate any concerns about predetonation. After going over the research with his fellow Hungarian Edward Teller, von Neumann suggested that this method of compression might also require less plutonium. If there was any chance that a bomb might be ready earlier and require less active material, Conant and Groves could not afford to pass it up. Conant knew there was only one man capable of leading the experimental effort into the complex implosion technique: George Kistiakowsky, chief of the NDRC's explosives division. Kistiakowsky had resisted Oppenheimer's pleas to join the Los Alamos lab full-time because he wanted to work only on weapons that would make a difference in the current war. But in the end, he allowed Conant, whose opinion was the only one that "really mattered," to persuade him to move to the mesa.

Parsons, free from the burden of nuclear research, began preparations for the combat use of the bomb. He assembled another ordnance team, headed by Norman Ramsey, one of Rabi's talented radar crew, and began making arrangements for full-scale drop tests of two basic bomb models with a modified B-29 at Muroc Army Air Base in California. The tests would allow them to obtain valuable ballistic data and determine the best procedures for dropping the bomb. For security reasons, Ramsey called the test dummies the "Thin Man" for the gun assembly, and the "Fat Man" for the implosion weapon. In his report, he noted that during their phone conversations the army air forces officers tried to make it sound as though they were "modifying a plane to carry Roosevelt (the Thin Man) and Churchill (the Fat Man)."

CHAPTER 16

One Fell Stroke

The essence of war is not slaughter but impressing your will upon the enemy.

—JBC to Vannevar Bush

As the Anglo-American high command perfected its plans for the invasion of Europe, Conant continued to face the very real possibility that the Germans would produce an atomic bomb before the Allies could. For all his expressions of optimism, he had far too much respect for Werner Heisenberg and the physicists at the Kaiser-Wilhelm Institute to count them out for a moment. Until he had proof to the contrary, he had to assume the Nazis were working on their nuclear program with the same feverish intensity as the Manhattan Project scientists.

What kept him awake at night was how little was known about Germany's progress toward a nuclear weapon. If nothing else, it made it impossible to estimate realistically how much time they had left to complete their own project. Their ignorance was a thorn in Conant's side that kept him unsettled and constantly on edge. He took some comfort in the idea that the enemy must be encountering the same baffling problems, observing in a private memorandum that "at least every difficulty that develops means probably an equal difficulty for the Germans!" His main concern was that the Nazis would stumble on to simple solutions to puzzles that Los Alamos was still struggling with; solutions that would propel them over the finish line first.

For months, the Reich had harped on its plan to use a secret scientific weapon in retaliation for Allied air attacks. On December 3, 1943, a Berlin radio broadcast declared that Germany would end the war "by one fell, drastic stroke," adding, "Mankind is not far from the point where it can blow up half the globe." Some of the refugee scientists at the Met Lab and Los Alamos were convinced the Germans were preparing to use atomic bombs against the United States or, more likely, England. One even urged Groves to make an official broadcast warning the American people of the danger of a nuclear attack—a possibility the general considered sufficiently remote that he rejected doing any such thing. "Although this was sometimes hard on our nerves," Groves acknowledged later, "it did keep us from ever becoming overconfident."

When the Manhattan Project assumed responsibility for all atomic intelligence in the fall of 1943, Conant and Groves agreed that their first priority must be to remain as informed as possible on the danger posed by German science. It was absolutely essential that they know what the other side might be capable of if their backs were to the wall. The steady stream of rumors from behind enemy lines stoked everyone's fears and suspicions but provided few details about the status of the German atomic program. (The Japanese did not concern them, not because they doubted their technical competence but because it would be too great an undertaking for their industry.) Early in the war, evidence of Germany's interest in making a bomb had surfaced when the Nazis occupied Norway in 1940 and seized the Norsk Hydro plant at Rjukan near Vemork, about sixty miles west of Oslo. The Germans turned the complex into a heavy water operation, and by September 1942, it was estimated that they were shipping 120 kilograms of the enriched water back to Berlin each month for experimental use. If they were able to stockpile enough heavy water, Germany could conceivably produce the plutonium it needed for an atomic bomb.

At the time, Conant and Bush recommended that Rjukan be bombed, but the British rejected the idea because they already had a secret sabotage operation in the works. Unaware of this, Conant persisted, and on December 9, 1942, he wrote Groves that the presumed German head start of a year or even eighteen months persuaded him that "every effort should be made by MID [Military Intelligence Division], ONI [Office of Naval Intelligence] and OSS, as well as the British Intelligence service, to obtain clues as to the German progress and their plans, with the view . . . to bombing the plants and laboratories where such work is in progress," emphasizing that they should "strain every nerve on the countermeasure side, which includes espionage and bombing."

The British struck first, with their Special Operations Executive (SOE) launching an extremely risky assault mission to destroy the Norsk Hydro heavy water plant on October 12, 1942. Bad weather doomed the already dangerous assignment: the two gliders transporting the British paratroopers crashed en route, killing many of the occupants and injuring the rest. The survivors were all captured by the Germans and executed. The attack was an unmitigated disaster, ending with a total of thirty-eight dead and alerting Nazi officials to the Allies' keen interest in heavy water. Determined to take out the plant, the British carried out an even more daring assault on February 17, 1943, with a nine-man team cross-country skiing into the site, scaling the icy ravine, and blowing up the heavy water electrolysis chambers. Although the British deemed the operation a success, the Germans repaired the damage with surprising speed and reactivated the plant.

The British operation, which Conant and Groves learned about by reading news dispatches from Oslo, caused them "some headaches," the general recalled, clearly aggrieved. One Swedish newspaper reported the successful sabotage and then went on to speculate about the importance of heavy water in attempts to break down the atom. The story was picked up by the London papers and then by the *New York Times*, which ran it with the lurid headline "Nazi 'Heavy Water' Looms as Weapon." This was the last thing the security-conscious Manhattan Project leaders needed.

Worried that the Norsk plant would soon resume production, Conant and Groves kept up constant pressure, which led the American Eighth Air Force to conduct a major bombing raid on Rjukan in November 1943. Even though it managed only two direct hits on the electrolysis plant, the Germans believed more attacks would follow, and dismantled the setup and moved it within the safety of their own borders. A few months later, a ferry carrying the remaining forty drums of Rjukan heavy water—roughly 3,600 gallons—destined for German research laboratories was sunk by commandoes, sending the precious cargo to the bottom of a mountain lake in Norway.

Eager to strike another blow against the Nazi bomb program, Groves asked Conant and Bush to investigate all the power plants in Germany that might be involved in heavy water production. When this task proved unwieldy—there were too many facilities that could easily be diverted to weapons work—Conant compiled a new list of important "S-1 targets" in Germany for army air forces bombers. Alarmed by new intelligence reports warning of a "German process" that sounded very much like atomic fission, he switched his attention from factories and power plants to research centers. Drawing on his intimate knowledge of the country, Conant identified the names of leading German scientists and the locations of chemistry laboratories where they were thought to be working on nuclear physics. At the top of his list were the Berlin laboratories of Otto Hahn and Werner Heisenberg, which he knew would be the beating heart of any German bomb effort.

On June 24, 1943, he wrote Bush that "the chances of seriously interfering with the German war effort by the demolition of targets 1 and 2 are very considerable." He also singled out the other branches of the Kaiser Wilhelm Institute spread throughout Germany as key sites, and, by extension, the scientists who ran them, but they were not as critical and could be attacked when convenient. Later the same day, Bush met with Roosevelt and told him the German targets had been pinpointed and "arrangements are now under way."

The focus on Heisenberg intensified with Bohr's arrival in the United States on December 6. He made it his personal mission to spread the word that the Germans were on a path to a bomb, and using Heisenberg's approach might be within reach of success. He had in his possession a drawing, given to him by his former friend and colleague in the fall of 1941, that he believed was evidence the Germans had figured out how to produce a chain reaction. During the two weeks he spent in Washington, Bohr confided his fears to British diplomats as well as to Supreme Court Justice Felix Frankfurter, who quietly conveyed them to the president. On December 27 Bohr and his son took the train to Chicago, where they were met by Groves. During the two-day trip to New Mexico, Bohr talked incessantly about German developments to Groves, who was seriously alarmed by the drawing he showed him.

On December 31 Oppenheimer convened an emergency meeting of the project's top scientists to consider whether Heisenberg's primitive sketch could be interpreted as a design for a German atomic bomb. The crude picture showed a box with horizontal lines or sticks coming out of the top that suggested control rods. "It was clearly a drawing of a reactor," recalled Bethe. "When we saw it, our conclusion was that these Germans were totally crazy—did they want to throw a reactor down on London?"* While no complete assurance could be given, Oppenheimer informed Groves that their considered opinion was that the arrangement of the materials suggested by the drawing would be "a quite useless military weapon." But the physicist Jeremy Bernstein, who has made a careful study of the Heisenberg sketch, maintains that the Germans were far from crazy. "If the people at Los Alamos had realized—which they didn't—that the Germans knew about plutonium, their concern about the German program, which was always considerable, might well have approached the panic level."

At a time of war, fear is contagious. Bohr's apprehensions, expressed repeatedly, accrued credibility and added to the project leaders' sense of urgency and concern that the Germans might be winning the race to the bomb. In late 1943 Groves summoned his security chief, Colonel John Lansdale, to his office and told him he had received a proposal that an attempt should be made to kidnap or assassinate Heisenberg. He said he had been advised that the removal of the brilliant German physicist would hurt or even cripple the Nazi bomb program and asked bluntly, "What do you think?"

Although Lansdale told him he thought any attack along those lines would almost certainly fail, Groves could not let go of the idea of disrupting Germany's atomic program by going after the nuclear scientist, according to Thomas Powers, author of a fascinating account of Heisenberg's wartime role. Groves had seen Conant's target list, and it coincided with similar ideas suggested by refugee scientists determined to prevent Hitler from getting his hands on a bomb. By late 1943, Groves and Bush were ready to make the case to Major General George Strong, the army's assistant chief of staff for intelligence, that an important goal of bombing the Berlin laboratories would be "the killing of scientific personnel employed therein"—meaning Hahn and Heisenberg.

Conant, according to Powers, "very probably knew" of the plot to eliminate Heisenberg, which over a period of months escalated from kidnapping to assassination, received high-level approval, and was assigned to the OSS. There is no record of whether he condoned the scheme that a year later led to an agent being sent to Zurich with instructions to shoot Heisenberg while he was delivering a physics lecture "if so much as a word suggested that the

---

* Aage Bohr has always disputed the claim that Heisenberg gave his father a drawing, and Jeremy Bernstein speculates that it may have been Bohr's idea of a reactor based on his discussions with Heisenberg and the German physicist J. Hans D. Jensen.

Wunderwaffe ["wonder weapon"] up Hitler's sleeve was an atomic bomb." Heisenberg never mentioned anything related to the bomb in his talk on December 18, 1944, so no action was taken, although the original proposal led to the German physicist being arrested on May 2, 1945.*

As Powers points out, it seems extraordinary that Conant and Bush, as civilian scientists, should have been asked by the military to name their co-equals in Germany with the express purpose of having them killed. Yet if there was a chance that eliminating one or two individuals could slow or halt the enemy's progress to a weapon, how could they do otherwise? Neither man ever wanted their involvement in the cold-blooded campaign to disrupt the German atomic program known, and both omitted it from their memoirs. It was not their proudest hour. But in the heat of war, with all the uncertainty about the imminence of a German bomb, "almost any effort to stop Heisenberg and Hitler would have been fully justifiable," writes Powers. "All we can say with fairness at this remove is that strange things may seem reasonable to men who know only enough to fear the worst."

As the plans for the June 1944 invasion of France began to take shape, another serious threat emerged: the possibility that the Germans might try to disrupt the Normandy landings by laying down a radioactive barrier along the beaches and approach routes, rendering them unsafe. If the Germans used ordinary explosive bombs containing radioactive material, and the Allied forces were unable to neutralize the contaminated area quickly, it could expose a large number of their troops, as well as civilians, to excessive radiation.

Groves worried that such a terrifying attack would have "disastrous results," quite apart from the possibility it could trigger a major panic across the Allied countries. As D-day drew nearer, however, he was no closer to reaching a decision about what to do about the problem, and all the conflicting advice he had been given left him no better off than when he started. "This was a time I was most appreciative of Conant's sound counsel," he recalled, noting that the calm, deliberate Yankee was "never one to become unduly excited over the wild conjectures that the fertile minds of some of

---

* Heisenberg was detained along with other German nuclear scientists at a British manor house called Farm Hill for six months and interrogated about how close they came to making an atomic bomb. Freed in 1946, he returned to Germany, where he lived and worked for another thirty years. The question of whether he attempted to build a bomb for Hitler, or consciously obstructed his country's atomic program, remains a subject of debate.

our people could produce, almost faster, it seemed, than we could disprove them."

Groves and Marshall asked Conant to head a special S-1 committee to assess the danger and develop countermeasures should the Germans engage in radiological warfare. In May 1943, Conant recruited Arthur Compton and Harold Urey to assist him, and together they conducted an intensive study of the use of radioactive materials as an offensive military weapon. In July, Conant submitted a preliminary report: "It now seems extremely probable that it will be possible to produce by means of a self-sustaining pile large quantities of radioactive materials with varying half-lives in the order of magnitude of twenty days." A week's output, he thought, distributed over two square miles, could incapacitate much of the population and necessitate evacuation. Compton was so frightened by the specter of a radiological attack that he urged that "we should be ready to 'reply in kind' . . . before Christmas if this is considered military strategy."

When Oppenheimer heard about Conant's inquiry, he told Groves that he and Fermi had already been working on an idea to poison German foodstuffs, probably a reference to beta-strontium, a highly toxic radioactive by-product of fission. He then wrote Fermi that he had received approval to talk to Conant about "the application that seemed to us so promising," but added with chilling pragmatism that it would not make sense to pursue it further "unless we can poison food sufficient to kill half a million men." Oppenheimer pursued the plan with Teller, but eventually the scheme ran into too many problems, and there is no mention of it in Conant's final report.

While he and his fellow committee members ultimately concluded the danger of a radiological attack was low—Conant, in contrast with the others, considered it "extremely unlikely"—they still recommended taking some precautionary measures to minimize its effects. Groves ordered these preparations as part of the highly secret Operation Peppermint, which provided for shipping portable Geiger counters to Britain, training officers in the use of detection equipment, and establishing channels for reporting any incidents promptly to avoid a panic. Army medical personnel in the European theater were instructed to report any symptoms of "unknown etiology." Along with signal and air officers, they were also told to look out for the unexplained fogging or blackening of photographic or X-ray film, a telltale sign of radiation exposure.

Not wanting to unduly alarm General Dwight D. Eisenhower, the supreme commander of the Allied Expeditionary Force, Groves instructed his aide,

Major Arthur V. Peterson, to acquaint him with the possibility the Germans could produce extremely effective contaminating agents, and could employ them without prior warning, but to tread softly and "emphasize our belief that they would not be used and the invasion plans should be made accordingly."

Groves's confidence in Conant's "sound counsel" is breathtaking. What if he was wrong? In the course of developing plutonium, the Germans were bound to have discovered the hazardous by-products produced by their reactors and to consider using them as a weapon to combat an invading army. Conant's opinion that they would not deploy these unreliable munitions was, at best, an educated guess, based on his analysis of the practical obstacles involved in handling radioactive material, and uniformly dispersing it over a designated area. But there were many possible forms of distribution, including spraying a persistent poison from low-flying planes or setting it off in land mines, which could also render streets, airfields, and rail yards uninhabitable. Operation Peppermint was concerned primarily with detection; the actual defensive measures were minimal.

Groves, of course, checked with Bush, who as usual sized up the situation much the same way Conant did. He had initially worried that radioactive contaminants or nerve agents might be used in combination with long-range rockets or V-1s—aerial photographs of the French coast had revealed large installations that looked like launch sites—but wrote Groves that he had come to the conclusion that it was too difficult and would not be an effective method. (Bush and Conant similarly believed it unlikely the Germans would initiate a gas attack, given the Allies had achieved air superiority, though a sixty-day supply of chemical bombs was sent to depots in England in case retaliatory operations had to be mounted.) Still, Eisenhower had to be informed. Bush, who traveled to England to brief him in person, had the unenviable task of explaining that while they had more or less ruled out the possibility of a toxic payload on Omaha Beach, there was still a good chance missiles might rain down on Plymouth and Bristol, the main staging areas for the invasion. "You scare the hell out of me," Eisenhower said to Bush when he was done, no doubt realizing it was his men who would pay the price if it turned out the scientists did not know their stuff.

On May 11, 1944, Eisenhower wrote Groves that he had carefully reviewed the situation, but since the Combined Chiefs of Staff had not officially brought it to his notice, he was assuming "on the present available intelligence, the enemy will not implement this project." Owing to the importance of maintaining secrecy "to avoid a possible scare," he had passed on the information to a very limited number of people, and no US or British commander participating in Overlord had been told. Moreover, he had not taken enough precautionary steps to "adequately counter enemy action of this nature."

When Groves read Eisenhower's letter, it must have given him a moment's pause. "I knew our advice had been fully accepted," he recalled in his memoir, "and that nothing more could be done except to pray that we had not made a mistake." Groves had assumed enormous responsibility in connection with the invasion, neglecting to inform the Combined Chiefs of Staff or US Joint Chiefs of Staff of the threat. It gave him, Conant, and the handful who knew about it "some bad hours" until they learned the Allied troops had made good their landing without encountering any radioactive interference.

Bush and Stimson were in a car headed for Capitol Hill when the first V-1 rocket was fired at London on June 13, in retaliation for the successful D-day landings the week before. After they had listened to the news on the radio, a dramatic report about the new kind of German flying bomb that had killed eight civilians and left a crater on a London street, Stimson put his hand on Bush's knee and asked, "Well, Van, how do you feel now?" But they were both thinking the same thing: the payload of the vengeance bomb had been a conventional explosive. No radiological products. No poison gas. "Very much relieved," was all Bush said.

The pressure did not let up that spring. At the same time he was trying to deal with the potential threat of radiological weapons on Allied territory and troops overseas, Conant had to cope with a series of discouraging setbacks on his own end. The plutonium manufactured in Oak Ridge, which finally began to reach Los Alamos in tangible quantities in early 1944, revealed for the first time an isotope with undesirable nuclear properties: plutonium-240, a strong spontaneous fissioner. Their problems reached a peak when Emilio Segrè's tests on plutonium confirmed their worst fears: it was not pure enough. The plutonium would fizzle out in a predetonation. Despite all their efforts and the development of the high-velocity cannon, plutonium would not work in the gun-type bomb. Oppenheimer broke the bad news to Conant on July 11. The bomb they had dubbed the Thin Man would never work. The disappointment in the room was palpable. It meant that all the plutonium coming from the giant pile at Hanford would not be reliable enough to use. The possibility of developing a plutonium weapon to defeat the Germans now seemed slim.

During a series of urgent meetings in Chicago on July 17, Conant consulted with Oppenheimer and Charles Thomas, who had come from Los Alamos, and then conferred with Groves and Fermi in an evening meeting. They reached an inescapable conclusion: the gun method for plutonium had to be scratched, eliminating the hoped-for shortcut to the bomb. Plutonium was useless unless an alternative design for a weapon could be found within a few months. The gloomy prognosis was reflected in the epitaph Conant scrawled across the top of Thomas's upbeat June 13 status report: "All to no avail, alas!"

Fortunately, there was an alternative, but it was far from finished. A small group at the laboratory had continued work on Neddermeyer's complicated implosion design and believed it could be achieved. When Conant talked to Oppenheimer, however, the latter was not optimistic about their chances of developing it quickly. The implosion program was floundering. Neddermeyer was systematic and difficult to work with and was continually in conflict with Parsons, who had doubted him from the beginning. As a navy ordnance officer, Parsons had his own set ideas about how things should be done. Kistiakowsky, a brilliant improviser, was caught in the middle and was so unhappy that he had asked to be released from the project. "The situation is a mess," Kisty had written after his first visit to Los Alamos. There was "a serious lack of mutual confidence between Parsons and Neddermeyer," and it was doubtful the former "believes in its success." Furthermore, Teller, who had been appointed head of a small implosion theory group, had lost interest in the task. He did not like working under Bethe and instead insisted on spending all his time on "the Super," the hydrogen weapon, which few believed would be developed in time to affect the war. Oppenheimer allowed Teller to go his own way, but a sign of his growing impatience was a little prayer he would sometimes mutter under his breath: "May the Lord preserve us from the enemy without and the Hungarians within."

By the time Conant returned to Los Alamos in July, he felt "the situation was desperate." The personality conflicts and turf battles—between "the most colossal egos" he'd ever encountered, he confided to Kisty—were dragging down the experimental effort at the very moment it had to be prosecuted vigorously. They had to make implosion work if there was to be any hope of developing an effective plutonium bomb. To step up the effort and avoid further disputes, the whole implosion operation would need to be completely overhauled and expanded.

Hoping for a fresh perspective, Conant and Oppenheimer went for a long hike in the mountains and began formulating a new plan of attack. Parsons would continue to head the Ordnance Division, but Kistiakowsky was put in charge of the new X (Explosives) Division dedicated to the difficult high-explosives development work, studying implosion dynamics and generally trying to figure out how to make the weapon do what they wanted it to. Robert Bacher was asked to run the G (Gadget) Division to investigate implosion experimentally and design the geometric sphere. Exercising great tact under the circumstances, Oppenheimer solved the management problem by easing Neddermeyer into the role of senior technical advisor, thereby improving the attitude and effectiveness of the entire unit. Morale received a much-needed boost when Fermi agreed to come in September and stay for the duration.

The injection of new blood—in the form of mathematician John von Neumann, physicist Luis Alvarez, fresh from the radar lab, and Commander Norris E. Bradbury, a Stanford University physicist with four years' experience at the Dahlgren Naval Proving Ground—helped them overcome some stubborn problems and move on. The development of "explosive lenses," suggested by James Tuck, a member of the British Technical Mission, and based on specially shaped charges designed to crack armor, finally generated the powerful series of shock waves necessary for successful implosion. The new method required exhaustive experimentation. Groves brought in reinforcements: six hundred young technicians, or SEDs (members of the US Army's Special Engineering Detachment), to help with the high-explosives development work and bomb construction.

As the laboratory girded itself for the final push, all the other divisions were reorganized and refocused on the fast-approaching deadlines. The Manhattan Project was continuing to expand and now cost $100 million a month. Results were essential. Everyone worked at a frenzied pace. The implosion experiments were ambitious, and with so much riding on them, Oppenheimer leaned heavily on Conant as they entered the home stretch, asking him to come to Los Alamos with greater frequency to help see the work through to the end. Conant's broad understanding and common sense would help keep them on track to the very last step and mediate any conflicting viewpoints that might threaten to disrupt their progress. "Your confidence in our future success is something that I would like to have checked against realities just as often as possible," Oppie confided, and, in a more heartfelt note, added, "I think the next months will inevitably be a time when we shall value your advice and help to a very special degree."

As the momentum of the work intensified, Conant could see the toll the pressure and anxiety were taking on Oppenheimer. He had shrunk to 113 pounds and was so painfully thin his shoulder blades poked through his shirt. To keep up his spirits, Conant sent letters of encouragement and sober, pedagogical words of praise: "Just a line to tell you once again how satisfactory I think everything is going at Y," he wrote after seeing how the personnel changes had revitalized the implosion program. "In all serious-ness, you are to be congratulated on the progress made and the organization as it now stands."

Conant advised Groves that Los Alamos should proceed with plans for the uranium gun-assembly bomb (Little Boy) and two kinds of implosion bombs (Fat Man), the first using uranium-235, and, as soon as they had it perfected, the second using plutonium. The implosion bombs would be low efficiency—Conant judged the blast would be the equivalent of only a few hundred tons of TNT, but at least they were a way of utilizing the atomic material they had produced at great expense.

On August 7, 1944, Groves presented Army Chief of Staff General Mar-shall with a new weapons timetable: several implosion bombs would be available between March and the end of June 1945, with a good chance for improved power. But if the development of the implosion bomb did not ful-fill "present expectations," they still had the gun-type bomb as a fallback. The Little Boy bomb was essentially completed—although they did not have enough U-235 to arm it—and he could state with assurance that it would be ready by August 1, 1945. The only problem was that since the gun assembly required large amounts of U-235, it would be possible to deliver only one, or at most two, additional bombs in 1945. They estimated its destructive effect would be roughly twice that expected of the low-powered implosion bomb. There was no longer any doubt that they would have weapons available for use; the only question was how efficiently the first models would work. While Groves's report was careful to point out that this schedule was based on "rea-sonable success with experiments yet to be conducted," he and his science advisors rather glossed over the fact that they had no idea when the plants would produce sufficient quantities of U-235 and plutonium for a weapon.

Either way, the revised timetable meant that in all probability, the atomic bomb would arrive too late for the German war. The summer of 1944 held out the promise of victory in Europe. On June 6, more than 150,000 Allied troops landed on the Normandy beaches, and, after weeks of bloody and relentless fighting, succeeded in gaining firm control of the peninsula. By the end of July, American soldiers had smashed through the enemy's defenses and won the costly battle for Saint-Lô, France. The German front was crumbling. On August 1 General George Patton's Third Army, which led the surge in northern France, began fanning out across the open country, racing for Paris. As terrible as the Allied losses had been, the Germans fared far worse, repeating a pattern that was becoming standard and giving the final outcome the feel of mathematical inevitability. Europe would be won by conventional means. It looked increasingly likely that if a bomb were ready—and if it were used—Japan would be its intended target.

Now that the tide was turning against the aggressors, it was no longer possible to delay decisions about the postwar world. Conant had been consumed with the bomb project, and it had been a good many months since he had made one of the belligerent speeches—demanding Germany's unconditional surrender, no stalemate, no negotiated peace—he had been known for in the early days of the war. But over the spring and summer of 1944, he found himself worrying that Americans were too optimistic about the future; too confident that international cooperation would be sufficient to prevent World War III. He did not share *Time* publisher Henry Luce's belief that at the war's end, the United States would automatically assume "leadership of the world," and inaugurate "the American Century." Stalin had made it clear at the December 1943 summit with FDR and Churchill in Tehran, Iran, and in his subsequent actions, that he would not be denied dominant influence in Eastern Europe. The Russian leader intended to play the part of world bully, extending his reach to the Baltic states and Italy, and ensuring that Poland never again fell into anti-Soviet hands.

America might be powerful, but cognizant as he was of how easy it would be for a country to secretly develop a bomb, Conant believed this was no time for the United States to soft-pedal foreign policy. He addressed a general warning to Harvard alumni in June, reviving what he described as his old interventionist "fight talk" and calling for a "decisive victory." Peace lay not in the vague resolutions of a united nations organization but in harsh, realistic measures that would prevent Germany and Japan from renewing their hostilities, and keep them "in check" for as long as fifty years—or until a new generation of leaders, untainted by Fascism or a desire for vengeance, could emerge.

Conant's views may have been influenced to some degree by the growing discontent of some of the Manhattan Project scientists. As usual, the restless souls at the Met Lab in Chicago were the loudest, with Szilard busily cataloguing their errors, as he put it to Bush, in order to "make a 'stink' after the war." They found fault with everything from Groves's repressive regime and Kafkaesque compartmentalization to Conant's brutish handling of the interchange with the British.

Rumors about costly delays became so widespread that at one point Roosevelt called Conant and asked him to deal with "a friend of Eleanor's," a young Met Lab physicist named Irving S. Lowen, who had gotten some "queer ideas" about what was going on. Lowen came to the OSRD's Washington offices and behind closed doors confided his disturbing discoveries, which Conant recognized as a rehashed version of the old "bill of complaints": the project was being poorly run, and it was slowing down the pace of the bomb work. Lowen ended his rant by saying he was determined to inform Roosevelt of this "almost treacherous situation."

It did not make the president's science advisor happy to learn there was so much "loose talk about the inadequacies of the top management." Conant knew that as an unenlightened chemist, he was regarded by many of the project physicists as deficient in his ability to understand atomic energy. He told himself that his critics "did not know the score," and that if security permitted him to bring them into the picture about the status of other processes and parts of the project, they might see things differently. Privately, though, he worried about the resentment building beneath the surface "because hundreds of young scientists felt left out."

His attempts to reassure the overwrought Chicago physicist failed. After Lowen repeated his story to a number of the First Lady's prominent Washington friends, Conant recalled, "the question was raised whether it was safe to leave him free to circulate his ideas?" Eleanor was worried enough to seek the advice of an old family retainer: Bernard Baruch. "I don't want to know anything," Baruch told Conant when he called about the young man's complaint. "I just want to know whether you are well informed and can assure me all is well." Conant assured his old rubber colleague that everything was being done that could be done "Your word is enough for me," Baruch replied. "I shall tell the lady to relax."

Prompted in part by the turbulent "spirit in Chicago," and the unrest triggered by the extreme secrecy that shrouded every aspect of the project, Conant began to consider the postwar political consequences of the bomb, and its domestic and diplomatic implications. At some point, it was going to have to be revealed to the world. He believed the Manhattan Project was "so significant it neither could or should be kept a secret," and had suggested a scientific summary of their work be prepared to be released after the war to help shape the public's—and Congress's—view of the revolutionary new weapon. The idea for the report emerged from conversations among Conant, Arthur Compton, and the Princeton physicist Henry De-Wolf Smyth, and resulted in Smyth being commissioned to write a book about the development of the bomb, *Atomic Energy for Military Purposes*, to be published after the war.

During an inspection trip to Los Alamos in August, Conant mentioned his concerns to Bush, who was just back from London, and they took advantage of the "complete privacy" of their surroundings to discuss at length the problems posed by atomic weapons and "what the policy of the United States should be when the war was over." They both knew the Chicago scientists were increasingly alarmed about the bomb's impact on the international scene and their belief that it would require a worldwide organization and complicated new controls to keep them out of the hands of the next generation of dictators. On the basis of that conversation and those that followed, they decided it was time to call the government's attention to the crucial need to devise effective policies to bring atomic power under national and international control.

On September 19, 1944, Bush and Conant addressed a letter to Stimson expressing their grave concerns about the alarming situation that would result if no US policy was developed before the bomb was dropped. "We cannot emphasize too strongly the fact that it will be quite impossible to hold essential knowledge of these developments secret once the war is over," they wrote. "Furthermore, we should like to emphasize that the progress of this art and science is bound to be so rapid in the next five years in some countries that it would be extremely dangerous for this government to assume that by holding secret its present knowledge we should be secure." They went on to advocate the release of a Manhattan Project history, along with the basic scientific information and domestic legislation to control atomic power. While they urged the importance of a treaty with Great Britain and Canada, they did not want America to align itself so closely with Britain as to jeopardize its future relations with the Soviet Union. With the first bomb still a year away from being delivered, Conant and Bush had only begun to formulate their ideas about international control, but they knew that the only alternative to a reasonable approach to Russia was a nuclear arms race.

On Friday, September 22, three days after they sent their letter, Roosevelt summoned Bush to a meeting in the Oval Office that exposed the wide gulf that had developed between the president and his atomic advisors when it came to the future of atomic power. Unbeknownst to them, FDR had been making his own forays into nuclear diplomacy. Bush found himself "very much embarrassed" to hear the president, in the presence of Lord Cherwell, who had just come from the second secret wartime conference in Quebec, holding forth on aspects of the bomb's effect on international relations that he had neglected to first review in private with his own experts. To Bush's growing dismay, it became clear that while the president still heeded their advice on administrative and technical matters, when it came to the bare-knuckle business of politics, he had no wish to consult his scientists. Roosevelt reserved solely to himself the right to make policy.

Roosevelt had begun the meeting by talking about the ideas of Niels Bohr, who had intentionally bypassed Bush and Conant in order to make his case to the president in person. Felix Frankfurter had brought him to the White House in late August, but Roosevelt was so distracted by what he saw as a possible security breach—the justice was not supposed to know about S-1—that it may have prejudiced him against the physicist. Bohr, who had a tendency to mumble and spoke in long, convoluted sentences, proceeded to urge that America and Britain inform Stalin about the bomb and make a generous offer to share its control if they hoped to avoid a disastrous arms race with the Soviet Union. He had made the same plea for postwar cooperation during an interview with Churchill in April and been roundly rebuffed. Roosevelt had been ambiguous in his response, but it was now apparent to Bush from the president's remarks that both leaders had flatly rejected Bohr's approach. (In fact, FDR had known for almost a year that the Russians were aware that the United States and Britain were working on a bomb, and both he and Churchill thought Bohr's proposals were so dangerous that while in Quebec they ordered surveillance of the Danish physicist to make sure he did not leak atomic secrets to the Soviets.)

In his meeting with Bush, the president touched on other aspects of his talks with Churchill at Quebec the previous week, stressing his belief in the "necessity for maintaining the British Empire strong" and that there should be complete interchange on all phases of atomic energy. What Roosevelt hinted at, but did not reveal, was that on September 19 at Hyde Park, he and Churchill had secretly signed an aide-mémoire pledging to continue their exclusive atomic alliance beyond the end of the war. Bush could only guess at the extent of the commitment, which both he and Conant opposed. But with Lord Cherwell present, as well as Admiral William D. Leahy, FDR's chief of staff, Bush felt it was not the time to probe further, or point out that it would be all but impossible to maintain an Anglo-American atomic monopoly after the war, as scientific discussions and publications about atomic energy would be inevitable. During the awkward ninety-minute meeting, the president also raised the issue of whether the atomic bomb should actually be used against Japan or used only as a threat after a demonstration in the United States. Bush replied that the question warranted careful consideration, "for certainly it would be inadvisable to make a threat unless we were distinctly in a position to follow it up if necessary." Roosevelt agreed.

Startled and upset by what he had heard, Bush apprised Conant of the unhappy state of affairs. Though Bush acknowledged they were not the president's "normal advisors" on international agreements or on postwar matters, they had been cut out of high-level diplomatic discussions about the bomb to a far greater degree than either of them had suspected. Both agreed that FDR had steered American atomic policy in the wrong direction, and it was imperative they try to reassert their influence. They hastened to alert Stimson to this "highly dangerous situation." He shared their forebodings but thought it was doubtful they would be able to hold the president's attention long enough to get through to him. He had had little luck getting him to discuss a number of issues on his own agenda.

Five days later, on September 30, Conant and Bush sent Stimson two memorandums along with a cover letter that conveyed their message in a few stark sentences. They wanted to be sure the seventy-seven-year-old secretary of war, who still liked to be called Colonel in honor of his time as a field artillery officer in France in 1918, grasped the magnitude of the new threat they would soon be facing. There was every reason to believe, they reported, that atomic bombs would be demonstrated before August 1, 1945. The blast damage would be equivalent to up to ten thousand tons of high explosives or a raid by a thousand B-29s. This was frightening enough, but, in the near future, loomed the hydrogen bomb, or "super-super" bomb, which was a thousand times more destructive. Every major population center in the world would lie at the mercy of the nation that struck first. It would be foolhardy to believe their present head start guaranteed their security or that secrecy offered lasting protection, as any nation with good scientific and technical resources could overtake them in three or four years. To head off this catastrophic competition, they proposed disclosing all but the manufacturing and military details of the bomb as soon it was demonstrated. "This demonstration," they wrote, "might be over enemy territory, or in our own country, with subsequent notice to Japan that the materials would be used against the Japanese mainland unless surrender was forthcoming." After the fighting was over, they proposed placing control of atomic weapons in the hands of an international agency.

Because the Bush-Conant memorandums, both in timing and tone, echo Bohr's advice to the US and British leaders, historians credit the Danish physicist with being the first to appreciate the political dangers posed by the bomb and to agitate for immediate diplomatic action. In his classic account of the origins of the arms race, *A World Destroyed: The Atomic Bomb and the Grand Alliance*, Martin J. Sherwin contends that Conant's and Bush's original proposals were "tentative" by comparison. Even by late September, they suggested "no diplomatic initiatives" likely to encourage international cooperation and never advocated that Roosevelt make any overtures to the Russians during the war, "as Bohr and the Chicago scientists had urged." But FDR's atomic advisors were nothing if not realistic about the American political system and what it would take to persuade the president and Congress to accept the idea of international control, and they believed that only a cautious approach had any chance of working. For better or worse, as Sherwin notes, "because of their position and present responsibilities, it was Bush and Conant who, inevitably, came to be cast in the role of brokers between the recommendations of the scientists and the inclinations of the policy makers."

There is evidence that by the spring of 1944, Conant had independently arrived at many of the same conclusions as Bohr but was not ready to advertise them. In a scribbled response to a Bush memo in mid-April, and in another private handwritten document dated two weeks later, Conant indicated that he, too, believed the only hope for humanity was a global association: "Alternatives[:] race between nations and in the next war destruction of civilization, or a scheme to remove atomic energy from the field of conflict."

The "scheme" Conant contemplated in his May 4 ruminations was a powerful fifteen-member international commission—which would include representatives from the United States, Britain, and the Soviet Union, and perhaps six other nations—that would have complete authority over all work on atomic energy conducted anywhere in the globe. After describing this hypothetical body, which would act as "trustees and custodians" of the nuclear arsenal—ensuring full inspections, scientific reciprocity, the end of military secrecy, and even something approaching a world government—he asked at the end, "What would be the result: Everyone would know where each nation stood???" But as biographer James Hershberg, who unearthed the document, observes, "The question marks perhaps express Conant's doubts that such radical ideas could ever be implemented." The fact that it remained a rough draft and was never circulated suggests that Conant "lacked the sense of urgency that drove Niels Bohr to all but plant himself on the doorsteps of 10 Downing Street and 1600 Pennsylvania Avenue."

Unlike Bohr, however, Conant was focused on making the bomb as fast as possible and had had little time for serious, orderly reflection on what would come afterward. But that was beginning to change. He recognized the need to speak out on postwar planning for Germany, one of the most controversial subjects at the Quebec Conference. A week after sending the bundle of memorandums to Stimson, he delivered a major speech on the disarmament of Axis countries, calling for dismantling their industry and converting them to pastoral economies. Addressing the Foreign Policy Association at the Waldorf-Astoria Hotel in New York on October 7, Conant declared that modern science and technology had "so transformed the art of war as to require us to rethink many of the problems involved in an international attempt to keep the peace." The mounting curve of aerial offensive power—from long-range bombers to V-1 rockets—meant that American cities were now vulnerable to a "sudden onslaught." For its own self-protection, the United States not only had to destroy the enemies' "engines of war," but also had to collaborate with other countries to prevent them from ever rearming again. "Only ignorance can lead one to deny the alternatives which face the country," he warned. "Either we must play our part in a world organization to preserve the peace, or we must convert this nation into an armed camp bristling with weapons."

While they waited for a response to their memos, Conant and Bush became increasingly apprehensive about the administration's attempts to map its postwar strategy without taking the bomb into account. The recently concluded Dumbarton Oaks Conference on a united nations organization had been a step toward greater cooperation but also a missed opportunity. They needed to begin laying the groundwork for their atomic energy agreement, which Conant believed could come about only gradually, "with a series of quid pro quos at every step." They decided to prod Stimson further and prepared a joint paper on deadly biological warfare, another weapon of mass destruction that could be developed in secret by an aggressor, which posed a threat to world peace. America and Britain were already exchanging information on biological warfare, Bush wrote Conant on October 24, and the United States could offer Russia a chance to participate, creating an opening or "entering wedge" for a similar proposal on atomic energy.

November passed in a blur of meetings and war business. Public discussion over what to do about postwar Germany continued to dominate the papers: Secretary of the Treasury Henry Morgenthau Jr. had proposed a plan forcing Germany to pay heavy reparations, partly through forced labor—but Conant did not like the vindictive tone and dropped out of the debate. Bush had to go to Europe, and the president, ill and exhausted from the chaotic last weeks of the 1944 election, was rarely in Washington. He had won a narrow victory over New York's governor, Thomas Dewey, but at considerable cost to his health. Postwar planning had to wait while Roosevelt recuperated at the "little White House" in Warm Springs, Georgia.

On December 8 Conant was summoned to a last-minute meeting with Groves, who was making his way back from Montreal to Washington. The general rushed directly from Union Station to the Cosmos Club to tell him the news: an Alsos team, part of Groves's military and scientific intelligence-gathering mission, had followed the Sixth Army into Strasbourg, France, and reported back that the German bomb program was far behind. Newly seized documents and interviews with captured scientists indicated that German research on nuclear fission had stalled. It seemed not to have progressed much beyond the stage reached by the Americans and British in 1940–41. So they were not facing an immediate threat from a German bomb.

For both men, the news came as a huge relief. But their elation was tempered by the realization that this was just one cache of papers, and the information would have to be analyzed thoroughly and nailed down by their experts on the ground. It was too early to assume they were out of the woods. They knew there were other laboratories, heavy water plants, secret pile operations, possibly even a centrifuge plant. Many of Germany's leading nuclear scientists were still at large—including Heisenberg. They could also not dismiss the possibility that this was a ploy, designed to divert their attention from the major effort being mounted elsewhere.

Later that same day, with still no response from the White House on their memos, Conant and Bush huddled with Harvey Bundy and Assistant Secretary of War John J. McCloy, both of whom were close to Stimson, and told them that planning for international safeguards for the bomb had to begin at once. Bush suggested that an advisory committee be appointed to consider postwar atomic matters. They all agreed that the time had come to let the State Department in on the secret. Edward R. Stettinius, a white-haired businessman who had only recently been named secretary of state—more for political reasons than for his nodding acquaintance with foreign policy—had not yet been informed about the Manhattan Project. The next day, December 9, Bundy met with Stimson and brought their suggestions to his attention. Four days later, Bush went over them with him again. But Stimson was not ready to commit himself. It was an exceedingly difficult decision, he said, and demanded enormous care.

Just before the close of the year, Conant and Groves returned to Los Alamos for a conference on the implosion group's progress. As they approached, they could hear the distant boom of explosions echoing in the proving grounds in the surrounding canyons. The most recent tests showed favorable results, but they were just beginning to experiment with different kinds of detonators. A lot of work still had to be done, and time was very short. Conant was so dubious about implosion's chances, he bet Oppenheimer that the gun weapon would be ready first. It was a pretty feeble wager. By then, both he and Groves were so discouraged, they had abandoned the idea of using the available U-235 in an implosion weapon and planned to assign it all to the gun bomb, which was as close to being a sure thing as you could get in untried technology. But the implosion assembly was so uncertain that after much debate that spring and summer, Oppenheimer had decided they would have a controlled test, even though Groves was annoyed at the prospect of squandering so much plutonium.

The New Year brought the first reports of real progress in implosion. In late February 1945 Conant and Groves went to Los Alamos for a comprehensive review of the best design options for the implosion bomb. An ingenious proposal made by Robert Christy, one of Oppenheimer's students, entailed using a smaller, solid core of plutonium—approximately the size of a grapefruit—that would theoretically be much easier to compress while still achieving criticality. The modifications involved in the Christy design were simple yet promised to produce enough compression for success. When the meeting was over, Oppenheimer, Groves, and the others left the room. Conant sat in contemplative silence, and Teller, who had also remained behind, heard him mutter, more to himself than anyone else, "This is the first time I really thought it would work." Teller stared at him in disbelief. "That was the first indication I had of how little confidence those in the highest scientific quarters had in our work," he recalled.

Kistiakowsky had further breakthroughs to report. Thanks to some very clever engineering and Luis Alvarez's invention of electric detonators, they had finally achieved the smooth, inward-moving spherical shock wave they needed to compress the core and get all of the explosive to detonate simultaneously. After this was confirmed in a second successful test on February 24, Groves announced the time had come to "freeze" the design for the implosion weapon. Even though the "Christy bomb" design with a solid core still needed to be proven experimentally in the weeks to come, it was incorporated in their thinking. Groves had set a deadline of August 1 for a bomb to be ready for combat use, and together they drew up a schedule of deadlines to solve the remaining difficulties and allow them time to stage a dry run.

The following month, planning began in earnest for the full-scale test of an implosion bomb. Oppenheimer, who had a flair for the dramatic, suggested the code name for the test project: Trinity. He later claimed the choice was inspired by one of John Donne's *Holy Sonnets*: the fourteenth, about death and the resurrection, or possibly another favorite poem that opens, "Batter my heart, three-person'd God." Oppenheimer was already thinking ahead: to their place in history, or perhaps a special corner of hell. So much of their work seemed macabre, the moral dilemmas about what they were doing grating their conscience like the sand in their teeth. This would be the culmination of all their efforts. If it worked, the tremendous demonstration of power they were planning in a desolate stretch of desert would change the world forever.

Oppenheimer asked the capable Harvard physicist Kenneth Bainbridge to take charge of all the arrangements for the Trinity test, scheduled for mid-July. He and Groves had already found a suitably isolated eighteen-by-twenty-four-mile tract of land in a barren desert that early Spanish settlers had dubbed Jornada del Muerto (Journey of Death). It was part of the Alamogordo Army Air Base, but far enough from the airfield to conduct the test shot safely; and some two hundred miles south of Los Alamos, which was close enough to facilitate the transportation of men and materials. To be on the safe side, the US Army secured an area four hundred square miles and posted No Trespassing signs along the dusty roads. Construction began on the test site, and Bainbridge selected a flat area he designated as zero point, where they would erect the hundred-foot steel tower on which the bomb would be detonated.

Because of the remaining fears of predetonation, and Grove's concern about wasting the only plutonium they had, they came up with the idea of testing the bomb inside a container. That way, if the bomb failed and a nuclear explosion did not take place, they would at least be able to recover some or most of the plutonium. The result was Jumbo, a giant 214-ton ellipsoidal steel tank with fourteen-inch thick walls, which they believed would be capable of withstanding the pressure created by the blast. It was hugely expensive to manufacture and, because of its monumental size and weight, had to be loaded onto specially reinforced railroad cars and then onto a custom-built sixty-four-wheel trailer to haul it to the site. By the time it arrived, however, more plutonium was available, and the timing and symmetry of implosion had improved enough that Jumbo was no longer needed. Instead, it was hoisted up a second steel tower eight hundred feet from zero point, a $500,000 monument to Groves's prudence. A third tower was built for a pre-atomic test: a practice run prior to Trinity, so the physicists could calibrate their instruments. Hundreds of crates of TNT were stacked on the twenty-foot-high tower's wooden platform. On May 7, 1945, the massive explosion—the most powerful in history at that point—produced a fireball and sent a mushroom cloud of smoke and dust fifteen thousand feet into the desert sky.

In a strange twist of fate, the "hundred-ton test," the dress rehearsal for Trinity, came on the last day of the European war. May 8 was V-E day, but for Conant, like most of the Manhattan Project scientists, the celebration was muted. Still reeling from Roosevelt's sudden death from a cerebral hemorrhage on April 12, he felt a sharp stab of disappointment that the wartime commander in chief had not lived to see the unconditional surrender of the German army. Back home in Cambridge, he told reporters he would not be making an address, nor would there be anything comparable to the mass rally at Sanders Theatre that had followed the Pearl Harbor attack. "The war is not over," he told them. Men were still fighting in the field, and they had a long way to go in their efforts to realize Roosevelt's aims in the Pacific.

An unassuming, little-known former senator from Missouri, unprepared and unsure of himself, was now the leader of the United States in a time of global war. By all accounts, Harry S. Truman had not even wanted to be vice president, and had accepted the nomination only reluctantly when Roosevelt told him his current vice president, Henry Wallace, had become a liability and the party needed his help to win. The newspapers portrayed

Truman as a man of character and integrity. Conant was not sure that would be enough in the present crisis. Roosevelt had been part of the genesis of the Manhattan Project, had personally approved it, and had been aware of the events that shaped its development and the decisions already taken. Truman would be coming in cold.

At noon on Wednesday, April 25, Stimson briefed the new president on the bomb. Then he brought in Groves, who was spirited into the West Wing of the White House via an underground passage to avoid reporters, to walk Truman through the report General Marshall had prepared on the status of the Manhattan Project. According to their timetable, the gun-type bomb would be ready by August 1. Another type of bomb, an implosion weapon, would be ready to test in July. They forecast that Fat Man would be available for combat before the end of summer. Japan was the designated target. For three quarters of an hour, the president listened to his senior military advisors lay out the facts about this "new force." Stimson, choosing his moment well, requested permission to establish a special select committee "charged with the function of advising the president on the various questions raised by our apparently imminent success in developing an atomic weapon." Truman told him to go ahead.

A week later, Truman signed off on the suggested membership of the Interim Committee, so named because Stimson assumed that after the war Congress would want to appoint a permanent commission to regulate atomic energy. Stimson would serve as chair, with the other members being Bush, Conant, Karl Compton, Undersecretary of the Navy Ralph A. Bard, Assistant Secretary of State William L. Clayton, and a personal representative of the president, whom they agreed should be James Byrnes, who had just resigned as director of the Office of War Mobilization. Stimson's alternate would be George L. Harrison, president of the New York Life Insurance Company and special consultant to the War Department. Stimson had finally succeeded in gaining approval for the advisory committee that Conant and Bush had been advocating. "Now we can start at work preparing for the many things that must be planned for S-1," he wrote in his diary, before sending out the invitations the next day.

When Conant learned of his appointment to the Interim Committee, he told Stimson he "doubted" whether he and Bush should represent the project scientists. There was a "growing restlessness" in the various laboratories, he wrote Stimson on May 5. Many of the men were extremely worried about the international problems arising from the use of the weapon, particularly in regard to Russia, which might be spooked into an arms race if they dropped the bomb in battle without prior notice. Unaware that he and Bush had been pressing the issue at the highest levels, the project scientists were convinced the OSRD leadership was woefully shortsighted when it came to national policy. Some of the Chicago contingent, headed by James Franck, were against the bomb's military use and were desperate to have their objections taken into account. If the United States were to use this means of "indiscriminate destruction" without prior warning, the Franck report argued, she would sacrifice her moral position in the world, precipitate an arms race, and "prejudice the possibility of reaching an international agreement on the future control of such weapons." They insisted that the only way to reveal this awful weapon to the world was "by way of demonstration in an . . . uninhabited area."

On top of everything, Niels Bohr had turned up at the OSRD's Washington headquarters brandishing the document on international control he had used during his conversation with Roosevelt, along with a new addendum inspired by the upcoming San Francisco conference to draft the United Nations charter, and was determined to bring it to the attention of responsible officials. Conant thought that it was "essential" they enlist the support of the scientific community to avoid "public bickering" among the experts after the bomb became public knowledge. Unless the administration did something to acknowledge their concerns, confusion and hysteria would fill the vacuum. The scientists had to be heard.

Conant told Stimson that if he were to serve on the committee, he had two conditions: first, he wanted to be allowed to show the Bush-Conant memorandums of September 30 to a few key project leaders to reassure them that Stimson was relaying their postwar concerns to President Truman; second, he would like some scientists to be allowed to present their views to the committee. Stimson told Conant he was needed on the committee and agreed to his requests. He was sympathetic to his arguments that they could not put off the scientists indefinitely and that the rumors were getting out of hand. In the last conversation he had with Roosevelt on March 15, they had discussed a report from Assistant Secretary of State James Dunn, who was troubled by talk of "extravagance in the Manhattan Project" and that "Vannevar Bush and Jim Conant had sold the president a lemon." Dunn suggested they bring in a body of "outside" scientists to review the situation because it "might become disastrous." Stimson dismissed it as a "nervous memorandum" and told the president as much. Still, he had come prepared with a list of the Nobel Prize winners and "practically every physicist of standing" who were backing up Bush and Conant on the project. It was a reminder, he later noted, that it was "always necessary to suppress the lingering doubts that such a titanic undertaking could be successful."

Stimson opened the first meeting of the Interim Committee on Wednesday, May 9, by soberly addressing the eight men gathered in his office at the Pentagon. "Gentlemen, it is our responsibility to recommend action that may turn the course of civilization." He went on to explain their broad mandate, which ranged from what would be said after the atomic attacks to what should be done about postwar research, developments, and controls. Groves, who was not a member of the committee but was invited to sit in on all the sessions, formed the distinct impression he was there "to make certain that the American people as well as leaders of other nations would realize that the very important decisions as to the use of the bomb were not made by the War Department alone but rather that [they] were decisions reached by a group of individuals well removed from the immediate influence of men in uniform."

Conant missed the second informal meeting on May 14 that saw approval of his scientific panel, with Oppenheimer, Fermi, Lawrence, and Arthur Compton as its members. Four days later, the committee reviewed the draft press releases that would go out after the bomb was dropped. William L. Laurence, the science editor of the *New York Times*, who was under contract to Groves, was asked to prepare the statements. They had no trouble with the two versions for release by the commanding officer of the Alamogordo Army Air Base, but Conant thought the seventeen-page presidential statement was too long, overly exaggerated, and sounded "phony." It was decided Truman should make only a brief announcement.

Foreign relations and the Russian situation took up most of the meeting, and especially interested Byrnes, who was soon to be named Truman's secretary of state, though it had not yet been announced. Byrnes had read the Bush-Conant memorandums and took issue with their judgment that the Soviet Union could catch up with the US atomic program in three to four years. Groves also disputed their estimate. Given his full knowledge of the enormous engineering feats that had been accomplished, and correspondingly dim view of Russian efficiency, he thought it would take a good twenty years. As Bush was absent, Conant defended their estimate, asserting that it would be unsafe to count on much more of a lead than a handful of years before the American atomic monopoly was broken.

At ten in the morning on May 31, the Interim Committee gathered at the Pentagon for the last crucial two days of deliberations. For the benefit of the scientific advisory panel, which had been asked to join them, Stimson gave a short opening speech, his voice tired and ragged. He wanted it understood that he and General Marshall were looking on the whole question of atomic energy "like statesmen and not merely soldiers anxious to win the war at any cost." He went on to assure the physicists that the committee did not regard the bomb "as a new weapon merely but as a revolutionary change in the relationship of man to the universe." The project might be "a Frankenstein" that would devour civilization or, if controlled, a means by which mankind could secure "the peace of the world." After technical presentations by Compton and Oppenheimer, there followed a lively debate about the need for ongoing atomic research to produce and stockpile materials for America to maintain its nuclear superiority; the prospects of international control, with Conant insisting on the necessity of inspections; and the problem of Russia.

At the luncheon that followed, Byrnes asked Lawrence about something he had said earlier in the morning about first providing the Japanese with "some striking but harmless" demonstration of the bomb. For the next ten minutes, they debated whether it would be possible to arrange "a nonmilitary demonstration of the bomb" that would result in the Japanese being so impressed by its destructive power that they would see the uselessness of continuing the war. "Various possibilities were brought forward," Arthur Compton noted in his account of the discussion, but "one after another," they were discarded:

> If a bomb were exploded in Japan with previous notice, the Japanese air power was still adequate to give serious interference. An atomic bomb was an intricate device, still in the developmental stage. Its operation would be far from routine. If during the final adjustments of the bomb the Japanese defenders should attack, a faulty move might easily result in some kind of failure. Such an end to an advertised demonstration of power would be much worse than if the attempt had not been made. It was now evident that when the time came for the bombs to be used, we would have only one available, followed

afterwards by others at all-too-long intervals. We could not afford
the chance that one of them might be a dud.

The possibility of a purely technical demonstration that would not destroy human lives was attractive, but no one could suggest a way to do it that
would be so convincing that it would end the war. A series of bloody, grind-
ing battles in the Pacific had marked the preceding months. On February
19 the invasion of Iwo Jima, one of the crucial final steppingstones to Japan,
resulted in a thirty-six-day siege that was one of the bloodiest in Marine
Corps history. Despite heavy naval and air bombardment, the Japanese dug
into bunkers deep within the volcanic rock, and the effort to drive them out
claimed the lives of 6,281 American marines, wounded another 19,000, and
killed most of the 21,000 Japanese defenders of the island. On April 1 the
Battle of Okinawa commenced, and by mid-May, thousands of American
soldiers had died in some of the worst fighting of the war. Though the Japanese Third Army was retreating, the island still had not been secured.* The
planned invasion of the Japanese mainland in November promised terrible
losses on both sides. Japan had never felt the conqueror's foot on her soil
and would mount a fierce defense. They had to find a way to end the slaughter once and for all. "We were keenly aware of our responsibility," wrote
Compton. "Experience of the determination of Japan's fighting men made
it evident that the war would not be stopped unless these men themselves
were convinced of its futility."

Oppenheimer could think of no solution "sufficiently spectacular" to
convince the Japanese that further resistance was pointless. He stressed that
the military use of the bomb was designed to induce surrender and that
"several strikes would be feasible." The "visual effect of an atomic bombing
would be tremendous," and would be accompanied by a "brilliant lumines-
cence" that would rise to the height of ten thousand to twenty thousand feet.
He estimated the number of deaths to be around twenty thousand, and the
"neutron effect of the explosion would be dangerous to life for a radius of at
least two-thirds of a mile."

To Conant, the bomb "seemed the ideal weapon for giving exactly the
shock to the Japanese which was required to bring about the surrender

---

* The Okinawa campaign would last eighty-two days, not ending until June 22. More than 13,000
American soldiers perished and almost 36,000 were wounded, while 70,000 Japanese soldiers were
killed. The highest toll was reserved for civilians caught in the crossfire: an estimated 100,000 to
150,000 Okinawan men, women, and children lost their lives.

before the bitter fighting of invasion should commence." He agreed with Compton that "nothing would be more disastrous than a prior warning followed by a dud." America had a meager supply of bombs, and "a maximum effect had to be obtained with the few at our disposal." It was a military necessity. The firebombing of their cities had not been enough to dissuade the Japanese from the dangerous course to which they had committed themselves. Dubbed "burn jobs" by Major General Curtis LeMay's Twentieth Air Force, they had been making low-altitude incendiary raids on the Japanese mainland and home islands with powerful new jellied petroleum bombs. Developed by Louis Fieser and a team of Harvard chemists working on secret weaponry for Conant's NDRC, they were designed to ignite white-hot conflagrations, spurting burning globs of a lava-like gel that stuck to the walls and roofs of the light wooden housing, consuming everything in its path. Over the course of a single night on March 9–10, 1945, the firebombing of Tokyo killed a hundred thousand, injured several times that many, and destroyed more than a quarter of the capital city. More than a million were left homeless.*

Given the devastation wrought by LeMay's B-29s, one committee member observed, "The number of people killed by the bomb would not be greater in general magnitude than the number already killed in fire raids." Just as had been the case in the latter stages of the European war, they were all aware that the steady heightening of the saturation bombing of Japan in recent months—much of it directed against urban areas—had been done in hopes that it would weaken the will of the warlords and Premier Kantaro Suzuki's government. The objective was a speedy victory, and civilian casualties had become a necessary evil, accepted by both the press and the public. Favorable articles about LeMay's "precision" bombing had appeared in the *New York Times, Time*, and *Newsweek*. An unabashedly gung-ho series in the *New Yorker* quoted LeMay's spokesman, St. Clair McKelway, explaining that the general's purpose in conducting the raids was "shortening this war." Bush, like Conant, felt sure the use of the atomic bomb would be "far less terrible than the fire raids on Tokyo, if it brought a quick end to the war, and would save more Japanese lives than it snuffed out."

Groves, who shared this military rationale, maintained that a real target

---

* The firebombing of Tokyo on March 9–10, 1945, and before it the bombing of Dresden, Germany, on February 13–15, 1945, are considered to be the most destructive attacks by conventional weapons in history, and have been roundly condemned.

with built-up structures would be the most effective demonstration. He had already convened a Target Committee, composed of Los Alamos scientists and ordnance specialists, to study seventeen urban or industrial Japanese areas. Groves had set as a "governing factor" that the targets chosen would be places that would "most adversely affect" Japanese morale, be military in nature—being either arsenals or garrisons—and relatively undamaged so that afterward they could definitely gauge the power of the bomb. Only Groves and Oppenheimer were members of both the Interim and Target committees and participated in the hastily convened meetings on site selection. Groves particularly wanted Kyoto, which thus far had been spared but had been identified as one of the most important military targets in Japan. Stimson ruled it out, and Truman, on hearing his reasons, agreed on the grounds that "it had been the capital of Japan and was a shrine of Japanese art and culture." The Target Committee would eventually settle on four cities, all major manufacturing centers: Hiroshima, Kokura, Nagasaki, and Niigata.

After considerable discussion of types of targets, the force of the explosion, and its desired effect, Stimson summed up the Interim Committee's conclusions: "We could not give the Japanese any warning; that we could not concentrate on a civilian area; but that we shall seek to make a profound psychological impression on as many of the inhabitants as possible." Conant suggested the "most desirable target" would be "a vital war plant employing a large number of workers and closely surrounded by workers' homes." There was no dissent, and Stimson took it as decided.

The following day, Friday, June 1, Stimson communicated the committee's formal recommendations to the president: the bomb should be used as soon as possible, the target should be a war plant surrounded by workers' homes, and it should be used without warning. The vote was unanimous.*

As Conant would observe years later, for all he and Bush had lobbied to become the president's nuclear advisors, they never foresaw their involvement in the "most important matter" before the Interim Committee—indeed the decision that historians would come to regard as the "hallmark" of their deliberations—"the use of the bomb against the Japanese." More tellingly, aware of its immense cost, awesome power, and profound mili-

---

* Secretary of the Navy Ralph A. Bard subsequently changed his mind about using the bomb against Japan without some "preliminary warning," and on June 27, 1945, submitted a memorandum expressing his reservations.

tary and diplomatic advantages, and assured of the wishes of the American public, they never questioned the basic assumption of *whether* it should be used at all.

While Truman and Stimson headed to Potsdam, Germany, for a meeting of the "Big Three" beginning July 17, 1945, Conant left for what he told his wife was a tour of West Coast facilities. Because of the uncertainty about the exact date of the Trinity test, the trip would put him in the geographical vicinity in the preceding days and allow him to be there at a moment's notice. After a meeting with Bush and Groves at Hanford, he made a quick detour on July 10 to Portland, Oregon, to see his youngest son, Ted, who had insisted on dropping out of high school to "join up" and was back on a brief layover before returning to the Pacific. The scrawny eighteen-year-old, who had poor vision and was partly deaf in one ear, had flunked the physical exam—he was classified as 4F—but the merchant marines were so short of skilled radio operators, they took him anyway.

Conant had been of two minds about his enlisting, but, in the end, the psychiatrist who was currently treating Ted convinced him it might do him some good. Hovering over them for years had been the "great danger" that the odd, socially awkward boy would never "find a place for himself in the world of men," as his dean at the Putney School had put it, and would end up in some kind of institution. According to Ted, who had been consigned briefly to Boston's McLean Hospital for observation, one Harvard doctor had recommended that he undergo a prefrontal lobotomy—a procedure that was gaining credence as a cure for a wide range of mental disorders, from depression, to schizophrenia, to mild retardation. It was also being used to treat an array of intractable behaviors, including homosexuality and uncontrollable disobedience in children. "My father would have none of it," recalled Ted, "and chose to send me off to war rather than cooking my brain." The merchant marines would either make him or break him.

While Jimmy was doing well in the submarine service and had already been promoted to lieutenant, Conant had been frankly skeptical that his youngest would be able to adapt to a life of duty and danger. According to Groves, the merchant marines were the "lowest of the low," and it would be hard going. Conant had not seen the rebellious youth for the better part of a year and had entertained few expectations for their reunion, but he wrote Patty that he was "pleased to report" that they managed to have a pleasant day:

I think for the first time, we got together on something approaching a mature and relatively unhampered basis. He has gained self-confidence to the degree necessary to allow him to drop his abnormal "bluff" and react essentially normally to situations. This makes discussion more profitable and interesting and much more realistic as to situations which involve him. He is still the same unusual kid, of course. Full of independence, energy, and projects. But his feet are very near the earth if not always on it, and he has a lot of nerve. The latter gets him by in the tough going of the merchant marines.

In short, I can report great progress and think the prognosis for the immediate future is excellent. I'm so glad I saw him and in a sense so relieved at what I found.

On Friday, July 13, Conant flew to San Francisco, where he rejoined Bush and Groves—the latter breaking his moratorium on project leaders flying together—and they went on to pick up Ernest Lawrence in Berkeley. The time for the test was now set for four in the morning on July 16, when there would be few witnesses to the flash from the explosion. While on the general's plane, Conant finished his letter about his visit with Ted, the heavy vibration of the plane making his handwriting more illegible than usual. Both boys were now on hazardous duty in the Pacific, which only added to his sense of urgency about completing the bomb. He and Groves would overnight in Pasadena and continue on to the Trinity site in the morning. Conant could say nothing of this to Patty, and simply closed the letter by apologizing for once again leaving her in the lurch, explaining, "This is an interesting trip, and I just had to take it, as you will see some day." There is nothing out of the ordinary in his tone, though the letter is more personal than most, and is signed affectionately, "your adoring Jim."

Their plane landed on the small Pasadena airstrip with a terrific thud, bringing everyone out of the operations office at a run. Among the group waiting to meet them was one of Conant's security officers, who remarked later that, if not the first, at least the second thought that flashed through his mind was: "How am I going to explain the accidental death of Bush, Conant, and Groves without publicity to the project and resulting breaches of security?" To avoid the incoming fog, they left early the next morning from March Field in Riverside, and, after landing in Albuquerque, drove the last 125 miles along the Rio Grande to Alamogordo. They arrived at base camp, about 9 miles from point zero, at about five in the afternoon.

The Project Trinity team had built a small desert laboratory, with its own administrative building, support facilities, and primitive living quarters for 125 military and scientific personnel. The test site consisted of a series of wood-and-concrete-slab bunkers covered by earth, which were built to protect the test instruments, generators, cameras, and personnel. The "gadget" had been raised to the top of the tower and was ready to go, a pile of mattresses stacked beneath it just in case the winch failed and it fell.

The mood at base camp was strained. Oppenheimer, looking drawn despite his tan, revealed that they might be in trouble. Bad news had come from Los Alamos. The test firing of the dummy rig, a twin for the Trinity explosive assembly except without the plutonium core, had not detonated properly. All indications were the Trinity bomb would be a dud. Stunned, Oppenheimer called an emergency meeting that quickly deteriorated into a shouting match. Kistiakowsky was identified as the "chief villain" and bore the brunt of their fury, with Oppie, Groves, and Bush taking turns grilling him for his incompetence and for jeopardizing months of hard work. "Everybody lectured me," Kistiakowsky recalled. "Only Conant was reasonable."

They spent a miserable night at the Albuquerque Hilton, all of them struggling to hide their dismay over the large number of generals and VIPs Groves had invited to observe the test. A call from Hans Bethe early the next morning revealed it was a false alarm. He had stayed up all night reviewing the data and discovered an error. The chances were good that the "gadget" would go off as planned.

Conant learned the Los Alamos physicists had set up a pool to take bets on the size of the explosion. "A few pessimists" wagered it would be a flop (0), with lowball bets by Oppenheimer (300 tons of TNT) and Kistiakowsky (1,400), all the way to a very optimistic Ed Teller, who believed the yield would be higher than 45,000 tons of TNT. Conant's own conservative figure was 4,400, but he decided as a project leader it would be bad form to participate.

When they returned to base camp Sunday evening, Oppenheimer greeted them, looking grim—there was more bad news. The weather forecast was distinctly unfavorable. After dinner, the winds picked up to thirty miles an hour, and the air grew heavy. A thunderstorm was threatening. The hundred-foot tower stuck out on the flat plain like a giant lightning rod. Many of the scientists were urging Oppenheimer to postpone the test, and he was being bombarded with advice from all sides about what should or should not be done. Some argued there might be a "reversal," with the swirling winds changing direction and blowing radioactive debris back onto the base camp. Others worried the rain might affect the electrical connections and increase the chances of a misfire.

Conant thought the atmosphere was "a bit tense, as might be expected," but Groves did not like it and felt everyone was dangerously keyed up. He pulled Oppenheimer into an empty office and listed all the reasons why the test had to happen. If the gadget got soaked, it might take days to dry out. Every hour of delay increased the risk of sabotage, and he had already ordered Kistiakowsky and two others to stand guard overnight at the tower. People's nerves had been pushed to the breaking point, and a delay would be unendurable. More to the point, the events at Potsdam prevented them from even considering calling it off. Conant and Bush, along with other leading scientists, had been pushing the president to advise the Russians that the United States was working on a bomb and expected to use it against Japan. Truman needed to know the results of Trinity to use in his negotiations with Stalin the next day. Oppenheimer said he understood, but spent the next few hours pacing and chain-smoking.

At around eleven o'clock, Groves told Oppie to go to bed and get some rest. Conant, who shared a tent with Bush and the general, found it impossible to sleep. "From 10:30 a.m. to 1 a.m. it blew very hard," he wrote in his diary, the tension and flapping canvas tent sides keeping him awake. "Then it poured for about an hour!" At one in the morning, Groves got up and drove out to the forward barricade to review the situation with Oppenheimer. Just after the rain stopped at 3:15, Rabi stuck his head in their tent and reported there had been "much talk of postponement," but after receiving the latest forecast, Groves had decided the test would take place at 5:00 a.m., by which point the storm would hopefully have passed. Conant and Bush threw on their clothes, gulped some coffee, and went outside. The sky was still overcast, but it was beginning to clear. Then word came that the test would be at 5:30 a.m.

At 5:10 a.m. Groves came back, and they prepared to view the shot from a trench carved into a slight rise near the camp, seventeen thousand yards from point zero. Fermi was at the same observation spot. He had irked Groves the night before by indulging in a bit of black-humored speculation about whether the bomb would "ignite the atmosphere" when detonated and blow them all to bits, a scenario first raised by Teller at the Berkeley conference and later laid to rest by Bethe. By bringing it up again only moments before the firing, Fermi was tempting fate in more ways than one. When the warning sirens blew, Conant and Bush took their positions on either side of the general. They had been instructed to lie belly down on the tarpaulin with their feet toward ground zero, and to look away at the start, and then look up, and to make sure to use the rectangle of dark green welder's glass they had been given to shield their eyes.

Through the loudspeaker nearby, they could hear physicist Samuel Allison count down the final seconds: "minus forty-five, minus forty, minus thirty, minus twenty . . ." After minus ten, there was an eerie silence, and Conant whispered to Groves that he "never imagined seconds could be so long." He kept his eyes open, staring at the horizon opposite the spot. "Then came a burst of white light that seemed to fill the sky and seemed to last for seconds. I had expected a relatively quick and bright flash. The enormity of the light and its length quite stunned me. My instantaneous reaction was that something had gone wrong and that the thermonuclear transformation of the atmosphere, once discussed as a possibility and only jokingly referred to a few minutes earlier, had actually occurred."

Blinded for a second, Conant rolled onto his back and raised his head slightly, viewing the fireball through the dark glass. It looked like "an enormous pyrotechnic display with great boiling of luminous vapors." Without thinking, he lowered his glass and watched the ball of gas turn into a large, expanding mushroom cloud, reddish purple against the predawn sky. After the initial roar, there was the deep rumbling sound of thunder as the blast reverberated in the distant hills. Then someone shouted, "Look out for the detonation wave!" but where they were, it only felt like a gust of hot wind forty seconds after zero. There were two secondary explosions, sending the cloud billowing upward. Conant turned to Groves and, at a loss for words, acknowledged their achievement with a silent handshake. Bush, who was on the general's other side, did likewise. As they got to their feet, Conant heard Groves mutter, "Well, I guess there is something in nucleonics after all." Then they heard the whole assembled group let out a spontaneous cheer.

Oppenheimer pulled up in his jeep, relief written all over his face. Groves congratulated him quietly. As they stood there, dazed but happy that their experiment had succeeded, the project leaders were mobbed by ecstatic scientists. The men came rushing in from the various shelters, hooting and hollering, slapping them on the back, and showering them with congratulations. The outburst was in its own way as violently intense as the eruption they had just witnessed. It was the sudden release of many months, even years, of pent-up emotions—of relief and hope, fear and exhaustion—a jubilant howl that the gadget had worked and their job was done.

The project leaders exercised more restraint. Although they were gratified that all their efforts, and the vast expenditures, had not gone to waste, their thoughts were already "wrapped up in the future," Groves recalled, and whether they could repeat that morning's performance and soon bring the war to an end. They had managed to prove that the plutonium implosion bomb worked, but that did not mean the next one would. Or that the completely untested uranium gun-type bomb would go off in combat—but that would have to be the first one deployed, as they had used up their entire supply of plutonium in the Trinity test, and it would take time to produce more fissionable material. As Conant put it later, "It was only a matter of probability that the first bombs used would be successful."

By then, the reports began coming in from all over. Kistiakowsky came over, covered in dust and grinning broadly. He had been standing at the South-10,000 bunker and said the force of the blast had "knocked him off his feet." Kisty had bet Oppenheimer a month's salary against $10 that the implosion device would work and was looking forward to collecting his winnings. The most exciting news was that the steel tower over Jumbo eight hundred yards away had "disappeared," Conant recalled. "This was unexpected and showed a very much more powerful effect than expected." Someone with binoculars located what looked like the remains of the twisted wreckage lying on its side. The blast scorched the heart of the test area, vaporizing the main tower and leaving a mile-wide swathe flattened and devoid of life. Later, two lead-lined Sherman tanks drove to zero point and discovered a vast sloping crater coated in molten gray-green glass formed from fused sand. There was no question they had achieved a nuclear reaction. Rabi won the pool: the test instruments showed that the force of the blast was around 18,600 tons of TNT. According to Teller, there was so much uncertainty that apart from himself, practically everyone bet too low, and Rabi admitted that he bet high only out of courtesy.

Later in the morning, they received more sobering reports. The scientists at the North-10,000 shelter had been forced to evacuate in a hurry when their meter went "off the scale." There was some radioactive fallout, but the level of toxicity, Conant wrote, proved "not serious." Still, the question of fallout would need closer examination. They had a network of men equipped with Geiger counters taking readings from the moving cloud. By eleven in the morning, they were faced with a security problem. With the "usual freakiness" of such explosions, the bomb had done little damage at base camp, or anywhere else nearby, but had cracked two plate glass windows in Silver City, New Mexico, 180 miles away. The blast had been much bigger than expected and was exciting the interest of reporters across the state. Groves approved a press release explaining that a remote ammunition dump had accidentally exploded. There was no loss of life, but weather conditions affecting the "content of gas shells" might make it necessary for the army to "evacuate temporarily a few civilians from their homes."

Before he left at noon, Conant ran into Sam Allison. The initial euphoria had faded, and the Chicago physicist looked distraught. "Oh, Dr. Conant," he said, as though just realizing that they had created a weapon of war. "They're going to take this thing and fry hundreds of Japanese!"

Conant drove to Albuquerque with Groves, Bush, Tolman, and Lawrence, and traveled on the general's plane to Nashville, where they spent the night. Groves had counted on holding meetings later that afternoon but recognized that "no one who had witnessed the test was in a frame of mind to discuss anything." On the way back, while the scientists talked over what they had seen, comparing notes on the world's first nuclear explosion, Groves turned his attention to the next phase of operations against Japan. A coded telegram had already been sent to Potsdam informing Stimson that the results of the "operation" were "satisfactory and already exceed expectations" and that "Dr. Groves was pleased." They could now start preparing for the transport of the components of the Little Boy bomb, along with the precious uranium—in two separate shipments, one by air and one by sea—to Tinian, the tiny Pacific island where the weapon would be assembled.

When Conant arrived at his Washington office the following afternoon, one of the first things he did was write up his account of the cataclysmic display in the desert for the OSRD files. There was no room for any soul searching or regret in his detailed eight-page report. A habit of a lifetime disinclined him from expressing his feelings and private fears, but he had been shaken to the core. A scientist to the last, he logged his clinical observations of the climax of the atomic project, noting only by way of conclusion its potential for global destruction:

"My first impression remains the most vivid, a cosmic phenomena like an eclipse. The whole sky suddenly full of white light like the end of the world. Perhaps my impression was only premature on a time scale of years!"

CHAPTER 17

A Changed World

The unleashed power of the atom has changed everything save our modes of thinking, and we thus drift toward unparalleled catastrophe.

—Albert Einstein

At eleven o'clock on the morning of August 6, 1945, radio stations began broadcasting a message from President Truman informing the American public that the United States had dropped an atomic bomb on the Japanese city of Hiroshima. Speaking in a stilted voice, with his flat Missouri inflections, he explained that the United States had "loosed" a weapon "harnessing the basic power of the universe." American and British scientists, working under the direction of the United States Army, had created the largest bomb in the history of warfare, adding "a new and revolutionary increase in destruction" to their arsenal. They were now prepared to obliterate every productive enterprise above ground in any city in Japan. The Potsdam ultimatum issued on July 26 had been designed to spare the Japanese people from "utter destruction," but their leaders had rejected it. If they did not accept American terms now, "they may expect a rain of ruin from the air, the like of which has never been seen on this earth."

Conant listened to the prepared statement with a mixture of pride and anguish. The White House announcement broke four years of silence, wrenching him from the clandestine cocoon of S-1 into the harsh glare of the spotlight. He had gone about the grim business of making weapons, carrying the tremendous secret burden foisted on him. He had achieved his objective: providing a weapon to end the war. It would eliminate the need for conquest by invasion, which the president's top military advisors estimated would save tens of thousands of American lives.

Conant did not doubt the "correctness of the action taken." The atomic bomb would force the Japanese Empire to bow to the Allies' superior power. The sooner Japan agreed to surrender, the sooner they could start working toward a stable peace. But at the same time, he could not help feeling a certain measure of dread. The bomb's efficient, deadly effect had been unleashed against the enemy—and it had been a terrible blow. Unless Japan acted quickly to sue for peace, more blows would follow. The components of Fat Man had already arrived at Tinian and were in the process of being assembled. A second plutonium bomb would be ready for use by August 24. Still more were in the pipeline: possibly another three in September and an additional seven in December. Truman had warned Japan that the retribution for continued resistance would be the annihilation of its industrial cities. Millions of leaflets carrying his warning were being dropped over the intended targets, instructing people to evacuate.

The next morning, Conant read his way through a stack of national newspapers. All of them dutifully printed the official history of the hitherto classified Manhattan Project—complete with his congratulatory handclasp with Groves after the Trinity test—supplied by the War Department. Truman, who had addressed the nation from aboard the USS *Augusta* as he sailed back from Potsdam, praised the atomic bomb as a technical triumph and a "marvel." It was the brainchild of many "scientists of distinction," who had worked together with their British colleagues to beat the Germans in the "battle of the laboratories" and win the race of discovery. "What has been done is the greatest achievement of organized science in history," the president declared, and it was done in an amazingly short time, "under pressure and without failure."

The laudatory language made Conant distinctly uneasy. He did not like seeing his name and face featured so prominently with the weapon that had decimated an entire city in a fraction of a second. The papers had gone to press before the details of the damage were known, but early estimates were that a greater part of Hiroshima had been gutted and the number of casualties might reach two hundred thousand—ten times Oppenheimer's estimate to the Interim Committee.* "Air became flame, walls turned to dust," reported the crew of the *Enola Gay* of the immolating blast. A monstrous column of smoke had erupted forty thousand feet into the sky, where it spilled into a huge, billowy mushroom cloud that hung over what was left of the teeming factory town. The poisonous radioactive particles had not yet settled, but when they did, those within a certain radius who escaped death would be burned, blinded, maimed, or diseased. Conant knew the American public would recoil from these horrors of war. He had seen it happen after World War I: the general rejoicing on the day of triumph, the relief that millions of troops would be coming home, and then, as memories of the suffering attending each additional day of war dimmed, the widespread repudiation of the weapons of mass destruction. He knew how quickly gratitude for victory abated in the face of such indiscriminate slaughter.

While the front-page stories celebrated the "Atom Age" and the "greatest scientific gamble" of all time, the editorial columns already contemplated the terrifying new chapter in human history. In an editorial entitled "The Haunted Wood," the *Washington Post* observed that most Americans responded to the revelations about the secret weapon "not with exultation but a kind of bewildered awe," wondering at the grotesque science-fiction fantasy they now found themselves in. Out of the wreck of the rational universe had come an invention whose development was driven by a race for survival but now threatened to doom civilization. With characteristic American optimism, Truman had announced "a new era in man's understanding of nature's forces," and predicted the day when atomic energy would replace coal, oil, and hydroelectric dams, but what was really necessary, the *Post* warned, was "a new era in the understanding of the nature of man, and whether it was really desirable for him to play with such toys as atoms. Otherwise the story of homo sapiens would become, as the late Lord Balfour once said, 'a brief and unpleasant episode in the history of one of the minor planets.'"

The *New York Times* foresaw an uncertain future dominated by a weapon with the gravest consequences. "Yesterday we clinched victory in the Pacific,

---

* As more information became available, the death toll at Hiroshima was estimated to be 100,000, with another 130,000 wounded and more than 8,000 missing. Those figures would increase steadily as the Japanese reported fatalities due to injuries and radiation exposure: the total number of deaths was approximately 140,000, with the five-year total estimated to have reached 200,000.

but we sowed the whirlwind," wrote the paper's military analyst Hanson Baldwin on August 7. "Certainly with such God-like power under man's imperfect control, we face a frightful responsibility."

From war-ravaged England, Winston Churchill, who had led his country to victory only to be defeated in July by Clement Attlee's Labour Party in the first general election since the war began, observed solemnly that the atom bomb, "more surely than the rocket, carries the warning that another world war would mean the destruction of all regulated life."

The comments reflected Conant's own growing sense of foreboding since Trinity. He, too, recognized the revolutionary character of atomic weapons and that without a means of control, such unprecedented power could overwhelm mankind. His main argument for the combat use of the bomb had been the need to prove its "devastating strength" to the world, so that warring nations would realize that the stakes had become too high and armed conflict too costly. Most Los Alamos scientists, from Bohr to Oppenheimer, had come to embrace the view that the bomb might bring an end to war itself. There could be no defense against such a destructive force. Once the nuclear threat went from scare propaganda to fearful reality, atomic energy could be used as an instrument of diplomacy in negotiations, and ensure worldwide cooperation in outlawing its military use and evolving peacetime applications for human welfare. Surely avoiding an arms race and future atomic wars, Conant and Bush had written to the Interim Committee days after the Alamogordo test, "must be the prime objective of every sane man."

All his hopes for the postwar situation depended on Japan's recognizing the larger significance of the weapon and conceding defeat immediately. Yet only a deathly silence came from the shattered island. Radio Tokyo was continuing to exhort people to defend the honor of their country and keep fighting. With so much riding on the bomb providing the necessary "shock" to compel the enemy's capitulation, Conant could hardly tear himself away from the radio. The strain of waiting was almost unbearable. If Japan did not respond soon, did not accept the Potsdam terms of unconditional surrender, the war would drag on to the bitter end, and any possibility of the weapon becoming an aid to peace would go up in smoke.

On August 8 Russia kept its promise to enter the war against Japan, sending a million troops into Manchuria to drive back the once-mighty Kwantung Army. It had long been believed that Soviet assistance in the Pacific would shorten the war, but it took Truman's whisper of a new weapon at Potsdam to seal their cooperation. The expert opinion was that the combination of Russian belligerency and the bomb would convince the Japanese that they were completely outmatched and enable the end-of-war advocates in the Suzuki government to begin negotiations. On Capitol Hill, there were complaints about Stalin's self-serving maneuver, timing his "Joey-come-lately" entrance after America's show of power and just before Japan's imminent collapse. Although he shared their cynical view of Moscow, Conant was counting on Russia's declaration to finally make the Japanese military leaders accept the humiliation of defeat. In view of the "hopeless odds," reported the *Times*, Washington was predicting an "early peace." The end was near.

Conant was not prepared for the terrible swiftness of the assault on Nagasaki. The implosion bomb disemboweled the imperial port city on August 9, digging a huge crater and destroying more than a square mile. As expected, the improved Fat Man bomb created a bigger blast than Little Boy—twenty-one thousand tons of TNT versus fifteen thousand—immediately rendering its predecessor obsolete. The death toll and magnitude of the damage would have been considerably greater except that dense fog hid the naval base, causing the bomb to be dropped two miles wide of its target. Twelve hours later, Nagasaki was still a mass of flames, a scorched ruin covered by a dense cloud of acrid smoke. The tall, black pyre, visible to reconnaissance pilots two hundred miles away, was thought to be the pulverized remains of the Mitsubishi Steel and Arms Works that had made the torpedoes used in the Pearl Harbor attack. According to Japanese news reports, the jammed shipbuilding yards and warehouses "crumbled and disintegrated under the devastating effect of the atomic bomb." Seventy thousand were instantly incinerated, the charred and blistered corpses "too numerous to be counted."

Conant had known, of course, that a second bomb was possible, even inevitable, though he did not take part in the final operational meetings held by Secretary of War Stimson, Groves, and Generals Marshall and Carl A. Spaatz, commander of the Twentieth Air Force. The scientists had been responsible for the development of the weapon, but the specific decisions about its deployment were a military matter—that had been understood from the beginning. There were no last-minute discussions in the seventy-five-hour interval following the Hiroshima attack in which to consider a second strike or its role in possibly hastening the end of the war. By that time, he noted in his memoir, they were already committed to an unswerving course, "and the detailed arrangements had been made for the use of a bomb as soon as enough material had been produced." The plans were locked in place and military protocols took over: the Tinian bomber command never received a direct order to destroy a second city, it simply carried out Groves's original directive, which included the instruction to deliver "additional bombs" to the designated targets as they became available and the weather permitted.

Whatever the psychological effect of the atomic bomb, General Spaatz was "taking no chances," he told reporters, keeping up the pressure on Japan by hitting it with another American secret weapon: napalm. At approximately the same time as the Nagasaki strike, thirty-eight thousand tons of "napalm bombs" were dropped on military installations in southern Kyushu. The previous day, 385 Superfortresses had carried out conventional bombing raids on another four industrial cities—having already laid flame to sixty—taking out chemical and steel factories in Wakamatsu, Tobata, Kurosaki, and Kokura, and, in what Spaatz described as a "mopping-up operation," leveled a major aircraft plant and arsenal in Tokyo. The new firebomb attacks were part of an intensified aerial assault meant to make the enemy yield, with fighter pilots vowing to "finish off" the murderous Japs. Conant winced at the bloodthirsty, racially tinged rhetoric, but he knew that for the combat forces, the pursuit of complete victory was more than justified by the treacherous attack on Pearl Harbor, the infamous Bataan Death March, and the brutal battles for Iwo Jima and Okinawa. The Pacific commanders were hell-bent on getting the job done and getting it done quickly, determined not to have to take on the tenacious Japanese soldiers, with their willingness to fight to the death, on their home turf.

On Thursday, August 9, Truman put out a special call to his top scientific and military advisors to attend a meeting at the White House to discuss what the public should be told about the bomb. Stimson postponed his Thursday morning press conference in order to attend, and Byrnes hurried over from the State Department building. They were dealing with what Groves described as a "royal foul-up" in the handling of the news stories from the Pacific, to say nothing of Spaatz's ill-advised comments on his mission. They had not adequately anticipated the enormous pressure from the newspapers for information about the atomic bombs, the impossibility of imposing restrictions on the coverage, and the difficulty of "clearing" all the dispatches from the large number of war correspondents in Guam. In short, they had been deluged, and chaos quickly ensued.

They were better prepared on the domestic front, thanks to Conant's foresight in having Henry Smyth's official report on the Manhattan Project ready for public consumption, edited carefully with an eye to security considerations, and giving credit where credit was due. One thousand copies had been printed using the Pentagon's production facilities and were locked in Groves's safe awaiting the president's approval.

From the beginning, Conant's argument in favor of issuing the *Smyth Report* was that the sudden revelation of the bomb would generate tremendous excitement and, along with it, all kinds of reckless and irresponsible statements by unrestrained scientists. Presenting the basic scientific facts would provide a basis for rational discussion, and the gesture of openness would make it easier to hold the line on important military secrets. At a meeting on August 2, Conant had persuaded both Groves and Stimson, along with their reluctant British allies, that publishing the document would appease the critics and possibly avoid further political agitation, with relatively little sacrifice. As to Stimson's concern that they might be divulging data that would assist the Soviet atomic effort, Conant had replied frankly that *Time* magazine could probably discover its entire contents in short order. After listening to all the arguments, Truman approved its immediate release.

The Sunday newspapers carried lengthy excerpts of the *Smyth Report*. Conant, who oversaw the writing and editing of the book at every stage, clearly had a hand in composing the preface that placed the "ultimate responsibility" for the nation's policy on its citizens, and trusted their ability to discharge their responsibilities wisely if informed by "a substantial group of engineers and scientific men who can understand such things and who can explain the potentialities of atomic bombs to their fellow citizens."

During the war, security requirements had meant that the decisions had to be made by only the scientists, the president, and a few advisors. In the postwar years, the nation would still face momentous decisions. If anyone was in a position to lead the way in the nuclear age, and grapple with the new dangers, Conant believed it was knowledgeable "scientific men" such as himself and Bush. While the bomb posed a serious threat, in the immediate future it would shift the balance of power substantially in favor of the United States. It was up to them to take advantage of the opportunity and find a way to achieve an international understanding to avert the catastrophe of nuclear warfare. He was eager to start shaping an atomic policy that might prevent the evils of his age from being repeated, even though privately he was less than sanguine that the weapon he had helped to create would lead to a world more fit for human habitation.

At breakfast time on August 10, Washington learned from Radio Tokyo broadcasts that Japan would accept the Potsdam Declaration provided that Emperor Hirohito could remain as sovereign ruler. This first word was unofficial, but Truman convened his military advisors for a nine o'clock morning meeting. Stimson wanted to make it as easy as possible for the Japanese to acquiesce and argued that retaining the emperor, a revered symbol of authority, might work to the Allies' advantage in the occupation. Byrnes was adamantly opposed and held out for unconditional surrender. While they debated a middle road, Truman decided against dropping the third atomic bomb—Los Alamos was already prepping another plutonium core—but ordered the Twentieth Air Force to continue its intensive firebombing campaign. Any concern Truman might have had that the American people would oppose retaining the emperor, whom the *New York Times* had only ten days earlier compared with Hitler, was erased by the overwhelming reaction of the troops in the field: "GIs in Pacific Go Wild with Joy," read the *Times* headline on August 10. "Let 'Em Keep the Emperor They Say."

Meanwhile, the militarists in the Japanese Cabinet were also dissatisfied with the terms and staged an unsuccessful palace coup to prevent the broadcast of the surrender. But by then, even the emperor recognized that the time for face-saving had passed. The reality was the country was already defeated: fifty-eight major cities had been laid to waste, nine million were wounded or homeless, and more than two million had died.

At noon on Tuesday, August 14, in a radio address to his subjects, who had never before heard his voice and could hardly understand his formal manner of speaking, the emperor stated that he had resolved to end the war "by enduring the unendurable and suffering what is insufferable." In his speech, Hirohito acknowledged the "new and terrible weapon" that had forced him to succumb:

"Should we continue to fight, not only would it result in an ultimate collapse and obliteration of the Japanese nation, but also it would lead to the total extinction of human civilization. Such being the case, how are we to save millions of our subjects, or to atone before the hallowed spirits of our Imperial Ancestors? This is the reason we have ordered the acceptance of the provisions of the Joint Declaration of the Powers."

At seven o'clock, Truman announced to the public that he had "received that afternoon a message from the Japanese government." It was as if the whole country had been holding its breath waiting for the news of surrender. In Washington, the first reaction brought a sudden hush, and then buildings began emptying of people as they poured into the streets and pushed through Lafayette Park in their rush to reach the iron fence outside the White House. The reaction grew in intensity as the exuberant crowd formed an impromptu parade up Fourteenth Street, accompanied by blaring automobile horns, backfiring trucks, ringing bells, and the growing roar of human voices raised in triumph and exultation. It was a bright, warm summer evening, and every restaurant and bar was packed with sailors, soldiers, Wacs, Waves, and government girls toasting the hard-won peace. The raucous celebration carried on until dawn. In the morning, the streets of downtown Washington were littered with broken bottles, tossed hats, and torn paper. Scattered everywhere were trampled copies of the late edition of the *Washington Star*, bearing the banner headline "The War Is Over."

Conant could not share in the unconditional jubilation that swept the nation. Tragically, peace in the Pacific did not come soon enough to spare his son, Jim, from harm. While attacking a Japanese convoy in the Luzon Strait, his submarine was spotted and driven down, and subjected to a depth charge assault of savage and sustained ferocity. Badly mauled, her position known to her attackers, the *Halibut*'s crew endured hours of desperate maneuvering before the enemy gave up, and the crippled sub finally surfaced in the dark and crept to the recently captured island of Saipan. Battered beyond repair, the *Halibut* was relegated to the scrap yard, but instead of being relieved of duty, her young deck officer was assigned to a new boat and ordered back to the war zone.* Just after he learned the bomb had been dropped, Conant received news that Jim had "cracked up" before going out on his sixth consecutive patrol and was in a hospital in Pearl Harbor. He was afflicted with what the doctor described as "a severe case of combat fatigue" and was being sent to a treatment facility on the Treasure Island naval base outside San Francisco.

"Coming just at this time, the news was a kick in the teeth," Conant wrote to his old friend Grenville Clark on August 17 in response to his letter congratulating him on the success of the bomb. "These psychoneurotic cases

---

* In 1946 James R. Conant was awarded the Silver Star medal for his performance as a torpedo data computer operator.

are bound to be long and distressing for all concerned," he noted resignedly, though he hastened to add that it was "nothing" compared with what others had suffered. Conant had already confided in Groves, who advised him that the "mental condition of being shell-shocked" was quite characteristic for anyone caught in the midst of an explosion, as was a certain lingering nervousness, and complete recovery could take as long as two years.

Stuck in Washington on official business, Conant telephoned Ted, who was on a layover in the Bay Area, and asked him to go see his brother. Unable to bring himself to discuss Jim's condition, Conant did not let on about the nature of his wounds. Nineteen-year-old Ted strolled into the hospital carrying a book and a bar of chocolate for the patient, and was directed down long corridors, and through heavier and heavier steel doors with reinforced glass, until he was surprised to find himself at the locked psychiatric ward. The desolate, hostile, hallucinating figure he saw in the padded cell bore almost no resemblance to the elegant, white-uniformed lieutenant who had proudly showed off his sub to him eighteen months earlier, giving him a playful thump as he clambered onboard. Jim saluted him and then began raging. He was spewing profanities—every foul word in a sailor's lexicon—all his fury and fitful accusations aimed directly at their parents. Shocked, Ted backed out of the room. It would be many years before he would forgive his father for sending him on a get-well visit without warning him that his brother was "stark-raving mad."

Every doctor's letter—and there were many—describing Jim's breakdown—and there would be more to come—was systematically shredded and discarded. Patty blamed his frayed nerves on the war and would not hear of any other cause, though she knew from her days as a hospital volunteer that the stress of prolonged combat could inflame existing neuroses. More than one psychiatrist would attempt to point out the history of mental illness in her family, to no avail. Denial was her way of coping. Conant went along with it, instinctively trying to shield her from any diagnosis that might add to her woes. He could barely cope himself. His personal stoicism ran too deep to countenance such a complete loss of self-control. He had pinned all his hopes on his firstborn, his favorite son and namesake. How could someone with such promise, with such a first-rate mind, become so emotionally unhinged? He simply could not fathom it. One psychiatrist would later remark to Ted that while he considered the Harvard scientist to be a brilliant man, he had never met anyone so obtuse about the complexities of the human brain.

Conant hid his grief and worry as best he could and threw himself into the problems of peace, campaigning for national and international atomic energy policies to protect the country from the hazards of nuclear warfare. Haunted by the proof of the almost limitless destructive force he had helped unleash, his worldview darkened. Truman had told the nation that the bomb was "too dangerous to be loose in a lawless world," and that was why America and Great Britain, who alone possessed the atomic "secret," must act as "trustees of this new force."

Conant could not have said it better, but he worried that the new administration failed to appreciate the far-reaching implications of the weapon, and lacked the moral vision and political maturity to plot a wise course. The president had made only a guarded mention of the bomb to Stalin at Potsdam, and the decision not to enlist the Russians in collaboration and control did not augur well for postwar cooperation. The abiding faith in the future that once led Conant to observe of the Manhattan Project that "only optimists would have willingly entered this Alice in Wonderland area of exploration," now gave way to new skepticism and distrust that there was any way to safeguard such great power. "The world is changed," Stimson had stated at the Pentagon press conference on August 9. "The result of the bomb is so terrific that the responsibility of its possession and its use must weigh heavier on our minds and on our hearts."

In the fall of 1945, responsibility for the bomb weighed very heavily on Conant. Returning to Harvard, and the pulpit of Memorial Church, at his greatest moment of personal triumph, he spoke in somber tones of the challenges of the postwar world. "For military courage, we must substitute civic courage," he explained at the opening day ceremony, addressing a student body filled with veterans. "Easy attitudes of complete cynicism on the one hand or Pollyanna optimism on the other are equally disastrous; it is a narrow and perilous knife edge [we] must walk."

There was a danger, which he had pointed to in a speech in 1943, that the principle "the end justifies the means," applied in a time of war to ensure a speedy victory, "could engender such conditions in our minds that we would be unable to preserve liberty when the time of peace had come." In the heat of struggle, a free nation might be forced to preserve its existence by measures that contradicted its founding principles—just as a battalion commander might have no choice but to resort to a ruthless human calculus to save his men, deciding to sacrifice a scouting party for the sake of the regiment. But in a time of peace, democratic countries had to repudiate the doctrine of the end justifies the means. America had to "reorient its sights" and struggle to find a way through the "shifting muddy ground" to the bedrock below—the basic ideals of equality and individual freedom it fought to preserve.

While Conant cautioned against "fear, panic, and foolish, short-sighted action" in his public speeches, privately he was wrestling with his own post-atomic jitters. The reverberations from the two bombs dropped on Japan were still rolling in from around the world, but the lesson driven home was that they had changed forever how war was waged. Doleful columnists were predicting "push-button wars" and pilotless "robot planes" that trivialized transoceanic distances and made American cities and industry vulnerable to a "hail of atomic charges." The significance of the atomic bomb as a military weapon lay in its compactness, in the tremendous power inherent in small volume. One B-29 carrying an atomic bomb was the equivalent of one or two thousand B-29s loaded to capacity with TNT. One plane could now do the work of an armada. "There was no defense against a surprise attack with atomic bombs," he warned.

Abandoning his usual cool detachment, Conant allowed himself to be caught up in the growing national paranoia. Only weeks after victory, he wrote War Department officials that atomic weapons were so effective they had to expect their use in the coming wars and begin paying serious attention to preparing for them. Inasmuch as laboratories and factories held the key to technical superiority, they would become the primary targets and would need to be defended. This "revolution in warfare" necessitated not only a change in military strategy but also a complete rethinking of postwar urban industrial planning if they wanted to survive an atomic attack, especially "the important problem of location of civilian industry and the nature of American cities."

The extent to which the scientist had come to fear his Frankenstein creation was evident to Harvard's chief librarian, Keyes DeWitt Metcalf, when Conant summoned him to his office in September and presented him with a strange, almost fanciful proposal to protect the crown jewels of knowledge that sounded like something straight out of H. G. Wells's *World Brain*.

"We are living in a very different world since the explosion of the A-bomb," Conant began, addressing the problem of what could be done in the event "much of our present civilization" was threatened with extinction. "We do not want to lose permanently a large part of civilization, as happened when Rome fell fifteen hundred years ago," he continued, noting that the "greatest disaster" associated with its downfall was the loss of a wealth of information that was then recorded only in manuscripts that were destroyed or lost. "It has seemed to me that in the world's present situation, it might be advisable to select the printed material that would preserve a record of our civilization for one we can hope will follow, microfilming it and making perhaps ten copies, and burying these in ten different places throughout the country."

Metcalf, who was married to Patty's first cousin Elinor, listened in astonishment to Conant's apocalyptic scenario and the secret precautions he was planning for the benefit of the survivors of World War III. "How many volumes would have to be copied, and what would it cost?" Conant asked. "How should the material be selected?" "How should it be organized?" Would Metcalf please look into the matter and get back to him in two weeks. Swallowing his dismay, the Harvard librarian did as he was asked and returned with a list of figures. In order to "preserve the material on which our present civilization is based," he reported straight-faced, they would need to film 500,000 volumes, averaging 500 pages each, or a total of 250 million pages. Ten sets would amount to 2.5 billion pages in all. He did not attempt to go into the huge costs.

"This would include the great literature of all countries that should not be lost, such as everything written by Shakespeare, Tolstoy, Dante, and Goethe," Metcalf advised, adding there would be no need to preserve more than a few of the thousands of volumes written about these writers and their works. This would also be true for other great authors of books about music, the fine arts, history, philosophy, economics, and—perhaps especially important—the sciences and all the new developments. It would be difficult to select the material, but he believed it could be done. That said, he thought it would be a "mistake" to go ahead with the project.

"It could not be done without the world learning about it," he told Conant. "Everyone would be so upset at the idea of such a catastrophe as the destruction of what we call our civilization that it would be unwise to undertake the task." After handing in his report, Metcalf heard "nothing more about it," and concluded that the normally levelheaded university president had only temporarily lost his bearings in the confusion of momentous events. In fact, Conant had concluded that in the event of a nuclear war, university libraries outside the major cities would most likely escape destruction, eliminating the need for the expensive project.

Conant was hardly alone in experiencing a kind of delayed reaction to the bombings. He and his fellow atomic scientists had lived with the fact of the weapon for years, had experienced what Ernest Lawrence called the "mighty thunder" at Alamogordo, so, unlike the public, they were not stunned by the news from Japan. For them, the psychological repercussions lay in their growing horror of the nuclear holocaust—the grisly scenes reported in the aftermath of the attacks, and the deadly long-term effects of radiation poisoning that emerged in the weeks and months that followed. And in the very real fear that it would happen again. Oppenheimer, according to an FBI report, was a "nervous wreck" after Nagasaki, the descriptions of the dreadful effects being no less painful for being expected. His moral uneasiness had begun after the first atomic explosion in the New Mexico desert, when the blinding light had brought to mind lines from the Hindu scripture the Bhagavad Gita: "Now I am become Death, the destroyer of worlds."

Many of the Los Alamos scientists experienced a deep personal "revulsion" at their part in killing so many Japanese civilians, especially in regard to the second attack, which seemed so unnecessary. Their initial pride in saving the lives of thousands of American and Allied soldiers faded quickly when, among the praise, the Vatican registered its disapproval, and other accusing voices condemned the United States' action as "barbarism," "mass murder," and "sheer terrorism."

Some managed better than others with the crush of ambivalent emotions, finding solace in the idea that the bomb was so decisive, so destructive, that it could not be used again—that "war was now impossible." The atomic era must and would see the banning of nuclear weapons. For his part, Enrico Fermi did not believe that technical advances in weaponry would frighten men into not waging war, but felt, as a scientist, that moving forward had been a necessity: "It is no good trying to stop knowledge." Ignorance was not an alternative. Besides, if they had not built the bomb, someone else would have soon enough, and then where would they be? Better that it end up in American hands. Still others regretted the bombings but felt they could not criticize, rationalizing that they had no say in political and military decisions. Teller regretted the loss of life, but his explanation of why he did not regret working on the weapons took the form of a single question: "What if we hadn't?"

For most, however, a sense of guilt, "felt more or less deeply, more or less consciously was there, undeniably," recalled Laura Fermi, who watched how her husband and the other scientists were changed by the knowledge of what they had done. "They assumed for themselves the responsibility for

Hiroshima and Nagasaki, and for the evils that atomic power might cause anywhere, anytime."

On September 1 Samuel Allison, speaking on behalf of seventeen atomic scientists gathered for a luncheon at the Shoreland Hotel in Chicago, expressed their sorrow and outrage at the "tragic use" made of their discovery, and criticized the dropping of the second bomb. With the future of the project uncertain, he used the occasion to protest their ongoing imprisonment in the semiluxurious military camp known as Los Alamos, and to plead for the free dissemination of scientific knowledge and unhampered research in nuclear physics. Unless the army removed the restrictions on their freedom, Allison declared, America's physicists would stage a strike and "begin an elaborate study of the colors of butterfly wings."

The butterfly wings remark, the first public manifestation of the rift between the project scientists and their military supervisors, received widespread coverage in the national press. "Scientist Drops A-bomb: Blasts Army Shackles" was the next morning's headline in the *Chicago Tribune*. Ten days later, James Franck and sixty-four other University of Chicago faculty members signed a petition protesting the military's failure to involve them in the decision-making process, and urging the president to share the atomic "secret" with other nations to avoid an armaments race. They also formed an association to "clarify and consolidate" the opinion of the scientists on the consequences of atomic power, with the hope of influencing policy. Similar groups were organized at other project sites, including the Association of Los Alamos Scientists—with its mordant acronym, ALAS—and more appeals for free interchange and international control were published, as the increasingly frustrated scientists lost faith that anyone in Washington understood the atomic predicament.

"This place is a bit of a madhouse," a harassed Bush wrote Conant from Washington in late September, what with the scientists up in arms, various bills on atomic energy coming up before Congress, and basic policy issues in a tangle. "I have a good deal of worry in my mind that I am having to handle important matters without the full mature consideration that their importance warrants," he added, noting that he "missed the times you and I could resolve difficult points by discussion."

Conant, who was back at Harvard full-time and feeling somewhat removed from the "center of affairs" in Washington, was more than happy to vent his opinions on the array of atomic issues stirring public and congressional controversy. He agreed that the atomic scientists should not be subject to rigid military censorship, and hoped that Truman would follow Bush's advice and approve "letting them loose." Open communication and the exchange of ideas were the lifeblood of their community. The imposition of compartmentalization and secrecy ran counter to everything they believed and was at the root of their pent-up resentments.

Even his own family had not escaped the "poison of deception," Conant would later note in his memoir, and he would pay dearly for the many lies he had told to cover his tracks. When he tried after Hiroshima to tell his wife about his role in building the bomb, she had turned away from him in cold fury and snapped, "What makes you think I would be interested?" He realized her anger reflected more than just the "years of frustration" at being kept in the dark. She had discovered a book of matches from the Santa Fe Chief in his suit jacket after a trip he claimed had taken him no farther than Chicago and believed that he was hiding an affair. It was a hurt that could not be undone with an apology.

With regard to the project scientists, Conant was aware that his stinginess with the truth had made him an object of considerable contempt and "hostility." But it could not be helped. Although he sympathized with their concerns about freedom of research, he did not hold with their confrontational—and often self-righteous—tone. Moreover, he felt that as he was still formally a member of several wartime committees, he had to abstain from publicly criticizing Groves and other government officials. In any case, he preferred to exert his influence anonymously by shaping policy in the councils of the executive branch. By now, discretion had become more than a habit, it was his modus operandi.

Conferring with Bush confidentially on the essential issues involved in the future of atomic energy and US–Soviet relations, Conant did not hesitate to speak his mind. He weighed in forcefully in letter after letter, alternately persuading and exhorting his old friend to go all the way in pushing for an international organization to control the bomb in his first major postwar address. The end of the war had brought to the surface the mounting differences between Russia and the West, and Conant was convinced they needed to act quickly to make Moscow accept an American plan for an atomic monopoly with the promise of sharing technical information as the incentive.

In July he and Bush had presented Stimson with a plan for a scientific commission under the United Nations Organization that provided for limited interchange with Russia—"to test out their good faith"—and stipulating that for at least five years, the agency would have no jurisdiction over American laboratories involved with manufacturing fissionable materials and bombs. The agreement would go into effect in stages, the quid pro quo for each stage being opening Russian laboratories to unlimited access by foreign scientists and then acceptance of unlimited inspection of all nuclear facilities. If all went well, and the inspection process was working, and frequent checks revealed the Russians were honoring the system, then and only then could they consider broadening the agreement so that all fissionable materials would be used only for the production of commercial power.

This gradual approach to sharing the atomic secret might be a hard sell, but there was no hope of obtaining a reliable agreement for proscribing nuclear weapons unless America was willing to get tough with its powerful ally. "I think your statement about not threatening the world with our present power will not stand up under careful analysis," Conant wrote Bush, reflecting the Truman administration's new policy of firmness. "It seems to me, you do essentially threaten or bargain if you do anything short of 'blandly giving away the secret,' and I think we should bargain and bargain very hard."

Conant sent Bush a copy of an extremely detailed six-page letter on the future of the bomb he had prepared as a kind of primer for Grenville Clark, who had organized a conference in Dublin, New Hampshire, for forty-eight prominent peace-seeking thinkers who were in favor of some form of "world government" to remedy what they saw as the fatal weaknesses of the United Nations. There had been a groundswell of public support for the idea, thanks to the powerful appeals by prominent figures, from Einstein to *Saturday Review of Literature* editor Norman Cousins, who insisted it was "world state or world doom," as the columnist Max Lerner put it.

While Conant could not attend the gathering in Dublin, he spent a weekend in late September at Clark's country retreat, Outlet Farm, where they "talked atomic bomb for five hours," according to Clark's diary. Conant, who confided he was thinking about stepping down as president of Harvard—presumably to devote all his energies to atomic energy—no longer believed a world government was the way to save the world and stressed the urgent need for a strong international authority to control the new weapon. The recommendations outlined in his letter, which was read aloud at the conference by US Supreme Court Justice Owen Roberts, bluntly called for realism and extreme caution in the dangerous new era in which Russia and other countries "could shortly have the bomb":

What has the future in store for us in the way of further scientific and technical advances? Much more destructive bombs, of that we may be sure . . . If we are to avoid a destruction of our modern arsenals, the industrialized areas, and a large number of civilians, we must avoid another major war. As a step in this direction, international control of the atomic bomb would help, and failure to control it would certainly work in the other direction. But an attempt to eliminate the atomic bomb as a weapon by international control seems to me to be a mistake. Any such proposal has a slim chance of working, confuses our military thinking (playing into the hands of the diehards in the army and navy), and does nothing to make another war less likely.

Without international control, and rigorous international inspection, he predicted, "We shall have a secret armament race, which to my mind can only have one eventual result: war." In a frightening assertion, which left a pall over the audience of educators, businessmen, lawyers, and journalists, he warned, "Throughout this letter, I have assumed that in another war atomic bombs will be used. For us to plan otherwise would be the height of folly."

The issue came to a head quickly with President Truman's message to Congress on October 3, promising to pursue with other nations an agreement "under which cooperation might replace rivalry in the field of atomic power," and asking for prompt passage of domestic legislation to take care of the situation in the United States. The administration's atomic energy bill, based on a proposal Conant and Bush had submitted to the Interim Committee the previous fall, was introduced to Congress immediately after Truman's speech in hopes of getting a warm reception. Their ideas had been developed into draft legislation by two War Department lawyers, Kenneth Royall and William Marbury, and while the general outline of the bill was recognizably the same—establishing a nine-man atomic energy commission with strong government support and leadership—the Royall-Marbury version called for continuing strict military control of atomic energy more or less at wartime levels.

Conant and Bush had wanted the agency to return to a peacetime status, ensuring complete publication of all current information on nuclear physics, limiting the commission's sweeping powers over basic research, and making it an all-civilian body. The release of technical data might shorten

Russia's road to the bomb by two years, but, on the other hand, it seemed the best way to avoid the greater risk of an arms race. They were overruled by the army's lawyers. Strong military representation was preserved, and it was very much a War Department bill that Robert Patterson, who had replaced Stimson as war secretary, hoped to get enacted hastily.

Patterson arranged for Senator Edwin C. Johnson of Colorado, the ranking member of the Military Affairs Committee, and Andrew Jackson May, chairman of the House committee, to rush it through public hearings in just five hours with the intention of sending it to the floors of both chambers by the end of the week. All four expert witnesses—Groves, Conant, Bush, and Patterson—testified that the extraordinary powers granted the proposed commission were necessary to control atomic energy, and nothing else would be enough to protect the nation's security and keep people from being poisoned or possibly blown up by careless experiments.

"The misuse of such energy, by design or though ignorance," Conant testified, struggling to convey the depth of his feelings about the potential threat, "may inflict incalculable disaster upon the nation, destroy the general welfare, imperil the national safety, and endanger world peace."

If Patterson was hoping that the project leaders' wartime record of accomplishments and aura of prestige would allow them the last word on the matter, he was sorely mistaken. No sooner had the experts finished than came an avalanche of outraged protests from a large contingent of Met Lab and Oak Ridge scientists who descended on Washington, convinced the restrictive measure was a drive by Groves to extend the Manhattan Project and his own dictatorial powers. Leo Szilard led the opposition, arguing that the army was trying to silence the scientists, and that the provisions for iron security were part of the military's plan to retain their monopoly on what the president called America's atomic "secret." But there was no secret to keep, scientist after scientist swore to reporters and legislators. The laws of nature could not be withheld for long, the workings of the atom belonged to the world, and the bill would just stifle scientific research and start an arms race.

The passionate outpouring moved the public, which stood in awe of these brilliant "Men Who Made the Bomb," as the project physicists were dubbed by the press. Men who seemed so young, as evidenced by the parade of boyish faces, bow ties, and crew cuts, and yet at the same time so sure of their subject—in contrast to the tired, old politicians. In response, Congressman May grudgingly reopened the hearings—for a day. Even though

Oppenheimer and the Compton brothers went on to endorse the bill as reasonable, and expressed confidence in Conant and Bush, tensions rose precipitously.

Eleven weeks after Hiroshima, little progress had been made toward either "international security or international morality," scolded the *New York Times*'s Hanson Baldwin. "They have been weeks of confusion and divided counsel, of lack of leadership, of claims and contradictions—and all the while, the atomic bomb has clouded the skies of tomorrow." Conant, who continued to demand the bill's immediate passage, increasingly became the focus of the scientists' wrath. Some felt betrayed by the NDRC chairman, believing he no longer had their interests at heart and was in league with the military officials. Those who had clashed with him during the war, including Szilard and Urey, were sharpest in their attacks, accusing both him and Bush of trying to retain their hold over atomic policy. Conant weathered the onslaught of criticism with his usual Yankee stiff upper lip, writing Bush that it "doesn't bother me in the least, but it does indicate in a small way just what a storm would have broken over our heads if the bomb hadn't gone off. I hope that thought cheers you up. It does me."

As the clamor continued into November, it was obvious that the May-Johnson bill was hopelessly stalemated. The president quietly withdrew his support. Congress, paralyzed by the fear and uncertainty that surrounded the entire subject of atomic power—"sweating at the very thought of legislating about it," mocked *Time* magazine—regarded the issue as "a monster that seemed to be getting bigger, more red-eyed, and more terrifying with every passing day." Seizing the opportunity, freshman senator Brien McMahon of Connecticut, who had managed to get appointed chairman of the Special Committee on Atomic Energy, held hearings throughout November and most of December to educate both the politicians and the public on the issues at stake. He succeeded in introducing an alternative bill calling for the creation of a purely civilian agency to administer America's research and weapons program. Groves's many objections to the McMahon Bill almost guaranteed that the scientists would enthusiastically embrace it, but their delight diminished when the much-amended bill, which finally passed the Senate in the spring of 1946, contained a powerful military liaison embedded in the framework of the Atomic Energy Commission. The Atomic Energy Act was passed by the House in July and signed into law on August 1, 1946.

Thus the battle lines were drawn in the quest for control of atomic energy, which some had called "the greatest challenge mankind ever faced." The heat of the conflict between the army and scientists over control of the bomb, and the special capacity of the military to preserve national security, had left the two camps in deep disagreement and greatly widened the ideological divide. Perhaps it was inevitable that such a critical postwar issue would ignite controversy and debate, but by arrogating responsibility for atomic policy to themselves, Conant and Bush reinforced the rank-and-file scientists' impression that they were once again being cut out of the decision-making process. Their detractors had no way of knowing about the pair's behind-the-scenes agitation for international control and growing misgivings about the Soviets' expansionist intentions. Karl Compton, in an attempt to smooth things over, stated that the May-Johnson bill had been prepared with the "wisest of motives" and "nothing of the sinister intent which some people, including a good many of our scientists, have suspected."

But the ill will that had dominated the prolonged dispute did not dissipate and would soon fuel future controversies. As Richard Hewlett and Oscar Anderson Jr., the authors of *The New World*, observed, "The same men who could command unquestioned support for a two-billion-dollar secret project a few months earlier were now looked upon as power-hungry connivers."

After the president's reluctance to exercise the powers of his office in the struggle for domestic control of atomic energy, Conant and Bush had little expectation that he would deliver on his promise to move forward on international control. They were dismayed by Truman's decision not to attend the meeting of the Council of Foreign Ministers in London in September 1945, and despaired at the news that Byrnes's negotiations with the Russians had been acrimonious and unprofitable. Byrnes was convinced, as Stimson put it, that "the implied threat of the bomb in his pocket" would give him leverage. He had wrongly assumed that America's atomic monopoly would "make Russia more manageable in Europe," and even enable him to demand geographical, political, and ideological concessions in exchange for the neutralization of the new weapon. Stimson had tried to warn him that unless the United States offered the Russians full partnership in developing atomic energy, it risked embittering relations and beginning "a secret armament race of a rather desperate character."

As his last act as a member of Truman's Cabinet, Stimson, his legendary reserves of strength finally beginning to ebb away, had prepared a three-page memorandum outlining his plan to approach Moscow directly about joining the United States and Britain in the effort to control the bomb. He believed an international organization would take too long to create and would never be taken seriously. The point was not whether the Russians got the bomb in five or twenty years, he argued, but whether they were "willing and cooperative partners among peace-loving nations of the world."

Conant and Bush agreed with Stimson, but they did not enjoy the same close relationship with the new secretary of state, or for that matter, the new president. They could no longer count on being consulted, let alone hope that their advice would be heeded. By then, it was apparent that the Interim Committee, the secret high-level group appointed to advise the president on nuclear energy, was being circumvented and Conant would soon resign from it. In late October he wrote Bush that he felt the time had come to "break his silence," adding, "It is getting to be a disgrace that the administration doesn't give the country 'a lead' on this issue."

Bush was equally exasperated. With the Anglo-American-Canadian atomic energy summit on the Potomac River approaching on November 11, and the bomb threatening to overshadow the talks, as it had in London, the administration seemed no better prepared on the subject. "I am very much disturbed at the handling of the matter of international relations on atomic energy," he complained to Conant on November 7, calling the situation "thoroughly chaotic."

With nothing to lose and everything to gain, Bush presented Byrnes with a document outlining the full-fledged international inspection and control policy that he and Conant had been working on in tandem for months. It laid out their step-by-step plan in greater detail than ever before, emphasizing that it would take many years to implement, and that the primary objective was to start Russia down the path to collaboration. Bush even included tactical advice, suggesting as a bold opening move that Truman should invite Russia to join the three Western powers in asking the United Nations to create a commission and charge it with disseminating scientific information in all fields, including atomic energy.

Lacking any real plan of their own, Truman and Byrnes proposed the Bush-Conant program almost to the letter to the British prime minster,

Clement Attlee, and his delegation—and to the Americans' great surprise, they accepted it. The Canadian prime minster, Mackenzie King, happy to be included as a full partner, was also amenable. After several more long days and nights of wrangling, and several more drafts, the White House called a press conference to announce the agreed declaration. On the morning of Thursday, November 15, an exhausted Truman, with the two prime ministers slumped at his side, read hoarsely from two legal-size pages: "We recognize that the application of recent discoveries to the methods and practice of war has placed at the disposal of mankind means of destruction hitherto unknown, against which there can be no adequate military defense, and in the employment of which no single nation can have a monopoly." They proposed that a UN commission be set up to formulate proposals for scientific exchange, for control adequate to ensure only peaceful uses of atomic energy, and to assemble a corps of inspectors to safeguard against violations. The agreement concluded that banishing the "scourge of war" could be achieved only "by giving wholehearted support to the United Nations Organization."

Conant was pleased with how the talks turned out, given the hasty and haphazard preparations. The three governments had agreed not to use their present knowledge as a threat, and had embarked on the program of international control that he and Bush felt was imperative. While the November 15 declaration did not include the direct approach to enlist Russian cooperation they had wanted, it also did not rule it out. At least now the United States government was publicly committed to taking the all-important "first steps" at the United Nations in January. Conant credited Bush's skillful leadership with carrying the day, but, in a nod to political realities, he sent Truman a telegram of congratulations and urged him to move rapidly to translate the agreement into action.

The Truman-Attlee-King agreement was intended to show that America did not wish to hold the atomic sword over the world, but Moscow chose to draw the opposite conclusion. The Soviet newspapers ran a rash of alarming stories implying that the Anglo-American bloc, armed with the atomic bomb, was intending to turn the United Nations against Russia. If the president and the secretary of state had any lingering doubts about approaching the Soviet Union, they were dispelled by the discord being stirred by the bad press. Recognizing the need for diplomatic intervention, Byrnes sent Soviet Foreign Minister Vyacheslav Molotov a cable on November 23 suggesting the moment was ripe for another gathering of the foreign ministers. Just as he had hoped, Molotov extended an invitation for a Moscow meeting, setting the date for December 15. When Bush fell ill with the flu, Conant, as one of the leaders of the Manhattan Project, was asked go in his place to help facilitate the negotiations. He just had time to visit his son Jim, who was recovering at Bethesda Naval Hospital, and tell him of his unexpected plans before rushing off to National Airport to catch his plane. Byrnes had assured him he would be back by Christmas, but Conant thought the man a "cheerful liar" and told Patty not to count on it.

Before he had agreed to join the delegation, Conant had sounded out Byrnes about his aims and was satisfied "his policy was that of paving the way for a scheme of international control and release of our information as the scheme develops." Worried about the risk of alienating the Russians, Conant was eager to secure Soviet support for the idea of a United Nations commission, and his fingers were "still crossed" on the promise of a scientific exchange to help win their cooperation. But Byrnes did not want to lose the advantage of secrecy. Catering to Conant's liberal inclinations to share all scientific information also invited trouble at home. Groves had insisted that American negotiators should offer no more than the exchange of basic scientific data, and felt so strongly about the issue that he sent Secretary of War Patterson a letter warning about the risks inherent in reciprocity. Secretary of the Navy James Forrestal had even graver doubts about the release of information until a firm agreement and safeguards were in place. The senators on the Foreign Relations Committee, and members of the Special Committee on Atomic Energy, already annoyed at being briefed at the last minute, had protested the presence of idealistic "college professors" in the delegation, arguing that it would surely lead to revelations of atomic data during the conference.

Conant got nowhere trying to convince Byrnes to initiate the scientific interchange before they left Moscow. It now seemed that they were poles apart. He could not persuade the secretary of state that it was not a matter of disclosing the "secret"—that it was only a question of a year or two before most of their technical information regarding the bomb reached the Soviets anyway by one route or another. As Conant had argued in a speech on December 3 at the Harvard Club in Boston, hinting at the case he would make to the Russians, fears about the time required before another nation would be ready to use atomic bombs—he estimated not fewer than five years but less than fifteen—were not as important as they first seemed. "The really crucial time interval," he warned, "is between today and the date on which the international political situation might become frozen in so ugly a pattern as to make impossible any control of the atomic bomb."

To the American delegation's amazement, however, the Russians showed little of their usual evasiveness and intransigence. No special inducements proved necessary. The agreement the foreign ministers reached followed the Truman-Attlee-King formulation. They ran into a little trouble when Molotov expressed concern about the language referring to proceeding "by stages," but when Byrnes argued it was central to the whole proposal, he withdrew his objections. It was also agreed that the UN commission report to the Security Council rather than to the General Assembly, and that the council deal with all matters affecting security. All told, there was far less difficulty over the proposal that the United Nations establish the Atomic Energy Commission than expected, and Byrnes apologized to the Harvard president for having dragged him into the icy depths of the Russian winter for no reason. Conant suspected Byrnes was more interested in scoring a public relations coup than in actually initiating atomic cooperation between the two nations, finding him "a little cynical about the whole business." Nevertheless, the conference was "headed for a large success," he noted in his diary, "but my fingers are still crossed on the bomb and will be until the commission is set up."

When he returned from his Christmas visit to the Soviet capital, Conant was of "good cheer." He still nursed the hope, expressed in a speech that November, that "very soon all the nations involved would agree to dismantle all their bombs." They could arrange to store the fissionable material or use it in the future in atomic power plants. He had faith that through the internationalism of science, they might yet avoid an arms race, although he knew better than to trust too much in the promises of the "dwellers of the Kremlin." His optimistic view of the future was reflected in a December 28 editorial in the *Boston Herald*, which called the Moscow agreement for the establishment of a UN commission the "most comforting news since the bomb fell on Hiroshima," and a sign that their leaders were transforming the technology of war into an instrument of peace.

Bush, who missed seeing Conant when he got back to Washington, was also feeling bullish about the future. "The outcome is excellent," he wrote his wartime partner and close friend in the New Year, his letter brimming with good humor. Looking back on the tumultuous events of the previous summer and fall, he reflected, "It seems to me that the way this whole thing has worked out is highly gratifying. It was about a year ago, or somewhat more, that you and I started down this path of creating an international arrangement along the lines that finally emerged. I had the satisfaction of the Attlee conference, and you have now had the Moscow affair, which are the final steps before the UN is launched. Of course, we can never know how successful UNO will be until some years have passed," he added, "but there is great satisfaction in the feeling that at least the whole show is started down the right path."

CHAPTER 18

Atomic Chaos

*His success [overseeing the Manhattan Project] does not
make Conant altogether happy. He considers control of the
Bomb the world's biggest job.*

—*Time* cover story on JBC, 1946

T he New Year did not bring relief from the atomic anxiety still gripping
the country. The hopeful spirit that followed the Moscow meeting soon
faded, drowned out by the incessant talk of the bomb that dominated the
radio, newspapers, and political platforms. The scientists' movement had
launched its crusade for international control. Earnest young chemists,
physicists, and engineers were fanning out across the country to lecture
people about the danger of atomic warfare, taking their pressing message
to churches, community associations, farmers' groups, labor unions, Elks
clubs, and the League of Women Voters. Editorial writers took up their
cause, and advice poured forth.

With everyone spouting different doomsday scenarios, an OSRD veteran summed up his colleagues' frantic response as "the atomic bomb is
just too dreadful, too awful, too-too-too—everybody must do something
about it quick!" A public opinion poll showed that a majority of Americans
agreed the US nuclear monopoly would be short-lived: 60 percent believed
the bomb secret was already known to other countries, and nearly half of
those surveyed expressed the fear that another world war was either certain
or possible in twenty-five years. *Time*'s annual "Man of the Year" issue fea-

tured Harry Truman on the cover, his image dwarfed by a huge mushroom cloud, one hand clamped to a lightning bolt. "In such a world," the magazine asked, "who dared be optimistic?"

Conant tired quickly of the media hysteria, which he considered to be on a low intellectual plane and counterproductive. There was too much misinformation. Too many ill-conceived schemes were being put forward. Yet in his speeches and comments to reporters, he, too, resorted frequently to dire warnings that people did not understand the "terrifying implications" of the new weapon and the urgent necessity of achieving international control of the atom to avoid the "nightmare of global war."

In opposing Truman's flawed proposal for a peacetime draft, he startled members of the House Military Affairs Committee by urging continuation of the existing Selective Service Act and vigorously promoting voluntary enlistment while they studied the new defense situation created by the atomic bomb, emphasizing that America needed to keep its army and navy strong "right now, at this minute, and in every way." While many prominent educators—and most parents—wanted the boys back home, Conant insisted they dare not let down their guard. Whether or not they could survive the "staggering blow" of a surprise nuclear attack was open to debate, he told the congressmen, but when it came to planning arms and manpower, "We must assume the worst: we have to assume that if the United States by any unhappy chance should find itself in such a position, it would fight on; we have to plan how to fight under these adverse conditions."

In speaking to the public about the bomb, Conant often equated his dilemma to that of a doctor with a diabetic patient shortly before the advent of insulin. If unduly alarmed, the patient could become so pessimistic that he might overindulge, possibly with fatal consequences. On the other hand, if the patient were not sufficiently impressed with the gravity of his condition, he might not obey the dietary rules and die as a result of similar recklessness—"not out of despair but out of indifference based on ignorance." If those same patients were made to realize the dangerous nature of their malady, however, they might learn to manage it, and be preserved until the discovery of insulin made their plight easier and their lives relatively safe. "If the American people are sufficiently aware of the extreme danger to our industrial civilization which is inherent in the new discovery," he told a gathering at the Harvard Club of Boston, "we may be intelligent and courageous enough to survive the peril." The analogy was not perfect, but he believed that if they could just find a scheme that was the "international equivalent of insulin," it might be possible to "evolve a world order which eliminates the major threat of war."

Conant's prescription for action got the White House's attention. On January 7, 1946, hours before leaving for London and the first meeting of the United Nations General Assembly, Secretary of State Byrnes telephoned to tell him he was appointing a committee to formulate American policy on international control of atomic energy and asked him to serve as one of the five members. Byrnes overrode any possible objections he might have by assuring him it was only a part-time commitment and would not interfere with his duties at Harvard. Conant had only just returned to the business of running the university, and by all rights it should have been his priority, but the question of what could be done about this terrifying new weapon could not wait.

Among the factors impelling him to take the job was that he would be in good company: Undersecretary of State Dean Acheson was named chairman of the committee, and the other members were Bush, Groves, and John J. McCloy, who had been one of Stimson's closest advisors in the War Department. Except for Acheson, an atomic neophyte, these were extremely competent men and capable of solving the problem of international control. All agreed on the necessity of a hardheaded, realistic, enforceable world agreement. At the suggestion of Acheson's assistant, a smart young lawyer named Herbert S. Marks, who observed that the all-star committee was perhaps "too grand" to have the time to work through all the material itself, a board of consultants was created to investigate and report on all the pertinent issues. David E. Lilienthal, an articulate and personable Chicago lawyer who had distinguished himself as head of the Tennessee Valley Authority, was made chairman, and he in turn recruited a group of seasoned hands: Chester Barnard, a leading figure in the business world, and three veterans of the Manhattan Project, Charles Thomas of Monsanto Chemical, Harry A. Winne of General Electric, and the man who knew more about the bomb than anyone, Robert Oppenheimer.

The consultants devoted six weeks of intensive labor to drafting their report, beginning with a crash course in nuclear physics guided by Oppenheimer. They presented their report to the Acheson committee on March 7. Their conclusion was that the only workable system of safeguards required an Atomic Development Authority with a worldwide monopoly on raw materials; control over all the dangerous activities in the field of atomic energy, from mining through manufacturing; as well as a commitment to continue nuclear research and development. They rejected most of the proposals that had been suggested immediately after Hiroshima, arguing that it was impossible to outlaw the weapons or effectively police atomic activities, because developments for peaceful purposes and for war were interchangeable. No inspection system would be seen as reliable, and rivalries and suspicions would inevitably result.

It was Oppenheimer, in a stroke of brilliance, who recognized that if a single international authority was the only authorized participant in the "dangerous activities"—such as operating separation plants for U-235 or large reactors for generating power—the problem became much easier to solve. If the dangerous activities were the sole province of the Atomic Development Authority, then all the "nondangerous power-producing piles" could be operated by individual nations under relatively moderate controls. The idea had immediate appeal, particularly by downplaying the agency's "cops" role and promoting a positive, dynamic future for atomic energy, and in so doing, enhancing the incentives for Russian cooperation. The board of consultants did not pretend it was a final plan—further study and negotiation were required—but it was "a place to begin; a foundation on which to build."

During two days of marathon discussions at Dumbarton Oaks, the Acheson committee members picked apart the report and requested revisions. Conant worried that the consultants had made the inspection process too easy, and insisted again on guaranteed freedom of access—the right to see any lab or plant anywhere, at any time. Bush wanted to specify the exact timing for turning over information to the international authority. They both understood the transition would have to be gradual and urged the panel to retain the idea of progressing toward disarmament in clearly defined "stages." They needed a plan, Conant stressed, that protected American interests but still convinced Russia and the other nations that the United States had no intention of using its nuclear monopoly to advance its global economic and political agenda. Despite their many differences, they managed to reach a consensus. On a damp, chill Sunday morning in mid-March, after copious cups of coffee, the Acheson group approved the report and sent it to Byrnes, calling it in a cover letter "the most constructive analysis of the question of international control we have seen and a definitely hopeful approach to a solution of the entire problem."

The so-called *Acheson-Lilienthal Report*, which was made public on March 28, 1946, was largely well received. The *Washington Post* praised the statesmanlike document for lifting the "Great Fear" that had descended over the world on August 6, 1945. As usual, the right-wing newspapers denounced it as a transparent scheme to give the bomb secret to the Russians. The columnist Dorothy Thompson dismissed it as an "Elysian daydream."

The report far exceeded the expectations of the scientists, who had been less than thrilled with the selection of Conant, Bush, and Groves, by then lumped together as part of oppressive officialdom. Like all the manifestos of the scientists' movement, the *Acheson-Lilienthal Report* was inspired by Bohr's original commitment to internationalize the atom and reflected the basic ideas in which they deeply and somewhat naïvely believed: confidence in the beneficent powers of science and that its practitioners could contribute significantly to a novel experiment in cooperation. The first sign of real progress since the setbacks on Brien McMahon's bill in December 1945, it was greeted with much relief and excitement. "We clasped the new bible in our hands and went out to ring doorbells," recalled William A. Higinbotham, the head of the Federation of Atomic Scientists.

Their hopes were dashed almost immediately when it was revealed that on the same day that the Acheson committee members and consultants reached a compromise, President Truman, without bothering to consult any of them, had asked Bernard Baruch to be the American representative at the United Nations Atomic Energy Commission (UNAEC). Conant, whose own name had been bandied about as a possible candidate for the job, was dismayed by the choice. Over the years, he had had many dealings with the crusty septuagenarian financier and would have preferred that such a difficult diplomatic task go to someone more nimble and less conservative. Baruch had been past his prime when they had been "park bench" colleagues—deaf in one ear and requiring a daily nap, and a team of "youngsters" to do the legwork—and that had been at the start of the war. Conant assumed that Byrnes and Truman felt that the "suspicions of many senators about scientists had to be allayed," and that they were counting on the elder statesman's "high prestige" to buy them credibility on Capitol Hill.

A furious Bush confronted Byrnes—who had reportedly suggested his fellow South Carolinian—and told him to his face that Baruch was completely unequal to the complexities of the task. The Old Man, as they called him, boasted of being almost entirely ignorant of the bomb, maintaining that all he needed to know was that it "went boom and it killed millions of people." When Oppenheimer heard that the formulation of international atomic policy had been entrusted to the vain, grandstanding Wall Street operator, he was crushed, saying later, "That was the day I gave up hope."

Truman was no fan of Baruch's. On the day he offered him the job, he noted caustically on his appointment sheet, "He wants to run the world, the Moon, and maybe Jupiter." But by then, any illusion of international magnanimity had evaporated, and on the key issues—especially the hard line toward the Russians—the two men were in agreement. As Truman put it, he was "tired of babying the Russians." His mistrust of the former ally had recently been reinforced by revelations of a Soviet espionage ring in Canada, resulting in the arrest of twenty-two suspects and inciting, over successive weeks of headlines, a near hysteria over Communist "atom spies" in America. Relations were further strained by Stalin's refusal to withdraw Russian troops from Iran, which they occupied jointly with the British, and his angry declaration that the uneven economic development in the West would split the capitalist world into "two hostile camps and war between them."

The Soviets' belligerence drew fire from America's favorite Englishman. Barely a month later, in March, Winston Churchill descended on Fulton, Missouri, and the defeated statesman delivered a ringing speech about the growing threat posed by the Russians. "From Stettin in the Baltic to Trieste in the Adriatic, an iron curtain has descended across the Continent," he proclaimed, echoing his celebrated wartime orations by calling on the "fraternal association of English-speaking peoples" to hold Soviet military expansion in check. He warned the Americans not "to entrust the secret knowledge of experience of the atomic bomb . . . to the world organization, while still in its infancy. It would be criminal madness to cast it adrift in this still agitated and un-united world."

The speech created such a furor that Truman was forced to claim that he had not had time to read an advance copy, even though he had stood by Churchill's side throughout, beaming from the rostrum. Acheson and Byrnes, still agitated by an eight-thousand-word telegram sent by George Kennan in the Moscow embassy characterizing the Russians as "fanatically" committed to the idea that there could be no "permanent peaceful coexistence" with the United States, took the Englishman's speech as a warning that it was high time to stand up to Stalin.

Conant, who largely accepted the image of an aggressive Russia that was fast becoming the new orthodoxy, deplored Churchill's "iron curtain" speech—the death rattle of Britain's shrinking empire—and worried it would be seen as a repudiation of the United States' attempt to work out a deal with the Soviets. It seemed like "rocking the boat," and might discourage the peacemakers' efforts to reach a nuclear settlement through diplo-matic initiatives and conciliatory gestures.

While Baruch did not blanketly accept Churchill's views, he took ex-ception to being saddled with the liberal-leaning *Acheson-Lilienthal Report*, which amounted to a statement of policy, and immediately began mak-ing alterations to the parts of the plan he viewed as too weak. Even more discouraging, he assembled a team of conservative cronies that included three banking associates, a former New York State racing commissioner, and Groves. The latter had already made it clear he thought the plan was a pipe dream, and persisted in the belief that the United States could corner the world's supply of high-grade uranium ore and thereby prevent any other nation from becoming a nuclear power. Such was the general skepticism about Baruch's commitment to international control that when he asked the scientists on the board of consultants to stay on, they refused to a man.

Conant also begged off politely, but he tried to use his influence to persuade Baruch of the Acheson-Lilienthal proposal's merits. His parting contribution was to recommend bringing in Richard Tolman as chief sci-entific advisor after Oppenheimer, who was the "logical" choice, objected to joining the Wall Street gang. (He eventually agreed to help.) Conant's only knowledge of the acrimonious behind-the-scenes struggle that devel-oped between the president's advocate and the creators of the report—at one point Baruch accused Acheson of secretly recording their telephone calls, which the latter denied heatedly—came from reading the *Bulletin of the Atomic Scientists* and listening to the complaints of colleagues fed up with "yes-yessing" the preening counselor. Apart from a few informal letters to Baruch urging flexibility, and warning him not to allow the talks to break down, Conant had no contact with the US delegation.

In the end, the American plan that Baruch presented at the opening session of the UNAEC on June 16 reflected the essentials of the Acheson-Lilienthal proposal, the one major change being on the question of enforce-ment: he demanded "immediate and certain punishment" for violators of the international agreement. Large-scale violations by a great power, as in the case of illegal work on atomic bombs, would be punished by war. Tru-man agreed with his stand on penalties and abolishing the veto power of the UN Security Council over such action, and assured his chief negotiator that he had his full backing. Addressing his fellow commission members, gath-ered in the elaborately decorated Hunter College gymnasium in the Bronx, the snowy-haired Baruch began with a dramatic warning even more dire than that of the scientists, his overblown, hortatory rhetoric intended for the history books:

> We are here to make a choice between the quick and the dead. That is our business.
>
> Behind the black portent of the new atomic age lies a hope which, seized upon with faith, can work our salvation. If we fail, then we have damned every man to be the slave of Fear. Let us not deceive ourselves: We must elect World Peace or World Destruction.

Back in Cambridge, Conant watched helplessly as Baruch played to the gallery, squandering any chance for the plan in endless posturing and propaganda harangues. After dispensing with the lofty goals, Baruch got straight to the point, insisting on the abolition of the veto. "If I read the signs aright," he said, "the peoples want a program not of pious thoughts but of enforceable sanctions—an international law with teeth in it." The Soviet response on June 19, delivered by Andrei Gromyko, who was all of thirty-six, did not explicitly reject the American approach but offered a counterproposal: a pledge by the participating nations never to use atomic weapons under any circumstances, and a moratorium on their possession and production.

Though the talks dragged on all summer, they had reached an impasse. Baruch was so preoccupied with punishments and the veto issue that he had gotten sidetracked, and Conant had the sickening feeling a precious opportunity was slipping away. The *New York Times* argued there was still a way to bridge the gap between the two positions. The editors of *Business Week* pleaded with the delegates to remain at the bargaining table for as long as it took: "Literally the fate of the world hangs on this attempt," they wrote. "Unless the United Nations Commission can arrest the drift of events, we are moving toward a horrible war. The commission must succeed . . . There is no alternative but atomic chaos."

A month later, Gromyko repeated his proposal, this time bluntly rejecting Baruch's position and, for that matter, the fundamental ideas of the Acheson-Lilienthal board. The president instructed the Old Man to "stand pat." Baruch, determined to emerge the recognized victor and portray the Soviets as obstructionists, never budged. Neither side ever altered its position. Truman believed the United States had what Baruch called the "winning weapon." America was ahead and would stay ahead by keeping the atomic "secret." They were never convinced by Conant's argument that they needed to share American know-how—they really did not believe another country could catch up anytime soon—nor did they believe that the informed diplomatic discussion he wanted was necessary to get down to brass tacks with the Russians. "The bitter truth," observed McGeorge Bundy, was that there was not at any time a serious effort to reach an accord: "In the forum to which, by agreement, they had referred the question—the largest threat to the human future ever known—the representatives of the two greatest powers in the world never undertook any direct negotiation."

Meanwhile, in mid-July 1946, Conant got a call from Acheson that the president would like to see him. A few weeks earlier, the Senate had finally passed and signed the McMahon Act authorizing the creation of the US Atomic Energy Commission, and he suspected Truman might offer him the chairmanship. His instincts proved correct, and, in a meeting at the White House, Truman expressed the hope that he would head the newly created agency. He had helped direct the wartime atomic project with brilliant success, and this responsibility would be as great as any shouldered in peacetime. Conant was sorely tempted. As the advisor to the president on all atomic energy affairs, he noted with anticipation, he would "be in a position of great influence on the future of the world."

Never one to act on impulse, Conant asked Truman for time to think it over. What was really keeping him from accepting was his "appraisal of the relative strength of the friends and enemies" he could expect to encounter if he took the job. He could be certain of the support of Bush, Oppenheimer, and the two Comptons, as well as Groves, but how many others who had been part of the Manhattan Project would rally around him? A few, at least, would be openly hostile. Byrnes had let him know that Leo Szilard would be at the front of the line. A considerable number of the younger men in Chicago would be right behind him.

The administration's attempt to railroad the May-Johnson bill through Congress had exacerbated the "accumulated dissatisfactions" among many of those who had toiled under the Bush-Conant management during the war years. The fact that they had both contributed to the scheme embodied in the May-Johnson bill, and both testified in its favor alongside Groves—whose attempts to perpetuate military control helped precipitate the scientists' revolt—had made them figures of suspicion. Contributing to Groves's declining reputation was the scandal over the army's senseless destruction of five Japanese cyclotrons in the final months of 1945, which had newspaper cartoonists conjuring up the spectacle of crude military "hatchet men" who could not distinguish between atomic weapons and important experimental research tools. The episode placed a permanent demerit by the general's name and hastened the end of his career. All in all, it was a pretty dismal picture. "For all I knew," the Harvard president recalled, "the entire scientific and technical manpower of the atomic energy establishments might have been just waiting until the war ended to become vocal in their condemnation of Conant, Bush, and Groves."

He felt unfairly tarred and feathered by his scientific fraternity. In his view, it was just plain wrong to claim the May-Johnson bill opened the way for the Atomic Energy Commission to be run by a military man—the scientists were convinced the army intended to install Groves, a possibility they could contemplate only with "extreme horror"—yet it was just this prejudice that had finally led Truman to have the bill killed. Realizing he was tainted by his association with Groves and no longer able to be effective, Conant had stood aside and let the storm over the legislation run its course. Now, confronted once again with this painful reality, he decided it would be the better part of valor to turn down the AEC job.

Conant was handicapped by virtue of being part of the atomic establishment. He was too much an insider, and privy to too many military secrets, to state publicly what he believed privately to be the case. He fervently believed that to eliminate the threat of war, the United States had to be willing to make concessions to the Soviet Union to secure some kind of nuclear alliance. Surely some kind of agreement, even an imperfect one, was better than nothing. But because he held back from criticizing Baruch—unlike Henry Wallace, who repeatedly attacked the banker's intransigence toward the Russians for discouraging rather than encouraging their cooperation—Conant appeared to have been converted to the administration's conservative policies. In fact, he was closer to most of the activists' way of thinking than they realized, and, as Alice Smith points out in her book *A Peril and a Hope: The Scientists' Movement in America, 1945–47*, deserved credit for "more liberal thinking on the implications of atomic energy and for calling official attention to them" than his critics were willing to grant.

He was deeply concerned about the militarization of atomic research, and had earlier refused a direct request from the secretary of war and the secretary of navy that he sit on the Joint Chiefs of Staff Evaluation Board for the first peacetime tests of the atomic bomb at Bikini Atoll in the Marshall Islands. From the beginning, the scientists' lobby protested that the timing of the tests—planned initially for May 15 but postponed until July by Truman so as not to interfere with Baruch's opening statement at the UNAEC—would be a tragic mistake at the very moment America was trying to persuade the world it was a nonaggressive country committed to peace. While Conant opted for a less confrontational tone, he wrote Patterson and Forrestal that he felt there was a "certain degree of incompatibility" between their push to further develop and refine the weapon for combat and his efforts to restrict its use, noting pointedly that his preference would be to "concentrate my attention on this phase of the problem."

On July 1 the United States set off its fourth atomic explosion. Two days later, just as the scientists predicted, *Pravda* declared that the Bikini test had "shattered faith" in the United States' intentions and proved it was interested in perfecting, rather than limiting, the weapon. Those who worried that the sight of another incandescent fireball might make atomic bombs seem less of a cosmic force and more like "just another weapon," as the *Times*'s William Laurence wrote, had their worst fears confirmed. This was compounded by a targeting error that resulted in disappointingly little damage—the blast sank only five of seventy-eight old battleships—inspiring some wags to dub the demo "No Atoll" or "Nothing Atoll." A second test, a subsurface explosion, was held on July 25 and yielded far more impressive results. A third, scheduled for September, was postponed indefinitely due to radioactive contamination of the target fleet—a hazard the scientists had warned of in advance—though this fact was withheld from the public at the time. The irony of the Bikini show was that while it looked like America was flaunting its atomic monopoly as a form of international blackmail, the original motivation for the tests lay in the fierce postwar rivalry among the services and the navy's insecurity that an army air force equipped with atomic weapons might render it obsolete.

On August 2 Conant telephoned the White House and declined the chairmanship of the Atomic Energy Commission. In a follow-up note to Truman, he wrote that it was a flattering proposition and blamed his obligation to Harvard, his usual excuse whenever he needed an out. After twice refusing major government posts, Conant reconciled himself to returning to academic life full-time. In his own mind, he had "turned his back" on any substantive role in the future of nuclear energy. "I really felt I was freed from the atom," he wrote, "and need not give the terrible prospects of an atomic arms race another thought."

But he was wrong to believe he could just walk away from the weapon he had brought into being. It was a responsibility he would never be free of, whether he liked it or not. If he was reluctant to recognize this fact, there were plenty in Washington who did, and they had no intention of letting him off the hook—or allowing his unquestioned expertise and competence go to waste. For its September 21, 1946, issue, *Time* put the fifty-three-year-old Harvard seer and "scientific celebrity" on the cover and reported that some of his former government colleagues wondered if Cambridge was the "most useful spot for him," adding that there was talk of his "presidential potentialities." The war-wrought scholar was the "No. 1 intermediary between the scientists, industrialists, and military," and the "indispensable link in building the Bomb," and he still had his work cut out for him. "His success in this role does not make Conant altogether happy. He considers control of the Bomb the world's biggest job."

A few weeks later, Conant received word from Bush that Truman wanted him to be a member of the high-level General Advisory Committee to the AEC, to provide counsel on a wide array of policy issues upon which the security and enrichment of the United States depended. David Lilienthal, who had agreed to serve as chairman of the AEC, would make the appointment official on January 1, 1947. From then on, the civilian AEC would take over from the Manhattan Project as custodian of the nation's atomic stockpile and empire of laboratories and manufacturing facilities. For better or worse, Conant was once again in the "atomic harness," and for a term of five years.

Bush, for one, was relieved to have him back in the fold. In a year when trust between the United States and the Soviet Union had steadily deteriorated, relations between America's atomic leaders were almost as badly frayed. The Baruch team and the Acheson-Lilienthal group had been at each other's throats for months. After Wallace followed up his attack on Baruch by giving a speech undercutting Byrnes's "get-tough" foreign policy, Truman had kicked the errant secretary of commerce and former vice president out of his Cabinet. Bush had been "very much disturbed" by the idea that Conant was becoming so frustrated with the administration's uncompromising stand toward the Russians that he might retreat from his public support of the Baruch plan, writing him on October 21 that "any indications whatever that we are willing to make any concessions at the present time would probably be fatal." If everyone rowed in different directions, and there were dozens of formulations, it could "wreck the scheme." This would play right into Moscow's hands, because its strategy was always "to create confusion, delay, and opposition on all sorts of technicalities with the expectation that they can wear us down."

Bush's letter is full of his conviction that it was incumbent on the official family to maintain a united front and manage public expectations in order to guide the country through this critical moment and secure a nuclear alliance. They needed to be "decidedly stiff in their attitude," he urged Conant, "and synthesize a steadfastness way beyond the ordinary." It was imperative that they adhere rigorously to the plan, even if it took "several years of wrangling of one sort or another" to induce the Soviets to acquiesce.

Conant, who was not in the habit of going against Bush, held the line. He was nothing if not steadfast. He, too, was fearful of diplomatic softness in this antagonistic postwar era that British novelist George Orwell and others had taken to calling the "cold war." In a wider sense, while he did not think the UN approach would amount to anything, Conant doubted the country was ready to hear the truth about the nuclear standoff that was just around the corner. In a speech that fall at a closed-door meeting at the National War College in Washington—a copy of which he sent to Bush with a note stating that he had been assured his remarks would be treated as "classified"—he outlined the necessary preparations for what he termed "the age of the Superblitz."

In his grim assessment of the future, within ten years' time, they would be living in a world in which two warring nations had stockpiles of bombs, and the "best" scenario he could imagine was that this simultaneous threat might prove to be an equalizer, producing an atomic "stalemate with both sides in a bad way." A new book, Bernard Brodie's *The Absolute Weapon: Atomic Power and World Order*, elaborated a similar theory of nuclear deterrence, but Conant, who had been mulling a treatise on the subject, did not put much faith in the threat of retaliation as a permanent fix. "In such an age, war may well be inevitable," he concluded. "It is hard to see a peaceful way out." It is unlikely that his gloomy predictions received a standing ovation.

On the last day of 1946, the UNAEC voted 10 to 2 to approve the American plan, with Russia and Poland in the negative. Baruch celebrated his hollow victory, but even he could see that it was the end of the road and resigned in early January 1947. Without the Soviet Union, the international-control effort was dead. The atomic policy that Conant and Bush had been advancing for more than two years had failed, and with it any chance of sparing mankind the dread of weapons of mass destruction and Armageddon. In retrospect, Conant realized the Russians were never going to give up the veto. And ultimately, the United States was never going to trade its all-important secret. The odds were always against a good outcome, given that neither nation was willing to abandon its atomic program.

When the UNAEC resumed its deliberations in the New Year, the propaganda battle continued, but Conant's last hope that they could build "a rickety bridge out of the shadow of the Superblitz" had collapsed. The arms race had begun.

By then, Conant's attention was already being diverted from concerns about security in a divided world to another more immediate cause for worry: the growing public backlash against the bomb. On August 31, 1946, John Hersey's "Hiroshima," a thirty-thousand-word account of the devastating effects of the first atomic attack on six ordinary Japanese civilians, had appeared all at once in a single issue of the *New Yorker*. The article, oddly tucked behind a lighthearted collage of summer pastimes, was a publishing sensation. The magazine sold out at the newsstand within hours. Reviewers hailed the piece as a classic, and reprint rights were requested from all over the globe. When the Book-of-the-Month Club rushed it out in hardback form two months later, it was a runaway bestseller. The ABC radio network preempted regular programming to broadcast a staged reading of the entire work by well-known actors in four half-hour segments.

In the era before television, no newspaper story or grainy black-and-white newsreel had the immediate and profound impact of Hersey's minutely observed report of the horrifying aftermath. In plain, unadorned prose, he described the human toll: "Their faces were wholly burned, their eyesockets were hollow, the fluid from their melted eyes had run down their cheeks. (They must have had their faces upturned when the bomb went off; perhaps they were antiaircraft personnel.) Their mouths were mere swollen, pus-covered wounds, which they could not bear to stretch enough to admit the spout of a teapot." More than ten thousand staggered burned and vomiting into the best hospital in town, "which was altogether unequal to such a trampling, since it only had 600 beds."

Among the many shocking aspects of the atomic blast Hersey brought into stark relief were the lingering effects of radiation poisoning, which meant that many of those lucky enough to find themselves alive in the smoldering city were sentenced to a slow, painful death. Within a few days, they developed a "rich repertory of symptoms"—nausea, fever, headaches, dizziness, diarrhea, nosebleeds, and fatigue—then their hair began to fall out in clumps, their gums swelled, and they developed bluish spots all over their bodies, a sign of hemorrhaging beneath the skin. The recurring waves of radiation illness that swept through Hiroshima and Nagasaki greatly compounded the suffering and tragedy, and added tens of thousands of civilians to the ever-rising casualty statistics.

While the Los Alamos scientists were aware to some degree of the danger posed by high doses of radiation—in a May 1945 memo, Oppenheimer predicted radiation emitted during detonation to be "injurious within a radius of a mile and lethal within a radius of about six-tenths of a mile"—they had had little time to study it in their rush to complete the weapon, and vastly underestimated the extent of the exposure and its devastating effects on the internal organs of the Japanese known as the *hibakusha*: the surviving victims of the bomb. Among the project scientists' many wrong assumptions, they presumed that those exposed to fatal doses of radiation would be killed by the blast before the penetrating gamma rays manifested in skin and bone.

For most readers, Hersey's graphic depiction of the radiation poisoning ravaging the bodies of Japanese civilians was their first introduction to this terrible unintended consequence of the atomic attacks. As a result of the strict censorship imposed by General Douglas MacArthur, the new supreme commander for the Allied powers and head of the US occupation in Japan, there had been almost nothing about radiation in the American press. Groves was convinced the Japanese claims of a new and deadly "A-bomb sickness" were a hoax, and other military leaders initially denied the reports or downplayed them as exaggerated and unsubstantiated. Hersey, a Pulitzer Prize–winning *Time* correspondent who spent three weeks in Hiroshima in the spring of 1946, succeeded in getting out the facts and figures on the dead and dying that government officials did not want printed for fear they would detract from their triumph.

After reading the article, Conant, who had just returned from a three-week vacation at his remote cottage in the White Mountains, became concerned that those facts might speak too loudly. He feared Hersey's article might amplify the awful effects of the explosion to the point of turning the public against the bomb, undermining its diplomatic potency and derailing the American effort to force the Soviets to accept international control. If the *New Yorker* piece served as a wake-up call to the "terrible implications" of the bomb, as the editors stated in a brief note in the front of the magazine, it might launch a heated public debate over the Hiroshima and Nagasaki attacks, and lead to a fundamental reassessment of the use of the weapon and justification of atomic warfare.

From the moment Hiroshima and his part in the Manhattan Project had become known, Conant had received countless letters from church leaders protesting the slaughter of innocents and attacking his "end-justifies-the-means" argument as a dangerous fallacy. After a presentation he gave at the Harvard Club of Manchester, New Hampshire, Bradford Young, an Episcopalian clergyman, wrote that he felt like they were all "war criminals." If there was no good reason why the new weapon could not have been demonstrated to the Japanese "as persuasively and harmlessly" as it was to Conant in New Mexico, then "the crime you helped us all commit was of the same stupendous order as the bomb."

Young also took exception to Conant's scientific detachment, which made it all seem that much more monstrous. "What bothered me," the reverend wrote, "was to see you preparing and participating in such a Godlike decision with apparently no sense of presumption, no fear and trembling, no feeling of tragic involvement in a horrible deed."

Conant allocated these sincere if, to his mind, naïve objections to the circular file. He disdained the scientists who "paraded their sense of guilt," carefully hid his own moments of disquiet, and continued to defend the use of the bomb, as he had poison gas, on the grounds that war created its own unique moral framework, insisting, "War is ethically totally different from peace."

He stuck to his fixed beliefs and saw no reason for further reflection until the spring of 1946, when suddenly the criticism gained in magnitude and meaning with the publication of a report on March 6 by a blue-ribbon panel of the Federal Council of Churches condemning the surprise bombings of Hiroshima and Nagasaki as "morally indefensible." Regardless of whether or not the atomic bomb shortened the war, the panel's twenty-two prominent Protestant ministers, theologians, philosophers, and historians concluded, the "moral cost was too high." Criticizing the "irresponsible use" made of the atomic bomb, and calling on American Christians to repent, they stated, "We have sinned grievously against the laws of God and the people of Japan."

This damning indictment did not sit well with Conant. Moreover, he was stung to find the name of Reinhold Niebuhr, whom he knew and respected, among the signatories. An evangelical preacher and social activist, Niebuhr was regarded as one of the most eminent theologians of his time. He was the author of a dozen books, including an unsurpassed work of political philosophy, *The Children of Light and the Children of Darkness*, about the struggle between the proponents of democracy and the forces of anarchy, and posited that it was morally acceptable to go to war to defend civilized values. Conant, who admired Niebuhr's stand against the isolationism and pacifism of the 1930s and support for the Allies during the war, and who recognized in his "Christian realism" a political pragmatism that mirrored his own—he was fond of quoting Niebuhr on the wise and courageous use of power, which he called "the triumph of experience over dogma"—had even tried to lure him to Harvard. Only hours after the council issued its call for repentance, Conant sent a strongly worded salvo to Niebuhr, questioning his moral judgment and arguing that there was no basis for condemning the atomic bomb so long as he accepted other weapons of mass destruction: namely, the strategic bombing of major European and Japanese cities that had laid waste to millions of lives during the war, the majority of whom were noncombatants.

"At the risk of having this letter considered a highly personal reaction by one who has a guilty conscience, I am writing you frankly about the report which you signed and which appeared in this morning's papers," he began, fairly bristling with indignation and firm in his denial of any need for contrition. Unapologetically attacking the council's logic, he reasoned that its line of argument taken to its conclusion was to "scrap all our armament at once," a plausible if not very realistic alternative, and distinctly out of character for Niebuhr, who'd consistently supported the use of the weapon to save the lives of American soldiers who would have otherwise perished on the beaches of Japan:

> If the American people are to be deeply penitent for the use of the atomic bomb, why should they not be equally penitent for the destruction of Tokyo in the thousand-plane raid using M69 incendiary which occurred a few months earlier. (I may say I was as deeply involved with one method of destruction as the other, so at least on these two points I can look at the matter impartially.) If we are to be

penitent for this destruction of Japanese cities by incendiaries and explosives, we should carry this point of view to the whole method of warfare used against the Axis powers.

Niebuhr sent a conciliatory reply, acknowledging the council's judgment "does not make sufficiently clear what was the conviction of most of us—that the eventual use of the bomb for shortening the war would have been justified." He maintained, however, that the United States would have been in a "stronger moral position had we published the facts about the instrument of destruction, made a demonstration of its effects over Japan in a nonpopulated section, and threatened the use of the bomb if the Japanese did not surrender." He also did not back down on the question of culpability. There was "too general a disposition to disavow guilt because on the whole we have done good—in this case defeated tyranny."

The heated exchange left Conant all the more convinced of the need to clarify the issue for the public at large. From the earliest days of the interventionist movement to the public unveiling of the Manhattan Project, and exemplified by his careful crafting of the *Smyth Report* explaining the scientific genesis and purpose of the new weapon, he had always been sensitive to the need to shape public opinion about the threat to national security and the necessary response. In his view, chronic controversy about the bomb could erode public confidence in the country's leaders as a united and resolute group and compromise their atomic diplomacy. The American people, "notoriously nondocile," as the playwright and FDR speechwriter Robert Sherwood once observed, had to be brought along every step of the way—whether it was casting aside isolationism, rising to the challenge of war, or accepting the responsibilities of a global power. In order to avoid being swamped by emotionalism and prevent a groundswell of antinuclear activism that could make the task of devising future policy that much more difficult, Conant felt the government needed to dictate the story of the bomb. Recognizing that history is written by the victors, yet always subject to challenge and the vicissitudes of time, he wanted to stake out the moral high ground—and more important, the judgment of posterity.

He was less than happy that among the people influencing Americans' early conceptions of atomic weapons were Hollywood executives. All that spring and summer, he had been fielding inquiries about Metro-Goldwyn-Mayer's *The Beginning or the End*, ostensibly the true story of the making of the bomb, which had Truman's blessing. It featured a cast of square-jawed movie stars playing the Manhattan Project's principals, including Hume Cronyn as Oppenheimer and Brian Donlevy—after Spencer Tracy turned down the role—as Groves.

Against his better instincts, Conant had already cooperated with a *The March of Time* newsreel documentary about the bomb after Bush had persuaded him that as its August release coincided with the UN negotiations and could be "very useful" in publicizing "the necessity for action looking toward international collaborative control." Conant had even agreed to reenact the congratulatory handshake after the Trinity test, posing prone on the faux-desert floor of a Harvard Square garage next to Bush and Groves and awkwardly clasping each man's proffered palm over and over for the cameras. Recognizing that the project leaders had to be involved with the MGM picture, if only to mitigate the potential damage, Bush reluctantly signed the release form. But Conant, who "never liked mixing the grim matter of atomic energy with Hollywood romance," stalled, only sending a letter stating he would *consider* signing if Bush did, just in case they needed to "take legal action."

It was the influential political commentator turned peace advocate Norman Cousins's blistering editorial demanding accountability for the "crime of Hiroshima and Nagasaki" in the September 14, 1946, *Saturday Review of Literature* that finally drove Conant to call Bush and suggest it was time to mount a defense. As an architect of the country's atomic strategy, Conant was incensed by the accusations that the bombings had been unnecessary and had been carried out to "checkmate Russian expansion." Singling out the "leaders" who approved the attacks, Cousins demanded answers for their "refusal to heed the pleas of the scientists against the use of the bomb without a demonstration" and surrender ultimatum, and the decision to doom two cities in a country that was already on its knees.

This last arrow found soft flesh. Only two days earlier, Admiral William F. "Bull" Halsey, commander of the Third Fleet during the war, had stated during a press conference that the bombings were a mistake because at the time they occurred Japan was on the verge of surrender. His remarks echoed the July report of the United States Strategic Bombing Survey on the effectiveness of Allied aerial attacks, which concluded that Japan would have been compelled to surrender before the end of 1945 and "in all probability" by November 1, "even if the atomic bombs had not been dropped, even if Russia had not entered the war, and even if no invasion had been planned or contemplated."

Conant found these reports deeply troubling. In light of all the evidence that had emerged in the past thirteen months, he had to concede that the defeat of Japan was inevitable: "That at the time of the Potsdam Conference, the signs of rapid deterioration of the Japanese situation were so clear as to be unmistakable to those who were privy to the latest intelligence." But what did it mean to say Japan's capitulation was inevitable? Though its army was beaten, how long would it take to break Tokyo's code of honor and political will? What if, as reported, a faction of the military insisted on continuing the fight because it did not believe the terms of unconditional surrender adequately protected the emperor's role as sovereign ruler, and its coup to topple the government had succeeded? How long would the war have raged on? Conant believed the argument that it was "unnecessary to use the bomb" was oversimplified and erroneous, and opened up "a whole spectrum of considerations, military and political."

After the ferocious battles for Iwo Jima and Okinawa, and mindful of the "terrible toll" of every additional day of fighting, Truman and Stimson— both World War I artillerymen—feared nothing more than the prospect of a long and bloody contest of ground forces.* "That nightmare was strong," recalled McGeorge Bundy, the son of Stimson's wartime assistant Harvey Bundy, who was helping the retired secretary of war with his memoir during the summer of 1946. The American leaders were "heavily affected by the fanatical tenacity of the Japanese on Okinawa and the demonstration of the willingness to die that was inherent in the kamikaze tactics newly adopted by Japanese fliers. What if this spirit, and not any rational calculation of odds against them, were to govern the decision of Japanese rulers?" They were disinclined to haggle with a regime that both FDR and Truman had denounced as criminal, and, as the latter told Churchill, did not have "any military honor after Pearl Harbor."

The president's military advisors recognized the possibility of a collapse from within, and the impact of Soviet entry, but they always came back to the conclusion that using the new weapon was the one way to end the war quickly. Their dread of a drawn-out denouement was intensified by the lesson the Allies had learned with the Germans: the way that Hitler's armies had fought on even after Patton swept across France, and surrender came

---

* As the historian Wilson D. Miscamble notes, "The losses in Hiroshima and Nagasaki assuredly were horrific, but they pale in significance when compared to the estimates of seventeen to twenty-four million deaths attributed to the Japanese during their rampage from Manchuria to New Guinea."

only when Germany was physically overrun. As General Marshall observed grimly of the March 1945 bombing raid on the Japanese capital, "We had a hundred thousand people killed in Tokyo in one night, and it had seemingly no effect whatsoever."

Churchill, like Truman and his advisors, could not conceive of withholding the weapon that would eliminate the need for the invasion and spare so many lives. "There was never a moment's discussion of whether the bomb should be used or not," he wrote later. "To avert a vast, indefinite butchery, to bring the war to end, to give peace to the world, to lay healing hands on its tortured peoples by a manifestation of overwhelming power at the cost of a few explosions seemed, after all our toils and peril, a miracle of deliverance."

Conant, who knew this to be the conviction of the men with command responsibility as the bomb became available, was impatient with after-the-fact assessments of Japan's readiness to surrender, dismissing such talk as "Monday morning quarterbacking." His only regret was that the bomb had not been completed earlier: "The difference between May and August 1945 was very large in terms of American casualties." And if the war had ended in May, the Red Army would not have been ready to take on Japan, and Russia would not have a claim to the spoils of victory. The whole postwar situation would have been very different. But it was probably inevitable that in the urgent atmosphere of the summer of 1945 the new president would seize on the new weapon to speed the end of the war. "Truman could have canceled the plans to drop the first bomb, of course, any time up to a few hours before the departure of the plane carrying the weapon which would destroy Hiroshima," Conant wrote. "He did not do so; neither Secretary Stimson nor any of his advisors recommended such a dramatic reversal of orders."

Conant saw no reason to second-guess their decision, but he did want to stifle the growing hue and cry. Given his proprietary feelings toward the Manhattan Project, he could not help taking some of the criticism personally. "I am considerably disturbed about this type of comment which has been increasing in recent days," he worried to his old wartime colleague Harvey Bundy, now back at his Boston law firm of Choate, Hall & Stewart, on September 23, enclosing a clipping of the Cousins editorial, complaining about Halsey's "unfortunate statement," and obsessing about a lone paragraph in the journalist Leland Stowe's new book about the failed effort to control the bomb, *While Time Remains*, which mentioned the "error of using it against the Japanese."

The problem, Conant continued in an uncharacteristically fretful and peevish three-page letter, was that the criticisms were coming not just from the "professional pacifists and . . . certain religious leaders," but also from the general public "taking up the same theme." Even if it was only a "small minority" of "verbally-minded" academics who were raising these questions, he was eager to reverse what he saw as a distressing trend. "This type of sentimentalism, for I so regard it, is bound to have a great deal of influence on the next generation."

He was particularly worried that doubts about the bomb could lead to a "distortion of history," and people could come to believe a main reason for the bombings—and certainly the one on Nagasaki—was to test the new weapons. There was a "danger," he warned, of repeating the revisionism that occurred after World War I, when it became "accepted doctrine among a group of so-called intellectuals" that America's entry into the conflict was a great mistake brought about by greedy arms makers. A return to this kind of prewar isolationism would only create more obstacles to promoting international control. To set the record straight and demolish any remaining doubts, Conant outlined his idea for an aggressive public relations offensive. "It seems to me of great importance to have a statement of fact issued by someone who can speak with authority," he began. "There is no one who could do this better than Mr. Stimson."

What Conant had in mind was a short article by the popular statesman "pointing out the conditions under which the decision was made and who made it." Annoyed at having the Chicago scientists' objections continually thrown in his face, he was also determined to show that some of the most senior and distinguished physicists had sat on the Target Committee and confirmed the decision to drop the bomb on Japanese cities. "I think it is important to show that while there was a small group of scientists who protested," he told Bundy, the scientific leaders of the movement raised no objections to the proposed plan. "On the contrary, you will remember that in the presence of Oppenheimer, Lawrence, Compton, and Fermi, there was a discussion of the actual target to be chosen. I think it unfair for the scientists by implication to try to dodge the responsibility for this decision."

He also thought Stimson needed to elaborate the reasons why the proposal at the "eleventh hour" to stage a demonstration in an unpopulated area was rejected, and show that the difficulties were discussed—the risk of a dud loomed large—and that the scientists' final conclusion was that they could find no acceptable alternative to military use. "I am quite unrepentant as to my own views about the matter," Conant assured Harvey Bundy:

"I expressed my views that the bomb should be used. I did so on the grounds (1) that I believed it would shorten the war against Japan, and (2) that unless it was actually used in battle, there was no chance of convincing the American public and the world that it should be controlled by international agreement. Nothing that has come to light since then has changed my opinion."

Conant's letter to Bundy—the contentious tone, continuous harping on the facts, and insistence that he felt no guilt for the bombings—suggests that he doth protest too much, that he was perhaps a man in desperate search of vindication. As the historian Barton J. Bernstein observed, Conant placed great faith in the idea that a full accounting of the events of 1945, presented publicly and persuasively by a revered figure such as Stimson, then in his eightieth year, would acquit him of any responsibility and "affirm the rectitude of the American leaders and of the A-bomb decision." Some modern historians, such as Paul Ham, like to cite Conant's denials of any moral qualms over Hiroshima as a sign of his "pride and utter lack of remorse." But it is worth noting that in his 700-page autobiography *My Several Lives*, Conant devotes just two and a half pages to the fateful decision. That such an abbreviated summary in no way reflects the agonizing internal debates, complex considerations, and uncertainty that resulted in one of the most terrible military actions ever undertaken by the United States would seem to speak less of pride than of pain.

Whether Conant was impelled to act by his uneasy conscience, concern for his reputation and that of his fellow bomb trustees, or a combination of the two, "the criticism of Hiroshima rubbed a raw nerve in this usually unemotional man," observed biographer James Hershberg.

Not content with marshaling Stimson's support, Conant ramped up the media blitz. He commissioned his old friend Karl Compton, who had just returned from Japan, to pen a parallel defense for the December issue of the *Atlantic Monthly* stating his conviction that dropping the bomb had avoided a costly invasion, brought the war to a rapid conclusion, and "saved hundreds of thousands—perhaps several millions—of lives, both American and Japanese." The bomb, he asserted, provided the Japanese government with a "face-saving argument" for those who wanted to battle on: "It was not one atomic bomb, or two, which brought surrender. It was the experience of what an atomic bomb will actually do, *plus* the dread of many more, that was effective."

"I think it's excellent, I have no suggestions or comments, only ap-

plause," Conant wrote after reading a copy in mid-October. He was especially pleased by the extra publicity it would receive as a result of Truman's
personal endorsement in the form of a letter to the magazine. He hoped it
would help offset the theatrical travesty produced by MGM, which Walter
Lippmann had previewed at an October screening and excoriated as "a bad
example of the vulgarization and commercialization of a great subject."

Outraged by the film's callous treatment of Truman's decision to bomb
Hiroshima—the president is shown as unhesitatingly giving the order, stating, "I think more of our American boys than I do of all our enemies"—
Lippmann wrote Conant, "I must say I am very much disturbed about its
effect abroad, for it will certainly be taken as official government propaganda in view of the fact that the film could not have been made without the
assistance of the War Department and leading scientists in the Manhattan
Project." Hoping to goad Conant into taking on the producers, he added
waggishly, "You appear in it impersonated by an actor who certainly doesn't
look like the president of Harvard University. If you have no other grievance
against the film, you certainly have a grievance against the fact that, whereas
as Groves has been transformed into a dashing, romantic cavalier, you have
been deglamorized in the most unfair way!"

Lippmann's protests, together with Truman's objections, succeeded in
getting the president's big scene reshot. (The film now includes mention
of sleepless White House nights.) Conant was not satisfied. Nervous about
the way he and the other project leaders were being presented, he placed
responsibility for their predicament "squarely" on the War Department
and Groves, who was paid $10,000 as a consultant (equivalent to $125,000
today). "Of course, the whole thing blows up Groves," Bush agreed. "It may
be the last straw that breaks the camel's back in the army, but I believe he
has no career there anyway. If I were in your place and the chap that depicts
you is a moth-eaten-looking individual, I would just not sign [the release]."

Betraying an intense concern for his public image even in this bland
and innocuous popularization, Conant instead moved to block the release
of the film. Turning to Baruch, he raised the possibility that *The Beginning
or the End* "might endanger the international solution of the atomic energy problem" and asked if he could find a way of having the film "kept out
of circulation." After many alterations to the script for historical accuracy
and emphasis, the banal final cut bored Lippmann almost as much as it
did moviegoing audiences. Conant skipped the star-studded Washington
premiere and cringed at the scathing reviews—*Time* noted its "cheery im-

becility"—taking some comfort in the fact that his character barely made an appearance.

Meanwhile, Harvey Bundy had heeded Conant's call to action. By early autumn, he had enlisted his son, "Mac"—now ensconced in a cottage behind the main house on Stimson's Long Island estate, Highhold—to serve as the former secretary's "scribe" and silent coauthor, and the two were busy digging out wartime diaries and memorandums and preparing the prescribed article. Conant had shrewdly advised against indulging in any polemics, and instead, inspired by Hersey's example, suggested that a matter-of-fact narrative might be a more powerful way to communicate. He also mobilized a group of his former A-bomb colleagues to provide assistance. Harvey Bundy, Harrison, Groves, and Interim Committee secretary R. Gordon Arneson all submitted drafts of valid A-bomb arguments to help bolster Stimson's case.

Since the job of defeating Japan appeared to require the heavy sacrifice of American youth, they agreed it should be a central tenet of their defense. War Department historian Rudolph Winnacker supplied the specific casualty estimates that would prove their point. He informed Stimson and McGeorge Bundy that the number of American troops killed in the European war had been 142,000, and the total US Army casualties (dead, wounded, and missing) in the entire Pacific war were 160,000. Prior to Hiroshima, those estimates had produced a final estimate of 132,500 to 220,000 casualties. (These figures do not include Army Air Force, Naval, and Marine Corps casualties.) What puzzles scholars is why the War Department did not provide them with the Joint War Plans Committee figures—planning documents probably shown to Stimson in mid-1945—which estimated that about 25,000 Americans would be killed if just the Kyushu invasion proved necessary, and about 46,000 would be killed and 170,000 wounded if both southern Kyushu and the Tokyo plain had to be invaded.

It is true that higher figures had been floated in the press. After Nagasaki, Winston Churchill declared that the bombings had saved well over 1.2 million Allied lives, including a million Americans. At the time, Groves acknowledged that Churchill's estimate was "a little high," though proud as he was of his contribution, he seemed to suggest it was only slightly less. Somehow, based on Winnacker's numbers, Stimson and Bundy arrived at what would turn out to be the single most controversial sentence in the final article bearing the former war secretary's name: "I was informed that [the two invasions] might be expected to cost over a million casualties to American forces."

That particular sentence did not fall to Conant's blue pencil, but many others did, and he sent a heavily edited manuscript back to young Bundy in late November, along with an eight-page letter full of suggestions from a skilled debater. "Eliminate all sections in which the secretary appears to be arguing his case or justifying his decision," Conant instructed. "It will be very hard for anyone on the other side to challenge this article if [it] deals almost entirely with the facts." He also wanted the piece to correct misinformation about the decision not to provide a demonstration or warning before actual combat use, rewriting the entire section himself. Stimson should also point out the "similarity in destruction" between the Tokyo fire raids and the atomic bombings. Conant suggested other revisions, including deleting "the problem of the emperor," as well as the whole issue of the future of nuclear arms, as they "diverted from the general line of argumentation." He had led the charge for the publication of the facts, but with typical arrogance felt he was best able to judge exactly how much transparency was good for the American public.

Stimson did not appreciate being put in the hot seat and was uncomfortable lending his name to what he called "the product of many hands." Unsure whether or not to go ahead with it, he solicited the advice of his longtime friend and confidant Felix Frankfurter, with whom he had shared his grave misgivings about the bomb back in 1945. "Jim Conant felt very much worried over the spreading accusation that it was entirely unnecessary to use the atomic bomb," he explained, adding he was the obvious choice to serve as the self-described "victim" who should defend the president's decision. But he was loath to argue the legitimacy of nuclear weapons and wondered if it might be better to wait until his memoir was ready, when he could include it in a discussion of his growing horror of war in the twentieth century. "I have rarely been connected with a paper about which I have so much doubt at the last moment," confessed Stimson, who was in poor health and could not help sparing a thought for his own legacy. "I think the full enumeration of the steps in the tragedy will excite horror among my friends who heretofore thought me a kindly old Christian gentleman but who will, after reading this, feel I am cold and cruel."

The justice, a strong proponent of using the bomb to end the war, telegraphed Stimson his support: "ARTICLE PROVES THAT CLEAR THINKING, DUTY TO RESTRICT LOSSES, AND WISE COURAGE DICTATED THE DECISION."

Conant was similarly enthusiastic after receiving an advance copy of the article in *Harper's* magazine, assuring Stimson in late January, "It seems to me just exactly right, and I am sure it will accomplish a great deal of good," adding that he was the "only one" who could have done it. "If the propaganda against the use of the atomic bomb had been allowed to grow unchecked," he explained, "the strength of our military position by virtue of having the bomb would have been correspondingly weakened," and that would scuttle any chance of international control:

> I am firmly convinced that the Russians will eventually agree to the American proposals for the establishment of an atomic energy authority of worldwide scope, *provided* they are convinced that we would have the bomb in quantity and would be prepared to use it without hesitation in another war.

Stimson's essay brilliantly achieved America's propaganda needs, highlighting the decisive role of the bomb in securing a humane victory, discounting the Soviet contribution to defeating Japan, and distracting attention from the political and strategic aims of American wartime policy—from keeping the Russians in line to the long-term diplomatic impact of nuclear fission—that had been foremost for himself and Bush from the start of the bomb effort and which were nowhere to be found in the eleven-page article.

"The Decision to Use the Atomic Bomb," which appeared in the February 1947 issue of *Harper's*, proved an extraordinary success, far exceeding Conant's expectations. The critical reception was overwhelmingly positive, and the piece was reprinted in hundreds of other magazines and newspapers around the world without charge, according to an editor's note, because of its "exceptional public importance." The *New York Times* commended the seminal article's historical contribution, noting, "Mr. Stimson shows [the reasoning of the War Department] was grim but irrefutable."

Truman also approved. Hoping to avoid ending up on the wrong side of history, he praised Stimson for clarifying the situation "very well," allowing him to reassure himself with the obfuscation—which over time has accrued the status of myth—in the *Harper's* piece that he had saved a million American fighting men compared with the fraction of lives lost in two Japanese cities that were devoted "almost entirely" to war work. In the years that followed, Truman usually placed the number at about half that, perhaps thinking it sounded more plausible, trotting it out whenever the critics piled on: "The men who were on the ground doing their jobs share my opinion that their lives and the lives of a half million other youngsters were saved by dropping the bomb."

Stimson's description of the thoughts and actions of American leaders leading up to the "decision" made for riveting reading and was all the more compelling because it seemed to be an open, honest first-person account based on his "clear recollection." In simple, eloquent prose, he asserted that American leaders had little alternative but to use atomic weapons to secure Japanese capitulation with the minimum loss of life on both sides. While he would not "gloss over" the death of "over a hundred thousand" Japanese at Hiroshima and Nagasaki, the decision to drop the bomb had been "carefully considered," an advance warning or demonstration had been deemed "impractical" and involved "serious risks," and, in the end, they were all agreed it was "our least abhorrent choice." He added somberly, "No man, in our position and subject to our responsibilities, holding in his hands a weapon of such possibilities . . . could have failed to use it and afterwards looked his countrymen in the face."

The article ended with a moving plea to abolish war:

In this last great action of the Second World War, we were given final proof that war is death. War in the twentieth century has grown steadily more barbarous, destructive, more debased in all its aspects. Now, with the release of atomic energy, man's ability to destroy himself is nearly complete. The bombs dropped on Hiroshima and Nagasaki ended a war. They also made clear that we must never have another war. This is the lesson men and leaders everywhere must learn, and I believe that when they learn it, they will find a way to lasting peace. There is no other choice.

Conant extolled Stimson's rhetorical tour de force in public appearances over the winter of 1946–47. He strove mightily to allay people's doubts about the necessity of the attacks on Hiroshima and Nagasaki—"We had no bombs to waste," he told audiences again and again—putting the best face on atomic weapons policy and maintaining a calm patriotic front despite the darkening nuclear reality. "I have certainly been well received so far," he wrote Patty, sounding weary but relieved as he plowed through a February speaking tour in the West.

Similarly, Stimson always supported Conant, whom he regarded as one of the more "realistic" scientific leaders, who did not flinch when the time came to make a tough call. As he informed the news commentator Raymond Swing that February, "President Conant has written me that one of the principal reasons he had for advising me the bomb must be used was that that was the only way to awaken the world to the necessity of abolishing war altogether. No technical demonstration, even if it had been possible under the conditions of war—which it was not—could take the place of the actual use with its horrible results."

Crowing about their essay's effectiveness in rebutting the damaging assertions of the A-bomb dissenters, Mac Bundy wrote Stimson, "We deserve some sort of medal for reducing these particular chatters to silence." The two would go on to collaborate on Stimson's 1948 memoir, *On Active Service in Peace and War*, in which the aging statesman attempted to further defend his role. The coauthors only succeeded in temporarily quieting the controversy. In time, the critics would rebound with a vengeance, challenging the exaggerated "over a million" casualty estimate and the authoritative explanation they sought to enshrine. As General Marshall would later observe, Stimson "generously took a greater share of responsibility than was fair" in attaching his name to the *Harper's* article.

While the Stimson essay probably remains to this day the single most influential account of the use of the bomb, revisionist historians from Barton J. Bernstein, to Gar Alperovitz, to Martin J. Sherwin have provided detailed analyses of why it is a misleading and deeply flawed version of the difficult choices facing the key members of Truman's inner circle. In his decisive study of their deliberations, Sean L. Malloy shows that by asserting that they had only two alternatives—a bloody invasion or the use of atomic weapons to compel surrender—Stimson and Bundy presented a virtually unassailable case in favor of dropping the bomb. To ensure continued public support, or at least acquiescence, Conant and the other unacknowledged contributors sought to exclude any unsettling connections between the decision to use the bomb against Japan and the diplomatic uses of the bomb in imposing their will on the Soviet Union. They also entirely elided the fundamental moral question of whether targeting cities—with either incendiaries or nuclear warheads—was ever legitimate when so many noncombatants would die in the process. Notably, Stimson never addressed why the Nagasaki bomb could not have been delayed.

The cold war historian James Hershberg reads into these omissions darker motives, and portrays Conant's campaign to defend the decision as vaguely conspiratorial, designed to manipulate public attitudes and conceal that the primary purpose of the bombings was to impress the Soviets and preserve the power of the American nuclear monopoly in the postwar years.

"Conant's reaction," he argues, "and that of others around him, revealed the depth of fear among those responsible for the birth and maintenance of America's nuclear policy that the lurking, inchoate, anomic terror of living in the strange new atomic age might coalesce into an unstoppable demand for the elimination of America's nuclear arsenal—or, almost as damaging, vitiate its diplomatic usefulness. Then as later, this antibomb sentiment was seen as playing into the hands of the Russians and their infernal, expedient demands for immediate nuclear disarmament."

What Conant, Stimson, and the other defenders aimed to do was shift the debate from the threat of the bomb to the threat of war. "America was heading into a period marked by US-Soviet rivalry, not one of global cooperation," contends Hershberg, "and if the negotiations were doomed, then it was time to resume the job of building atomic weapons, not dismantling them."

McGeorge Bundy, who went on to become a respected scholar and policy maker, maintains that Conant's and Stimson's motives were simpler—and more honorable. They wanted to reassure Americans that the decision had been judiciously conceived, that the overriding purpose was to shorten the war, and at the same time dramatically announce the age of nuclear weapons and the need to control the atom to avoid future wars. If they "claimed too much for the process of consideration," as Bundy acknowledged in his own reckoning of the decision in 1988, perhaps it was because this "preemptive purpose," along with the compulsive secrecy, had made them slow to explore the various options: warnings, demonstrations, targets, and diplomatic leverage. "What is true—and important—is that these same decision makers were full of hope the bomb would put new strength into the American power position," he wrote. "They would have been most unusual men if they had thought it irrelevant" and ignored the weapon's diplomatic advantages in dealing with the Russians and helping to cement the peace.

Above all, they wanted to build Americans' confidence that the government could be trusted to make wise choices about nuclear weapons, both in the recent past and in the present, and continue to advance what they believed to be sound policy. "The bomb did not win the war, but it surely was responsible for it ending when it did," concluded Bundy. "To those who cheered at the time—and they were the vast majority—that was what mattered most. The bomb did shorten the war; to those in charge of its development, that had been its increasingly manifest destiny for years."

CHAPTER 19

First of the Cold Warriors

Dr. Conant is a man who has no doubts about the superior-
ity of the democratic beliefs he is defending. It is this un-
shaken and unshakable belief which makes him unafraid.

—Saturday Review

It was Harvard's first full commencement since the end of the war. Behind the traditional mace bearer, General George C. Marshall, revered as the "organizer of victory" and five months into his tenure as Truman's secretary of state, led the procession of 1947's doctoral candidates and dignitaries making their way into the Yard. For the past two years in a row, Marshall had been too busy to come to Cambridge to claim his degree, and right up to the final week in May, it had seemed he might send his regrets. Then, on May 28, he had casually informed Conant that he would be present for the 1947 ceremony. Although unable to give a formal address, he would "be pleased to make a few remarks in appreciation of the honor and perhaps a little more." He gave no indication he had anything else in mind, not even at the dinner at the president's mansion the night before, and Conant had gone to bed unaware he had anything so "epic making" planned. But word of Marshall's appearance at the university leaked—Dean Acheson had tipped off a handful of journalists, worried that the press might doze through the academic exercises and not give the story the play it deserved—and that morning's *New York Times* reported, "He is expected to deliver a speech that perhaps will include an important pronouncement on foreign affairs."

The crowd of fifteen thousand did not expect to see history made. They had simply come to see one of the country's most admired soldiers and statesmen. As it turned out, however, Marshall chose that fine June afternoon at Harvard to launch his massive European Recovery Program, a $17 billion transfusion that would become known as the Marshall Plan. After a few polite preliminaries, the old general fumbled for the speech in his jacket pocket and for the next twelve minutes rarely looked up from the prepared text he read from the podium.

"I need not tell you, gentlemen, that the world situation is very serious," he began, speaking softly and at times inaudibly. Marshall explained the fundamental issues at stake in simple terms: Europe was in crisis. Ten years of war had destroyed its cities, factories, mines, and railroads, amounting to the "dislocation of the entire fabric of the European economy." The poverty and chaos would lead to further political and social disintegration unless they broke the "vicious cycle" and restored people's confidence in the future of their countries and in Europe as a whole. The consequences for the United States, and the "possibilities of disturbances arising as a result of the desperation," should be apparent to all. While he never specifically mentioned the Soviet Union, it was clear the danger to the European democracies came from the rapacious Russians, who were setting up dictatorships in all the territories they had occupied during the war and subverting political cohesion in the region. "It is logical," Marshall stated, "that the United States should do whatever it is able to do to assist in the return of the normal economic health in the world, without which there can be no political stability and no assured peace."

The reception Marshall's address received across the Atlantic brightened Conant's outlook considerably, though he later confessed he had not immediately grasped its significance, in part due to the dull monotone of the general's delivery. The American press missed its importance as well and failed to accord the event front-page coverage. But when British Foreign Secretary Ernest Bevin heard portions of the speech the following morning on BBC radio, he knew at once that it was far more than just an aid bill and called it a "lifeline to sinking men" that "brought hope where there was none."

At home, Walter Lippmann, an unofficial administration advisor, hastened to explain to his readers the strategy of using American prosperity to curtail Soviet influence. If the purpose of the Truman Doctrine, announced in March, was a quick $400 million fix to shore up the faltering pro-Western regimes in Greece and Turkey, then the Marshall Plan was a far-reaching comprehensive economic and political aid program designed to get Europe back on its feet and combat the spread of Communism. The genius of Marshall's design was that because it offered a helping hand to everyone—extending the offer of assistance to Germany as well as the Eastern Europeans already under Soviet influence—and encouraged the Europeans to draw up their own plan for an economic coalition, no one could accuse America of having malign intentions. "Our financial intervention in Europe would almost certainly be purged of the suggestion we were treating Europe as a satellite continent in our contest with the Soviets," Lippmann wrote, "and even in Moscow our real intentions would surely become clearer."

To Conant, Marshall's initiative was exactly what was needed. He immediately enlisted in the newly formed Committee for the Marshall Plan and campaigned for Truman's policy of aid to Europe. The lure of an American loan could be the first step in a rapprochement with Russia and lay the foundation for a workable atomic agreement. Marshall's inspiring vision of a new inclusive international order was certainly an improvement over the adversarial tone of the Truman Doctrine. In his effort to get a tightfisted Congress to pay for putting down the Communist-led rebellion in Greece, Truman had resorted to messianic rhetoric, depicting the precipitous two-power rivalry as an inexorable clash between opposing ways of life, culminating in his declaration that it must be the policy of the United States to "support free peoples who are resisting attempted subjugation by armed minorities or by outside pressures." The president's talk of an ideological showdown—and possible military countermeasures—marked a dangerous turn in the administration's response to the Soviet threat and left Conant so distressed about future nuclear negotiations that it caused him "to lose almost all the hope" to which he still clung.

The cautious optimism that flickered briefly in the six weeks following Marshall's speech was snuffed out completely at the end of June when Soviet Foreign Minister Molotov stalked out of the Paris Peace Conference, dragging the reluctant Eastern Europeans with him. Stalin denounced the Marshall Plan as economic imperialism—"a ploy" to "infiltrate European countries." The Russians promptly organized a Communist trading bloc and brought their territories under more rigid control. The Marshall Plan had envisaged a united Europe without a dividing line, "but the men in the Kremlin would not have it so," Conant lamented, and instead lowered the Iron Curtain "on one side of the Continent." All they could do now was hope that "one day it might rust away."

In the July 1947 issue of *Foreign Affairs*, George Kennan, the American chargé d'affaires in Moscow, outlined the administration's new hardline policy of "containment" aimed at confronting Soviet encroachment. The Russians were bent on tyrannical rule, and in their incessant quest for world power would try to fill every "nook and cranny" unless countered by an "unanswerable force." Soviet Communist expansion could best be "contained by the adroit and vigilant application of counterforce at a series of constantly shifting geographical and political points." Lippmann labeled it a "strategic monstrosity." The appearance of Kennan's latest anti-Soviet pronouncements—although only signed by "X"—in the influential journal was tantamount to an official announcement that the White House was adopting a tougher stance. The State Department planners had concluded that diplomatic negotiations with such an implacable foe were pointless.

Conant was not ready to concede that a settlement with Moscow was a lost cause. Increasingly in the minority among his peers, he still believed there were real advantages to allaying Stalin's suspicions and working toward some form of agreement to outlaw the proliferation of atomic weapons. Unlike the Nazis, he did not think the Soviets were intent on conquering the world. Rather, he saw the Russian armies hidden behind the Iron Curtain as "defensive," fearful of a revived Germany and tightening their grip on Eastern Europe out of a sense of insecurity and conviction that the West was intent on cheating them out of the valuable territories and trading areas they regarded as their rightful fruits of victory. If the Russian rulers could be convinced that the United States and the Western democracies were not going to "disintegrate in a whirlpool of internal troubles"—the standard Marxist-Leninist critique of capitalism—but were instead strong, prosperous, and united, they might decide it was in their interest to remove the "sword of Damocles that now hangs over all industrialized nations." As long as American and European leaders did not deviate from the goal of international control, Conant still believed they could rein in the nuclear arms race.

Over the summer, he mounted a last-ditch effort to break the deadlocked negotiations with the Russians, advancing a bold, new plan for disarmament that removed the whole atomic energy enterprise from the equation. Appointed by General Frederick H. Osborn, the new US representative to the UN Atomic Energy Commission (UNAEC), to serve as one of a select group of consultants to the US atomic control negotiators, Conant began lobbying behind the scenes for a moratorium on all nuclear power development. For there to be any chance of enlisting Russian cooperation, he argued, the

United States had to propose prohibiting all atomic power development for a period of time, until it could clearly specify exact stages for sharing all of its atomic information and disposing of its nuclear fuels, with the ultimate objective of eliminating its stockpile of atomic bombs.

Not only did Conant's idea flout the AEC's latest public relations campaign, spearheaded by its chairman David Lilienthal, to sell the public on the peacetime promise of atomic energy, a number of his fellow atomic consultants doubted the wisdom of destroying the United States' reserve of nuclear fuels, especially given the chronic uranium shortage. Oppenheimer, who was also a consultant to the UNAEC, warned that the Soviets were closed off to any cooperative venture and that to keep negotiating was "unwise" and "exceedingly dangerous to the American position." He urged breaking off all negotiations.

Undaunted by the negative reception, Conant stubbornly continued what historian James Hershberg calls his "against-the-wind battle to promote his own radical, alternative plan to save international control," even though his closest nuclear collaborators, Bush and Oppenheimer, found his assertions increasingly hard to accept. Conant spent his August vacation in the Canadian Rockies strengthening his argument on long, rigorous eighteen-mile hikes. Patty did not find the pastime the least bit relaxing and arranged to turn an ankle so she could skip the forced marches.

At the start of September, Conant departed for a speaking tour on the West Coast more determined than ever to do everything he could to avert the looming collision with the Soviets. Looking into his "crystal ball," he told an audience at the Commonwealth Club of San Francisco that he could see a time when the division between the West and the Communists would be more or less complete, and they might reasonably look forward to a period of stability—not peace, exactly, but an "armed truce" for many years to come. This "balance of power" could be preserved as long as America remained courageous and firm in its resolve.

"A divided world is now upon us," he asserted. "It seems to me the height of folly to assume that the division is permanent or of a kind that precludes friendly intercourse across the line—and the height of foolishness to maintain that the division must lead to war." Although he could not talk openly about his controversial moratorium plan, he emphasized that he remained committed to the possibility of a pact with Moscow.

In his second annual appearance at the National War College on October 2, Conant, feeling less constrained in front of a military audience, went even further and suggested that it would be much better for the security of the United States if there were no nuclear weapons or their equivalent anywhere in the world. "I do not believe the benefits of atomic energy are worth the price," he stated bluntly. "Atomic fuels can be too readily turned into atomic bombs to be safe for the civilized world to handle. A self-denying ordinance is needed . . . People who have a mania for suicide aren't permitted to use razors," he concluded with unaccustomed harshness. "If the human race has this mania, perhaps we had better put all this atomic fuel underground."

As news of his controversial War College remarks circulated in Washington, Conant discovered that his call for a moratorium on all atomic development was making waves. Lilienthal, already annoyed by Conant's frequent comments discouraging hope of any substantial peacetime uses of atomic energy for decades to come, condemned his plan to eliminate nuclear power as counter to the basic premise of scientific progress and likened it to "trying to put the genie back in the bottle." Over lunch, he tried to tactfully counsel Conant against publicly promoting such an idealistic—and unrealistic—idea. In the end, not wanting to be "written off as soft-headed," Conant agreed to shelve his scheme, conceding that perhaps this was not the moment to be making such a generous offer to the Soviets.

The coup in Czechoslovakia in February 1948 doomed Conant's hopes for a nuclear alliance. The Russians installed a Kremlin puppet as prime minister, and hundreds of government leaders who had supported democracy were purged from the government and imprisoned. The last independent country in Eastern Europe had succumbed to Soviet pressure. If France or Italy were to fall next, all of Western Europe would be threatened. With their stricken economies close to collapse, it might be a matter of only weeks before the Communist parties were able to seize control. The contest between East and West had become "alarmingly clear and grim." Any "lingering doubts" Conant had about the administration's adversarial foreign policy were gone. Moscow's brutal course of action converted him into "one of the first of the Cold Warriors."

The Prague coup, Truman told the country in a nationwide radio address on March 17, "sent a shock through the civilized world." The president asked Congress to approve the Marshall Plan and introduce the draft again. Conant applauded the administration's decision to come to the aid of Europe but did not see the sense in fanning the public's war fears. While many of his contemporaries in Washington were in a state of near panic—Lippmann wrote a column predicting the "showdown" Truman had prophesied was upon them—Conant did not think the Soviets were about to march west. Speaking to the Boston Rotary Club a few days later, he tried to be deliberately upbeat, maintaining calmly that the Russians were not looking for a fight and the crisis would pass. "Conant Sees: No War, but Armed Truce," reported the *Boston Globe*.

But privately, he was increasingly pessimistic about the chances of peacefully settling the quarrel with Moscow, especially if the Russians were intent on making Europe the heart of the struggle. After listening to the president's speech, Conant dashed off an intemperate letter to Bush—"you being the only person in the administration I know well enough to blow off to"—venting his frustration at the "tremendous amount of fuzziness in the present planning."

"It is all very well to talk of being prepared, mobilizing, strong from a military point of view, et cetera," he began his rant, "but just what does this add up to in terms of strategy?"

> But what annoys me more comes in your area as a planner from a scientific point of view. It is the failure to show the importance of our meeting on a manpower basis the Russian military potential in Europe. Our only chance of balancing their threat with an equal one is by means of an air offensive, including use of the atomic bomb . . .
>
> I think that knowledge on the part of the Russians that they would have to trade devastation in their own country for the privilege of marching to the channel would make them stop and think.

Careful even in the heat of anger, Conant advised his longtime confidant to toss his tirade in the "wastebasket, or better, the incinerator" immediately after reading it.

Galvanized by the frightening events in Czechoslovakia, Conant found himself returning to the role he had played on the eve of World War II: once again using his national stature to issue a clarion call for intervention, both economic and military. "The proper pattern for preventing the outbreak of another global war involves readiness to answer coercion by the use of force," he declared, only slightly tempering his new tough line on defense by asserting that it should be "coupled with a willingness to negotiate at any time on matters of broad policy." He now saw the need for mobilization; for maintaining conventional ground forces in Europe to match Russia's vast army of three to four million men, for alliances and spheres of influence, and for "ideological and political thrusts supported by military." When a blue-ribbon committee led by Karl Compton recommended universal military training, Conant supported it publicly despite its shortcomings and joined a citizens' committee led by prominent university presidents urging Congress to pass the necessary legislation.

By the spring of 1948, preparedness had become a matter of urgency, all the more so given the gravity of the situation in Berlin. At the Potsdam Conference in 1945, Berlin had been divided by the victorious Big Four into four separate zones of military occupation, and the Western sectors were now vulnerable to Russian attack. Over the past year, the fate of Germany had become a flash point in the increasingly tense postwar negotiations between the Soviets and the West, with the Russians demanding $10 billion in punitive reparations for the damage caused by the Nazi invasion and scorched-earth retreat of the Wehrmacht, as well as joint control over the iron and steel industries in the Ruhr.

As the situation worsened, the United States, Britain, and France announced they were integrating their occupation zones. With frictions frighteningly high, the Western Allies issued a new currency. The Soviets immediately denounced the move as completing the split of Germany, and the same day imposed a land blockade around Berlin, cutting off all supplies to the American, British, and French sectors of the city, and leaving 2.3 million citizens and the Allied troops without food, coal, and other basic necessities. The Americans and British responded with a counterblockade, stopping all rail traffic from their zones into East Germany. They then began a huge airlift operation to supply the crucial Western outpost—an all-important symbol of democracy—inside the Communist East. But Truman stopped short of a military confrontation. It was an election year, a tight one, and he was never going to get the American public to back a war with Russia in order to rescue Berlin, the capital of a country they had defeated only three years ago.

Conant, who was putting the finishing touches on a new book about the need to reform America's public schools, entitled *Education in a Divided World: The Function of the Public School in Our Unique Society*, quickly added an introduction that amounted to a call to arms. Strengthening the defense of Europe to stop a Soviet advance had to be a top priority, he urged, acknowledging implicitly that the atomic bomb might not serve as a deterrent and that Stalin might be tempted to test America's willingness to use the destructive weapon in Europe. He advocated the creation of a universal military training system, enrolling every boy of eighteen or high school graduate in a national militia for a period of ten years. "Since Russia might on short notice overrun Europe with her armies (which as far as we know may be mobilized to spring forward at any moment), our balanced strength must be equally ready to strike. How? With what? From where?" he demanded, warning of the country's diminished military capacity and urging the administration and Congress to begin preparing an "overall strategic plan" to offset the Russian challenge. "Once our military answer to a possible military thrust [from across the Iron Curtain] is definite and convincing, a real stalemate will be evident to all clear-minded men even in Soviet Russia."

Truman's proposal for a universal military training bill was defeated, and Congress hastily reenacted the Selective Service Law in response to the war scare. To Conant, the stopgap measure gave little thought to the means of raising an army and awakened his old concerns about the fairness of granting certain college students deferments, worrying it would inevitably result in charges of favoritism and corruption. The most "scrupulously honest" method would be for all young men between eighteen and twenty-two to be obliged to serve, with a lottery system selecting the number required to keep the military up to strength. To his mind, the nation's real defense depended on nuclear retaliation—atomic weapons delivered by B-29 Superfortresses—not on a large infantry. This threat had been made explicit at the peak of the Berlin crisis, when America dispatched a fleet of sixty B-29s to Britain, destined for permanent bases in Europe within range of the Soviet Union. It was a ruse—while described as "atomic-capable" in the government press, the planes actually carried no atomic weapons—but there was no mistaking the message it sent Moscow.

With the success of the airlift, the prospect of war diminished, though it did not mean the end of the cold war. "There has been a definite crystallization of American public and congressional opinion over the Berlin issue," Marshal declared with satisfaction, noting the country was now "unified in its determination not to weaken in the face of pressure." Conant's sharp anti-Soviet rhetoric and hardened attitude toward national security was in keeping with the United States' new antagonism toward Russia and Communism. To his mind, containment had been tested and proven. The transferring of B-29s to forward bases for strategic nuclear bombing was a sign of the United States' readiness and resolve to fight should the crisis escalate.

But Washington's response to the standoff had also revealed a lack of clarity concerning a long-term solution to the threat posed by Russia. He worried the country's dangerous swing to the right and the rising anti-Communist hysteria might lead to a misguided public discussion about using its stockpile of nuclear weapons to "do something foolish on the international scale."

As the November 1948 presidential election approached, and rumors and portents of war dominated the headlines, Americans seemed dissatisfied with their "accidental president." Growing doubts about Harry Truman's handling of international developments and ongoing domestic turmoil were undermining public confidence in his ability to do the job. High taxes, inflation, industry strikes, and increasing controversy about Communist sympathizers in the federal government had allowed the Republicans to recapture the House and the Senate in the 1946 midterm elections. Back in power after fourteen years, the Republicans were in a fighting mood, and no political figure would prove more forceful in his attacks than the thirty-seven-year-old junior senator from Wisconsin, Joseph P. McCarthy. A Marine Corps veteran and self-proclaimed war hero, he had garnered popular support by promising to "clean up the political mess" in Washington, particularly the administration's failure to protect the government from enemy infiltrators and spies.

It seemed all but certain that the Republicans would repeat their success. As part of the conservative backlash, they were out to show that Roosevelt's New Dealers were "soft on Communism" and that Truman's government was riddled with traitors and fellow travelers, with the current Progressive Party candidate, Henry Wallace, FDR's former vice president, being a prime example. There was talk of the "treason of Yalta," as GOP right-wingers criticized the secret wartime agreements that had led to the division of Eastern Europe, occupation zones in Germany, and the ceding of territorial rights to Russia in the Far East. Thomas E. Dewey, the Republican nominee, tried to avoid the mudslinging, but in the final weeks he hopped on the Reds-in-the-government bandwagon. All the major papers predicted a Dewey sweep, and Conant was resigned to reporting to yet another nuclear neophyte.

In the end, however, the public defied the polls, as Truman won comfortably. "The American people admire a man with courage even if they don't always agree with him," wrote Drew Pearson in his November 2 syndicated column, struggling to make sense of the stunning political upset.

To Conant, it meant continuity. The Democrats were back in control of Congress and its committees. He was relieved to be carrying on with the same men who had gotten their heads under the tent years ago. Despite the many new Republican faces in Congress and on the AEC, the president still trusted the "firm hands" of his wartime atomic statesmen with charting the nation's nuclear future. As one of the wise men on the AEC's powerful General Advisory Committee (GAC), and chair of the weapons subcommittee, Conant—along with Bush and Oppenheimer—was one of the government's "nuclear oracles," accorded the highest security clearance and access to the most sensitive defense and national security documents. At the same time, he was head of the Committee on Atomic Energy for the Joint Research and Development Board, coordinating R&D for the army and navy on a continuing peacetime basis, and responsible for reviewing all atomic programs as well as research into other weapons of mass destruction, including biological and radiological warfare. President Truman had awarded him the Medal for Merit, the highest civilian award, and the Bronze Oak Leaf Cluster for military service. He had been made a commander of the Legion d'Honneur by France and an honorary commander of the British Empire by Britain in 1948. The *Atlanta Constitution* named him first among the "Five Greatest Living Americans" based on his achievements in the field of education and "tremendous contributions to the winning of both our great wars."

The late 1940s were a period of intense, almost frenetic activity, which Conant pursued with his usual prodigious energy. No longer content with a wholly academic life in Cambridge, he admitted to being drawn to the more exciting and "glamorous" high councils of government, where he could "engage all sorts of enemies in the thickets of Washington." At the peak of his powers, he brought his enormous self-confidence to bear on the largest conflicts of his day: confronting the nuclear age, cold war competition, the spread of Communism, domestic reactionaries, and class divides. Conceding reluctantly that Russia was not ready for atomic control at the present time, he believed the United States had to build up its nuclear arsenal to maintain the military balance of power, and placed his hopes for the future in a patient foreign policy anchored to the bedrock principles that informed his view of America's imperial role. To the degree that the United States demonstrated its unique doctrine of equality of opportunity was no mere myth or legend, it might become an "exportable commodity" that could contribute to the stability of the other nations even as it advanced their own democracy along its historic path. "Conant tried to find in the practical world of daily affairs solutions to the deep cleavages in twentieth-century American and European society," observed historian Samuel Bass Warner Jr. "At the height of his powers, enriched by the experience of being a university president for more than a decade, and now with five years as a national science advisor as well, he rushed from committee to lecture platform to writing desk, trying to ease major public problems."

Oppenheimer, who had achieved the same Olympian heights and even more outsize fame as the celebrated "Father of the A-bomb," had not made the transition to the peacetime corridors of power as smoothly. During his first face-to-face interview with Truman, he had failed to hide his conviction that the president had missed his chance to avert nuclear war by not being open with the Russians at Potsdam, and then punctuated his appearance with the bizarre confession "Mr. President, I feel I have blood on my hands." Truman had been so infuriated by the remark that he told Acheson, "I never want to see that son of a bitch in this office ever again," and even six months later, he was still ranting about the "cry baby scientist."

Oppenheimer had also succeeded in offending many influential military and government figures with his mournful, quasi-religious remarks after the bombings, only just managing to redeem himself in their eyes with his important contribution to the Acheson-Lilienthal plan. Arrogant and enigmatic, he had a knack for making enemies—chief among them J. Edgar Hoover, director of the FBI—and was fortunate to still count Conant as a strong ally. The two wartime leaders had forged an unshakable bond, and Conant did not think twice about going to bat for his old friend during the renewed security investigation that followed his appointment as chairman of the General Advisory Committee of the AEC, after Conant had ducked the job, citing an already heavy workload.

With anti-Communist sentiments running high in the winter of 1947, the AEC confirmation hearings had been particularly vicious. Senate Republicans had a field day interrogating Truman's five nominations for the commission leadership, disparaging the scientists' "leftist" sympathies and "Communist tendencies," even branding the affable Lilienthal an "appeaser of Russia," according to the conservative Washington Times-Herald. Conant had been forced to put aside his own personal differences with Lilienthal—who had angered him by criticizing the release of the Smyth Report as the "principal breach of security since the beginning of the atomic energy project"—and defend him from Tennessee senator Kenneth D. McKellar's outrageous questions about his Austro-Hungarian parentage, "Americanism," and "Communist proclivities." Lilienthal finally won Senate approval on April 9, but the nastiness of his lengthy inquisition had not boded well for Oppenheimer, whose appointment to the GAC put him back in the FBI's crosshairs.

In early March 1947, just when Lilienthal's drawn-out ordeal was coming to an end, J. Edgar Hoover had a special messenger deliver a thick file of "derogatory information" about Oppenheimer to the AEC. One of the provisions of the McMahon Act was that all AEC employees who had been cleared to work on the Manhattan Project had to be investigated by the FBI, so agents had reinterviewed dozens of Oppie's old friends and colleagues and gathered information for a fresh dossier. The file revealed that both Oppenheimer and his brother, Frank, were alleged to be members of the Communist Party, and as both had extensive knowledge of the bomb, this could present a security risk. In addition, it rehashed all the material dug up by the FBI during the war about Kitty Oppenheimer's radical past, her Communist first husband, and Oppenheimer's dubious conduct in spending a night in June 1943 with Jean Tatlock, a former lover with a history of Communist sympathies. The most damning piece of information was that sometime in January or February of that year, Oppenheimer had been approached by his leftist friend Haakon Chevalier and asked to leak secret information about the bomb, and that he subsequently gave inconsistent accounts of this exchange in interviews with security officers, while always maintaining that he had refused to pass information. Although Oppenheimer's statements were at times vague and conflicting, there was no proof of his complicity in any espionage scheme.

On Monday, March 10, Conant, who happened to be in Washington for a meeting on atomic matters at the Pentagon, found the shocked leaders of the fledgling agency in Lilienthal's office poring over the contents of Oppenheimer's FBI file. One look at their stony faces told him they had concluded they had to take the allegations seriously. After Lilienthal summarized the findings, Conant told them that he was not especially concerned. Both he and Bush, who had also received an urgent summons, went on to explain that none of the information was new: Oppenheimer's left-wing tendencies had been known to General Groves at the time of his selection to head the bomb laboratory in the fall of 1942, and the various allegations had been discussed and dismissed then. Both men stressed that Oppenheimer's "brilliant and driving leadership" and outstanding postwar advisory role had "clearly demonstrated his loyalty," and that losing him would be a serious setback for the atomic program. Such was Conant's admiration and affection for his Los Alamos colleague that immediately after the war he had made Oppenheimer a very attractive offer to come to Harvard. He thought the world of him and had been profoundly disappointed when the sought-after physicist chose instead to accept the directorship of the Institute for Advanced Study at Princeton, despite Oppie's fond assurances of his "regret" at not having Conant as his "boss in the times to come."

The five AEC commissioners were in a quandary about what to do about the FBI material. If word of the dismaying information contained in Oppenheimer's file made its way back to the Senate committee, the whole confirmation process would be plunged back into the sewer of innuendo and speculation from which they were just emerging. On the other hand, Hoover was clearly concerned enough to bring the report to their attention, even phoning Lilienthal to express the hope he would give personal attention to the matter. The FBI had devoted hours of interviews and untold days of technical surveillance to accumulating the evidence against the controversial Berkeley physicist. At first glance, the AEC members felt there was enough there to "seriously impeach" Oppenheimer's reputation. They decided they had no choice but to inform the president of the FBI's suspicions. Truman, who was caught up in the crises in Greece and Turkey, was too preoccupied to meet with them. Instead, he referred them to his White House counsel, Clark Clifford, who, much to their relief, saw no reason to pursue the matter.

To help Oppenheimer's case, Conant wasted no time marshaling his forces, obtaining statements from Secretary of War Patterson and Groves vouching for the Los Alamos director, and providing his own glowing testimonial:

> I can say without hesitation that there can be absolutely no question of Dr. Oppenheimer's loyalty. Furthermore, I can state categorically that, in my opinion, his attitude about the future course of the United States in matters of high policy is in accordance with the soundest American tradition. He is not sympathetic with the totalitarian regime in Russia, and his attitude toward that nation is, from my point of view, thoroughly sound and hardheaded. Therefore, any rumor Dr. Oppenheimer is sympathetically inclined toward the Communists or toward Russia is an absurdity.

His impassioned championing of Oppenheimer, reaffirmed by Bush and Groves, allowed the physicist to skate through the vetting process. On August 11, 1947, despite weeks of sensational newspaper stories about his brother's Communist past, the AEC unanimously agreed to approve Oppenheimer for a "Q" clearance granting him access to all of the nation's atomic secrets.

In the interim, however, Truman announced an onerous federal loyalty program in an effort to deflect Republican accusations of Communist influence in the government. The disclosures of the Russian spy ring in Canada in 1946 had sent twenty people to trial in Ottawa and provided demonstrable proof of Soviet espionage. Forced to act, Truman's Executive Order 9835 required that all federal employees had to be of "complete and unswerving loyalty to the United States" and should be screened for "activities and association" that might be disloyal, including membership in or affiliation with any organization designated as "totalitarian, Fascist, Communist, or subversive."

Having scored their first victory, the Republicans continued to use the national anxiety over loyalty and security to hold Truman's feet to the fire and taunt Democrats for failing to curb Communist infiltration and keep the country's atomic secret safe. Groves, called before Congress to testify about security practices at the AEC, created a stir by blaming the breaches on an unnamed power and "its misguided and traitorous domestic sympathizers." While his intention was to discredit civilian control of atomic energy and return it to military control, the resulting furor over secrecy gave new impetus to the House Un-American Activities Committee (HUAC) investigations of bomb spies.

Conant's wartime allegiances did not extend to the increasingly unreasonable Groves, whose persistent challenging of international control and efforts to retain custody of the Manhattan Project's nuclear arsenal had succeeded in alienating many of his former scientific colleagues. By early 1948, Groves, who had been appointed chief of special weapons as well as the army representative on the Military Liaison Committee, was locked in a bitter feud with David Lilienthal over his stewardship of the AEC, and had allowed his bulldog tenacity to get the better of his judgment. He finally went too far, reportedly leaking documents to Congress that led to the AEC being charged with what the newspapers termed "incredible mismanagement."

The "Groves situation" had grown sufficiently problematic that Conant was summoned to a meeting in mid-January with Secretary of Defense

James Forrestal for the purpose of deciding how to dislodge the driven officer. Recognizing the need for change at the top, Conant had earlier written a "Personal and Confidential" letter to Oppenheimer plainly stating that the only way to end the internal strife and create an efficient, well-run weapons bureaucracy was to push aside Groves, asking for anonymity from everyone considering the "drastic nature of the proposals in so far as personalities are concerned." In the course of their four-hour meeting with the defense secretary, Conant, Bush, and Oppenheimer debated the awkward business of relieving someone of such colossal stature, but all three insisted that "Groves must get out."

The general, who knew his days in the army were numbered, saved them the ordeal of a head-on confrontation by announcing his intention to retire. From Conant's point of view, it was the best outcome—no one, not even Groves, could be allowed to impede the proper functioning of the nation's atomic energy program. In the years that followed, he continued to speak highly of the general's oversight of the Manhattan Project, and the two remained on friendly terms.

Right to the end, Groves remained convinced the Russians were still as much as twenty years away from an atomic bomb, telling a reporter at his last press conference in February 1948 that he was "not a bit worried." Conant was not willing to bank on that "military insurance." Twice in the past year, the country had been on the brink of war, despite its nuclear hegemony. Moreover, the inevitability of a Soviet bomb meant that America's atomic monopoly was rapidly disappearing, "like a cake of ice on a hot sunny day." Groves had been unwavering in his advocacy of more, bigger, and better bombs, and while Conant would not miss him, he wished that American policy makers, conflicted about whether to emphasize military action or deterrence, would evolve as clear and consistent a position on atomic warfare. He worried that the United States' military strategy was increasingly reliant on the atomic blitz, and what he saw as a dangerous—and potentially disastrous—tendency to want to capitalize on the country's short-term advantage.

Returning to the National War College that fall, Conant spoke out against the right-wing "preventive war" movement—the "Let's smash 'em now before they're ready" chorus—which wanted to rush into war with the Soviets while they were still unable to respond in kind. Some of the country's most renowned government officials and military leaders—Generals LeMay and Spaatz were among the most vocal proponents—were pressing for a preemptive attack against the Soviet Union, insisting that the one sure way to prevent nuclear war was to strike the first blow and overcome the enemy arsenal before it was launched. Even William Laurence, the respected science writer for the *New York Times*, wanted to force the Soviets to accept nuclear disarmament through an ultimatum, and if they rejected the American demand, "their nuclear plants should be destroyed before bombs could be produced." Conant dissented strongly, arguing that such a panicked approach would lead us to "develop a Machiavellian foreign policy culminating in our launching a surprise attack on the Soviet Union or declaring war for the sole purpose of waging destruction which would negate the very premise on which our culture rests."

In his speech, Conant posed the "ugly question" that had haunted him since the black day he was drafted into weapons work as a young chemist: "how to reconcile the doctrine of military force—killing men in war—with a moral purpose?" The only way to make sense of this apparent paradox was to understand the distinction between the ethics of war and the ethics of peace that must be the "fundamental postulate" of their democratic society. "The citizens of the United States, while abhorring war, nevertheless believe it is *not always wrong*," he told his military audience. "They have a deep-seated conviction, however, that war is always totally different morally from peace."

It was true, of course, that history was full of examples of freedom being gained by the successful use of force: the liberties of the early settlers of New England had been secured by Oliver Cromwell's soldiers, who overpowered the church and the king. But once won, Conant maintained, freedom "can be protected only by adherence to those moral principles which were repudiated in its achievement." The moment society failed to adhere to this moral distinction, it fell prey to Communists and fanatics, "men so dedicated to a cause that they did not scruple to use violence as an adjunct to political action." Presenting a reformulated version of his ends-versus-the-means doctrine, he contended that initiating an air-atomic offensive against Russia would be no better than waging a holy war: "only those who believe they are divinely led or that history is on their side can maintain that the issue between themselves and their opponents demands the rules of war should operate even in time of peace."

America, Conant argued, had to deliberately refrain from such desperate measures. What was really needed in response to the Russian threat was conscription, a buildup of conventional forces, and the courage to walk "a perilous knife edge" between providing the nation with adequate military protection while preserving the strength of America's unique free and open society.

Forrestal was so impressed with Conant's critique of the preventive war movement that he urged him to prepare a version of his talk for the *Atlantic Monthly*, and personally contacted the editor, Edward Weeks, about publishing it. Flattered to have the Pentagon chief as his patron, Conant agreed and arranged to have it declassified. "Force and Freedom" appeared on the cover of the January 1949 issue, featuring an artist's imaginative rendition of Conant, a fiery atomic blitz under way in the background, pondering the nation's chances of survival in World War III. Forrestal, who was sent an advance copy, raved about the article. The *Washington Post* reprinted it in full, accompanied by a large photograph of Truman pinning the service medals on Conant while a beaming Bush looked on. The article was read and extolled at the highest levels of government, enhancing Conant's reputation as an intellectual leader and moral guide in what he called "these confused and gloomy days."

Between January 1949, when Truman announced his intention to provide military aid to Western Europe, and April 4, when the North Atlantic Treaty was signed in Washington, it was as if every competing faction of the army, navy, and air force was using the press to promote its atomic delivery system and convince the public and Congress that it deserved a hefty increase in funding to defend against Soviet aggression. From Conant's perspective, the disclosures about nuclear weapons—including an alarming leak in March of a presentation to the Joint Chiefs of Staff showing that seventy strategic targets in Russia were within range of the new B-36 bombers—were the most distressing.

When, in the midst of this mess, Forrestal asked him to chair a panel of eight prominent civilians charged with reexamining the government's nuclear secrecy policy, Conant agreed with alacrity. At the heart of the matter was the delicate question of what information about weapons of mass destruction—atomic, biological, chemical, and radiological—the public was entitled to know for the purposes of education and approving national policy, and what was not suitable for release. Forrestal had been prodded into action by the growing press criticism of excessive government secrecy, specifically the suppression of a report on the Bikini tests, and renewed pressure for the United States to articulate an official statement on employing atomic weapons in the event of war.

On April 7 Conant convened the first meeting of the "Fishing Party," as his top-secret committee was known, the code name serving as an apt comment on the Truman administration's leaky ship. The high-powered group—which included Dwight D. Eisenhower, then president of Columbia University, and John Foster Dulles, a New York lawyer with political ambitions, and several industrialists—met at the Pentagon a few times that spring and summer, but was sharply divided about what information should be released, with the ultraconservative members convinced that neither the American public nor Congress could be trusted with the facts of these new weapons and their operational use. Adept as he was at battling military bureaucracies, Conant, who was in favor of a more open information policy, could not overcome the entrenched secrecy. He had been especially concerned about the closed-door debate over the hydrogen superbomb— which Teller and others had pushed since 1942 and which he opposed—and felt that it merited public release as it was more sensitive politically than technically. He was overruled. The H-bomb, still on the drawing boards, would remain classified. Truman, who insisted that everything connected to America's nuclear arsenal be as closely held as possible, did not intend for it to become an issue of public discourse.

The Fishing Party's final report, submitted to Compton on October 15, 1949, was a poor compromise that protected the H-bomb from public discussion and careful, responsible criticism, and continued, in the words of Conant and his pro-release colleagues, "the present haphazard methods of keeping the American people informed whereby the public receives its information on these critical matters through a process of osmosis involving intentional or unintentional 'leaks' to the press by individuals with access to classified data." Although he earned high marks for his handling of the difficult assignment, Conant wrote Compton that he was "not very proud of the results," feeling he had failed to make the positive changes Forrestal had mandated.

Meanwhile, the Republican rancor that followed Truman's election had made Washington a treacherous place. Forrestal, exhausted and under constant venomous attacks in the columns—Drew Pearson imputed that he had been advising Dewey on foreign affairs and was disloyal—was forced to resign at the end of March. The muckrakers in Washington bore down, delving into his Wall Street background and personal life, hinting darkly about corruption and conflict of interest. Forrestal, who was undergoing treatment after a nervous breakdown, killed himself two months later, leaping out of a window on the sixteenth floor of Bethesda Naval Hospital. Conant was appalled. It was the same hospital where his son had spent months recovering after the war. Jim had regained the balance of his mind and was doing better now, but it had been a close-run thing.

Conant felt oppressed not only by the death of the vanquished defense secretary but also by the developments in his own backyard that signaled the ugliness was spreading to the academic realm. The conservatives in Congress, bent on domestic revenge, had decided the best way to undermine Truman was not to attack his global policy of "containing" the Soviet Union—both the Marshall Plan and the Berlin Airlift were working—but to focus on the "fifth column" eating away at the heart of the United States. The exaggerated claims of Communist subversion that Conant had thought would be a "passing excitement" had not died down, and it now appeared that Truman's second term would be plagued by an endless series of "Red Scare" scandals.

HUAC had been busy: there was the espionage investigation into physicist Edward Condon, identified as "one of the weakest links" in the country's atomic security; the probe of the motion picture industry and subsequent jailing of the "Hollywood Ten," who refused to answer questions about their political affiliations, claiming immunity under the First Amendment; and allegations by Elizabeth Bentley that one of FDR's aides, Lauchlin Currie, had been among the purveyors of secrets to the Soviets. But none of these cases would impact Conant as directly as the cause celebre born of Bentley's evidence, and that of her fellow Communist informer Whittaker Chambers, a *Time* magazine editor, that a former high-ranking State Department official named Alger Hiss was a Russian spy.

As soon as he heard the astonishing accusations against Hiss, a distinguished president of the Carnegie Endowment for International Peace, Conant felt a frisson of unease. While he had never crossed paths with the Harvard Law graduate, he knew of him and from the beginning was "certain that he was an innocent victim of a vicious Red hunt." Not only had the tall, patrician forty-four-year-old Hiss clerked for Justice Oliver Wendell Holmes on the recommendation of Felix Frankfurter, but also his oldest friend and fiercest defender was William Marbury, the War Department lawyer with whom Conant had collaborated in drafting the May-Johnson Act in the summer of 1945. Since then, Marbury had become a close friend, and Conant had put the up-and-coming Baltimore lawyer's name forward as a member of the Harvard Corporation, the conservative Brahmin inner sanctum he had vowed to infuse with new blood before the war got in the way. His nomination of Marbury—a non-Bostonian who had not even attended Harvard College—kicked off yet another of those consuming and prolonged battles that Conant despised. Though he prevailed in getting his choice confirmed, the fierce struggle damaged his relationship with the governing boards and added to his growing discontent with his old job. So when Marbury appeared at Hiss's side before HUAC in August 1948, and Hiss categorically denied being a Communist and insisted he had never met Chambers, Conant cheered them on from Cambridge. Many Harvard alumni testified to Hiss's character and helped cover the cost of his defense.

When Hiss was called back for a second round of questioning, a relentless first-term congressman from California named Richard Nixon succeeded in shaking his story that he and Chambers were barely acquainted. Conant suddenly became very concerned. He and Grenville Clark, who was especially upset by Hiss's crumbling credibility, summoned Marbury to a meeting at 17 Quincy Street on the evening of Sunday, September 12, to discuss the case. At first, no one had believed the rumpled, slightly disreputable journalist's claims about the handsome, well-spoken Harvard lawyer who had been one of FDR's valued advisors. It helped that Hiss had friends in high places, and that even Truman, who tended to regard all Communist smears as politically inspired, denounced the HUAC hearings as a "red herring." But now they told Marbury the hearings had gone too far. Failure to refute Chambers's allegations might be taken as an admission of guilt and, worse still, might open the floodgates to a torrent of similar charges against academic and political figures until, Conant warned, "nobody is safe."

Both he and Clark counseled Marbury to act aggressively to clear Hiss's name and sue Chambers for libel. On September 27 Marbury filed Hiss's defamation suit seeking $50,000 in damages. In response, Chambers led two HUAC investigators to the rear garden of his Maryland home and retrieved a cache of incriminating documents and microfilm hidden in a scooped-out pumpkin. The day Nixon displayed the "pumpkin papers" at a crowded press conference, Marbury knew the slander suit was lost. Hiss's indictment followed, embroiling Marbury and Harvard in the lurid, melodramatic trial—which ended in a hung jury in July 1949—and retrial, which hypnotized the public, Congress, newspaper reporters, and radio commentators for months. In January 1950 Hiss was convicted on two counts of perjury. Still protesting his innocence, he was sentenced to five years in jail.

Chastened by the outcome, Conant was no longer sure what to believe. It had begun to look like Hiss had been a party member and possibly leaked some documents, even if they were of small consequence. "After the conviction, it was hard to maintain that there was no possibility of Communists being in positions of responsibility," he recalled. The ordeal convinced him that espionage, sabotage, and spilled secrets would be a fact of life under the armed truce. Reasonable precautions had to be taken. "Careful security checks," he noted, "were certainly in order."

Long before he heard the final verdict in the Hiss case, Conant had begun to worry about the ramifications of radicalism abroad on universities and how they could "preserve their integrity during this period of warring ideologies." He had been greatly influenced by Stimson's argument against allowing Communists to teach, set forth in a 1947 *Foreign Affairs* article that concluded, "those who now choose to travel in company with American Communists are very clearly either knaves or fools . . . are either to be tolerated in an academic community?"

At Harvard, Conant struggled to find a way to walk a middle line between protecting the "spirit of tolerance" he had long espoused, while maintaining that universities should not be "ivory towers" cut off from the problems of their age, and should be responsive to the government's needs in perilous times. For the past three years, he had lobbied tirelessly for the dissemination of scientific knowledge and greater freedom of research, even renouncing lucrative classified government contracts at Harvard on the grounds that such a close partnership with the military, while necessary during the war, was in peacetime "highly inadvisable" for an institution dedicated to free investigation. Striving to make the university more relevant in global affairs, he founded the Russian Research Center, underwritten by a grant from the Carnegie Corporation, to fill what he saw as the pressing need for Soviet experts to advise the State Department, military, and Central Intelligence Agency on their cold war adversary.

Even as anti-Communist feeling intensified, he steadily, stubbornly championed free speech, defending liberal professors such as China expert John King Fairbank, under attack from the right for acknowledging Mao Tse-tung's legitimacy, and the astronomer Harlow Shapley and literary critic F. O. Matthiessen, who were both maligned as "pinkos" for their involvement in Henry Wallace's third-party campaign in 1948. Despite vehement opposition from the Overseers, Conant backed tenure and promotion for the iconoclastic young economist John Kenneth Galbraith, whose Keynesian views and New Deal politics were particularly obnoxious to the conservative bankers on the board. For his trouble, Conant was condemned by the National Council of American Education for harboring what it called "reducators" at Harvard, singling him out along with seventy-six faculty members allegedly engaged in disloyal activities. The reactionaries in Congress piled on, pointing out other Communists with institutional ties to the "Kremlin-on-the-Charles."

Refusing to be intimidated, Conant argued that interference with academic freedom "as a consequence of panic" could have "most disastrous" effects on the universities. "There is no doubt," he warned, "a dark shadow has been cast upon our institutions of advanced education by the unfortunate turn of events in the postwar world." Free inquiry was "the bedrock on which the scholarly activities of a university are founded. No compromise with this principle is possible even in the days of an armed truce."

Arthur Schlesinger Jr., a young associate professor of government at Harvard, called on political and intellectual leaders to follow in Conant's footsteps to stop the purges, praising the university president for his firm stand in defending the right of professors to hold unpopular ideas, and for having faith in "the value of our freedoms" and the willingness to do what was necessary to save them. "We need courageous men to help us recapture a sense of the indispensability of dissent," Schlesinger wrote in his 1948 treatise *The Vital Center: The Politics of Freedom*, citing Conant's opposition to the Massachusetts teachers' loyalty oath bill twelve years earlier, "and we need dissent if we are to make up our minds equably and intelligently."

Like Schlesinger, Conant deplored the Communist witch hunt—and corresponding fear and paranoia—but at the same time felt they could not afford to underestimate the danger in the Russian threat. The list of organizations reportedly penetrated and manipulated by agents on behalf of the Soviet Union was expanding steadily, from the State Department and Foreign Service to labor unions and liberal-leaning publications. (In a headline-grabbing case, six people associated with *Amerasia* magazine had been arrested and accused of stealing documents for the Chinese Communists.) With the country increasingly polarized, and under pressure from right-wingers eager for even more repressive measures, Conant reacted with characteristic caution, on the one hand deploring "the overemphasis on 'loyalty'" and vigorously criticizing the attacks on educators and academic freedom, while on the other acknowledging that as a country "we would be well advised to be on guard." At the same time, however, he tacitly embraced the language of Truman's loyalty regulations. "We must be realistic about the activities of agents of foreign powers," he stated repeatedly. While the government should employ only "persons of intelligence and discretion," it was important that "any steps we take to counteract the work of a foreign agent within our borders do not damage irreparably the very fabric [of democracy] we seek to save."

Disturbed by the headlines generated by the Condon espionage hearings, and widespread rumors that Manhattan Project scientists had passed secrets during the war, Conant urged Alfred Richards, president of the National Academy of Scientists, to act to nip the scandal in the bud. Conant recommended adopting tighter security regulations, especially a new, stricter clearance policy for personnel handling classified data. Those suspected of being a "poor security risk," because they were either naïve or indiscreet, could not be trusted and should be transferred to a less responsible position. He also strove to provide procedural protections for those deemed temperamentally unsuitable, so they would not be unduly "penalized, stigmatized, deprived of livelihood, or exposed to public shame."

But his reformer's zeal, combined with his desire to make certain the atomic program remained above reproach, drove him toward a dogmatism that he would later regret. "The government, in resolving doubts on these matters about employees, including scientists, must settle the case in favor of the government rather than the individual," Conant asserted. "If a shadow of a doubt exists, the individual should be prevented from having access to confidential information." The academy adopted the tougher standard on February 3, 1949, and Conant sent it to Truman with "the hope that you will find it of interest and possible usefulness."

By the spring of 1949, with the anti-Communist crusade extending to the classroom, Conant resorted to what Schlesinger and many of his liberal Harvard colleagues viewed as an "extreme measure" to protect the educational system from the pernicious investigations. HUAC had sent a letter to eighty-one colleges demanding lists of textbooks currently in use in the fields of literature, economics, history, political science, and geography. After working to defeat another Massachusetts loyalty oath bill proposed by State Assistant Attorney General Clarence Barnes the previous year, Conant now backtracked on that principled stand and gave in to the watchdogs, hoping that by throwing them a bone he could prevent the wholesale banning of books and blacklisting of professors.

On June 9 the *New York Times* announced, "Eisenhower and Conant in Group Barring Communists as Teachers," the two university presidents joining eighteen other prominent educators in signing a statement declaring that membership in the Communist Party involved "adherence to doctrine and disciplines completely inconsistent with the principles of freedom on which American education depends." Belonging to a movement characterized by conspiracy and deceit, the Education Policies Commission's (EPC) fifty-four-page pamphlet *American Education and International Tensions* concluded, rendered an individual "unfit to discharge the duties of a teacher in this country."

It was a calculated, cynical tactic that Conant, as one of the leaders of the EPC, justified as pragmatic politics. The move showed how far he was willing to go to protect the independence of the university and keep the FBI from becoming a fixture on campus. He knew it would be too far for some and that the die-hard civil libertarians would judge him harshly, noting, "A lot of people would say I sold myself down the road to the reactionaries."

Complicating matters, Conant had enlisted the help of Grenville Clark in fending off Frank B. Ober, a wealthy, conservative Harvard Law alumnus who as a state legislator had sponsored the Maryland Subversive Activities Act of 1949, and that spring launched a campaign to end all financial contributions to the university until all the radical professors were discovered and fired. Conant was willing to fire avowed Communists, but he would do without Ober's money before he got into the business of trying to "ferret out" clandestine party members, convinced that policing professors could seriously damage the university. Clark responded to Ober's complaints with a double-barreled twelve-page letter-cum-legal-brief reaffirming the university's refusal to censure its faculty for unpopular views, stating categorically, "Harvard cannot be influenced at all to depart from her basic tradition of freedom by any fear that gifts will be withheld."

Unfortunately, the publication of the EPC's strong statement barring Communist teachers coincided with the *Harvard Alumni Bulletin*'s reprinting of the Clark-Ober letters, exposing Conant's somewhat inconsistent stands on academic freedom and placing him, he later admitted, in "an almost indefensible position." Seeking to explain himself, to both the faculty, which approved of the EPC's anti-Communist policy two to one, and the students, who were opposed by the same margin, he gave a talk to the university on June 22.

"In this period of a cold war," he told them, "I do not believe the usual rules as to political parties apply to the Communist Party." Drawing a distinction between heresy and subversion, he likened Communists to a group of spies or saboteurs in an enemy country. Sticking to his statement that he would not knowingly appoint "card-holding members of the Communist Party" to the teaching profession, and calling the ban the "single exception which is the unique product of this century," he then concluded with his usual ringing rhetoric: "As long as I am president of the university, I can assure you there will be no policy of inquiring into the political views of members of the staff."

Harvard's battles with HUAC were far from over, and Conant's stern opposition to faculty members who took the Fifth Amendment to avoid self-incrimination continued to aggravate critics. But even the gadflies on the *Crimson* conceded that he came up with the "answer to end all answers to the 'iffy' question" in an interview after the commencement exercises of Yeshiva University, where he received an honorary degree. When asked what he would do if a member of the faculty walked into his office and announced his allegiance to Moscow, Harvard's president, exasperated by the vexing issue, retorted, "I would send for a psychiatrist."

Conant made other accommodations during this fraught period that indicate his actions were often ruled by expediency and that his support of academic freedom was not as unfaltering as it ought to have been. "Conant talked one way and acted another," was author Sigmund Diamond's withering description of the Harvard president's conduct when, under pressure from the Carnegie Corporation, he acquiesced in the forced resignation of a young radical historian from the Russian Research Center, H. Stuart Hughes, the grandson of Chief Justice Charles Evans Hughes. In his book *Compromised Campus: The Collaboration of Universities with the Intelligence Community, 1945–1955*, Diamond contends that Conant allowed the CIA to vet members of the Russian center—modeled on the research and analysis branch of the OSS—so that it became "the locus of a fruitful collaboration between the intelligence agencies and Harvard," hoping this cooperation would be a way of keeping Hoover at bay while still maintaining good relations with the government and preserving all those lucrative research grants. There is little evidence of Conant's direct personal involvement in the CIA and FBI collaboration that Diamond alleges, although it could be argued that his willingness to look the other way was bad enough.*

In desperate need of "some peace and quiet," the Conants left for their annual August sojourn in the Canadian Rockies, eager to escape the summer heat and boiling controversy. As was her habit, Patty fretted about their holiday plans and whether there was enough to do to keep her husband occupied during his time off. "I always feel dubious about vacations with Jim because he is theoretically 'against' them, and expects so much from any outlay of his precious time that I'm never sure that the best-laid plans will turn out satisfactorily," she wrote her mother. At the end of their first week, she was relieved to report that "after the usual early stages of suspended judgment," he seemed to be enjoying himself, and was so absorbed in his geopolitical contemplations and outdoor exertions that "the days aren't long enough. I'm also grateful that the fish are cooperating," she added, "something one can't always count on!"

With his bad back forcing him to retire from what he thought of as "real" climbing, Conant had to settle for long all-day rambles in the wilderness, losing himself in the unspoiled alpine meadows and measureless solitude. Earlier in the summer, on a drive from Berkeley to San Francisco with the physicists Ernest Lawrence and Luis Alvarez, he had intimated that he was "burned out" and was finding his duties as an atomic advisor increasingly burdensome. When Lawrence tried to engage him on the subject of radiological warfare, Conant raised his hands to stave him off, saying in effect that he had "done his job during the war" and was too old and tired to be exploring new weapons of mass destruction. Disillusionment, fatigue, and the failure to achieve any kind of international cooperation had worn him down and dimmed his enthusiasm for nuclear policy.

That July marked the fourth anniversary of Trinity. Just days after the test, full of plans for the future, Conant had jotted down a list of "personal ambitions" on a scrap of blue Harvard stationary: "What JBC would like to do before death or senility overtakes him." There were books he wanted to write: on chemistry, the philosophy of science, poetry, and public educa-

---

* Lest anyone accuse him of having a secret axe to grind, Sigmund Diamond disclosed that he was dismissed from Harvard by McGeorge Bundy in 1954, a year after Conant's retirement, because he refused to talk to the FBI about his and former associates' ties to the Communist Party.

tion. A course he wanted to teach on Critical Phases in the Advancement of Knowledge. Subjects he wanted to study intensively—the seventeenth century—with an eye to still more books. All he had managed was *Education in a Divided World* and another slim volume, *On Understanding Science: An Historical Approach*, an attempt to give readers a better understanding of modern achievements by providing a basic grounding in the trial-and-error nature of experimental inquiry. The previous fall, in a break with a long-standing Harvard tradition that its presidents did not teach, he had actually taught a course based on the book. Still, four years had passed, and he had hardly made a dent in the list.

There were also fences to mend. He was trying to spend more time with Patty and had promised to dine with her at home twice a week. He had been far too preoccupied and had left her "holding the bag" after their son's breakdown, to an unfair extent. This was also the first time in many years that they were sharing their holiday with Ted, now twenty-three, on summer break from Swarthmore College, where he enrolled after being discharged from the merchant marines. Father and son were still uneasy in each other's company, but they had a shared passion for the mountains, and the lofty summits and vast expanses gave them a fresh perspective and seemed to allow for their own "armed truce," however temporary. Patty was pleased to see them "having an experience of shared exhilaration and companionship that is unique to both of them."

Acknowledging the bumpy road they had traveled to get here, she confided to her mother, "You can imagine how happy it makes me to see them having such fun together—with all the pressures of 17 Quincy St. far away." With their oldest son seeming more like himself every day, and starting a new job as a reporter in Chicago, she felt for once that all was right with the world. "Our vacation has been a great success," she scribbled at the end of her last letter on September 4. "Jim & I have never known such uninterrupted sunshine."

CHAPTER 20

A Rotten Business

When I am in Washington, it seems as though I were in a
lunatic asylum.

—JBC to Bernard Baruch

In September 1949 Conant was en route to Cambridge, after his annual swing through the California Harvard Clubs, when he was summoned from his railroad car to receive an urgent telephone call from Washington. Picking up the receiver, he heard a voice relay the message—scrambled by the usual OSRD shorthand—he had dreaded since the start of the arms race in 1945: "They have it." An American B-29 weather reconnaissance plane on routine patrol over the North Pacific had picked up a radioactivity count that was higher than usual. Laboratory analysis confirmed the presence of fission isotopes. By September 19, Bush's hastily organized panel of experts concluded that the Soviet Union had successfully tested an atomic bomb.

On September 23 Truman made a terse announcement: "We have evidence that within recent weeks an atomic explosion occurred in the USSR." The president wisely decided to conceal Washington's shock and alarm, and, in an effort to minimize public anxiety, endeavored to put the Soviet explosion in context, explaining that the basic facts of nuclear fission were available for all nations to exploit, and that it had been known the American monopoly would eventually be broken. Conant had been certain the Russians would get there, just not this soon. Unlike Bush and Groves, who had always dismissed his fear of a rival in the race, he had given a great deal of thought to this day. The Russian achievement demonstrated once and for all the futility of secrecy. The balance of power was now a balance of terror, but it did not alter his attitude toward the Soviet challenge: the two countries were still locked in a stalemate, and it was more evident than ever that they must work toward international control, with the long-term goal of gradual disarmament.

The news of Russia's accomplishment sent a collective shiver through the closed community of nuclear physicists and weapons experts, touching off an intense inner struggle over the correct response to the new Soviet threat. The immediate reaction of most of Conant's peers was that the United States should accelerate its atomic program to increase its lead over the Soviet Union, with some advocating they move aggressively to develop a hydrogen bomb. America's current stockpile of atomic warheads numbered about two hundred, with technical advances having increased the explosive power achievable by a factor of five or more. The Joint Chiefs of Staff had already put forward a proposal that summer to expand the production of weapons and fissionable material, including a hugely improved fission bomb equivalent to five hundred thousand tons of TNT. But now that the Soviets had caught up, the question was whether this would be enough to maintain the National Security Council strategy of "overwhelming superiority" and continue to act as a deterrent to war.

This question added sudden urgency to the discussion of the hydrogen bomb and sent Edward Teller and Ernest Lawrence scurrying to Washington to launch a campaign to persuade the president to mount a crash program to develop what some viewed as the ultimate winning weapon. AEC commissioner Lewis Strauss, the lone conservative Republican appointee, articulated their position. "The time has come to make a quantum jump in our planning," he wrote, arguing that only the most powerful offensive weapons could provide a reliable defense against Soviet domination. "We should now make an intensive effort to get ahead with the Super . . . that is the way to stay ahead."

Conant was quickly drawn into the center of the debate when Strauss urged Truman to consider inaugurating a thermonuclear weapons program, and the president referred the issue to the AEC's General Advisory Committee. Horrified at the prospect, Conant took prompt personal control of the H-bomb opposition, impressing on Oppenheimer, as chairman of the GAC, that the correct response to the Soviet threat would be to reinvigorate the existing atomic program, not rush into a breakneck effort to build the still hypothetical superbomb. It was strategically wrong, to say nothing of the moral arguments against building a weapon capable of almost unlimited destruction. Oppenheimer, who also had reservations about the much more powerful fusion bomb, attempted to rein in an excited Teller when he called hours after the announcement of the Soviet test. "Just go back to Los Alamos and keep working," he told him curtly, then added, "Keep your shirt on."

Teller was stung by Oppenheimer's hostile reaction. An insistent advocate of the Super since 1942, Teller was not going to give up the chance to explore the new weapon and possibly lead his own bomb laboratory. He had been aghast when Oppenheimer had dropped by his Los Alamos office the day after peace was declared in August 1945 and informed him, "With the war over, there is no reason to continue work on the hydrogen bomb." Teller's traumatic childhood memories of the Fascist persecution of Jews in Hungary had made him a ferocious anti-Communist, and he equated national security with maximum firepower. He found Oppenheimer's nonchalant attitude almost frightening. His feelings were complicated by jealousy—the October cover of *Life* touted the tall, handsome physicist as the "No. 1 Thinker on Atomic Energy"—and deep resentment that Oppenheimer was regarded as "Father of the Atomic Bomb." Now he saw a chance to be father of the hydrogen bomb, and realize his ambition to develop the new weapon and make certain the United States maintained its nuclear superiority.

Teller found an eager ally in Lawrence, who was also politically "at the opposite end of the spectrum" from most of the members of the GAC and was in search of a new role—and new source of funding—for his cyclotrons. The Berkeley physicist had listened with rapt attention as a confident Teller explained that the hydrogen bomb was feasible: the project would require large quantities of tritium (a form of heavy hydrogen) that would in turn require the construction of a huge production reactor using heavy water instead of graphite as a moderator. It would take a big, concerted effort—comparable to the Manhattan Project—to produce such a big bomb. Lawrence, galvanized by the challenge, recruited his colleague Luis Alvarez to the cause, and they left to meet with Teller in Los Alamos on Friday, October 7, 1949. Then they flew directly to Washington that weekend and threw themselves into whipping up military and congressional support for their plan. David Lilienthal, who like Conant believed that dependence on the atomic arsenal created a "false sense of security," was revolted by the "bloodthirsty" trio's ardor for a weapon of such awful power.

From the start, the GAC had been divided about the feasibility and advisability of the Super. Conant had made no secret of his views, speculating grimly about how many H-bombs it would take to contaminate the atmosphere and the possible global effects of the radioactivity generated by a few gigantic blasts. On one occasion, he muttered to fellow committee member I. I. Rabi that developing the weapon would "only louse up the world still more." He loathed Lewis Strauss. The irritating, self-important Wall Street banker's appointment to the AEC was one the main reasons he had turned down the chairmanship. Aware that Oppenheimer was carefully weighing all the alternatives before making such a far-reaching policy decision, Conant sought to exert his influence. He wrote a letter elaborating the reasons he was against any all-out effort that might disrupt the Los Alamos atomic program in favor of a weapon of such dubious feasibility, stating emphatically that the crash program to build the Super would go ahead "over my dead body."

When Oppenheimer met with Teller and Hans Bethe to discuss the issue at his office at the Institute for Advanced Study in Princeton on Friday, October 21, he reportedly read or showed his visitors Conant's letter, possibly hoping to dampen their enthusiasm without venturing an opinion. Bethe, who was still undecided, was struck by Conant's very strong feelings, and that both the tone and content of the letter revealed that he and Oppenheimer were in close contact—apparently sharing and reinforcing each other's doubts about the weapon, which they viewed as qualitatively different from the atomic bomb.

Teller, troubled by Conant's vehement opposition, recalled that one phrase from the letter stuck in his mind afterward: "over my dead body." In an interview in his office at the Lawrence Livermore National Laboratory in 2003, shortly before his death at the age of ninety-four, Teller admitted to being very upset by Conant's resistance to the H-bomb and concerned that Oppie would follow his lead. "They wanted to stop me," he recalled. Suddenly becoming very agitated and growing red in the face, he said that the hurt and anger of his subsequent rift with Conant were still painfully fresh. "Why did he have to say 'over my dead body'?" he demanded, pounding the arms of his wheelchair. "Why did he say that?"

Still unsure of the military value of the Super, let alone its cost and deliverability, Oppenheimer wrote Conant that same Friday, explaining that he was not sure "the miserable thing" would work, nor that the weapon— which was too large to be portable—could "be gotten to a target except by

ox cart." He was worried that "this thing appears to have caught the imagination, both of the congressional and military people, as the answer to the
problem posed by the Russian advance":

> It would be folly to oppose the exploration of this weapon. We have
> always known it had to be done; and it does have to be done, though
> it appears to be singularly proof against any form of experimental
> approach. But that we become committed to it as the way to save the
> country and the peace appears to me full of dangers.
>
> We will be faced with all this at our meeting, and anything that
> we do or do not say to the president will have to be taken [sic] into
> consideration. I shall feel far more secure if you have had an oppor-
> tunity to think about it.

Oppenheimer had difficulty rounding up all the members of the GAC—he
delayed the meeting for weeks so that Conant and Fermi could attend—and
was not able to convene the crucial meeting to consider an expanded effort
on the H-bomb until the weekend of October 28. Conant missed the Friday session in which George Kennan, equally opposed to the Super, filled
the panel in on the State Department's view of the Soviet situation. Kennan
argued that Russia, still struggling to rebuild its ravaged industry after the
war, might not want to commit millions to a costly weapons program and
might be willing to negotiate an arms agreement that ensured neither side
developed the hydrogen bomb. The Soviets preferred nonmilitary means of
expansion, relying on political pressure, subversion, and economic blackmail. They might not proceed with the Super if the United States did not.
When Conant arrived in Washington that evening, he was given a summary
of the talk by Bethe and his other Los Alamos colleagues. Bethe, after talking to Teller and Oppenheimer, had decided he would not participate in an
intensive H-bomb effort—even for the victors, the blast and radioactive effects of such a weapon would render the world not worth living in.

At ten o'clock the next day, a damp, gray Saturday morning, Conant
joined the seven other members of the General Advisory Committee—
Oppenheimer; Fermi; Rabi; Cyril Smith; Lee DuBridge, the Rad Lab director who was now president of Caltech; Hartley Rowe, a division head of
the NDRC; and recent addition Oliver Buckley, president of Bell Labs—
gathered in room 213 of the heavily guarded AEC headquarters building on
Constitution Avenue. Only Glenn Seaborg, who was in Sweden, was absent.

He sent Oppie a somewhat vague letter stating that he would "have to hear some good arguments before [he] could take on sufficient courage to recommend not going toward such a program."

The morning was taken up by a military briefing with the Joint Chiefs of Staff, headed by General Omar Bradley, one of the senior battle commanders during World War II and regarded by his peers as a master tactician. Bradley felt the Soviet Union could not be allowed to have the Super first but conceded that the H-bomb's military advantage over a stockpile of atomic weapons was "mostly psychological." At noon, they broke for lunch, and went off in small groups to a restaurant nearby. Oppenheimer voiced his reservations about developing the hydrogen bomb and his concern that the Russians, spurred by the US lead in fission weapons, would develop their own with possibly catastrophic results. When Luis Alvarez, who had been unable to stay away, saw that the group was siding against the Super, he realized his dream of a Berkeley heavy water reactor was dead and departed angrily for California.

Later that afternoon, Oppenheimer went around the table and asked each member of the committee to express his view on the course of action the nation should take. Conant spoke out most forcefully against the hydrogen bomb, drawing on what he described later as a combination of "political and strategic and highly technical considerations" to drive home his point. During a lengthy, searching discussion of the moral implications of building a weapon up to a thousand times more destructive than the Hiroshima bomb, and the danger its very existence posed to humanity as a whole, the Harvard scientist looked "almost translucent, so gray," Lilienthal wrote in his journal that night, noting that Conant came out "flatly against it 'on moral grounds.'" At one point, Conant turned to him and confided that the proceedings gave him an uneasy feeling of déjà vu. "The whole discussion," he said, recalling the controversy over the atomic bomb, "makes me feel I was seeing the same film, and a punk one, for the second time."

During the long, intense day of deliberations, Conant held sway over the group. Older and more senior than most of his colleagues, he had held high command during the wartime project, second only to Bush, and bore a heavy burden of responsibility for ushering in the atomic bombs that had been used against two Japanese cities. He had been Oppenheimer's mentor for many years, and his powerful moral arguments against using nuclear weapons on such a massive scale had a profound effect on the physicist, who despite his misgivings was still on the fence about foreclosing the Super as a military option. It was "a result of Conant's intervention," Oppenheimer conceded some years later, that he decided to take a stand against the H-bomb. By the end of the afternoon, Oppenheimer found there was a "surprising unanimity of opinion," and suggested they retire to begin drafting their reports and reconvene the next morning.

The committee members spent the bulk of Sunday discussing and writing their reports. The main report was written by Oppenheimer (aided by John Manley) and was signed by all eight members of the GAC present. It consisted of two sections, each compressed into two typewritten pages: part one recommended that high priority be given to developing atomic weapons for tactical purposes, urging an increase in the production of reactors, isotope-separation plants, and fission bombs; part two was devoted to the Super, with the conclusion that a crash program could conceivably overcome the formidable theoretical and engineering problems, giving it "a better than even chance of producing a weapon in five years." However, when it came to the question of what *should* be done with regard to the superbomb, which was estimated to have an explosive effect "some hundreds of times that of fission bombs," they all expressed the hope that the development of thermonuclear weapons could be avoided.

The authors confronted head-on the question of what would be involved in actually using the weapon: because of its size, the Super could not be deployed "exclusively for the destruction of military or semimilitary purposes," they concluded. "Its use therefore carries much further than the atomic bomb itself the policy of exterminating civilian populations." The eight men agreed unanimously that "it would be wrong at the present moment to commit ourselves to an all-out effort towards its development."

As to how the government should proceed to prevent development of the Super, the committee split 6 to 2, resulting in two appended statements. The majority opinion, written by Conant (and signed by Buckley, DuBridge, Rowe, Smith, and Oppenheimer), favored a complete and unconditional commitment not to develop the weapon: "We believe a superbomb should never be produced," they asserted. The nation's stockpile of atomic weapons would provide a "comparably effective" means for retaliation. "The extreme dangers to mankind inherent in the proposal wholly outweigh any military advantage that could come from this development . . . a superbomb might become a weapon of genocide."

Conant attempted to end on his usual optimistic note: "In determining not to proceed to develop the superbomb, we see a unique opportunity of providing by example some limitations on the totality of war and thus elimi-nating the fear and arousing the hope of mankind."

The minority opinion, written and signed by Fermi and Rabi, was that this commitment never to produce the Super should be "conditional on the response of the Soviet government." The United States should first ask Rus-sia and the nations of the world to join in a "solemn pledge" renouncing hydrogen weapons and promising not to proceed. They, too, viewed the ex-traordinary destructiveness of the H-bomb as repellant, calling it "necessar-ily an evil thing considered in any light."

It had been a grueling weekend, charged with emotion, impassioned de-bate, and an overriding sense of what was at stake for the future. Hurrying for the evening train to Boston, Conant felt drained. He hoped he was suc-cessful in forestalling the development of a weapon that surpassed the atom bomb in becoming a "weapon of genocide." He had called for declassifying sufficient information on the Super to enable public discussion and debate on such an irrevocable decision. But he knew there was no guarantee that the AEC would follow their advice or that the scientists' opinions would be enough to dissuade the military from its faith in overwhelming superiority.

On Monday morning, October 31, Lilienthal called to congratulate Conant on the decision to forswear the Super, convinced that his unswerv-ing opposition had been the decisive factor. Fortified by the GAC's report, Lilienthal wanted to find a way to translate the scientists' opposition to the H-bomb into a broad statement of national policy. But he soon discovered that several members of the AEC board were critical of the report, with one caustically dismissing the policy of "renounce and announce." Teller and Lawrence, two "experienced promoters," as Oppie called them, had been busily rallying support among the air force generals to speed work on all the bombs the AEC labs could crank out, especially the Super. Ten days later, the members of the AEC, still sharply divided, submitted their disparate views to the president. Unable to reach consensus, they urged Truman to seek further advice. The president handed off the problem to a three-man committee composed of Dean Acheson, who had replaced the ailing Mar-shall as secretary of state, Secretary of Defense Louis Johnson, and AEC chairman David Lilienthal.

Over the course of the fall, the secret debate over the fate of the Super continued to rage in back rooms across Washington, with the weapon's avid supporters writing letters to the president and lobbying sympathetic sena-tors, arguing that the H-bomb was essential to the United States' margin of safety. As the historian Herbert F. York has pointed out, the argument was between "hawks" and "superhawks," for the simple reason no "full-fledged doves" were granted the necessary clearances. Prominent nuclear scientists from Los Alamos and Berkeley became missionaries for the project. MIT president Karl Compton wrote the president that in the absence of an international agreement, the work on the Super must proceed; that the Russians were equally capable of developing such a weapon, and the United States could not allow such an implacable enemy to pull ahead. Senator Brien McMahon, chairman of the Joint Committee on Atomic Energy, pressed his case by letter, and then in person, arguing that given Russia's vast armies, America had no alternative but to rely on strategic airpower, and with the Super, they could not miss. "If we let Russia get the Super first, catastrophe becomes all but certain," he warned. "Whereas if we get it first, there exists a chance of saving ourselves." Strauss sent a long letter supporting McMahon's analysis and conclusion that the United States should proceed "with all possible expedition to develop thermonuclear weapons."

Realizing that a decision on the Super had to be made before the secret debate hit the papers, Acheson invited Conant for lunch on January 8, 1950. He had all but made up his mind. The Joint Chiefs had signed a memorandum stating it would be "intolerable" to let the Russians get the weapon first, and, after reading their report, he saw no alternative to the H-Bomb development going forward. Louis Johnson was all for it. Out of respect for the eminent Harvard scientist, however, Acheson gave him one last hearing, but finally found him unpersuasive.

"After listening to Conant, it would be very easy to arrive at the opposite conclusion," he noted in his journal the following day, "except in arguing against the position I had come to, he admittedly could not suggest an alternative." From day one, the scientists had granted they would have to "start with the assumption that the Russians were working on it also." Acheson's lasting impression was not of the power of Conant's logic—"neither the maintenance of ignorance nor the reliance on perpetual good will seemed to me a tenable policy"—but what he later described in his recollection of the debate as the "immense distaste for what one of them, the purity of whose motive could not be doubted, described as 'the whole rotten business.'"

On January 31, at a regular meeting of the GAC, Lilienthal tipped the committee members to Truman's decision to authorize work on "all forms of atomic weapons, including the so-called hydrogen or superbomb." Conant and his colleagues had been resoundingly overruled. It was more than just a defeat on a policy issue, it was on *the* policy issue—the one with the gravest significance for the nation's future, and the fate of the world. In terms of the immediate fallout, Conant realized the GAC's influence had been downgraded and its members' individual standing as advisors impaired. Despite a presidential gag order instructing no one to talk about the polarizing H-bomb debate, Conant, the *New Yorker* reported in its Letter from Washington column on February 11, created considerable anxiety "when he called attention to the conflicts of opinion among the scientists and questioned the competence of lay officials to determine which opinions are sound and which are not."

No one outside their inner circle knew the full meaning of what had been decided, and Conant felt impotent—and something close to desperation—that the immensely important question of whether or not to embark on the H-bomb would never be put before the American people. In Washington's bipolar state, every assertion of a scientific or political nature had quickly bred a counterassertion, so that it was not really information, as the *New Yorker* observed, but "anti-information." Despondent, several of his GAC colleagues contemplated resigning. Acheson had been so worried that Conant might quit or lodge a public protest if things did not go his way that he had tried to counsel restraint over lunch, reportedly telling him, "For heck's sake, don't upset the apple cart." It showed how little he knew the man. Conant was too much the "good soldier" to resign, as he later told a friend, explaining that he and Oppenheimer still felt obliged to "do what we could to carry out orders of the president."

For weeks, Conant had been receiving disturbing reports about the aspersions being cast on the scientists blocking the Super, including rumors that some Pentagon officials thought they wielded too much influence. The entrenched us-and-them mentality that had characterized the US approach to relations with the Soviet Union for so long now extended to the bitter dispute between those who were for and against the H-bomb. The possibility of a detrimental debate in the press had hastened Truman's decision, but as time wore on, it was apparent the Super's supporters were not going to let the issue drop, their attitude attaining a kind of vindictive quality. "The majority's flat recommendation against *any* development of the H-bomb was what enraged the opposition," observed McGeorge Bundy.

Their animus was fueled in part by the public response, with a Gallup survey showing that Americans overwhelmingly favored attempting an H-bomb, and in part by the larger political climate. Just four days before

Truman's final decision, the German-born British physicist Klaus Fuchs confessed to being a Soviet spy, throwing the government—and the entire nuclear program—into a state of panic. Fuchs had been given top security clearance at Los Alamos, was an editor of the twenty-five-volume classified *The Los Alamos Primer*—a summary of all the research carried out—and had sat in on some of Teller's early H-bomb sessions. By the time British intelligence agents from MI5 confronted him in London, he was working at Harwell, the center of England's nuclear weapons research. The extent of the damage he had done was more than Conant, bilious at the thought, could begin to fathom.

Teller, who took Truman's decision as a personal triumph, parked himself in Washington with an eye to becoming the administration's new "No. 1" atomic expert. But like a dog with a bone, he could not let the disagreement over the Super go. One morning he argued so emotionally in favor of thermonuclear weapons that General Kenneth D. Nichols, the army's residing nuclear authority, finally asked him why he was still "worrying about the situation so much?" Teller responded with fierce conviction, "I'm worrying about the people who should be worrying about it."

Fear of the Russians had driven the arms race and now it drove an all-out attack on Communist spies in the government. The Soviet menace dominated the news, and the screaming headlines inflamed the public's imagination. Playing on popular anxieties, Senator Joseph McCarthy gave a speech on February 9, 1950, in Wheeling, West Virginia, claiming he had a list of some two hundred "Communists in government." Republican Red-baiters carried the attack to the Truman administration, pillorying Acheson for standing by Hiss after his January conviction, and calling for the secretary's head. In an effort to blame Acheson and the Democrats for the cold war reversals and loss of China to the Communists, after the defeat of the American-backed Nationalists in 1949, McCarthy declared Acheson a "bad security risk." He rose in the Senate to inquire if the secretary was going to defend other unidentified Communists in the government. Right-wing elements in Congress and the military exploited the frenzy to further the HUAC investigations of subversion among the scientists and to discredit the H-bomb opponents.

Conant was apprehensive that the house cleaning might include the GAC scientists who were now out of step with official presidential policy to develop the Super. He wrote Oppenheimer on February 14, warning him the H-bomb lobby was up to no good, and enclosed a copy of a letter a reporter had slipped him disclosing that a Republican senator on the Joint Committee on Atomic Energy (JCAE) was spreading the story that the GAC had voted negative on the H-bomb "on moral grounds." What neither man knew was that on February 6, in a secret JCAE hearing, the subject of Haakon Chevalier's wartime approach to Oppenheimer to pass secrets to the Soviets had come up in the course of a general discussion of security matters, and a thorough review of the thick Oppenheimer file had begun.

By then, McCarthy's noisy antics had so convulsed Capitol Hill that any reasoned debate or discussion was impossible. Conant, whose expertise and judgment were still required as the nuclear program ramped up, was finding it increasingly difficult to function as an advisor and express an independent opinion in such a frantic, topsy-turvy environment. "When I am in Washington, it seems as though I were in a lunatic asylum," he wrote Bernard Baruch. "However, I am trying to keep my sanity and will do what I can with the others."

In the spring of 1950, Conant received an unexpected—and—bitter blow. The head of the nominating committee of the National Academy of Sciences had contacted him and asked if he would be willing to replace the retiring Alfred Newton Richards as president of the prestigious organization. Conant had been approached three years earlier, but he had only just returned to Harvard then, and the timing was bad. He was delighted to be asked again. The idea of being anointed leader of national science policy and ascending to such an honored and influential seat had fresh appeal. But at what he had been led to believe would be a pro forma meeting on April 24 to approve his nomination, a California chemist suddenly took the floor and drafted Detlev W. Bronk as a candidate for president, and was quickly seconded by another chemist. The unprecedented move outraged Conant's friends, who registered their protest. After a heated debate, a vote was taken: the tally was 77 to 71 for Bronk. While everyone at the meeting waited, Bush phoned Conant at William Marbury's Baltimore home, where he was dining, and explained the situation. Caught off guard, and humiliated, Conant told Bush to withdraw his name.

"They ganged up on him," was how George Kistiakowsky put it years later, still angry that the double cross came without warning. "They were a small but secretly well organized group of little men who resented Jim's wartime leadership. The rest of us were unaware of what was being organized and thus were unable to demonstrate in good time the strong support which, in fact, would have been his." The "revolt" was staged by a handful of

West Coast chemists who had nursed a grudge since what they regarded as the NDRC chairman's "excessively authoritarian" reign and, in recent years, had grown jealous of his close ties to Oppenheimer.

Aware of the "sensitive personality" that lay beneath his friend's brisk, businesslike façade, Kistiakowsky was one of the few who knew how deeply wounded Conant was by the betrayal, recalling it as "the most painful incident of Jim's life as a science leader." Conant tried to put a good face on it, telling people he was "too busy to give the position the attention it deserved." He would go on to become chairman of the National Science Foundation and play an important role in developing policy and procedures in support of basic research, but the experience soured him on the scientific community, now so riven by internal battles that he no longer recognized it. The "old guard" was changing: the postwar divisions had been deepened by the acrimonious debate over the H-bomb, and a new, rising militarist faction was drowning out the voices of the dissenting atomic scientists.

On June 22, 1950, Conant presided over Harvard's commencement exercises, repeated his usual hopeful sentiments about society's transcendent values, and went home to pack for a much-anticipated trip to Scotland. The following morning, he woke up with a sharp, throbbing pain in his abdomen. Patty called the family physician, and the next thing he knew he was on the operating table and "in the hands of the surgeons." The fifty-seven-year-old Harvard president was suffering from acute diverticulitis, and doctors at Massachusetts General Hospital opened him up and removed six inches of his large intestine.

Three days later, North Korea's People's Army marched across the thirty-eighth parallel into South Korea. The Korean War was nearly a week old before Patty would allow her husband to see a newspaper, giving him her own cursory summation of the surprise Communist attack. Trying to make sense of what had happened, Conant could suppose only that the Soviets never expected North Korean aggression in such a faraway land to incite such a swift American response. Instead, the State Department had requested a special session of the UN Security Council, which unanimously condemned North Korea's action. The next day, June 27, the UN endorsed military aid to South Korea, and Truman ordered US forces to assist as part of what he termed a "police action" in order to avoid acknowledging that he had gone to war. On June 30, with the South Koreans in full retreat, Truman dispatched American ground troops.

To Conant, sitting in his hospital bed, it was as if "the whole international situation had altered" in the space of a few days. For the first time in history, the United States was defending terrain not vital to America's self-interest. He worried that Washington had made a much more irrevocable commitment than it realized, setting itself on a course that could bring the United States into direct confrontation with both China and Russia. Although he had never had a chance to form an opinion "unbiased by the fait accompli," Conant cautiously approved the president's action as the "right decision." He dispatched notes of support to Truman and Acheson, who earlier that week had sent telegrams expressing concern for his health. Patty shooed away all visitors, amazed by "the number of relative strangers who want to get in and sit by his bedside!" She blamed Truman's telegrams, writing her mother that they "so impressed the nurses that nothing is too good for Jim."

By mid-August, after a month convalescing at his summer cottage in Randolph, New Hampshire, Conant was desperate to "trade ideas" about the international situation with someone other than his wife. A neighbor, the prominent Boston judge R. Ammi Cutter, invited him to dinner with Tracy Voorhees—until recently the undersecretary of the army—who also had a summer home nearby. Voorhees filled him in on the alarming state of affairs, implying that Secretary of Defense Louis Johnson's budget cuts had stripped the American armed forces, leaving them woefully underequipped and understaffed and completely unprepared for war. Conant worried it was no exaggeration: the manpower shortage was a subject he had spoken out about again and again. He also knew that in this struggle, the United States' nuclear arsenal was "irrelevant." While it was "too secret" to discuss with Cutter and Voorhees, he thought "no sane man would advocate the use of the bomb now that the Russians had one of their own."

As the invalid headed back to bed at the end of the evening, he called over his shoulder to Voorhees to start organizing a "citizen's lobby" along the lines of those they had all joined in 1940. "From what I have just heard, the country is asleep," he told them. "You should wake it up."

A month later, the military situation had progressively deteriorated—along with Conant's health, the onset of peritonitis requiring a second surgery. By the end of September, the UN army was hanging on to only a small bit of the Korean peninsula. The conflict in Asia terrified European leaders, who viewed the Communist invasion as a direct challenge to the United States, and worried it was the beginning of world anarchy. What was to stop the Soviets from taking advantage of the diversion and moving against the West in Europe? Conant believed the strengthening of ground forces in Europe was imperative to preserve the "global stalemate" and avoid a third world war.

Unable to travel, he wrote letters and worked the phones, contacting as many people as he could to galvanize support for greatly expanding the existing Selective Service System to funnel men into the armed forces. In early October he helped found the Committee on the Present Danger (CPD), joined by Vannevar Bush and ten other prominent East Coast educators and former government officials, aimed at ratcheting up military spending, organizing emergency mobilization for war, and beating back the isolationist propaganda of Herbert Hoover and Republican senator Robert Taft. They sent their proposal to General Marshall, who Truman had pulled out of retirement and made secretary of defense after firing Louis Johnson. Marshall promptly responded by letter, acknowledging their initiative as "an undertaking of great importance," and suggested a meeting.

Three days after Thanksgiving, the Chinese launched a full-scale assault in Korea, forcing the US Eighth Army to retreat in chaos. The prospect of defeat in Korea motivated Conant to write a seven-page memorandum, published the following month as an article in *Look* magazine, warning of "the extreme peril the free world faces," and demanding the immediate conscription of three and a half million men. Raising such a large army would require mandatory military service for two years for all eighteen-year-old men, with absolutely no deferments or exemptions, and large tax increases to pay for it. He submitted a plan for compulsory military service to Marshall, aware that the only thing less popular at the time with Congress was continuing aid via the Marshall Plan. He recognized that the sacrifice required to support such a huge increase in military spending could test the limits of public support. "The price is high, but it must be paid," he argued— it was "the only chance of averting a war of world dimensions." Eisenhower, the new supreme commander of the North Atlantic Treaty Organization (NATO) forces, needed all the help he could get, and he sent Conant a note of encouragement: "Your memorandum rings the bell with me!"

The Committee on the Present Danger made its public debut at a press conference at the Willard Hotel in Washington on December 12. A grim-faced Conant fielded questions from reporters, maintaining with measured toughness that despite the United States' efforts at peace, the Soviets were intent upon precipitating World War III. "The bitter fact," he stated, "is that our country has again been thrust into a struggle in which our free existence is at stake; a struggle for survival. We have no time to lose."

Scanning the next morning's favorable headlines, Conant thought their timing was just right and the launch was "a success." But the isolationist critics had heard the draft song once too often from the familiar peddlers of crisis: "same old salesmen," they complained, convinced the Truman administration was throwing good money after bad in Europe.

On February 7, 1951, following Eisenhower's speech to the joint session of Congress on his return from a fact-finding mission to Europe, Conant gave a nationwide radio address calling for all-out mobilization just short of war to counter the Soviet threat. He opened with the dramatic declaration "Fellow citizens, the United States is in danger." He hammered away at the Soviet Union and its insatiable appetite for expansion, citing the fact that its military power was mounting, both in terms of the bomb and most types of modern weaponry, and that its allies were ready to gain their ends by force.

The "preservation of a free America," as Eisenhower had put it, required that the United States defend Western Europe and furnish it with arms, military equipment, and men on the ground. Employing the martial rhetoric he had refined during the interventionist campaign a decade earlier, Conant tried to prepare the American public for "a new period—a highly disturbing and dangerous period," one that would involve standing by Europe the next twenty to thirty years and would require a vast program of rearmament and mobilization. Consciously wrapping himself in "Eisenhower's mantle," as he put it, Conant echoed the general's statement that these measures were necessary in order to "build a secure wall for peace," hoping to create an atmosphere of intensity that would help win support for their expanded system of conscription and increased foreign aid.

With the outbreak of hostilities in Korea, Conant became, as the historian Richard Norton Smith put it, "the coldest of cold warriors." He fell in line with the Truman administration's view that only a major military buildup could ensure the future security of the United States, a policy expressed in *National Security Council Report 68 (NSC-68)*, a secret document largely prepared by Paul Nitze, a wealthy forty-three-year-old Harvard-educated Wall Street banker who was George Kennan's successor as the State Department's director of policy planning. Nitze was convinced that the "Kremlin's design for world domination" depended on "the ultimate elimination of any effective opposition," and that it would work inexorably to achieve "sufficient atomic capability to make a surprise attack on us." Acheson and Nitze, and Truman's military advisors, were sophisticated and knowledgeable and were not drawn into what the historian Robert Dallek calls McCarthy's "uncritical militancy"—a rabid, impulsive anti-Communist response. "But they were held in thrall by the experience of World War II and the failed appeasement policies that gave the Nazis and Japanese license to run wild in Europe and Asia—at least until they encountered a superior force."

Conant was more moderate than Truman's military chiefs, but he was "deeply troubled by the unwillingness of American people to recognize the inherent threat in the international situation" and did not hesitate to remind them of the imminent danger to sell the public on the defense plan he thought the country needed to avoid "global war." He was a persistent and energetic propagandist for the defense of Europe, cajoling an ever-longer list of East Coast luminaries to join his cause, including Oppenheimer, former OSS chief William Donovan, speechwriter Robert Sherwood, *New York Times* vice president Julius Ochs Adler, and CBS broadcaster Edward R. Murrow. He went on the air with Murrow to push universal military service and to criticize Truman's executive order of March 31, 1951, allowing deferments for college students, which Conant charged was "undemocratic." He convinced other renowned nuclear scientists to make radio broadcasts about how the bomb was no longer a sufficient deterrent to the Soviet threat. On April 4 the Senate finally voted its approval of deploying troops to defend Europe, committing four divisions (a total of a hundred thousand men) to the Continent. The draft that Congress passed was nowhere near as universal as Conant had originally proposed, and it included many exemptions, but he always regarded the CPD's role in arousing the country to the cold war crisis among his most "cherished" victories.

By October, armistice talks were under way in Korea. The war had not spread to China, and the "present danger" was much less obvious than it had been when Conant founded the committee. He thought there was "a good chance" of avoiding World War III as long as Europe remained strong; only with a large offensive force as a deterrent to a Soviet advance could the global stalemate hold. "What we had to guard against," he brooded, his gloomy outlook on the future convincing him of the need for continued vigilance against Communist aggression, "was a lapse of public opinion into the mood of complacency which had been present before the Korean War began."

When his five-year term with the GAC ended that summer, Conant retired from government service, ending his long run as one of the nation's most influential science advisors. With Oppenheimer, another charter member, also leaving the committee at the same time, it was the end of an era. Meanwhile, the government's crash program to build a thermonuclear weapon was nearing completion. Los Alamos was finalizing its preparations for the first full-scale test of a hydrogen bomb, based on a design by Teller and Stanislaw Ulam, on November 1. Conant wanted no part of building an arsenal of H-bombs. He was relieved to be through with nuclear politics, noting in his diary: "10½ years of almost constant official conversations with a bad business now threatening to become really bad!!!"

On November 4, 1952, Eisenhower, standing as a Republican, was elected president, with Nixon as his running mate. In one of the biggest landslides since FDR's reelection in 1936, they swept into office. Conant and his CPD colleagues had actively supported Eisenhower over his Democratic opponent, and many were being rewarded with positions in the new administration. On Sunday evening, December 21, he took the night train from Cambridge to New York for a meeting with the president-elect but was unable to sleep. "My mind was focused on one fact: I had been offered the post of the United States high commissioner for Germany and had practically accepted."

Actually, Conant, three months shy of sixty, was not quite sure where things stood. He had turned down the job when Acheson had first sounded him out about it a year earlier. John J. McCloy, the current high commissioner, had been anxious to retire and had recommended the Harvard president as his replacement. Although Conant had admitted to being ready to leave Harvard, he had hemmed and hawed to such a degree before finally declining that he doubted he would "ever hear of the matter again." He had regretted his decision almost immediately and, after discussing it with Patty, made up his mind that "if by any chance the opportunity again arose, I should seize it." Shortly after Eisenhower's election, he read that the high commissioner's job was open again, but it seemed unlikely that the incoming secretary of state, John Foster Dulles, would renew the offer. According to the newspaper speculation, anyone in any way connected to Acheson was seen as suspect. Still, as Conant prepared for the next morning's meeting, he could not help wondering whether he would be asked to serve. "I could not entirely banish from my thoughts the bare possibility that fate might give me a second chance."

On Monday Conant had lunch with Eisenhower at the Commodore Hotel and spent two hours briefing him on the Committee on the Present Danger's latest proposals for increased military and economic aid to the Allies. Just as they were finishing their meal, Eisenhower turned to Dulles, a tall, severe-looking man, and prompted, "Foster, don't you want to talk to Jim about Germany?" After they excused themselves and went into an adjacent room, Dulles offered him the high commissioner's post. It would be a term of at least four years, he said, adding, "You won't be much good to us for a year until you have shaken down in the job."

In his typically forthright fashion, Conant brought up his political liabilities, including his recent controversial stand against state funding for parochial schools—his argument that they were divisive of the social fabric had antagonized Catholics—which might affect his confirmation by the Senate. He also felt obliged to mention that while he favored the demilitarization and denazification of Germany, he had "grave doubts" about the administration's plans to rearm the country. Impatient, Dulles brushed aside his reservations. "Well, we don't have to agree on everything," was his gruff response.

As Conant boarded the five o'clock train for Cambridge, he was elated. "The Day! Oh Boy!" he scribbled in his diary that night. "Where will I be 4 years from now? Heaven knows, but at least not in *this* job." He was done with Harvard. He could hardly believe it.

The next day, Dulles telephoned to seal his appointment. "You are hooked," he said. "There is nothing in the objections you raised."

Moments later, McCloy called to urge him to accept and impress upon him the importance of the job at this critical juncture. In a divided Europe, Germany—still under Allied and Soviet occupation—was on the front lines of the ideological struggle, and the key to whether there would be war or peace in the world. When the Federal Republic of Germany was founded in 1949, the hope was that this would be the beginning of a new era of reconciliation and reconstruction, reintegrating the war-torn country into the democratic European community, and that this new Germany would dedicate itself to the defense of the West. Its purpose was to become a strong partner in the cold war NATO alliance, the breastplate against Communist aggression. If continental unification could be achieved, the president wrote, "all lesser" problems facing Europe "would disappear."

Now Eisenhower was calling on Conant to complete the transition from military to civilian control and to conclude the recognition of the Federal Republic of Germany, or West Germany, as a sovereign state—as well as its rearmament as part of the European Defense Community (EDC), which was a cornerstone of the administration's European policy. The treaties had been signed in May 1952 but not yet ratified and were "hanging fire." As the Berlin crisis had showed, a misstep could provoke the Russians and ignite another East-West showdown. The sooner he got to Bonn, McCloy told him, the better. Dulles was doing what he could to "rush through" Conant's appointment, and he would be on the first plane after being cleared by the Senate.

He and Patty began making plans for their new life. It was not the Cabinet post that her ambitious young suitor had promised during their courting days, but as good as. She was giddy with excitement and immediately began brushing up on her rusty German, which, she reminded him, had always been much better than his. On Christmas Eve a warm note arrived from "Ike" expressing his gratitude at Conant's "readiness to help. I scarcely need tell you," Eisenhower added, "what a great satisfaction it is to know that you will be on the team." He agreed to "keep the matter completely under cover" until Conant had a chance to inform the governors of the university. Three days later, another letter came from Eisenhower: "How delighted I am with the prospect of having you with us," he wrote. "I find myself almost bursting with the desire to tell my friends about our good fortune in this regard."

Conant spent the weekend writing notes to old friends he wanted to tell personally and present some justifications for his decision, ahead of the White House announcement. Twenty years in the Harvard trenches, he wrote George Kistiakowsky, was "long enough to serve a sentence for youthful indiscretion."

In the hectic days that followed, McCloy called several times to say that speed was of the essence. Conant did not have to be persuaded. He was in a hurry to go. He hated "lengthy farewells," and his innate horror of fuss made him want to get the mawkish scenes behind him as fast as possible. It had not been a hard decision. As he told his old friend Bill Marbury when he tendered his resignation, he was "tired of exercising the same muscles." After two decades at the helm of Harvard, Conant was tired of passing the collection bucket around the Brahmin elite, tired of complaints about his controversial political stands, tired of the bureaucratic battles. Just the previous spring, two major rows tried his patience, the first over his opposition to state funding for parochial schools, and the second over his reorganization of the slumping football program and "firing without warning" the director of athletics—both of which earned him more brickbats than plaudits.

Even his critics had to concede that despite his playing "hooky" to a great degree during the war years, Conant had been an inventive, modernizing president, ushering in the era of "Big Science" and introducing a series of significant improvements and additions that had transformed Harvard from a provincial school to a leading national university. His National Scholarship program opened the college to needy students from all parts of the country, setting a precedent that other leading American universities would soon follow, while his tenure reform and system of ad hoc committees to oversee permanent appointments—so resented at the time—kept the faculty robust and guaranteed that talent would continue to converge there. His relentless focus on merit broadened the student body and weakened the quota system designed to limit the admission of Jewish and African American students. In establishing the Nieman Fellowship, he sought to elevate the standards of journalism by bringing reporters to Harvard to pursue further studies. Conant created the Littauer School of Public Administration to enable government officials to study policy, and transformed the Harvard School of Education into one of the major training centers for public school administrators. The Harvard report *General Education in Free Society*, published in 1945, became the blueprint for college curricula and, along with the required "general education" courses, influenced the next two generations of students and professors. Under his stewardship, Harvard's endowment grew from $138 million to $290 million—few presidents could hope to leave a richer legacy.

That fall, *Newsweek* had put him on the cover as the undisputed leader of American education, but noted of his controversial tenure, "being a seer is no guarantee of wholesale approval." For his part, Conant felt he had given Harvard his all and was ready for a fresh challenge.

On New Year's Day Conant broke the news to the Harvard Corporation. His announcement, he recorded in his diary, was greeted with "thunderous silence." Informing the Overseers two weeks later proved anticlimactic. A heavy New England snowstorm cut down on attendance, and a morning radio broadcast carried the story. He explained that the Corporation had made him president emeritus from September 1, 1953—he would be sixty, the age at which the by-laws allowed him to retire—and granted him a leave of absence until that date. "I shall be leaving Harvard permanently," he concluded, metaphorically shutting the door behind him.

His sudden departure shocked observers of the national scene from Cambridge to Washington. "Even in a period of surprises, the resignation of President James Bryant Conant and his acceptance of the highest American diplomatic post at Bonn will startle many," opined the *Boston Daily Globe*. "Conant has been, during the last 20 years, so bright a star in the galaxy of American educators, particularly in the realms of science, that it is difficult to think of him as a moveable body."

It was not, however, a complete surprise on Harvard's campus. His tête-à-tête with Eisenhower in New York just before Christmas had not gone unnoticed, and rumors abounded. The Harvard community had its own insular view of Conant's latest globetrotting enterprise, which it did not necessarily perceive as graduating to greater glory. "It seemed ten steps down," commented McGeorge Bundy, whose name was already being mentioned as a possible successor, "for the president of Harvard to merely run Germany."

The editorials on his appointment, from the *New York Times* to the *Tribune*, applauded him for putting his country's problems before Harvard's, and praised a life dedicated to defending democracy and the principles of freedom. For once, the *Crimson* was not critical: "Conant reached greatness," wrote the editors. "His courage, his calm and modest determination, and his sense of high purpose have infected all those whom he has touched. Now these same qualities have called him to a new task, and certainly it too is a crucial one. We cannot pass judgment on his choice, nor can we doubt its wisdom. But we cannot deny a sense of personal loss, because we are students in America and because we are Harvard students."

Hundreds of letters and telegrams came from prominent alumni, fellow educators, and public figures across the country paying tribute to his achievements, mourning the passing of an era, and hailing Eisenhower's new envoy as the man of the hour. A few bemoaned his leaving while Joe McCarthy's congressional investigations still hung like a dark cloud over Harvard, and begged him to stay and continue to fight. "You alone could give altitude to the opposition and courage to the quavering academes," wrote Agnes E. Meyer, an influential journalist and education activist who was married to *Washington Post* publisher Eugene Meyer.

But his wartime colleagues understood the urge to buckle on new armor and slay new dragons. "The next time I see you, I will click heels and salute!" cheered Bush in an ironic reference to the Fascist forces that would need to be eradicated once and for all if democracy were to flourish in Germany. Oppenheimer, too, recognized the lure of such a momentous challenge, exclaiming to a colleague, "Typical of the physical scientist! To give up something very difficult so as to try the impossible!"

Conant said much the same thing when he attempted to explain his abrupt exit to Percy Bridgman, the laboratory partner with whom he had just missed inventing synthetic rubber all those years ago. "I would like to be frank with an old friend," he wrote, "and to say that one of the primary reasons for my undertaking the difficult assignment is the feeling that I wanted to try my hand at one more tough task before I die."

CHAPTER 21

Man of the Hour

At a time when the whole European treaty system and the prog-
ress toward European unification hang in the balance, there is
urgent need of a man of impressive stature in that strategic post.
President Conant is just the man to fill the need.
                    —*New York Times* editorial, January 13, 1953

For Conant, the diplomatic assignment felt like coming full circle. "Germany has been a thread running all through my life," he told a reporter as they toured the bombed-out ruins of Berlin, the former capital of Germany, now divided and under four-power control, and located 110 miles within what used to be the Soviet zone of occupation and was now the German Democratic Republic (GDR). When the Federal Republic was formed in 1949, Bonn became the de facto headquarters of the West German government, but Berlin remained the de jure capital and all-important symbol of resistance. Conant liked to make a show of driving through the Eastern sector in the high commissioner's shiny black Cadillac sedan, with the American and High Commission flags flying from its front fenders, as a way of letting Berliners—and the Russians—know he was there.

After playing a leading role in the devastating military defeat of Germany, he had returned as its defender, not conqueror. This new partitioned nation now stood at the very heart of the cold war conflict. Conant's task was to restore order in the hotly contested region and protect it from the Russians, who had registered their displeasure at the proposed European Defense Community (EDC) by sealing off the East German border and imposing on the Western sector of Berlin what was known as the "little blockade," to distinguish it from the big blockade that precipitated the Berlin crisis of 1948. Frightened of being forever trapped in the Communist bloc, East Germans were finding subterranean routes through the Russian barriers and converging on West Berlin at the rate of three thousand a day. On top of the scores of refugees, the prospect of rearmament was the cause of enormous uncertainty, as was the fate of Berlin itself, to be determined by separate negotiations between the East and the West. After having spoken out so much about a strong Europe being the key to the defense of the free world, Conant could not help feeling there was a certain "symmetry" to his coming back to bring the emerging Federal Republic solidly into the Western democratic alliance and NATO.

He had been thrown right into the thick of things. Between the day that Eisenhower named him high commissioner for Germany and his arrival in Bonn on February 11, through his CIA briefing and hostile grilling before the Senate Foreign Relations Committee, it was exactly a month. He had expected McCarthy to give him trouble—the usual charges about Harvard being "soft on Communism"—but the Wisconsin senator had remained strangely silent. Instead, most of the questions had come from Republican senators who zeroed in on his infamous claim in the *Atlantic* that he favored the "complete redistribution of property every generation." They demanded to know if Conant's refusal to investigate radicals on Harvard's faculty meant their German counterparts would be able to "pull the wool over his eyes."

What swung the two-day confirmation hearing in his favor was that Eisenhower, who had courted McCarthy just enough to win his endorsement for the presidency, exerted pressure on the junior senator from Wisconsin not to hold up the appointment. McCarthy, who by his own admission was gearing up for an "all-out fight," had researchers digging into every phase of Conant's career, even asking a sharp young Yale author named William F. Buckley Jr. to prepare a speech that would help scuttle his nomination. After Ike dispatched Nixon to drive home his message, McCarthy backed down, writing Eisenhower that even though he was "much opposed to Conant," he would not carry it to the Senate floor because he did not "want to make a row." Massachusetts senator Leverett Saltonstall, his college classmate, also came to Conant's aid and helped to push through his confirmation as the last order of business on Friday, February 6.

He was sworn in the very next day, wearing in the lapel of his best dark suit the rosette representing the Medal for Merit awarded to him for his wartime contributions. It was all done with a minimum of formality, Saturday morning not being the usual time for such a ceremony. Seventy-two hours later, "loaded down with information," he left for Germany on a plane from New York. It all happened so quickly that Patty was not finished with her packing and household arrangements and had to follow on a later flight. When the celebrated American scientist-turned-diplomat picked up his wife at the Frankfurt airport on February 12, his welcoming embrace—"Der Kuss!"—was captured by dozens of photographers and made the front page of newspapers around the world. The press was friendly, their questions bland. Conant was amused by "such rapid changes in fortune." He was now a diplomat and "no longer a controversial figure."

Returning to Germany after an absence of twenty-three years, Conant had no idea what to expect. He was not sure what the lingering effects of Hitler's regime might be, or, as he put it to a journalist, "how many Nazis might still be hiding under the bushes." He no longer thought of the Germany of old but of "Germany as a bulwark" against any Soviet plans to expand its Communist regime.

As high commissioner, he was in effect military governor of West Germany, inheriting the mantle passed down by Eisenhower himself, who had taken charge when it was a shattered country on the brink of mass starvation. After Ike, with short intervals when the post was held by deputies, came the formidable General Lucius D. Clay, and then the banker John J. McCloy, who used his almost dictatorial powers to promote democracy and lay the groundwork for the booming economic revival of West Germany by dispensing almost $3 billion worth of Marshall Plan funds. At the same time, Conant was also chief of the US Mission in West Berlin.

There were now two Germanys, with two capitals, two currencies, and two ideologies, and the escalating tensions with the Russians had all but doomed West German Chancellor Konrad Adenauer's hopes for reunification. While Conant privately accepted the logic of a divided Germany, Secretary of State Dulles had warned that the fall of the pro-American Adenauer government would be "disastrous," so the new high commissioner was pledged to plug the revered seventy-seven-year-old leader's campaign for unity and do all he could to make sure he won reelection.

The situation was confusing from the outset, and Conant's first challenge was to complete the job the State Department thought it had already accomplished: get the West Germans and the French—who could not quite bring themselves to believe in the rapprochement—to put aside their ancient feuds and ratify the European Defense Community (EDC) treaty, which would create a continental army of two million men. As soon as the pact was signed, it would abolish the High Commission, restore normal diplomatic relations between the United States and Germany, and lead to the exchange of ambassadors. Conant was convinced that the sooner he could end the occupation and establish West Germany as a sovereign nation, with its own army, the better it would be able to defend against the peril on its own doorstep. For the United States, advancing West Germany's postwar path "from pariah to partner" was pragmatic national self-interest: a peaceful, prosperous Germany, integrated in Europe and aligned with America, preserved German industry and resources for the West and ensured order.

The problem was that although all parties proclaimed their desire for an independent West Germany, it quickly became apparent that each nation had its own agenda, and one sticking point followed another. The Soviets, still suffering the effects of years of ferocious struggle against the Wehrmacht, did not want to see their old foe rearmed and had responded to the proposal for a European force—and inclusion of West German units—with dire threats. In recent months, they had begun making good on those threats, blocking the boundary between East and West Germany by slapping up barbed wire, a death strip, watchtowers, and sentries. The terror increased as some of the first attempts to cross the border were met not by arrests but by shooting. As panic set in, fugitives from East Germany began pouring into Berlin, where there were no border controls restricting movement between the sectors, making it the last escape route. What had started as a trickle of people seeking asylum was expected to swell to a hundred thousand a month by spring, and would soon overwhelm the refugee center. Faced with the possibility the influx might reach "staggering numbers," straining West German resources beyond their limits, the nervous new high commissioner reported to Dulles that the "danger of epidemics," as well as "riots and disturbances inspired either by general discontent or Communists" could not be discounted.

The future of Germany was one of Eisenhower's most important foreign policy challenges, and Berlin, as the flash point for US-Soviet tensions, was the political and diplomatic battlefield. Conant had been instructed to make it immediately clear that the United States would stay in Berlin, come what may, and continue to protect and feed its 2.25 million citizens and burgeoning refugee population. Within a week of his arrival, he boarded the high commissioner's private three-car train—once the plush quarters of Nazi leader Hermann Göring—and traveled through the bleak, snow-covered

Soviet zone to the "outpost of freedom." West Berlin's mayor, Ernst Reuter, met him on the platform and drove him around the still-demolished city.

Berlin presented a "fantastic, grim picture," mile after mile of hollow, blackened shells of buildings and barren land—a far cry from the vibrant, elegant metropolis Conant remembered. Hundreds of thousands of homes had been flattened and factories burnt to the ground. There were food shortages, and the black market flourished. They were looking at an enormous reconstruction job. In his first radio broadcast on February 18, he promised to continue to facilitate Berlin's recovery and keep funneling the dollars needed to rebuild its decimated industry and create jobs, predicting that as the strength of the West increased, Communism would retreat, and "the frontiers of freedom would peacefully expand." The exodus of skilled workers from the Communist regime—those refugees who were "voting with their feet"—was already imperiling East Germany's economy, and he feared that Moscow's policy of diverting funds to military efforts might further impoverish the area and mean "a slow death for millions of Germans."

At his first staff meeting at the American Mission in Berlin, Conant was confronted with two pressing questions: "When will the Russians seal off their sector completely?" and "What will we do then?" They were afraid they would soon be boxed in. The new high commissioner assured them that he would not falter in his determination to protect US claims to free access, but he had no real answers. "I found a stark sense of reality shaping my thoughts as I listened to the speculation about the future course of events," he recalled, full of foreboding as he contemplated the inevitable cycle of escalating Soviet threats and US counterthreats and where it all might lead.

In his first months on the job, Conant got a crash course in diplomacy. To his dismay, he discovered that many of the headaches of the High Commission were not dissimilar to the administration problems he had dealt with at Harvard, and had to do with balancing the complicated, and often competing, interests of the military, the Foreign Service, and the intelligence bureaucracies. He was responsible for running RIAS, the American radio station in Berlin, which was seen as a highly effective propaganda infiltration into the Soviet zone, and also facilitated the collection of intelligence data and recruitment of sources and agents. The CIA, which had a large station in Berlin, had made it abundantly clear it expected to be given a wide berth for its anti-Soviet propaganda efforts and covert operations behind the Iron Curtain. (One of the most ambitious, Operation Gold, was masterminded by Dulles's brother, CIA head Allen Dulles, who ordered a phone-tapping tunnel dug between West and East Berlin in 1954 and operated it for about a year before the Soviets unearthed it and held a press conference exposing the American skullduggery.)

Conant, who stuck to the "need to know" rule he had operated under during the war, advised CIA officials that he wanted to learn the minimum about their espionage activities. He was skeptical about psychological warfare, especially what the State Department termed "psychological offensives" aimed at rolling back Communism rather than merely containing it. Dulles was convinced that if the United States kept the "pressure on, psychological and otherwise," it could "force a collapse of the Kremlin regime or else transform the Soviet orbit from a union of satellites dedicated to aggression, into a coalition for defense only." This was especially true for East Germany, where the Eisenhower administration was operating a food relief program designed to win over the population and aggravate antagonism toward the Soviets. On more than one occasion, Conant quashed dodgy CIA schemes—including a plan to drop food packages in the Eastern zone by way of balloons—that he considered reckless and that might end in bloodshed. The objective of American policy with regard to the Soviet zone, he wrote Dulles, at least as he understood it, was "to keep the pot simmering but not bring it to a boil." Political and economic cooperation served containment and was the slow but steady way to win the cold war.

What he had not expected, however, was that even in Germany his "chief anxieties were to be the consequences of working for the federal government in the McCarthy era." Conant had long regarded McCarthy as a ruthless demagogue who, like Hitler, used the "big lie" technique to impose his will. While at Harvard, he had the luxury of condemning McCarthy and his followers from a safe distance, but now that he was a high government official—and on a target list that already included Acheson, Marshall, and other former Cabinet officials—Conant found it more difficult to maintain his "calm aloofness."

He had been horrified when McCarthy accused Marshall of being a Communist appeaser when he became secretary of defense, and the president-elect had said nothing to defend his wartime commander. Once Eisenhower took office, he continued to placate the powerful senator, giving him too much of a "free hand" with the State Department, and appointing his enforcer, R. W. Scott McLeod, as head of security. When McCarthy set his sights on the US Information Service (USIS), it was clear to Conant that there was going to be trouble. Dulles, eager to score points with McCarthy, and a virulent anti-Communist in his own right, immediately dismissed a number of career Foreign Service officers. Conant had hardly had a chance to get settled in Bonn when a State Department order crossed his desk requesting the resignation of a staff aide, Charles Thayer, whom McCarthy had deemed a "security risk."

Conant was dismayed at the extent to which the campaign of vilification was affecting their conduct of foreign policy. "Something approaching a state of war existed between the McCarthy forces and the majority of the staff of the Washington office of the State Department," he recalled. "There was spying and counterspying going on." When he tried to probe who within the agency was working with or for the senator, he discovered "that there were not only wheels within wheels, as is usual in a complex government organization, but that some of the wheels were spinning counterclockwise."

One way or another, McCarthy continued to make Conant's life difficult. In March ominous cables from Washington reported that subversive books had been found in the USIS libraries in Europe, known as America Houses, and that the censored volumes would have to be removed—*deshelved* was the odious official term—in accordance with department policy. A team of inspectors—two McCarthy henchmen, Roy Cohn and G. David Schine—descended on Bonn, interrogated members of the embassy staff, and held an embarrassing press conference in which they made all sorts of unfounded charges. The resulting media flap did not reflect well on the new high commissioner, who missed the excitement, as he was escorting Adenauer on his first official trip to Washington to plead for $250 million for refugee relief. "If there was one subject on which the former president of Harvard should have had his mind made up, books should have been it," scolded the *Saturday Evening Post*, calling the book-removal rumpus regrettable and Conant an "amateur diplomat."

Conant had received a message warning of the impending raid as he was boarding the plane but chose not to stay and defend his patch. It was an embarrassing blunder, and another blow to staff morale, already at an all-time low because of the uncertainty caused by the security crackdown and the impending cutbacks when the occupation came to an end. Conant summed up his rocky start in his private journal on May 31, 1953: "Well, the HICOG [high commissioner of Germany] part of the job has turned out so far to be the most difficult and least pleasant. Having inherited a large organization in process of contraction without a real head for nearly a year, the personnel problem would have been bad in any case. With the 'goings on' in Washington, a bad situation has become so bad as to be almost funny were it not so tragic for some people."

His failure to quarrel openly with Washington regarding the dismissal of a handful of veteran diplomats led the American reporters based in Bonn to conclude that the new Dulles-Eisenhower appointee was "too cautious and cagey." Conant was bothered by the poor reviews but felt powerless to reverse them. Always too rigid in his interpretation of the rules, he felt he was no longer a private citizen who was free to speak his mind or get on his moral high horse when he felt like it. He was the president's personal emissary, there to dutifully carry out the policy handed down from above. Dulles had impressed on him that in his new post he would be expected "to play ball with the administration in every way." Conant was beginning to wish he had heeded his old friend A. A. Berle's warning that if he took the job as high commissioner, he would be little more than a "glorified messenger."

There was little glory in his appearance before the Senate Appropriations Committee in June 1953, where he turned in an uncharacteristically timid performance. Unaware that the previous day Eisenhower had spoken out against the book purges in a speech at Dartmouth College, Conant allowed himself to be cornered and browbeaten by McCarthy into a mumbled quasi-acceptance of the "deshelving" policy, and engaged in an unedifying exchange in which he appeared to clear the senator of the charge of being a "book burner." It was only after they broke for lunch and he learned of Eisenhower's critique of the censorship campaign—a direct shot at McCarthy—that Conant understood that the senator had been out for revenge. Aware that the congressional investigations of subversion were filling the front pages, Conant, as a new envoy to Germany, had spent the morning trying to keep his answers as bland and uncontroversial as possible. As a result, he had unwittingly allowed McCarthy to win the first round.

By the afternoon session, assured that a robust rebuttal would not be frowned on by the White House, Conant stood his ground and repeatedly defended his information officers against charges they were Communist sympathizers. Infuriated by his witness's firmer tone, a bullying, blustering McCarthy finally resorted to insults, calling him a "kindly old professor who isn't doing his job very well as high commissioner." Conant did not respond to the taunts except to give a small, tight smile. By drawing McCarthy's fire and shielding his employees, he managed to salvage his performance and put himself back in the press's "good graces." Writing in the *New York Herald Tribune* that August, Stewart Alsop (who shared the column with his younger brother Joseph Alsop) gave the high commissioner credit for trying to do his bit to end the "reign of stupidity," noting that "after a natural initial period of uncertainty, Conant has let it be known that he is prepared to back loyal subordinates to the hilt."

On June 11 he presided over his final Harvard commencement and met the university's very earnest, very Episcopalian new president, Nathan Pusey, who appeared promising enough "but with different ideas." As Conant headed for the airport after giving the alumni address, it hit him that this was really the end of his life in Cambridge. He would not return to haunt the campus in his dotage like Lowell.

By the time he got back to Germany, the tensions that had been building all winter had erupted in East Berlin. On June 17, 1953, more than sixty thousand German workers rose up against their Soviet oppressors, venting their anger in a violent demonstration. The Russians moved quickly to suppress the rebellion before it turned into a revolutionary movement. Soviet troops, supported by tanks, crashed through the lines and fired on the workers, who were armed only with stones and cudgels. More than 125 men and women were killed in the course of riots in different cities and towns across the GDR—19 in East Berlin alone—and thousands were arrested.

When Conant finally reached Berlin, four days later, an uneasy quiet had settled on the still smoldering streets, and part of the city was under martial law. Allied officials had said nothing about the brutal Soviet assault, while Washington vetoed anything but "sympathy and asylum." Strikes and unrest pervaded the spring, and Berliners looked to the high commissioner to do something as the representative of *the* occupying power, but his hands were tied: action could be taken only jointly by the three Allied high commissioners.

With no coherent policy, he found the job of maintaining American credibility, and West German confidence, maddening, to say the least. Washington's restrained response pointed not only to the Eisenhower administration's unwillingness to provoke a military confrontation with the Soviet Union but also to the profound disagreements between the three occupying forces in the West. Joseph Stalin's death on March 5, 1953, had done nothing to mitigate what a recent National Security Council report called the "irreconcilable hostility" between the Eastern bloc and the non-Communist world. Although Conant continued to push for the lowering of border barriers, the uprising had deepened the schism between East and West, and he was pessimistic about making any headway with the new leadership in the Kremlin.

In the September 1953 German election, Adenauer, who, as Conant put it, "had virtually run on an American ticket," won a decisive victory at the polls, with a mandate to carry on his policy of "Westintegration" another four years. The green-and-white flag of "European unity" was unfurled beside the banner of West Germany on Schaumburg Palace, the chancellor's official residence in Bonn. The Communists and right-wing neo-Nazi splinter groups hardly made a showing at the polls and were thoroughly discredited. Adenauer's surprising success marked a turning point in Germany's political future: according to a Department of State analysis, "no single party has ever before won a majority of the seats in the German lower house in a free election, and even Hitler," in 1933, "received only 43.9 percent of the popular vote." Dulles excitedly told Conant that the chancellor's "personal influence" was now "enhanced to a point where it will be difficult— and perhaps undesirable—to deal with the German problem except on the basis of treating him as a full partner." They hoped Adenauer's landslide, which Eisenhower told French premier Joseph Laniel marked the "triumph of democracy and common sense," would finally push the French into line on the EDC.

In January 1954 Conant helped organize the Berlin Conference, the first four-power meeting since the outbreak of the Korean War, to consider a solution to the "German problem." Its unstated purpose was to find a way of convincing the French that rearming of the Germans was a necessity and the treaty establishing a European army must be ratified. French approval hinged on the outcome of an extremely fraught domestic political debate, and it seemed doubtful, given the widespread public anxiety that a revitalized Germany might rise up once again and threaten Europe. But with their own military situation in Indochina worsening steadily, the French wanted Dulles's help in securing a settlement that would include Communist China and were willing to negotiate. The rearmament issue also met with resistance within Germany, where it inspired strong opposition from those still distrustful of their own military, triggered heated debate on its constitutionality, and fueled the vociferous "Without Me" movement of young men refusing to enlist. The Russians rejected the agreement as a harbinger of permanent division.

Dulles, an EDC true believer from his first days in office, was committed to West German military and economic integration with Europe, and as a means of binding the region to America. If the EDC failed, he wrote Conant in a personal note at the suggestion of the president, "the resources which the United States in its own enlightened self-interest has been pouring into Europe will be wasted." Conant believed there was only an "off-chance" of achieving any of the Berlin meetings' stated goals, but he invested vast amounts of time and effort into drawing up the documents put before the four foreign ministers. The conference ran true to his predictions, and after everything was said and done, none of the major issues was resolved, making it a useless exercise.

Conant spent the winter campaigning for an independent, rearmed West Germany, arguing that the move toward European integration was the best way to achieve peace. But with each side jockeying for power, he was growing increasingly worried that if the squabbling continued much longer, far less constructive alternatives would gain credence. Elements within Adenauer's coalition, angered by France's foot-dragging, were making noises about creating a German "national army" instead of the multinational EDC force. He was leery of any scheme that would lead to an Anglo-American military evacuation and leave the coal- and industry-rich Ruhr Valley vulnerable to the Russians. Conant warned Eisenhower and Dulles that "even a remote possibility" that this could occur would be dangerous, given the political instability of the country, and was "thoroughly alarmed."

Frustrated by the endless delays, shifting demands, and disturbing signs of growing nationalistic fervor in both France and Germany, his patience was wearing thin. "What growling dogs they both are," he complained to his diary. "Can this European business be made to work by the present bunch of politicians unless the Russians scare them more? I am in my Robert A. Taft mood," he added, empathizing briefly with the diehard isolationist.

The intensifying fight over the EDC pushed Conant to brave Dulles's disapproval, and, in a rare departure from the official line, he gave a speech in Frankfurt on March 31, 1954, in which he baldly stated that West Germany should become a sovereign state whether or not six "little European countries" ratified the treaty. "No reaction from Washington as to my 'calculated indiscretion,'" he noted in his diary, but Conant was pleased his sharply worded statement had gotten everyone's attention, reassured the restive German public, and added impetus to the ratification process. France, of course, immediately took offense. Though the State Department tried to characterize Conant's remarks as personal, his statement was construed as a direct threat to France's veto power over German rearmament. Despite

Conant's sortie into pressure diplomacy, and taking to the newspapers and radio to exhort the European leaders to vote for ratification, it looked like the EDC was a lost cause.

Two weeks later, on April 17, he flew back to the United States for a final stand in what promised to be another losing battle: testifying in Oppenheimer's defense before the Atomic Energy Commission's specially convened security hearing. Oppenheimer was threatened with the removal of his military security clearances and stood accused of various indiscretions—namely, friendships with members of the American Communist Party—by zealous proponents of the hydrogen bomb. Conant had dreaded this day since receiving a letter on March 22 from Oppenheimer's distinguished New York attorney, Lloyd Garrison, seeking both a written testimonial to his client's character and loyalty and his promise to appear as a supporting witness. Conant had already fought and won an earlier skirmish with J. Edgar Hoover over whether the left-wing physicist was fit to have access to classified information, and, after a review, his clearance had been upheld.

Conant thought it was probably inevitable with the "atmosphere of fear in Washington" that Oppenheimer's past would catch up with him again. But this was a much graver situation, not the least because it was so public, with the newspapers printing the AEC's charges, and McCarthy's televised probe of a Communist cover-up in the US Army heightening the climate of suspicion. Three days before the AEC security hearing was set to begin, McCarthy gave an interview denouncing Oppenheimer for deliberately delaying work on the hydrogen bomb, and claiming the only reason he himself was not pursuing an investigation was because of assurances from "top administration officials that this matter would be gone into in detail."

Conant worried that the "notorious senator" was setting the stage for what promised to be a tawdry political sideshow. He also worried that his absence from the Washington scene, and waning influence in the scientific community, meant that he was no longer in the same position to protect Oppenheimer from the powerful forces aligned against him. Even before Conant had left for his new job in Germany, the whispering campaign against Oppenheimer was growing louder and more vicious. The bitter split over the H-bomb, exacerbated by Teller's relentless lobbying for a second nuclear weapons laboratory, had emboldened Oppenheimer's antagonists in the FBI, the air force, and amid the bigger bomb proponents at Los Alamos and in the halls of government. They wanted him out of the way, and would stop at nothing to ruin his reputation and topple him from his lofty perch atop the nuclear hierarchy.

Conant knew that his and Oppie's efforts at nuclear restraint over the past decade had earned them enemies. He had not forgotten the chilling conversation with Oppenheimer and Lee DuBridge in the spring of 1952, when they had agreed it was time to watch their backs. "Some of the 'boys' have their axe out for three of us on the GAC of the AEC," Conant had later noted in his diary. Nor had he forgotten the "dirty words" being said about Oppie at the time, and the fact that his political promiscuity, in light of the country's present anti-intellectualism, made him an easy target. After the Soviets tested their first hydrogen bomb in August 1953, Oppenheimer's critics had stepped up their attacks, arguing that he had been wrong in his advice against the H-bomb, and suggesting that his call for arms control and dialogue had been motivated by disloyalty and the desire to disclose military secrets to the Russians.

It was Vannevar Bush, during a January visit to Bonn, who told Conant that the slur campaign against Oppenheimer had finally succeeded in eroding Eisenhower's trust in his chief nuclear advisor. At the urging of Lewis Strauss, the new chairman of the AEC, and General Kenneth Nichols, the AEC's general manager, the president had secretly ordered that a "blank wall" be erected between Oppenheimer and all atomic secrets. Strauss was in the hawkish Teller camp, but his personal animosity toward the arrogant former Los Alamos director went far beyond policy differences. Showing off before a Senate panel, Oppenheimer had made a fool of the investment banker—making an isotope joke that exposed his ignorance—and Strauss's hatred of him had festered ever since. On December 21, 1953, Strauss and Nichols informed Oppenheimer that he was now regarded as a security risk, and his clearance had been suspended. They then handed him an eight-page letter listing the charges on which the suspension was based, consisting largely of the "derogatory material" dredged up from his FBI file. But rather than resign quietly and avoid a hearing, as they had hoped, Oppenheimer insisted on being given the opportunity to clear his name.

After all Oppie had done for his country, after all he had achieved, Conant could not believe the AEC would proceed against him. He was determined to help defend his old friend from retaliation by a group of ambitious rivals. Moreover, he was outraged by the suggestion that Oppenheimer's opposition to thermonuclear weapons in any way impugned his patriotism, especially as recent events—the imminent prospect of a Soviet Super—had confirmed their sickening foreboding about Russia's ability to duplicate their accomplishments. In his view, Truman's decision to proceed with the development of the H-bomb had been a disaster, and they were now committed to a renewed arms race and stockpiling ever more dangerous nuclear weapons. He supposed the fact that they had been right made them even more suspect.

"I have no apologies whatsoever for the position I took and to which all the other members [of the GAC] subscribed in general," Conant asserted in a letter to Bush in late March. "Indeed, I think I was as much a leader of this point of view as any person." But he had no illusions about what he was up against. Even before the hearing began, he questioned the competence of the three members of the Personnel Security Board—Gordon Gray, Thomas A. Morgan, and Ward V. Evans—to fairly assess the enormously complicated technical and military defense issues involved in the H-bomb decision, complaining to Bush that they could not possibly "pass judgment on the wisdom or lack of it of the GAC recommendations in 1949." It did not help that all three were decidedly conservative: Gray, the chairman, was the former secretary of the army, now president of the University of North Carolina; Morgan was chairman of the Sperry Corporation; Evans, a retired chemistry professor, had served on AEC security panels in the past and had a track record of denying clearances.

Adding to Conant's misgivings was Dulles's negative reaction to his confidential note alerting him of his intention to appear at the hearing in support of Oppenheimer. Immediately cabling Conant that "factors unknown to you make [an appearance] undesirable," Dulles followed up with an "eyes only" letter warning him off in no uncertain terms:

> There is the general feeling in White House circles that it would be a good deal better if you did not become publicly involved in the matter. I do not mean to indicate there is any evidence to throw doubt on the gentleman's loyalty, and I do not think that any effort will indeed be made to prove disloyalty, at least as far as the executive is concerned—I cannot vouch for what might happen in Congress. However, there is considerable evidence of laxity and poor judgment and, in some cases, lack of veracity.
>
> I thought you ought to know this.

There was never any question in Conant's mind that he would testify on Oppenheimer's behalf, even though he was almost sick at the thought of the coming ordeal. When he stepped off the plane in New York, the press corps was waiting for him. The papers were full of stories about the extraordinary closed-door sessions and reports that he had flown in from Germany to appear before the Security Board on behalf of the man he had chosen to supervise the atomic bomb project. Conant dodged their questions and headed straight for Washington to meet with the secretary of state. In a brief meeting with Dulles on Monday, April 19, the two "covered Germany in 15 min" before moving on to the real business at hand. "Told him I had no choice but to testify at Oppenheimer hearing," Conant reported in his diary. "He said I should know this might destroy my usefulness to govt. I said I quite realized this and he only had to give the word and I was through."

The next afternoon, he walked into the drab little hearing room of the AEC's Temporary Building III to affirm Oppenheimer's fitness to serve the government. He took the stand, raised his right hand, and swore to tell the truth, and then sat facing the three men on the Personnel Security Board, who were positioned around a big, horseshoe-shaped table. Asked if he had a comment on the AEC's December 23 letter listing the charges against Oppenheimer, Conant, in an admittedly "aggressive mood" that reflected his anger at the farcical proceedings, replied that he had read it and thought that it must have been "carelessly drafted." The way it was worded, he observed caustically, he, too, would be ineligible for government service because he strongly opposed—"as strongly as anybody else on that committee"—the development of the hydrogen bomb. Describing the AEC's reasons for doubting Oppenheimer as almost a "caricature" of the kind of sound argument he was accustomed to, he went on to pick apart the logic of its contention that Oppenheimer's opposition to the H-bomb was detrimental to the interests of the United States. "The record is quite the contrary," he stated emphatically, and proceeded to read into the record all the things Oppenheimer had done and said that were "detrimental to the Soviet Union."

During cross-examination, Conant kept to short, clipped responses. He was too practiced a witness to be easily manipulated by the AEC's skillful attorney, Roger Robb, and refused to be drawn into making contradictory statements or to rise to digs about why he and his fellow atomic advisors exceeded their authority by giving advice on military strategy. "Nobody has to take the advice if they don't want to," was Conant's calm rejoinder. "It turned out they didn't." He was unwavering in his defense of Oppenheimer's loyalty and insisted that his failure to report the so-called Chevalier incident—when he was approached for security information to pass on to Russian scientists—was insignificant. "He had nothing else but conversation with the man," Conant asserted. Nor did he alter his view of Oppenheimer's record of "effective actions against the Soviet Union."

But Oppenheimer's behavior, as described in the AEC indictment, *had* been a bit odd: first in delaying several months before reporting the incident and then in declining to name Chevalier as the person who had approached him. Conant wobbled only once, when Ward Evans posed the hypothetical question of what someone should do if approached for security information, and pressed for the answer he wanted, "Wouldn't you have reported it just as quickly as you could?"

"I think I would have, yes," faltered Conant, who had helped foster the national security mentality that now threatened to entrap Oppenheimer. "I hope I would have; let us put it that way."

Sensing his discomfort, Robb broke in and exploited the opportunity to further discredit Oppenheimer by implying that the discrepancies in the physicist's account of the Chevalier exchange with counterintelligence officials amounted to intentional deceit. "When you did report it, Doctor," Robb asked pointedly, "you would have told the whole truth about it?"

"I hope so."

Satisfied, Robb had the last word: "I am sure you would."

Afterward, Conant was "not very happy" about the AEC's lawyer's prosecutorial style, which he compared with a "belligerent corporal," and reported his concerns to Eisenhower. From what Conant had seen and heard, the AEC charges and proceedings seemed so stacked against Oppenheimer that there was virtually no chance he would prevail. The president said he had "prayed it would come out okay, but doubted it."

Conant also shared his concerns that Oppenheimer's resistance to the H-bomb was included in the AEC indictment, creating the impression that he was being punished for his opinion. Later in the day, Eisenhower wrote Conant a brief note explaining that "no criticism" was directed toward Oppenheimer because of his opposition to the H-bomb—"that opinion was recited merely to give background to certain other allegations to the effect that, even after the decision to produce had been made by the highest possible authority, the Doctor [Oppenheimer] departed from his proper role as advisor and attempted to slow down development." Eisenhower apparently had second thoughts about that assertion, as he decided against sending the note to Conant, though he sent a copy to Strauss.

Conant departed for Germany before the hearing concluded, but he had heard enough gossip around town to leave him thoroughly depressed about the outcome. "Washington very tense!" he reported in his diary. Roger Adams, the foreign secretary of the National Academy of Sciences, confided over lunch at the Cosmos Club that the academy members were "divided" on Oppie and that "the California gang of chemists said he was a security risk." Others such as Bush, Rabi, DuBridge, and Jack McCloy were furious. Privately, many of them blamed Teller and the "scientists in the other camp" for starting the trouble by circulating rumors. Conant agreed but reserved some of his anger for the White House, which could have avoided the "first-class mess."

On May 27 the board issued its report, recommending 2 to 1 to strip Oppenheimer of his security clearance. In fantastically contorted prose, the majority report, signed by Gray and Morgan, concluded that Oppenheimer was a "loyal citizen," but that his "continuing conduct and associations" re-flected a serious disregard for security, and that his views regarding the hy-drogen bomb program were "sufficiently disturbing as to raise a doubt as to whether his future participation . . . would be clearly consistent with the best interests of security." It was Ward Evans, the only scientist, who pointed out the paradox inherent in their finding him loyal but a security risk: "To deny him clearance now for what he was cleared for in 1947, when we must know he is less of a security risk now than he was then, seems hardly the proce-dure to be adopted in a free country." A month later, the five AEC commis-sioners confirmed the Security Board's judgment by a vote of 4 to 1. Again, it was the lone scientist, Henry DeWolf Smyth, who dissented. Strauss, the least impartial member of the panel, wrote the majority report for the AEC, which explained why it was laced with suspicion and vitriol.

The verdict ended Oppenheimer's government service. Compounding his disgrace was the government's sudden decision to publish the full tran-script of the hearings in June, violating its assurances to Oppenheimer and all the witnesses that it would be kept confidential. To make sure that public sentiment was in its corner, the AEC even provided the press with a guide to the 992-page document highlighting the passage in which Oppenheimer admitted the original story he told security officers about the Chevalier in-cident was a "tissue of lies." From a public relations standpoint, it allowed the government to control the story, contrast the orderly AEC inquiry with McCarthy's kangaroo court, and cast its actions in the best possible light.

But for Conant, it was one betrayal too many. Oppenheimer had made mistakes, said things he should not have, certainly, but he had done nothing to deserve a public lynching. Notwithstanding his belief that the proceedings were never justified in the first place, "They were not at all what they were supposed to be: a hearing on the merits of a fine man," Conant told an interviewer years later, his anger still palpable. He would never forgive Teller, whose complaints about Oppie's attitudes and actions had formed the basis of the charges that he was a security risk, and whose devastating testimony made the government's case.

"It was an outrageous business from beginning to end," Conant said, adding heavily, "a thing of a very unfortunate nature."

As the Oppenheimer tragedy played out in Washington, Conant was engaged on another front by the looming failure of the EDC. By the spring of 1954, the French had moved from confusion to a full-blown state of crisis after the loss of Indochina, the last vestige of their colonial empire, to the Communist-trained Vietnamese nationalist forces. At the Geneva Conference in July, Vietnam was temporarily divided along the seventeenth parallel between the Communist North and the South. As the French government fell to a vote of no confidence, Conant gloomily contemplated the "fatal day" of their EDC vote, aware that a great opportunity was slipping away. "The free world seems to be coming apart at the seams, and the European movement," he wrote, "is very sick indeed." On August 31, the day after the French National Assembly finally killed the EDC—"D-day or Defeat Day," as he called it—Conant met with Adenauer, who was "shattered." Two full years of exhausting international diplomacy had "gone up in oratorical smoke," jeopardizing the future of NATO and throwing the Western alliance into doubt. "What will happen?" Conant worried to his diary that night. "Anyone's guess?"

Dulles, who eight months earlier had warned that defeat of the EDC would force an "agonizing reappraisal" of American commitments, now called the situation "a crisis of almost terrifying proportions." Eisenhower, who considered German rearmament crucial to his strategic design, dispatched Dulles to London in October to talk to the NATO representatives and find a way to break the deadlock. It was Britain's new prime minister, Anthony Eden, who picked up the pieces and resolved the differences, though Conant was convinced Dulles's "threatening attitude had a good deal to do with Eden's putting forward the plan." The French finally agreed to restore West German sovereignty after nearly a decade of occupation and authorize the creation of a German army, permitting the Federal Republic to play a role in the defense of Europe. In return, Adenauer assured France that Germany would limit its military contribution to NATO to twelve divisions and 1,300 aircraft, forgo missiles and naval vessels, and renounce its right to manufacture atomic, biological, and chemical weapons. At the end of a long, hard week spent hammering out the details, Conant headed back to Bonn. Though it seemed almost miraculous, they had at last reached an agreement on German rearmament.

The day before Christmas, Conant was listening to the morning news on Armed Forces Radio when he heard the French National Assembly had again voted to reject the accords. Weary and disheartened, he was in no mood to attend the holiday party that evening at the French High Commission. Trying to put a good face on it, he and Patty sipped champagne through gritted teeth and attempted polite small talk. No mention was made of that morning's stunning setback. When a high-ranking French general turned to Conant and commented in excellent English, "Oh, you are the high commissioner for Germany. The Germans are a most difficult people," Conant could not help himself and indulged in a rare outburst of temper, snapping, "To us Americans, all Europeans seem difficult people!"

To his immense relief, two days before the New Year, the French National Assembly voted 287 to 260 *for* the agreements. It had taken months of "incredibly torturous" negotiations to get France to bow to the inevitable. The three new accords were signed in Paris on March 27, 1955, securing the future of Western Europe. In his journal that Sunday, Conant dashed off one line: "So it seems that at long last the Paris treaties are ratified." The announcement of the new independent Germany was not accompanied by any noisy celebrations or parades. Conant and Adenauer handled it quietly, aware of the strong opposition east of the Elbe River, where the eighteen million Germans who lived outside the borders of the Federal Republic viewed it as the last nail in the coffin of reunification.

On May 5 the Allied occupation would come to an official end. The ceremony for the formal exchange of ambassadors of the new sovereign nation was scheduled for noon. Each of the high commissioners had been instructed to arrive at the reception rooms in full evening attire, accompanied by five members of staff, likewise in white tie and tails. Two days before the historic occasion, a cable came from Washington: the Senate Foreign Relations Committee had not yet approved Conant's appointment as ambassador of the Federal Republic. His wrath "boiled over": because of bureaucratic incompetence, he would be left "diplomatically naked" at the stroke of twelve.

The holdup, as he soon learned, was due to a last-minute appeal from a former chief justice of the Allied High Commission Court of Appeals in West Germany, William Clark, who harbored a grudge against Conant for having amended the law of the occupation tribunal in a way that circumvented his authority and, he believed, led to his being dismissed from the bench.* In the end, a red-faced Conant explained his predicament to German officials and attended the grand celebratory dinner, though he lacked the proper credentials. Nine days later, he became ambassador to Germany after being approved unanimously by the Senate committee, a thumping endorsement that, under the circumstances, the *New York Times* called "tantamount to a tribute to Conant's role as a diplomat."

Following the Geneva Summit in July, there was a slight thaw in East-West relations. The new Soviet leadership agreed to sign the Austrian Peace Treaty, making that country independent but neutral, on the Swiss model, with its own defense forces. Eisenhower was delighted, hailing it as another small crack in the Iron Curtain. While little progress had been made on the key issues of disarmament, European security, and German reunification, the Soviets had shown a willingness to negotiate, which made for a refreshing change.

In an effort to reduce tensions and minimize the danger of a surprise nuclear attack, Eisenhower had unveiled at the summit his "open skies" proposal to open the airspace above the United States and the Soviet Union to inspection flights by each country. His plan called on each side "to give each other a complete blueprint of our military establishments, from beginning to end, from one end of our countries to the other." The Russians were not interested. Nikita Khrushchev, the new secretary of the Communist Party, was convinced it was an espionage plot. But Eisenhower continued to promote the "spirit of Geneva," telling congressional leaders that after ten years of relentless, hostile cold war rhetoric, both nations had taken a step

---

* Clark pursued his grievance in a libel suit in the United States District Court but died before it could be settled.

back from the arms race and horrifying prospect of nuclear Armageddon. Conant, who saw no sign the Russians were serious about disarmament, thought the summit was a "fraud, from beginning to end," and dismissed the whole exercise as political theatrics. His suspicions were confirmed when two weeks after the conference, the Russians embarked on a series of H-bomb tests.

By his fourth year in Germany, Conant had become a popular figure, often fondly referred to in the press as "Professor Atom," his scientific learning commanding more respect than his statesmanship. He had rapidly improved on his chemist's German and spoke the language fluently, with a freewheeling approach to grammar and a flat Boston accent that endeared him to the local citizenry. He was conscientious about performing what he called his "goodwill tours," visiting every large and medium-size city in the country, stopping by refugee camps, Red Cross centers, and orphans' homes, attending bull sessions with editors and beer evenings with local politicians, lecturing at schools and listening to the concerns of teachers and their pupils. He was particularly proud of the new Free University of Berlin, which had started in a warehouse a handful of years earlier and now occupied a resplendent modern campus paid for with Ford Foundation money. In his frequent addresses to college students, he tried to "accentuate the positive," talking about the way Germans had repudiated Hitler and rebounded under enormously trying circumstances, calling them the "commandos of the Cold War."

On the subject of Nazism, however, he became vehement, insisting it was an "abomination," a "monstrous aberration," a terrible crime not only against Europe but also against the best and lasting traditions of the German people themselves. Some neo-Nazism still existed on the fringes, and there was a certain cynicism about party politics that, if it became too pervasive, could degenerate into nihilism, but he did not believe in the lazy truism that history was doomed to repeat itself. "The spirit of free Germany is the spirit of people who have turned their back on the Nazi past," he declared, hailing the Nuremberg trials and their tragic record of Nazi war crimes as a guidepost to a future ruled by law, not force. Once again resolutely turning his hopes to education, he argued that any educated society, "given half a chance," would choose freedom over tyranny, and self-government under law. He attributed his optimism to his conversations with the younger generation, whom he credited with an amazing resilience and a real eagerness to move beyond the rubble of yesterday to a better tomorrow.

Now that the Federal Republic had been ushered into the Atlantic fraternity, and the country was "on its way," Conant felt his mission had been accomplished, and he began looking forward to returning home and resuming his career as an educator. Only weeks after the new independent Germany was born, he began planning his next act. John W. Gardner, the new president of the Carnegie Corporation, had written to him, stating that he was just the sort of compelling communicator and "effective crystallizer" they were looking for to tackle some aspect of the problems facing American education. He could do anything that interested him, and Gardner would underwrite it with a "blank check." Conant leapt at the offer and immediately began making notes for an ambitious study of American high schools. "He was absolutely clear in his mind what he wanted," recalled Gardner, who met him for lunch that spring during one of the ambassador's flying visits to Washington, and told him the offer stood and there was no need to make a hurried decision. But Conant had made up his mind, confiding that he would in all likelihood resign his post at the end of Eisenhower's term, following the 1956 presidential election. "He had thought it through," marveled Gardner, who happily closed the deal then and there. "I might have known he never goes off half-cocked."

Conant's impatience to wind up his diplomatic career stemmed from his dissatisfaction with the job and his growing dislike of Dulles. Though Conant had a grudging respect for his nerve and negotiating skills, the Wall Street lawyer was reluctant to delegate power and tended to treat his envoys like the lowly office boys in his old firm. The secretary of state was a polarizing figure. Like Conant, none of the ambassadors who came through Bonn were "very favorably inclined towards him." His personal feelings aside, however, it was Dulles who was the prime mover of American foreign policy, and his position was only strengthened after Eisenhower's heart attack in September 1955. For months afterward, he was the reigning figure in the administration, guaranteeing there would be no change in his extremely hands-on approach to diplomacy.

No doubt Conant also sensed that he had fallen out of favor with Dulles, who took a dim view of his independent forays into cold war diplomacy. Once the treaties had been ratified, and the Soviets saw there was no longer any chance to divide the Western Allies, the tensions over Berlin increased dramatically, as did the friction between Conant and his boss. The trouble started when the Soviets' puppet regime in East Germany arbitrarily imposed exorbitant tariffs on the autobahn in and out of West Berlin and then announced its intention to halt all barge traffic, which Conant considered "tantamount to blackmail." When he told Dulles and Adenauer that the lifelines into free Berlin were being threatened, they brushed aside his concerns, recommending it be left in "German hands." Instead, Conant took matters into his own hands, lodging official protests and pushing back against the Soviets' blatant attempts to gain control of the city.

Things came to a head with the nuisance arrest of two US congressmen, Representatives Edward P. Boland of Massachusetts and Harold C. Ostertag of New York, on November 27, 1955. The two American VIPs had been on a sightseeing trip in the Soviet zone of Berlin and on their return were detained at gunpoint at the border crossing by East German police on the grounds they had used their car's radio telephone in violation of GDR laws. When the Soviet Berlin commander refused to accept a United States protest of the incident because East Berlin was part of the GDR and no longer subject to occupation rule, Conant decided he could not allow the "grossly discourteous and threatening conduct" to go unchallenged. He hopped on his private train to Berlin and then defiantly drove deep into the Soviet sector in his official car with the Stars and Stripes flying as a symbol of American determination not to abandon the divided city. At a crowded news conference later that afternoon, he explained that his impromptu road trip was intended to provide "visible proof" the United States would remain in Berlin.

The US ambassador's dramatic stunt made headlines back home: "Conant Defies Reds," reported the December 3 *New York Herald Tribune*, including a photo of him grinning broadly beneath his homburg. Editorial writers commended Conant's refusal to be bullied by the Soviets, and several congressmen wrote to express their appreciation. Dulles, however, was not pleased with his heroics. Several days later, Conant received a patronizing reprimand from one of the assistant secretaries, reminding him "decisions could only be made in Washington." Unrepentant, Conant felt no reply was necessary.

Distrust had dogged the Conant-Adenauer relationship from the start, and it grew considerably worse over the next year. Proposals calling for a substantial reduction in US Army manpower had rekindled the aged chancellor's nightmares of an American withdrawal from Europe. The so-called Radford Plan (named for its advocate, Admiral Arthur Radford, chairman

of the Joint Chiefs of Staff) was part of the administration's New Look Doctrine, which approved the use of nuclear weapons in limited war situations,
thus reducing the need for maintaining large conventional forces. This deliberate shift to nuclear deterrence over local defense forces was, in Dulles's
words, the modern way to get "maximum protection at a bearable cost."

Now that West Germany had won the right to rearm, Dulles wanted the
Federal Republic to move ahead quickly with its plan to build its own half-
million-man army and impose a mandatory two-year conscription, in order
to relieve the United States of the expense of keeping reserve troops. Frustrated by Adenauer's leisurely pace, Conant was under orders to expedite
the military buildup. The whole plan was almost derailed when the German
press reported that NATO's secret Carte Blanche exercise, designed to simu-
late its response to a Soviet attack, culminated in a mock nuclear battle with
335 enemy devices exploded on West German soil and five million casualties. Needless to say, this frightening preview of Dulles's strategy of "massive
retaliation" as a means of defense against Communist aggression did not go
over well, and, along with the anticipated cutbacks in American land troops,
was exploited by Adenauer's political opponents.

The chancellor was doubly angry because he believed he had been deliberately left in the dark regarding the impending troop reductions, and
Conant could not blame him: "Somebody in Bonn really smelled what the
real situation was." Almost from the beginning, US officials had planned to
rearm Germany and pull out the American troops, but if "any hint of such
a thing" had got back to the country's leadership, they never would have
cooperated. Although uncomfortable with diplomatic subterfuge, Conant
went along with it: "We were dealing with a very, very delicate situation in
which hypocrisy verging on straight prevarication was about the only thing
that could be used." Despite Conant's determined efforts to assuage the
chancellor's fury, Adenauer retaliated by refusing to honor his agreement
with the Americans to put through a two-year draft; instead, he cut the size
of the German army down to 350,000 and reduced the duration of the conscription period to twelve months. As a result, rearmament proceeded even
more slowly. "What irony," Conant scribbled in his diary. "First we were
afraid the Germans would rearm, and now we are afraid they won't!"

Dulles tried to soothe the chancellor, but by then their friendship had
foundered. Rather than blame himself, Dulles blamed Conant and decided
what was needed was a new face in Bonn. For months, he had been fielding
complaints that the Harvard scientist was too "textbook" in his approach to

foreign relations. Dulles tended to agree, regarding the brisk, businesslike Conant as too reserved and, while lofty in argument, lacking in "political touch." He had nothing of the courtier about him and had failed to forge the desired bond of intimacy with Adenauer that would strengthen US-German ties.

When Dulles had first suggested to the president that perhaps a change might be in order, back when the German High Commission was abolished in the spring of 1955, Eisenhower had rebuffed him, replying by memo, "I prefer to appoint Conant." Now Dulles changed tacks. On July 16, 1956, he approached Eisenhower about possibly transferring Conant to Rome, a post currently occupied by the flamboyant Clare Boothe Luce, who was known for her lavish entertaining. Earlier in the day, Dulles had joked with his aides about whether the notoriously tightfisted Yankee could afford Italy, remarking that he "probably would not operate on the extravagant style of Mrs. Luce." Eisenhower had his doubts. After reviewing the available ambassadorships, Dulles then suggested India, and Ike readily approved the plum assignment.

Conant, who was spending his annual summer leave at his rustic cottage in Randolph, New Hampshire, was surprised to receive a message from the tiny North Country Inn, located a mile away, that the secretary of state was trying to reach him. (Since they were there for barely a month and did not want to be disturbed, he had not bothered to have the phone connected.) Filled with visions of the "major catastrophe" that would require his urgent attention, he jumped in the car and sped down the road. He braced himself for the news from Washington, picking up the hotel phone just off the lobby, a far-from-private spot. Without any introduction, Dulles said: "The president and I would like to have you go to India as the United States ambassador." Conant gasped, mostly in horror—India held no attraction, nor did the prospect of another four years under Dulles. When the secretary insisted he give it serious consideration, Conant politely agreed.

As he "tramped the mountain trails" over the next few days, he took stock of his situation. It was obvious he was being "pushed out" of his German post. He was not sure who was behind the intrigue or to what degree the president was even aware of it, "but it didn't matter." By then, he had come to realize that it was not that he had been unsuccessful in the job as much as unnecessary. Dulles had never wanted a strong, opinionated ambassador and preferred to lock horns with Adenauer himself, one old bull to another. A few days later, Conant called the White House and said no.

Dulles told him to take another week, he was just tired, and asked him to come to Washington to talk it over with the president. Conant was flattered by the invitation but begged off. What the telephone call had made clear was that whether Eisenhower was reelected in November or not, his days in the diplomatic corps were coming to an end.

His final months were marked by a series of crises and a growing gap between American rhetoric and the reality of the world situation. The Suez Canal crisis blew up in late July, when Egyptian president General Gamal Abdel Nasser announced he was nationalizing the canal after months of tensions with Britain, France, and Israel. The prospect of war between the US's Allies and the influential Middle Eastern power, and the possibility the Soviets might intervene to assist Nasser, forced Eisenhower, who was still recovering from abdominal surgery, back into command. When Conant paid a visit to the Oval Office on September 7 before returning to Germany, he found the president looking tired and troubled, grappling with the difficult question of how to deal with Egypt's nationalist leader. "How to cut Nasser down to size without war or uniting the Arabs?" was how Eisenhower defined the dilemma, though Conant knew that, unlike Dulles, at the deepest levels, his old friend was categorically opposed to the use of military force.

With US and NATO officials distracted by the Suez affair, the Russians moved into Budapest on November 1, crushing the uprising in the Hungarian capital and overthrowing the government. While Conant was digesting this report, Moscow delivered to Bonn a threatening note warning that London and Paris were vulnerable to nuclear attack if they continued down the path of aggression. "What sounded like a herald of World War III from the Kremlin came last night," Conant recorded in his diary, more frightened than he cared to admit. "We are quite uncertain what the future has in store."

Amid the chaos of events and news that Dulles had undergone surgery, Conant offered to stay on in Berlin until the spring. It would accommodate the secretary's convalescence for what turned out to be colon cancer and give Eisenhower, who had easily won reelection, more time to find a suitable replacement. But on January 10, 1957, he was somewhat startled to receive a sealed letter from Dulles accepting his resignation effective as of February 15, coinciding with a planned trip to the United States for a series of speaking engagements. It took another two weeks for the White House to issue the official announcement, leaving Conant to wonder if at the last minute there had been "a difference of opinion at the State Department." The president sent a letter expressing his "deep personal regret" that Conant was leaving and thanked him for his outstanding work in seeing the return of Germany to "its rightful place in the family of nations." On a more personal note, Eisenhower added that he would miss his old friend's "wise counsel on which I drew so frequently."

Conant, who had been taken aback by his abrupt dismissal, was sorry to be leaving in such a hasty and undignified fashion, but on later reflection, he felt almost relieved. He was eager to be finished with his ambassadorial duties so that he could plunge into his new work. The press had sniffed out his Carnegie project and broke the story the moment his resignation was announced, igniting something of a bidding war for his services. There were the usual rumors that he would go into politics, and the *Boston Herald* named him as a possible running mate for Vice President Nixon in the 1960 presidential election.

In their final weeks in Bonn, the Conants attended the requisite round of farewell parties, received more parting gifts than they knew what to do with, and bid good-bye to their embassy staff, "quite a heart-rending business," Patty reported to her mother. On February 19 they flew to New York and took up residence in the Algonquin Hotel, their temporary address until they decided where to settle. After living in official housing for more than a quarter century, they had no place to call home.

CHAPTER 22

Warrior Educator

What will be needed is not more engineers and scientists,
but a people who will not panic and political leaders of
wisdom, courage, and devotion, with capacity for solving
intricate human problems. Not more Einsteins, but more
Washingtons and Madisons.

—JBC to President Eisenhower

In the summer of 1957, Edward R. Murrow made a special trip to Randolph, New Hampshire, to see Conant, who had recently returned from a two-month sojourn in Switzerland. They had known each other since the war and were old friends, and had joined forces on the Committee on the Present Danger. The last time they had seen each other was in the fall of 1953, when the CBS broadcaster had interviewed Germany's new high commissioner in front of the Brandenburg Gate in Berlin. The interview had made news because a border incident had taken place while the cameras were rolling, capturing the dramatic scene as West German police used their nightsticks to turn back a group of young Communists who were trying to cross into the Western sector.

Sitting on the porch of Conant's summer home and sipping lemonade, they laughed at the memory of the sensational headlines and caught each other up on the more prosaic events in their lives. Both men were older and grayer, a touch more austere in appearance, but neither had changed much, each still as tough and lean as winter lobster. Murrow, whose hard-hitting reports had helped lead to the downfall of Joseph McCarthy, hosted his own weekly television show on CBS called *See It Now*, which covered important issues as well as profiles of famous actors, musicians, and newsmakers. He had conducted an interview with Oppenheimer, and one with Truman in 1955 in which the president admitted that dropping the bomb had not been a difficult decision—the hard choice had been to intervene in Korea, which started a war. Murrow was intruding on Conant's holiday to see if he could persuade him to cooperate with a program about his remarkable career of public service, which the *Washington Post* had hailed as that of a man "who could indeed be called a leader of leaders." It would cover his pioneering Manhattan Project role, activities as a nuclear policy maker, and contributions to the defense of Germany, as well as his perspective on the arms race and their chances of imminent extinction.

Conant turned him down flat, his twinkly good humor gone. He did not want a documentary highlighting his wartime service. Nor would he appear in *See It Now*'s upcoming two-part series on atomic energy. He took no pride in the creation of the atomic bomb because of the ongoing threat to the world posed by nuclear weapons. He had no wish to revisit that part of his life. Fortunately, he had been active on other fronts—as a chemist, university president, and statesman. Now, at age sixty-four, he intended to devote his remaining time—"as long as I can write and talk"—to education in a time of revolutionary change. He was in the midst of organizing a major study of the nation's public high schools, which he believed were the "vast engine of democracy" and the American way of life. It was backed by a generous $350,000 grant from the Carnegie Corporation, which had rented him offices at 555 Fifth Avenue in New York, footed the bill for a small staff of former principals and professors, and arranged for what in military terms was called "logistical support" from the Educational Testing Service (ETS) of Princeton, which he'd helped start and served for years on the governing board.

His plan of attack remained unchanged: assign the most talented people to the research study, identify the best formula for change, apply the ideas in a test case, and make the results public in an effort to foment action. After Labor Day, he would begin inspecting as many schools across the country as possible, observing classrooms and interviewing students, teachers, and administrators. He intended to devote a year to his exploration, and would publish his findings and recommendations in book form. He envisioned other education initiatives down the road, and other books. What he did not say in so many words, but perhaps did not need to, was that he intended this work to be his legacy—not the bomb.

He would remain gun-shy about subsequent efforts to chronicle his storied career. He rebuffed a similar approach from CBS's Eric Sevareid and rejected his publisher's initial suggestion that he write about his life, stating his "strong prejudice against people who wrote autobiographies." Conant was ultimately persuaded to write a memoir of his Harvard presidency, but it was so dry and devoid of personal detail that after reading the finished manuscript, his editor had to request the inclusion of at least a few mentions of his wife and children.

It was not simply that he was averse to examining his actions and motivations; he had a genuine horror of delving into the past. Conant had spent most of his married life trying to keep his family's private tragedies out of public view, in part out of a sense of self-preservation, and in part to protect his wife from further heartache. His fear of exposure had increased in proportion to his fame. Over the years, he had gone to great lengths to preserve the carefully curated image of a proper Boston family that he and Patty presented to the world. No matter how hard he tried, however, he was powerless to prevent the inherited maladies of the Richards family from wreaking havoc with their lives. While in Germany, he and Patty had been rocked by the news of the suicide of her youngest brother. In November 1953, just before Thanksgiving, Thayer had thrown a topcoat over his pajamas and driven to the railway station near his home in Blacksburg, Virginia, and then laid down on the tracks. He was forty-eight.

Conant attributed his death to the same endogenous depression that twelve years earlier had claimed Patty's brother Bill. Despite a fortunate start, Thayer's life had been full of disappointment. He had wanted to be a naval architect but ended up teaching design at Virginia Polytechnic Institute, and in recent years had struggled to support his wife and twin boys. Bankrupted by his wife's breakdowns and hospitalizations, and having begged money from family and friends until they cut him off, he had finally buckled under the weight of debt and despair. Conant, hoping to keep it out of the press, decided against returning home for the funeral. Patty wrote her grief-stricken mother how "brave and wise" she was in coping on her own and for "carrying your burden very gallantly." She assured her that she "need not worry too much about Thayer's boys," both juniors at Harvard, as they appeared "intelligent, well-balanced and happy-natured." But by then, of course, there was every reason to worry. Faced with this latest evidence of her family's genetic predisposition to mental illness, Conant feared there was a very real risk the disease was being passed down from one generation to the next.

Perhaps for this reason as much as for any past difficulties, Conant remained wary of his adult sons. He was always braced for bad news. On the surface, Jim, a reporter in the Montreal office of *Time*, seemed to be stable and making a go of it as a journalist, but there were ominous signs of strain. He had married a pretty young woman, Norice O'Malley, with a four-year-old daughter. Raised a strict Catholic, her parents had managed to have her first marriage annulled and had adamantly opposed another ill-conceived union, and refused to attend the wedding. In rapid succession, the couple had a daughter and a son of their own. When Jim and his young family had visited Randolph that summer, they did not appear to be coping well. Jim was moody and tired from working long, unpredictable reporters' hours. He was drinking more than he should and chain-smoked as if his life depended on it. Patty was too besotted with her grandchildren to notice, but Conant, who did not miss much, was concerned that the demands of the job, lack of sleep, and three small children might be his son's undoing. He sent Jim off with a hefty check and hoped it would ease some of his financial worries. With advancing age had come the inevitable regrets about his inadequacies as a father, and Conant, following his father-in-law's example, used money as a means of assuaging his guilt.

As usual, the news about Ted was even more troubling. Through the diplomatic grapevine, they received word that their younger son, who had been living in South Korea on and off since the war in 1950, was planning to elope after a whirlwind two-week romance. They had scarcely seen him in recent years and knew little about his life beyond the fact that he had been working in the television and film unit of the United Nations and various offshoot information agencies, and was trying to establish himself as a documentary filmmaker. He had spent his last dime—and more than a few of theirs—to finance *Children in Crisis*, about the youngest victims of the Korean War, which had won an award at the 1955 Berlin Film Festival. Before they could register their objections, a cable arrived from Ted informing them that it was all decided and casually describing his intended, Ellen Psaty, as "an attractive, intelligent American girl." After tying the knot in a civil ceremony in the Seoul mayor's office, they would be taking off on a two-month honeymoon in Southeast Asia. He could not have made it any plainer that their presence was not required. A telegram from Alice Dowling, the wife of the US ambassador to South Korea, Walter "Red" Dowling, who had been Conant's deputy in Bonn, furnished the details that the bride was an art historian, an assistant professor at the University of Georgia, and "possessed of a great deal of social charm." Far from assuaging Patty's doubts, the Dowlings' wire convinced her that the woman in question had latched onto her son because of his last name and they would all pay dearly for it in the end. Ted still seemed determined to spite them at every turn.

It seemed they had come home to all the problems they had left behind and then some. In September 1957 Miriam Richards died at the age of ninety-one. Distraught and still mourning, Patty went to Cambridge to pack up her mother's apartment in the Hotel Continental, where she stumbled across letters and diaries disclosing details about her brothers' illness and a continued debate with a succession of doctors over what was the cause— nature or nurture. Filled with rage and pain, she spent weeks reading and ripping up her mother's tortured introspection, stuffing armloads of papers down the incinerator chute of their New York apartment in Manhattan House, at 200 East Sixty-Sixth Street. "My mother suffered all her early life from 'nervous prostration,'" Patty confided to a friend, explaining that her "gifted brothers" had never really found themselves and "ended in suicide." Her husband had been her tower of strength through it all: "I have my much more realistic and earthy spouse to thank that I turned out fairly normal!" But the letters had reopened old wounds and left her wobbly and more needy than ever. Conant could not bear the way she martyred herself to her family, enshrined her father, and wallowed in misery.

Making matters worse, Patty was finding it difficult to adjust to the everyday realities of civilian life. She had enjoyed the perks of having a large household staff since moving into the Harvard president's mansion in 1933, and, as she complained to a friend, was really no longer very "domestic minded." She had reveled in the luxury of their subsidized embassy existence—the butler, maids, cooks, drivers, secretaries, and solicitous aides who catered to their every need—and missed the endless distractions of the diplomatic social merry-go-round. Their New York routine was comparatively dull, and until they found a competent "daily" to cook and clean, they were forced to eat most of their meals out at one of their clubs: the Century, Metropolitan, Harvard Club, and Patty's favorite, the Cosmopolitan Club. Conant, who relished his independence, quite liked fending for himself and boasted of becoming "master of the two-minute boiled egg." Patty jokingly despaired that he would be content to "live like a monk."

Unlike his wife, Conant did not miss official life. He wrote Patty not to expect him to accept another ambassadorial post "unless you force me to it," adding for good measure, "I would be perfectly happy if I never attended another formal dinner party the rest of my days! Ditto for cocktails." If he initially had misgivings about the amount of travel involved in visiting some fifty-five schools in eighteen states over the academic year, he came to see it as a way to banish all the melodrama from his life. Work was his deliverance. It was a relief to go on the road.

He was on his fourth or fifth school when the news flashed on October 5, 1957, of Russia's unexpected coup in launching Sputnik, the first man-made satellite to orbit earth. Sputnik came as a shock to the United States and touched off a wave of hysteria that the Soviets had stolen the technological lead, with conservative critics blaming the lag in science on serious structural flaws in American public schools. The erosion of the US atomic advantage, highlighted by the Soviets' successful test of an intercontinental ballistic missile a month earlier, meant that Soviet nuclear warheads could now reach American soil. Edward Teller went on television and announced gravely that the United States had lost "a battle more important and greater than Pearl Harbor." A stream of prominent scientists and military leaders bemoaned the fact that the United States had conceded technical superiority to the Russians, and warned that the country had to catch up in what was now a "tough competitive race."

The deep sense of national humiliation, and anxiety over the alleged intellectual inadequacy and "softness" of American society, led to a big push to overhaul the education system, with teachers looking to Moscow for new methods and models, much less panaceas. Conant counseled President Eisenhower not to overreact to the exaggerated threat and steered him away from creating a crash science education program, believing excessive reliance on technology and technocrats could hurt the country. "Those now in college will before long be living in the age of intercontinental ballistic missiles," he telegrammed Eisenhower, revealing a skepticism of the narrow agenda of the new generation of cold war leaders. "What will be needed is not more engineers and scientists, but a people who will not panic and political leaders of wisdom, courage, and devotion, with capacity for solving intricate human problems. Not more Einsteins, but more Washingtons and Madisons."

Facing charges of unpreparedness, Eisenhower was under pressure to reactivate a major research-and-development effort along the lines of the OSRD and place it under the control of a "qualified citizen such as Ex-Pres Conant of Harvard," as a *Boston Globe* editorial urged. Eisenhower announced he would appoint a full-time science advisor to the president to help lead the counteroffensive against Russia. He asked William T. Golden, a respected financier-turned-dollar-a-year man who had first suggested the idea to Truman, to interview likely candidates, beginning with Conant. "He displayed no interest in returning to science activism," recalled Golden, who had a long conversation with the former wartime leader and considered him "too opinionated and set in his ideas to fulfill the role." Conant was still adamantly opposed to the hydrogen bomb, as well as to biological and chemical warfare, and maintained that the "missile gap"—he refused to believe the Russians had any real advantage in ICBMs—was a myth. He admitted to working "on the arbitrary assumption that there will be no war for a year or more," but did not seem very hopeful another world conflict could be avoided.

To appease his critics, Eisenhower agreed to a buildup of nuclear weapons, and appointed James Killian, the president of MIT, to the post, and under his direction assembled the President's Science Advisory Committee to provide crucial counsel on the missile program as well as the space race. George Kistiakowsky, the committee's missile expert, tried to persuade Conant to take part but found him unsympathetic to the alarmist response to the Soviet muscle flexing.

While pooh-poohing the rush to build bomb shelters and expand the missile program, Conant appreciated that the furor over Sputnik had made education a top national priority. In 1958 Eisenhower put forward the National Defense Education Act, a shrewdly titled piece of legislation authorizing increased federal aid to public schools and ushering in a huge program of student loans for college, aimed particularly at those majoring in math, science, and foreign languages, all fields relevant to national security. Amid the scramble for brainpower, critics were calling for raising educational standards in American schools to keep up with the Russians, while others, such as Admiral Hyman G. Rickover, the developer of the nuclear-powered submarine, believed imposing "tough" training of talented youth was so central to the fate of the nation that he advocated the European system of segregating the brightest, university-bound students in special academies. School board superintendents and principals all over the country were clamoring for answers to questions about how their curriculum should be reorganized and how to improve instruction in science, math, and foreign languages. In terms of stimulating public interest in his study, Conant noted, the "timing was perfect."

If the Carnegie Corporation was betting that by recruiting a figure of Conant's stature it would mean the nation must take notice of his school report, it paid off. His book *The American High School Today: A First Report to Interested Citizens*, published in February 1959, spent weeks on the bestseller list—unusual for a book about education—and sold fifty thousand copies in its first three months. It garnered high praise from critics, gave impetus to extensive school reforms, and landed him on the cover of *Time* as "The Inspector General" of US public schools. (His fourth appearance on the cover was "a rare record" for someone who had never held elected office.) The postwar baby boom was propelling an enormous expansion in American education, and no one was better positioned to lead the way forward than Conant, the magazine's publisher declared, "who has done more than any other educator to throw Sputnik's red glare where it belongs—on the US public schools."

Conant's slim book supplied the answers the country was looking for in twenty-one specific reforms that were elegant in their simplicity and rejection of extremes. Essentially optimistic about the basic pattern of American schools, he saw no need for "radical changes" and instead urged numerous improvements in the identification and nurturing of talent to serve the nation. He flirted with controversy only in his assertion that too little was being done for gifted pupils: the top 15 percent who were the country's secret weapon in the ballyhooed competition with Russia. He attributed the lower enrollment of able girls in math and science courses to parental and societal influences, and urged additional guidance counseling to help focus career goals at an earlier age. His prescription was to have all students tested at an early age and provided with two tracks, so that those with greater aptitude could move on to advanced-level courses and enter college ahead of the game. The SAT, which he helped to create and was instrumental in establishing as the world's largest-scale intelligence testing program for college admissions, would help with this "sorting-out process" and would serve as a democratizing force.

Repeating the same themes that had once jolted Harvard, he argued against a caste-conscious system that would separate the intellectual elite and entrench social antagonisms, and recommended shared homerooms and citizenship courses to promote integration and cohesion. For the same reason, he believed the excessive development of private and parochial schools could be dangerously divisive. He sought to galvanize students of all classes and races across the board, arguing that "equality of esteem" was every bit as essential as equality of opportunity. He did not believe everyone should attend a four-year college and was a staunch supporter of junior colleges and vocational programs. "Each honest calling, each walk of life," he argued with his unassailable faith in public education, "has its own elite, its own aristocracy based on excellence of performance."

These were ideas Conant had delineated as far back as the early 1940s, in an unpublished book titled *What We Are Fighting to Defend*, in which he first set down his vision of a distinctive American meritocracy, with social mobility and opportunity for all. In Conant's Jeffersonian vision of American education, *Time* reported, a comprehensive high school should be a shared experience of community; a "melting pot" that not only served the academically talented but also mixed children of all social backgrounds and intellectual abilities, and provided training to each student geared to his or her needs. "A modern industrial nation needs more than a few brains: it has to uplift talent at every level. It cannot afford technological unemployables—spiritually, politically, or economically." The best way to beat the Soviets was to lead by example; to show that democracy was better than dictatorship, and this required a public school system that furthered all the hopes and aspirations of a free society.

Conant was so "intensely focused, to the point of being blindered, on the idea of a class-bound present," according to Nicholas Lemann, author of a history of the SAT, that he failed to detect the obvious flaw in his plan to build a classless society "by relentlessly classifying everyone." He did not foresee that an entire industry would spring up to help students, who could pay for it, achieve higher test scores in order to get into elite colleges, and the SAT would end up inhibiting diversity. Or that as a consequence of this flagrantly unfair competition, the intellectual elite would be resented at least as much as they were admired for the work, scheming, and investment that propelled them to the top of the educational—and societal—heap. For such a dogged realist, Lemann contends, Conant was naïve—"touchingly naïve, or willfully naïve, or just unpardonably naïve"—not to realize he was creating "a new kind of class system even more powerful than the old one."

Conant never thought he had all the answers. Ever the pragmatist, he always regarded the SAT as a work in progress, not the be-all and end-all it became. He saw his reforms as a first set of attainable goals in what should be an ongoing dynamic process. But he persevered, marshaling all the forces available to him to solve the problem of social inequity, convinced of his mission to make democracy work by revitalizing the education system, in the same way the drafters of the Constitution sought to safeguard the goals of the American Revolution. His educational doctrine helped shape many of the basic meritocratic ideas and attitudes that Americans now take for granted: the principle that admission to college should be based not on family background but on talent and achievement; the necessity of need-blind, full-aid admissions; and the policy of colleges and universities to rely on the SAT as a way to expand the pool of candidates outside the traditional geographic and socioeconomic regions of recruitment.

"Conant believed that admissions policy was a weapon in the battle against Communism," observed cultural critic Louis Menand, noting that both his educational philosophy and political ideology were conditioned by the cold war. "Conant helped create the atomic bomb; he also helped to create the SAT. Americans born after 1945 were raised in the shadow of both."

Conant's campaign for American intellectual and ideological leadership gained momentum as the cold war heated up. On November 27, 1958, Soviet Premier Nikita Khrushchev provoked a new Berlin crisis by demanding that the United States and Western Allies pull their forces out of West Berlin within six months, reviving fears of a superpower clash. Khrushchev demanded that West Berlin be converted into a demilitarized "free city." If the Allies did not accept his proposal and get out of Berlin, the Soviet Union would sign its own peace treaty with the GDR and end the Allied occupation unilaterally. "Berlin is the testicles of the West," Khrushchev stated at the time, testing US resolve. "Every time I want to make the West scream, I squeeze Berlin." Eisenhower dismissed Khrushchev's threats in a terse statement but was perturbed to hear that the French foreign minister thought some kind of "low-level" recognition of the GDR might be preferable to risking war. At the president's direction, Dulles was on his way to Brussels to formulate a unified NATO response, but before leaving, he asked for input from the three past US high commissioners to Germany.

Conant, who had long predicted that Khrushchev would venture close to war to get his way, believed the Western powers should hold their ground and warn Moscow they had no intention of relinquishing their responsibilities for the freedom and safety of the people of West Berlin. "I am still firmly of the opinion that no negotiation of any sort should be opened with the German Democratic Republic," Conant advised Dulles, who was fully prepared to send in troops to honor their commitment to a free Berlin. "And I hope that the first public statement of the Western position will make it plain that we will use force if necessary to ensure that West Berlin remains under the control of the present freely elected government, and likewise we will use force if necessary to ensure that the city is supplied *as at present*."

As the Berlin crisis kept the West on edge, and Khrushchev's high-stakes play resulted in a flurry of diplomatic activity, Conant fielded a number of offers from Eisenhower and others to return to government service. He was offered the opportunity to head or participate in commissions on foreign economic aid and national goals. Various lobbying groups also sought to enlist his support, including many members of the rebooted Committee on the Present Danger (CPD-II) who felt the Berlin situation was a ticking time bomb that could escalate into the use of nuclear weapons. Conant declined all the invitations, preferring to focus all his efforts on education. The Soviets' six-month deadline came and went, and they decided not to push their ultimatum. But with a four-power conference planned for that summer in Geneva to try to resolve the Berlin situation, Conant continued to speak out on the need to stand firm and not yield to Khrushchev's posturing and propaganda. Believing that too many Americans were unaware of the gravity of the East-West battle, he joined Bush in forming a new citizens group, the Committee to Strengthen the Frontiers of Freedom.

On July 5, 1959, *Parade* magazine featured a silver-haired, bespectacled Conant on the magazine's cover in front of an American flag, publishing what it called "an Independence Day message from a great patriot answering Khrushchev's boast that the future belongs to Communism." In his "Open Letter to America's Grandchildren," Conant, the great gladiator for democracy, endeavored to be the steadying hand he had been over the past two turbulent decades, restoring faith in the public school system, reassuring a new generation that their country would win the cold war, and dispensing soothing advice on how to survive "the long protracted struggle between two cultural patterns that seems to lie ahead." He had played the same role so many times before, during so many crises, that the phrases all had a familiar ring: "Patience and yet more patience, strength and wisdom to handle strength—all these we shall need in abundant measure," he counseled. "This nation, having arrived at the point in history where the words 'foreign policy' take on new meaning, must traverse that narrow knife edge which divides supineness from belligerency."

Although he had shifted his sights from world affairs to the classroom, it had not altered his view of the cold war competition with the Russians. Looking ahead ten years, Conant predicted the nation would be living in a "fearful world" dominated by rockets. "There is one essential for our survival," he declared in a speech upon receiving the Woodrow Wilson Award for Distinguished Service, "and that is that we possess an invulnerable system of retaliatory power and that the Soviets believe the system to be invulnerable." To defend its freedom, the United States had to keep up its military spending in order to maintain a rocket system able "to deliver thermonuclear weapons to such an extent and in such a way that at least three-fourths of the industrial complexes of the Soviet Union would be utterly destroyed." He was increasingly concerned with the role of education in preserving society and the need to nurture the vital democratic institutions of the nation to guard against totalitarianism.

He did everything he could to shake the country out of its complacency—none of his contemporaries did more—but Conant had no new ideas to offer, observed the historian Sam Bass Warner Jr., just the same pleading to maintain the nuclear freeze until the cold war thawed. "What emerged from Conant's tireless efforts," he wrote of the spent warrior, "was not a discovery of alternatives but an endless defense." Conscious that he had pounded the same drum for more than two decades, Conant sounded a little melancholic when he told an interviewer, "It is easy to be defeatist about the prospects for peace and freedom and to forecast global war. I have ventured to do otherwise with all sincerity." Quoting his beloved Jefferson, he told reporters, "The price of liberty is eternal vigilance." In the nuclear age, it was the price of survival.

He had reluctantly agreed to serve as a consultant to the National Security Council Planning Board, a one-day review of highly classified material, when a medical emergency in March 1959 landed him back in the hospital. A small benign tumor was removed from his thyroid gland, and he was on doctor's orders to reduce his workload. He was still recovering at home in New York when a panicked call came from Norice that Jim had suffered a complete nervous breakdown. It was a reoccurrence of the mania, phobias, and suicidal thoughts that had been brought on by combat stress during the war. Conant and his wife canceled a planned trip to England and rushed to Montreal to see their son. They were unprepared for the pathetic condition they found him in: frothing, delusional, paranoid, and wildly agitated. Jim was diagnosed with manic depression, known today as bipolar disorder. The doctors assured them that with rest, therapy, and medication, the symptoms would abate, but when they left their son on the mental ward that afternoon, they were both in an anguished state.

After two months in the hospital, Jim was discharged. He was "released in fragile health," recalled his cousin and Exeter classmate Gregory Henderson, and before long "the shadows came back, uninvited." Over the next eighteen months, Jim would have two more acute breakdowns and was in and out of the hospital. The treatments then available—isolation, electric shock therapy, and the powerful tranquilizer Thorazine—could calm his excited state but could not control the manic "cycles," the massive highs and miserable lows, which struck with alarming frequency. Conant consulted the finest doctors in the country, talking to specialists at McLean Hospital in Boston, Payne Whitney in New York, and Silver Hill in Connecticut, as well as a world-renowned psychiatrist in Switzerland.

On the advice of his old friend Dr. Lawrence Kubie, he sent Jim to Sheppard Pratt, a small private psychiatric hospital in Baltimore. Kubie, who had closed his New York practice to become the hospital's director of psychotherapy, had a reputation for being extremely good at courting the rich and famous, and counted the playwright Tennessee Williams among his former patients. Patty told Ted that Sheppard Pratt, with its rolling green lawns and country club look, was preferable to the other asylums because it was where the novelist F. Scott Fitzgerald had sent his wife, Zelda, when she periodically "went to pieces." As was so often the case, Conant indulged his wife's fantasy that it was a genteel place to heal for the literary set. "He was more concerned for her peace of mind," said Ted, disgusted by what he viewed as his father's concern with reputation, and reliance on the Harvard old-boy network, rather than "doing what was best for their son."

They were celebrating Christmas at Ted and Ellen's new house in Winchester, Massachusetts, in 1961 when they received word that Jim's estranged wife, who had been battling depression, had attempted suicide. With both parents in the hospital at the same time, the children had taken refuge at the neighbors'. Conant spent the next two weeks flying back and forth to Montreal, arranging for Norice's hospitalization and scrambling to find a live-in nanny to look after the three young children. Lawyers were hired, trust funds set up, and a psychiatrist appointed to supervise the care of the entire family, effectively removing him from the equation. Conant quickly packed his wife off to Germany for an extended holiday to help put the wretched business behind her. "After that, he washed his hands of the whole mess," said Ted. "He did not want my mother disturbed, he did not want their life disrupted any more than it already had been. It was out of sight, out of mind."

Jim would recover and resume work on a Baltimore newspaper, but he struggled with the crushing apathy induced by the drugs. He was still "on the edge," Conant jotted in his diary in the dispassionate tone of a scientist observing the anomalies of the brain, noting that his son's moods were still decidedly on the "manic side."

Jim's life slowly unraveled. "He tried to slug it out in those lower depths," recalled Henderson, who visited him in places he "never knew existed," filled with the homeless and criminally insane, "the jetsam companions this Harvard president's son was cast among." His illness robbed him of everything, leaving in its wake "lonely apartments, dissolved marriages, and children adrift from any real home." He was increasingly unkempt, his tweed jacket tattooed with cigarette burns, fingers stained yellow with nicotine. When in the grip of mania, Jim drank to excess—a dangerous cocktail when mixed with heavy medication—and wandered the streets arguing with his demons, telephoned at all hours of the night, and repeatedly reported his brother to the FBI as a Communist agent, resulting in more than one follow-up investigation.

Conant and his wife were appalled by Jim's steady deterioration. After one harrowing episode, when he went off the rails at their summer retreat in Randolph and disappeared in the night, a neighbor, Judge R. Ammi Cutter, had to drive all over the countryside looking for him. He pulled Jim out of a local bar and called an ambulance to cart him back to Sheppard Pratt. Patty, mortified by all the gossip, had reached her limit and refused to allow him to return. "It's all very well for us to go through the dread and anxiety we have lived with so long—that's our lot!—but we have inflicted enough on the Randolph community," she wrote her husband. Then she softened her tone, adding dismally, "I'm afraid I can't see his problems very objectively anymore."

Jim's downward spiral took an emotional toll on the extended family, especially the Conants' youngest son, who was terrified he would "go the same way" as his brother and uncles. After Jim's breakdown in 1959, Ted and his wife received a letter from Dr. Kubie informing them there was no need to be concerned about the mental health of their offspring—one-year-old James and a new baby daughter, Jennet—and stating categorically that Jim's condition was not caused by genetic factors. It was obvious Conant had asked Kubie to write the letter to put their fears to rest, but his glib assurances had the opposite effect. "I wondered what the hell kind of mad family I had married into," Ellen recalled. "Here I was a new mother with two small children condescendingly being told, 'Don't worry, dear.' It was frightening. I thought that none of them were living in the real world." Ted was increasingly tense, and at times worryingly wrought up, the smallest setbacks sending him into an uncontrollable rage. Ellen was convinced her husband's problems were rooted in his relationship with his rigid, judgmental father. "The tragedy of Ted's life is that he felt he had to revolt against what he admires most in his heart," she told her mother-in-law angrily, demanding to know how such an acclaimed educator could have been such an inadequate parent. "His admiration for [his father] and all he stands for is boundless," yet the two could "barely speak to one another."

Turning his back on an ill wind, Conant concentrated on his work. In his new incarnation as "educational statesman," he kept up a "cruel pace," one journalist observed, visiting 125 more schools over the next year, giving speeches and interviews, running for planes and buses, sleeping in bad hotels, and eating lukewarm chicken lunches in an endless succession of cafeterias. The second installment of his Carnegie study, *Slums and Suburbs: A Commentary on Schools in Metropolitan Areas*, completed in 1961 and "written in wrath" at the conditions he found in Philadelphia, Chicago, Saint Louis, and Detroit, ignited a firestorm with his warning that ghetto schools were woefully inadequate and that the equivalent of "social dynamite" was building up in the big cities, especially in the African American community. Unless prompt action was taken to improve slum schools, and unless there were "drastic changes" in the advancement and employment prospects of African American youth, he feared the "dangerous social situation" would "explode." To add a cold war rationale to his wake-up call, Conant argued that not only was this social injustice unacceptable, it left inner-city children more vulnerable to the "relentless pressures" of Communism: "What can words like 'freedom,' 'liberty,' and 'equality of opportunity' mean for these young people?" he asked.

The landmark 1954 Supreme Court decision *Brown v. Board of Education* had outlawed segregation in public schools, and by the early 1960s, the country had embarked on a painful struggle to attain the equality of opportunity Conant had long espoused. It was a huge step in the right direction, but there was continued resistance across the country, and Conant was impatient for change. "These situations call for action, not hairsplitting arguments," he argued, insisting that ignoring racial inequality would put the nation at risk. He was sounding the alarm again, only this time for the children for whom his meritocratic solutions did not apply. "For the first time the reserved, understating New England scientist and university administrator appeared moved to anger," observed the *New York Times*. "He has seen the underprivileged slums and the prestige-obsessed over-privileged suburbs. The sight offended his sense of justice as much as his ideology."

Slums and Suburbs, published in 1961, made headlines at a time when the civil rights movement was at its peak. While some reviewers lauded the book as trenchant and prophetic, Conant infuriated black leaders, who seized on his criticism of "token integration"—the transporting of pupils across large cities—as tacit approval of the "separate but equal" doctrine and condemned his views. He had argued that a better long-term strategy would be to spend more money to upgrade inner-city schools and the sur-rounding area, "to bring the schools closer to the needs of the people in each neighborhood," and invest in better housing and business opportunities. His demand that pupils be taught "marketable skills"—any real vocational training that could lead to jobs and be a vehicle of opportunity—was mis-interpreted as an attempt to create what one critic called "an army of shoe-shine boys." After the National Association for the Advancement of Colored People (NAACP) challenged his assertion that the real issue was "not racial integration but socioeconomic integration," Conant resigned himself to the fact that the issue was already so inflamed he could make little headway, and retreated. By the time the Signet edition was issued in paperback in 1964, he had revised his views, and stated he had been wrong to oppose busing.

Accustomed by now to shrugging off attacks, he quickly turned his at-tention to the education of teachers, despite a colleague's admonition that it would make the past disputes "seem as nothing by comparison." Undeterred, Conant kicked the "hornets' nest," writing a stinging critique of traditional teacher training—alienating many of his peers in the process. Calling the existing certification system "scandalously remiss," he proposed making ac-tual teacher performance in the classroom the major criteria for licensing public school teachers, and recommended significantly reducing theoretical courses in teaching methods. He cited the glaring shortcomings turned up by his study, expressing alarm that more than one third of all seventh- and eighth-grade mathematics classes in the country were taught by teachers with less than two college courses in the subject. He went on to declare the certification system "bankrupt," referred to education extension courses as

"Mickey Mouse" offerings, and labeled the teachers who took them to earn easy credits "opium smokers."

Those who hoped Conant might be mellowing with age were in for a surprise. He was more outspoken than ever, his tone magnificently sulfurous. All his books were calls to action, and even his establishment opponents had to acknowledge they were of "unequaled impact," attributing his success to his "missionary zeal" and willingness to crisscross the country popularizing for his reforms. He was driven by his "burning faith in the American social experiment," said Frank Keppel, one of Conant's closest Harvard colleagues and Carnegie advisor. "He did not enjoy controversy, but was often involved in it. His sense of responsibility simply drew him to move ahead." A *Los Angeles Examiner* columnist quoted Conant's favorite motto, which for many years hung on the wall behind his desk in the Harvard president's office: "Behold the turtle—he makes progress only when he sticks his neck out." "He hasn't pulled his neck in yet," the writer observed. "That's the kind of man he is, and the attitude is implicit in his every word and gesture."

After writing six books in six years and running through $1 million of Carnegie Corporation financing—all the royalties were plowed back into research—Conant found himself feeling restless again. Anticipating the outcry that would accompany the publication of his last installment, 1963's *The Education of American Teachers*, he decided it might be a good time to get out of town. In the habit of thinking several moves ahead, he already had a plan. A brief trip to Berlin in 1962 had started him thinking about the future now that the Soviets had erected a wall dividing the city. The Iron Curtain, which had been "transparent" in his time as ambassador, was now made of concrete and topped with barbed wire—a constant reminder of the cold war. No longer could one say, as he had done so often as high commissioner, that Berlin was the "showplace of democracy." Nikita Khrushchev's immediate purpose was to put a stop to the humiliating exodus of East Germans to the West, but the perimeter had a profound impact on the isolated city, surrounded by Russian troops. To Conant, "The armed East German police who looked from watchtowers over the wall provided proof that the potentialities of a third world war were ever present."

The youthful American president, John Fitzgerald Kennedy, who ran on post-Sputnik fears and the mythical "missile gap," had won office with his promise of a reinvigorated defense policy. But for a week after the wire fence was rolled out and work started on a more permanent partition in August 1961, Kennedy made no public protest over the Berlin Wall, casting doubt on America's pledge to protect the "outpost of freedom." West Berliners were understandably furious that the Americans had not knocked down the wall. They felt betrayed and abandoned. They had seen their city torn in half, had their freedom curtailed, and in some cases had been cruelly separated from family and friends. In an attempt to boost morale, Berlin's mayor, Willy Brandt, was planning an ambitious project to turn free Berlin into a major cultural center. Conant was approached about lending his prestige to a new Pedagogical Center that would make Berlin the leading city in Europe in the field of education. When he returned to New York, he wrote a memorandum on the tense political situation in Berlin at the request of the Ford Foundation, mentioning the planned education center. Before long, Conant was asked to go back under the foundation's auspices to help build the center and strengthen the German-American friendship.

On June 26, 1963, a few weeks after he and Patty arrived in Berlin, Kennedy came through on a much-anticipated state visit. It was a bright, unseasonably warm summer day, and they decided to join the quarter million Berliners who were gathering downtown to hear the American president's address from the balcony of the town hall. "There are many people in the world who really don't understand, or say they don't, what is the great issue between the free world and the Communist world," Kennedy told the cheering throngs. "Let them come to Berlin." When he told his audience "in the world of freedom, the proudest boast is, "*Ich bin ein Berliner*," pronouncing the German words in his strong Boston accent, Conant could not help smiling. He experienced the tremendous rush of recognition and gratitude that surged through the crowd and felt that Kennedy's speech had done a great deal to restore their belief that America stood with them. "The president went very far in committing himself emotionally to the Berliners," he noted in his diary, pleased by the clear statement of US support, and seeing it as a continuation of the solidarity with the German cause he had voiced during his years there. "'If one wants to understand the modern world, let him come to Berlin.' Excellent and moving sentiments with which I not only heartily agree but could claim to have anticipated."

The following week, the White House announced that for his outstanding contributions to science and education, Conant would be awarded the Presidential Medal of Freedom, the highest award given by the government to civilians. President Kennedy would bestow the medals in a ceremony on

December 6, 1963. Patty excitedly made plans for their trip to Washington, with friends offering to organize a party in his honor. On November 22, just before they were due to leave for the United States, Conant was at the closing banquet of a teachers' conference at the Hotel Kempinski when the manager approached and whispered in his ear in German that Kennedy had been shot. Stunned, and racked with anxiety and horror, he struggled to remain composed and asked to be kept informed of any developments. Moments later, the manager returned and "with a despairing gesture" told him the president was dead. Out of respect for their American guests, their German hosts and dinner companions stood and observed a moment of silence for the slain president. He and Patty stumbled blindly through the lobby, in a hurry to be away.

They sat up half the night listening to the news on the radio. Outside, tens of thousands of Germans took to the streets in a torchlit procession, "full of sorrow and worry." It was impossible not to think of Kennedy's enormous impact on Berlin, as well as the "spirit of optimism" that followed his successful confrontation of Khrushchev over the Cuban Missile Crisis in October 1962, and how that "new spirit" mounted still higher after his triumphant visit. The next morning, they joined other stricken members of the diplomatic community at a military service. The brightness of the day contrasted sharply with the somber nature of the occasion, and when two buglers sounded the first melancholy notes of taps, both he and Patty felt it "went right through our hearts."

He was struck by the force of the emotion, considering that he had never particularly liked Joe Kennedy Sr., and they had often butted heads, especially when his youngest son, Edward "Ted" Kennedy, was expelled from Harvard for cheating on a Spanish exam during his sophomore year. "I found myself asking myself why I, a cold, reserved New Englander and not a personal friend, should have been so overcome last night and at the ceremony this morning," he wrote his old friend Tracy Voorhees. "I felt, still feel, the way I did the afternoon of Pearl Harbor. I don't know the answer myself, but almost all of free Berlin feels the same way."

Conant assumed the award ceremony would be canceled, but when word came that it would be taking place as scheduled, he and Patty flew at once to Washington. On the morning of December 6, Conant and his wife went to the White House, where the mood was a strange mixture of "sadness and festivity." A touching note of congratulations from Robert F. Kennedy, a Harvard student in the Conant era like his brothers, added to the poignancy of the day. They gathered in the State Dining Room, where the new president, Lyndon B. Johnson, opened by saying that despite the shameful events of two weeks earlier, this was a moment of great pride. He presented Conant with the medal with special distinction, and read the citation: "Scientist and educator, he has led the American people in the fight to save our most precious resource—our children." It felt a bit like old home week, with Felix Frankfurter and Jack McCloy collecting white stars at the same time.

Conant returned to Berlin for what would turn out to be a two-year stay. German bureaucracy moved at such an excruciatingly slow pace that by the fall of 1964, when construction on the new building was supposed to have begun, no stone had been turned and no money allocated. By now an old hand at intimidating bureaucrats, he knew the one sure way to get results was to shine a light on the problem. He told the mayor "politely but firmly" that if the necessary funds were not voted, and he had to leave Berlin with nothing accomplished, "neither the collapse of the brilliant plan or my own frustration would go unnoticed." Conant got the funds. When he finally left for America in May 1965, the center was on its way to becoming a reality. Brandt, who had become a good friend, likened Conant's critical role in rallying support for the project to that of a "fleet in being" which never had to fire a shot yet was the decisive factor in the confrontation.

His sabbatical in Germany may not have been as productive as he had hoped, but it afforded ample time for what he described as "leisurely reflection." It was impossible to turn a corner of that historic city without starting a train of reminiscences. "As I ticked off the dates of modern history in my mind," he recalled, "I almost always found myself starting with a picture of that placid world which started to go to bits just when I graduated from college in 1914. It seemed inconceivable that Americans could have ever been so aloof from international affairs and so self-righteous as we were then." On his return from Europe, Conant, who had cranked out several more books on education reform, planned to embark on his last book project: his memoir. He told his editors he expected it would fill several volumes. In the fall of 1964 he had turned down a job offer from Sargent Shriver, director of the Peace Corps and the newly created Office of Economic Opportunity, to lead and direct the troops on the educational front of the Johnson administration's War on Poverty. His excuse was his age, though he later agreed to join the advisory council. The truth was that apart from speaking out on the education issues he felt most strongly about, he was ready to step off the public stage.

On the way home, he and Patty stopped off in Paris, where he intended to treat his wife to a grand holiday, when a sudden spell of weakness caused by an irregular heart rhythm landed him in the hospital. He spent two weeks in the American Hospital undergoing tests and receiving intravenous medication. Released in late June, he flew straight to New York and checked himself back into the hospital. He was put on a regimen of digitalis and other medications, but was cautioned against any rigorous exercise. His heart condition meant no more hiking the steep mountain trails of New Hampshire. He was still absorbing this piece of bad news when Patty, who had also been under the weather, was diagnosed with colon cancer. She underwent immediate surgery, and the malignant tumor was removed. They caught the cancer before it had spread, but the operation left her with a colostomy bag. Weak and dejected, Patty could not face yet another house search and move in what she called their "lone wolf existence," changing countries and addresses every few years. They spent most of the next three months convalescing in a succession of hotels and seaside resorts, "picking ourselves up by our bootstraps." In October they settled in a new apartment in Manhattan House, and Conant began work on his memoir.

He spent mornings writing at home in his study. He had two unlisted phone numbers, one reserved for calls to the Princeton office of the Educational Testing Service, over which he spent hours dictating drafts of the chapters of his book, and another so that he could talk "uninterruptedly" to various VIPs, as Patty put it to a friend. He did not like to go into Carnegie's New York office because he had "too many visitors." He felt better but tired easily, and to Patty's dismay, he cut back on their social engagements in order to conserve his energy for work. He refused to return to Randolph now that hiking was off-limits. "He can't bear to look at those peaks," she confided, "and be condemned to the one easy walk in our neighboring woods, which bored him to extinction last summer." When John S. Dickey, the president of Dartmouth, offered him a chair, they sold the remote cottage and looked for some place to buy in the college town of Hanover, New Hampshire. Cautious to the end, Conant bought a neat white house a quarter mile from Mary Hitchcock Memorial Hospital and around the corner from his cardiologist.

The further he got with his memoir, the more dubious he found the enterprise. One of his Harper & Row editors urged him to risk enough of himself to write "an autobiography with my heart on my sleeve instead of the history which I started out to write," he reported to a colleague at Carnegie, which was underwriting his latest effort. "Whether she or I will win this struggle remains to be seen." He was honest enough with himself to know that his strictly factual account left out a great deal—most of his work on the Manhattan Project, except where he felt obliged to address published accounts of certain incidents—and skimped on a number of Harvard scandals.

The book, *My Several Lives: Memoirs of a Social Inventor*, came out in early 1970 and was reviewed widely. The general consensus was summed up by one headline, "Good Man, Dull Book." One reviewer saw beyond the exhaustive account of accomplishment—fighting three wars, two hot, one cold; transforming Harvard; rearming Germany; reforming the education system; and authoring twenty-one books—to something the author himself might have missed: "Mr. Conant called his book the memoirs of a social inventor. In fact, his major social invention may turn out to be the invention of himself as a social influence."

In the preface, by way of an apology for the immodest hawking of his achievements, Conant wrote: "The White Knight in *Through the Looking Glass* is the model for all egotistical inventors." He went on to explain that the Lewis Carroll novel had a special significance in his life: the night before he was born, his older sisters, eager to know whether their new sibling would be a brother or sister, had made their aunt promise to leave their favorite book open on the table to the telltale page. So it happened that he was born "under the sign of the White Knight."

This was the story he recounted to his grandchildren when he read aloud to them from the book, the same dog-eared first edition in its frayed red cloth cover that had been his as a boy. It would require little imagination to believe that Conant, in his later years, was also driven by the desire to embody the nobler definition of the white knight: the beleaguered champion who rides to the rescue. He spent the last decade of his life trying belatedly to fill that role for his family. He struck a fragile truce with Ted—strained at times by fierce arguments over Vietnam, which he publicly supported along with Eisenhower and Truman—helping his son's career in educational television, offering financial support, and reveling in the role of "Grandpa." He found it easier to relate to his grandchildren than to his own children, flying all five youngsters—sans parents—to Hawaii to celebrate his eightieth birthday and tour Pearl Harbor in 1973.

He tried, and failed, to reconcile himself to Jim's disturbed state, put off by his Puritan fatalism and a kind of squeamishness. In the end, he distanced himself, relying on a growing list of doctors and lawyers to perform what Ted called the necessary "triage." Jim's latest doctor attributed the manic depression to a hereditary chemical imbalance, and prescribed a new drug called lithium, which had proven effective in Europe in cases of treatment-resistant depression. Jim was started on the experimental psychiatric medication before it was legally available in the United States, but the huge doses had debilitating side effects. His condition stabilized, and he was able to hold down a job as chief editorial writer for the *Baltimore-News American*, though he still suffered manic episodes that led to relapses, hospitalizations, a second divorce, and declining health. Compounding the tragedy, both of Jim's biological children would be diagnosed as bipolar, continuing the sad saga into the next generation. When Jim died at the age of fifty-seven on a rundown ward of the Veterans Administration Hospital in Washington, his cousin noted that in his later years, there had been "flickers of bitterness" at the perceived neglect. "What Jim would have liked is some affirmation of caring," he said, "for all he promised and tried so hard to be."

A few weeks after his memoir was published, Conant had an unexpected reunion with Bush and Groves in Washington, when the three pillars of World War II received the Atomic Pioneer Award for their contributions to the development of nuclear weapons. The current chairman of the AEC, Glenn Seaborg, felt that the honor was long overdue and that some of the unpopular stands they had taken with regard to postwar nuclear development may have prevented them from getting the recognition they deserved. On February 27, 1970, President Nixon bestowed the gold medals. During an informal conversation in his office, the president asked, "Were you all convinced before the first device was set off that it was going to work?" The question elicited an amused response. "Oh no," Bush said, grinning. Conant agreed, adding with a mischievous nod at his colleagues, "These two gentlemen were going to get the blame." After teasing Bush and Groves for not having run out to buy his book, Conant gave them each a signed copy with the fond inscription: "With grateful memories of the days we worked together so pleasantly and effectively."

In a radio interview, Conant admitted that as an old man his thoughts often strayed back to the early days, but not to the Manhattan Project. "I do not look back on that with any pleasure," he said. "It was a tough job. What

I look back on with pleasure is when I was a young carefree professor of chemistry doing my own research." When asked about the difficult decisions he was forced to make on the wartime committees, the seventy-seven-year-old scientist became querulous, almost but not quite acknowledging there were some that still gnawed at his soul.

"Well, the whole fact that the atomic bomb turned out to be what it was, and all the arguments about whether it should have been dropped," he said wearily, his voice trailing off, "I'm never free from that." The power and influence thrust on him by the government he had tried to use as a force for good by becoming an apostle for education. Having changed the subject, he was off again, lecturing his interviewer about financing elementary education in New Jersey, which he predicted would be a major problem in the next ten to twenty years.

Conant was philosophical about all the criticism, writing to George Kistiakowsky in the spring of 1972 that he was not discouraged by the "negative voices about science." Progress could not be stopped, and most nostalgia for a less complicated time was, in his view, misplaced. "A lot of people think they would rather live in the 18th century than today," he mused, using the slightly mocking tone he always employed when pointing out the hypocrisy of the establishment. What they usually had in mind "without admitting it" was being one of the privileged few with their own farm and a retinue of servants. "But if one lists all the technological changes since 1800," he added, "I think not one of us would be willing to go without."

The letter echoed what he wrote in his book *On Understanding Science: An Historical Approach*, shortly after the war:

> The natural tendency of people to recoil with horror from all thought of further scientific advance because of the implications of the atomic bomb is to my mind based on a misapprehension of the nature of the universe. As I watched the secret development of the atomic bomb through four years of the war, I often thought of the work being done at the same time . . . of the then-secret research on penicillin, on DDT, on antimalarial drugs, on the use of blood plasma, and realized how much these scientific advances meant for the future of mankind. I often thought of Emerson's famous essay on the Laws of Compensation:
>
> "With every influx of light comes new danger . . . There is a crack in everything God has made. It would seem there is always the vin-

dictive stroke, this kick of the gun, certifying that the law is fatal; that in nature nothing can be given, all things are sold."

Over the next few years, Conant became increasingly frail. His deafness made conversation difficult, and he spent his days reading, becoming increasingly silent and withdrawn. He was in the middle of Theodore Sorensen's biography of Jack Kennedy, making meticulous notes in the margins in a shaky hand, when he suffered the first of a series of strokes in the summer of 1977. For a man of his exacting intellect, the confusion that descended was the ultimate indignity. He died at the age of eighty-four in a nursing home in Hanover, New Hampshire, on February 11, 1978.

Despite Patty's protests, Conant had insisted on a private burial with no religious service, so he was quietly interred in the Richards' family plot in Mount Auburn Cemetery in Cambridge. Whether he wanted to spend all of eternity surrounded by her crazy relatives is open to debate, but he lost that battle. At a small, decidedly unostentatious service at Harvard in April, George Kistiakowsky, among others, paid tribute to the soft-spoken man who had made an indelible mark on the century, and said good-bye to a "cool Yankee who could be a warm friend."

In the weeks that followed, Patty received hundreds of letters and telegrams from scientists, educators, politicians, and heads of state mourning the loss of an American original and the end of an era. But among the handful she saved, and treasured, was a brief note from their old friend the patrician lawyer and novelist Louis Auchincloss, who had been part of a monthly "round table" discussion group with Conant in New York, and knew the private man who was accessible to only a chosen few. "Never again," he wrote, "can we expect to find the same combination of humor and wisdom and gentle kindness with a seemingly infinite knowledge of the hard old world and its ways."

After Conant's death, a *New York Times* editorial noted that "to say that he was the last of his breed would be too defeatist a view of America's future. But it is only realistic to acknowledge that a vacancy exists. There is not now at any major university a leader concerned with the whole of American education. The nation could use a successor in the line that led from Jefferson to Eliot to James Bryant Conant."

The title of the editorial was "The Conant Vacancy."

ACKNOWLEDGMENTS

I am greatly indebted to my parents, Ellen and Theodore R. Conant, for giving me access to all of my grandparents' private papers, correspondence, diaries, journals, scrapbooks, and photographs. They were enormously generous with their time, patiently sitting for countless interviews and fielding endless probing, sometimes painful, questions. My father's passing midway through the process, at age 89 in October 2015, made his contribution all the more precious. I would also thank my brother, Jim, for his forbearance as usual. And I must acknowledge my cousin, Clark Conant, a psychologist, for her kindness in helping me to shine a light on the dark corners of our family history and contribute to the story of how far we have come in understanding bipolar disorder, and how far we still have to go.

I am grateful to numerous historians and scholars in various fields whose works helped me in the writing of this book: James B. Conant's autobiography, *My Several Lives: Memoirs of a Social Inventor*, which in turn was informed by the investigations of two graduate students in the School of Education at the University of Wisconsin, Charles Biebel and William M. Tuttle Jr., who wrote their doctoral theses about different aspects of Conant's career, and had the benefit of his assistance. A third thesis, by Jeanne Amster at Harvard's School of Education, was also very helpful. An undergraduate thesis by James Hershberg for Harvard College which grew into a massive study of cold war atomic policy, *James B. Conant: Harvard to Hiroshima and the Making of the Nuclear Age*, was also an invaluable resource. Over the last twenty years, and three books on the Manhattan Project, I have been the recipient of wisdom and guidance from many of my grandfather's friends and fellow scientists, all of whom took the time to share their memories—both good and bad—and spoke with touching confidence and candor. I must single out for special thanks George and Elaine Kistiakowsky for first helping me to find my way, and Philip Morrison for his inexhaustible humor and insight. They are sorely missed.

A book of this kind requires a tremendous amount of archival research, and I was helped immeasurably by my wonderful and dedicated colleague Ruth Tenenbaum, who was with me every step of the way over this long, arduous journey. Her ability to unearth the unexpected and track down the most obscure documents and scraps of information never ceases to amaze me. Her encouragement in low moments will never be forgotten. I also benefitted from a very able researcher in Christopher Edling, a Columbia University MFA student, who ransacked hundreds of hours of oral histories. I must also recognize the research staff at Harvard's Pusey Library for their unstinting efforts in plumbing Conant's extensive archive. I would also like to acknowledge all the able people connected with the Atomic Heritage Foundation, especially Nathaniel Weisenberg. For his scientific expertise, and for taking the time to scrutinize my creaky chemistry, I must thank the brilliant Charles Sawyers. Ann Daly's assistance at CBS was above and beyond the call of duty.

My thanks as always to Alice Mayhew, who has been the driving force behind all five of my books. I count myself fortunate to have the support of Jonathan Karp and the entire S&S team, with a special nod to Stuart Roberts for staying on top of so many loose ends. My literary agent, Kristine Dahl, has been a rock for more than twenty-five years. On the home front, Cavelle Sukhai provided what my grandfather liked to call the necessary "logistical support" without which our troop would surely have floundered. Dear friends have provided support of every other kind. A shout-out to all those who went over the final draft of the manuscript with a fine-tooth comb. Above all, I must thank my husband and son for enduring yet another World War II book. You were cheerful and willing participants, listened to my stories again and again, and you have my love and gratitude.

ABBREVIATIONS

Frequently cited people and sources are identified by the following abbreviations.

AM	*Atlantic Monthly*
BDG	*Boston Daily Globe*
BG	*Boston Globe*
BH	*Boston Herald*
BL	Bancroft Library, University of California
BMB	Bernard M. Baruch
CCR	Carnegie Corporation Records
CFP	Conant Family Papers
CUOH	Columbia University Oral History
DDE	Dwight D. Eisenhower
DDEL	Dwight D. Eisenhower Library
EOL	Ernest O. Lawrence
GRC	Grace "Patty" Richards Conant
GTR	Greenough Thayer Richards
HC	*Harvard Crimson*
HLS	Henry L. Stimson
HST	Harry S. Truman
HUA	Harvard University Archives
JBC	James Bryant Conant
JBCPP	James Bryant Conant Personal Papers
JBCPRESP	James Bryant Conant Presidential Papers
JFD	John Foster Dulles
JRO	J. Robert Oppenheimer
LRG	Leslie R. Groves

LOC	Library of Congress
MSL	*My Several Lives* by James B. Conant
MTR	Miriam Thayer Richards
NA	National Archives
NDRC	National Defense Research Committee
NY	*New Yorker*
NYHT	*New York Herald Tribune*
NYT	*New York Times*
OSRD	Office of Scientific Research and Development
PUOH	Princeton University Oral History
TFAR	*Twenty-Fifth Anniversary Report* by James B. Conant
TRC	Theodore "Ted" Richards Conant
TU	Tufts University
TWR	Theodore William Richards
VB	Vannevar Bush
WL	Walter Lippmann
WP	*Washington Post*
WTR	William "Bill" Theodore Richards
YU	Yale University

Notes

Chapter 1: Atomic Pioneer

1 *"Here sits a man . . ."*: JBC's descriptions of the Moscow mission and Christmas Eve dinner at the Kremlin in Moscow are taken from his handwritten seventeen-page diary covering the events from December 10 to December 29, 1945, JBCPP, HUA. There are numerous firsthand accounts of Molotov's famous toast at the Kremlin dinner on December 24, 1945: JBC's memoir, *My Several Lives*; Charles E. Bohlen, *Witness to History, 1929–1969*; James F. Byrnes, *All in One Lifetime* and *Speaking Frankly*; George F. Kennan, *Memoirs, 1925–1950*.

1 *"There is no foolishness . . ."*: JBC Moscow diary, December 20, 1945, JBCPP.

2 *"anxious to speak to him . . ."*: MSL, 476.

4 *"If we fail to approach them . . ."*: Robert L. Messer, *The Making of a Cold Warrior*, 138.

5 *"only trying to be pleasant"*: Byrnes, *Speaking Frankly*, 267.

5 *"speak of secret matters," "Here sits a man . . ."*: JBC Moscow diary, December 24, 1945. Also see "Conant: Werk eines Mannes," *Der Spiegel*, March 25, 1953.

6 *"Comrade Molotov . . . ," "Here's to Professor Conant"*: JBC Moscow diary, December 24, 1945.

6 *"humorous remarks," "But I can say . . ."*: Ibid.

6 *"a shrewd but kindly . . . ," "Those were fine words . . ."*: Ibid.

7 *"There in the banquet hall . . ."*: Bohlen, *Witness to History*, 249.

7 *"pinned their hopes"*: MSL, 483.

7 *"crass nationalistic movie . . ."*: JBC Moscow diary, December 25, 1945.

8 *"unfavorable evidence"*: MSL, 483.

8 *"time, but not too much . . . ," "There is no defense . . ."*: DBG, December 12, 1945, MSL, 488–89.

8 *"One thing has been as clear . . ."*: Ibid.

9   *"social inventor"*: Ibid., xv.

9   *"potentialities for destruction"*: Ibid, 304.

10 *"The verdict of history . . ."*: Ibid.

CHAPTER 2: A DORCHESTER BOY

11 *"He is manly . . ."*: D. O. S. Lowell to J. G. Hart, May 4, 1910, JBC file, Office of the Registrar, HUA.

11 *"proper Bostonian"*: MSL, 3; JBC, "A Guide to Public Education for the Conscientious Citizen," unpublished manuscript, foreword, 2, CCR.

11 *"missed the boat"*: Author recollection.

12 *"I'm studying . . ."*: Kermit Roosevelt, "Harvard's Prize Kibitzer," pt. 1, *Saturday Evening Post*, April 23, 1949, 72.

12 *"He had a chip on his shoulder . . ."*: Interview with Martha "Muffy" Henderson Coolidge.

12 *"best people"*: John P. Marquand, *The Late George Apley*, 215–19.

12 *"Ever since he was eight . . ."*: *Boston Sunday Post*, May 1, 1933.

12 *"Dorchester Boy . . ."*: BG, May 20, 1933.

13 *"may as well have been . . ."*: Interview with John B. Fox Jr., a historian, former senior advisor to the dean of the Faculty of Arts and Sciences of Harvard College, and author of an unpublished history, *The Faculty of Arts and Sciences at Harvard University, 1686–1933*.

13 *"only the most intrepid . . . ," "country seats," "streetcar suburbs"*: Douglass Shand-Tucci, *Ashmont*, 12.

13 *"a Boston man . . ."*: *Boston Sunday Post*, May 14, 1933.

13 *"The Lowells speak . . ."*: Roosevelt, "Harvard's Prize Kibitzer," 39.

14 *"a single Harvard sheepskin," "For Harvard to 'marry' . . ."*: *Boston Sunday Post*, May 14, 1933.

14 *"boiling"*: Ibid.

14 *"color" pieces*: Roosevelt, "Harvard's Prize Kibitzer," 39.

14 *" 'Skid' and 'Spike' "*: BDG, May 15, 1933.

14 *"intimate details," "You may be sure . . ."*: Esther Conant to JBC, June 19, 1933, CFP.

14 *"Science and Puritanism . . ."*: George Kistiakowsky, eulogy of JBC, 1978, 1, CFP.

15 *"No matter what . . ."*: John W. Gardner, "Reminiscences," Carnegie Corporation of New York, 2, 1998, CCR.

15 *"natural aristocracy"*: Thomas Jefferson to John Adams, October 28, 1813, *The Adams-Jefferson Letters: The Complete Correspondence Between Thomas Jefferson and Abigail and John Adams*, edited by Lester J. Cappon, Vol. 1 (Chapel Hill: University of North Carolina Press for the Institute of Early American History and Culture, Williamsburg, VA, 1959).

15 *"pioneer life"*: MSL, 3.

16 *Salters' Company*: Clifford K. Shipton, *Roger Conant*, 10. Includes detailed account of early Conant family history and launching of the Puritan commonwealth at Salem.

16 *Naumkeag*: Ibid., 59.

16 *"prudent moderation," "city of peace"*: William Hubbard, *A General History of New England, from the discovery to MDCLXXX* (Boston: Charles C. Little and James Brown, 1923), 110–13.

16 *cordwainer*: *BG*, May 20, 1933.

17 *"The family was poor . . . ," "not pleasant," "one bright spot"*: MSL, 7.

17 *"the grand but simple lady . . .":* Ibid.

17 *"Made on the Massachusetts South Shore"*: *BDG*, May 22, 1933.

17 *"special faith," "Here was to be found . . .":* MSL, 9–10, and descriptions of early family life, 7–12.

19 *"a regiment of women"*: MSL, 8–11.

20 *"Trinitarian doctrines"*: Ibid.

20 *"What my mother approved . . .":* Ibid.

20 *disliked the dull curriculum*: Charles DeWayne Biebel, "Politics, Pedagogues and Statesmanship," 12.

21 *"possible threats"*: JBC, "A Guide to Public Education."

21 *"built for bicycles," "horse-and buggy age"*: MSL, 6, 4.

21 *"full swing"*: MSL, 7.

21 *"scourge of the community"*: Interview with John B. Fox Jr.

21 *"Our own homes . . .":* JBC, "A Guide to Public Education," 2–3.

22 *"I must have breathed . . .":* Ibid.

22 *"Of this, I was quite certain . . .":* MSL, 5.

22 *"marvel," "standard equipment," "monkeying"*: MSL, 14.

22 *"It may be that my love . . .":* JBC, "A Guide to Public Education."

22 *"an applied chemist"*: MSL, 15.

23 *"cold winter afternoons . . .":* JBC Diary, JBCPP.

23 *"Young Edison . . .":* *NY*, June 3, 1933.

23 *"silent and nose-holding awe"*: Biebel, "Politics, Pedagogues and Statesmanship," 16.

23 *"out batting a baseball . . . ," "pedant"*: *BG*, May 14, 1933.

23 *"Sintific"*: JBC to James Scott Conant, July 10, 1904, CFP.

23 *"It was agreed . . .":* JBC, "A Guide to Public Education." Detailed descriptions of Conant's early schooling and high school years can also be found in Biebel, "Politics, Pedagogues and Statesmanship"; Jeanne Ellen Amster, "Meritocracy Ascendant"; and William M. Tuttle Jr., "James B. Conant, Pressure Groups, and the National Defense." Roxbury Latin entrance exam: *BSG*, March 14, 1933, and *NY*, September 12, 1936, 23. JBC, "A Guide to Public Education," foreword.

24 *"college was either for those . . .":* Ibid., 5.

24 *"Must do work in penmanship"*: School report, JBCPP.

25 *"towhead with a Dutch cut . . .":* *Boston Sunday Post*, May 14, 1933.

25 *one of Black's disciples*: MSL, 18.

25 *"You don't expect . . .":* *BG*, May 16, 1933.

25 *"prompt signs of facility"*: *BSG*, March 14, 1933.

26 *"skeptical"*: MSL, 17.

26 *"backbone"*: *BSG*, March 14, 1933.

26 *"an exciting business . . .":* MSL, 16–17.

26 *"By the way . . .":* Ibid.

27 *"Why don't you try . . .":* Ibid.

27 *"unusual mental power"*: N. Henry Black to J. G. Hart, May 3, 1910, JBC file, Office of the Registrar, HUA.

27 *"My career was now clearly marked . . ."*: MSL, 17.

27 *"GREAT!!!"*: JBC 1908 diary, JBCPP. JBC to Marjorie "Midge" Conant, March 31, 1908. JBCPP.

27 *"I, James Bryant Conant"*: JBC grade card, JBCPP. Amster, "Meritocracy Ascendant," 28.

28 *"considering his extraordinary ability"*: MSL, 17–18.

28 *"boy chemist"*: N. Henry Black to TWR, May 18, 1910, JBC file, Office of the Registrar, HUA.

28 *"just so many hurdles . . ."*: JBC, "A Guide to Public Education," 8.

28 *"ballast"*: BH, May 9, 1933.

28 *"I doubt if any schoolteacher . . ."*: MSL, 15.

29 *"In regard to Mr. James Bryant Conant . . ."*: N. Henry Black to J. G. Hart, May 3, 1910, JBC file, Office of the Registrar, HUA.

29 *"practically lived in the library"*: Roxbury Latin, *Tripod* (Boston: Roxbury Latin School, June 1910), 15, JBCPP, HU.

30 *"God damn you," "Lucille . . ."*: BH, May 14, 1933. *Tripod*, February 1910, 4–5.

30 *"Congratulations my very dear boy . . ."*: Marjorie Conant to JBC, June (undated), 1910, CFP.

30 *"'Jim' has been with us . . ."*: *Tripod*, June 1910, 15.

30 *"headed to Cambridge"*: Boston Tribune, June 4, 1910.

30 *"We certainly hope . . ."*: *Tripod*, June 1910, 15.

31 *"star boy"*: N. Henry Black to TWR, May 18, 1910, JBC file, Office of the Registrar, HUA.

31 *"misgivings," "The enjoyment . . ."*: MSL, 24.

CHAPTER 3: A HARVARD MAN

32 *"Grottlesexers"*: Millicent Bell, *Marquand*, 61. Cleveland Amory, *The Proper Bostonians*, 299.

32 *"other than alphabetically"*: Amory, *The Proper Bostonians*, 297.

32 *"heart's desire"*: Ibid., 294.

33 *"aristocracy to which the sons . . ."*: William Allan Neilson, *Charles W. Eliot: The Man and His Beliefs* (New York: Harper, 1926), 20–21.

33 *"solidarity . . ."*: Henry Aaron Yeomans, *Abbott Lawrence Lowell*, 119.

33 *"collegiate way of living," "King's 'Guide to Cambridge' . . ."*: Samuel Eliot Morison, *Three Centuries of Harvard*, 419.

33 *"mistaken laissez-faire"*: Ibid., 421.

33 *"Gold Coast"*: Ibid., 419. John T. Bethell, *Harvard Observed*, 22–24.

33 *"Divisions of wealth . . ."*: As quoted in Morison, *Three Centuries of Harvard*, 420.

34 *"the aristocrats controlled the places . . ."*: John Reed, "Almost Thirty," *New Republic*, 332–33.

34 *"Mrs. Mooney's Pleasure Palace"*: BH, May 14, 1933. BDG, May 23, 1933.

34 *"pose as that of an outsider . . ."*: Interview with John B. Fox Jr.

35 *"In vain are freshmen..."*: Morison, *Three Centuries of Harvard*, 421.

35 *"a greaseball," "He was part..."*: Bell, *Marquand*, 62.

36 *"morning-after party"*: BDG, May 23, 1933.

36 *Two-Beer Dash*: HC, June 12, 1952.

36 *"a grand sense of humor"*: BH, May 14, 1933.

37 *"club material," "sophomore sifters"*: Amory, *The Proper Bostonians*, 297.

37 *"He was brilliant..."*: Amster, "Meritocracy Ascendant," 35.

37 *"nose thumber..."*: Bell, *Marquand*, 17.

38 *"outer gravity"*: Pringle, "Profiles: Mr. President," pt. 1, *NY*, September 12, 1936, 23. Amster, "Meritocracy Ascendant," 36.

38 *"Smile, damn it, smile!"*: JBC diary 1911–1912, JBCPP.

38 *"handling," "demur and go his own way"*: Merle Borrowman, "Conant, the Man," *Saturday Review of Literature* 46 (September 21, 1960): 58.

38 *"fate of more than one..."*: MSL, 35.

38 *"time-consuming operation"*: JBC diary 1911–1912, JBCPP. *MSL*, 24.

38 *"FINIS!..."*: JBC diary, April 7, 1911, JBCPP.

39 *"the minimum amount of work...," "only be awake..."*: BG, May 8, 1933.

39 *"punched"*: JBC diary 1911–1912, JBCPP.

39 *"nearly wrecked a half-year of work"*: MSL, 24.

39 *"Big Punch!..."*: JBC diary 1911–1912, JBCPP. Amster, "Meritocracy Ascendant," 36–38.

40 *"beneath consideration"*: Bell, *Marquand*, 60.

40 *"Not one of us was genuinely solvent..."*: Amster, "Meritocracy Ascendant," 38.

40 *"all the effort worthwhile," "sophisticated"*: MSL, 24–25.

40 *"class segregation," "more than anything else..."*: HC, January 1, 1912.

41 *"like [Woodrow] Wilson did..."*: Amory, *The Proper Bostonians*, 307.

41 *"the modern spirit"*: Reed, "Almost Thirty."

41 *"whole collegiate future"*: MSL, 23.

42 *"Groups are like ready-made clothing," "C is the gentleman's grade"*: Morison, *Three Centuries of Harvard*, 343, 441.

42 *"The college..."*: Ibid., 444.

43 *"concentrated," "three-year plan"*: MSL, 23.

43 *"grand strategy"*: Ibid., 30–31.

43 *"primal mysteries of the universe,"* Sheldon Jerome Kopperl, *The Scientific Work of Theodore William Richards* (PhD diss., University of Wisconsin, 1970), 16, 71.

43 *"Unless one aimed at a degree"*: MSL, 28–31.

43 *"dedicated to things"*: Ibid.

44 *"abhorred disagreement"*: Ibid.

44 *"To him, the advancement..."*: Ibid.

44 *"Only those who have seen him..."*: JBC, "Elmer Peter Kohler, 1865–1938," National Academy of Sciences *Biographical Memoir*, 1952, 270, 274, 268.

45 *"a series of scientific adventures"*: Ibid.

45 *"wanted to be a physical chemist"*: MSL, 32–34.

45 *"strategist," "tactician"*: Ibid.

45 *"solidity," "commonsense judgments"*: MSL, 34.

45 *"Swiss guide," "mastery of technique"*: JBC, "Elmer Peter Kohler," *Biographical Memoir*, 274.

45 *"What was intended"*: MSL, 32.

46 *"knock the puck around," "I had to work"*: *Boston Sunday Post*, May 14, 1933.

46 *"She is an angel," "Made a fool of myself"*: JBC diary 1912–1913, JBCPP.

47 *"She decided to tell . . . ," "big"*: Ibid.

CHAPTER 4: NO-MAN'S-LAND

48 *"Men who would otherwise"*: Bethell, *Harvard Observed*, 68–69.

49 *"[It] came with all the blackness"*: JBC, "When May a Man Dare to Be Alone?" JBCPP.

49 *"pyrotechnic patriotism"*: HC, May 15, 1915.

49 *"complete neutrality"*: BG, March 6, 1915.

49 *"not only pro-Ally"*: MSL, 41.

49 *"bosom friends"*: JBC, "When May a Man Dare to Be Alone?" Also Tuttle, "James B. Conant," 39.

49 *"despised all things German"*: JBC, "Theodore William Richards, January 31, 1868–April 2, 1928," National Academy of Sciences *Biographical Memoir*, Vol. 44, 1974, 251–68.

49 *"Such reversal of sentiment"*: MSL, 41.

49 *"expression of personal opinion"*: HC, October 13, 1914.

50 *"The professors were losing their minds"*: Virginia Spencer Carr, *Dos Passos*, 34.

50 *"cut dead," "When I heard someone"*: MSL, 41.

50 *"frenzied rooter"*: JBC, "When May a Man Dare to Be Alone?"

50 *"swing the sympathy . . ."*: MSL, 42. Lusitania dead: Bethell, *Harvard Observed*, 70.

50 *"where the big scientists were"*: Biebel, "Politics, Pedagogues and Statesmanship," 20–21.

51 *"Nineteen-fifteen was the year . . . Organic chemists were in demand"*: MSL, 42.

51 *"What I learned about steelmaking"*: Ibid., 39.

52 *"committed organic chemist"*: Ibid., 33.

52 *General Leonard Wood*: A detailed description of Harvard's First World War contribution can be found in Bethell, *Harvard Observed*, 72. See also Morison, *Three Centuries of Harvard*, 450–60.

53 *"Harvard ought to take the lead"*: Theodore Roosevelt, "Harvard and Preparedness," *Harvard Advocate*, December 8, 1915, 57–58.

53 *"showing more emotion . . . ," "I adhered to the other camp"*: MSL, 47.

53 *"less than popular"*: Martin D. Saltzman, "James Bryant Conant: The Making of an Iconoclastic Chemist," *Bulletin of the History of Chemistry* 28, no. 2 (2003): 86.

54 *"Though, of course . . ."*: MSL, 43–44.

54 *"On paper, it was easy"*: Ibid.

54 *"comfortable bankroll," "meager salary"*: Ibid.

55 *"a form of pioneering . . ."*: Harvard College class of 1914, TFAR, 164.

55 *"cautious chlorination"*: Kathryn Steen, *The American Synthetic Organic Chemicals Industry: War and Politics, 1910–1930* (Chapel Hill: University of North Carolina Press, 2014).

55 *"startling letter," "By what seemed to me": MSL*, 44, 47.

56 *"All would have been saved"*: *Newark Evening News*, November 27, 1916. See also *Newark Evening News*, November 28 and 29; *BG*, November 28, 1916; *BG*, May 26, 1933.

56 *"Because I had not even seen . . .": MSL.*

57 *"The account Loomis gave"*: Ibid.

57 *"permanent mark"*: Ibid., 44–45, 51.

57 *"greenness," "move up in a year or two"*: Ibid., 45.

58 *"The spectacle"*: Ibid., 47.

58 *"It is a fearful thing . . . ," "The world must be made safe"*: *NYT*, April 3, 1917.

58 *"The chief reason . . . ," "Teaching was no place"*: *MSL*, 47.

CHAPTER 5: THE CHEMISTS' WAR

59 *"We were not soldiers . . .":* Pringle, "Profiles: Mr. President," pt. 1, 24.

59 *"My friends were . . .": MSL*, 48.

59 *"There seems to be"*: JBC to George Kelley, March 26, 1917, JBCPP. Also Amster, "Meritocracy Ascendant," 43.

59 *"To wait until . . .": MSL*, 48.

60 *"When the United States entered"*: *BG*, May 19, 1933.

60 *"A beautiful vision . . . ," "If I can find a copy"*: JBC to GTR, July 4, 1917. CFP.

61 *"only remotely related"*: *MSL*, 48.

61 *"You're crazy!"*: Pringle, "Profiles: Mr. President," pt. 1, 24. *MSL*, 48.

61 *"since everything German"*: *MSL*, 49.

61 *"poison bombs"*: *NYT*, April 24, 1915. For details of attack at Ypres, see Gerard J. Fitzgerald, "Chemical Warfare and Medical Response During World War I," *American Journal of Public Health* 3 (April 2008): 611–12.

61 *"The smoke was suffocating"*: *Boston Sunday Globe*, April 26, 1936. Also in Bethell, *Harvard Observed*, 70–71.

62 *"poison or poisonous weapons"*: Fitzgerald, "Chemical Warfare and Medical Response."

62 *"cynical and barbarous," "as soldier," "an Army . . .":* "Sir John French on the Use of Poison Gas at the Second Battle of Ypres, 15 June 1915," in Charles F. Horne, ed., *Source Records of the Great War*, Vol. III (New York: National Alumni, 1923).

62 *Leonardo da Vinci and forerunners of chemical weapons*: L. F. Haber, *The Poisonous Cloud*, 15. For a history of German development of chemical weapons, 22–40. Also Fitzgerald, "Chemical Warfare and Medical Response." Description of mustard gas, effects and response: Brigadier General Alden H. Waitt, *Gas Warfare*, 29–33.

63 *"king of the battle gases"*: Fitzgerald, "Chemical Warfare and Medical Response," 617.

64 *"helps to cheer us up"*: JBC to GTR, March 8, 1918, CFP.

64 *scientific steps*: Haber, *The Poisonous Cloud*, 111. Detailed account of competing methods to produce mustard gas, 112–15.

65 *thirty tons of mustard gas a day*: W. Lee Lewis to editors of the *Chicago Chemical Bulletin*, January 1919, 5.

65 *"It was an extraordinary performance"*: Haber, *The Poisonous Cloud*, 168.

66 *"Cambridge and Harvard"*: JBC to GTR, March 8, 1918, CFP.

66 *"brewing"*: Pringle, "Profiles: Mr. President," pt. 1, 24. Also Fitzgerald, "Chemical Warfare and Medical Response," 9–10.

66 *"rather anomalous"*: JBC to GTR, March 8, 1918, CFP.

66 *"I will have to postpone . . . ," "I certainly envied her"*: JBC to GTR, July 1918, CFP.

67 *"highly secret operation"*: MSL, 49.

67 *"great American gas"*: JBC, TFAR, 165.

67 *"Captain Lewis"*: Joel A. Vilensky, *Dew of Death*, 3–28.

68 *"so sick"*: Ibid.

68 *"The contents of the flask"*: Ibid.

68 *"desensitize"*: Ibid.

68 *G-34 and "methyl"*: Ibid.

69 *"the premier of them all"*: Wilder D. Bancroft, "Lewisite," *Chemical Bulletin* 6 (June 1919): 154. Willoughby plant site description: General Electric Company, *The National in the World War*, 214–18. See also *Willoughby Republic*, November 18, 1918. "Our Super-Poison Gas," *NYT Magazine*, April 20, 1919. *BDG*, May 27, 1933.

70 *"mousetrap"*: BDG, May 27, 1933.

70 *"new form of rubber"*: Vilensky, *Dew of Death*, 48.

71 *"A-a-ll up!"*: General Electric, *The National in the World War*, 218.

71 *"Everybody respected him"*: BG, May 27, 1933.

71 *"revolutionary changes"*: General Electric, *The National in the World War*, 182.

71 *"The fields of France"*: Tuttle, "James B. Conant," 11–12.

71 *"disastrous attempt"*: MSL, 51.

71 *"slightest indication"*: Pringle, "Profiles: Mr. President," pt. 1, 24.

72 *"unbelievable accomplishment . . ."*: Cleveland Plain Dealer, November 28, 1918.

73 *"Here Is the Big Story"*: Willoughby Republican, November 29, 1918.

73 *"Now We Know"*: Willoughby Independent, December 5, 1918.

73 *"pilot production," "no appreciable quantity"*: TFAR, 165.

73 *"many doubts . . . open to question"*: MSL, 49.

73 *"commercial production"*: Vilensky, *Dew of Death*, 52.

73 *"ten tons a day"*: NYT Magazine, April 20, 1919.

73 *"72 times deadlier"*: Ibid. Cleveland Plain Dealer, June 15, 1919.

73 *"dew of death"*: Vilensky, *Dew of Death*, 56.

74 *"Death Valley"*: NYT, March 17 and November 29, 2012.

74 *"the deadliest poison ever known"*: NYT, May 25, 1919; WP, May 26, 1919; Cincinnati Tribune, May 25, 1919.

74 *"first on the list"*: Frank Parker Stockbridge, "War Inventions That Came Too Late," *Harper's* 139 (1919): 828.

74 *"For quantity"*: W. Lee Lewis, "How the American Chemists Silence Germany," *Chemical Bulletin* 6 (January 1919): 6.

74 *"merciful," "One pound of chloropicrin"*: Ibid.; Thomas Ian Faith, "Under a Green Sea," 52. Also see Vilensky, *Dew of Death*, 58.

75 *"stupendous"*: Lewis, "How the American Chemists Silence Germany," 5.

75 *"I think poison gas"*: U.S. Committee of Military Affairs, *Reorganization of the Army*, August 1919.

75 *"a gift," "To me, the development . . .": MSL*, 49–50.

76 *"moral"*: Ibid.

76 *"cruel" and "savage"*: Faith, "Under a Green Sea," 54.

76 *"carried wherever the wind"*: Thomas Ian Faith, *Behind the Gas Mask*, 58.

76 *"chain of reasoning," "old-fashioned," "civilian casualties": MSL*, 49–52.

76 *"highly unattractive task . . . ," "carrying the title of 'Professor'. . .":* Ibid.

77 *"strange adventure in applied chemistry": TFAR*, 165.

77 *"As head of a team . . . ," "alone on a high pedestal," "cherished . . .": MSL*, 51–52.

CHAPTER 6: AIR CASTLES

78 *"Naturally, I was impressed . . .":* John R. Tunis, "John Harvard's Biggest Boy," *American Magazine*, October 1933, 20.

78 *"moved upstairs"*: Ibid.

79 *"it already had a chemist . . .":* Amster, "Meritocracy Ascendant," 43.

79 *"The army and powers that be . . .":* Lawrence V. Redman, *Chemical Bulletin* 6 (January 1919): 4.

79 *"Would you be willing to consider . . .":* Ibid.

79 *"so rockbound in your provinciality . . .":* Tuttle, "James B. Conant," 15.

79 *"I'm going to marry a girl . . .":* Tunis, "John Harvard's Biggest Boy."

80 *"most impressive," "very nice and simple . . . ," "As usual . . .":* GTR diary, January 4, 1919, CFP.

80 *"caste system"*: Tuttle, "James B. Conant," 13.

80 *"waltz onto the stage"*: Interview with Martha "Muffy" Henderson Coolidge.

81 *"splendid playing . . .":* William James to TWR, July 13, 1892, CFP.

81 *"highly cohesive, rarified world . . .":* Jean Strouse, *Alice James: A Biography* (Boston: Houghton Mifflin, 1980), 91.

81 *"unusual," description of unorthodox upbringing*: JBC, "Theodore William Richards," National Academy of Sciences *Biographical Memoir* 44, 251–86.

82 *"Four publications . . .":* Ibid., 255.

82 *"The work had been strenuous . . .":* TWR, "Retrospect," *Vecko-Journalen*, (undated) 1914, CFP.

83 *"morbid views and dark forebodings"*: Martha Davis Richards to TWR, August 1, 1903.

83 *"nervously sensitive," "dark prospect"*: Martha Davis Thayer to TWR, July 31, 1903, CFP.

83 *"He was too bright . . .":* Anna Matlock Richards to MTR, January 1896, CFP.

83 *"vital elements," "vital life"*: MTR to Anna Matlock Richards, (undated) 1896, CFP.

83 *"your disease of ethics . . .":* Charles Loeser to MTR, September 6, 1894, CFP.

84 *"standards," "quality"*: Interview with Martha "Muffy" Henderson Coolidge.

84 *"stern Yankee household"*: GRC diary, 1910, CFP.

84 *"an overwhelming sense . . .":* GRC diary, October 11, 1910.

84 *"as a spur"*: GRC diary, April 27, 1914.

84 *"university people," "swells"*: GRC diary, June 14, 1914.

84 *"distracting task of making money . . ."*: TWR, "Retrospect."

84 *"The habit of attempting . . ."*: JBC, "Theodore William Richards," *Biographical Memoir*, 258.

85 *"defective"*: Sir Harold Hartley, "Theodore William Richards Memorial Lecture," April 25, 1929, CFP.

85 *"My long imprisonment . . ."*: GRC diary, August 17, 1910, CFP.

85 *"cross, selfish, and quarrelsome"*: GRC diary, October 18, 1910.

85 *"overstudy"*: TWR to Kenneth G. T. Webster, chairman of the Academic Board of Radcliffe, May 10, 1916, GRC papers, Radcliffe Institute for Advanced Study, Schlesinger Library, Cambridge, MA.

85 *"genius"*: Interview with Martha "Muffy" Henderson Coolidge.

86 *"narrow existence"*: GRC diary, 1916, CFP.

86 *"chiefly Papa's advisees"*: GRC diary, June 20, 1913.

86 *"Sometimes I'd feel . . ."*: GRC diary , October 2, 1918.

86 *"stuck," "And now, of all times . . ."*: Ibid.

86 *"all the ardor"*: GRC diary, January 4, 1919.

86 *"wholly unimpressed . . ."*: John H. Finley, eulogy for GRC, 1985, CFP.

86 *"believe in it . . . ," "great comfort"*: GRC diary, January 4, 1919, CFP.

87 *"blind alley," "wallowing in the laboratory," "pay dirt"*: MSL, 53.

87 *"so many irons in the chemical fire"*: JBC to GRC, July 27, 1920, CFP.

87 *"down east," "a mirage . . ."*: JBC to GRC, August 31, 1920, CFP.

87 *"shout"*: Ibid.

88 *"I still have a strong taint . . ."*: Ibid., August 13, 1920.

88 *"too much influenced . . ."*: Ibid., July 27, 1920.

88 *"fine-grained," "I realize only too well . . . ," "clash," "possible difference . . ."*: Ibid., September, 27, 1920.

88 *"paper offensive," "miserable performance"*: Ibid., September 21, 1920.

88 *"Accepted him finally . . ."*: GRC diary, September 24, 1920, CFP.

88 *"dark fears and timid doubts"*: Ibid., September 26, 1920.

88 *"passed the line of decorum"*: JBC to GRC, September 30, 1920, CFP.

88 *"cheapness" and "dissipation"*: Ibid., September 27, 1920.

89 *"conquer"*: Ibid., September 30, 1920.

89 *"a few false moves," "in the spirit of joviality . . . ," "The whole question . . ."*: Ibid.

89 *"Let our love for each other . . ."*: Ibid., October 10, 1920, CFP.

89 *"stormy month"*: GRC diary, October 22, 1920, CFP.

89 *"It's no use . . ."*: JBC to GRC, October 15, 1920, CFP.

89 *"Engaged again for the final time"*: GRC diary, October 22, 1920, CFP.

90 *"vague fear," "vanish again"*: JBC to GRC, October 25, 1920, CFP.

90 *"A heavenly hour alone . . ."*: GRC diary, March 18, 1921, CFP.

90 *"excellent match"*: Norris Hall to JBC, undated, CFP.

90 *"Why shouldn't I be looking . . ."*: JBC to GRC, December 2, 1920, CFP.

90 *"There's no question . . ."*: Interview with John B. Fox Jr.

90 *"You're certainly one lucky fellow . . ."*: JBC to GRC, March 31, 1921, CFP.

91   *"It didn't seem dreary . . . ," "a sort of halo," "goggles," "It was all most lovely . . ."*: MTR to Edith Henderson, April 19, 1921, CFP.

91   *"always dress attractively . . . ," "Jim's air-castles"*: GTR diary, January 27, 1921, CFP.

CHAPTER 7: THE SPECIALIST

92   *"Gambling on the stock market . . ."*: JBC to GRC, June 29, 1930, CFP.

92   *"with the more or less explicit . . ."*: MSL, 55.

92   *"delightful time"*: JBC to Esther Conant, July 3, 1921, CFP. The letter is reprinted in *MSL*, 55–56 and all quotes describing that trip are taken from there, including JBC's regret about Germany being excluded because it was "tainted by war guilt."

93   *"slip in"*: MSL, 56.

93   *"Almost alone among American chemists . . ."*: Caryl P. Haskins, draft eulogy, 1978, CFP.

93   *"restless soul"*: MSL, 52.

93   *"one of the most brilliant . . ."*: BDG, December 24, 1931.

93   *"the best years"*: MSL, 59.

94   *"almost a point of honor . . ."*: As quoted in Martin Saltzman, "James Bryant Conant and the Development of Physical Organic Chemistry, *Journal of Chemical Education* 49, no. 6 (June 1972): 411.

94   *"open mind," "calculated gambler"*: Paul F. Douglass, *Six upon the World*, 338.

94   *"He spanned the whole spectrum . . ."*: G. B. Kistiakowsky and F. H. Westheimer, "James Bryant Conant, 1893–1978," *Biographical Memoirs of the Royal Society* 25 (November 1979): 212.

95   *"scientific imagination"*: Pringle, "Profiles: Mr. President," pt. 2, September 19, 1936, *NY*, 23.

95   *"The combination of hemoglobin . . ."*: MSL, 61.

95   *"searching logic"*: Paul D. Bartlett, "James Bryant Conant, 1893–1978," National Academy of Sciences *Biographical Memoir* 34 (1983): 95.

95   *"the state of oxidation . . . ," description of oxidation experiments*: MSL, 61.

95   *"foreign field"*: Ibid.

95   *"When I read your paper . . ."*: Ibid.

96   *"Teaching is certainly the thing . . ."*: GRC to her parents, April 17, 1923, CFP.

96   *"a bit small"*: MSL, 58.

96   *"draughts," "Jim and I . . ."*: GRC to MTR, (undated) 1922, and March 20, 1923, CFP.

97   *"overapprehensiveness," "Jewish doctor"*: WTR to MTR, November 7, 1932, CFP.

97   *"borrow trouble"*: MTR diary, undated, CFP.

97   *"the perfect husband . . ."*: GRC to MTR, October 6, 1921, CFP.

97   *"be prompt . . ."*: GRC 1924–25 diary, undated, CFP.

97   *"Patty did not have a practical bone . . ."*: Interview with Martha "Muffy" Henderson Coolidge.

97   *"Jim wants perfection . . ."*: GRC 1924 diary, CFP.

98   *"invidious remarks," "the servant question . . ."*: GRC to parents, June 4, 1925, CFP.

98   *"screed," "I have an incorrigible impulse . . ."*: GRC 1924 diary, CFP.

99 *"bantering sense of humor"*: Tuttle, "James B. Conant," 16.

99 *"straightness . . ."*: John H. Finley, JBC eulogy, 1978, CFP.

99 *"do my bit . . . ," "conservative and parrot-minded . . . ," "vulgar"*: GRC to MTR, October 6, 1921, CFP.

99 *"a wider view . . . ," "too shy"*: MSL, 65.

100 *"Which will make eight in all . . ."*: GRC to TWR, July 10, 1924, CFP.

100 *"You are a thoughtful . . ."*: GRC to TWR, January 9, 1925, CFP.

100 *"a most sadly defeated . . ."*: GRC to parents, March 9, 1925, CFP.

100 *"fearfully bad"*: GRC diary, March 4, 1925, CFP.

100 *"horrible Socialist burgermeisters"*: Ibid.

101 *"It seems like dragging . . . ," "the center of discontent"*: GRC to parents, March 9, 1925, CFP.

101 *"That's all very well . . . ," "Such sentiments . . ."*: MSL, 68.

101 *"when friendly intercourse . . ."*: TFAR, 165.

102 *"The rivalry among universities . . ."*: MSL, 71–73.

102 *"massive contributions," "elaborate and tricky"*: Ibid.

102 *"impressive output"*: Ibid.

102 *"[Jim] is simply delighted . . ."*: GRC to parents, March 9, 1925, CFP.

102 *"father of chemical warfare," "anathema"*: MSL, 630.

103 *"curious"*: Ibid.

103 *"a great discovery"*: Ibid., 60.

103 *"He paid me the greatest . . ."*: Ibid., 630.

104 *"a most attractive offer"*: MSL, 74.

104 *"The sky's the limit"*: JBC to GRC, March 16, 1927, CFP.

104 *"anxious to avoid anything . . . ," "foolish," "They will end . . . ," "hardly regard such a fate . . ."*: MSL, 74–75.

105 *"neck and neck"*: GRC to MTR, January 8, 1932.

105 *"superacidity" experiments*: Kistiakowsky and Westheimer, "James B. Conant," 212.

106 *strong impetus to progress*: F. H. Westheimer, "James Bryant Conant: March 26, 1893–February 11, 1978," *Organic Synthesis* 58 (March 1978): vi–xi.

106 *"He was among the group . . ."*: Ibid.

106 *"magnetic attraction for budding chemists"*: Kistiakowsky, eulogy of JBC, 1978, CFP.

106 *"He was a very, very energetic . . ."*: Oral history interview with Paul D. Bartlett, July 18, 1978, Niels Bohr Library.

107 *"a constant stimulus . . ."*: Bartlett, "James Bryant Conant," *Biographical Memoir*, 106.

107 *"without ever removing his eye . . ."*: James Hershberg, *James B. Conant: Harvard to Hiroshima*, 54.

107 *"living in his laboratory," "never bear to be separated . . ."*: BH, May 14, 1933.

107 *"turned his face to the wall . . ."*: Interview with Martha "Muffy" Henderson Coolidge.

107 *"nervous load . . ."*: JBC, "Theodore William Richards," *Biographical Memoir*.

108 *"hustling scholars"*: Melvin Maddocks, "Harvard Was Once, Unimaginably, Small and Humble," *Smithsonian* 17 (September 1986): 160.

108 *"synthetic carbonated beverages"*: Amster, "Meritocracy Ascendant," 52.

108 *"play the market," "the depression days . . ."*: MSL, 115.

108 *"even my closest friends . . ."*: Michael J. Halberstam, "James Bryant Conant: The Right Man," *HC*, June 19, 1952. Voting record detailed in JBC, "A Guide to Public Education," 15.

109 *"professional chemist," isoprene, "monopoly on the production . . . ," "pang"*: MSL, 77, 62–63.

109 *"sharp insight"*: Borrowman, "Conant, the Man," 58.

110 *"overpowering amount . . ."*: GRC to MTR, January 8, 1932, CFP.

110 *"refrain from the use . . ."*: *Chemical Bulletin.*

110 *"Jim was the sensation . . ."*: GRC to MTR, November 29, 1931, CFP.

110 *"I came to think of Conant . . ."*: Bartlett, "James Bryant Conant," *Biographical Memoir*, 106.

111 *"Of course, the more talk . . ."*: GRC to MTR, October 2, 1931, CFP.

111 *"highly strung"*: Ibid., July 8, 1930.

111 *"I have been a little shocked . . ."*: GRC to JBC, June 13, 1930, CFP.

112 *"a bit neurasthenic"*: GRC to MTR, November 13, 1930, CFP.

112 *"fairly blush"*: GRC to Marjorie Conant, February 20, 1933, CFP.

112 *"problems"*: GRC to MTR, November 22, 1931, CFP.

112 *"nervous strain," "irritable streaks," "I pounce on him . . ."*: GRC diary, December 17, 1928, CFP.

112 *"somewhat unmanageable"*: GRC to MTR, July 3, 1930, CFP.

112 *"It's all right . . ."*: JBC to GRC, June 17, 1930, CFP.

112 *"collection," "Marjorie withstood the shock . . ."*: Ibid., June 29, 1930.

113 *"queer and unremunitive"*: Ibid., July 15, 1930.

113 *"I hadn't realized . . ."*: Ibid., June 29, 1930.

CHAPTER 8: THE DARK HORSE

114 *"1933 was quite a year . . ."*: As quoted in Robert Shaplen, "Sabbatical," *NY*, October 3, 1958.

114 *"mouth shut"*: James B. Conant, "Shall We Shoot Him First or Interview Him?" *Harvard Bulletin*, October 5, 1970, 21.

114 *"abdicating from chemistry"*: Pringle, "Profiles: Mr. President," pt. 1, 20.

114 *"somewhat piqued"*: MSL, 83.

115 *"a little circle of seven men . . ."*: *BG*, November 27, 1932.

115 *"the most exclusive club . . ."*: Pringle, "Profiles: Mr. President," pt. 2, 23.

115 *"outsider"*: *NYT*, May 9, 1933.

115 *"the chilling effects . . ."*: Amster, "Meritocracy Ascendant," 54.

115 *"Back Bay Lear"*: Richard Norton Smith, *The Harvard Century*, 64.

116 *"Shall the institution of learning . . ."*: *New York World-Telegram*, April 15, 1935.

116 *"declared without question"*: MSL, 81.

116 *"material rather than intellectual growth"*: Pringle, "Profiles: Mr. President," pt. 1, 20.

117 *"negative views," "mediocre men"*: MSL, 82.

117 *"A university was a collection . . ."*: MSL, 83.

117 *"unduly critical"*: Ibid., 82.

118 *"I rather doubted . . . ," "My wife . . ."*: Ibid.

118 *"crossing the Atlantic . . ."*: Smith, *The Harvard Century*, 103.

119 *"deist"*: MTR diary, CFP.

119 *"attractive personality"*: Amster, "Meritocracy Ascendant," 57.

119 *"hardest boiled alumni . . ."*: BSP, May 14, 1933.

119 *"safer and surer . . . ," "The more I . . ."*: Amster, "Meritocracy Ascendant," 58.

119 *"rescue the college . . ."*: MSL, 107.

120 *"good authority"*: MSL, 67.

120 *"The Cambridge atmosphere . . ."*: GRC to Marjorie Conant, February 20, 1933, CFP.

120 *"ENJOYED YOUR LETTER . . ."*: JBC to GRC, March 29, 1933, CFP.

120 *"a fool," "poor choice"*: MSL, 87–90.

121 *"It was painfully evident . . ."*: Ibid.

121 *"They said you wanted . . ."*: Ibid.

121 *"Parting with chemistry . . ."*: JBC, "An Account of the Year 1933," CFP. And Biebel, "Politics, Pedagogues and Statesmanship," 39.

121 *"I hope events will prove . . ."*: Hershberg, *Harvard to Hiroshima*, 75.

121 *"dark horse," "weak acids and bases"*: HC, May 8, 1933; BG, May 8, 1933; NYT, May 9, 1933.

122 *"used to flee . . ."*: NYT, May 28, 1933.

122 *"ease, accessibility . . . ," "stuffed shirt"*: BH, May 11 and 12, 1933.

122 *"An admirable choice"*: *Boston Post* and *Boston Globe*, May 9, 1933.

122 *"a man who to a large extent . . ."*: HC, May 9, 1933.

122 *"100 percent a scientist," "enigma"*: NYT, May 14, 1933.

122 *"I don't in the least . . . ," "The trouble is that Jim . . ."*: WTR to GRC, May 11, 1933, CFP.

122 *"few illusions, "the most thankless job . . . ," "If the president . . ."*: JBC to Marjorie Conant, May 17, 1933, JBCPP.

123 *"brain trust"*: John T. Bethell, "Frank Roosevelt at Harvard," *Harvard Magazine*, November–December 1996.

123 *"relieved at the outcome"*: Ken Murdock to JBC, undated, CFP.

124 *"serene mysteries of the laboratory . . . ," "You idolize Jim's chemistry . . ."*: MTR diary, May 14, 1933.

124 *"wonderful wife . . ."*: JBC to GRC, May 17, 1933, CFP.

124 *"out of danger"*: MSL, 99.

124 *"better half"*: JBC's favorite term for GRC, author recollection.

124 *"I am very happy"*: JBC to GRC, May 17, 1933, CFP.

124 *"A clear-cut social philosophy," "handle educational problems . . ."*: Tuttle, "James B. Conant," 24.

125 *"declare war"*: MSL, 91.

125 *"cranky New Englander," "The magic of words . . . ," "education is not something . . ."*: JBC, "A Guide to Private Education," 15.

125 *"a good excuse"*: MSL, 107.

125 *"have a minute," "but behind the intimated . . ."*: BH, September 6, 1933.

126 *"Today more than ever . . ."*: JBC, "Address to Freshmen," September 9, 1933, reprinted in NYT, September 10, 1933.

126 *"You and I are both facing"*: Ibid.

126 *"wretched temperance punch"*: Samuel E. Morison, "The Installation of President Conant," JBCPRESP, HUA.

126 *"No Pomp"*: *Boston Traveler*, October 10, 1933.

127 *"cold-fish chemist"*: Halberstam, "James Bryant Conant: The Right Man."

127 *"even the most collegiate . . ."*: JBC to Marjorie Conant, May 17, 1933, JBCPP.

127 *"Politically and intellectually . . ."*: Smith, *The Harvard Century*, 109.

127 *"That's what all the ballrooms . . ."*: Pringle, "Profiles: Mr. President," pt. 2, 27.

128 *"The hard reality . . ."*: GRC to Marjorie Conant, June 23, 1933, CFP.

128 *"Remember! You can never afford . . ."*: GRC diary, fall (undated) 1933, CFP.

128 *"I have been . . . ," "loaded down with cares . . ."*: GRC diary, August 29, 1934.

128 *"Negro question," "exaggerated prejudices . . . ," "Jim says . . ."*: GRC diary, November 16, 1935.

129 *"Jim has all this . . ."*: GRC diary, February 27, 1934.

129 *"the only way to keep . . ."*: GRC diary, May 19, 1934 or 1935.

129 *"looked into the matter . . . ," "New Deal . . ."*: Halberstam, "James Bryant Conant: The Right Man."

129 *"Never set foot . . ."*: Smith, *The Harvard Century*, 109.

129 *"I thought we had come . . ."*: Pringle, "Profiles: Mr. President," pt. 1, 20.

130 *"something more than a New England school . . ."*: Theodore H. White, *In Search of History: A Personal Adventure* (New York: Harper, 1978), 41, 43.

130 financial pressures of the times, *"There is a limit . . . ," "Whether one was a liberal . . ."*: MSL, 116, 119.

131 *"were men, not buildings"*: NYT, January 24, 1936.

131 *"We should be able to say . . . ," "artificial barriers," "nearest my heart"*: MSL, 129.

131 *"exclusivity . . ."*: MSL, 122.

132 *"sliding-scale"*: Amster, "Meritocracy Ascendant," 117.

132 *"a promising device"*: MSL, 131.

133 *"burned with a fierce disapproval . . ."*: Nicholas Lemann, *The Big Test*, 21.

133 *"science with limited possibilities . . ."*: Ibid., 5–6.

133 *"State of the University . . ."*: Biebel, "Politics, Pedagogues and Statesmanship," 60.

133 *"a truly national university . . ."*: JBC, *Annual Report, 1932–1933*, 1–5, JBCPRESP, HUA. NYT, January 29, 1934.

133 *"If we fail . . ."*: Biebel, "Politics, Pedagogues and Statesmanship," 61.

133 *"too obviously sacred"*: MSL, 136.

133 *"Under James Conant . . ."*: "Chemist at Cambridge."

134 *"best brains"*: H. I. Brock, "Conant States His Creed for Harvard," *NYT Magazine*, March 18, 1934, 3; "Chemist at Cambridge."

134 *"quality, not quantity"*: NYT, January 29, 1934.

134 *"High character"*: Jerome Karabel, *The Chosen*, 148.

134 *"the privilege of higher education . . ."*: Robert van Gelder, "Dr. Conant's Triple Life," *NYT Magazine*, July 20, 1941.

134 *"mistaken philanthropy . . ."*: Amster, "Meritocracy Ascendant," 94.

134 *"to ensure a permanent career . . ."*: Pringle, "Profiles: Mr. President," pt. 1, 24.

134 *"inbreeding among tenured faculty . . ."*: Amster, "Meritocracy Ascendant," 96.

134 *"has a clear vision . . ."*: Brock, "Conant States His Creed for Harvard."

135 *"conduct under stress," "the liar . . . ," "to expect the worst . . ."*: MSL, 86.

135 *"The presidency is an awful job . . ."*: As quoted in MTR diary, May 1, 1934, CFP.

135 *"a novel investigation"*: Kistiakowsky, eulogy of JBC.

136 *"the times"*: MTR diary, fall–winter 1933, CFP.

136 *"He is tense inside . . . ," "Jim is so pessimistic . . ."*: Ibid.

CHAPTER 9: UNEXPECTED TROUBLES

137 *"To begin with . . ."*: Louis Mertens, *Robert Frost: Life and Talks-Walking*, 241.

137 *"This is an age of dictators . . ."*: Brock, "Conant States His Creed for Harvard."

137 *"Age of Conant"*: Halberstam, "James Bryant Conant: The Right Man."

137 *"a healthy clash of ideas"*: DBG, June 22, 1934. JBC, "Free Inquiry or Dogma?" *Atlantic Monthly*, April 1935, 439.

138 *"unexpected troubles"*: MSL, 139.

138 *"It will be a sad day . . ."*: BH, BG, NYT, June 21 and 22, 1934. *Harvard Alumni Bulletin* 36 (July 6, 1934).

138 *"Down with Hitler! . . . ," "Fascist butchers!"*: Ibid. JBC, Memorandum III, "Hitler Comes to Power," 7, JBCPP, MSL, 41. Also see a detailed chronicle of Hanfstaengl at Harvard in William M. Tuttle Jr., "American Higher Education and the Nazis: The Case of James B. Conant and Harvard University's 'Diplomatic Relations' with Germany," *American Studies* 20, no. 1 (Spring 1979): 49–70 (hereafter Tuttle, "AHE and the Nazis"). Also John Sedgwick, "The Harvard Nazi," *Boston Magazine*, March 2005.

139 *"an immense, high-strung . . ."*: William L. Shirer, *Berlin Diary*, 17.

139 *"the man who has saved Germany . . ."*: Harvard College class of 1909, TFAR, 277.

139 *"The German Storm"*: Tuttle, "AHE and the Nazis," 55.

139 *"greatest anticipation," "flabbergasted"*: NYT, March 29, 1934. HC, September 24, 1934.

139 *"Dr. Hanfstaengl Scholarship," "perennial love . . ."*: Original letter in JBCPP.

139 *"Beware of Nazis Bearing Gifts"*: Smith, *The Harvard Century*, 118.

140 *"has risen to distinguished station . . ."*: HC, June 13, 1934.

140 *"Hanfstaengl appeared large . . . ," "I bring you greetings . . . ," "My response was cold . . ."*: JBC, "Hitler Comes to Power," 7.

141 *"To me the answer . . . ," "Hitler's henchmen . . . ," "We are unwilling . . ."*: MSL, 143–44.

141 *"Bully for Harvard"*: Smith, *The Harvard Century*, 119.

141 *"Harvard Rebuffs Dr. Hanfstaengl . . ."*: DBG, October 4, 1934.

141 *"one of the finest pages . . ."*: BH, October 5, 1934.

141 *"so curt and caustic . . ."*: HC, September 24, 1934.

141 *"public relations problem"*: TFAR, 166.

141 *"translate the wild and whirling . . ."*: Peter Conradi, "Opinion," NYT, November 30, 2004.

141 *"authentic voice . . ."*: NYHT, May 19, 1933. Ronald Steel, *Walter Lippmann and the American Century*, 331.

142 *"not alone in his reticence"*: Tuttle, "AHE and the Nazis," 66.

142 *"danger of controversy"*: MSL, 115.

142 *"But as a university president . . ."*: Tuttle, "AHE and the Nazis," 66, 52.

143 *"mix up charity and education . . ."*: Ibid. JBC's original letters to Grenville Clark, November 14, 1933, Harold Laski, November 3, 1933, and E. K. Bolton, September 13, 1933 are all in JBCPRESP, HUA.

143 *"I have not seen many men . . . ," "imported people . . ."*: Tuttle, "AHE and the Nazis."

143 *"Our London representative . . ."*: Morton Keller and Phyllis Keller, *Making Harvard Modern*, 155.

143 *"certainly very definitely . . ."*: Stephen H. Norwood, *The Third Reich in the Ivory Tower*, 39.

143 *"rather against bringing . . ."*: Keller, *Making Harvard Modern*, 155.

144 *"I doubt if we can use him . . ."*: Ibid.

144 *"failure of compassion"*: Tuttle, "AHE and the Nazis," 54.

144 *"beloved Law School"*:

144 *"We're in a kind of a hole . . .", "pathological case," "insulting a friendly government . . . ," "If I were not President . . ."*: Hershberg, *Harvard to Hiroshima*, 87.

144 *"significant contribution"*: JBC, "Hitler Comes to Power," 11.

145 *"not very pleasant," "new order"*: MSL, 143.

145 *"I'm not in it . . ."*: Boston Transcript, September 17, 1933. JBC, "Hitler Comes to Power," 5.

145 *"open to their approaches?"*: MSL, 143.

145 *"judgment on the Nazis"*: Ibid.

145 *"In at least two foreign countries . . ."*: JBC, "Free Inquiry or Dogma?" 436–42.

146 *"The suppression of academic freedom . . . ," "spirit of inquiry . . ."*: JBC, School and Society 42 (July 13, 1935): 41. "Harvard Present and Future," *Harvard Alumni Bulletin* 38 (April 10, 1936).

146 *"the case for a sharp refusal . . . ," "Even if one despised . . ."*: MSL, 146.

147 *"ancient ties"*: HC, March 3, 1936.

147 *"shower of abuse," "weighed the pros and cons," "strongly anti-Nazi," "No one seemed to remember . . ."*: MSL, 146.

147 *"perhaps too gentle"*: Keller, *Making Harvard Modern*, 157.

148 *"Weltanschauung," "pronounced a lot of nonsense . . ."*: Ibid.

148 *"What my views would have been . . ."*: Tuttle, "AHE and the Nazis," 72–74.

148 *"endeavor"*: Ibid.

148 *"diplomatic relations," "the dilemma of those abroad . . . ," "a friendly act . . ."*: JBC, "Tenth Anniversary of Amerikahaus in Munich," *State Department Bulletin* 34 (February 27, 1956).

149 *"barbarity"*: MSL, 213.

149 *"dangerous follies"*: Ibid., 434.

149 *"traitor to his class," "rancorous and almost hysterical . . ."*: John T. Bethell, "Frank Roosevelt at Harvard," *Harvard Magazine*, November–December 1996.

149 *"This country is being run . . ."*: Ibid.

149 *"quizzed . . . ,"*: Smith, *The Harvard Century*, 126.

150 *"worthwhile experiment"*: Halberstam, "James Bryant Conant: The Right Man."

150 *"A public servant . . ."*: *HC*, June 12, 1935.

150 *steady procession of Harvard visitors*: Bethell, "Frank Roosevelt at Harvard."

150 *"We appear to be entering . . . "*: JBC, *President's Report, 1934–35*, 8, PBCPP. Amster, "Meritocracy Ascendant," 87.

151 *"The presence or absence . . ."*: Ibid.

151 *"academic New Deal . . ."*: Brock, "Training Leaders: A Test for Colleges," *NYT Magazine*, June 16, 1934, 15.

151 *"less than pleased"*: *MSL*, 153.

151 *"stump speech"*: JBC to A. Lawrence Lowell, March 9, 1936, JBCPRESP, HUA.

151 *"Having to introduce a man . . ."*: *MSL*, 153.

151 *"Mr. Franklin D. Roosevelt . . . ," "about ten minutes . . ."*: Bethell, "Frank Roosevelt at Harvard."

151 *"which was that of a schoolmaster . . ."*: *MSL*, 153.

152 *"Damn"*: Bethell, "Frank Roosevelt at Harvard."

152 *"very bad politics . . ."*: JBC to A. Lawrence Lowell, March 12, 1936, JBCPRESP, HUA.

152 *"ca'm jedgment," "incredible among cultured men . . ."*: Bethell, "Frank Roosevelt at Harvard."

152 *"increasing suspicion . . ."*: *MSL*, 448.

152 *"Red professors," "disloyal to our American ideals," "Raw Deal"*: Milton Mayer, *Robert Maynard Hutchins: A Memoir* (Berkeley: University of California Press, 1993), 147–49.

152 *"hot beds of radicalism"*: *NYT*, January 20, 1935.

153 *"It is being said . . . ," "we must also have . . ."*: JBC, "Free Inquiry or Dogma?"

153 *"kind of academic declaration . . ."*: *NYT*, January 20, 1935.

153 *"more militant"*: *NYT*, March 9, 1935.

153 *"hopeless," "Take Oath or Quit"*: *MSL*, 451–52.

153 *"It is out of the question . . . ," "dunking his promising defense . . ."*: Ibid.

154 *"obnoxious law"*: Ibid.

154 *"dangerous precedent"*: Ibid.

154 *"This is admittedly a time . . ."*: JBC, "The Endowed University in American Life," March 20, 1936, JBCPP.

154 *"first step in the same direction . . ."*: Amster, "Meritocracy Ascendant," 107.

154 *"black shadows surrounded . . ."*: *MSL*, 151.

155 *"the equivalent of an inaugural address"*: *MSL*, 149.

155 *"Early History of Harvard"*: "Harvard's James B. Conant," *Time* 28 (September 28, 1936): 23.

155 *"Such a gathering as this . . ."*: JBC's tercentenary oration is reprinted in *MSL*, 651–58.

155 *"a wave of anti-intellectualism . . ."*: *MSL*, 651.

156 *"alumni were sorely troubled . . ."*: Bethell, "Frank Roosevelt at Harvard."

156 *"As proud as he might be . . ."*: "Harvard's James B. Conant," *Time* 28 (September 28, 1936): 26.

156   *"Conant's way of soaking the rich . . ."*: Ibid., 24.

156   *"President of Harvard . . . to do his will," "own innovation"*: Pringle, "Profiles: Mr. President," pt. 2, 24–25.

157   *"polling the jury"*: Ibid.

157   *"up or out"*: Amster, "Meritocracy Ascendant," 97.

157   *"the modern equivalents . . . ," "I told Conant once . . ."*: Mertens, *Robert Frost*, 241.

157   *"full of petty malice"*: Arthur M. Schlesinger Jr., *A Life in the Twentieth Century*, 122.

157   *"slide-rule administrator"*: Douglass, *Six upon the World*, 366; Halberstam, "James Bryant Conant: The Right Man."

157   *"waves of criticism . . ."*: Pringle, "Profiles: Mr. President," pt. 2, 25.

157   *"cruel necessity"*: Brock, "Conant States His Creed for Harvard."

CHAPTER 10: THE ACID TEST

158   *"A laboratory is not the ideal . . ."*: Irwin Ross, "The Tempest at Harvard," *Harper's* 81 (October 1940): 549.

158   *"sop"*: GRC diary, winter 1936–1937, CFP.

159   *"make the best of a bad prospect," "walking uphill"*: MSL, 195–98.

159   *"excellent condition"*: Ibid.

159   *"internal wrestling match . . . ," "The twenty-four hours . . ."*: Ibid.

160   *"collective security"*: For FDR's policy of collective action, see Barbara Rearden Farnham, *Roosevelt and the Munich Crisis: A Study of Political Decision-Making* (Princeton, NJ: Princeton University Press, 1997), 60–65.

160   *"By the horror . . ."*: JBC, "When May a Man Dare to Be Alone?"

160   *"hatreds of the moment," "welter of words . . ."*: Ibid.

161   *"The acid test . . ."*: JBC, "Addresses to Harvard Freshmen," *Harvard Alumni Bulletin* 1 (September 28, 1934).

161   *"gangster rule," "armed aggression," "man on the street"*: MSL, 212–13.

161   *"not only bitterness . . ."*: Shaplen, "Sabbatical."

161   *"quarantine the aggressors"*: Farnham, *Roosevelt and the Munich Crisis*, 65.

161   *"boil to the surface"*: MSL, 209.

162   *"I was neither an isolationist . . ."*: Ibid.

162   *"make the world safe . . ."*: JBC, "Education and Peace," June, 18, 1938, JBCPP.

162   *"I believe it is easy . . . ," "I do not believe . . . ," "war to end war"*: JBC to Archibald MacLeish, June 18, 1937, Archibald MacLeish Papers, LOC.

163   *"poisoned"*: MSL, 218.

163   *"Lion from Idaho"*: Joseph Martin Hernon, *Profiles in Character: Hubris and Heroism in the U.S. Senate, 1789–1996* (New York: Routledge, 2016).

164   *"I am beginning to think . . ."*: JBC to Walter Lippmann, August 12, 1938, Lippmann papers, YU.

164   *"criminal error"*: MSL, 213.

164   *"the problem of evil . . ."*: JBC, Chapel Address, October 1938.

164   *"cause of stopping Hitler . . . I was tortured"*: MSL, 212–13.

164   *"barbaric spirit of the German government . . ."*: *School and Society* 48 (November 26, 1938): 678.

164 *"struck a note of fear . . ."*: JBC, "Hitler Comes to Power," 10.

165 *"We went to Conant's office . . . ," "dollar for dollar"*: *Harvard Magazine*, September–October 2006. Also JBC, "Hitler Comes to Power," 10.

165 *"the humanitarian basis of democracy . . . ," "appreciate greatly . . ."*: Ibid.

165 *"Committee on Scientific Aids . . ."*: Vannevar Bush, *Pieces of the Action*, 32 (henceforth POTA).

166 *"With Munich fresh . . ."*: TFAR, 164.

166 *"No,"* Compton told him: Tuttle, "James B. Conant," 86.

166 *"[It] seems to me . . ."*: JBC to Archibald MacLeish, September 7, 1939, Archibald MacLeish Papers, LOC.

167 *"cash and carry"*: MSL, 215.

167 *"The paramount issue . . ."*: Tuttle, "James B. Conant," 90.

167 *"silver-tongued orators"*: Beatrice Bishop Berle and Travis Beal Jacobs, eds., *Navigating the Rapids, 1918–1971: From the Papers of Adolfe A. Berle* (New York: Houghton Mifflin Harcourt, 1973), 258.

168 *"one-man minor operation . . ."*: MSL, 213.

168 *"earning an unenviable place . . ."*: MSL, 214.

168 *"strongly in favor of repeal . . ."*: Tuttle, "James B. Conant," 93, 97.

169 *"pulled their punches"*: MSL, 215.

169 *"phony war"*: Hernon, *Profiles in Character*, 157.

169 *"Nobody could be sure . . ."*: MSL, 215.

169 *"almost revolutionary force"*: Ibid.

169 *"Resignations are threatened . . ."*: *Harvard Progressive*, October 1939. "To Save Harvard," *Time*, October 16, 1939, 68.

169 *"I feel quite as though war . . ."*: Hershberg, *Harvard to Hiroshima*, 117.

170 *"crack research men"*: "To Save Harvard."

170 *"solely on grounds . . . ," Magna Charta*: *Time*, June 5, 1939, 36.

170 *"no choice"*: MSL, 163.

170 *"the Leverett House gang"*: Smith, *The Harvard Century*, 135.

171 *"stubborn streak"*: Smith, *The Harvard Century*, 133.

171 *Magna Charta, "flexibility"*: Ross, "The Tempest at Harvard," 547. For a full description of the whole Walsh-Sweezy affair, see 544–52.

171 *"Mirror, mirror," "A laboratory is not the ideal . . ."*: Ibid., 548–49.

172 *"slap in the face"*: MSL, 170.

172 *"you could have heard . . ."*: Smith, *The Harvard Century*, 137.

172 *"knockdown fight," "I had no stomach for apologizing"*: MSL, 169–70.

172 *"sounded unanimous"*: Ibid.

173 *"close to being vindictive"*: Ibid.

173 *"An accumulation of prejudices . . ."*: Ibid.

173 *"We saw so little of him . . ."*: Interview with Theodore R. Conant.

173 *"soft"*: Ibid.

174 *"soothing holidays"*: JBC to GRC, summer 1938, CFP.

174 *"children should be seen . . ."*: Interview with Theodore R. Conant.

174 *"little savages," "I seem to have to ask . . ."*: GRC to MTR, September 1, 1940, CFP.

174 *"a Goody Two-shoes"*: Interview with Theodore R. Conant.

174 *"extremely repressed"*: GRC diary, February 6, 1937, CFP.

174 *"reserved, conscientious . . ."*: GRC diary, May 17, 1938.

174 *"disastrous," "Ted is so far from . . ."*: GRC to Marjorie Conant, February 20, 1933, CFP.

175 *"tool of Wall Street"*: Interview with Theodore R. Conant.

175 *"Commie"*: DBG, April 14, 1938.

175 *"bad for business," "horror of the housekeeper . . ."*: Interview with Theodore R. Conant.

175 *"Lord Haw-Haw," "all over the Yard . . ."*: MTR diary, May 1940, CFP.

175 *"Hitler's favorites," Germany Calling*: Interview with Theodore R. Conant.

175 *"Ted has been living . . ."*: GRC diary, February 25, 1939, CFP.

176 *"inferiority complex"*: GRC to MTR, 1941, CFP.

176 *"quackery"*: Interview with Theodore R. Conant.

176 *"intense and continuous solicitude . . . ," "spoiled imp"*: JBC diary, January 15, 1940, JBCPP. The entry, written in pencil in GRC's handwriting, had been erased but is legible.

176 *"conflict of claims"*: GRC diary, April 15, 1936, CFP.

176 *"checking up . . ."*: GRC diary, November 16, 1935.

176 *"You have definitely changed . . ."*: GRC diary, April 15, 1936.

176 *"I think none the less . . ."*: MTR diary, torn page, undated, CFP.

177 *"mean machine," "struggle"*: GRC diary, September 9, 1938, CFP.

177 *"relapsed," "spell of the vapors . . ."*: GRC diary, February 6, 1937.

177 *"entirely* negative . . . ," *"unworthy, selfish . . ."*: GRC diary entries covering the years 1936–1938, CFP.

177 *"never come back," "There's poison in my will . . . ," "I inject a little bit . . ."*: GRC diary, July 19, 1938.

177 *"vicarious pleasure," "rosier than they have seemed"*: JBC to GRC, July 7 and 28, 1938, CFP.

177 *"plateau of contentment," "emotional indigestion"*: JBC to GRC, February 27 and August 29, 1934.

178 *"The war engulfed all of us . . ."*: MSL, 203.

CHAPTER 11: A PRIVATE CITIZEN SPEAKS OUT

179 *"It is not too late . . ."*: JBC, "Immediate Aid to Allies," May 29, 1940, *Speaking as a Private Citizen: Addresses on the Present Threat to Our Nation's Future* (Cambridge, MA: Harvard University Press, 1941).

180 *"W. T. Richards Ends Life . . ."*: NYT, January 31, 1940.

180 *"family only"*: JBC diary, February 2, 1940, JBCPP.

180 *"died by his own hand"*: "William Theodore Richards," Memorial, Vicennial Report of the class of 1921, Harvard College.

180 *"real progress toward restored health . . . ," "at once accepted it"*: MTR letter, with instructions it be sent out to "intimate friends," undated 1940, CFP.

180 *"a card at the Athenæum . . . ," "a fatal flaw . . ."*: Interview with Theodore R. Conant.

180 *"beyond any doubt . . ."*: "William Theodore Richards," Memorial, Vicennial Report.

181 *"died of an overdose . . ."*: MTR letter to be sent to "intimate friends:" MTR letter, undated 1940, CFP.

181 *"They thought Bill was a bit gaga . . ."*: Interview with Martha "Muffy" Henderson Coolidge.

182 *Howard M. Ward*: Willard Rich, *Brain-Waves and Death*.

183 *"brazen hussy"*: Ibid.

183 *"steamed up"*: JBC to EOL, May 30, 1940, JBCPP.

184 *"A ton of uranium . . ."*: Willard Rich, "The Uranium Bomb," unpublished manuscript, CFP.

185 *"To make a uranium bomb . . ."*: Ibid.

185 *"play down"*: McGeorge Bundy, *Danger and Survival*, 34 (henceforth *DAS*).

185 *"extremely powerful bombs . . ."*: Ibid., 35–36.

185 *"revolutionize civilization"*: Rich, "The Uranium Bomb."

186 *"great nose for unusual news,"*: MSL, 299.

186 *"outlandish," "no better than"*: Interview with Theodore R. Conant.

186 *"I conceded the argument . . ."*: Ibid.

187 *"without pause or interruption," "now at hand . . ."*: JBC, "Humanity's Experiment with Free Institutions," September 26, 1939, JBCPP.

187 *"listened intently . . ."*: GRC to MTR, September 26, 1939, CFP.

187 *"so inimical . . . ," "tasks at home," "Gigantic steps in preparedness . . ."*: JBC, "Humanity's Experiment with Free Institutions."

188 *"I hope you are making progress . . ."*: Hershberg, *Harvard to Hiroshima*, 116.

188 *"We were all drawn together . . ."*: POTA, 33.

188 *"a highly technical struggle"*: Ibid.

189 *"We all agreed . . ."*: MSL, 224.

189 *"get in and help," "No, be realistic"*: JBC diary, May 17, 1940, JBCPP.

189 *"bad point of view . . ."*: JBC diary, July 9, 1940.

189 *"immediate aid," "rearm at once," "I shall mince no words . . ."*: JBC, "Immediate Aid to the Allies." WP, May 30, 1940.

190 *"not an easy one to uphold"*: HC, June 12, 1940.

190 *"From that moment . . ."*: Douglass, *Six upon the World*, 372.

190 *"Let your voice be heard"*: JBC, "Immediate Aid to the Allies."

190 *"Venture to wire . . ."*: MSL, 218.

190 *"Was semi-officially assured . . ."*: Tuttle, "James B. Conant," 111.

190 *"thinking along these lines"*: FDR to JBC, June 8, 1940, JBCPRESP, HUA.

190 *"very favorable . . ."*: JBC diary, June 1, 1940, JBCPP.

190 *"coming out for FDR . . ."*: Smith, *The Harvard Century*, 141.

191 *"sneers," "barrage of dead cats," "I am getting used to the volleys . . ."*: JBC to Archibald MacLeish, May 30, 1940, JBCPP.

191 *"intellectual leadership"*: NYT, June 13, 1940.

191 *"fifth best-dressed man . . ."*: JBC diary, February 13, 1940. DBG, February 13, 1940.

191 *"common touch . . ."*: HC, February 13, 1940.

191 *"colds in Cambridge . . ."*: BH, February 13, 1940.

191 *"the opponents of force . . ."*: NYT, June 11, 1940.

191 *"We as a people . . .":* NYT, June 13, 1940.

192 *"O.K.—FDR":* James Phinney Baxter 3rd, *Scientists Against Time,* 14–19. This book tells the official story of the history of the NDRC and OSRD. Also Robert E. Sherwood, *Roosevelt and Hopkins: An Intimate History* (New York: Harper, 1948), 153–56; JBC diary, June 14, 1940, JBCPP.

192 *"Will you be a member?," "Is it real," "Are you to head . . .":* MSL, 235; Baxter, *Scientists Against Time,* 15.

192 *"four horsemen":* Baxter, *Scientists Against Time,* 71; JBC diary, June 18, 1940, JBCPP.

193 *"the mood was anything . . . ," "the equivalent of helping . . . ," "Hurry as they might . . .":* MSL, 239.

193 *candidates would have to be cleared:* Baxter, *Scientists Against Time,* 15; MSL, 241.

194 *"faute de mieux":* JBC diary, June 25, 1940, JBCPP.

194 *"Jim will definitely . . .":* GRC to MTR, July 14, 1940, CFP.

195 *"revolutionary":* MSL, 236–37.

195 *"felt ill at ease":* JBC diary, July 3, 1940, JBCPP.

195 *"never straighten up":* MSL, 204.

195 *"go on the air," "He said Cousin Eleanor . . . ,":* JBC diary, June 29, and July 4, 7, and 8, 1940.

196 *"save himself":* Ibid.

196 *"extremists," "four jumps ahead":* MSL, 220.

196 *"great scheme":* JBC diary, August 4, 1940, JBCPP.

196 *"this utterly aimless war":* DBG, September 25, 1940.

197 *"wave of the future":* Schlesinger, *A Life in the Twentieth Century,* 242.

197 *"British plutocrats":* Olson, *Those Angry Days,* 283.

197 *"cold-blooded efficiency . . .":* James R. Conant '40, Class Oration, *Phillips Exeter Bulletin,* July 1940, 6.

197 *"quite 'shocking,' " "an overstatement of 'hard-boiled' ":* JBC diary, June 23, 1940, JBCPP.

197 *"booed and hissed":* JBD diary, June 18, 1940.

197 *"fantastic nonsense," "Harvard was in bitter contention . . .":* Schlesinger, *A Life in the Twentieth Century,* 244–45.

198 *"Mass airplane attacks . . .":* JBC diary, August 12, 1940, JBCPP.

198 *"The importance of physicists . . .":* MSL, 241.

198 *"stupidity of the FBI":* JBC diary, August 7, 1940.

198 *"fundamental physico-chemical study . . .":* JBC diary, July 18, 1940, JBCPP.

199 *"next moves":* JBC diary, July 25, 1940.

199 *"pretending to be away . . .":* Ibid., July 15, 1940.

199 *"almost overpowering emotional reaction":* MSL, 227.

199 *"finest hour," "aid to allies," "I certainly put my heart . . .":* MSL, 225, 220–21.

199 *"What is the worst possibility . . .":* JBC, September 24, 1940, as quoted in MSL, 221.

200 *"a real exchange of information . . .":* JBC diary, October 9, 1940, JBCPP.

200 *"Navy and Army faces . . .":* Ibid.

200 *"Rad Lab":* Jennet Conant, *Tuxedo Park: A Wall Street Tycoon and the Secret Palace of Science That Changed the Course of World War II* (New York: Simon & Schuster, 2002), 138.

200 *"Your boys are not going..."*: Dallek, *Franklin D. Roosevelt*, 250.

200 *"thus preserving political neutrality!..."*: JBC diary, November 5, 1940, JBCPP.

201 *"private citizen"*: JBC, "Speaking as a Private Citizen," 3.

201 *"We shall be rightly condemned..."*: Ibid.

201 *"the best we can hope for..."*: Smith, *The Harvard Century*, 145.

201 *"No fan mail"*: JBC diary, November 21, 1940, JBCPP.

201 *"So large a proportion ... ," "advantageously insisted upon ..."*: Tuttle, "James B. Conant," 214.

201 *"I am much disturbed..."*: JBC to FDR, December 16, 1940, *MSL*, 228.

202 *"168 signees more to come"*: JBC diary, December 26, 1940, JBCPP.

202 *"Conant-Douglas round-robin"*: Tuttle, "James B. Conant," 238.

202 *"short of war," "lifeline," "Aid to the allies..."*: *MSL*, 229, 225–26.

202 *"muzzled," "row developed ..."*: JBC to Grenville Clark, December 3, 1940, JBCPP. Tuttle, "James B. Conant," 242.

203 *"united front"*: Ibid.

203 *"Publicly, I think..."*: JBC to Grenville Clark, December 31, 1940, as quoted in *MSL*, 228.

203 *"make it the settled policy..."*: JBC to FDR, December 26, 1940, JBCPP.

203 *"inform the American people..."*: FDR to JBC, December 1940, JBCPP.

203 *"fireside chat," "great arsenal of democracy"*: *MSL*, 228.

203 *"magnificent"*: JBC to Grenville Clark, December 31, 1940, JBCPP. Also quoted in *MSL*, 228.

203 *"very effective..."*: JBC diary, December 29, 1940, JBCPP.

204 *"I have been very encouraged..."*: JBC to Grenville Clark, December 31, 1940.

204 *"this country is singularly fitted..."*: FDR to VB and JBC, ordering the creation of the NDRC, June 15, 1940, NDRC file, Bush Papers, NA.

204 *"pessimistic about the long..."*: JBC diary, June 29, 1940, JBCPP.

204 *"Expressed my views..."*: Ibid.

204 *"dangerous man"*: *MSL*, 223.

204 *"no reference to Harvard"*: JBC diary, January 2, 1941, JBCPP.

204 *"heavy deans"*: Smith, *The Harvard Century*, 142.

204 *"wonder..."*: JBC diary, December 20, 1940.

CHAPTER 12: MISSION TO LONDON

206 *"To the sorely pressed..."*: *POTA*, 42.

206 *"Am sailing for England..."*: JBC to Marjorie Conant, Friday, February 14, 1941, CFP.

206 *"gala," "might well be the gay 20s ... ," "dignified though conservative..."*: JBC's typed and edited diary of his mission, "Trip to England—1941," JBCPP (henceforth JBC MTE diary). The trip is also chronicled in *MSL*, 248–71.

207 *"recent scientific information..."*: Ibid.

207 *"Conant Heads Mission to London"*: Ibid.

207 *"As president of Harvard..."*: *NYT*, February 16, 1941.

207 *"little or no enthusiasm"*: JBC MTE diary, 12.

207 *"No Conant tea..."*: As quoted in *Harvard Alumni Bulletin* 43, February 22, 1941.

207 *"Winston: 'One lump . . . '"*: Ibid.

208 *"I feel very strongly . . ."*: JBC to VB, December 13, 1940, NDRC files, NA.

208 *"ill-advised," "I feel that this may be . . ."*: JBC MTE diary, December 20, 1940.

208 *"conspiracy"*: Ibid.

208 *"war from the skies . . ."*: MSL, 249.

208 *"probably not more than one . . . ," I believe actions . . ."*: JBC to Frank Jewett, December 27, 1940, JBCPP.

209 *"grand job"*: FDR to VB, February 4, 1941, NDRC files, NA.

209 *"courage of his convictions"*: BH, February 17, 1941.

209 *"He was very anxious . . . ," "Yes, of course . . . ," "proof"*: JBC MTE diary.

209 *"He has made some of the most forceful . . ."*: NYT, July 20, 1941.

210 *"It is like granting a man . . . ," "dictatorship-war-bankruptcy . . . ," "the New Deal's triple A . . ."*: Tuttle, "James B. Conant," 250, 246.

210 *"stooge"*: Ibid., 253.

211 *"Hitler's soldiers are proponents . . ."*: JBC testimony, Hearings Before the Committee on Foreign Relations, United States Senate, S. 275, a Bill Further to Promote the Defense of the United States, part 3, February 11, 1941. Also NYT, February 12, 1941.

211 *"Democracy was finished"*: David Nasaw, *The Patriarch: The Remarkable Life and Turbulent Times of Joseph P. Kennedy* (New York: Penguin Press, 2012), 498.

212 *"New England caution," "subtle flattery . . ."*: MSL, 224–25.

212 *"I saw a stouthearted population . . ."*: MSL, 248.

212 *"the ideal emissary"*: POTA, 42.

213 *"messenger of hope"*: MSL, 248.

213 *"The job is really important . . ."*: JBC to GRC, March 4, 1941, reprinted in MSL, 256.

213 *"obviously tired and grumpy"*: JBC MTE diary, 42.

213 *"let himself go"*: MSL, 254.

213 *"This bill has to pass . . ."*: William Manchester and Paul Reid, *The Last Lion*, 312.

213 *"such a profound ignorance . . ."*: MSL, 254.

214 *"We don't want your men . . . ," "habit of quoting . . ."*: JBC's MTE diary, and MSL, 253–55.

214 *"calculated quotient of righteous anger, "monster bomb," "to address such dastardly technologies . . ."*: Manchester and Reid, *The Last Lion*, 304.

214 *"any new form of explosive," "the Prof," "Uranium is continually halving . . ."*: Ibid., 305.

215 *"exploiting uranium . . ."*: MSL, 274–76.

215 *"no responsible statesman . . . ," "had succeeded," "American news very discouraging . . ."*: MSL, 254–55.

215 *"your great president . . ."*: JBC as quoted by GRC to Marjorie Conant, May 13, 1941, CFP.

215 *"the gratitude of the British . . ."*: JBC MTE diary, 44.

216 *"what shall I talk to him about? . . ."*: MSL, 253. Also Manchester and Reid. *The Last Lion*, 306.

216 *"the maximum time . . ."*: JBC MTE diary.

217 *"first real Blitz . . . ," "cross between fireworks"*: JBC to GRC, March 8, 1941, reprinted in MSL, 255–57. Also described in JBC's diary.

217 *"Six Bombs dropped . . . ," "lovely but heavy":* Ibid.

218 *"wild idea," "most important . . . ," "electronic battalion," "Conant scheme":* JBC MTE diary, 60–62, 69–70; *MSL,* 269–70.

218 *"One thing they do better . . . critical point":* JBC to VB, March 16, 1941, NDRC files, NA.

218 *"not many men . . . enormous difference":* JBC to VB, March 20, 1941, NDRC files, NA.

218 *"If you accept this line of argument . . . years or longer":* Ibid.

219 *"Here he was ahead of his time . . .":* Baxter, *Scientists Against Time,* 122–23.

219 *"brass hats":* JBC to VB, March 16, 1941, NDRC files, NA.

219 *"clearly conveying secret information," JBC's conversation with Lindemann:* MSL, 277–78, "grave offense" on 271.

220 *"If I were to stay here . . .":* JBC to GRC, March 25, 1941, reprinted in *MSL,* 264–65.

221 *"Here we are . . . ":* Manchester and Reid, *The Last Lion,* 328–29.

221 *"intensity of my feelings . . .":* Ibid.; *MSL,* 266.

221 *"immediate objective," "could not be won at all":* Ibid.

221 *"radio magic," "almost totally ignorant":* JBC MTE diary and *MSL,* 270.

222 *"marvelous progress . . .":* Henry L. Stimson diary, April 25, 1941, YU.

222 *embarrassing position, pet scheme":* MSL, 271, and Baxter, *Scientists Against Time,* footnote, 123.

222 *"As one Harvard graduate . . .":* JBC meeting with FDR, *MSL,* 267–69.

222 *"trusting to luck":* James MacGregor Burns, *Roosevelt: The Soldier of Freedom (1940–1945)* (Orlando, FL: Harcourt, 1956), 91–92.

222 *"If we could preserve our freedom . . .":* JBC, "When Shall America Fight?" June 15, 1941, *Speaking as a Private Citizen.*

223 *"cold, hard facts":* DBG, May 28, 1941.

223 *"Friends of freedom everywhere . . .":* JBC to FDR, 1941.

223 *"any man or state . . . ," "equally detestable":* DBG, July 1, 1941. *NYT,* July 1941.

224 *"The thing that worries me . . .":* JBC to Grenville Clark, 1941.

224 *"No voice is louder . . .":* BG, July 21, 1941.

224 *"persistent rumor":* NYT, June 15, 1941.

224 *"certain great authors," "continuation of the liberal . . .":* Amster, "Meritocracy Ascendant," 149–52.

224 *"Jefferson's ideal," "our common heritage . . . ," "The Objectives . . .":* Ibid.

CHAPTER 13: WAR SCIENTIST

226 *"You say you are convinced . . .":* AQ; OSRD Records, NA; Baxter, *Scientists Against Time,* 124.

227 *"won the confidence of President Roosevelt . . .":* Henry L. Stimson and McGeorge Bundy, *On Active Service in Peace and War,* 465.

228 *"light a fire":* Herbert Childs, *An American Genius,* 311. *MSL,* 274–75.

228 *"almost completely negative," "only hinted at . . .":* MSL, 278.

228 *"so important," "To me, the defense . . . ," "talked in excited tones . . .":* Ibid.

228 *"rough job," "prime efforts":* VB to EOL, July 14, 1941, EOL Papers, BL.

229 *"I have been putting a lot of thought . . .":* Ibid.

229   *"when I retailed to him . . .": MSL*, 279–80.

230   *"It can be made to work . . . ," "complete faith," "reversal in attitude"*: Ibid.

230   *"more significant"*: Ibid.

230   *"practically irresistible," "counterthreat"*: Childs, *American Genius*, 315. JBC, "A History of the Development of the Atomic Bomb," 1943, unpublished manuscript, CFP (henceforth JBC, Secret History). Also in OSRD Records, NA.

230   *"critical mass," "We have now concluded . . ."*: The *MAUD Report*, 1941, Outline of Present Knowledge, pt. 1, general statement, www.atomicarchive.com. Also see Richard G. Hewlett and Oscar E. Anderson, Jr., *The New World*, 42 (henceforth *TNW*).

230   *"unprecedented violence," "justify the scheme . . ."*: Ibid.

231   *"With the news from Britain . . . ," "about the question . . ."*: JBC, Secret History, 21.

231   *"discreet inquiries," "amazed and distressed"*: Mark Oliphant, "The Beginning: Chadwick and the Neutron," *Bulletin of Atomic Scientists* 38, no. 10 (December 1982): 17.

231   *"gossip among nuclear scientists . . . ," "all-out advocates"*: JBC, Secret History, 19, 24.

232   *"Though the factual evidence . . .": MSL*, 280.

232   *"practical feasibility," "We just [cannot] afford . . ."*: Arthur H. Compton, *Atomic Quest*, 8 (henceforth *AQ*). The pivotal meeting is described in dramatic detail in *AQ*, 6–10.

232   *"If such a weapon"*: Ibid.

233   *"Ernest, you say . . ."*: Ibid.

233   *"If you tell me this is my job"*: Ibid.

233   *"Top Policy Group," "deeply involved in the atom . . .": MSL*, 280–81.

233   *"A fission bomb . . ."*: Ibid.

234   *"all-out" American effort, "high responsibility . . ."*: *TNW*, 71, 52.

234   *"full steam ahead": MSL*, 281.

235   *"speedy and complete victory"*: DBG, December 9, 1941. *Harvard Alumni Bulletin* 44, December 13, 1941, 209–13.

235   *"rush of hot anger"*: JBC, "What Victory Requires," December 22, 1941, *Speaking as a Private Citizen*.

235   *"Some defeatists have said . . ."*: DBG, December 9, 1941.

236   *"the mobilization of young men . . ."*: JBC, *President's Report, 1940–1941*, JBCPP.

236   *"organizing some kind of a superintelligence service . . ."*: Keller, *Making Harvard Modern*, 163.

236   *"Conant's Arsenal"*: "Conant's Arsenal," *Time*, August 31, 1942. See Bethell, *Harvard Observed*, 137–54, for a detailed description of Harvard's wartime transformation and contribution.

236   *"Of what goes on behind . . ."*: JBC, *President's Report, 1940–1941*, 4, JBCPP.

236   *"The last thing in the world . . ."*: JBC as quoted by John Finley, Memorial Address, April 2, 1978, CFP.

237   *"forward the national goal . . ."*: JBC, "Total War," in Amster, "Meritocracy Ascendant," 138.

237   *"catastrophic possibilities . . . ," "spreading the gloom": MSL*, 280.

238   *"how the devil . . ."*: Harvey Bundy Oral History, CUOH.

238   *"The Germans can never win . . ."*: Harvey H. Bundy, "Remembered Words," *Atlantic Monthly*, March 1957, 57.

238 *"learn to think offensively . . . in utmost secrecy"*: WP, December 23, 1941. JBC, "What Victory Requires."

238 *"armed alliance of free societies . . ."*: Ibid.

239 *"The country had been at war . . . ," "There will be no need . . ."*: JBC, Secret History, 31.

239 *"not yet been seen . . . ," "largely unknown"*: MSL, 282.

240 *"this was Conant . . . ," "Glenn Seaborg is a very competent . . ."*: AQ, 71.

240 *"near certainty," "magnificent achievement"*: MSL, 282.

240 *"really an afterthought"*: AQ, 71.

241 *"exciting events"*: AQ, 78–79.

242 *"In guiding these discussions . . ."*: AQ, 71, 78–79.

242 *"recurring question"*: MSL, 284.

242 *"a heavy burden"*: POTA, 59.

242 *"When called on in May . . ."*: Baxter, Scientists Against Time, 434.

242 *"betting heavily," "All five methods," "Anything less . . . unconsciously"*: JBC to VB, May 14, 1942, VB-JBC files, NA. Also in Baxter, Scientists Against Time, 434.

243 *"determining," "They cannot be far behind . . ."*: Ibid.

243 *"Why nearly two years' delay?"*: MSL, 285.

243 *"VB—O.K.—FDR," "when necessary . . ."*: Ibid.

244 *"Take the necessary action"*: NCBT, 10.

244 *"all too little," "Like the need for speed . . ."*: JBC, "The Mobilization of Science for the War Effort," American Scientist 35, no. 2 (April, 1947).

244 *"natural aristocracy"*: Borrowman, "Conant, the Man," 58–60.

245 *"only a few elderly . . ."*: GRC to MTR, September 29, 1941, CFP.

245 *"doghouse"*: Interview with Theodore Richards Conant.

245 *"inefficiency, mismanagement . . ."*: William M. Tuttle Jr., "The Birth of an Industry: the Synthetic Rubber 'Mess' in World War II," Technology and Culture 22, no. 1 (January 1981): 37.

246 *"fearless, independent . . ."*: NYHT, July 27, 1942.

246 *"investigate the whole rubber situation"*: Tuttle, "The Birth of an Industry," 54.

246 *"a little bit disappointed . . ."*: MSL, 309.

247 *"Let me handle . . ."*: Tuttle, "James B. Conant," 330.

247 *"thankless task"*: NYHT, July 27, 1942.

247 *"No, sir . . ."*: Tuttle, "The Birth of an Industry," 54. Jordan A. Schwarz, The Speculator: Bernard M. Baruch in Washington, 1917-1965 (Chapel Hill: University of North Carolina Press, 1981), 389–96.

247 *"Unquestionably, the very best . . ."*: Ibid. NYT, August 2, 1942.

247 *"getting the mostest rubber fastest"*: Tuttle, "The Birth of an Industry," 55.

248 *"park bench committee"*: "Three Men on a Bench," Time, August 17, 1942. Schwarz, The Speculator, 389.

248 *"keep our armed forces . . . ," "bullying through . . . no middle course"*: Tuttle, "James B. Conant," 334–35.

248 *"overlapping and confusing authority," "rubber administrator"*: Ibid.

248 *"almost too good . . ."*: JBC to BMB, August 11, 1944, as quoted in Tuttle, "The Birth of an Industry," 65.

248 *"the incantations . . ."*: Schwarz, *The Speculator*, 394–95.

248 *"excellent"*: Tuttle, "The Birth of an Industry," 58.

249 *"What about you, Dr. Conant? . . ."*: Tuttle, "James B. Conant," 336.

249 *"a plan"*: Ibid.

249 *"It's all in there . . ."*: NYHT, September 11, 1942. MSL, 348.

CHAPTER 14: A COLOSSAL GAMBLE

250 *"To my mind . . ."*: JBC to LRG, December 9, 1942, JBCPP. Hershberg, *Harvard to Hiroshima*, 163.

250 *"grand scale," "Napoleonic approach," "desperate need for speed"*: JBC to VB, May 14, 1942, VB-JBC files, NA.

251 *"scientific aspects"*: TNW, 71–73.

251 *"the whole thing . . ."*: POTA, 61.

251 *"threatened to negate"*: MSL, 288.

252 *"near rebellion"*: AQ, 109.

252 *"too soon by one or two . . ."*: TNW, 79–80. Baxter, *Scientists Against Time*, 436.

253 *"cool reception"*: POTA, 61.

253 *"very seriously," "abrupt and lacking in wit"*: VB to JBC, September 17 and 21, 1942, JBCPP. VB to Harvey Bundy, as quoted in Leslie M. Groves, *Now It Can Be Told*, 20 (henceforth NCBT). Stanley Goldberg, "Groves Takes the Reins," *Bulletin of the Atomic Scientists* 48 (December 1992): 32–36, 38–39.

253 *"I fear we are in the soup"*: Ibid. Also see Richard Rhodes, *The Making of the Atomic Bomb*, 427.

253 *"unwieldy"*: NCBT, 24.

254 *"perform miracles"*: MSL, 294.

254 *"Conant had always been"*: General Leslie Groves, pt. 1, interview by Stephane Groeff, Atomic Heritage Foundation, "Voices of the Manhattan Project," January 5, 1965, http://manhattanprojectvoices.org/oralhistories/leslie-groves-interview.

255 *"weakest horse"*: TNW, 102; for a detailed technical description of all five competing methods, 85–115.

255 *"boggled"*: MSL, 291.

255 *"champagne dinner," "elephants with a peashooter"*: TNW, 102, 91. AQ, 151.

256 *"delayed," "a marginal fraction," "breaking out of control"*: AQ, 137–38.

257 *"in the middle of Chicago," "disturbed," "too late"*: MSL, 289.

257 *hazard of war*: JBC, Secret History.

257 *"unwarranted risk"*: MSL, 289.

257 *spoil the weapon*: TNW, 109.

258 *"rather fuzzy state . . ."*: Ibid.; Hershberg, *Harvard to Hiroshima*, 162.

258 *"Now is the time for faith," "It isn't faith we need . . ."*: AQ, 68.

258 *"Our Italian navigator . . . ," "Is that so . . ."*: MSL, 290. AQ, 144.

259 *"Everyone landed safe . . ."*: Ibid.

259 *"time schedule . . . "*: JBC to LRG, December 9, 1942, JBCPP. Hershberg, *Harvard to Hiroshima*, 163.

260 *"an uncertainty either way . . ."*: TNW, 114–15.

260 *"To my mind . . .":* JBC to LRG, December 9, 1942. Hershberg, *Harvard to Hiroshima,* 163.

260 *"Conant has the gambling spirit . . .":* Baxter, *Scientists Against Time,* 434.

261 *"totally unprepared":* Jonathan B. Tucker, *War of Nerves,* 41.

261 *"lewisite was first discovered . . .":* Tuttle, "James B. Conant," 12.

261 *"How many years before . . .":* JBC, "The Fight for Liberty in Peace and War," January 10, 1943, *Harvard Bulletin* 45, no. 7 (January 16, 1943): 236–39.

262 *"jaundiced eyes":* MSL, 294.

262 *"founded on possibilities":* NCBT, 19.

262 *"long-haired scientists":* AQ, 113.

262 *"Doctor," "Professor":* Childs, *American Genius,* 335.

262 *"soundness of his reasoning":* NCBT, 45.

262 *"more drastically guarded . . .":* FDR to JRO, June 29, 1943, LOC.

262 *"reliable information," "we have become convinced . . . ," "verify":* Thomas Powers, *Heisenberg's War,* 161–63.

263 *"The amount of bare-faced lying . . .":* MSL, 297.

264 *"be of direct use":* Ray Monk, *Robert Oppenheimer,* 313.

265 *"I am not a Communist . . .":* Nuel Phar Davis, *Lawrence and Oppenheimer,* 154.

265 *"through the back door":* Monk, *Robert Oppenheimer,* 321.

265 *"a necessary nuisance . . . investigation":* JBC to EOL, January 30, 1942, EOL Papers, BL.

266 *"Whoever gets this first . . .":* Hershberg, *Harvard to Hiroshima,* 158; Davis, *Lawrence and Oppenheimer,* 154; Peter Michelmore, *The Swift Years,* 69–71.

266 *"Oh! . . . Oh! . . . Oh my goodness!":* Hershberg, *Harvard to Hiroshima,* 158.

266 *"complete ban":* MSL, 297.

266 *"compartmentalization":* Robert S. Norris, *Racing for the Bomb,* 11.

266 *"the desirability of asking Oppenheimer . . .":* EOL to JBC, March 26, 1942, VB-JBC files, NA.

266 *coordinator of rapid rupture,* "wisdom and firmness": AQ, 127.

267 *"showed a refined, sure . . . ," "unforgettable," "intellectual power . . .":* Monk, *Robert Oppenheimer,* 332.

267 *"Status of the Bomb," "150 times energy . . . ," "Estimate devastation of area . . . terminated":* Rhodes, *The Making of the Atomic Bomb,* 421.

267 *"tremendous intellectual capacity," "knew everything . . .":* NCBT, 61.

268 *"strongly impressed . . .":* AQ, 129.

268 *"down-to-earth":* NCBT, 61.

268 *"None of them were go-getters . . .":* Jennet Conant, *109 East Palace: Robert Oppenheimer and the Secret City of Los Alamos* (New York: Simon & Schuster, 2005), 36.

269 *"a lovely spot":* Alice Kimball Smith and Charles Weiner, *Robert Oppenheimer,* 236.

269 *"This is the place":* Conant, *109 East Palace,* 34.

270 *"showed any great enthusiasm":* NCBT, 61.

270 *"To most physicists . . .":* Rhodes, *The Making of the Atomic Bomb,* 449.

270 *"prestige among his fellow . . .":* NCBT, 62–63.

270 *"it became apparent . . . ," "snag," "His background included . . .":* Ibid.

270 *"duration of the war . . . greeted"*: JRO to JBC, November 30, 1942, JRO Papers, LOC. Also see Smith and Weiner, *Robert Oppenheimer*, 247–48.

271 *"The job we have to do . . ."*: Ibid.

271 *"Oppenheimer saw this faculty . . . policy matters"*: Hershberg, *Harvard to Hiroshima*, 167.

271 *"wondering whether we have found . . . on the idea"*: Ibid.

272 *"None of us would come"*: John S. Rigden, *Rabi*, 150–51.

272 *"the discussion of which . . . speed required"*: Ibid.

272 *"on a strictly civilian basis," "Through Dr. Conant"*: Groves-Conant Letter to Oppenheimer, February 25, 1943, Atomic Heritage Foundation, info@atomicheritage.org.

273 *"great experience . . ."*: NCBT, 150–51.

273 *"patience, courage . . . need and want"*: Hershberg, *Harvard to Hiroshima*, 169.

273 *"Uncle Jim"*: Michelmore, *The Swift Years*, 168.

273 *"We are addressing this letter . . . instrument of war"*: Monk, *Robert Oppenheimer*, 344–45.

274 *"fragment of a strange scientific history," "This highly secret . . . to be achieved"*: JBC, Secret History, 1, and pt. 2, 16–17, 30.

274 *"unforeseen block," "How many times . . . explosion"*: Ibid.

275 *"What the future a year hence . . . ," "this scientific delirium tremens"*: Ibid.

CHAPTER 15: UNEASY ALLIANCES

276 *"The price of greatness . . ."*: "Harvard Welcomes Mr. Churchill," *Harvard Alumni Bulletin* 46, no. 1 (September 18, 1943): 18.

276 *"President Conant of Harvard . . ."*: H. G. Wells, "New Americans," *Collier's*, February 5, 1938.

276 *"A good many million . . ."*: J. Z. Jacobsen, "An American Radical: President Conant of Harvard Believes a New Program Is Essential for Us," *Fact Magazine*, May 1943, 25.

276 *"tempting fate," "post-victory era," "larger maladjustment, " "when it is not necessary . . . radical philosophy," "we may well sow . . . $25, 000 mark"*: JBC, "Wanted: American Radicals," *Atlantic Monthly* 171, no. 5 (May 1943): 41–45.

278 *"splendid successor . . . worthy of note"*: Editorial note, ibid., 41.

278 *"this is not a dignified . . ."*: Karabel, *The Chosen*, 160.

279 *"a destructive sort of chap . . ."*: Ibid., 158–59.

279 *"disagreeable cold . . . extreme mood"*: Ibid. Also see Hershberg, *Harvard to Hiroshima*, 178.

279 *"potent and refreshing . . . schoolmaster"*: WSJ, April 23, 1943.

280 *"Conant for President"*: JBC scrapbook, CFP.

280 *"the stew continues . . ."*: JBC to GRC, June 29, 1943, CFP.

280 *"stirred up a hornet's nest . . . ," "crisis"*: Karabel, *The Chosen*, 160.

280 *"By the time you read this . . . may be wrong"*: JBC to GRC, August 7, 1943, CFP.

281 *"it won't hurt my feelings . . ."*: JBC to GRC, August 12, 1943.

281 *"coordinated or even jointly conducted"*: TNW, 270.

281 *"very glad," "in complete accord"*: DAS, 98–99.

282 *"nebulous"*: JBC to VB, December 14, 1942, NDRC files, NA.

282   *"essentially responsible to anyone . . ."*: Hershberg, *Harvard to Hiroshima*, 180.

283   *"wasting his time"*: Ibid. For a detailed history of Anglo-American nuclear agreement, see *TNW*, 263–77.

284   *"come as a bombshell . . ."*: Martin J. Sherwin, *A World Destroyed*, 76.

285   *"a sombre decision"*: Sherwood, *Roosevelt and Hopkins*, 105.

285   *"astounding," "sit tight"*: *TNW*, 274.

285   *"renew, in an inclusive manner . . ."*: Ibid.

285   *"bawling him out . . . arrangement," "Very well . . ."*: *POTA*, 281–82.

286   *"review"*: Ibid.

286   *"interested only in fighting . . . make you a proposition"*: *POTA*, 283.

286   *"all sorts of trouble"*: Ibid.

286   *"to fruition . . ."*: *TNW*, 278.

287   *"heavy sense of responsibility . . ."*: *DAS*, 101–2.

287   *"But if Bush, Conant, and Groves . . ."*: Ibid., 109.

287   *"a most interesting though strenuous . . ."*: JBC to GRC, August 7, 1943, CFP.

287   *"The Quebec Agreement . . . Nazi foe"*: *TNW*, 279.

288   *"Confidential," "Academic meeting"*: "Harvard Welcomes Mr. Churchill," 11.

289   *"I am once again in academic groves . . ."*: Ibid., 18.

289   *"the blitz was running hard"*: Ibid.

289   *"The price of greatness . . . all will fail"*: "Harvard Welcomes Mr. Churchill," 18, 13.

289   *"national public relations job"*: JBC to GRC, September 22, 1943, CFP.

290   *"typical"*: Roosevelt, "Harvard's Prize Kibitzer," 2.

290   *"How did I do, Mother?. . . best"*: GRC, "A Brief Visit from a Great Man or a Hostess Remembers," unpublished reminiscence of Churchill visit, 1943, CFP.

290   *"the empires of the future . . . ," "The twentieth-century struggles . . ."*: *MSL*, 289.

291   *"most optimistic . . ."*: JBC to GRC, August 7, 1943, CFP.

292   *"atomic explosions"*: Powers, *Heisenberg's War*, 241.

294   *"the gadget"*: Conant, *109 East Palace*, 105.

294   *"the Super"*: *TNW*, 240.

295   *"gun method"*: *MSL*, 292–93. *TNW*, 235.

295   *"implosion method"*: Ibid. For a detailed technical description of the development of the two methods, see *TNW*, 235–54.

296   *"engineering"*: John Bass, *The Moment in Time: The Manhattan Project*, documentary film, University of California, 2008.

296   *"The reason why I am here today . . ."*: Lawrence Badash, Joseph O. Hirschfelder, and Herbert P. Broida, *Reminiscences of Los Alamos*, 71.

297   *"it might be regarded . . ."*: *NCBT*, 162.

297   *"intrinsic explosibility"*: *TNW*, 240.

297   *go-ahead signal*: *MSL*, 291.

298   *"fast" neutrons*: *TNW*, 240.

299   *"really mattered"*: Badash, Hirschfelder, and Broida, *Reminiscences of Los Alamos*, 49.

299   *"Thin Man," "Fat Man," "modifying a plane . . ."*: Rhodes, *The Making of the Atomic Bomb*, 481.

CHAPTER 16: ONE FELL STROKE

300 *"the essence of war..."*: JBC to VB, May 9, 1945, JBCPP.

300 *"at least every difficulty..."*: JBC, Secret History, pt. II, 17.

301 *"by one fell, drastic stroke..."*: NYT, December 3, 1943.

301 *"Although this was sometimes..."*: NCBT, 187.

301 *"every effort should be made..."*: JBC to VB, December 9, 1942. Powers, *Heisenberg's War*, 209.

301 Germans occupied Norway ... seized Norsk Hydro plant: Norris, *Racing for the Bomb*, 281–84.

302 *"some headaches"*: NCBT, 188.

303 *"S-1 targets," "German process"*: Powers, *Heisenberg's War*, 209–10.

303 *"the chances of seriously interfering...," "arrangements are now under way"*: Ibid.

303 *"It was clearly a drawing...," "a quite useless military weapon," "If the people at Los Alamos..."*: Jeremy Bernstein, "The Drawing or Why History Is Not Mathematics," *Physics in Perspective* 5, iss. 3 (September 2003): 2–7.

304 *"What do you think?"*: Powers, *Heisenberg's War*, 250.

304 *"the killing of scientific personnel..."*: Powers, *Heisenberg's War*, 251.

304 *"very probably knew"*: Ibid, 537-38.

304 Aage Bohr's dispute: Bernstein, "The Drawing or Why History is Not Mathematics," 6.

304 *"if so much as a word..."*: Ibid., 399.

305 *"almost any effort to stop..."*: Ibid., 252.

305 *"disastrous results," "This was a time ... disprove them"*: NCBT, 200.

306 *"It now seems extremely possible..."*: Barton J. Bernstein, "Radiological Warfare: The Path Not Taken," *Bulletin of the Atomic Scientists* 41 (September 1985): 45–46.

306 *"the application that seemed ... half a million men"*: Powers, *Heisenberg's War*, 354–55.

306 *"extremely unlikely"*: NCBT, 200. Hershberg, *Harvard to Hiroshima*, 201.

306 Operation Peppermint, *"unknown etiology"*: NCBT, 201–5.

307 *"emphasize our belief..."*: Ibid.

307 *"You scare the hell out of me"*: POTA, 307.

307 *"on the present available ... of this nature"*: NCBT, 205.

308 *"I knew our advice"*: Ibid., 206.

308 *"some bad hours"*: Ibid., 199.

308 *"Well, Van, how do you feel...," "Very much relieved"*: POTA, 307.

308 Thin Man problems: TNW, 251.

309 *"All to no avail, alas!"*: Ibid.

309 *"The situation is a mess..."*: Monk, *Robert Oppenheimer*, 429.

309 *"May the Lord preserve us..."*: Conant, *109 East Palace*, 231.

309 *"the situation was desperate"*: MSL, 293.

309 *"the most colossal egos"*: George Kistiakowsky, "James B. Conant, 1893–1978," *Nature* 273, no. 5665 (June 29, 1978): 793–95.

310 *"explosive lenses"*: Badash, Hirschfelder, and Broida, *Reminiscences of Los Alamos*, 50–52.

310 *"Your confidence in our future..."*: JRO to JBC, August 3, 1944, as quoted in Smith and Weiner, *Robert Oppenheimer*, 278–79.

311   *"Just a line to tell you . . .":* JBC to JRO, October 20, 1944, ibid., 287.

311   *"present expectations," "reasonable success":* TNW, 252.

312   *"leadership of the world," "the American Century":* Steel, *Walter Lippmann*, 404.

312   *"fight talk," "decisive victory":* Tuttle, "James B. Conant," 371–72.

313   *"a friend of Eleanor's," "queer ideas," "bill of complaints," "almost treacherous situation":* MSL, 295–96.

313   *"loose talk about the inadequacies":* Ibid.

313   *"did not know the score . . . felt left out":* Ibid., 296–99.

313   *"the question was raised . . . ," "I don't want to know . . . lady to relax":* Ibid.

313   *"spirit in Chicago":* Ibid., 295.

313   *"so significant it neither could . . .":* Sherwin, *A World Destroyed,* n122.

314   *"complete privacy . . .":* MSL, 300.

314   *"We cannot emphasize . . . should be secure":* VB and JBC to HLS, September 19, 1944, AEC document, quoted in Hershberg, *Harvard to Hiroshima,* 204. MSL, 300.

315   *"very much embarrassed":* Sherwin, *A World Destroyed,* 122–25.

315   *"necessity for maintaining . . . ," "for certainly it would be . . .":* Ibid.

316   *"normal advisors," "highly dangerous situation":* Ibid.

316   *"This demonstration . . .":* TNW, 329.

317   *"tentative," "no diplomatic initiatives . . . scientists had urged," "because of their position . . .":* Sherwin, *A World Destroyed,* 122, 127, 116.

317   *"Alternatives[:] . . . stood???," The question marks . . .":* Hershberg, *Harvard to Hiroshima,* 198–200.

318   *"so transformed the art of war . . . bristling with weapons":* JBC, "The Effective Disarmament of Germany and Japan," October 7, 1944, JBCPP. *NYT,* October 8, 1944. Tuttle, "James B. Conant," 377–78.

318   *"with a series . . .":* JBC to Major George Fielding Eliot, January 29, 1945, JBCPP. Tuttle, "James B. Conant," 380.

319   *"entering wedge":* VB to JBC, October 24, 1944, Bush-Conant file, NA.

320   *"This is the first time . . .":* Edward Teller with Judith Shoolery, *Memoirs,* 202–3.

321   *"freeze," "Christy bomb":* Conant, *109 East Palace,* 264. James P. Delgado, *Nuclear Dawn,* 50.

321   Trinity, *"Batter my heart . . . ,"* macabre: Rhodes, *The Making of the Atomic Bomb,* 571–72.

321   Jornado del Muerto, *No Trespassing signs, zero point:* Conant, *109 East Palace,* 236–38. For a detailed description of Trinity test, see Delgado, *Nuclear Dawn,* 53–59.

322   *"hundred-ton test":* Ibid., 56.

322   *"The war is not over . . .":* HC, May 8, 1945.

323   *"new force," "charged with the function . . .":* Stimson and Bundy, *On Active Service,* 616.

323   Interim Committee, *"Now we can start . . .":* Ibid. HLS diary, May 2, 1945, HLS Papers, YU.

323   *"doubted," "growing restlessness":* MSL, 300.

324   *"indiscriminate destruction . . . uninhabited area":* Daniel J. Kevles, *The Physicists,* 335.

324   *"essential," "public bickering":* JB to HLS, May 1945, HLS Papers, YU.

324 *"extravagance in the Manhattan Project . . . might become disastrous," "nervous memo-randum . . . be successful"*: Stimson and Bundy, *On Active Service*, 615–16. HLS diary, March 15, 1945, HLS Papers, YU.

325 *"Gentlemen, it is our responsibility . . ."*: David McCullough, *Truman*, 390.

325 *"to make certain . . ."*: Norris, *Racing for the Bomb*, 389.

325 *"phony"*: TNW, 354.

326 *defended their estimate*: MSL, 301.

326 *"like statesmen and not merely . . . peace of the world"*: HLS diary, July 21, 1945.

326 *"some striking but harmless . . . ," "a nonmilitary demonstration . . . ," "Various possibili-ties . . . ," "might be a dud"*: AQ, 238–39.

327 *"We were keenly aware . . ."*: Ibid.

327 *"sufficiently spectacular . . . two-thirds of a mile"*: Ibid. Monk, *Robert Oppenheimer*, 447.

327 *"seemed the ideal weapon . . . at our disposal"*: JBC to McGeorge Bundy, November 30, 1946, HLS Papers, YU.

328 *"burn jobs"*: Life, August 20, 1945.

328 *"the number of people killed . . ."*: Sherwin, *A World Destroyed*, 207–8.

328 *"precision"*: DAS, 66.

328 *"shortening this war"*: St. Clair McKelway, "A Reporter with the B-29's," *NY*, part III, June 23, 1945.

328 *"far less terrible . . ."*: POTA, 62–63.

329 *"governing factor," "most adversely affect"*: DAS, 63.

329 *"it had been the capital . . ."*: McCullough, *Truman*, 436.

329 *"We could not give the Japanese," "most desirable target . . ."*: Sherwin, *A World De-stroyed*, 302.

329 *without warning*: DAS, 73.

329 *"most important matter . . ."*: MSL, 302.

330 *"join up," "4F"*: Interview with Theodore Richards Conant.

330 *"great danger . . ."*: John Parks to JBC, March 30, 1945, CFP.

330 *"My father would have none . . ."*: Interview with Theodore Richards Conant.

330 *"pleased to report . . . what I found"*: JBC to GRC, July 13, 1945, CFP.

331 *"This is an interesting trip . . ."*: Ibid.

331 *"How am I going to explain . . ."*: NCBT, 290.

332 *"chief villain," "Everybody lectured me . . ."*: Badash, Hirschfelder, and Broida, *Reminis-cences of Los Alamos*, 59.

332 *"A few pessimists"*: JBC, "Notes on the 'Trinity' Test held at Alamogordo bombing range," VB-JBC file, OSRD, NA (henceforth JBC, "Notes on Trinity"). Reprinted in its entirety in Hershberg, *Harvard to Hiroshima*, 758–61.

333 *"reversal"*: NCBT, 9291–93.

333 *"a bit tense . . ."*: JBC, "Notes on Trinity."

333 *"From 10:30 a.m . . ."*: Ibid.

333 *"ignite the atmosphere"*: NCBT, 296–97.

334 *"minus forty-five . . ."*: JBC, "Notes on Trinity."

334 *"never imagined seconds . . ."*: NCBT, 438.

334   *"Then came a burst . . . actually occurred"*: JBC, "Notes on Trinity."

334   *"an enormous pyrotechnic display . . . wave,"* *"Well, I guess there is something . . ."*: Ibid.

335   *"wrapped up in the future"*: NCBT, 298.

335   *"It was only a matter . . ."*: JBC to McGeorge Bundy, November 30, 1946, HLS Papers, YU.

335   *"knocked him off his feet"*: Badash, Hirschfelder, and Broida, *Reminiscences of Los Alamos*, 60.

335   *"disappeared . . . expected"*: JBC, "Notes on Trinity."

335   *"off the scale,"* *"not serious"*: Ibid.

336   *"usual freakiness,"* *"content of gas shells . . ."*: NCBT, 301.

336   *"Oh, Dr. Conant . . ."*: Davis, *Lawrence and Oppenheimer*, 240.

336   *"operation . . . pleased"*: Norris, *Racing for the Bomb*, 406.

336   *"My first impression . . ."*: JBC, "Notes on Trinity."

CHAPTER 17: A CHANGED WORLD

337   *"The unleashed power . . ."*: Nancy Peterson Hill, *A Very Private Public Citizen*, 169.

337   *"loosed . . . on this earth"*: NYT, August 7, 1945. McCullough, *Truman*, 455.

338   *"correctness of the action . . ."*: MSL, 302.

338   *"marvel . . . without failure"*: NYT, August 7, 1945.

339   *"Air became flame . . ."*: "The War Ends," *Life*, August 20, 1945.

339   *"Atom Age,"* *"greatest scientific gamble"*: BDG, August 7, 1945.

339   *"The Haunted Wood,"* *"not with exultation . . . minor planets"*: WP, August 7, 1945.

339   *"Yesterday we clinched victory . . ."*: NYT, August 7, 1945.

340   *"more surely than the rocket . . ."*: Winston Churchill, "Potentialities of the New Weapon—Warning for the Future," radio address, August 10, 1945.

340   *"devastating strength"*: JBC to Harvey Bundy, November 30, 1946, JBCPP.

340   *"must be the prime objective . . ."*: JBC and VB to the Interim Committee, July 18, 1945, as quoted in Hershberg, *Harvard to Hiroshima*, 236.

341   *"Joey-come-lately,"* *"hopeless odds . . ."*: NYT, August 9, 1945.

341   *"crumbled and disintegrated . . ."*: NYT, August 20, 1945.

341   *"and the detailed arrangements . . ."*: MSL, 303.

342   *"additional bombs"*: LRG's directive to General Carl Spaatz, July 23, 1945, as quoted in NCBT, 308; McCullough, *Truman*, 457.

342   *"taking no chances,"* *"napalm bombs"*: NYT, August 9, 1945.

342   *"mopping-up operation,"* *"finish off"*: "The War Ends."

342   *"royal foul-up,"* *"clearing"*: NCBT, 346–47.

343   *"ultimate responsibility . . . fellow citizens"*: Henry DeWolf Smyth, *Atomic Energy for Military Purposes: The Official Report on the Development of the Atomic Bomb Under the Auspices of the United States Government, 1940–1945* (Princeton, NJ: Princeton University Press, 1945), vii.

343   *"scientific men"*: Ibid.

344   *"GIs in Pacific . . ."*: NYT, August 10, 1945.

344   *"by enduring the unendurable . . . Declaration of Powers"*: Delgado, *Nuclear Dawn*, 115.

345 Halibut's *crew*: Admiral I. J. Galantin, *Take Her Deep! A Submarine Against Japan in World War II* (Chapel Hill, NC: Algonquin Books, 1987), 223–248.

345 *"cracked up," "A severe case . . ."*: Hershberg, *Harvard to Hiroshima*, 239.

345 *"Coming just at this time . . ."*: Ibid.

346 *"mental condition of being shell-shocked"*: General Leslie Groves, interview, "Voices of the Manhattan Project."

346 *"stark-raving mad"*: Interview with Theodore Richards Conant.

347 *"too dangerous to be loose . . ."*: *NYT*, August 10, 1945.

347 *"only optimists would have willingly . . ."*: JBC, Secret History, 33.

347 *"The world is changed . . ."*: *TNW*, 416.

347 *"For military courage . . ."*: JBC, "From War to Peace," *HC*, September 28, 1945. *Harvard Alumni Bulletin*, October 6, 1945, 81.

347 *"could engender such conditions . . ."*: Ibid. Also see JBC, "The Fight for Liberty in Peace and War."

348 *"fear, panic, and foolish . . ."*: JBC, "From War to Peace."

348 *"push-button wars," "robot planes . . ."*: "The Atom Bomb and Future War," *Life*, August 20, 1945.

348 *"There was no defense . . ."*: JBC, speech to the Cleveland Chamber of Commerce, *HC*, November 23, 1945.

348 *"revolution in warfare . . ."*: Hershberg, *Harvard to Hiroshima*, 241.

348 *"We are living in a very different . . ."*: Keyes Dewitt Metcalf, *My Harvard Library Years, 1937–1955* (Cambridge, MA: Harvard University Press, 1988), 116–17.

349 *"How many volumes . . . ," "preserve the material . . ."*: Ibid.

349 *"This would include . . ."*: Ibid.

349 *"It could not be done . . . nothing more about it"*: Ibid.

350 *"mighty thunder"*: Delgado, *Nuclear Dawn*, 61.

350 *"nervous wreck"*: Monk, *Robert Oppenheimer*, 475.

350 *"Now I am become Death . . ."*: Delgado, *Nuclear Dawn*, 63.

350 *"revulsion"*: Alice Kimball Smith, *A Peril and a Hope: The Scientists Movement in America, 1945–47* (Cambridge, MA: MIT Press, 1965), 77.

350 *"barbarism," "mass murder," "sheer terrorism"*: "Opinion," *Time*, August 20, 1945.

350 *"war was now impossible"*: Smith, *A Peril and a Hope*, 77.

350 *"It is no good trying . . ."*: Laura Fermi, *Atoms in the Family*, 244.

350 *"What if we hadn't?"*: Teller, *Memoirs*, 216.

350 *"felt more or less deeply . . . anywhere, anytime"*: Fermi, *Atoms in the Family*, 245.

351 *"tragic use . . ."*: *Chicago Tribune*, September 2, 1945.

351 *"begin an elaborate study . . ."*: *TNW*, 423.

351 *"Scientist Drops A-bomb . . . ," "clarify and consolidate"*: Ibid. Smith, *A Peril and a Hope*, 88–89.

351 *"This place is a bit . . . discussion"*: VB to JBC, September 24 and October 1, 1945, VB-JBC file, OSRD, NA.

351 *"center of affairs . . . letting them loose"*: JBC to VB, October 4, 1945, VB-JBC file, OSRD, NA.

352 *"poison of deception"*: MSL, 298.

352   *"What makes you think . . ."*: Interview with GRC.

352   *"years of frustration"*: MSL, 299.

352   *"hostility"*: Ibid.

352   *"to test out their good faith"*: TNW, 412.

353   *"I think your statement . . ."*: JBC to VB, October 4, 1945.

353   *"world government," "world state . . ."*: Paul Boyer, *By the Bomb's Early Light*, 34–35.

353   *"talked atomic bomb . . ."*: Hill, *A Very Private Public Citizen*, 162.

353   *"could shortly have the bomb . . . the height of folly"*: Hershberg, *Harvard to Hiroshima*, 247.

354   *"under which cooperation . . ."*: TNW, 426.

355   *"The misuse of such energy . . ."*: Ibid., 431.

355   *"Men Who Made the Bomb . . ."*: Byron S. Miller, "A Law Is Passed: The Atomic Energy Act of 1946," *University of Chicago Law Review* 15, no. 4 (Summer 1948): 800.

356   *"international security . . ."*: Smith, *A Peril and a Hope*, 174.

356   *"doesn't bother me . . ."*: JBC to VB, October 23, 1945, VB-JBC file, OSRD, NA.

356   *"sweating at the very thought . . ."*: "Hold That Monster," *Time*, November 19, 1945.

357   *"the greatest challenge . . ."*: TNW, 428.

357   *"wisest of motives . . . ," "The same men who could command . . ."*: Ibid., 435.

357   *"the implied threat of the bomb . . ."*: Ibid., 417.

357   *"make Russia more manageable . . ."*: Sherwin, *A World Destroyed*, 202.

357   *"a secret armament race . . ."*: TNW, 419.

358   *"willing and cooperative partners . . ."*: Ibid.

358   *"break his silence . . ."*: JBC to VB, October 23, 1945, VB-JBC file, NA.

358   *"I am very much disturbed . . ."*: VB to JBC, November 7, 1945, VB-JBC file, NA.

359   *"We recognize that the application . . ."*: TNW, 464–65.

359   *"first steps"*: JBC to Harry S. Truman, November 15, 1945, VB-JBC file, NA.

360   *"cheerful liar"*: JBC Moscow diary, December 10, 1945, JBCPP.

360   *"his policy was . . . ," "still crossed"*: Ibid., December 24, 1945.

360   *"college professors"*: TNW, 473.

361   *"the really crucial time . . ."*: JBC, "National Defense in the Light of the Atomic Bomb," December 3, 1945, JBCPP. JBC gave a similar talk, "Conant on the Bomb," at the Cleveland Chamber of Commerce on November 20, 1945.

361   *"by stages"*: TNW, 476.

361   *"a little cynical . . . ," "headed for a large success . . ."*: JBC Moscow diary, December 24, JBCPP.

361   *"good cheer," "dwellers of the Kremlin"*: MSL, 486–87.

361   *"most comforting news . . ."*: BH, December 28, 1945, reprinted in MSL, 487.

361   *"The outcome is excellent . . . down the right path"*: VB to JBC, January 2, 1945, VB-JBC file, NA.

CHAPTER 18: ATOMIC CHAOS

363   *"His success . . ."*: "Harvard's James Bryant Conant: Chemist of Ideas," *Time*, September 23, 1946, 60.

363   *"the atomic bomb is just too dreadful . . ."*: Smith, *A Peril and a Hope*, 228. Public opinion poll: Boyer, *By the Bomb's Early Light*, 22.

364 *"In such a world . . ."*: "The Presidency: A Policy Is Born," *Time*, December 31, 1945.

364 *"terrifying implications," "nightmare of global war"*: JBC, "National Defense in the Light of the Atomic Bomb."

364 *"right now . . . adverse conditions"*: JBC testimony, Committee on Military Affairs, House of Representatives, 79th Cong. 1st Sess., part 1, "Universal Military Service Hearings," November 8–December 19, 1946.

364 *"not out of despair . . . major threat of war"*: JBC, "Conant and the Bomb," November 20, 1945, *Harvard Alumni Bulletin*, December 8, 1945.

365 *"too grand"*: DAS, 159.

365 *Atomic Development Authority*: Ibid.

365 *"dangerous activities . . . ," "cops," "A place to begin . . ."*: TNW, 536, 540.

366 *"stages," "the most constructive analysis . . ."*: DAS, 161.

366 *"Great Fear," "Elysian daydream"*: TNW, 558.

367 *"We clasped the new bible . . ."*: Smith, *A Peril and a Hope*, 335.

367 *"youngsters"*: Tuttle, "James B. Conant," 330.

367 *"suspicions of many senators . . ."*: MSL, 493.

367 *"went boom . . ."*: Gregg Herken, *The Winning Weapon*, 161.

367 *"That was the day . . ."*: Monk, *Robert Oppenheimer*, 500.

368 *"He wants to run the world . . ."*: DAS, 162.

368 *"tired of babying the Russians . . ."*: Ibid., 176.

368 *"atom spies"*: Smith, *A Peril and a Hope*, 308.

368 *"two hostile camps . . ."*: Steel, *Walter Lippmann*, 427.

368 *"From Stettin in the Baltic . . . un-united world"*: Ibid., 428.

368 *"fanatically," "permanent peaceful coexistence"*: Ibid., 433. Also Kennan, *Memoirs*, 292–95.

368 *"rocking the boat"*: MSL, 506.

369 *"logical"*: Ibid., 493.

369 *"immediate and certain punishment"*: DAS, 165.

370 *"We are here . . . World Destruction"*: Smith, *A Peril and a Hope*, 338.

370 *"If I read the signs . . ."*: TNW, 577.

370 *"Literally the fate of the world . . ."*: Boyer, *By the Bomb's Early Light*, 56.

370 *"stand pat," "winning weapon," "The bitter truth . . ."*: DAS, 166–69.

371 *"be in a position of . . ."*: MSL, 494.

371 *"appraisal of the relative strength . . . ," "accumulated dissatisfactions"*: Ibid., 494–95.

372 *"hatchet men"*: Smith, *A Peril and a Hope*, 303.

372 *"For all I knew . . ."*: Ibid., 497.

372 *"extreme horror"*: Ibid.

372 *"more liberal thinking . . ."*: MSL, 301; Smith, *A Peril and a Hope*, 15.

373 *"certain degree of incompatibility . . ."*: Hershberg, *Harvard to Hiroshima*, 264.

373 *"shattered faith"*: Smith, *A Peril and a Hope*, 340.

373 *"just another weapon"*: Delgado, *Nuclear Dawn*, 157.

373 *"Nothing Atoll . . ."*: Ibid., 154.

374 *"turned his back . . ."*: MSL, 499.

374 *"scientific celebrity . . . world's biggest job"*: "Harvard's James Bryant Conant: Chemist of Ideas," 53, 60.

374 *"atomic harness"*: MSL, 500.

374 *"get-tough"*: TNW, 601.

374 *"very much disturbed . . . wear us down"*: VB to JBC, October 21, 1946, VB-JBC file, NA.

375 *"decidedly stiff . . ."*: Ibid.

375 *"cold war"*: George Orwell, "You and the Atomic Bomb," *London Tribune*, October 19, 1945.

375 *"classified," "the age of the Superblitz"*: Hershberg, *Harvard to Hiroshima*, 273.

375 *"in such an age . . ."*: Ibid.

376 *"a rickety bridge"*: Ibid.

376 *"Their faces were wholly burned . . . 600 beds"*: John Hersey, *Hiroshima* (New York: Random House, 1946), 51–52, 24–26. Boyer, *By the Bomb's Early Light*, 205.

377 *"rich repertory of symptoms"*: Hersey, *Hiroshima*, 110.

377 *"injurious within . . ."*: Susan Southard, *Nagasaki: Life After Nuclear War* (New York: Viking Penguin, 2015), 107.

377 *hibakusha*: Hersey, *Hiroshima*, 110.

377 *"A-bomb sickness"*: Ibid.

378 *"terrible implications"*: "To Our Readers," NY, August 31, 1946.

378 *"war criminals . . ."*: Hershberg, *Harvard to Hiroshima*, 282–83.

378 *"What bothered me . . ."*: Ibid.

378 *"paraded their sense of guilt . . . ," "war is ethically . . ."*: JBC to Muriel Popper, June 21, 1968, JBCPP. Amster, "Meritocracy Ascendant," 150.

378 *"morally indefensible . . . people of Japan"*: Boyer, *By the Bomb's Early Light*, 202.

379 *"Christian realism," "the triumph of experience . . ."*: Paul Elie, "A Man for All Reasons," *Atlantic Monthly*, November 2007.

379 *"At the risk . . . Axis powers"*: Hershberg, *Harvard to Hiroshima*, 284.

380 *"does not make sufficiently clear . . . defeated tyranny"*: Ibid., 285. For Niebuhr's full reply, see James G. Hershberg, "A Footnote on Hiroshima and Atomic Morality: Conant, Niebuhr, and an 'Emotional' Clergyman, 1945–46," *December 2002 Newsletter*, George Washington University.

380 *"notoriously nondocile"*: Robert E. Sherwood, *Roosevelt and Hopkins: An Intimate Story* (New York: Harper, 1948), 437.

381 *"very useful . . ."*: VB to JBC, July 18, 1946, JBCPP.

381 *"never liked mixing . . . legal action"*: Hershberg, *Harvard to Hiroshima*, 285–86.

381 *"in all probability . . ."*: Barton J. Bernstein, "Seizing the Contested Terrain of Early Nuclear History: Stimson, Conant, and Their Allies Explain the Decision to Use the Atomic Bomb," *Diplomatic History* 17, iss. 1 (January 1993): 35–72. JBC's efforts to shape popular opinion about the use of the bomb is also examined in James Hershberg, "James B. Conant, Nuclear Weapons, and the Cold War," 117–80.

382 *"That at the time . . . and political will"*: MSL, 302.

382 *"terrible toll," "That nightmare . . . physically overrun"*: DAS, 61.

382 *"The losses in Hiroshima and Nagasaki . . .":* Wilson D. Miscamble, *The Most Controversial Decision,* 114.

383 *"There was never a moment's discussion . . .":* Robert Dallek, *The Lost Peace,* 128.

383 *"Monday morning quarterbacking":* JBC to Harvey Bundy, September 23, 1946, JBCPRESP, Harvey Bundy correspondence, HUA.

383 *"The difference between . . .":* MSL, 303.

383 *"Truman could have canceled . . .":* MSL, 303.

383 *"I am considerably disturbed . . . against the Japanese":* JBC to Harvey Bundy, September 23, 1946.

384 *"professional pacifists . . . next generation":* Ibid.

384 *"distortion of history . . . Mr. Stimson":* Ibid.

384 *pointing out the conditions . . . for this decision":* Ibid.

384 *"eleventh hour," "I am quite unrepentant . . .":* Ibid.

385 *"I expressed my views . . .":* Ibid.

385 *"affirm the rectitude":* Bernstein, "The Decision to Use the Bomb," 36.

385 *"pride and utter lack . . .":* Paul Ham, *Hiroshima, Nagasaki,* 466.

385 *"the criticism of Hiroshima . . .":* Hershberg, *Harvard to Hiroshima,* 282.

385 *"saved hundreds of thousands . . . effective":* Karl T. Compton, "If the Atomic Bomb Had Not Been Used," *Atlantic Monthly* 178 (December 1946): 54–56.

385 *"I think it's excellent . . .":* Bernstein, "The Decision to Use the Bomb," 44.

386 *"A bad example . . . ," "I must say I am . . . most unfair way":* Walter Lippmann to JBC, October 28, 1946, JBCPRESP, HUA.

386 *"squarely":* JBC to Walter Lippmann, November 1, 1946, JBCPRESP, HUA.

386 *"Of course, the whole thing . . .":* VB to JBC, November 4, 1946, VB Papers, LOC.

386 *"might endanger the international . . .":* Hershberg, *Harvard to Hiroshima,* 291.

386 *"cheery imbecility":* "The New Pictures," *Time,* February 24, 1947.

387 *"scribe":* DAS, 92. Winnacker's casualty figures: Winnacker to Stimson, November 12, 1946, as quoted in Bernstein, "The Decision to Use the Bomb," 50. For more on the making of the myth of "over a million" US casualties, see Gar Alperovitz, *The Decision to Use the Atomic Bomb,* 458–97.

387 *"a little high":* Barton J. Bernstein, "A Postwar Myth: 500,000 U.S. Lives Saved," *Bulletin of the Atomic Scientists,* June/July 1986, 38.

387 *"I was informed":* Bernstein, "The Decision to Use the Bomb," 50.

388 *"Eliminate all sections . . . line of argumentation":* JBC to McGeorge Bundy, November 30, 1946, Henry L. Stimson Papers, YU.

388 *"the product of many hands . . . cold and cruel":* Bernstein, "The Decision to Use the Bomb," 50–51.

388 *"ARTICLE PROVES . . .":* Ibid.

388 *"It seems to me just exactly . . . another war":* Ibid.

389 *"Mr. Stimson shows . . .":* NYT, February 2, 1947.

389 *"very well," "almost entirely":* Bernstein, "The Decision to Use the Bomb," 55.

389 *"The men who were on the ground . . .":* Miscamble, *The Most Controversial Decision,* 116.

390 *"clear recollection . . . countrymen in the face":* HLS, "The Decision to Use the Atomic Bomb," *Harper's* 194 (February 1947): 97–107.

390 *"In this last great action . . . There is no other choice"*: Ibid.

390 *"We had no bombs . . ."*: HC, February 14, 1947.

390 *"I have certainly . . ."*: JBC to GRC, February 15, 1947, CFP.

390 *"realistic," "President Conant has written . . ."*: Bernstein, "The Decision to Use the Bomb," 57.

391 *"We deserve some sort of medal . . ."*: Ibid.

391 *"generously took a greater share . . ."*: Sean L. Malloy, *Atomic Tragedy*, 161.

392 *"Conant's reaction . . . immediate nuclear disarmament"*: Hershberg, *Harvard to Hiroshima*, 304.

392 *"America was heading into a period . . ."*: Ibid.

392 *"claimed too much . . . ," "preemptive purpose," "What is true . . . thought it irrelevant"*: DAS, 88–89.

392 *"the bomb did not win the war . . ."*: Ibid., 93.

CHAPTER 19: FIRST OF THE COLD WARRIORS

393 *"Dr. Conant is a man . . ."*: *Saturday Review*, January 8, 1949.

393 *"organizer of victory"*: Henry Kissinger, "Reflections on the Marshall Plan," *Harvard Gazette*, May 22, 2015.

393 *"be pleased to make a few remarks . . ."*: Bethell, *Harvard Observed*, 185–86.

393 *"epic making"*: Hershberg, *Harvard to Hiroshima*, 321.

393 *"He is expected to deliver . . ."*: NYT, June 5, 1947.

394 *"I need not tell you . . . no assured peace"*: George C. Marshall, the Marshall Plan, George C. Marshall Research Library, www.marshallfoundation.org/marshall/the-marshall-plan.

394 *"lifeline to sinking men . . ."*: Kissinger, "Reflections on the Marshall Plan."

395 *"Our financial intervention . . ."*: Steel, *Walter Lippmann*, 441–42.

395 *"to lose almost all the hope . . ."*: MSL, 306.

395 *"a ploy . . ."*: Kissinger, "Reflections on the Marshall Plan."

395 *"but the men in the Kremlin . . . might rust away"*: JBC, "Education and the Prospects of World Peace," September 8, 1947, JBCPP.

396 *"nook and cranny," "unanswerable force . . . political points"*: Steel, *Walter Lippmann*, 443.

396 *"strategic monstrosity"*: Wilson D. Miscamble, *George F. Kennan and the Making of American Foreign Policy, 1947–1950* (Princeton, NJ: Princeton University Press, 1992), 66.

396 *"defensive," "disintegrate in a whirlpool . . . ," "sword of Damocles . . ."*: JBC, "Education and the Prospects of World Peace."

397 *"unwise," "exceedingly dangerous . . ."*: Richard G. Hewlett and Francis Duncan, *Atomic Shield*, 268.

397 *"against-the-wind battle . . ."*: Hershberg, *Harvard to Hiroshima*, 323.

397 *"crystal ball," "armed truce," "A divided world . . ."*: JBC, "Education and the Prospects of World Peace."

398 *"I do not believe . . . atomic fuel underground"*: Hershberg, *Harvard to Hiroshima*, 341.

398 *"trying to put the genie back in the bottle"*: Ibid., 347.

398   *"written off as soft-headed"*: JBC, *Education in a Divided World*, 28.

398   *"alarmingly clear and grim"*: Ibid.

398   *"lingering doubts"*: MSL, 506.

398   *"one of the first of the Cold Warriors"*: Tuttle, "James B. Conant," 385.

398   *"sent a shock . . . ," "showdown"*: Steel, *Walter Lippmann*, 450.

399   *"Conant Sees . . ."*: BG, March 18, 1948.

399   *"you being the only person . . . present planning"*: JBC to VB, March 19, 1948, JBCPP.

399   *"But what annoys me . . . stop and think"*: Ibid.

399   *"wastebasket"*: Ibid.

399   *"The proper pattern . . ."*: JBC, *Education in a Divided World*, 219–20.

400   *"ideological and political thrusts . . ."*: Ibid. Also *MSL*, 521.

401   *"Since Russia might . . ."*: Ibid.

401   *"scrupulously honest"*: MSL, 359.

401   *"atomic-capable"*: Herken, *The Winning Weapon*, 253.

401   *"There has been a definite . . ."*: Isaacs and Downing, *Cold War*, 79.

402   *"do something foolish . . ."*: JBC, "Some Problems of an Armed Truce," March 24, 1948, JBCPP. Hershberg, *Harvard to Hiroshima*, 364.

402   *"accidental president," "clean up the mess . . ."*: Dallek, *The Lost Peace*, 219–20, 224.

402   *"soft on Communism," "treason of Yalta"*: Ibid., 217–25. Also see Philip M. Stern, *The Oppenheimer Case*, 115–16.

402   *"The American people admire . . ."*: McCullough, *Truman*, 715.

403   *"firm hands"*: Hewlett and Duncan, *Atomic Shield*, 8.

403   *"nuclear oracles"*: Richard Terry Sylves, *Nuclear Oracles: A Political History of the General Advisory Committee of the Atomic Energy Commission, 1947–1977* (Ames: Iowa State University Press, 1987).

403   *"Five Greatest Living Americans . . ."*: *Atlanta Constitution*, July 27, 1949.

403   *"glamorous . . ."*: MSL, 494.

403   *"Conant tried to find the practical world . . ."*: Sam Bass Warner Jr., *Province of Reason*, 233–34.

404   *"Father of the A-bomb"*: Stern, *The Oppenheimer Case*, 107.

404   *"Mr. President, I feel . . . ," "cry baby scientist"*: Conant, *109 East Palace*, 343–44. Monk, *Robert Oppenheimer*, 493–94.

404   *"leftist," "Communist tendencies," "appeaser of Russia"*: Hewlett and Duncan, *Atomic Shield*, 7–9.

404   *"Americanism," "Communist proclivities"*: Ibid.

405   *"derogatory information"*: Stern, *The Oppenheimer Case*, 101.

405   *"brilliant and driving leadership"*: Ibid.

406   *"regret . . ."*: Smith and Weiner, *Robert Oppenheimer*, 163.

406   *"seriously impeach"*: Stern, *The Oppenheimer Case*, 101.

406   *"I can say without hesitation . . . is an absurdity"*: Hershberg, *Harvard to Hiroshima*, 318.

407   *"complete and unswerving loyalty . . ."*: Stern, *The Oppenheimer Case*, 105.

407   *"its misguided and traitorous . . ."*: Herken, *The Winning Weapon*, 273.

407   *"incredible mismanagement"*: Ibid., 242–43.

407 *Groves situation*: Ibid., 273.

408 *"Personal and Confidential . . ."*: JBC to JRO, January 5, 1948, JBCPP.

408 *"Groves must get out"*: Norris, *Racing for the Bomb*, 502.

408 *"not a bit worried"*: Herken, *The Winning Weapon*, 243.

408 *"military insurance"*: JBC, "Force and Freedom, "*Atlantic Monthly*, January 1, 1949.

408 *"like a cake of ice . . ."*: WP, April 25, 1947.

408 *"preventive war," "Let's smash 'em now . . ."*: JBC, "Force and Freedom."

409 *"their nuclear plants . . ."*: William L. Laurence, "How Soon Will Russia Have the A-Bomb?," *Saturday Evening Post*, November 6, 1948.

409 *"develop a Machiavellian foreign policy . . ."*: "JBC, "Force and Freedom."

409 *"ugly question . . . different morally from peace"*: Ibid.

409 *"can be protected only . . . in time of peace"*: Ibid.

409 *"a perilous knife edge"*: Ibid.

410 *"these confused and gloomy days"*: JBC, "Force and Freedom."

411 *"Fishing Party"*: Hershberg, *Harvard to Hiroshima*, 385.

411 *"the present haphazard methods . . ."*: Ibid.

411 *"not very proud"*: Ibid., 390.

412 *"passing excitement"*: "Text of Conant's 'Red Scare' Talk," *DBG*, June 23, 1949.

412 *"one of the weakest links"*: David Caute, *The Great Fear*, 471.

412 *"certain that he was an innocent victim . . ."*: MSL, 561.

413 *"red herring"*: McCullough, *Truman*, 652.

413 *"nobody is safe . . ."*: Hershberg, *Harvard to Hiroshima*, 428.

413 *"pumpkin papers"*: Caute, *The Great Fear*, 60.

414 *"After the conviction . . . certainly in order"*: MSL, 561, 454.

414 *"preserve their integrity . . . ," "those who now choose . . ."*: Ibid.

414 *"spirit of tolerance"*: Ibid.

414 *"highly inadvisable . . ."*: JBC, "Education and the Federal Government," December 12, 1946, JBCPP.

414 *"pinkos"*: Bethell, *Harvard Observed*, 188.

415 *"reducators"*: Smith, *The Harvard Century*, 181.

415 *"Kremlin-on-the Charles"*: Bethell, *Harvard Observed*, 188.

415 *"as a consequence of panic . . . armed truce"*: WP, January 21, 1948.

415 *"the value of our freedoms . . . intelligently"*: Arthur M. Schlesinger Jr., *The Vital Center*, 210.

415 *"the overemphasis on 'loyalty' . . . ," "We must be realistic . . . we seek to save"*: WP, January 21, 1948.

416 *"poor security risk . . . exposed to public shame"*: Hershberg, *Harvard to Hiroshima*, 437.

416 *"The government . . . confidential information," "the hope that you . . ."*: Ibid.

416 *"extreme measure"*: Schlesinger, *Innocent Beginnings*, 491.

417 *"A lot of people would say . . ."*: MSL, 457.

417 *"Harvard cannot be influenced . . ."*: Ibid., 455.

417 *"an almost indefensible position"*: Ibid., 457–58.

418 *"In this period of a cold war . . . members of the staff"*: Ibid.

418   *"answer to end all answers . . . ," "I would send . . .":* Ibid., 459.

418   *"Conant talked one way . . .":* "Conant & the FBI," Sigmund Diamond letter to the editor, *New York Review of Books*, October 20, 1994.

418   *"the locus of a fruitful . . .":* Sigmund Diamond, *Compromised Campus*, 50–51.

419   *"some peace and quiet . . . can't always count on!":* GRC to MTR, August 11, 1949, CFP.

419   *"burned out," "done his job during the war":* Hershberg, *Harvard to Hiroshima*, 470.

419   *"personal ambitions . . .":* JBC, handwritten list of future plans, July 19, 1945, JBCPP.

420   *"having an experience . . .":* GRC to MTR, August 29 and September 2, 1949, CFP.

420   *"You can imagine how happy . . . uninterrupted sunshine":* Ibid.

CHAPTER 20: A ROTTEN BUSINESS

421   *"When I am in Washington . . .":* JBC to BMB, February 24, 1950, BMB Papers, PU.

421   *"They have it":* Kenneth P. O'Donnell, "Professor in a Hot Spot," *Saturday Evening Post*, September 5, 1953, 141.

421   *"We have evidence . . .":* NYT, September 24, 1949.

422   *"overwhelming superiority":* DAS, 204.

422   *"The time has come . . .":* Ibid.

423   *"Just go back to Los Alamos . . .":* Monk, *Robert Oppenheimer*, 565.

423   *"With the war over . . .":* Conant, *109 East Palace*, 344.

423   *"false sense of security":* Herken, *The Winning Weapon*, 306.

423   *"bloodthirsty" trio:* Hewlett and Duncan, *Atomic Shield*, 385.

424   *"only louse up the world . . .":* "I. I. Rabi: Man of the Century," *A Walk Through the Twentieth Century with Bill Moyers*, Moyers & Company, PBS, New York, aired July 25, 1984.

424   *"over my dead body":* Edward Teller interview, 2003. Stern, *The Oppenheimer Case*, 138.

424   *"They wanted to stop me . . . Why did he say that?":* Edward Teller interview.

424   *"the miserable thing . . . think about it," "have to hear some good arguments . . .":* Stern, *The Oppenheimer Case*, 139, 137.

426   *"mostly psychological":* Hewlett and Duncan, *Atomic Shield*, 382.

426   *"political and strategic . . .":* Richard Polenberg, *In the Matter of J. Robert Oppenheimer*, 385–87.

426   *"almost translucent, so gray . . . ," "flatly against it . . . for the second time":* David E. Lilienthal, *The Journals of David E. Lilienthal*, 581.

427   *"a result of Conant's intervention":* Hershberg, *Harvard to Hiroshima*, 475.

427   *"surprising unanimity":* Hewlett and Duncan, *Atomic Shield*, 383.

427   *"a better than even chance . . . ," "some hundreds of times . . .":* Ibid., 383–84. DAS, 208.

427   *"it would be wrong . . .":* Ibid.

427   *"We believe a superbomb . . . hope of mankind":* Ibid.

428   *"conditional on the response . . . ," "necessarily an evil thing . . .":* Ibid.

428   *"renounce and announce," "experienced promoters":* Ibid., 537, 378.

429   *"hawks," "superhawks," "full-fledged doves":* Herbert F. York, *The Advisors*, x.

429   *missionaries for the project:* Ibid., 390.

429   *"If we let Russia . . . ," "with all possible expedition . . .":* DAS, 211, 222.

429 *"intolerable"*: Ibid.

429 *"After listening to Conant . . ."*: Hershberg, *Harvard to Hiroshima*, 481.

429 *"start with the assumption . . . ," "immense distaste . . ."*: DAS, 218, 216.

429 *"all forms of atomic weapons . . ."*: WP, February 1, 1950.

430 *"when he called attention last week . . ."*: "Letter from Washington," *NY*, February 11, 1950, 50.

430 *"anti-information"*: Ibid.

430 *"for heck's sake . . ."*: Polenberg, *In the Matter of J. Robert Oppenheimer*, 86.

430 *"good soldier . . ."*: Hershberg, *Harvard to Hiroshima*, 482.

430 *"The majority's flat recommendation . . ."*: DAS, 216.

431 *"worrying about the situation . . ."*: Rhodes, *The Making of the Atomic Bomb*, 768.

431 *"Communists in government," "bad security risk"*: Dean Acheson, *Present at the Creation*, 362–64.

432 *"on moral grounds"*: Hershberg, *Harvard to Hiroshima*, 483.

432 *"When I am in Washington . . ."*: JBC to BMB, February 24, 1950, BMB Papers, PU.

432 *"They ganged up on him . . ."*: George Kistiakowsky to GRC, May 1, 1980, CFP.

432 *"the revolt . . . WWII"*: MSL, 499.

432 *"sensitive personality," "the most painful . . ."*: George Kistiakowsky to GRC, May 1, 1980.

433 *"too busy . . ."*: MSL, 499.

433 *"in the hands of the surgeons"*: Harvard College class of 1914, TFAR.

433 *"police action"*: NYT, June 30, 1950.

434 *"the whole international situation . . . ," "unbiased by the fait accompli . . ."*: MSL, 507–8.

434 *"the number of relative strangers . . ."*: GRC to MTR, three letters in July 1950, CFP.

434 *"trade ideas," "irrelevant . . . of their own"*: MSL, 508.

434 *"citizen's lobby"*: Jerry W. Sanders, *Peddlers of Crisis*, 61.

434 *"From what I have just heard . . ."*: MSL, 508.

435 *"global stalemate"*: JBC, "The Present Danger," February 7, 1951, JBCPP.

435 *"an undertaking of great importance"*: MSL, 511.

435 *"the extreme peril . . . ," "the price is high . . ."*: "A Stern Program for Survival," *Look* magazine, December 19, 1950, 33–35.

435 *"Your memorandum rings the bell with me!"*: Hershberg, *Harvard to Hiroshima*, 503.

436 *"a success," "same old salesmen"*: MSL, 512, 526.

436 *"Fellow citizens . . . ," "preservation of a free America . . . dangerous period"*: JBC, "The Present Danger."

436 *"Eisenhower's mantle," "build a secure wall . . ."*: MSL, 516.

436 *"the coldest of cold . . ."*: Smith, *The Harvard Century*, 184.

436 *"Kremlin's design . . ."*: Dallek, *The Lost Peace*, 298.

437 *"uncritical militancy . . . ," "But they were held"*: Ibid., i, 299.

437 *"deeply troubled by the unwillingness . . . global war"*: JBC, "The Present Danger."

437 *"undemocratic," "cherished"*: MSL, 527, 519.

437 *"present danger"*: Ibid.

437 *"a good chance of avoiding . . ."*: WP, February 11, 1951.

437 *"What we had to guard against . . ."*: MSL, 519.

438 *"10 ½ years..."*: JBC diary, June 1, 1952, JBCPP.

438 *"My mind was focused...," "in the not too... give me a second chance"*: MSL, 533–35.

439 *"Foster, don't you want to talk...," "Well, we don't have to agree..."*: Ibid.

439 *"The Day! Oh Boy!..."*: JBC diary, December 22 and 23, 1952, JBCPP.

439 *"You are hooked"*: MSL, 68.

439 *"all lesser" problems..."*: Deborah Kisatsky, *The United States and the European Right*, 51.

440 *"hanging fire," "rush through"*: Ibid., 536, 538.

440 *"readiness to help... in this regard"*: DDE to JBC, December 24 and 27, 1952, CFP.

440 *"long enough to serve..."*: JBC to George Kistiakowsky, January 6, 1953, CFP.

440 *"lengthy farewells"*: HC, January 22, 1953.

440 *"tired of exercising..."*: Smith, *The Harvard Century*, 186.

441 *"firing without warning"*: Bethell, *Harvard Observed*, 191.

441 *"hooky"*: Paul Buck as quoted in Keller, *Making Harvard Modern*, 163.

441 *"being a seer..."*: "U.S. Education's No. 1 Man," *Newsweek*, September 22, 1952, 73.

441 *"thunderous silence"*: JBC diary, January 1, 1953, JBCPP.

441 *"I shall be leaving..."*: Smith, *The Harvard Century*, 186.

442 *"Even in a period..."*: BDG, January 1953, CFP.

442 *"It seemed ten steps down..."*: Smith, *The Harvard Century*, 186.

442 *"Conant reached greatness... Harvard students"*: Crimson farewell, reprinted in *Harvard Bulletin*, January 24, 1953.

442 *"You alone could..."*: Agnes E. Meyer to JBC, January 14, 1953, CFP.

442 *"The next time I see you..."*: VB to JBC, January 9, 1953, CFP.

443 *"Typical of the physical scientist!..."*: Hershberg, *Harvard to Hiroshima*, 648.

443 *"I would like to be frank..."*: JBC to Percy Bridgman, January 1, 1953, CFP.

CHAPTER 21: MAN OF THE HOUR

444 *"Germany has been a thread...," "little blockade," "symmetry"*: Robert Shaplen, "Sabbatical," 142, 138, 151.

445 *"soft on Communism," "complete redistribution...," "pull the wool"*: MSL, 539–41. "President Conant Testifies," *Harvard Alumni Bulletin*, February 21, 1953.

445 *"much opposed to Conant... make a row"*: Jean Edward Smith, *Eisenhower*, 585.

446 *"loaded down with information...," "such rapid changes... controversial figure"*: MSL, 545.

446 *"how many Nazis...," "Germany as a bulwark"*: Shaplen, "Sabbatical," 152.

446 *"disastrous"*: JBC interview with Gordon Craig, August 9, 1965, John Foster Dulles Oral History Project, PUOH.

447 *"from pariah to partner"*: Kisatsky, *The United States and the European Right*, 27.

447 *"staggering numbers," "danger of epidemics... discontent or Communists"*: JBC to JFD, February 27 and March 5, 1953, as quoted in Christian Ostermann, "The United States, the East German Uprising of 1953, and the Limits of Rollback," Cold War International History Project, Woodrow Wilson International Center for Scholars, December 1994, 10.

448 *"outpost of freedom"*: MSL, 556–57.

448 *"fantastic, grim picture"*: Ibid.

448 *"the frontiers of freedom. . . ," "voting with their feet," "a slow death . . .*": *NYT*, February 13, 1953.

448 *"When will the Russians . . . course of events"*: MSL, 557.

448 *"headaches"*: Ibid., 551.

449 *psychological warfare, "the pressure on . . . for defense only," "to keep the pot simmering . . ."*: Ostermann, "The United States, the East German Uprising of 1953," 13.

449 *"big lie," "calm aloofness," "free hand," "security risk"*: MSL, 561, 563–64.

450 *"Something approaching . . . spinning counterclockwise"*: Ibid.

450 *deshelved, "If there was one subject . . ."*: O'Donnell, "Professor in a Hot Spot," 32–33.

450 *"Well, the HICOG . . ."*: JBC diary, May 31, 1953, JBCPP.

451 *"to play ball with . . ."*: MSL, 576.

451 *"glorified messenger"*: A. A. Berle Sr. to JBC, January 18, 1953, CFP.

451 *"book burner"*: MSL, 555–56.

451 *"kindly old professor . . ."*: O'Donnell, "Professor in a Hot Spot," 32.

451 *"good graces," "reign of stupidity . . ."*: MSL, 578.

452 *"but with different ideas"*: Smith, *The Harvard Century*, 190.

452 *"sympathy and asylum"*: Thomas Powers, *The Man Who Kept Secrets: Richard Helms and the CIA* (New York: Pocket Books, 1979), 55–56.

452 *"irreconcilable hostility"*: Monk, *Robert Oppenheimer*, 619.

453 *"had virtually run . . . ," "Westintegration," "no single party . . . ," "personal influence . . ." "triumph of democracy . . ."*: Kisatsky, *United States and the European Right*, 55–56.

453 *"German problem"*: MSL, 603.

454 *"the resources of which the United States . . ."*: Hershberg, *Harvard to Hiroshima*, 672.

454 *"off-chance"*: MSL, 603.

454 *"national army . . . thoroughly alarmed"*: JBC to JFD, November 13, 1953, JFD Papers, DDEL.

454 *"What growling dogs . . ."*: JBC diary, March 2, 1954, JBCPP, HUA.

454 *"little European countries," "No reaction from Washington . . ."*: JBC diary, April 1, 1954.

455 *"atmosphere of fear . . ."*: MSL, 562.

455 *"top administration officials . . ."*: Polenberg, *In the Matter of J. Robert Oppenheimer*, xvii.

455 *"notorious senator"*: MSL, 566.

456 *"Some of the 'boys' . . . ," "dirty words"*: Monk, *Robert Oppenheimer*, 579.

456 *"blank wall"*: Polenberg, *In the Matter of J. Robert Oppenheimer*, xvii.

457 *"I have no apologies . . . ," "pass judgment . . ."*: JBC to VB, March 26 and April 1, 1954, JBCPP.

457 *"factors unknown to you"*: Hershberg, *Harvard to Hiroshima*, 679.

458 *"covered Germany in 15 min . . . I was through"*: JBC diary, April 19, 1954, JBCPP.

458 *"aggressive mood," "carelessly drafted"*: MSL, 501. JBC's testimony is quoted in the full transcript of the hearings in Polenberg, *In the Matter of J. Robert Oppenheimer*.

459 *"not very happy"*: JBC diary, April 19, 1954, JBCPP.

459 *"belligerent corporal"*: JBC as quoted in John C. Landers, "An introduction to an interview with James B. Conant: The Manhattan Project as seen by Dr. Conant, and Commentary on the unprecedented and what it has left us," March 8, 1974, Harvard University, HUA (henceforth JBC OH/Landers).

459 *"prayed it would come out . . ."*: JBC diary, April 26, 1954, JBCPP. Hershberg, *Harvard to Hiroshima*, 680.

459 *"No criticism . . ."*: DDE to JBC, unmailed draft, April 26, 1954. See Hershberg, *Harvard to Hiroshima*, 680. Also see Stephen E. Ambrose, *Eisenhower the President*. Vol. 2 (New York: Simon & Schuster, 1984), 167.

460 *"Washington very tense! . . . scientists in the other camp"*: JBC diary, May 23, 1954, JBCPP.

460 *"first-class mess"*: JBC to Bill Marbury, as quoted in Hershberg, *Harvard to Hiroshima*, 681.

460 *"loyal citizen . . . interests of security," "to deny him clearance . . ."*: Polenberg, *In the Matter of J. Robert Oppenheimer*, xxv, xxviii.

460 *"tissue of lies"*: Ibid., xxviii.

461 *"It was an outrageous business . . ."*: JBC OH/Landers.

461 *"fatal day," "the free world . . . ," "D-day or Defeat Day"*: JBC diary, July 29, July 10, and August 30, 1954, JBCPP.

461 *"shattered"*: JBC interview with Gordon Craig.

461 *"gone up in oratorical smoke . . ."*: MSL, 588.

461 *"What will happen? . . ."*: JBC diary, August 31, 1954, JBCPP.

461 *"agonizing reappraisal," "a crisis of almost terrifying . . ."*: Townsend Hoopes, *The Devil and John Foster Dulles: The Diplomacy of the Eisenhower Era* (Boston: Little, Brown, 1973), 249.

462 *"threatening attitude . . ."*: JBC interview with Gordon Craig.

462 *"Oh, you are the high commissioner . . ."*: MSL, 588–89. JBC diary, March 27, 1955, JBCPP.

462 *"incredibly torturous," "So it seems that at long last . . ."*: Ibid.

463 *"boiled over," "diplomatically naked"*: MSL, 590.

463 *"tantamount to a tribute . . ."*: DBG, May 6, 1955. MSL, 593.

463 *"open skies," "to give each other . . ."*: Smith, *Eisenhower*, 667.

463 *"spirit of Geneva"*: Hoopes, *The Devil and John Foster Dulles*, 300.

464 *"fraud, from beginning to end"*: JBC interview with Gordon Craig.

464 *"Professor atom," "goodwill tours," "accentuate the positive"*: O'Donnell, "Professor in a Hot Spot," 141–42.

464 *"commandos of the Cold War," "abomination," "monstrous aberration," "the spirit of free Germany . . . given half a chance"*: Ibid., 140–42.

465 *"on its way"*: Ibid.

465 *"effective crystallizer"*: John W. Gardner, "Reminiscences," CCR.

465 *"blank check," "He was absolutely clear . . . goes off half-cocked"*: Ibid. MSL, 615.

465 *"very favorably inclined . . ."*: JBC interview with Gordon Craig.

466 *"tantamount to blackmail"*: NYT, May 6, 1955.

466 *"German hands"*: MSL, 604.

466 *"grossly discourteous . . . ," "visible proof"*: BH, December 5, 1955.

466 *"decisions could only be made . . ."*: MSL, 608.

467 New Look Doctrine, *"maximum protection . . . ," "massive retaliation"*: Hoopes, *The Devil and John Foster Dulles*, 198–99.

467 *"Somebody in Bonn . . . only thing that could be used"*: JBC interview with Gordon Craig.

467 *"What irony . . ."*: JBC diary, July 3, 1955, JBCPP.

467 *"textbook," "political touch"*: Kisatsky, *United States and the European Right*.

468 *"I prefer to appoint Conant," "probably would not operate . . ."*: Hershberg, *Harvard to Hiroshima*, 695.

468 *"major catastrophe," "The president and I would like. . . ," "tramped the mountain trails," "pushed out"*: MSL, 615.

469 *"How to cut Nasser down . . ."*: JBC diary, September 7, 1956, JBCPP.

469 *"What sounded like a herald . . ."*: Ibid., November 5–7, 1956.

469 *"a difference of opinion . . ."*: MSL, 617–18.

470 *"deep personal regret . . . drew so frequently"*: DDE to JBC, reprinted in *NYT*, January 29, 1957.

470 *"quite a heart-rending business"*: GRC to MTR, February 27, 1957, CFP.

Chapter 22: Warrior Educator

471 *"what will be needed . . ."*: JBC to Sherman Adams for DDE, November 10, 1957, JBCPP.

471 Murrow visit: Interview with Theodore R. Conant.

472 *"who could indeed be called . . ."*: WP, January 14, 1954.

472 *"as long as I can write . . ."*: Amster, "Meritocracy Ascendant," 193.

472 *"vast engine of democracy," "logistical support"*: JBC, "A Guide to Public Education for the Conscientious Citizen," foreword, unpublished manuscript, CCR.

473 *"strong prejudice . . ."*: JBC, "Notes on Writing an Autobiography," unpublished manuscript, May 22, 1969, 1, CCR.

473 *"brave and wise . . . boys"*: GRC to MTR, December (undated), 1953, CFP.

474 *"an attractive, intelligent . . . ," "possessed of a great deal . . ."*: As quoted by GRC to MTR, August 27 and 30, 1957, CFP.

475 *"My mother suffered . . . fairly normal!"*: GRC to Jean Demos, February 22, 1968, CFP.

475 *"domestic minded"*: GRC to Jean Demos, fall 1957, CFP.

475 *"master of the two-minute . . ."*: JBC to GRC, October 22, 1957, CFP.

475 *"live like a monk"*: GRC to Jean Demos, fall 1957, CFP.

476 *"unless you force me . . . Ditto for cocktails"*: JBC to GRC, October 2, 1957, CFP.

476 *"a battle more important . . . ," "tough competitive race"*: Isaacs and Downing, *Cold War*, 155.

476 *"softness"*: Ibid.

476 *"Those now in college"*: JBC to Sherman Adams for DDE, November 10, 1957, JBCPP.

476 *"qualified citizen . . ."*: BG, November 5, 1957.

477 *"He displayed no interest . . ."*: Interview with William Golden.

477   *"on the arbitrary assumption . . ."*: William Golden's private notes on conversation with JBC, courtesy of William Golden.

477   *"tough"*: "The Inspector General," *Time*, September 14, 1959, 74.

477   *"timing was perfect"*: MSL, 621.

478   *"a rare record," "who has done more . . ."*: "A Letter from the Publisher," *Time*, September 14, 1959.

478   *"radical changes," "sorting-out process"*: "The Inspector General," 70–79. Amster, "Meritocracy Ascendant," 223.

478   *"equality of esteem," "Each honest calling . . ."*: Ibid.

479   *"a melting pot," "A modern industrial nation . . ."*: Ibid.

479   *"intensely focused . . . the old one"*: Lemann, *The Big Test*, 47.

480   *"Conant believed that admissions . . ."*: Louis Menand, *American Studies*, 92.

480   *"free city," "Berlin is the testicles . . ."*: Smith, *Eisenhower*, 744.

480   *"low-level"*: Ambrose, *Eisenhower*, 502.

480   *"I am still firmly . . . supplied as at present"*: JBC to JFD, December 10, 1958, as quoted in Hershberg, *Harvard to Hiroshima*, 715.

481   *"Open letter to America's Grandchildren . . . supineness from belligerency"*: "A Stirring Message for Independence Day," *Parade*, July 5, 1959, 4–5.

482   *"fearful world," "there is one essential . . . utterly destroyed"*: JBC, "The Defense of Freedom," November 12, 1959, JBCPP.

482   *"What emerged from Conant's . . ."*: Warner, *Province of Reason*, 234.

482   *"It is easy to be defeatest . . ."*: BDG, September 6, 1951.

483   *"released in fragile health . . ."*: Gregory Henderson, "For Jim Conant," typed transcript of memorial remarks, August 29, 1981, CFP.

483   *"went to pieces," "He was more concerned . . ."*: Interview with Theodore R. Conant.

483   *"After that, he washed his hands . . ."*: Ibid.

484   *"manic side"*: JBC diary, January 1–4, and scattered mentions throughout spring 1962, JBCPP.

484   *"He tried to slug it out . . . any real home"*: Henderson, "For Jim Conant."

484   *"It's all very well . . . objectively anymore"*: GRC to JBC, November 9, 1964, CFP.

484   *"go the same way," "I wondered what the hell . . ."*: Interview with Ellen Conant.

485   *"The tragedy of Ted's life . . ."*: EC as quoted by GRC to JBC, October 27, 1958, CFP.

485   *"educational statesman," "cruel pace"*: NYT, October 17, 1961.

485   *"written in wrath," "social dynamite . . . these young people?"*: Ibid.

485   *"These situations call for action . . ."*: JBC, *Slums and Suburbs*, 21.

486   *"For the first time . . ."*: Fred M. Hechinger, "Conant: A New Report by the Schools' Mr. Fixit," a review of JBC's *The Comprehensive High School: A Second Report to Interested Citizens*, NYT, March 5, 1967.

486   *"token integration," "separate but equal"*: MSL, 622–23.

486   *"to bring the schools closer . . . marketable skills," "army of shoeshine boys"*: Hechinger, "Conant: A New Report by the Schools' Mr. Fixit."

486   *"not racial integration . . ."*: Atlanta Daily World, October 26, 1961.

486   *"seem as nothing"*: JBC, "A Guide to Public Education for the Conscientious Citizen," foreword, unpublished manuscript, CCR. MSL, 624.

486 *"hornets' nest"*: JBC to GRC, September 12, 1963, CFP.

486 *"scandalously remiss"*: *NYT*, September 15, 1963.

486 *"bankrupt," "Mickey Mouse," "opium smokers"*: Ibid. Also JBC, *The Education of American Teachers* (New York: McGraw-Hill, 1963).

487 *"unequaled impact," "missionary zeal"*: *NYT*, September 15, 1963.

487 *"burning faith in the American . . ."*: Frank Keppel, as quoted in Torsten Husen, "Encounters with James B. Conant—Harvard President and Defender of Public School," Project Muse, 87.

487 *"Behold the turtle . . ."*: *Los Angeles Examiner*, March 16, 1960.

487 *"transparent," "The armed East German . . ."*: *MSL*, 624.

488 *"There are many people . . . Ich bin ein Berliner"*: Isaacs and Downing, *Cold War*, 155.

488 *"The president went very far . . . claim to have anticipated"*: JBC diary, June 26, 1963, JBCPP.

489 *"with a despairing gesture"*: JBC Planner, November 22 and 23, JBCPP.

489 *"full of sorrow and worry"*: JBC Diary, November 22, JBCPP.

489 *"spirit of optimism," "new spirit," "went right through our hearts"*: JBC, "Report to President of the Ford Foundation" (Report on two years in Berlin) 5, CCR.

489 *"I found myself asking . . ."*: JBC to Tracy Voorhees, November 29, 1963, JBCPP.

489 *"sadness and festivity"*: JBC diary, December 6, 1963, JBCPP.

490 *"Scientist and educator . . ."*: *BG*, December 7, 1963.

490 *"politely but firmly . . . unnoticed," "fleet in being"*: *MSL*, 628–29.

490 *"leisurely reflection . . . as we were then"*: Ibid.

491 *"lone wolf existence," "picking ourselves up . . ."*: GRC to Jean Demos, January 25, 1968, CFP.

491 *"uninterruptedly . . . too many visitors"*: Ibid., December 5, 1965, CFP.

491 *"He can't bear to look . . ."*: Ibid., October 16, 1967.

492 *"an autobiography . . ."*: JBC to E. Alden Dunham, April 17, 1967, CCR.

492 *"Good Man, Dull Book"*: John Leonard, review of *My Several Lives: Memoirs of a Social Inventor*, *NYT*, March 4, 1970.

492 *"Mr. Conant called his book . . ."*: Harold Taylor, review of *My Several Lives: Memoirs of a Social Inventor*, *NYT Book Review*, March 22, 1970.

492 *"The White Knight . . . ," "under the sign . . ."*: JBC, *My Several Lives*, xvi.

493 *"triage"*: Interview with Theodore Conant.

493 *"flickers of bitterness," "What Jim would have liked . . ."*: Henderson, "For Jim Conant," typed transcript of memorial remarks, August 29, 1981, CFP.

493 *"Were you all convinced . . . ," "Oh no," "These two gentlemen . . ."*: *Los Angeles Times*, February 28, 1970.

493 *"With grateful memories . . ."*: Inside page of Groves's copy, generously given to the author by a reader.

493 *"I do not look back . . . my own research"*: "James Bryant Conant," Douglas P. Cooper Distinguished Contemporaries Collection, WNYC. January 1, 1970.

494 *"Well, the whole fact . . . never free from that"*: Ibid.

494 *"negative voices about science . . . willing to go without"*: JBC to George Kistiakowsky, June 23, 1972, CFP.

494 *"The natural tendency . . . all things are sold"*: JBC, *On Understanding Science*, xii–xiii.

495 *"cool Yankee . . ."*: George Kistiakowsky, "James B. Conant: Chemist and Statesman of Science," James Bryant Conant: A Remembrance," memorial address, April 4, 1978, CFP.

495 *"Never again . . ."*: Louis S. Auchincloss to GRC, February 14, 1978, CFP.

495 *"to say that he was the last . . . The Conant Vacancy"*: *NYT*, February 14, 1978. Also Frank Keppel, "Mr. Conant's Influence on Education," James Bryant Conant: A Remembrance," memorial address, April 4, 1978, CFP.

SELECTED BIBLIOGRAPHY

BOOKS

Acheson, Dean. *Present at the Creation: My Years in the State Department.* New York: W. W. Norton, 1969.

Alperovitz, Gar. *Atomic Diplomacy: Hiroshima and Potsdam.* Rev. ed. New York: Penguin Books, 1985.

———. *The Decision to Use the Atomic Bomb.* New York: Random House, 1995.

Amster, Jeanne Ellen. "Meritocracy Ascendant: James Bryant Conant and Cultivation of Talent." PhD diss., Harvard University, 1990.

Amory, Cleveland. *The Proper Bostonians.* New York: E. P. Dutton, 1947.

Bacher, Robert F. *Robert Oppenheimer, 1904–1967.* Los Alamos, NM: Los Alamos Historical Society, 1999.

Badash, Lawrence, Joseph O. Hirschfelder, and Herbert P. Broida. *Reminiscences of Los Alamos, 1943–1945.* Boston: Reidel, 1980.

Balogh, Brian. *Chain Reaction: Expert Debate and Public Participation in American Commercial Nuclear Power, 1945–1975.* New York: Cambridge University Press, 1991.

Baxter, James Phinney, III. *Scientists Against Time.* Boston: Little, Brown, 1947.

Bell, Millicent. *Marquand: An American Life.* Boston: Little, Brown, 1979.

Bernstein, Barton J., ed. *The Atomic Bomb: The Critical Issues.* Boston: Little, Brown, 1976.

Bethell, John T. *Harvard Observed: An Illustrated History of the University in the Twentieth Century.* Cambridge, MA: Harvard University Press, 1998.

Biebel, Charles DeWayne. "Politics, Pedagogues and Statesmanship: James B. Conant and the Public Schools, 1933–1948." PhD diss., University of Wisconsin, 1971; Ann Arbor, MI: University Microfilms, 1971.

Bohlen, Charles E. *Witness to History, 1929–1969.* New York: W. W. Norton, 1973.

Boyer, Paul. *By the Bomb's Early Light.* New York: Pantheon, 1985.

Bradford, Gov. William. *Bradford's History "Of Plimouth Plantation."* Westminster, MD: Heritage Books, 2008.

Brophy, Leo P., and George J. B. Fisher. *United States Army in World War II: The Technical Services. The Chemical Warfare Service: Organizing for War.* Washington, DC: Center of Military History, 1989.

Bundy, McGeorge. *Danger and Survival: Choices About the Bomb in the First Fifty Years.* New York: Random House, 1988.

Bush, Vannevar. *Science—The Endless Frontier.* Washington, DC: US Government Printing Office, 1945.

———. *Pieces of the Action.* New York: William Morrow, 1970.

Byrnes, James F. *Speaking Frankly.* New York: Harper, 1947.

———. *All in One Lifetime.* New York: Harper, 1958.

Carr, Virginia Spencer. *Dos Passos: A Life.* Evanston, IL: Northwestern University Press, 1984.

Caute, David. *The Great Fear: The Anti-Communist Purge Under Truman and Eisenhower.* New York, Simon & Schuster, 1978.

Childs, Herbert. *An American Genius: The Life of Ernest Orlando Lawrence.* New York: E. P. Dutton, 1968.

Compton, Arthur H. *Atomic Quest: A Personal Narrative.* New York: Oxford University Press, 1956.

Conant, James B. *Our Fighting Faith: Five Addresses.* Cambridge, MA: Harvard University Press, 1942.

———. *On Understanding Science.* New Haven, CT: Yale University Press, 1947.

———. *Education in a Divided World.* Cambridge, MA: Harvard University Press, 1948.

———. *Science and Common Sense.* New Haven, CT: Yale University Press, 1951.

———. *Modern Science and Modern Man.* New York: Columbia University Press, 1952.

———. *Germany and Freedom: A Personal Appraisal.* Cambridge, MA: Harvard University Press, 1958.

———. *Slums and Suburbs.* New York: McGraw-Hill, 1961.

———. *My Several Lives: Memoirs of a Social Inventor.* New York: Harper, 1970.

Dallek, Robert. *Franklin D. Roosevelt and American Foreign Policy, 1932–1945.* New York: Oxford University Press, 1995.

———. *The Lost Peace: Leadership in a Time of Horror and Hope, 1945–1953.* New York: Harper, 2010.

Davis, Nuel Pharr. *Lawrence and Oppenheimer.* New York: Simon & Schuster, 1968.

Delgado, James P. *Nuclear Dawn: The Atomic Bomb from the Manhattan Project to the Cold War.* New York: Osprey, 2009.

Diamond, Sigmund. *Compromised Campus: The Collaboration of Universities with the Intelligence Community.* New York: Oxford University Press, 1992.

Douglass, Paul F. *Six upon the World: Toward an American Culture for an Industrial Age.* Boston: Little, Brown, 1954.

Faith, Thomas Ian. "Under a Green Sea: The U.S. Chemical Warfare Service 1917–1929." PhD diss., George Washington University, 2008; Ann Arbor, MI: University Microfilms, 2008.

———. *Behind the Gas Mask: The U.S. Chemical Warfare Service in War and Peace.* Urbana: University of Illinois Press, 2012.

Fermi, Laura. *Atoms in the Family.* Chicago: University of Chicago Press, 1954.

Fries, Amos A., and Clarence J. West. *Chemical Warfare: History of the US Army's Development and Use of Poison Gas Weapons in World War One.* New York: McGraw-Hill, 1921.

Gaddis, John Lewis. *Strategies of Containment: A Critical Appraisal of Postwar American National Security Policy.* New York: Oxford University Press, 1982.

General Electric Company, National Lamp Works. *The National in the World War, April 6, 1917–November 11, 1918.* Cleveland: General Electric Co., 1920.

Gilpin, Robert. *American Scientists and Nuclear Weapons Policy.* Princeton, NJ: Princeton University Press, 1962.

Giovanitti, Len, and Fred Freed. *The Decision to Drop the Bomb: A Political History.* New York: Coward-McCann, 1965.

Goodchild, Peter. *J. Robert Oppenheimer: Shatterer of Worlds.* Boston: Houghton Mifflin, 1980.

Groves, Leslie M. *Now It Can Be Told.* New York: Da Capo Press, 1962.

Haber, L. F. *The Poisonous Cloud: Chemical Warfare in the First World War.* New York: Oxford University Press, 1986.

Ham, Paul. *Hiroshima, Nagasaki: The Real Story of the Atomic Bombings and Their Aftermath.* New York: St. Martin's Press, 2014.

Harris, Seymour E. *Economics of Harvard.* New York: McGraw-Hill, 1970.

Herken, Gregg. *The Winning Weapon: The Atomic Bomb in the Cold War, 1945–1950.* New York: Alfred A. Knopf, 1980.

Hershberg, James G. "Ends vs. Means: James B. Conant and American Atomic Policy 1939–1947." BA thesis, History Department, Harvard University, 1982.

———. "James B. Conant, Nuclear Weapons and the Cold War, 1945–1950." PhD diss., Tufts University, 1989.

———. *James B. Conant: Harvard to Hiroshima and the Making of the Nuclear Age.* New York: Alfred A. Knopf, 1993.

Hewlett, Richard G., and Oscar E. Anderson, Jr. *The New World: A History of the United States Atomic Energy Commission.* Vol. I, *1939–1946.* University Park: Pennsylvania State University Press, 1962.

Hewlett, Richard G., and Francis Duncan. *Atomic Shield: A History of the United States Atomic Energy Commission.* Vol. II, *1947–1952.* University Park: Pennsylvania State University Press, 1969.

Hill, Nancy Peterson. *A Very Private Public Citizen: The Life of Grenville Clark.* Columbia: University of Missouri Press, 2014.

Hubbard, William. *A General History of New England, from the Discovery to MDCLXXX,* 1848. Boston: Arno Press, 1972.

Isaacson, Walter, and Evan Thomas. *The Wise Men: Six Friends and the World They Made.* New York: Simon & Schuster, 1986.

Karabel, Jerome. *The Chosen: The Hidden History of Admission and Exclusion at Harvard, Yale, and Princeton.* New York: Houghton Mifflin, 2005.

Keller, Morton, and Phyllis Keller. *Making Harvard Modern: The Rise of America's University.* New York: Oxford University Press, 2001.

Kennan, George F. *Memoirs, 1925–1950.* Boston: Little, Brown, 1967.

Kevles, Daniel J. *The Physicists.* New York: Alfred A. Knopf, 1978.

Kisatsky, Deborah. *The United States and the European Right: 1945–1955.* Columbus: Ohio State University Press, 2005.

Kunetka, James W. *City of Fire: Los Alamos and the Birth of the Atomic Age, 1943–1945.* Rev. ed. Albuquerque: University of New Mexico Press, 1979.

Lamont, Lansing. *Day of Trinity.* New York: Atheneum, 1965.

Lanouette, William, with Bela Szilard. *Genius in the Shadows: A Biography of Leo Szilard, the Man Behind the Bomb.* New York: Charles Scribner's Sons, 1992.

Lemann, Nicholas. *The Big Test: The Secret History of the American Meritocracy.* New York: Farrar, Straus and Giroux, 1999.

Lilienthal, David E. *The Journals of David E. Lilienthal: The Atomic Energy Years, 1945–1950.* New York: Harper, 1964.

Malloy, Sean L. *Atomic Tragedy: Henry L. Stimson and the Decision to Use the Bomb Against Japan.* Ithaca, NY: Cornell University Press, 2010.

Manchester, William, and Paul Reid. *The Last Lion: Winston Spencer Churchill, Defender of the Realm, 1940–1965.* New York: Little, Brown, 2012.

Marbury, William L. *In the Catbird Seat.* Baltimore: Maryland Historical Society, 1988.

Marquand, John P. *The Late George Apley.* New York: Grosset & Dunlap, 1936.

———. *H. M. Pulham, Esquire.* Boston: Little, Brown, 1941.

McCormick, John. *George Santayana: A Biography.* New York: Alfred A. Knopf, 1987.

McCullough, David. *Truman.* New York: Simon & Schuster, 1992.

Menand, Louis. *American Studies.* New York: Farrar, Straus and Giroux, 2002.

Mertins, Louis. *Robert Frost: Life and Talks-Walking.* Norman: University of Oklahoma Press, 1965.

Messer, Robert L. *The End of an Alliance: James F. Byrnes, Roosevelt, Truman, and the Origins of the Cold War.* Chapel Hill: University of North Carolina Press, 1982.

———. *The Making of a Cold Warrior: James F. Byrnes and American-Soviet Relations, 1945–1946.* Chapel Hill: University of North Carolina Press, 1982.

Michelmore, Peter. *The Swift Years: The Robert Oppenheimer Story.* New York: Dodd, Mead, 1969.

Miscamble, Wilson D. *George F. Kennan and the Making of American Foreign Policy, 1947–1950.* Princeton, NJ: Princeton University Press, 1992.

———. *The Most Controversial Decision: Truman, the Atomic Bombs, and the Defeat of Japan.* New York: Cambridge University Press, 2011.

Monk, Ray. *Robert Oppenheimer: A Life Inside the Center.* New York: Doubleday, 2012.

Morison, Samuel Eliot. *Three Centuries of Harvard, 1636–1936.* Cambridge, MA: Harvard University Press, 1936.

Morrison, Philip. *Nothing Is Too Wonderful to Be True.* Woodbury, NY: American Institute of Physics Press, 1995.

Nichols, K. D. *The Road to Trinity.* New York: William Morrow, 1987.

Norris, Robert S. *Racing for the Bomb: General Leslie R. Groves, the Manhattan Project's Indispensable Man.* South Royalton, VT: Steerforth Press, 2002.

Norwood, Stephen H. *The Third Reich in the Ivory Tower: Complicity and Conflict on American Campuses.* New York: Cambridge University Press, 2009.

Olson, Lynne. *Those Angry Days: Roosevelt, Lindbergh, and America's Fight over World War II, 1939–1941.* New York: Random House, 2013.

Polenberg, Richard, ed. *In the Matter of J. Robert Oppenheimer: The Security Clearance Hearing.* Ithaca, NY: Cornell University Press, 1991.

Powers, Thomas. *Heisenberg's War: The Secret History of the German Bomb.* New York: Alfred A. Knopf, 1993.

Rhodes, Richard. *The Making of the Atomic Bomb.* New York: Simon & Schuster, 1986.

Rich, Willard. *Brain Waves and Death.* New York: Charles Scribner's Sons, 1940.

Rigden, John S. *Rabi, Scientist and Citizen.* New York: Basic Books, 1987.

Sanders, Jerry W. *Peddlers of Crisis: The Committee on the Present Danger and the Politics of Containment.* Boston: South End Press, 1983.

Santayana, George. *The Last Puritan: A Memoir in the Form of a Novel.* New York: Charles Scribner's Sons, 1936.

Schlesinger, Arthur M., Jr. *The Vital Center: The Politics of Freedom.* Boston: Houghton Mifflin, 1949; repr. ed., New York: Da Capo Press, 1988.

———. *A Life in the Twentieth Century: Innocent Beginnings, 1917–1950.* New York: Houghton Mifflin, 2002.

Shand-Tucci, Douglass. *Built in Boston: City and Suburb, 1800–1950.* Amherst: University of Massachusetts Press, 1988.

———. *Ashmont: An Historical Guide to Peabody Square, Carruth's Hill, and Ashmont Hill and the Architecture of Edwin J. Lewis, Jr. and John A. Fox.* Dorchester, MA: Dorchester Historical Society, 1991.

Sherwin, Martin J. *A World Destroyed: Hiroshima and the Origins of the Arms Race.* New York: Vintage, 1987.

Shipton, Clifford K. *Roger Conant: A Founder of Massachusetts.* Cambridge, MA: Harvard University Press, 1944.

Shirer, William L. *Berlin Diary: The Journal of a Foreign Correspondent, 1934–1941.* New York: Alfred A. Knopf, 1941.

Smith, Alice Kimball. *A Peril and a Hope: The Scientists' Movement in America, 1945–47.* Cambridge, MA: MIT Press, 1965.

Smith, Alice Kimball, and Charles Weiner, eds. *Robert Oppenheimer: Letters and Recollections.* Cambridge, MA: Harvard University Press, 1980.

Smith, Jean Edward. *Eisenhower: In War and Peace.* New York: Random House, 2012.

Smith, Richard Norton. *The Harvard Century: The Making of a University to a Nation.* New York: Simon & Schuster, 1986.

Steel, Ronald. *Walter Lippmann and the American Century.* Boston: Little, Brown, 1980.

Stern, Philip M. *The Oppenheimer Case: Security on Trial.* New York: Harper, 1969.

Stimson, Henry L., and McGeorge Bundy. *On Active Service in Peace and War.* New York: Harper, 1947.

Teller, Edward, with Judith Shoolery. *Memoirs: A Twentieth-Century Journey in Science and Politics.* Cambridge, MA: Perseus, 2001.

Truman, Harry S. *Memoirs.* Vol 1, *Year of Decisions.* Garden City, NY: Doubleday, 1955.

———. *Memoirs*. Vol 2, *Years of Trial and Hope, 1946–1952*. Garden City, NY: Doubleday, 1956.

Tucker, Jonathan B. *War of Nerves: Chemical Warfare from World War I to Al-Qaeda*. New York: Pantheon, 2006.

Tuttle, William M., Jr. "James B. Conant, Pressure Groups, and the National Defense, 1933–1945." PhD diss., University of Wisconsin, 1967; Ann Arbor, MI: University Microfilms, 1970.

Vilensky, Joel A. *Dew of Death: The Story of Lewisite, America's World War I Weapon of Mass Destruction*. Bloomington: Indiana University Press, 2005.

Waitt, Brigadier General Alden H. *Gas Warfare: Smoke, Flame, and Gas in Modern War*. Washington, DC: Infantry Journal, 1944.

Warner, Sam Bass, Jr. *Province of Reason*. Cambridge, MA: Harvard University Press, 1984.

Yeomans, Henry Aaron. *Abbott Lawrence Lowell 1856–1943*. Cambridge, MA: Harvard University Press, 1988.

York, Herbert F. *The Advisors: Oppenheimer, Teller, and the Superbomb*. Stanford, CA: Stanford University Press, 1976.

Zachary, Pascal G. *Endless Frontier: Vannevar Bush, Engineer of the American Century*. New York: Free Press, 1997.

MANUSCRIPT COLLECTIONS

Bancroft Library, University of California, Berkeley: Ernest O. Lawrence Papers; Alfred Loomis Interview Transcript.

Carnegie Corporation of New York Records. Columbia University, Rare Book and Manuscript Library.

Conant Family Papers, Hanover, NH: Books, diaries, letters, journals, scrapbooks, and photographs of the members of the Thayer, Richards, and Conant families; also many of James B. Conant's personal papers and correspondence; private collection entrusted to Jennet Conant.

Dartmouth College Library, Hanover, NH: Grenville Clark Papers.

Dwight D. Eisenhower Library, Abilene, KS: Eisenhower's Prepresidential Papers and Presidential Papers; John Foster Dulles Papers; Gordon Gray Papers.

Franklin D. Roosevelt Presidential Library, Hyde Park, NY: President's Personal File; Harry Hopkins Papers; President's Secretary File.

General Records of the Department of State, 1763–2002, RG59, National Archives.

Harvard University Archives, Pusey Library: James B. Conant Personal Papers, Diaries, Speeches, and Presidential Papers; Theodore William Richards Papers.

Harvard University Law School, Langdell Library: Felix Frankfurter Papers.

Library of Congress: Joseph Alsop Papers; Vannevar Bush Papers; Archibald MacLeish Papers; J. Robert Oppenheimer Papers.

Massachusetts Institute of Technology, Cambridge, MA: Vannevar Bush Papers; Karl T. Compton Papers.

Princeton University, Mudd Library: Bernard M. Baruch Papers; Harold Dodds Papers; John Foster Dulles Papers; James Forrestal Papers; David E. Lilienthal Papers.

Records of the Federal Bureau of Investigation (FBI), 1896–2008, RG65, National Archives.

Records of Leslie R. Groves, RG200, National Archives.

Records of the Manhattan Engineering District (MED), RG77, National Archives.

Records of the National Defense Research Committee (NDRC), RG227, National Archives.

Records of the National Science Foundation, RG307, National Archives.

Records of the Office of Scientific Research and Development (OSRD): Bush-Conant files; James B. Conant, "A History of the Development of the Bomb," RG227, National Archives.

Records of the Research and Development Board, RG330, National Archives.

Records of the Secretary of War, RG107, National Archives.

Records of the US Atomic Energy Commission (AEC), RG326, National Archives.

Records of the US High Commissioner for Germany, Washington National Records Center, Suitland, MD, RG466.

Records of the US Joint Chiefs of Staff, RG218, National Archives.

Tufts University, Medford, MA: Vannevar Bush Papers; Edward R. Murrow Papers.

Washington University, St. Louis, MO, University Libraries, Department of Special Collections: Arthur Holly Compton Personal Papers.

Yale University, Sterling Library: Dean G. Acheson Papers; Walter Lippmann Papers; Henry L. Stimson Papers.

ORAL HISTORY TRANSCRIPTS

American Institute of Physics, Niels Bohr Library, College Park, MD: Niels Bohr; Robert F. Bacher; Paul D. Bartlett.

Columbia University Oral History Research Office Collection: Paul Buck; Harvey H. Bundy; Vannevar Bush; James B. Conant; John W. Gardner; William L. Lawrence; Henry L. Stimson; Henry A. Wallace.

Princeton University, John Foster Dulles Oral History Project: James B. Conant.

RADIO AND TELEVISION

CBS News Archives, CBS News Reference Library, New York: James B. Conant interview transcripts and DVDs, *CBS Reports, Face the Nation, Person to Person, See It Now.*

INDEX

ABOUT THE AUTHOR

Jennet Conant is the author of four bestselling books about World War II: *A Covert Affair: Julia Child and Paul Child in the OSS*; *The Irregulars: Roald Dahl and the British Spy Ring in Wartime Washington*; *109 East Palace: Robert Oppenheimer and the Secret City of Los Alamos*; and *Tuxedo Park: A Wall Street Tycoon and the Secret Palace of Science That Changed the Course of World War II*. She was a general editor of *Newsweek* magazine, and has written for *Vanity Fair*, *GQ*, *Esquire*, and the *New York Times*. She lives with her husband and son in New York City and Sag Harbor.

PHOTO CREDITS